Clearing and Settlement in Europe

Clearing and Settlement in Europe

by

Dermot Turing, MA (Cantab), DPhil
Solicitor

Bloomsbury Professional

Bloomsbury Professional Ltd, Maxwelton House, 41–43 Boltro Road, Haywards Heath, West Sussex, RH16 1BJ

© Dermot Turing 2012

Bloomsbury Professional is an imprint of Bloomsbury Publishing plc

A CIP Catalogue record for this book is available from the British Library.

ISBN: 978 1 78043 110 9

Typeset by Phoenix Photosetting Ltd, Chatham, Kent
Printed and bound by CPI Group (UK) Ltd, Croydon, CR0 4YY

FOREWORD

In recent years the structure for effecting financial market transactions, often referred to as the financial markets infrastructure, has become an area of growing interest for practitioners, policy makers and researchers. Such interest has stemmed from the structural changes in global finance – greater volumes of cross border transactions, as well as the creation of integrated financial areas like the Eurozone.

Such is the importance of financial markets infrastructure that the latest (failed) attempt by the European Commission to deeply reform the system to make it more efficient, given the freedom to trade, the presence of a single currency and the development of a uniform set of rules, has arguably been blocked by a political opposition fearing the such reform would have created a large and very competitive financial system in the continent of Europe.

The post trading system is made of two pillars: laws and contracts on one side as well as information and communication technology on the other. Dermot Turing's book focusses squarely on the first pillar. It is the first piece of work tackling all legal and regulatory aspects of post-trading and, as such, it represents a valuable contribution. This book is to be recommended to all who want to understand the working of the financial system and its likely evolution ahead of us.

Alberto Giovannini
Chief Executive Officer of Unifortune and former chief policy advisor of the European Commission's Clearance and Settlement Advisory and Monitoring

PREFACE

2012 is an interesting time to be writing about clearing and settlement. After many years of neglect, being regarded somewhat distastefully as the 'plumbing' of the financial markets, it is now slowly being acknowledged that the post-trading industry is one in which financial firms make money, and one in which risk issues need careful management. Reliable clearing, payment and settlement structures are perceived to be essential to enable financial firms to withstand shocks. A great deal of the cost of trading and cross-border investment is, rightly or wrongly, attributed to the processes of clearing and settlement. For all these reasons, the subject has deserved more thorough and coherent study than it has received in legal literature.

The absence of any harmonising law, a state of affairs which held until very recently, has in part been to blame. The law relating to infrastructures such as central counterparties (CCPs), central securities depositories (CSDs) and payment systems was left to the discretion of member states, leaving a patchwork of inconsistent practices. Initiatives to iron out the differences at the European level have had mixed success:

- Professor Giovannini's first report on the barriers obstructing efficient cross-border clearing and settlement was issued in 2001.
- The European Commission debated during 2002-2006 whether to have a directive on the subject, but decided on a voluntary Code of Conduct. The Code can be credited with an observed reduction of costs for investors. It has also encouraged interoperability between CCPs.
- Various industry bodies attempted to agree common ground-rules in a number of other areas, notably corporate actions processing.
- In other areas, such as the question of whether infrastructures should consolidate, compete, exist in vertical silos or be not-for-profit utilities, no consensus has emerged notwithstanding ten years of debate. Attempts to consolidate have faced formidable regulatory difficulties.
- Target2-Securities is intended to eliminate national settlement differences at a stroke, but is taking an age to become operational.

And so the cacophony of national rules and practices identified by Prof Giovannini is still, obstinately, in place.

The financial crisis of 2008 has brought the spotlight to bear on central counterparties and clearing, and that crisis has also catalysed a revival of the European legislative effort. Some 20 years after the first comprehensive EU directives relating to financial services, harmonised legislation is coming into force on the essential post-trade services which underpin systemic and economic stability. In March 2012, the European Council and European Parliament agreed a Regulation on CCPs and a draft Regulation on CSDs was put into the legislative process. The influential Committee on Payment and Settlement Systems issued its definitive Principles for Financial Markets Infrastructures in April 2012. This book aims to explain these legislative measures and put them into their proper context.

The new laws need to dovetail with a long tradition of practice, which itself gives rise to complex risk management questions. Examples can be found in approaches to liquidity, collateral arrangements, outsourcing, corporate actions, securities lending, regulatory capital and tax. Those topics are not peculiar to the world of clearing and settlement, although they need fresh analysis in that context. But some particularly troublesome questions arise which are specific to post-trade operations, and on these literature has been relatively sparse; they include default management, 'client clearing', protective insolvency legislation, failure of infrastructures, and interoperability between them. These subjects all deserve fuller coverage and discussion than they have been allowed before.

So, the aims of this text are, first, to describe what happens in clearing and settlement, and the roles of (and risks assumed by) the various participants in the post-trade marketplace. Secondly, the law applicable to infrastructures, how they are regulated, and the other topographical features of their legal landscape are explored in detail. In third place, the legal and practical aspects of risk management and operations of infrastructures are looked at. Finally, the risks faced by participants in payment, clearing and settlement systems – the agent banks – are explored, along with practical and operational issues which they face in their roles.

LEGISLATION IN THE PIPELINE

Tradition dictates that an author of a book should explain that the law is stated as at such-and-such a date. For anyone writing during a period of frenetic change, it is a challenge to fix such-and-such with any degree of usefulness. To enable readers to understand how things are at the time they are reading the book, the approach taken has been to look ahead in time as far as possible, but to make it clear whenever the adoption of future legislation has been anticipated.

So, with some editorial trepidation, the scheme followed in this book is this: the law is stated as at 1 June 2012, with the exceptions mentioned below where legislation is still in the pipeline at that date.

(1) Final text for the Regulation on OTC derivatives, central counterparties and trade repositories (EMIR, Regulation (EU) No 648/2012 of 4 July 2012) is available, but had not then been published in the Official Journal of the European Union. EMIR is treated as being in force, even though that had not occurred on 1 June 2012.

(2) The Financial Services Bill 2012 is in the House of Lords, having completed its passage in the House of Commons. The text relies on the version of the Bill presented to the Lords (HL Bill 25) and assumes that this will have been implemented into law in that form.

(3) The proposal for a Regulation on improving securities settlement in the EU and on central securities depositories (2012/29 (COD)) – the CSD Regulation – has begun its journey through the EU's legislative process. Substantial modifications to the European Commission's proposal can be expected. The text cites the European Commission's proposal, but does so in a way which makes it clear that the commentary refers to the proposal only, not the final text, whenever that is agreed.

(4) The replacement legislation for the Banking Directive (2006/48/EC) and the Capital Adequacy Directive (2006/49/EC) – a proposed Capital Requirements Regulation, and a proposed Credit Institutions Directive (2011/202 and 203 (COD)) – is mid-way through inter-institutional negotiation as at 1 June 2012. The replacement legislation will also include the European adoption of the Basel III prudential accord. In this case, rather

than cite the European Commission's proposed legislation as issued in July 2011, which will have been changed both substantively and, to the annoyance of readers, with numerous changes to article numbers, the approach has been to refer wherever feasible to the equivalent existing provision in the Banking or Capital Adequacy Directives. Readers are invited to find the new location of these provisions once carried into the new legislation by using a table of destinations which is likely to be annexed to the final version of the new Regulation. Where the new Regulation includes Basel III material not included in the previous directives, the approach has been to cite (exceptionally) the European Commission's proposed legislation as issued in July 2011. Where significant modification of the Commission's proposal was already being debated or agreed by 1 June 2012, the evolution has been taken into account as far as possible. On the same subject, the Basel Committee had consulted for a second time on the capital adequacy requirements arising from clearing members' exposures to CCPs. As at 1 June 2012 the final pronouncement has not been issued.

(5) The Markets in Financial Instruments Directive (MiFID, 2004/39/EC) is also due to be replaced by a Regulation and a Directive (2011/296 and 298 (COD)). These instruments are also mid-way through the European legislative process on 1 June 2012. Again the approach taken has been to refer to the old MiFID, referring where necessary to the European Commission's proposal as issued in October 2011 for material which was to be introduced by the new legislation.

(6) Preliminary work for a Securities Law Directive, consulted on in 2009 and again in 2010 by the European Commission Services, has not by 1 June 2012 shown signs of being adopted formally by the Commission as a proposal for legislation. Where the possible future directive might be relevant to an issue discussed in the text, this is indicated.

(7) The European Commission's proposal for a Recovery and Resolution Directive (2012/0150 (COD)) was issued on 6 June 2012. This will make a significant difference to the procedures for rescuing or resolving ailing banks, and the way that agent banks and infrastructures approach counterparty risk management. The proposals are likely to be substantially modified during their passage through the European legislature, and their full impact has not been explored, notwithstanding occasional references in the text.

(8) Various items of Level 2 legislation are due to be created to supplement and add detail to EMIR. If the legislative timetable is adhered to, these ought in large part to be issued during the second half of 2012.

(9) Various other pieces of legislation, of minor importance for the text, appear to be stuck in the pipeline as at 1 June 2012. These include proposals for renewed versions of the Investor Compensation Schemes Directive (97/9/EC); the Deposit Guarantee Directive (94/19/EEC); and the Savings Tax Directive (2003/48/EC).

ACKNOWLEDGMENTS

Many people have contributed to this book, and the ideas in it, in many ways: notably Sarah Berry, Simon Chamberlain, Diana Chan, Liz Cramb, Tim Daniels, Anita Gaspar, Andy Hill, Marie Julien, Ruben Lee, Julia Milosh, Sarndra Rouse, Merrie Witkin and Yesha Yadav. The partners at Clifford Chance have made themselves, their thoughts, and the resources of the firm, available over many years. My family has shown commendable toleration while this has been in preparation.

However, special thanks are due to Jeffrey King of Citi Transaction Services, who suggested that this book should be written, and whose patient teaching has helped me understand much of what happens in the world of clearing and settlement.

The opinions and errors are of course mine alone.

Dermot Turing
St Albans, UK
June 2012

CONTENTS

Table of Cases

Table of Statutes

Table of Statutory Instruments

Table of European Legislation

Table of Abbreviations

Acronyms abound. Many will be familiar to readers but some will not. It is annoying to have to search for the place earlier in a text where an acronym is defined, so a central table may be of assistance; here it is. It is not comprehensive, but picks out the most frequently used acronyms, regardless of their likely familiarity. Where the text explains the term, a cross-reference is given.

ACH	automated clearing house **section 2.28**	ECB	European Central Bank	OTC	over-the-counter
CCP	central counterparty **section 2.2**	EMIR	Regulation (EU) No 648/2012 of the European Parliament and of the Council of 4 July 2012 on OTC derivatives, central counterparties and trade repositories	OTF	organised trading facility **section 3.6**
CLS	Continuous Linked Settlement **section 2.37**	ESMA	European Securities Markets Authority	Part VII	Part VII, Companies Act 1989 **section 8.10**
CPSS	Committee on Payment and Settlement Systems	FMI Principles	Principles for Financial Market Infrastructures **section 6.41**	RRRs	Financial Services and Markets Act 2000 (Recognition Requirements for Investment Exchanges and Clearing Houses) Regulations 2001

Table of Abbreviations

CSD	central securities depository **section 2.16**	FSA	Financial Services Authority (UK)	RTGS	real-time gross settlement **section 2.33**
DNS	daily net settlement **section 2.30**	GCM	general clearing member **section 2.8**	SFD	Settlement Finality Directive
DVP	delivery versus payment **section 15.2**	MiFID	Markets in Financial Instruments Directive	T2S	Target2-Securities **section 2.22**
EBA	1) European Banking Authority; cf 2) EBA Clearing (where EBA used to stand for Ecu/Euro Banking Association)	MTF	multilateral trading facility **section 3.5**	USRs	Uncertificated Securities Regulations 2001

1 Introduction to Clearing and Settlement

CLEARING AND SETTLEMENT IN HISTORICAL PERSPECTIVE

1.1 Entering into a transaction has a certain thrill – the knowledge that you have secured a fabulous price for an unworthy asset or snapped up a precious thing for a song. But, as on-line shoppers know, the cost and inconvenience of postage and packing needs to be brought into account before the celebrations begin – for no transaction is over until the courier bearing the parcel is outside the door and the payment is in the bank. This book is about the 'postage and packing' of financial transactions.

Decades ago, securities were in paper form and payments were dependent on paper drafts and cheques as well. In the UK, securities settlement required delivery of share certificates and stock-transfer forms; the number of shares on the certificate might not match the number traded; title was recorded by company registrars many days after the trade was agreed; there was no simultaneity of delivery and payment. With the volumes of new shares being traded following the wave of privatisations in the 1980s, the UK market began to feel like the US had in the paper crunch some years before.

> 'The back offices of US securities brokers were not able to handle the sharp increase in trading volumes. The number of "fails", ie failures to deliver securities on the settlement date, soared in consequence, and so did losses from errors at brokerages. ... Declining revenues at a time when costs continued to rise resulted in the failures of many brokerage houses. ... The Securities and Exchange Commission (SEC) initially reacted to the back office problems by shortening the trading day in August 1967 and in early 1968, but with little effect. In the 1970s, the SEC imposed a compulsory surcharge on the commissions paid on small trades in order to prop up the income of brokerages, but even so expenses of the leading securities firms substantially exceeded income and sizeable backlogs remained. ... A 1973 report by the New York Stock Exchange found that three out of 10 investors had experienced lost or late-delivered securities.'[1]

As recently as 1993, the Economist wrote: 'London's share settlement is an acknowledged mess. It takes up to two weeks to settle trades, as 800,000 bits of paper are shuffled around. Electronic settlement should speed up and

---

[1] Ledrut, E and Upper, C, 'The US Paper Crunch 1967–1970' (December 2007) BIS Quarterly Review

rationalise the process.'[2] This comment heralded the introduction of CREST as the electronic settlement system for UK-listed company shares. Securities are now held in dematerialised, book-entry form; cash obligations are settled across the books of banks; and, more generally, payment by cheque is being phased out in many countries.

Clearing and settlement processes have been streamlined and centralised. Centralised settlement systems mean that it is no longer necessary for a buyer of shares to get in touch with the keeper of the shareholders' register for the company which issued the shares in order to have his ownership legally registered. Clearing systems cut down the paperwork so that buys and sells can be netted, and reduce the risks associated with broker bankruptcy. Computerisation and standardisation speeds everything up so that delivery and payment can occur together, and post-trade processes are no longer a log-jam giving rise to settlement failures and triggering bankruptcies.[3]

CLEARING AND SETTLEMENT DEFINED

1.2   For a person entering into the subject of clearing and settlement, the terminology – particularly the meaning of 'clearing' – is bewildering. Before making a detailed study of the subject, achieving clarity of defined terms is essential. Understanding the functions carried out by the different participants in the post-trade process is the key to understanding the terminology. This book cannot expect to change people's habits, though, so it is important for the reader to remember that other people may use terms in a different sense.

Table 1.1   Comparison of Terminology

Securities terms

European Central Bank glossary[4]	European Commission	Legislation
Clearing: the process of transmitting, reconciling and, in some cases, confirming transfer orders prior to settlement, potentially including the netting of orders and the establishment of final positions for settlement.	*Clearing*: the process of establishing settlement positions, including the calculation of net positions, and the process of checking that securities, cash or both are available.[5] *Clearing* is the process that occurs between trading	*Clearing* means the process of establishing positions, including the calculation of net obligations, and ensuring that financial instruments, cash, or both, are available to secure its exposures arising from those positions.[6]

---

2   The Economist (US), 27 November 1993.
3   See Knott, R, and Mills, A, 'Modelling risk in central counterparty clearing houses: a review' (December 2002) Bank of England Financial Stability Review, p 162
4   European Central Bank, *Glossary of terms related to payment, clearing and settlement systems* (December 2009), http://www.ecb.eu/pub/pdf/other/glossaryrelatedtopayment clearingandsettlementsystemsen.pdf
5   European Commission services, *Draft Working Document on Post-Trading* (May 2006), http:// ec.europa.eu/internal_market/financial-markets/docs/clearing/draft/draft_en.pdf
6   Commission Decision relating to Clearstream, Case COMP/38.096 – Clearstream (Clearing and Settlement) (July 2009) OJ C165/7

European Central Bank glossary	European Commission	Legislation
Sometimes this term is also used (imprecisely) to cover settlement. For the clearing of futures and options, this term also refers to the daily balancing of profits and losses and the daily calculation of collateral requirements.	and settlement. Clearing ensures that the buyer and the seller have agreed on an identical transaction and that the seller is selling securities which it is entitled to sell.[7] *Central counterparty clearing*: the process by which a third party interposes itself, directly or indirectly, between the transaction counterparties in order to assume their rights and obligations, acting as the direct or indirect buyer to every seller and the direct or indirect seller to every buyer.[8]	
Settlement: the completion of a transaction or of processing with the aim of discharging participants' obligations through the transfer of funds and/or securities. A settlement may be final or provisional.	*Book-entry settlement*: the act of crediting and debiting the transferee's and transferor's accounts respectively, with the aim of completing a transaction in securities.[9] *Settlement* is the final transfer of securities from the seller to the buyer and the final transfer of funds from the buyer to the seller, as well as the relevant annotations in securities accounts.[10]	*Settlement* means the completion of a securities transaction with the aim of discharging the obligations of participants through the transfer of funds or securities.[11]

7 European Commission services, *Draft Working Document on Post-Trading*

8 Regulation (EU) No 648/2012 of the European Parliament and of the Council of 4 July 2012 on OTC derivatives, central counterparties and trade repositories (EMIR), art 2(3)

9 European Commission service, *Draft Working Document on Post-Trading*

10 Commission decision relating to Clearstream

11 European Commission, *Proposal for a Regulation of the European Parliament and of the Council on improving securities settlement in the European Union and on central securities depositories (CSDs), etc*, (March 2012) COM(2012) 73 final, http://eur-lex.europa.eu/LexUriServ/LexUriServ.do?uri=CELEX:52012PC0073:EN:PDF, art 2(1)(2)

Payment terms

European Central Bank glossary	European Payments Council	Legislation
Automated clearing house (ACH): an electronic clearing system in which payment orders are exchanged among participants (primarily via electronic media) and handled by a data-processing centre.	*Clearing* is the process of transmitting, reconciling, and confirming payments of different types and the establishment of a final position for settlement either on an individual transaction basis or on a periodic basis for aggregated or netted positions.[12]	
Payment scheme: a set of interbank rules, practices and standards necessary for the functioning of payment services.	The *Scheme* establishes a set of interbank rules, practices and standards to be observed by Participants who adhere to the Scheme.[13]	*Payment scheme* means a single set of rules, practices, standards and/or implementation guidelines agreed between [payment service providers] for the execution of payment transactions across the Union and within Member States, and which is separated from any infrastructure or payment system that supports its operation.[14]
Payment system: this term has two meanings: 1) in some cases, it refers to the set of instruments, banking procedures and interbank funds transfer systems which facilitate the circulation of money in a country or currency area; 2) in most cases, it is used as a synonym for 'funds transfer system'.		*Payment system* means a funds transfer system with formal and standardised arrangements and common rules for the processing, clearing and/or settlement of payment transactions.[15]

12 European Payments Council, *PE-ACH/CSM Framework* (June 2008), http://www.europeanpaymentscouncil.eu/knowledge_bank_download.cfm?file=EPC170-05%20v1%20 2%20CSM%20Framework%20approved.pdf

13 European Payments Council, *SEPA Credit Transfer Scheme Rulebook version 5.1* (November 2011), http://www.europeanpaymentscouncil.eu/knowledge_bank_download. cfm?file=EPC125-05%20SCT%20RB%20v5.1%20Approved.pdf

14 Regulation (EU) No 260/2012 of the European Parliament and of the Council of 14 March 2012 establishing technical and business requirements for credit transfers and direct debits in euro, etc, art 2(7)

15 Regulation 260/2012, art 2(6)

European Central Bank glossary	European Payments Council	Legislation
Settlement: the completion of a transaction or of processing with the aim of discharging participants' obligations through the transfer of funds and/or securities. A settlement may be final or provisional.	*Settlement* is an act that discharges the obligations created through the clearing process with respect to liabilities between participating Scheme Participants.[16]	

Step 1 – matching

1.3   Two traders meet in electronic space, or, in some markets, on a physical trading floor, and believe they have struck a bargain, say to buy some shares at a given price, with payment and delivery to take place in accordance with the conventions applicable to the market in which they are operating. To be sure that they have indeed reached a binding agreement, there needs to be some mechanism to ensure that each has the same understanding as the other about their transaction. A difference of view on the essential terms of the bargain means that there is no binding contract.[17] Essential terms, in this context, will include the price; the number of shares; and the ISIN or other identification number of the shares. In most markets or trading contexts, the other terms of the bargain will be incorporated expressly under exchange or trading platform rules, or implied by market convention if they are notorious, certain and reasonable.[18] Even some of the essential economic, variable, terms may be generated automatically by the trading system – for example when a trader clicks on a particular offer to accept it, the economic terms will have been evident from the screen.

Nonetheless the need to ensure that the parties are 'ad idem' requires a *matching* process to weed out perceived trades where there was, in fact, no agreement. Matching systems are discussed in more detail in **section 4.2**. Matching can be defined as 'the process of reconciliation of transaction details, to ensure there is agreement on these details'. This definition closely follows the definition given by the European Commission's draft Working Document on Post-trading[19] to the term 'verification'.

Note, however, that 'matching', as defined above, does not include any process for repair of defective data or resolving discrepancies. Under English regulatory law,[20] an activity which 'brings about' a bargain between two trading persons is likely to be characterised as akin to broking, and providers of matching services will wish to heed the distinction between reconciliation (reporting a failure of matching) and intervention (resolving the mismatch, and thus bringing

---

16 European Payments Council, *PE-ACH/CSM Framework*
17 There are many cases; but see *Sudbrook Trading Estate v Eggleton* [1983] 1 AC 444 (failure to agree price); *Frederick E Rose (London) v William H Pim Jnr & Co* [1953] 2 QB 450 (failure to agree on type of goods sold)
18 *Cunliffe-Owen v Teather and Greenwood* [1967] 1 WLR 1421
19 European Commission services, *Draft working document on post-trading* (May 2006), http://ec.europa.eu/internal_market/financial-markets/docs/clearing/draft/draft_en.pdf
20 Financial Services and Markets Act 2000 (Regulated Activities) Order 2001, SI 2001/544, art 25(1)

about the trade). Regulation of post-trade activities in the United Kingdom is discussed further in **section 4.25**.

Step 2 – clearing

1.4   'Clearing' is the most over-used and least-understood term in post-trade services. To understand its purpose, it is probably best to begin with the world of payments, and a short history lesson.

> 'Every profession and every line of business, as well as every trade, develops its own peculiar terms and phrases. Those who become familiar with the routine of the business or the profession use these terms among themselves with a degree of precision and certainty of meaning which sometimes is difficult for one outside of the group to comprehend. The usage in this regard by banks and clearing-houses is no exception to the general rule. ... The term "to clear" ... takes on a broader meaning, and the only adequate conception of it is afforded by a view of the actual operations of a clearing-house ... '.[21]

This was written in 1900, by Mr James G Cannon, Vice-President of the Fourth National Bank of the City of New York, on the subject of bill- and cheque-clearing systems. Unfortunately usage has not got much more precise in the intervening century, and his comments retain their appropriateness today.

Nevertheless, what Cannon described as the functions of a clearing house is useful to show the current received usage of the term 'clearing'. In the clearing of cheques, representatives from banks which had taken in cheques from payee customers would gather together at a central location – the clearing house – and pile up the cheques drawn on each other bank. The other banks' representatives would exchange these piles of cheques, assess their validity, and agree the balances due between the banks. So far, this process does not need to involve a process of 'multilateral netting', or the striking of a single balance due to or from each participating bank; but indeed the settlement of the balances struck between the banks was done, in clearing houses both in the United States and in London, by reaching a single sum payable to or from all of the other participating banks. These settlement balances would typically be paid to the clearing house itself in the form of cash, with the clearing house acting as agent for the participating banks.[22]

1.5   These functions may still be observed nowadays, and may be automated – so that they are performed by an automated clearing house or ACH. ACHs are creatures found only in the clearing and settlement of payment transactions, but the functions of a clearing house in relation to post-trade activities regarding securities transactions are equivalent:

- the delivery and payment obligations of the participants are aggregated;
- a single net balance in respect of each type of obligation is struck for each participant;
- the net balances are settled with the clearing house.

On the other hand, one can identify some differences between clearing of payments and the clearing of securities transactions:

---

21 Cannon, J, *Clearing-Houses, Their History, Methods and Administration* (1900), republished by Lighting Source as ISBN 978-1-44462-475-5, p 3–4
22 Cannon, pp 35ff, 331ff

- a securities clearing house may have no role in the validation of the obligations of the participants;
- a securities clearing house will not normally act as the participants' agent, but instead become the counterparty – the central counterparty – in respect of the participants' trading;
- a securities clearing house will usually have an enhanced role in managing counterparty risk, in particular by taking margin and operating a default management mechanism if a participant fails.

Returning briefly to payment systems: the functions of 'clearing', as just described, and of 'settlement', which will be explicated below, can be provided by a single system. This is because only payment obligations are involved. There is no reciprocal exchange of one valuable thing for another in a payment system. Once the system has calculated who owes what to whom, it is only one step away from settling those obligations. Exchange-of-value systems have to be more complex than that: once the clearing system has calculated what the net delivery obligation of a participant is for a particular class of securities, and what the net payment obligation (or entitlement) of the same participant is, there are two obligations to be settled, and the likelihood is that different infrastructures will be engaged in the settlement process for the different obligations.

1.6   However, in the post-trade securities world, 'clearing' and 'settlement' need to be kept separate. 'Clearing' is what central counterparties (CCPs) do. A CCP would historically, at least in the context of futures transactions, have been called a 'clearing house', and indeed 'clearing organization' is the terminology still used in the Dodd-Frank Act to denote a CCP.[23] However, in the securities clearing context, ambiguity persists in the usage of the word 'clearing'. No doubt following the lead of ACHs established for clearing of payment transactions, the providers of securities settlement services described their activities as 'clearing', and the operator of the UK equities settlement system (CREST – operated by a company with the word 'Euro*clear*' in its name) is a 'recognised clearing house' under the Financial Services and Markets Act 2000.[24] 'Clearing' is, however, a misleading and unhelpful term to use for the activities of a *settlement* system. In this book, the term 'clearing' is not used for settlement services, except in some specific contexts (such as 'Model B Clearing'[25]) where even more confusion would follow from adopting a new term which is not recognised by any market participant. Avoiding ambiguity is essential, particularly as 'clearing' of derivatives products is now mandated by law, and clarity is needed over that thing which must legally now be done.

Definitively, then: *clearing* of securities transactions is the activity carried out by central counterparties to manage counterparty risk arising between parties to a transaction up to the moment of settlement. Taking a simple equities trade, what the CCP does is to interpose itself contractually between the buyer and seller, so that it becomes buyer to the seller and seller to the buyer. The process by which this is done is described further in **sections 2.3–2.4**. This interposition enables the CCP to offer two benefits to each of its participants. First, it can provide to any one participant multilateral netting of their whole book of trades, regardless

---

23   For example: Dodd-Frank Wall Street Reform and Consumer Protection Act of 2010, s 725
24   See the FSA register under the confusing heading 'Exchanges'.
25   See **section 18.26**

of their original counterparty: a trader who has sold 90 securities to party A at 10 am and then purchased 80 securities from party B at 10.15 am would prefer to settle only the net delivery obligation of ten securities; this can be done if the trades are cleared by the CCP, because the trader's counterparty for both original transactions is the CCP, which can net off the delivery obligations and prices against each other. (The reason that settlement systems are called 'clearing houses' is that settlement systems, like payment systems, can also perform this multilateral netting service, although there may be *British Eagle* risk in their doing so – see **box 2.1**). The second benefit which a CCP offers to its participants is a shield against counterparty default. How they do this is discussed extensively in **Chapter 14**. But the point here is that because the CCP is now the buyer for every sale transaction and the seller for every purchase, each participant faces only the CCP as its continuing counterparty. CCPs thus centralise all counterparty risks for each market they clear; and because of that, they call for margin and take other protective steps to ensure they can handle that concentration of exposure.

1.7   The confusion in defining 'clearing' is heightened because CCPs' membership eligibility criteria are tough – so many traders cannot deal directly with the CCP, having to engage the services of a 'general clearing member' (GCM) instead – who provides the trader with a 'clearing' service. So the trader now finds that the GCM is buyer for every sale and seller for every purchase, and the GCM sits in the middle between the trader and CCP in what is now becoming a chain of sales and purchases. GCMs' functions are, however, very similar to those of CCPs[26]: they can multilaterally net down the positions of each trader client with all the client's counterparties; and they assume counterparty risk, and so try to protect themselves against client defaults by calling margin and through other measures. The distinction between the GCM and the CCP is that the CCP is the *central* counterparty, which always faces GCMs and self-clearing traders (called individual clearing members or ICMs), whereas GCMs always have an asymmetry: in one direction they face their clients (traders), in the other they face the CCP. Both CCP and GCM are engaged in 'clearing', but without the CCP no clearing can take place.

1.8   'Clearing' can thus be characterised as the process whereby a person becomes interposed between two parties to a transaction, so that, as regards each party it has assumed the rights and obligations of the other party under that transaction. This definition may be compared with the definitions given by the European Commission's draft Working Document on Post-Trading, as set out in **table 1.1**.

The Commission's suggested definition of 'clearing' fails to capture the essence of clearing as described above. Calculation of settlement positions may be done by agencies such as data repositories which merely report to their participants on their net obligations without providing any assurance of the legal effectiveness of the netting process. CCPs and GCMs, which are intimately involved in 'clearing' in most market participants' minds, are not concerned with 'checking' that securities and cash are available – that is their clients' obligation – though by assuming the role of counterparty on a transaction they will become obliged to *deliver* the securities and *pay* the cash, not just check their availability. Settlement systems (whose functions may sometimes be

---

26 See **section 2.10**

called clearing) will check the availability of securities or cash before effecting a settlement, but to describe this essential part of a settlement function as 'clearing' is to perpetuate the confusion between clearing and settlement. The definition of clearing proposed by the Commission should therefore be rejected.

The definition proposed for 'central counterparty clearing' is closer to the mark, though still open to some criticism, as (particularly following the abolition of the concentration rule[27]) there are many ways to trade a particular instrument, so that even a 'central' counterparty will not often capture the whole of the trading in that instrument. What makes it 'central' is that, for a given population of market users, there is no other person carrying out clearing who deals only with GCMs and ICMs; or, to put the same point in different terms, there is no other person taking on counterparty risk in respect of more transactions (as originally entered into).

So, what distinguishes a CCP is not so much what it does (clearing) as who it does clearing for (GCMs and ICMs); it is not necessary to define clearing in terms of the activities of CCPs. The term 'clearing house' would generally be used to describe a CCP, rather than a GCM; but in some geographies 'clearing house' can include GCMs, so this term is avoided in this book.

1.9 Various other terms can be encountered, so a short glossary of these is set out below.

(1) *OTC clearing.* This phrase refers to 'clearing', in the sense defined above, for over-the-counter derivatives. The roles of the parties are no different from the case clearing of transactions which were entered into on an exchange or trading platform, except in three main respects: (i) the risks associated with the derivative product are likely to differ from an exchange-traded product; (ii) the derivative is likely to be cash-settled, so that settlement of delivery obligations will usually not be an issue; (iii) EMIR obliges many parties to ensure that their trades are cleared.[28]

(2) *Client clearing.* Some persons, being ineligible, cannot become members of CCPs. Yet EMIR may require them to clear certain trades, as discussed in **section 5.9**. It is possible for a non-member to retain a GCM to comply with EMIR; in some cases the GCM may also be the client's counterparty to the derivative trade. Where the GCM is also the counterparty the structure of the transaction is slightly unusual, as described in **section 2.15**. Further, where a party to a trade is a 'client', the opportunity for transfer of its positions and margin to a new GCM will be given under EMIR.[29]

(3) *Bilateral clearing.* This phrase refers to the *absence* of 'clearing' in the sense used in this book. Bilateral 'clearing' means that the parties to the transaction have not used a CCP to manage their counterparty risk. Instead they will typically have a netting agreement such as an ISDA master agreement with or without a credit support annex.[30] This arrangement will achieve netting and margining, and so has effects similar to 'clearing'. But to call it clearing is a misuse of terminology, as multilaterality and the interposition of a new counterparty are essential ingredients of 'clearing' in

---

27 See **section 3.2**

28 Regulation (EU) No 648/2012 of the European Parliament and of the Council of 4 July 2012 on OTC derivatives, central counterparties and trade repositories; see **sections 5.8ff**

29 See **section 6.29(3)**

30 International Swaps and Derivatives Association, *2002 ISDA Master Agreement* (January 2003), http://www.isda.org/publications/isdamasteragrmnt.aspx

its true sense. To call it bilateral *netting* would be more accurate and draw a better distinction against the *multilateral netting* function of a person carrying out *clearing*.

1.10   A final word on the subject of clearing may once again come from Mr James G Cannon. 'Occasionally the words "clearance" or "clearances", which, properly employed, designate space or distance, are used in the place of "clearing" and "clearings". Their employment in the place of the latter is not justified by general usage nor by the real meaning of these forms of the word.'[31] Hoorah: what was true in 1900 remains so today.

Step 3 – settlement

1.11   Whether or not a trade is cleared, the parties' obligations must be discharged by the buyer making a payment and the seller (assuming the trade involves the transfer of non-cash assets, rather than being purely cash-settled) making a delivery. Settlement can thus be defined as 'the process of effecting delivery or payment so as to discharge an obligation'.

This definition contrasts with the European Commission approach,[32] which defines 'book-entry settlement' as 'the act of crediting and debiting the transferee's and transferor's accounts respectively, with the aim of completing a transaction in securities'. This formulation may be open to criticism, because 'completing' is not a term of art, and aiming for it is too feeble (by contrast with the finality implicit in discharge of an obligation) and, if anything, restates the problem using a different word. More practically, the Commission's approach overlooks the possible involvement of more than one account-provider.

1.12   Settlement will usually occur by means of the transfer of entitlement to cash or assets across the books of a settlement system, which is responsible for keeping definitive records of entitlement. Ultimately, the definitive arbiter of entitlement to cash is the central bank for the currency concerned. Of course, most people do not have accounts at the central bank, and their entitlement to cash is represented by credits to bank accounts or cash accounts provided for them by other intermediaries. Payment systems provide the machinery by which payment obligations are settled (that is to say, by which payments are transferred); often payment systems are operated by central banks. For securities the functional equivalent of the central bank is typically a central securities depository (CSD), though this is not invariably the case. In particular, it is possible for the role of the person keeping the records which definitively establish the ultimate root of title to be distinct from that of the person providing the securities settlement system – the machinery by which title to securities is transferred. (**Section 2.16** looks in more detail at CSDs and title. **Chapters 9** and **10** are also concerned with entitlements to cash and securities held via an account provided by an intermediary, and the difference between this and cash and securities held directly at a central bank or CSD.)

As with clearing, not all traders will be eligible to participate directly in payment or settlement systems, and where this is the case they will need to hire

---

31   Cannon, pp 4–5
32   European Commission Services, *Draft Working Document on Post-Trading* (May 2006), http://ec.europa.eu/internal_market/financial-markets/docs/clearing/draft/draft_en.pdf

a service provider. To return to the European Commission's draft definition, it is possible for the trader to have a securities account and a cash account with his custodian bank, who will in turn participate in the securities settlement system and hold accounts at the central bank and the CSD in order to effectuate transfers of cash and securities across the definitive books of those institutions. Using the Commission's definition it would not be possible to say whether settlement occurred when the book entries were made at the central bank and CSD in relation to the custodian as account holder, or when the custodian made the entries on its own books in favour of the trader. Yet only one of these steps will be effective to discharge the obligation of the trading party with finality.[33]

1.13 Defining a CSD is more challenging. Dr Ruben Lee says that 'two aspects are commonly believed critical. First, a CSD is an entity that holds securities centrally either in certificated or dematerialised form. Second, a CSD enables the central transfer of ownership of securities, namely settlement, typically by means of book-entry transfer between securities accounts maintained on an electronic accounting system.'[34]

1.14 Historically, settlement services have been called 'clearing' services. Settlement functions on the London Stock Exchange, before the introduction of a rule compelling members to clear their trades through a CCP, were carried out by 'clearing firms' who (if they were Model B clearers) guaranteed to the market counterparty that their client would perform its obligations.[35] A 'clearing agreement' may therefore have nothing to do with participation in a CCP, but may be synonymous with a 'settlement services agreement'.

The settlement process can have features which resemble multilateral netting carried out by CCPs. Older settlement systems operate through a process called daily or cyclical net settlement[36] which net down the payment and delivery obligations of each participant. This methodology is subject to greater risk than the more modern real-time gross settlement, so nowadays the activities performed by settlement systems look more distinguishable from those of CCPs.

PAYMENT SCHEMES AND PAYMENT SYSTEMS

1.15 The structure of clearing and settlement of payments closely mirrors that discussed above in relation to securities transactions. Terminology is, again, confusing, with the phrases 'payment schemes' and 'payment systems' sometimes (but wrongly) being used as if they were synonymous. Nonetheless, while the risks assumed by the various participants in payments processing may differ from those applicable to participants carrying out equivalent functions in securities transaction processing, there are visible parallels. The overall 'payments system' can be divided into three stages: the generation of payment instructions; clearing; and settlement. There is an astonishing array of payment methodologies, though, which makes the analysis of the payments system and

---

33 Finality is considered in detail in **section 9.16**
34 Lee, R, *Running the World's Markets: The Governance of Financial Infrastructure* (Princeton University Press, 2011), ISBN 978-0-691-13353-9, p 23
35 Rules 10.13 and 10.14 of the old LSE rules, now repealed. See **section 18.26** for present-day Model B clearing services
36 See **section 2.30**

its substructures highly complex. Added to that, there are different patterns of payment usage in different countries,[37] and national concepts and solutions do not travel easily.

Creation of payment instructions

1.16 In the United Kingdom, the Payments Council has noted the following means of making a payment: cash, cheque, direct debit, direct credit, mobile payment, cards, and wholesale (interbank) transfer.[38] Apart from payments in cash, there are statutory rules, contractual rules and market conventions which govern the creation, formatting, transfer, receipt and processing of payment instructions. These rules create obligations for each of the participants in the payments process. It is therefore rather challenging to generalise about those obligations and to lay down hard principles which apply to all methodologies. It is, however, possible to distinguish the *creation and formatting* of payment instructions from the subsequent processes, which follow from the instructions, and bring about the *clearing or settlement* of the payment instructions. That distinction allows the formal separation of 'payment schemes' (responsible for instructions) from 'payment systems' (responsible for clearing and settlement). Examples of payment 'schemes', in this narrower sense, are the SEPA credit transfer and direct debit schemes for euro payments overseen by the European Payments Council.

1.17 The phrase 'payment system' thus typically means an organisation (which can include a consortium of banks acting under a commonly agreed rulebook) providing a clearing system or a settlement infrastructure. So, for example, the Office of Fair Trading defined a payment system as 'the shared part of an end-to-end process that offers an account-based transfer service between two final customers and two different banks'.[39] This would, as the OFT intended, capture 'the UK's money transmission clearing schemes ... and ... debit, credit, and ATM card networks.' A more useful definition is given by the glossary prepared by the Committee on Payment and Settlement Systems: 'a payment system consists of a set of instruments, banking procedures and, typically, interbank funds transfer systems that ensure the circulation of money.'[40]

Clearing and settlement

1.18 The meaning of 'clearing' and 'settlement' can be deduced from the discussion above in relation to securities. Settlement involves the discharge of the payment obligation, and thus implies the transfer of cash (or creation of an asset, such as an obligation owed by a commercial bank, which the parties accept as being functionally equivalent to the receipt of cash) to the payee. Clearing of

---

37 See for example Tumpel-Gugerell, G, *The Single Euro Payments Area in a Global Context* (January 2008), Speech, http://www.bis.org/review/r080123d.pdf

38 National Payments Plan (May 2008), http://www.paymentscouncil.org.uk/files/payments_files/national_payments_plan_may_2008.pdf

39 Office of Fair Trading, *UK Payment Systems* (May 2003), http://www.oft.gov.uk/shared_oft/reports/financial_products/oft658.pdf

40 Bank for International Settlements, *A glossary of terms used in payments and settlement systems* (March 2003) http://www.bis.org/publ/cpss00b.pdf?noframes=1

payments, however, does not necessarily involve the assumption of obligations to the whole market-place, as it does in relation to clearing of securities. The functions of an ACH were described in **sections 1.4–1.5**: it is possible, indeed it may be common, for an ACH to compile a schedule of the net payment obligations of the clearing system's participants inter se, and inform each of them of their net obligation or entitlement, without itself providing the central mechanism for exchange of the cash necessary to discharge those obligations. On the other hand, the ACH may be able to supplement its 'clearing' activity – the striking of net balances – with settlement functionality, for example where it can provide an account into which net payers pay in their net balances and from which the ACH can remit sums to net recipients.

1.19 Thus the phrase 'automated clearing house' denotes a clearing system which computes the settlement obligations of its participants on a multilaterally-netted basis, and then provides a file of net amounts to a central bank across the books of which transfers of cash balances can occur to settle those net obligations. The Euro Banking Association's EURO-1 clearing system historically followed this model. More recently, the trend for large-value payments has been to switch their methodology for settlement towards real-time gross settlement,[41] thereby reducing the process of multilateral netting as part of the settlement process; ACHs thus typically serve the high-volume, low-value retail payments market, dealing with payroll, corporate dividends, interbank reckoning-up from use of ATMs and so forth.

1.20 To a large degree the distinction between clearing and settlement in pure payments processing is of academic interest only. This is because, unlike clearing and settlement of securities transactions, regulatory guidance on payments infrastructure treats all payment systems – that is, both clearing and settlement – as subject to the same standards.[42] The important distinction is between payment schemes and payment infrastructures.

Separation of schemes from infrastructures

1.21 Competition is a powerful force in Europe as regards the shape of financial markets infrastructure. In a report into the banking industry in the United Kingdom,[43] Sir Don Cruickshank 'concluded that there were profound competition problems and inefficiencies associated with payment systems in the UK. The report found that the underlying economic characteristics of the systems did not deliver price transparency, good governance, non-discriminatory access, efficient wholesale pricing and innovation.'[44] Various initiatives were put in hand to improve the competitiveness of payment systems. These included a separation of the infrastructure service provider formerly owned by the provider of the UK Bacs payment schemes. A report prepared by VocaLink, the infrastructure provider, explains:

---

41 See **section 2.33**
42 See **section 6.41(1)** in particular and **Chapter 6** generally
43 Cruickshank, D, *Competition in UK Banking: A Report to the Chancellor of the Exchequer* (March 2000) http://www.hm-treasury.gov.uk/fin_bank_reviewfinal.htm
44 Office of Fair Trading, *UK Payment Systems* (May 2003), http://www.oft.gov.uk/shared_oft/reports/financial_products/oft658.pdf, para 1.5

'On the 1st December 2003, the governance structure of BACS and its owner-participants was fundamentally changed:

- The schemes and infrastructure components of BACS were placed in separate companies with no management linkage. ...

- The scheme company, named BACS Payments Schemes Limited ("BPSL"), representing the "buy side" in the clearing system, is now free to appoint any infrastructure provider it so wishes to operate its schemes.

- The "sell side", the infrastructure company [now VocaLink] is now able to provide payments infrastructure and other services freely to payments schemes and other potential users of its services in domestic and international markets, and to do so on a fully commercial, for-profit, basis.'[45]

This model has been followed in continental Europe too. Euro payment infrastructures are operated and governed independently: the European Payments Council, which is responsible for the payment schemes making up the Single Euro Payments Area, explains as follows:

'Separation of the Scheme from Infrastructure
The Scheme provides a single set of rules, practices and standards and is separate from any infrastructure that supports its operation. The Scheme is implemented by individual banks and (potentially multiple) infrastructure providers. Infrastructure providers include [clearing and settlement mechanisms] of various types and the technology platforms and networks that support them. Infrastructure is an area where market forces prevail, based on the decisions of banks. The result is that the interbank processing of credit transfers is provided on a consistent basis by multiple CSMs, chosen by individual banks as the most appropriate for their needs, but based on a single set of rules, practices and standards, as defined by the Scheme.'[46]

CONSTRUCTION OF EUROPE'S POST-TRADE INFRASTRUCTURE

1.22 Various influences have helped shape the infrastructure of clearing and settlement in Europe since the beginning of the century. These are rooted in a desire for efficiency and a desire for stability. Stability has been the predominant force in shaping payment systems, whereas efficiency has battled with stability for dominance in post-trade issues relating to securities. Latterly, as clearing of OTC derivatives became prominent as a political topic, other forces entered the fray.

---

45 Bacs Limited, *A New Legal Framework for Payments in the Internal Market – A Response Submitted to the Commission of the European Communities* (February 2004), http://ec.europa. eu/internal_market/payments/docs/framework/2004-contributions/bacs_en.pdf

46 European Payments Council, *SEPA Credit Transfer Scheme Rulebook*, version 5.1 (November 2011), http://www.europeanpaymentscouncil.eu/knowledge_bank_download. cfm?file=EPC125-05%20SCT%20RB%20v5.1%20Approved.pdf, s 1.5

Payment systems

1.23   Starting with the Lamfalussy[47] and Allsopp[48] reports, the concern of regulatory authorities has been to assure the safety of payment systems and their durability in a financial crisis. In November 1990, the Committee on Payment and Settlement Systems of the Bank for International Settlements (CPSS) issued a report of a committee chaired by Baron Lamfalussy, setting forth standards to be adhered to by prudently managed 'interbank netting schemes'. The risk being addressed was the danger of unwinding settlements in a system operating under a net settlement structure.[49] A second risk of similar gravity was settlement risk: the danger that one participant pays but receives nothing in return. This risk was addressed in 1996 by a seminal report of a CPSS committee chaired by Mr Peter Allsopp on settlement risk in foreign exchange transactions. Noting that 20 years had elapsed since the failure of Bankhaus Herstatt, with all that had entailed in settlement risk,[50] the CPSS called for action by the banking industry to address the problem. In due course this led directly to the establishment of the CLS system, described in **section 2.37**.

The trend since these reports has been to replace net settlement schemes with real time gross settlement structures and to encourage the development across the globe of a legal framework supporting finality of settlement of payments. These changes were largely completed in Europe at the beginning of the century, and since then there has been little interference at a policy level with the shape of payment systems. Politically, the scene has instead been dominated by European monetary and currency union, and the requirements of that great project to create payment schemes and payment systems which transcend national boundaries: the replacement of the patchwork TARGET system with TARGET2,[51] and the development of the single euro payments area[52] and associated payment systems to support it.

Securities settlement

1.24   Pressure for change in settlement systems for securities has, by contrast, come from the users of the industry. Paper crises and the need for efficient settlement structures to assist the wider economic needs of the nation have led countries to develop structures and legal rules to enable title to securities to be transferred as simply as cash balances, that is over the electronically-maintained books of a central securities depository (CSD).

International guidance on standards has been led by consortia of industry participants, notably the International Securities Services Association[53] and the

---

47 Bank for International Settlements, *Report of the Committee on Interbank Netting Schemes of the Central Banks of the Group of Ten countries* (November 1990) http://www.bis.org/publ/ cpss04.pdf

48 Bank for International Settlements, *Settlement Risk in Foreign Exchange Transactions* (March 1996) http://www.bis.org/publ/cpss17.pdf

49 See **box 2.2**

50 See **box 2.3**

51 See **section 2.35**

52 See European Payments Council, *Making SEPA a reality: the definitive guide to the Single Euro Payments Area* (September 2009) http://www.europeanpaymentscouncil.eu/knowledge_ bank_detail.cfm?documents_id=183

53 International Securities Services Association, *Recommendations 2000* (June 2000) http://www. issanet.org/pdf/rec2000.pdf

Group of Thirty.[54] The standards have focused primarily on efficiency, but with due regard to limitation of risk, in particular strengthening the linkage between transfer of title to securities and the payment (DvP or delivery versus payment). There has been official interest in risk management and safety, with the CPSS in particular issuing recommendations in 2001[55] and periodically following these up.

Since the creation of CSDs and the eurozone, the spotlight has, as with payments, been turned to the elimination of national silos so as to create a single European trading area for securities. Various structures have been tried and commented on: in particular, creating links between CSDs, and the Target2-Securities initiative of the European Central Bank, establishing a single settlement platform to be shared by all participating CSDs. These solutions are intended to enable CSDs to compete for business: competition is a powerful force in European post-trade services,[56] and nowhere is its influence more strongly felt than in the provision of central counterparty clearing services.

Clearing

1.25 Central counterparties (CCPs) have existed for many years. Largely because of the long tenor of the transactions concerned, their role was until the late 20th century focused on the listed derivatives (futures) markets: most futures exchanges would own or operate a clearing house (CCP), though in London some horizontal consolidation happened with the London Clearing House clearing for a clutch of exchanges, at one stage including the derivatives markets operated by the London International Financial Futures and Options Exchange, the London Metal Exchange, the London Commodity Exchange and the International Petroleum Exchange of London. For cash equities markets, there seemed little need to introduce clearing through a CCP. Pre-settlement counterparty risk was limited in duration, and structures were in place to ensure that stock exchange participants' obligations were underwritten by adequately robust institutions.

Beginning at the turn of the century this logic came under challenge. Increased volumes were one factor: having a CCP would allow for greater efficiencies in settlement, as a result of netting; this efficiency gain, coupled with the safety element introduced by having a CCP specialising in containment of counterparty risk, was enough to offset the additional cost of having clearing. The London Stock Exchange moved itself to a cleared structure in 2001. The arguments in favour of clearing for cash equities markets were not wholly clear: the Group of Thirty reported:

> 'At the clearing level, the key issue that the industry has to tackle is whether to establish CCPs. These have undoubted benefits in terms of reducing both cost and risk, but they are also costly to establish and maintain, and the cost-benefit equation will be different in each market. The Steering Committee expects that in most markets the benefits of using a CCP are likely to

---

54 Group of Thirty, *Global Clearing and Settlement: A Plan of Action* (January 2003)
55 Bank for International Settlements, *Recommendations for Securities Settlement Systems* (November 2001) http://www.bis.org/publ/cpss46.htm
56 See **Chapter 7**

outweigh the expense, but does not consider it wise to prejudge the outcome of a full and thorough analysis in specific markets.'[57]

Another paper noted a handful of potential *negative* effects on financial stability if a CCP were introduced: risk concentration, contagion, moral hazard as CCPs may be too big to fail, information asymmetry as participants would not have data about the CCP, limits on the CCP's liability, and the risk of a race to the bottom if CCPs compete with each other on risk issues.[58] These arguments have been more fully developed as, more recently, debate has taken place on the merits of compulsory clearing of OTC derivatives.[59] Nevertheless, with the influence of the International Securities Services Association and the European Securities Forum (ESF), momentum gathered to roll out the clearing model across Europe's cash equities markets.

The question, however, was how. Should there be a single CCP for Europe, as argued by the ESF,[60] or should CCPs compete for business? Competition should reduce costs, but, as explained in **section 7.24(2)**, industry infrastructure is subject to network effects and tipping, such that the most likely outcome (given a level playing-field) would be a single provider of central clearing services which had crowded out any others. But Europe's playing-field is not level, and national champions reign in their countries, and sometimes in their region. So, in July 2007, there were nine CCPs operating in the EU;[61] at the start of 2010, the European Association of CCP Clearing Houses listed 20 members, of which 17 were in the EEA.[62] Part of the reason for the plethora of providers is that some CCPs are in common ownership with CSDs or exchanges. Another complication is that interoperability links between CCPs are extremely difficult to forge,[63] so that participants wishing to choose different CCPs have not been allowed a real choice and high quality CCPs have not been able to win business in markets where they are not the incumbent. The official policy of the European Commission is in favour of competition;[64] but the voice of the integrators was hard to quell,[65] including in their number even the European Parliament, still arguing for a single pan-European CCP as late as August 2009.[66]

57 Group of Thirty, *Global Clearing and Settlement: A Plan of Action* (January 2003)

58 Ripatti, K, *Central counterparty clearing: constructing a framework for evaluation of risks and benefits* (December 2004), Bank of Finland Discussion Paper No.30, http://papers.ssrn.com/sol3/papers.cfm?abstract_id=787606

59 See **Chapter 5**

60 European Securities Forum, *EuroCCP: ESF's Blueprint for a Single Pan-European Central Counterparty* (December 2000)

61 Kalogeropoulos, G, Russo, D, and Schönenberger, A, 'Link Arrangements of Central Counterparties in the EU – Results of an ESCB Survey' in *The Role of Central Counterparties* (European Central Bank/Federal Reserve Bank of Chicago, July 2007), http://www.ecb.eu/pub/pdf/other/rolecentralcounterparties200707en.pdf, p 50

62 http://www.eachorg.eu/each/EACH_information/?contentId=11976

63 See **sections 13.17ff**

64 European Commission Communication, *Clearing and Settlement in the European Union – the way forward* (April 2004), COM(2004) 312 final, http://eur-lex.europa.eu/LexUriServ/LexUriServ.do?uri=CELEX:52004DC0312:EN:HTML

65 European Securities Services Forum, *A Vision for Integrated Post-Trade Services in Europe* (August 2009) http://essf.sifma.org/publications/documents/ESSF%20Post%20Trading%20Vision%20Paper%20final%20version%20Aug09.pdf

66 European Parliament Directorate-General for Internal Policies, *Clearing and Settlement in the EU* (August 2009), IP/A/ECON/ST/2008-31 PE 416.242

The Giovannini barriers and beyond

1.26 In 2001, a committee chaired by Professor Alberto Giovannini carried out an investigation into cross-border clearing and settlement in the European Union. The committee identified 15 barriers to efficient clearing and settlement of cross-border trades, attributable to the fact that separate clearing and settlement systems had developed nationally, each with the objective of serving their local market.[67] (A 'cross-border securities transaction' involves a market participant buying or selling securities issued outside their home country.)

1.27 The European Commission issued two Communications on clearing and settlement, setting out its vision for resolving the problems highlighted by Prof Giovannini.[68] The European Commission concluded in its Second Communication that four policies should be pursued: 'liberalisation and integration' of securities clearing and settlement systems – that is, the enablement of rights of choice and access; application of competition policy to address restrictive market practices; a common regulatory framework for financial stability and investor protection, 'leading to the mutual recognition of systems'; and the implementation of appropriate governance arrangements.

Table 1.2   Legal measures to dismantle the Giovannini barriers

	Barrier description	Whether alleviated by T2S	Whether solution (partly) legal	Legal measures	Date of enactment
1.	National differences in information technology and interfaces used by clearing and settlement providers	Y		None	
2.	National clearing and settlement restrictions require use of multiple systems	Y	(Y)	EMIR CSD Regulation	2012 ?
3.	Differences in national rules relating to corporate actions, beneficial ownership and custody	Y	Y	MiFID (re custody) Shareholder Voting Rights Directive Securities Law Directive	2004 2007 ?
4.	Absence of intra-day settlement finality	Y	Y	Settlement Finality Directive	1998

---

67 Giovannini, A, *Cross-Border Clearing and Settlement Arrangements in the European Union* (November 2001) http://ec.europa.eu/internal_market/financial-markets/docs/clearing/first_giovannini_report_en.pdf

68 European Commission, *Clearing and settlement in the European Union – Main policy issues and future challenges* (May 2002), COM(2002) 257 final, http://eur-lex.europa.eu/LexUriServ/LexUriServ.do?uri=CELEX:52002DC0257:EN:HTML; European Commission, *Clearing and Settlement in the European Union – The way forward* (April 2004), COM(2004) 312 final, http://eur-lex.europa.eu/LexUriServ/LexUriServ.do?uri=CELEX:52004DC0312:EN:HTML

	Barrier description	Whether alleviated by T2S	Whether solution (partly) legal	Legal measures	Date of enactment
5.	Practical impediments to remote access to national clearing and settlement systems	Y		MiFID EMIR CSD Regulation	2004 2012 ?
6.	National differences in settlement periods			CSD Regulation	?
7.	National differences in operating hours and settlement deadlines	Y		None	
8.	National differences in securities issuance practice			None	
9.	National restrictions on the location of securities		Y	CSD Regulation	?
10.	National restrictions on the activity of primary dealers and market makers		(Y)	None	
11.	Domestic withholding tax regulations serving to disadvantage foreign intermediaries		Y	Withholding Tax Recommendation	2009
12.	Transaction taxes collected through a functionality integrated into a local settlement system		(Y)	None	
13.	Absence of an EU-wide framework for the treatment of interests in securities		Y	Securities Law Directive	?
14.	National differences in the legal treatment of bilateral netting for financial transactions		Y	Financial Collateral Directive Recovery and Resolution Directive	2002 ?
15.	Uneven application of national conflict of law rules		Y	Settlement Finality Directive Financial Collateral Directive Securities Law Directive	1998 2002 ?

The Commission also set up a 'legal certainty group' and a 'fiscal compliance group' to tackle specific Giovannini barriers, sponsored the development of a Code of Conduct by infrastructures,[69] created a 'monitoring group' to report on behaviour under the Code of Conduct, and a 'clearing and settlement advisory and monitoring expert group' (CESAME) to work on removal of the Giovannini barriers. Much of this was done in order to avoid having a directive on clearing and settlement; without legislation, rights of choice and access proved to be unattainable, ex-post competition enforcement was incapable of dismantling national silos, a unified regulatory framework was non-existent, and governance arrangements were dictated nationally by local regulators. European legislation was eventually put forward for adoption in 2010. It is difficult to see how the changes recommended by Prof Giovannini could be achieved without it.

Continuing evolution

1.28   The advances and changes to infrastructures developed over the first years of the 21st century thus have not created a settled new world. Such rapid evolution was bound to lead to tension and a struggle for survival of the fittest. Further consolidation, rearrangement and development are unavoidable. The concerns expressed at the beginning of the century that clearing and settlement were expensive and under-regulated continue to be heard; in particular, a continuing belief that post-trade services in Europe are very expensive by comparison with the US lies at the heart of much policy thinking, notwithstanding that the various studies done are difficult to interpret.

1.29   Some comments might be made on the question of costs. First, comparison of methodologies merits a whole thesis of its own: it depends who you ask and what you are asking about.[70] Secondly, there are many possible explanations for the US-EU differential, ranging from a fragmented, nationally-focused marketplace in Europe to inherent market differences rooted in investor behaviour, trading styles, pension planning, and economic cohesion. Clearing and settlement have remained predominantly single-state activities in Europe, whereas in the US they have since the mid-1970s been carried out country-wide. Thirdly, the differences between the EU and the US are important, even if they exist more in perception than experience: the sense that Europe is behindhand is a powerful force for change.

Change, therefore, has continued to be a defining characteristic of the clearing and settlement industry in Europe. Competition has been invoked as a traditional – perhaps over-used – remedy for reduction of costs. **Chapter 7** explores in more detail the role which competition policy has played in shaping European clearing and settlement infrastructure. In the early years of the century, cost and competition policy were in the ascendant: with attacks on interbank processing fees for processing payments, challenges to the position of ICSDs, development of multiple centres of liquidity for trading, and encouragement of interoperability to facilitate competition in clearing and settlement. Clearing

---

69   http://ec.europa.eu/internal_market/financial-markets/docs/code/code_en.pdf
70   Oxera Consulting, *Methodology for monitoring prices, costs and volumes of trading and post-trading activities* (July 2007) http://ec.europa.eu/internal_market/financial-markets/docs/clearing/oxera_study_en.pdf

and settlement are not risk-free activities, but cautious attention to risk control increases cost. But then there was a financial crisis, which allowed a more balanced philosophy of infrastructures, risk and regulation to emerge, as well as a clutch of new legislation. EMIR has imposed rules on capital, structure and governance of CCPs. A new code of laws has eliminated many, if, alas, not all, areas of legal uncertainty about securities held in accounts. And internationally accepted standards of safety in payment, securities settlement and clearing systems have received quasi-legislative status in Europe.

Table 1.3 Studies of post-trade costs

Study	Cost of clearing and settlement in Europe	Cost of clearing and settlement in the US	Observations
CEPS, 2001[71]	€ 2.98 per transaction	€ 2.77 per transaction	'Operating income per transaction' for securities settlement systems was assessed. With International Central Securities Depositories and without netting the differential was more acute: € 3.10 in Europe compared with € 0.40 in the US
Niels et al, 2001[72]	€ 4.43 per transaction	€ 0.41 per transaction	'Income per transaction' data taken from published accounts of infrastructure providers
NERA, 2004[73]	€ 0.35–0.80 per transaction	€ 0.10 per transaction	Study of tariffs charged by infrastructure providers for equities trades
Oxera, 2009[74]	€ 0.43–2.44 per transaction	No data	Survey of broker-dealers' reports on costs of clearing and settlement for equities trades
Oxera, 2011[75]	€ 0.36 per transaction	No data	Survey (for equities trades) of revenues received by service providers and costs experienced by users divided by transaction number

---

71 Lannoo, K, and Levin, M, *The Securities Settlement Industry in the EU: Structure, Costs and the Way Forward* (December 2001), Research Report, Centre for European Policy Studies, ISBN 92-9079-362-7

72 Niels, G, Barnes, F, and van Dijk, R, 'Unclear and Unsettled: The debate on Competition in the Clearing and Settlement of Securities Trades' (December 2003) ECLR 634

73 NERA Economic Consulting, *The Direct Costs of Clearing and Settlement: an EU-US Comparison* (June 2004) Corporation of London, City Research Series Number 1, http://secure-uk.imrworldwide.com/cgi-bin/b?cg=downloadsedo&ci=cityoflondon&tu=http://217.154.230.218/NR/rdonlyres/0A6216E8-6153-44F3-B1EA-55FFA4CB19C2/0/BC_RS_clearsettle_0406_FR.pdf

74 Oxera Consulting, *Monitoring prices, costs and volumes of trading and post-trading services* (July 2009), http://ec.europa.eu/internal_market/financial-markets/docs/clearing/2009_07_ec_report_oxera_en.pdf, para 7.2.2

75 Oxera Consulting, *Monitoring prices, costs and volumes of trading and post-trading services* (May 2011), MARKT/2007/02/G, Report prepared for European Commission DG Internal Market and Services, http://ec.europa.eu/internal_market/financial-markets/docs/clearing/2011_oxera_study_en.pdf

Giovannini revisited

1.30   After a period of more than ten years, the Giovannini barriers are due for re-assessment. A review was carried out by the European Commission's Expert Group on Market Infrastructures in 2011 (the EGMI Report).[76] The review summarises developments and the then state of the post-trade market, but notes that progress has in fact been poor. Professor Giovannini is quoted as saying:

> '[T]he political economy of the reform of EU financial market infrastructure has the following characteristics:
> - like monetary reform, it is an arcane subject with little genuine political appeal;
> - like other forms of international liberalizations, the gainers are dispersed and largely unaware of what is going on, let alone the potential gains of the reform;
> - the industry of financial markets infrastructure is not all against reform, but many actors feel threatened by it (many protected markets would disappear);
> - the intensely technical nature of the reform hinders the power of initiative of authorities;
> - the consultations process allows de-facto over-representation of post-trading industry interests.
>
> These conditions would lead to predictions that broadly match the actual outcome so far: reform has been very slow; all fundamental aspects of reform, that is the legal and regulatory framework that would allow true consolidation and integration of post-trading service providers, are still to start in a significant way. In other words, since the interest groups with relatively more effective influence on policymaking are ambivalent about the gains from liberalization (some certain market advantages would be lost), since policymakers are not under pressure to move forward, and may well be concerned about undesired and unforeseen effects of reform, progress has been very slow.'[77]

The EGMI Report ends with three policy options offered for the further consideration of the European Commission: re-booting Giovannini; designing a frictionless infrastructure from scratch; and a halfway measure. Perhaps the most interesting vision is that of the frictionless infrastructure, which would comprise the following elements:

- a standardised trading and clearing system;
- a small number of utility CCPs;
- inclusion of CCPs in resolution planning for systemically important institutions;
- transparency on transaction costs.

The other two policy proposals set forth an agenda of largely industry-led objectives designed to relieve further the barriers identified by the original Giovannini report, and studies to examine issues such as insolvency protections, infrastructures to support loan and bond markets, and vertical silos.[78] However,

---

76 Expert Group on Market Infrastructures (EGMI), Report (October 2011), http://ec.europa.eu/internal_market/financial-markets/docs/clearing/egmi/101011_report_en.pdf
77 EGMI Report, p 29
78 See **section 7.20**

the EGMI Report did not appraise the continuing relevance of the Giovannini recommendations. In that regard, the following observations might be made:

(1) The tension between policy designed to improve market structure and policy designed to facilitate fair competition is poorly handled. Competition policy sometimes obstructs market development, either through an excess of dogmatism (multiple CCPs are considered desirable regardless of the risk and complexity of interoperability arrangements[79]) or through an excess of zeal (standard-setting, which is necessary to create harmony, can be thought dangerous owing to the penal powers of the Commission[80]). Without coherence and proper balance of these policy forces, development will be inhibited.

(2) National incumbents continue to dominate the scene. Single markets should not need single-nation solutions. But the dominance of national infrastructures is a force for conservatism and confuses debate. One example is whether 'vertical silos' are desirable, since the 'for' arguments may be protectionism disguised in stability and safety clothing.

(3) On the other hand, national legal differences create real barriers, some of which are difficult to pull down, where the desire to invoke national protectionism is absent. 'Choice of CSD' for issuers will remain out of reach in practice until a clean dividing line is drawn between corporate law (the internal affairs of an issuer) and investment law (the trading and post-trading affairs).[81] This question, which is Giovannini Barrier 9 (location of securities), is the most challenging of the barriers still in place at the time of the EGMI Report.

(4) Further work is needed on some legal reforms actually carried out. In particular the Financial Collateral Directive[82] and the proposed Securities Law Directive[83] ought to have achieved a more reliable code of laws for how to acquire ownership, and how to acquire a security interest, in securities held in an account at an intermediary such as an agent bank. Unfortunately, the law and practice on this topic remains mysterious, complex, expensive to understand and encrusted with national differences. Furthermore, the Securities Law initiative is at risk because of the desire of policy-makers to add controversial investor-protection objectives into the law rather than focus on its central 'law of property' objective.

(5) Some types of infrastructure are systemically as vital as clearing and settlement infrastructures. Communications and matching service providers are examples. Barriers, which may be less visible than those identified by Giovannini, can also arise in these sub-sectors of the post-trade space. Control of data and its flow continue to determine who is allowed to provide post-trade services. For example, the need for access to transaction feeds has been identified as a necessity to enable competition among post-trade service providers to take place.[84]

---

79 See **Chapter 13**
80 See **section 7.28**
81 Cf **section 10.24**
82 Directive 2002/47/EC of the European Parliament and of the Council of 6 June 2002 on financial collateral arrangements; see **sections 8.25ff**
83 See **section 10.8**
84 See **sections 4.6–4.13**

(6) Finally, the marketplace will undoubtedly change further as a result of the introduction of mandatory clearing for OTC derivative transactions.

OTC DERIVATIVES CLEARING

1.31 Following the financial disasters of 2007–2008, central counterparties became regarded as saviours of the day. The various CCPs which had handled the default of Lehman Brothers were deemed to have performed well, and the stability which their processes had engendered was seen as a benefit which could be extended to other areas of financial business, in particular credit default swaps.[85]

The European Commission urged derivatives trading firms to develop clearing solutions for credit derivatives, and obtained a written commitment[86] to make clearing via a CCP possible for these products. By July 2009, Internal Market and Services Commissioner McCreevy was able to announce:

'Back in October 2008, I called upon the industry to reduce the risks inherent in the credit default swaps market, in particular by moving the clearing of these contracts onto a European central counterparty (CCP). The financial crisis highlighted a number of problems in the credit default swaps market, especially where transparency, market concentration and risk mitigation were concerned. Clearing through central counterparties is key to improving risk management and to increasing the stability of the financial system. I am pleased that the extraordinary efforts by the industry and service providers have made it possible that two European CCPs are starting to clear these products now, with a third aiming to launch its service by the end of the year. The existence and the use of more than one CCP is essential for the proper development of a safe and competitive environment.'[87]

That, however, marked the beginning, not the end. The debate on the merits and implementation of clearing of OTC products merits a discussion of its own, which is reserved for **Chapter 5**.

---

85 See the European Commission's Communications *Ensuring efficient, safe and sound derivatives markets* (July 2009), COM (2009) 332 final http://eur-lex.europa.eu/LexUriServ/LexUriServ.do?uri=COM:2009:0332:FIN:EN:PDF and *Ensuring efficient, safe and sound derivatives markets: future policy actions* (October 2009), COM (2009) 563 final http://eur-lex.europa.eu/LexUriServ/LexUriServ.do?uri=COM:2009:0563:FIN:EN:PDF

86 International Swaps and Derivatives Association, letter to Commissioner McCreevy (March 2009), http://ec.europa.eu/internal_market/financial-markets/docs/derivatives/2009_02_17_isda_letter_en.pdf

87 European Commission, press release IP/09/1215 (July 2009), http://europa.eu/rapid/pressReleasesAction.do?reference=IP/09/1215&format=HTML&aged=0&language=EN&guiLanguage=en

2 What happens in Clearing and Settlement

2.1   This chapter is about infrastructures and their participants. Having established the terminology of clearing and settlement, the next objective is to describe who does what, and how: the essential functions of a CCP, a CSD, and a payment system, the roles which the agent banks which participate in those systems carry out, and where this leaves the end-user clients whose transactions are submitted to them for clearing and settlement.

CLEARING

2.2   Clearing requires the involvement of a CCP.[1] The principal role of the CCP in a securities transaction is to become buyer to every seller and seller to every buyer. (In a derivatives transaction, the position is similar: the CCP will become Party A to every Party B and Party B to every Party A – taking an interest rate swap as example, the CCP will become the fixed rate payer to the floating rate payer, and floating rate payer to the fixed rate payer.)

Novation

2.3   The process by which the CCP becomes the counterparty to the original parties to a trade is typically by novation. Novation is appropriate where the original clients have a binding contractual relationship with each other from the moment that their transaction details are inputted into the relevant trading system and matched. When this is the case, to replace each other as counterparty, the original contract between the traders needs to be torn up and replaced by two new contracts, one between the seller and the CCP and the other between the CCP and the buyer. This is the model in use by CCPs such as LCH.Clearnet for SwapClear[2] and Eurex Clearing for OTC transactions,[3] for example.[4]

---

1   See **section 1.6**
2   LCH.Clearnet Limited, *General Regulations* (February 2012), http://www.lchclearnet.com/rules_and_regulations/ltd/, reg 48
3   Eurex Clearing AG, *Clearing Conditions* (March 2012), http://www.eurexclearing.com/download/documents/regulations/clearing_conditions/clearing_conditions_en.pdf   number 1.2.2(2)
4   Cf **section 14.19**

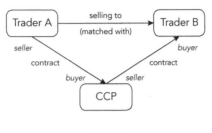

Fig 2.1

Open offer

2.4   An alternative to novation is 'open offer.' This technique was used by the now-defunct foreign exchange clearing house ECHO, and is used by Eurex Clearing for exchange-originated transactions.[5] Open offer is simpler than novation, in that there is never a binding contract between the two original clients: the trading and matching system rules, coupled with the rules of the CCP, provide that a matched bargain gives rise to the two contracts between seller and CCP and between buyer and CCP. The open offer structure, under English law, relies on the doctrine set forth in the well-known (if rarely read) case of *Carlill v Carbolic Smoke Ball Co,*[6] under which a binding contract can be achieved if one party (here, the CCP) states openly that it is willing to be contractually bound if the other party (here, either of the original clients) performs certain acts. The open offer idea is, however, not peculiar to English law of contract and should be effective under other legal systems.[7]

Multilateral netting

2.5   The impact of the CCP becoming interposed into every transaction is that the number, and size, of each participant's transactions will be reduced by a process of multilateral netting. This is shown in **figure 2.2**, which takes a rather artificial example of only three trades in the same security for settlement on the same day between three participants. Multilateral netting may thus be regarded as a primary function of a CCP, and sometimes CCPs have been characterised by reference to this aspect of their operations.[8] Although a modern clearing house acts as central counterparty – taking on the contractual performance obligation vis-à-vis each participant – it was not always so.

Clearing houses carry out a useful role in optimising the efficiency of settlements, and for this it is not necessary for the clearing house to become counterparty to each of its members' transactions. On one view, the function of a clearing house is to perform the calculations necessary for the multilateral netting process, without assuming contractual responsibility for the deliveries. Back in the 19th century, the clearing house could optimise deliveries among traders so as to avoid the inefficiencies if each pair of contracting parties had

---

5   Eurex Clearing Conditions, number 1.2.2(1)
6   [1893] 1 QB 256, CA
7   Cf Zweigert, K, and Kötz, H, *Comparative Law* (3rd Edn translated by Tony Weir, Oxford University Press, September 1995), ISBN 0-19-826859-9, ch 26
8   See **sections 1.5–1.6**

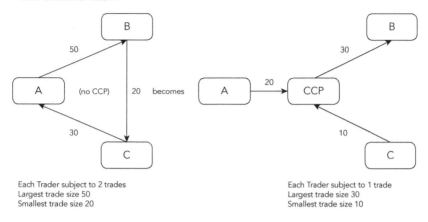

Trader A sells 50 to Trader B
Trader B sells 20 to Trader C
Trader C sells 30 to Trader A

Each Trader subject to 2 trades
Largest trade size 50
Smallest trade size 20

Each Trader subject to 1 trade
Largest trade size 30
Smallest trade size 10

Fig 2.2

Table 2.1   Why multilateral netting reduces recovery for the unsecured creditors of a defaulter

Position for B's liquidator and creditors with and without multilateral netting based on scenario of figure 2.2

B's assets and liabilities without multilateral netting	B's assets and liabilities with multilateral netting
Assets: A owes 50 to B Liabilities: C is owed 20 by B	Assets: CCP owes 30 to B Liabilities: none
C also has to pay up the 30 he owes to A, and as a creditor of B's estate is entitled to a dividend on the 20 owed by B	C's original obligation to pay 20 to B is netted along with the 30 C owes to A C therefore pays a net 10 to the CCP
Outcome: B's liquidator gets 50 for the estate C pays 30 immediately and has to wait for the hope of a recovery from B's estate	Outcome: B's liquidator gets 30 for the estate, so the estate is worse off C has immediate satisfaction and no loss – C is not treated as a creditor as C's position is handled outside the estate

both to deliver and receive. If the clearing house were to have control of the settlement process, it could determine that the more efficient outcome would be for the deliveries to be arranged as if there were a CCP, simply by informing the participants about what should be delivered and to whom; or, better still, by accepting the net deliveries-in and arranging for the net deliveries-out to take place at its premises.[9]

---

9   Cf Kroszner, R, 'Central Counterparty Clearing: History, Innovation and Regulation' in *The Role of Central Counterparties* (European Central Bank/Federal Reserve Bank of Chicago, July 2007), http://www.ecb.eu/pub/pdf/other/rolecentralcounterparties200707en.pdf, pp 30–35

2.6   While it is certainly possible for a clearing house to calculate and restate the participants' obligations without becoming contractually bound on their transactions – that is, without becoming a CCP – it is not self-evident that this form of clearing will be legally effective in the event of default by a participant. The effectiveness of a multilateral netting scheme for which the clearing house was not a CCP was tested in the *British Eagle* case (see **box 2.1**). The objection, which struck down the multilateral netting arrangements in use there, was that the distribution of the insolvent participant's assets gave a better return to the other participants in the arrangements than to creditors generally, and that was contrary to the policy of the insolvency laws. The same objection might be made in respect of any clearing house arrangement, but a clearing house which becomes central counterparty has a defence available: because it is the counterparty as principal to all of the insolvent participant's trades, it is merely trying to strike a net balance *bilaterally* with the insolvent participant, and there is no unfairness to creditors provided that the mechanisms for interposing the clearing house as CCP, and for bilateral netting between the clearing house and the insolvent participant, are both effective and can withstand a supervening insolvency.

Box 2.1   Case study – the *British Eagle* case

British Eagle was an airline which participated in a multilateral netting scheme operated by the International Air Transport Association (IATA) to deal with the criss-crossing payment obligations which arise between airlines which carry each other's passengers, for example when passengers switch flights. IATA would carry out a monthly tally of what each airline owed each other participating airline, calculate a net sum due to or from each airline, and oversee the collection and distribution of the amounts thus calculated. British Eagle went into liquidation and its liquidator objected to the operation of the IATA scheme, asserting that its operation was contrary to the mandatory scheme of distribution of a company's assets in a winding-up. By a majority of 3–2 the House of Lords agreed.[10]

The problem with the IATA set-up was that it could lead to a better outcome for the surviving participants than if they had retained their original obligations and entitlements (see **table 2.1** for a model illustration as to how this might arise). The enhanced benefit for participants, achieved at the expense of the other creditors of the insolvent participant, was the feature which was contrary to the insolvency rules.

IATA subsequently modified its rules, so that the clearing house became a CCP, and in a more recent airline insolvency case the multilateral netting system was upheld by the Australian courts.[11]

---

10 *British Eagle International Air Lines v Compagnie Nationale Air France* [1975] 1 WLR 758, HL
11 *Ansett Australia Holdings Limited v International Air Transport Association* [2006] VSCA 242, Victoria Court of Appeal

2.7   Across Europe, insolvency codes are likely to have difficulties with multilateral netting systems similar to those explored in *British Eagle* because of the detriment to the general body of creditors caused by what is essentially a private mini-liquidation. The solution of converting to bilateral netting through interposing the clearing house as principal contracting party may not be available in respect of participants which are wound up under other systems of law. To overcome the difficulty arising from insolvency law objections, CCPs will wish to seek protection under an internationally-recognised legislative measure designed to insulate market infrastructures from interference by liquidators or insolvency laws, such as the Settlement Finality Directive.[12]

CLEARING MEMBERS

2.8   Where an original party to a trade is not a direct participant in the CCP it may be necessary to hire a third party to act as its 'general clearing member' (GCM). The terminology refers to the historical practice whereby members of exchanges were either members of the CCP (thus 'clearing' members *of the exchange*) or not ('non-clearing-members'). Non-clearing members of exchanges (NCMs) need to hire a third party to clear for them if the exchange requires that all trades be cleared; a clearing member willing to clear other members' trades as well as its own will be a 'general' clearing member. Nowadays many transactions do not originate on exchanges and participation in a CCP may not be linked to membership of any exchange, so that 'GCM' may be something of a misnomer when it merely denotes participation in a CCP with a view to providing access to the CCP for persons who are not CCP participants. Nevertheless, EMIR adopts similar usage: participants in CCPs are referred to as 'clearing members', even though there may be no other class of 'member' of the CCP. It may also be noted that a GCM may not actually indulge in trading activity at all – it may specialise in clearing and (where permitted) decline membership of any exchange.

2.9   A GCM may be needed by a trader because the criteria for participation in the CCP are likely to be tougher than those for participation in a trading platform. This is because the CCP is taking on counterparty risk with each new participant it admits to its select club, and its first line of defence against that risk will be in those criteria.[13] On the other hand, members of the exchange or trading platform which can meet the CCP's criteria can (if they choose to do so) 'self-clear', thus being dubbed 'individual clearing members' (ICMs) of the exchange.

Internalised clearing by GCMs

2.10   As clearing becomes more popular, more stress is placed on GCMs, which to a degree centralise counterparty risk in a similar manner to CCPs. Because a GCM provides services to several NCMs, the possibility arises that one NCM may be selling to another NCM using the same GCM. Depending on how the CCP handles such transactions, the CCP may be cut out of the clearing

---

12 Directive 98/26/EC of the European Parliament and of the Council of 19 May 1998 on settlement finality in payment and securities settlement systems; see **sections 8.18ff**
13 See **section 14.12**

process altogether, as shown in **figure 2.3**. If the CCP nets off the transactions immediately where the same GCM is on both the 'buy' and 'sell' sides, the transaction will completely disappear as far as the CCP is concerned. The remaining transactions of a GCM, which remain on the books of the CCP until an opposite transaction is registered or settled, is described as the GCM's 'open interest' in transactions of that type. The immediate netting of opposite trades at the CCP, which leaves the GCM as sole clearer for the open interest in all the transactions effected between its own clients, in effect 'internalises' part of the clearing within the GCM.[14] A risk issue which (in theory) arises when there are very few GCMs in a market is that a GCM which has a very attractive service offering might even find itself taking on more counterparty risk than a CCP.

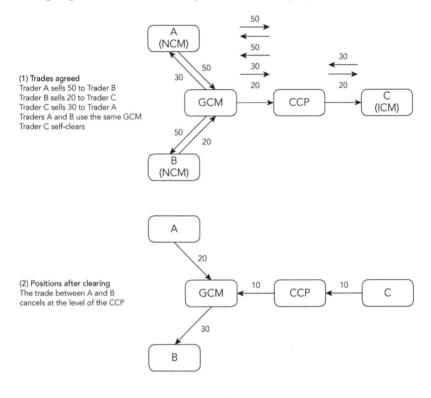

(1) Trades agreed
Trader A sells 50 to Trader B
Trader B sells 20 to Trader C
Trader C sells 30 to Trader A
Traders A and B use the same GCM
Trader C self-clears

(2) Positions after clearing
The trade between A and B
cancels at the level of the CCP

Fig 2.3

2.11   The total disappearance of trades from a CCP where a GCM is shared by buyer and seller is not an inevitable outcome. Whether this is the result will depend on the CCP's practices and procedures. It may be possible for a CCP to adopt a practice of calculating margin on a 'gross' basis – ie without netting off opposite transactions in the same security or financial product for the same delivery date – but in practice most CCPs appear to calculate margin obligations

---

14 See also Committee of European Banking Supervisors, *Report on the outcome of CEBS's call for evidence on custodian banks' internalisation of settlement and CCP-like activities* (April 2009), http://www.eba.europa.eu/getdoc/cdc06b31-83ac-4fac-9969-a6eb265b659d/Report-on-the-outcome-of-the-call-for-evidence-on-.aspx

in respect of each account, rather than each transaction.[15] So a fundamental question is whether the trades done by one client would be booked to the same account as another client's (in which case they can disappear through netting) or whether they are kept separate. Here the CCPs allow the creation of separate accounts for different customers of the GCM, but do not appear to envisage that as the normal situation.[16]

(A further distinction must be made in relation to settlement instructions. Even though margin is calculated on a net basis per account, it may be that transactions are settled gross. This will occur if the settlement instructions are generated by the platform and sent direct to the CSD, rather than being generated by the CCP. In such a case the CSD may carry out its own netting to reduce the number of criss-crossing settlements.)

GCMs are principals, not agents

2.12 Do not be misled by the treatment in this book of GCMs alongside 'agent banks'. First, as will be shown, GCMs are not agents, at least not in the technical legal sense. Secondly, there is no reason why a GCM needs to be configured as a bank, though that might in practice facilitate the provision of GCM services such as the extension of credit. However, the risk profile of clearing services can conveniently be assessed at the same time as other transaction services – and the service providers for settlement and payment services are commonly referred to as 'agent' banks.

2.13 A GCM will ordinarily act as principal, even if it is hired by a client to provide a clearing service. If the GCM were a mere agent, that could compromise the CCP's counterparty risk management process. A CCP may depend on a strict doctrine that all its participants must deal with it as principal, because this achieves certainty in three principal areas:

(1) *Contractual responsibility.* The CCP will need to know who is responsible for performance of the contractual obligations it is owed in respect of each transaction. Given that the CCP's risk management begins with the selection of suitable persons as participants – whether as GCM or ICM – it would be rash to allow an agency structure to put the CCP into contractual relations with weaker NCMs or other clients of its participants. The rules of CCPs are explicit about the contractual responsibility of their participants.[17] Furthermore, LCH.Clearnet Ltd's General Regulation 1, which specifies the principal-to-principal basis for dealings, explains that the CCP's responsibilities are owed to no person other than the member. However, the principal-to-principal basis for clearing has not prevented actions under which clearing firms have been alleged to act as agents.

---

15 See, for example, LCH.Clearnet Ltd, *General Regulations*, reg 5; Eurex Clearing AG, Clearing Conditions, Number 3.1

16 See LCH.Clearnet Ltd, *General Regulations*, reg 5(c); Eurex Clearing AG, Clearing Conditions, Number 4.2; LCH.Clearnet SA, Clearing Rulebook (March 2012), http://www. lchclearnet.com/Images/Rule%20Book%20published%20on%2008032012_tcm6-44081.pdf, art 3.2.2.6

17 See LCH.Clearnet SA, Clearing Rulebook, s 2.2.3; Eurex Clearing AG, Clearing Conditions, Number 1.3.

In *Limako BV v H Hentz & Co Inc.*[18] Hentz acted as broker to Limako. Limako sold 64 cocoa options. Hentz, as the exchange member, sold 64 options on the exchange. All 64 options were exercised on the due date by the clearing house, but Hentz only told Limako immediately about the exercise of 20, so Limako instructed Hentz to sell the cocoa held against the remaining 44, which they did. Later, Hentz told Limako that the other 44 options had also been exercised, and the question for the court was whether Hentz or Limako should suffer the loss suffered on the buy-in of replacement cocoa to meet the obligations due under these 44 options. The Court of Appeal upheld Limako's contention that Hentz dealt with them in regard to the options as principal; although Hentz, as broker, was an agent 'to go into the market in order that the price may be fixed and the option thus given content. But at that point Hentz's agency ceases. They are in all other respects principals...'.

See also *Brandeis (Brokers) Ltd v Herbert Black,*[19] in which it was said that 'a broker is not an agent for an undisclosed principal in the sense of creating a contractual relationship between the parties involved in the back-to-back contract, but in all other respects the substance of the relationship is much more closely akin to that of agency than of buyer and seller at arm's length.' What seems clear is that being treated by CCPs as principals does not preclude brokers from owing agent-like duties to their clients. A distinction might need to be drawn, however, with Model B clearing agents,[20] who assume responsibility vis-à-vis the client's market counterparty for the client's performance (but not the other way round), and with *del credere* agents in international trade activity, who assume responsibility for the counterparty's performance in favour of the agent's client, but not the other way round.

(2) *Margin*. A GCM must take responsibility not just for the performance of the contract itself but also for the timely payment or delivery of margin. A GCM who is only an agent would be able to hide behind the operational inefficiency of his principal; this would ruin the effectiveness of the CCP's risk management. A GCM thus needs to have access to sufficient liquidity to cover any gap, temporary or permanent, which its client may experience in funding.

(3) *Set-off*. Wherever set-off is allowed by insolvency regimes it is almost always essential that there be 'mutuality' between the obligations being set off – that is, that they are owed by two counterparties to each other, and that the counterparties are acting in the same capacity in respect of both obligations. Agency can thus be fatal to mutuality.[21] Indeed, the reason for the decision in *British Eagle* was that IATA had acted as agent for the participating airlines; if it had acted as principal, there would surely have been no difficulty with its scheme.

2.14 Accordingly, the chain of contractual relationships can become elongated, as there are more principal-to-principal units arising out of the novation (or open offer) process, as illustrated by **figure 2.4**. Protecting CCPs

---

18   1979] 2 Lloyd's Rep 23 (CA)
19   [2001] All ER (D) 342
20   See **section 18.26**
21   *Richardson v Stormont Todd & Co Ltd* [1900] 1 QB 701

by means of the principal-to-principal dealings rule is fine, but when the GCM is insolvent, protection which the CCP has built for its own well-being may be unhelpful to the client. There is a need for special protection, such as segregation and portability rules, which enable the CCP to look beyond its participant to the client in such cases. CCPs profess that they will try to transfer a client's positions in the event of a GCM's insolvency, though they do not promise to do so.[22] Transfer and look-through arrangements are for exceptional circumstances, since the CCP will regard its participants (GCMs and ICMs), not their clients, as the persons on whom the CCP takes risk. The reasons for the difficulties in effecting transfer, and the solutions which may be available, are examined in **sections 14.47ff**.

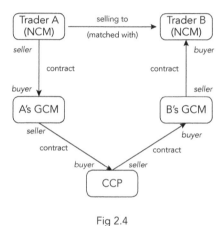

Fig 2.4

OTC derivatives and client clearing

2.15   A final explanation in the context of clearing is called for by the introduction of mandatory clearing of OTC derivatives transactions under EMIR. Where a transaction must be cleared,[23] it may be that one party to the transaction is not a participant in a CCP, and needs to engage the services of a GCM to satisfy its clearing obligation. This could lead to a chain of back-to-back transactions as in **figure 2.4**. A more subtle variant, however, arises where the non-participant's counterparty is itself a participant in the CCP and can take care of the clearing itself. In order to do so, the participant/counterparty will put on an additional hat: that of GCM for the client. It will thus face the CCP in two capacities: that of counterparty to the cleared transaction, in which capacity the transaction appears in its 'house' account at the CCP, and that of GCM to the client in respect of the same transaction, in which capacity the transaction appears in its 'client' account. It will be noted that the effect of client clearing is that both parties to the transaction will be required to post initial margin to the CCP; even if the client's counterparty is able to perform the clearing function, the need for both sides of the bargain to be margined will still arise.

---

22   LCH.Clearnet Ltd, Default Rules, r 6(g); Eurex Clearing AG Clearing Conditions, Part 9; LCH.Clearnet SA Clearing Rulebook, art 4.5.2.5
23   See **sections 5.8ff**

Client clearing

(1) Client and counterparty agree transaction terms

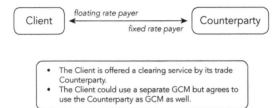

- The Client is offered a clearing service by its trade Counterparty.
- The Client could use a separate GCM but agrees to use the Counterparty as GCM as well.

(2) Transaction is cleared

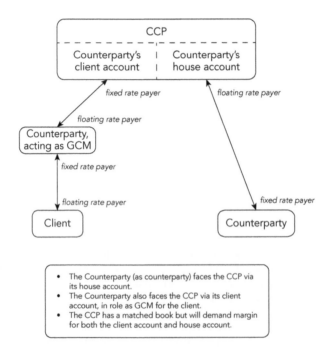

- The Counterparty (as counterparty) faces the CCP via its house account.
- The Counterparty also faces the CCP via its client account, in role as GCM for the client.
- The CCP has a matched book but will demand margin for both the client account and house account.

Fig 2.5

SETTLEMENT – CSDs

2.16   The function of a CSD can only be understood in a historical context. In days when the value of securities was embedded in the paper constituting the security (what in Germany is referred to as *Wertpapier* and in English is sometimes incorrectly called a 'document of title'), it made sense to store the securities in vaults, and to have a central depository maintain a record of who was entitled to them. In this way, the CSD (1) held the ultimate record of entitlement and (2) undertook responsibility for carrying out transfers of entitlement when ownership of the securities was intended to change hands. These remain the core functions of CSDs.

The proposed Regulation on CSDs[24] defines the essential functions of a CSD as operating a securities settlement system and either or both of 'initial recording of securities in a book-entry system ("notary service")' and 'maintaining securities accounts at the top tier level ("central maintenance service")'. In relation to these activities, the following explanation has been given:

'The CSDs serve three core functions:

1. the "notary function" that starts at the issuance of securities and ends when they are reimbursed
2. the "settlement function" through which securities are paid and delivered every time they change hands following a trade on organised or even OTC venues, and
3. the "central safekeeping" function, which may also form part of this triptych. ...

The "notary function" of CSDs lies somewhat in between corporate law and financial law ... [the European legislator] has however to regulate the notary function in order to ensure that there are no more securities circulating with their settlement participants than there were actually issued ...

'The "settlement function" is as important, since the Securities Settlement Systems (SSS) operated by the CSDs have a systemically important nature ...

'The "central safekeeping" function works as a linchpin between the two previous functions. Both the "notary" and the "settlement" functions require in practice the recourse to "securities accounts" for the initial creation of the securities and for their settlement between participants to the SSS.'[25]

Notwithstanding the views thus expressed, the core functions of a CSD are only two in number: the root-of-title function and the settlement function. The root-of-title function is a combination of the notary and safekeeping roles described, but it is misleading to suggest that these could be split apart. The issuer-facing aspect of maintaining the integrity of the issue, described as the 'notary' function, is inseparable from 'safekeeping' in the sense of providing a register of entitlement to the securities credited to accounts of CSD participants. Another safekeeping function may be the physical holding of a document, for example where title to the securities depends on it, but in such a case this is also a necessary component of the root-of-title role, and not somehow to be treated as separate.

2.17   The following comments may also be made:

(1) *Root of title.* A fundamental question for investors – for their very ownership of securities depends on it – is who is responsible for operation of the definitive record of entitlement to the securities. The importance of this title-management function cannot be overstated: inefficiency or operational failure by the operator can lead to expropriation of innocent

---

24 European Commission, *Proposal for a Regulation of the European Parliament and of the Council on improving securities settlement in the European Union and on central securities depositories etc,* COM(2012) 73 final, http://eur-lex.europa.eu/LexUriServ/LexUriServ. do?uri=CELEX:52012PC0073:EN:PDF (March 2012)

25 Terret, M-E, 'Harmonisation of CSD legislation' (July 2011) European Commission DG Internal Market and Services, Unit MARKT/G2 Info-letter on post-trading, Issue 3, http:// ec.europa.eu/internal_market/financial-markets/docs/infoletter/2011_july_en.pdf, p 10

investors. Having the role carried out centrally by an adequately regulated infrastructure is self-evidently a worthwhile policy objective.

Alternative arrangements have existed. A company may maintain its own register of shareholders, but it is inefficient for each security to have its own idiosyncratic system for recording and transfer of ownership. Abolition of paper crunches in each country requires a movement to dematerialisation of title records, or at least immobilisation of documents of title into a central securities depository.[26] Securities which are not shares may not be well-suited to the corporate-register option: for example, title to Eurobonds is recorded at one of the ICSDs.[27]

Ordinarily it makes sense for the operator of the settlement system also to be the provider of the central register of entitlement – the register of people who own the securities. However, this is not invariably the case. The root-of-title function of a CSD is in effect that carried out by a company's registrar, who maintains the official list of shareholders for the company's investor-relations and corporate governance purposes. In some countries, however, the roles of registrar and CSD may be distinct: in the United Kingdom a company's shareholder register may be maintained not solely at CREST but also by the company's registrar.

(2) *Central role.* Any accounts in which securities are held may be capable of constituting records of entitlement, even if they are not provided by a CSD.[28] Those accounts would not, however, be 'central', if they do not serve the whole market: it is, for example, possible for a custodian to provide such accounts, and even carry out settlements of securities transactions without any change taking place at the root-of-title register.[29] But an essential characteristic of a CSD is that it carries out similar roles for the whole market – ultimately all investors depend on the central set of records provided by the CSD as to ownership of the securities, and for the central settlement system operated by the CSD to carry out transfers between accounts in order to give effect to changes in ownership.[30] The proposed Regulation's concept of the 'top tier level' is designed to give effect to the notion of centrality.

(3) *Other functions.* It may be noted that the European Commission has not regarded it as a defining characteristic of CSDs that they should actually act as a depository at all. Other functions of CSDs, such as being involved in corporate actions processing, fails coverage, or provision of credit for the purposes of facilitating settlement, are considered to be ancillary functions.[31]

2.18   In the United Kingdom, the Uncertificated Securities Regulations 2001[32] (USRs) set out the legal rules under which CREST, the UK CSD operated by Euroclear UK & Ireland (EUI), carries out its functions. The central provision of the USRs is that the 'Operator register of members' – that is, the set of records maintained at CREST by EUI – takes precedence over the entry of a person's name in a company's own register of members, in respect of shares

26 Cf proposed Regulation on CSDs, art 3
27 See **section 2.24**
28 See **section 10.27**
29 See **section 2.21**
30 Cf European Commission Services, *Draft Working Document on Post-trading* (May 2006), http://ec.europa.eu/internal_market/financial-markets/docs/clearing/draft/draft_en.pdf, para 2.1.3
31 Proposed Regulation on CSDs, Annex
32 SI 2001 No. 3755

held in uncertificated form.[33] The CSD therefore maintains the 'root of title' – the ultimate record of ownership, than which there is no better title. While the USRs make only limited provision for transfer between accounts maintained by the CSD, the context of the USRs is for the Operator to be approved by the Treasury to operate a 'relevant system', which is a 'computer-based system, and procedures, which enable title to units of a security to be evidenced and transferred without a written instrument.'[34]

2.19   In carrying out its settlement function, a CSD will accept transfer instructions from participants – in the course of a day, many thousands of securities of the same type may need to be transferred either from or to the name of a single participant. A CSD may operate by collecting in all the transfer instructions in respect of each security in advance, and reducing them to a net delivery obligation or receive entitlement by a process of multilateral netting. It will immediately be seen that such a procedure would involve *British Eagle* risk, particularly as the CSD is unlikely to assume the role of central counterparty (although that may be the case in some countries). Some form of protection against insolvency challenge will be needed where a CSD adopts this structure. Alternatively, a CSD may transfer securities gross by acting upon each transfer instruction separately. CREST allows for either approach.[35] The 'net' (DNS) and 'gross' (RTGS) methods for acting upon instructions are discussed further in relation to settlement of payment obligations at **sections 2.30ff**.

Agent banks

2.20   Given that CSDs operate the ultimate register of ownership it is important to protect the integrity of that register. Accordingly, only certain persons are accorded the privilege of giving instructions to the CSD to effectuate transfers of ownership. In the United Kingdom, such instructions are referred to as 'properly authenticated dematerialised instructions',[36] the sending of which requires authorisation under the Financial Services and Markets Act 2000.[37] An investor thus has a choice: to hold its securities directly in EUI, and to obtain authorisation, or to hire a duly authorised person to give instructions on its behalf. Indeed, the hiring of an authorised person may go further, so that the investor does not even hold its securities in its own name, but uses its intermediary as a custodian so that both the holding and the instructing are carried out by the intermediary.

Such intermediaries are sometimes referred to as 'agent banks', though there is no requirement in English law for the regulated activities of 'giving dematerialised instructions' or 'safekeeping and administering investments' to be carried out by banks. More commonly such intermediaries will be called 'custodians', though it can be seen that a settlement agent – a person who is engaged for the purposes of giving dematerialised instructions – need not have custody of the investments at all.

---

33   USRs, reg 24(3)
34   USRs, regs 2(1) and 4(1); cf **sections 11.21ff**
35   See Euroclear, *Enhancing CREST: January 2008 – Competitive Clearing for the London Stock Exchange in CREST* (September 2007), https://www.euroclear.com/site/publishedFile/ enhancing-crest-compclear-Jan08_tcm87-119403.pdf?title=Enhancing+CREST+Competitive +Clearing+for++London+Stock+Exchange+in+CREST, p 16
36   USRs, reg 35
37   Financial Services and Markets Act 2000 (Regulated Activities) Order 2001, SI 2001 No. 544, art 45

Agent banks will often have custody of their clients' assets – that is to say, will hold legal title to the assets themselves, but acknowledging that they do so as trustee on behalf of their clients who retain beneficial ownership[38] – but it is also possible for the agent bank to act as 'account operator'. Under an account operator arrangement, the agent bank does not in any sense hold the securities, but simply carries out the activity of giving dematerialised instructions. The account operator approach balances one policy objective of allowing investors direct ownership of their assets, without taking custody risk on an agent bank, with another, which is to ensure that dematerialised instructions (which can alter ownership rights and are potentially of systemic importance) are given only by those who are subject to regulatory oversight.

Internalised settlement

2.21 Custodian banks might, in theory, be able to 'internalise' the process of settlement in a similar manner to the 'internalisation' of clearing described at **section 2.10**. If both buyer and seller of securities happen to have custody accounts at the same agent bank, it should be possible to arrange for the obligation to deliver securities to be settled simply by an internal book transfer across the common custodian's books. (Indeed, this is what would be expected in the case of a cash transfer between account-holders at the same bank. In such a case the transfer would be referred to as an 'on-us' settlement.)

There has, however, been some controversy over internalised settlement. There are a number of reasons, some of which are less edifying than others. A debate took place between agent banks, who claimed that market infrastructures such as CSDs were encroaching on their position in the market by acting as intermediaries, and others who claimed that the distinction between infrastructures and agents who provide access to infrastructures was artificial.[39] The European Commission's early efforts to understand the dynamics of the post-trade marketplace tended to see everything which followed the trade as part of a single 'clearing and settlement system' – the agent banks were thus part of the system. Whether in practice 'internalised settlement' was easy to do is a matter of conjecture: when settlement instructions originate at the trading platform, it would require special intervention by the agent bank to identify and extract from the ordinary settlement process those trades where coincidentally both buying and selling parties happened to be clients, as well as the operational capability to see that it acts for both buyer and seller so that instructions to the CSD can be cut out of the settlement process. Whether there was a policy problem with internalised settlement was not clarified. After a flurry of studies and commentaries,[40] the issue seems not to have been considered in need of legislative intervention in the proposed CSD Regulation.

---

38 Cf **section 10.4**
39 Cf **section 7.19**
40 See, for example, Citigroup, *The Optimal Market Structure for Clearing and Settlement in the EU* (July 2004), http://ec.europa.eu/internal_market/financial-markets/docs/clearing/2004-consultation/citigroup_en.pdf; Chan, D, et al, *The Securities Custody Industry* (August 2007), European Central Bank Occasional Paper No 68, http://www.ecb.eu/pub/pdf/scpops/ecbocp68.pdf; Committee of European Banking Supervisors, *Report on the outcome of CEBS's call for evidence on custodian banks' internalisation of settlement and CCP-like activities* (April 2009), http://www.eba.europa.eu/getdoc/cdc06b31-83ac-4fac-9969-a6eb265b659d/Report-on-the-outcome-of-the-call-for-evidence-on-.aspx

Target2-Securities

2.22   Target2-Securities (T2S) is an initiative of the European Central Bank intended to remove some of the national differences between settlement practices in different CSDs. 'T2S will provide harmonised delivery versus payment (DvP) settlement in central bank money in a variety of currencies for almost all heavily traded securities circulating in Europe.'[41] Of the 15 Giovannini barriers discussed in **section 1.26**, T2S is expected to alleviate no fewer than six.[42]

The introduction of T2S does not in theory affect the basic functions of CSDs as described above. Rather, T2S provides a settlement engine to which participating CSDs will outsource the transfer functionality of the CSD, leaving the ultimate record of ownership function, and the legal responsibility for operating the central securities settlement system, with the CSD. CSDs are then to be free to offer enhanced investor and issuer services ('asset servicing') alongside their guardianship of title. This much is the theory. However, in practice T2S will take over the registers of the CSDs during daylight hours, so that the records held within the T2S engine will actually hold the final record of title, and T2S provides the settlement engine itself, leaving the CSDs with no vital components for their basic statutory function.

2.23   It is unclear how the introduction of T2S will alter the landscape. The following comments may be made.

(1) The introduction of a single platform may eliminate the raison d'être of national CSDs, thus facilitating consolidation. Yet that is an idealistic view, paying inadequate regard to the idea of CSDs as symbols of national identity to be protected by their governments. CSDs, having outsourced their primary functions to T2S, will need to look for other activities to vitalise their existence. CSDs will find business development challenging, since the proposed Regulation on CSDs limits the business which CSDs will be permitted to do.[43]

(2) The single platform may allow CSDs to offer one-stop settlement services for securities issued in many countries. This is because CSDs participating in T2S must comply with eligibility criteria,[44] which are designed to provide a level competitive playing-field, and force participating CSDs to offer accounts to other CSDs. In this way interoperability is assured. But, in practice, interoperability among CSDs requires intermediation.[45] Intermediation involves additional cost, as the intermediary will wish to take its fee; and intermediation by CSDs implies encroachment on the competitive space occupied by agent banks, which may be controversial.

---

41 European Central Bank, *T2S – Settling without borders* (November 2009), http://www.ecb.eu/pub/pdf/other/settlingwithoutborders_t2sbrochure112009en.pdf?1438a8761205a512ed5fef97467ba3e8, p 15

42 See **table 1.2**

43 Recital (20) and art 14(2

44 Decision of the European Central Bank of 16 November 2011 establishing detailed rules and procedures for implementing the eligibility criteria for central securities depositories to access TARGET2-Securities services (2 December 2011), ECB/2011/20, OJ L 319/117

45 See **section 13.46**

(3) T2S itself may introduce cost. As service provider to CSDs, T2S will charge a fee; CSDs will not be viable as businesses unless they charge more.[46]

ICSDs and common depositories

2.24 International Central Securities Depositories carry out the same role as CSDs, except that they do so for 'homeless instruments'. They were established to serve the Eurobond market – that is, bonds issued by corporate issuers for international investors, typically in a non-domestic currency. Eurobonds, unlike domestic securities, do not have a natural CSD, but again they were once paper-based and securely deposited either with the Morgan Guaranty Trust Company in Belgium or Cedel in Luxembourg. The function of the ICSDs, backed by provisions of local legislation assuring ownership rights to investors, was to maintain a register of entitlement to the deposited instruments.

Once the two ICSDs had established themselves and were acting in competition, the question arose as to how an account-holder at one ICSD could transfer title to Eurobonds to an account-holder using the other ICSD. This classic problem of interoperability required two developments: first, the opening by each ICSD of an account with the other; and secondly, that the paper instrument constituting the bond itself be held by a neutral third party who could maintain a root-of-title record as to the number of units/bonds held by each ICSD at any given time. The neutral third party is known as the 'common depository' for any particular issue of bonds, and the mechanism between the ICSDs which rebalances their respective accounts at the common depository is often referred to as the 'bridge' between the ICSDs.

What this leads to is the conclusion that the ICSDs may be international, but neither is truly 'central' nor is it a 'depository'. As with much terminology in clearing and settlement, the name is of historical interest but can engender confusion. The ICSDs are certainly infrastructures, but serve the wholesale markets and are operated as private enterprises. This feature may be a valid distinction from the national CSDs, which guard title to shares which are invested in by the retail public, and which have historically been either in state ownership or closely supervised by national regulators as a matter of domestic public policy.

The role of the ICSDs has expanded rather beyond Eurobonds. The provision of securities accounts for their members is the central feature of their services, and this function can be put to many uses. These include traditional securities intermediation – effectively providing custody services in relation to securities for which the home (or issuer) CSD is elsewhere; collateral management; and settlement of other international securities such as global depositary receipts.

DvP

2.25 Securities settlement is, however, more complex than mere delivery and acceptance of securities between accounts at the CSD. Unless the transfer of securities is free-of-payment, there will need to be a countervailing payment

---

46 Cf Lannoo, K, and Valiante, D, *Integrating Europe's Back Office – 10 years of turning in circles* (June 2009), ECMI Policy Brief No 13, http://www.ceps.eu/ceps/download/1673

between participants too. The CSD would typically not be responsible for the payment leg of securities settlements, but will be connected to a payment system which will take care of this. The need for a connection between the CSD and the payment system involves analysis of the risk that delivery and payment may not be simultaneous or mutually conditional – the question whether there is settlement risk. The analysis of this is developed at **sections 15.2ff**. In the meantime, it is appropriate to consider the types and functions of payment systems.

TYPES OF CASH TRANSFER SYSTEMS

2.26 As observed in **section 1.16**, a distinction should be drawn between payment 'schemes', which set out the standards, rules and obligations for creation and transmission of payment instructions, and 'payment systems' which bring about the clearing and settlement of payment obligations. Again, as with clearing and settlement of securities transfer obligations, infrastructures bringing about discharge are of various types, which ought first to be considered.

2.27 The following types of payment system may be identified.

(1) *Automated Clearing House (ACH)*. Automated clearing houses are functionally similar to CCPs, in that they amalgamate and net payment obligations (though, crucially, they do not assume counterparty risk). A typical retail-payments system, such as Bacs in the United Kingdom, operates as a netting system with daily (or possibly more frequent) processing cycles. Details of the proposed payments are submitted to a central processing hub, which calculates a net payment due between each pair of participants. The net payment will take account of all payments due to flow in each direction between those participants. Sophisticated algorithms may be deployed to reduce the payment flows by identifying circular payments (X is due to pay 100 to Y; Y is due to pay 150 to Z; Z is due to pay 90 to X; 90 can be eliminated from the circle leaving net payments of 10 from X to Y and 60 from Y to Z). But in a 'pure ACH' model the payment system itself neither receives nor makes any payment. It generates a set of net payment obligations owing between its participants, which then need to be settled, typically by transfers across the books of the central bank using the central bank's RTGS. (See **sections 2.28–2.29**.)

(2) *Real-Time Gross Settlement System (RTGS)*. Wholesale and large-value transfer systems operate by causing a debit of the payer participant's account and a credit to the payee participant's account on the books of the payment system operator. Typically, though not invariably, the operator is a central bank. Settlement of the payment obligations is achieved through these book transfers. (See **sections 2.33–2.34**.)

(3) *Multilateral Netting System (DNS)*.[47] A more advanced type of ACH provides a settlement function. As with a regular ACH, a DNS system will calculate all the payments due from each participant, and all the payments due to each participant, and net them off against each other, leaving a single net pay-in or pay-out for each participant for each cycle. In this case, the net payment obligations must be settled with or via the central hub, so a payment system operating as DNS system will need to hold an account at

---

47 See **section 2.30** for explanation of the acronym

a bank, typically a central bank, to and from which transfers representing the net payments can be made. A corollary of this is that the payment system operator may receive deposits from its participants, even if on a very short-term basis, and will therefore expose its participants to credit risk on the payment system operator itself. The EBA's EURO-1 system operates in approximately this manner, though the German law 'single obligation structure' leaves each participant not with a claim on the system operator but a claim on the other participants jointly (but not severally).[48] (See **sections 2.30–2.31**.)

(4) *Exchange of Value System.* Finally, where both parties to a transaction have payment obligations, it may be necessary to have a settlement system similar to a CSD which can move value in two opposite directions simultaneously. This would occur, for example, where a foreign exchange transaction is being settled, so that party A pays currency ψ to party B at the same time as party B pays currency ϕ to party A. The prime operator of this type of system is CLS. (See **sections 2.37–2.39**.)

ACHs

2.28   First, then, it is appropriate to look at the role of the ACH. An ACH is a 'clearing' system which assists bulk transfers of payments. Employers who need to pay employees, make dividend payments to investors, or run periodic settlement of outstanding invoices will wish to settle their obligations by providing a composite electronic file to their bank which contains the payees' bank details and the amounts concerned. Suppliers who collect payments from customers by direct debit will also wish to use the electronic file method for instructing their bank about the collections. To process each of these relatively small payments individually would be inefficient; an ACH interposing itself between the banks can collapse the multiple payment obligations into (typically) a net pay-in or net receipt by each bank, coupled with full information for the receiving banks (or, in the case of direct debit collections, the paying banks) of the accounts to (from) which the payments are due to be made. As with a CCP, the ACH model depends on the effectiveness of multilateral netting. (See **figure 2.2**.)

The role of the ACH can be illustrated by that of EURO-1, the multilateral large-value payment system for euro payments managed by EBA Clearing. EURO-1 is a net settlement system. It handles credit transfers and direct debits. Payment obligations are combined into a 'single obligation' – a pay-in or pay-out amount representing the net payment in respect of all other participants in the system, which automatically adjusts upon processing of each payment message sent or received by a participant. Balances are settled at the end of the day by payments into or out of a settlement account provided for EBA Clearing at the European Central Bank, unless the participating bank is required to pre-fund its settlement account. EBA Clearing also operates the 'STEP1' and 'STEP2' payment systems, which respectively enable banks which do not participate directly in EURO-1 to exchange payments with each other, and provide pan-

---

48 ECB, *Payment and Securities Settlement Systems in the European Union* (the Blue Book) (August 2007), http://www.ecb.eu/pub/pdf/other/ecbbluebookea200708en.pdf, vol 1, p 43; Kokkola, T, (ed), *The Payment System* (European Central Bank, September 2010), ISBN 978-928990632-6, http://www.ecb.eu/pub/pdf/other/paymentsystem200909en.pdf, pp 180–182

European reachability for bulk credit and debit transfers in euro. Both STEP1 and STEP2 rely on EURO-1 as their infrastructure.[49]

2.29 While multilateral netting is at the heart of an ACH's operations, one contrast with the operations of a CCP should be highlighted. ACHs do not ordinarily take counterparty risk on their participants. Thus, while ACHs do modify payment obligations, they do not typically collect margin or need elaborate default rules to expunge unsettled transactions from their books. A participant with a net pay-in obligation (referred to as a participant with a short position) may be in breach of the rules and may cause an unwind of settlements if it does not pay, but the victims of non-performance will be the other participants in the ACH rather than the ACH itself. The effect of non-performance in netting systems is, however, a troublesome issue, which will now be examined.

DNS systems

2.30 Payment systems relying on multilateral netting are commonly known as 'DNS' systems, originally standing for 'daily net settlement' or, because netting cycles may be completed more frequently than daily, 'deferred net settlement' or 'designated-time net settlement'. DNS Systems have various drawbacks:

(1) In the event of a payment default by a participant, there will be a net shortfall in funds. Unless one participant can be prevailed upon to provide the missing funds, it may be necessary for all the settlements in the system to be unwound.

(2) To minimise the risk of an unwind, the system may require participants to make available liquidity to plug a non-payment by a defaulter and, to minimise the risk to participants, may impose strict position limits. Another solution is to calculate the net pay-in of each participant, and to require prior payment-in from each participant before commencing the netting cycle; but this slows down the performance of the system and does not allow the continuous re-balancing of obligations which a sophisticated system like EURO-1 can provide. Yet another approach is to require participants to lock up collateral with the system operator. However, the method most commonly used is control at the gate: only the most robust banks are allowed to participate directly in the system.[50]

(3) The legal robustness of multilateral netting cannot be relied on in all jurisdictions, giving rise to the possibility that a liquidator of a failed participant (whether or not a net payer) seeks to unwind settlements, by invoking the *British Eagle* principle.[51] Designation under the Settlement Finality Directive[52] should protect the system and its participants from such an attack, but it cannot provide missing money.

---

49 European Central Bank website (May 2010), http://www.ecb.int/paym/market/payinfr/large/html/index.en.html and EBA Clearing website, https://www.ebaclearing.eu/Legal-basis-N=E1_Legalbasis-L=EN.aspx; Kokkola, pp 180–183
50 Kokkola, p 181
51 See **box 2.1**
52 See **section 8.19**

Box 2.2   Case study – the collapse of Barings and the ECU clearing

'The unforeseen collapse of Baring Brothers at the end of February 1995 caused a problem in the ECU clearing. On Friday, 24th February one clearing bank had sent an ECU payment instruction addressed to Barings' correspondent for a relatively small amount for value on Monday, 27th February. After the appointment of an administrator to Barings on 26th February the sending bank sought to cancel the instruction but it found that the rules of the ECU clearing did not permit this; moreover, the receiving bank was legally unable to reverse the transaction. As it turned out, the sending bank happened to find itself in an overall net debit position in the clearing at the end of the day. Under pressure of time the bank agreed to cover that position by borrowing from a long bank, so enabling the settlement of more than ECU 50 billion in payments between the 45 banks participating in the clearing eventually to be completed on the due date.'[53]

What is going on here? Barings' correspondent was a net payer-in in the ECU clearing but unwilling to perform owing to the risk it was taking on its now insolvent client. A small unperformed pay-in obligation due from the sending bank jeopardised the whole clearing until the loan was made. The loan from the long bank (a net payee-out) created a new payment obligation in favour of the clearing bank which could cancel out the clearing bank's short position; now there was no shortfall of money in the system compared with pay-in obligations of the participants. So far, so good.

The 'solution' adopted to ensure that the payments went ahead was, however, a fudge. The long bank had to lend to the recalcitrant sending bank – taking credit risk on a bank which, although itself not insolvent, was known to be exposed to Barings and to be unwilling to perform its own obligations in the clearing. The loan made through the system meant that the long bank did not achieve full payment of its entitlements as net recipient and therefore did not achieve finality of settlement. That could have caused liquidity problems for the long bank. What is not answered is how the situation would have resolved if none of the long banks had been willing to step up with a loan.

2.31   Not all payment obligations are cleared through an ACH, and even an ACH needs to arrange for settlement of the net payments into or out of the system. At some point, cash needs to change hands. But the mysterious process of 'transfer' of cash needs elaboration. Unless someone is going to stuff wads of paper currency into their pockets and walk up the street, 'transfer of cash' will involve account entries at banks.[54] The process was analysed by Staughton J in *Libyan Arab Foreign Bank v Bankers Trust Co,*[55] in which the Libyan Bank demanded payment of $131m standing to the credit of their account with Bankers Trust.

---

53   Bank for International Settlements, *Settlement Risk in Foreign Exchange Transactions* (March 1996), http://www.bis.org/publ/cpss17.pdf?noframes=1, p 8
54   Cf **Chapter 9**
55   1989] QB 728

'An account transfer means the process by which some other person or institution comes to owe money to the Libyan Bank or their nominee, and the obligation of Bankers Trust is extinguished or reduced pro tanto. "Transfer" may be a somewhat misleading word, since the original obligation is not assigned (notwithstanding dicta in one American case which speak of assignment); a new obligation by a new debtor is created.'

The judge went on to describe three methods by which an account transfer might be effected: by both payer and payee having accounts at the same bank, which could effect a book-entry 'transfer' by simultaneous credit and debit of the payee's and payer's accounts ('correspondent transfer'); by credit to the account of a third party who banked with Bankers Trust (the payer bank) ('in-house transfer'); and by a complex set of transfers via intermediaries, whereby for example payer banks with B, who banks with C, and payee banks with E who banks with D, and C and D each have accounts with a Federal Reserve bank, with credits and debits being made at each stage in the chain ('complex account transfer'). But the point was that any of these methodologies required that 'sooner or later, if cash [notes and coins] is not used, there must be an in-house transfer at an institution which holds accounts for two beneficiaries, so that the credit balance of one can be increased and that of the other reduced.'

2.32 Payment systems are mechanisms for distilling the many payments due between account-holders at different banks into aggregate net payments which will ultimately be discharged through book transfers. Payments infrastructure thus ultimately depends on the existence of banks where any payment obligation can be settled through account transfer – that is, absent any other bank with which all the participants hold accounts, the central bank.

RTGS systems

2.33 Central banks may arrange for payments to be processed by a settlement system of the DNS type, or, more commonly, rely on real-time gross settlement (RTGS) methodology.[56] The principle behind RTGS is that each payment obligation is separately and immediately processed, subject only to the payer having a sufficient balance, and participants make or receive a separate payment into or from the system for each payment. Payers must pay in or borrow in order to fund each payment; if payer has no funds in the system at the time of the payment, payer may borrow (subject to provision of collateral) or the payment will fail. The principal drawback of RTGS systems is that they are very intensive users of liquidity. Unless some kind of optimisation algorithm is used, a payer may have to wait for all payments to which it is entitled to settle in its favour before it can settle any of its own obligations. So RTGS systems need someone to 'prime the pump', by crediting their account with sufficient funds to start the chain of settlements going, to avoid the system freezing up.

2.34 Modern RTGS systems use a complex set of queuing rules, netting and 'circles processing' to eliminate such blockages. Queuing rules ensure that transactions are processed in the order which minimises the amount of liquidity

---

56 Fry, M, 'Risk, cost and liquidity in alternative payment systems' (February 1999) Bank of England Quarterly Bulletin, http://www.bankofengland.co.uk/publications/quarterlybulletin/risk.pdf, p 78

needed.[57] Netting rules will allow mutual bilateral payment obligations to be settled by a transfer of only the net amount due. Circles processing identifies money moving in a circle (A owes B 60, B owes C 50, C owes A 70) where elimination of the circular payment reduces the liquidity required (if A pays B 10 while simultaneously C pays A 20, and all three payment obligations are then discharged). Typically a circles processing algorithm involves, on a small scale, multilateral netting (in this example, A's account will be credited with a net payment of 10, B's account will be credited with a net payment of 10, and C's account will be debited with a net payment of 20, with all three entries happening simultaneously). RTGS algorithms may also take circles processing one step further and operate, in very short timescales, DNS-type multilateral nettings.

Nevertheless, RTGS systems will usually be coupled with a formal borrowing arrangement to enable smooth running. Central banks depend on repo facilities to do this without damaging monetary policy. In the eurozone, the situation is more complex because there are multiple central banks, and the possibility arises of providing repo collateral to a different central bank from that which is providing liquidity. Euro settlement arrangements are provided through TARGET-2, and cross-border repo collateral via CCBM2, which are centralised facilities under the oversight of the European Central Bank.

TARGET-2 and CCBM2

2.35 TARGET-2 is not truly a settlement system. It is, rather, a settlement engine. When an account-holder at one national central bank (NCB) wishes to transfer funds for the account of another account-holder, the processing of debits and credits to the accounts of the participants is effected by software (TARGET-2) provided at the ECB.[58] In effect, the NCB has outsourced to the ECB the responsibility for providing the engine driving its settlement process. Each NCB in the eurozone has done the same thing, with the advantage that all settlements in euro will be done in a common manner and subject to the same procedural rules and standards.

2.36 CCBM2 is the mechanism by which an NCB can provide liquidity to its own participant even if that NCB itself holds no collateral at all for the participant in question.[59] 'CCBM' stands for 'correspondent central bank model', implying that another NCB would receive the collateral on behalf of the liquidity-providing NCB, acting as its correspondent bank and collateral agent. CCBM2 develops this notion by standardising the operational processes and technical requirements, and centralising the collateral management engine within the ECB. CCBM2 also allows for collateral posted by a participant with any NCB to be reallocated or released, so as to minimise the amount of securities which are locked-up as collateral for liquidity purposes.[60]

---

57 See Fry, pp 82-83 for an example
58 European Central Bank, *Information Guide for Target2 Users* (October 2009), http://www.ecb. int/paym/t2/shared/pdf/infoguide_V3_1_0.pdf
59 For information and documents, see http://www.ecb.eu/paym/ccbm2/html/index.en.html
60 European Central Bank, *Target2 and CCBM2: Drivers of efficient liquidity management* (September 2009), slide presentation, http://www.ecb.int/paym/coll/coll/ccbm2/pdf/ Presentation_Sibos_2009_on_TARGET2_CCBM2_fin.pdf?58052020a91ebd068eb5e75b3603 aa7b

---

Box 2.3   Case study – Bankhaus Herstatt and settlement risk

'On 26th June 1974 the Bundesaufsichtsamt für das Kreditwesen withdrew the banking licence of Bankhaus Herstatt, a small bank in Cologne active in the FX market, and ordered it into liquidation during the banking day but after the close of the interbank payments system in Germany. Prior to the announcement of Herstatt's closure, several of its counterparties had, through their branches or correspondents, irrevocably paid Deutsche Mark to Herstatt on that day through the German payments system against anticipated receipts of US dollars later the same day in New York in respect of maturing spot and forward transactions. Upon the termination of Herstatt's business at 10.30 a.m. New York time on 26th June (3.30 p.m. in Frankfurt), Herstatt's New York correspondent bank suspended outgoing US dollar payments from Herstatt's account. This action left Herstatt's counterparty banks exposed for the full value of the Deutsche Mark deliveries made (credit risk and liquidity risk).'[61]

'Herstatt risk' is the name sometimes used to describe any situation where the reliability of DvP (delivery versus payment, or in the foreign exchange context, payment versus payment or PvP) is not assured. The parties bear 'principal' or 'gross' settlement risk on each other, because of the risk that the first party to perform pays away the full gross amount of the transaction, and may get nothing at all in return. This is far more serious than 'net' or 'market' risk, which occurs where either the countervalue was received but is less valuable than what was disposed of, or neither party performed at all (in which case the non-defaulting party has lost only the replacement cost of the transaction).

CLS

2.37   The CLS system was established specifically to address the problem of settlement risk in foreign exchange transactions. 'CLS' stands for 'continuous linked settlement', which describes the two central notions which underlie CLS: payment-versus-payment (PvP) on a real-time gross basis.

At the moment of settlement, a foreign exchange transaction requires one bank to transfer X amount of one currency in return for a transfer of Y amount of another currency. Before CLS, this could not be done without one bank taking the risk that it would pay in full and receive nothing in return, because the other bank had failed before making its payment. This problem materialised in actuality in the case of the failure of Bankhaus Herstatt in 1974, giving rise to the inevitable spate of litigation.[62] It is perhaps remarkable that it took 25 years for the problem to find a solution.

---

61   Bank for International Settlements Committee on Payment and Settlement Systems, *Settlement Risk in Foreign Exchange Transactions* (March 1996), http://www.bis.org/publ/cpss17.pdf?noframes=1, p 6
62   See for example *Momm v Barclays Bank* [1977] QB 790

The solution is a bank, CLS Bank International, which provides settlement accounts for each of its 60 participants.[63] Once Bank A has the amount which it is to pay credited to its account, and Bank B has the amount which it is to pay credited to its account, then CLS Bank can simultaneously debit and credit the two accounts so that both banks' obligations are discharged at exactly the same moment. Thus, settlement risk is eliminated, except inasmuch as both Banks A and B are taking credit risk on CLS Bank while their currency is deposited there.

2.38 In practice it is slightly more complicated than this. Participants submit to CLS in advance of settlement day a file with the transactions which they propose to settle for their own account and for their clients. CLS responds to each participant with a pay-in and withdrawal schedule for each currency, and the participant must pay in to its account at CLS, via the large-value transfer system for funds denominated in each pay-in currency, the requisite amount. CLS Bank thus needs to have an account at the central bank for each participating currency, in order to be able to receive pay-ins and from which to disburse pay-outs. For the euro, which is a currency with many central banks, CLS has an account with the European Central Bank.[64]

CLS operates complex algorithms for optimising settlement, including circles processing and partial settlement, and relying on the credit balance of a participant in one currency as collateral to cover an overdraft in another currency in order to allow settlements to take place which might not otherwise be possible. Clearly a participant will be unable to withdraw funds if they are still acting as collateral, or if overall CLS has an insufficient amount of that currency because it is still awaiting a pay-in from another participant.[65]

2.39 CLS should be distinguished from a CCP. Foreign exchange contracts are not novated to CLS Bank in the way that they were historically novated to ECHO, a CCP set up specially for clearing of such trades, or as in LCH. Clearnet's ForexClear service.[66] CCPs are designed to manage counterparty defaults in the period between trade and settlement: they are less well-suited to handle settlement risk, that is the danger in an exchange-of-value transaction that Party X performs in full, then Party Y defaults before it has performed at all. CLS, by contrast, is designed specifically to address settlement risk, but not pre-settlement risk. CLS does not have a close-out mechanism and does not take margin to help participants replace lost value on transactions which a failed counterparty will no longer perform. However, it has been noted that CLS does

63 CLS Group, News Article (May 2010), http://www.cls-group.com/Media/Pages/NewsArticle. aspx?id=57

64 European Central Bank, *Explanatory memorandum on the recommendations concerning CLS payments in euro* (February 2001), http://www.ecb.int/paym/pdf/pol/clsmemo.pdf

65 Hills, B, and Rule, D, 'Counterparty credit risk in wholesale payment and settlement systems' (November 1999) Bank of England Financial Stability Review, p 107; Mägerle, J, and Maurer, D, *The Continuous Linked Settlement foreign exchange system (CLS)* (November 2009), Swiss National Bank Report, http://www.snb.ch/en/mmr/reference/continuous_linked_settlement/ source; Kokkola, pp 183–186

66 LCH.Clearnet, *LCH.Clearnet receives Regulatory non-objection to launch OTC FX clearing* (March 2012), Press release, http://www.lchclearnet.com/Images/2012-03-13%20 ForexClear%20Press%20Non%20Objection_tcm6-61145.pdf

perform some of the ancillary functions that a CCP might undertake, such as trade matching and netting of pay-in and pay-out amounts.[67]

Direct and indirect participation

2.40 The operator of a system which settles payments is evidently exposed to risk, particularly if the participant becomes insolvent. Criteria for participation in systems will therefore aim to exclude from membership any applicant which might introduce an excessive amount of risk.[68] And, as explored in **section 7.11**, competition law will expect the criteria for membership of any system which amounts to an infrastructure to be transparent, non-discriminatory, and justifiable in terms of objectivity and proportionality. Accordingly, many financial institutions and end-users of payment and settlement services will find themselves unable to meet the requirements for direct participation in a system, and will therefore need to hire a direct participant to provide them with access. The risk is thereby shifted from the operator of the system to the direct participant, which will under system rules be exclusively responsible for the obligations inherent in its participation and the settlement instructions which it submits.

Another reason why one financial institution may need to hire another in order to access a payment or settlement system is cost. Even where a bank is able to meet the eligibility criteria for direct participation, the volume of settlements processed in the relevant currency may not merit the investments required for direct participation. In such cases indirect participation may be preferable notwithstanding the counterparty risk being assumed.

2.41 The position of a direct participant providing access services to a payment system can be regarded as formally analogous to that of an internalising GCM, discussed at **section 2.10**, in that the direct participant may be operating, on a larger or smaller scale than the system itself, a payment or settlement system in its own right. This problem is referred to as 'tiering'.[69] The direct participant that agrees to provide an access service will therefore wish to have regard not just to the risk issues ordinarily inherent in providing settlement services to a client,[70] but also to the extent to which it is itself providing a multilateral netting system, with the regulatory and special risk implications that brings. In particular, the United Kingdom Treasury has power under section 184 of the Banking Act 2009 to 'specify' an inter-bank payments system as a 'recognised system', which would have the effect of subjecting the system to the regulatory regime described in **section 11.3**. There is no requirement for a recognised system to be an infrastructure: it is sufficient that the system is of systemic importance.[71]

2.42 Indirect participants will also appreciate that indirect access to a system will involve the indirect participant taking risk on the access provider.

---

67 Manning, M, Heath, A, and Whitelaw, J, 'The Foreign Exchange Market and Central Counterparties' (March 2010) Reserve Bank of Australia Bulletin, http://www.rba.gov.au/publications/bulletin/2010/mar/8.html
68 See **section 16.12(1)**
69 See **section 11.5**
70 See **Chapter 18**
71 Banking Act 2009, s 185(1)

Direct participants may wish to point to the protection given to 'participants' in settlement systems which are designated under the Settlement Finality Directive, but that protection is only available in respect of the defaults of other *participants* in the system.[72] Indirect participants can, in theory, be granted protection,[73] but only if they themselves are regarded as of systemic importance. To identify any institution as systemically important is practically the same as saying the institution is 'too big to fail', and before the Financial Stability Board developed a practice of publishing a list of systemically important financial institutions,[74] there was limited appetite for branding banks as 'systemically important' in Europe.[75]

---

72 See **section 16.7**

73 Settlement Finality Directive, art 2(f)

74 Financial Stability Board, *Policy Measures to Address Systemically Important Financial Institutions* (November 2011), http://www.financialstabilityboard.org/publications/r_111104bb.pdf

75 European Commission, *Evaluation report on the Settlement Finality Directive 98/26/EC (EU25)* (March 2006), COM (2005) 657 final/2, http://ec.europa.eu/internal_market/financial-markets/docs/settlement/evaluation_report_en.pdf, p 6

3 Trading

BEFORE THE POST-TRADE

3.1   Without a trade there is no need for post-trade services. A brief overview of trading structures will provide context to the discussion of post-trade issues, as in some respects the manner in which the trading is done shapes and constrains the post-trade services too.

3.2   There are essentially two ways in which a trade in any product can be carried out: either privately (usually referred to as over-the-counter (OTC)) between buyer and seller, who have to seek each other out, or hire brokers to do so; or in an organised marketplace. In some European countries it was considered undesirable to have trading OTC, presumably because private trading impairs the process of price discovery: in those countries it was mandatory for equities trading for retail customers to be carried out on an official stock exchange. This practice – of limiting retail transactions to regulated markets – was known as the 'concentration rule', and was expressly permitted by the Investment Services Directive (ISD)[1] until its repeal in 2007.

3.3   In other countries, such as the United Kingdom, trading was permitted outside the stock exchange, but an OTC trade carried out by a member of the stock exchange would be treated as an on-exchange trade for certain purposes such as price transparency.[2] Rules such as these had three principal effects:

(1) The cleanliness of the market and the quality of service provided to investors was under the supervision of the stock exchange, which had a regulatory role. For example, to take the United Kingdom again, it is a condition of recognition as a 'recognised investment exchange' that the exchange 'must ensure that business conducted by means of its facilities is conducted in an orderly manner and so as to afford proper protection to investors,' and it 'must be able and willing to promote and maintain high standards of integrity and fair dealing ... in the course of using the facilities provided by the exchange.'[3] By concentrating the trading, and in particular control over the disclosure of prices formed by intermediaries, into the hands of the stock exchange, a high degree of integrity could be assured in respect of the stock-exchange's officially published prices of securities;

---

1   Council Directive 93/22/EEC of 10 May 1993 on investment services in the securities field
2   Cf London Stock Exchange, *Rules of the London Stock Exchange* (February 2012), http://www.londonstockexchange.com/traders-and-brokers/rules-regulations/rules-lse.pdf, r 3000
3   Financial Services and Markets Act 2000 (Recognition Requirements for Investment Exchanges and Clearing Houses) Regulations 2001, SI 2001/995, Schedule, paras 4(1) and 6(1)

and consequently investors could be assured of 'best execution' of their orders without the need for excessive scrutiny of the conduct of brokers.

(2) Data relating to the price of securities traded on an official exchange was firmly under the control of the exchange. Exchanges' income derives partly from charging trading fees, and partly from selling information about stock prices and movements.

(3) Post-trade clearing and settlement structures were geared around the exchange as the fount of trading. Operational arrangements were set up so as to ensure efficient communication between the exchange and the clearing and settlement infrastructures. In some countries, this was achieved by co-ownership of the trading and post-trading infrastructures; in others, by devising straight-through-processing methodologies. In still others, specific local-market arrangements could be added into the system – for example the tax (stamp duty or stamp duty reserve tax) due on transfers of securities in the United Kingdom is monitored by CREST.[4]

THE COMPETITION IMPERATIVE

3.4   In 1996, concentration rules were in place in Belgium, France, Italy, Spain, Portugal and Greece.[5] But anything which has a monopolistic appearance will be under competition scrutiny in Europe, and trading infrastructures are no exception. In a review of 2000, the European Commission remarked:

'The concentration rule of Art. 14(3) of the ISD offers Member States the option of requiring the execution of transactions in certain financial instruments on a "regulated market". This provision was intended to enhance investor protection by limiting "off-market" transactions to professional investors. However, trading in financial instruments could be artificially diverted to a particular regulated market. Investor protection is better served by appropriate provisions addressed to market participants acting on behalf of investors, and by strict enforcement of "best execution" requirements. In order to avoid arbitrary or disproportionate restrictions on competition between "regulated markets", it may be appropriate to examine the continued rationale and/or present form of the "concentration rule". Article 15(5) ISD empowers Member States to restrict the establishment of new markets on their territory. ... However, the current provision should be reviewed to ensure that it is not used to obstruct the activities of "regulated markets" authorised by partner country authorities.'[6]

3.5   In countries which did not have a formal concentration rule, alternative trading methods and venues began to develop. When the Investment Services Directive came up for review, a regime permitting 'multilateral trading facilities' (alternative trading venues) and internalised execution was expressly introduced, with a view to injecting competition among providers of execution

---

4   See **section 22.5**
5   European Commission, 'Investment Services Directive: A European Passport available to investment firms from 1 January 1996' (February 1996) Single Market News, http://ec.europa.eu/internal_market/smn/smn02/s2mn13.htm
6   European Commission, *Upgrading the Investment Services Directive (93/22/EEC)* (November 2000), Communication to the European Parliament and the Council, COM(2000)729 final, http://eur-lex.europa.eu/LexUriServ/LexUriServ.do?uri=COM:2000:0729:FIN:EN:PDF, p 14

venues.[7] In the result, the Markets in Financial Instruments Directive (MiFID,[8] which replaced the ISD), contained various options for trading, which must be recognised by member states:

(1) *Regulated markets.* The old-style stock exchange is called a 'regulated market' in MiFID, and twelve articles of MiFID are devoted to their regulation and duties.[9] Regulated markets provide services going beyond those of alternative trading platforms, in that they must have rules relating to the admission to trading (and removal from trading) of financial instruments.[10] As will be seen, the transparency obligations of competitor trading venues depend on whether an instrument has been admitted to trading on a regulated market, so the position of regulated markets remains essential notwithstanding any fall in their market share of trading activity. Regulated markets also have to ensure that financial instruments which they admit to trading are capable of being traded in a fair, orderly and efficient manner, and that transferable securities are freely negotiable.[11] Finally, regulated markets have to allow a degree of choice over clearing and settlement arrangements to their participants.[12]

(2) *Multilateral trading facilities.* Alternative trading venues where more than two brokers can come together collectively to hunt out the best price are inelegantly termed 'multilateral trading facilities' (MTFs) in MiFID. An MTF is defined as a multilateral system, operated by an investment firm or market operator, which brings together multiple third-party buying and selling interests in financial instruments – in the system and in accordance with non-discretionary rules – in a way that results in a contract.[13] The central difference between an MTF and a regulated market is that MTFs are regulated in the same way as investment firms (brokers), rather than being subject to their own regulatory regime. However, the regime for investment firms is supplemented in the case of MTFs by rules dealing with issues such as pre- and post-trade transparency of prices, trading processes, admission of participants and choice of clearing and settlement arrangements,[14] so the distinctions are in practice not so great as might be imagined. The transparency obligations regarding prices applied only to shares, and depended on the instrument being admitted to trading on a regulated market.

(3) *Dark pools.* Regulators were, however, given the power to exempt a regulated market or MTF from the obligation to publish pre-trade bid and offer prices 'based on the market model or the type and size of orders.'[15] This opt-out facilitated the development of 'dark pools' where unusual orders, which might otherwise have to be executed sub-optimally because the other market participants would quickly see what was going on in a 'lit' venue, could still be carried out.

---

7   See European Commission, *Communication from the Commission to the European Parliament and the Council – Upgrading the Investment Services Directive (93/22/EEC)* (November 2000), http://ec.europa.eu/internal_market/securities/docs/isd/2000/com-provision_en.pdf, p 3

8   Directive 2004/39/EC of the European Parliament and of the Council of 21 April 2004 on markets in financial instruments, etc

9   MiFID, arts 36–47

10 MiFID, arts 40, 41

11 MiFID, art 40(2)

12 MiFID, art 46; see also **section 7.21**

13 MiFID, art 4(1)(15)

14 MiFID arts 14, 26, 29, 30, 35

15 MiFID, arts 29(2) and 44(2)

(4) *Systematic internalisers.* A systematic internaliser is an investment firm which, on an organised, frequent and systematic basis, deals on its own account by executing client orders outside a regulated market or an MTF.[16] In other words, a systematic internaliser is a broker whose volume of buy or sell orders in respect of particular stocks is so large that it can match buyers and sellers. Systematic internalisers dealing in shares traded on a regulated market are obliged to publish firm quotes for orders up to standard market size. However, the take-up of systematic internaliser status was very low,[17] presumably because the obligation to publish quotes was onerous and nothing in MiFID prevented a broker from matching buyers and sellers without systematically publishing quotes.

BEYOND MiFID

3.6   However, an important omission from MiFID's formal regulatory structure was a regime for broker crossing networks. Owing to the absence of prohibition in MiFID of operating a matching system, brokers have been able to establish their own private 'broker crossing networks' in which buying clients and selling clients can trade with each other without their order going near an exchange or MTF. Brokers operating these arrangements had to comply with the best execution rule, which would ordinarily require that the execution price obtained for the client was no worse than if the broker had executed on its usual selection of public execution venues. Yet there are adverse implications for price transparency if trades are privately executed in such arrangements. The proposed revision of MiFID thus intends to introduce a new category of 'organised trading facility' or OTF, which will be obliged to comply with pre- and post-trade transparency rules. The European Commission stated, in distinguishing OTFs from systematic internalisers:

'(7) In order to make European markets more transparent and to level the playing field between various venues offering trading services it is necessary to introduce a new category of organised trading facility (OTF). ... The new category includes broker crossing systems, which can be described as internal electronic matching systems operated by an investment firm which execute client orders against other client orders. ... It shall not include facilities where there is no genuine trade execution or arranging taking place in the system, such as bulletin boards used for advertising buying and selling interests, other entities aggregating or pooling potential buying or selling interests, or electronic post-trade confirmation services.

'(8) This new category of organised trading facility will complement the existing types of trading venues. While regulated markets and multilateral trading facilities are characterised by non-discretionary execution of transactions, the operator of an organised trading facility should have discretion over how a transaction is to be executed. Consequently, conduct of business rules, best execution and client order handling obligations should apply to the transactions concluded on an OTF operated by an investment firm or a market operator. However, because an OTF constitutes a genuine trading

---

16 MiFID, art 4(1)(7)
17 European Commission Services, *Review of the Markets in Financial Instruments Directive (MiFID)* (December 2010), Public Consultation, http://ec.europa.eu/internal_market/consultations/docs/2010/mifid/consultation_paper_en.pdf, para 2.4

platform, the platform operator should be neutral. Therefore, the operator of an OTF should not be allowed to execute in the OTF any transaction between multiple third-party buying and selling interests including client orders brought together in the system against his own proprietary capital. This also excludes them from acting as systematic internalisers in the OTF operated by them.'[18]

3.7   Clearly there is a diversity of methodologies, but for the purposes of a study of clearing and settlement arrangements they can be grouped into two sets: multilateral venues, such as regulated markets (exchanges) and MTFs, and single-firm arrangements typified by the OTF and systematic internaliser. This distinction is important for an understanding of how clearing and settlement instructions originate and can be carried out. In the first type, clearing and settlement instructions are typically generated by the platform, and sent directly to the clearing and settlement system operators. Systematic internalisers may act as buyer to the seller and vice versa – in effect carrying out a mini-CCP type role – obviating the need for clearing. Operators of single-firm trading environments may be able to effect settlement of the trades they arrange between clients by holding client assets in custody, and achieving settlement by book transfer on its own books. This process is called 'internalised' or 'on-us' settlement;[19] but in practice the coincidence between custodianship and broking is infrequent, so a more usual model is for each client to have to make its own settlement arrangements. Settlement would be achieved by generation of bespoke settlement instructions sent via the client's custodian, where applicable, to the CSD.

Finally, mention should be made of two other features of the post-MiFID trading environment: smart order routing technology and direct market access by clients.

Smart Order Routing

3.8   With the proliferation of trading venues and a requirement to achieve best execution for clients, firms need to be able to search around the various possible venues for best prices, and indeed to seize price opportunities for themselves in relation to their own proprietary trading activities. Smart order routing enables this type of scanning to take place and for orders to be sent automatically for execution at the optimum venue. Smart order routing can, however, be complicated. A large sale order may be received by a firm which has another client which has an unfilled order to buy the stock. One option is to split up the large sale and attempt to cross the sale and purchase orders; another is to execute the sale order in small units on the relevant regulated market (or, if more than one, one of them) or an MTF; a third is to expose it to a dark pool; a fourth may be to bargain bilaterally with other brokers who may operate BCNs or act as systematic internalisers or market-makers. If the order, or part of it, is routed to another broker's BCN it may move out into the hands of a third broker who might execute in a regulated market or MTF rejected by the smart

18 European Commission, *Proposal for a Regulation of the European Parliament and of the Council on markets in financial instruments etc* (October 2011), COM(2011) 652 final, http://eur-lex.europa.eu/LexUriServ/LexUriServ.do?uri=COM:2011:0652:FIN:EN:PDF, proposed recitals (7) and (8)

19 Cf **section 2.21**

order routing software of the first broker. For clearing and settlement practice, none of this complexity matters, provided that each step is clearly demarcated in terms of who the counterparty to the trade is, and the price, ISIN and size are reconciled.

Direct Market Access

3.9   Sophisticated clients such as hedge funds may be eager to seize momentary price advantages in fast-moving markets, advantages which would be lost if they had to submit orders to a broker who executes the order in the traditional manner. Clients like these have demanded and been given 'direct market access', which enables them to enter directly into transactions at the relevant venue, without the intervention of the actual venue participant. The participant remains responsible for the client's trading, in terms of market orderliness and ensuring that arrangements are in place enabling the client's positions to be cleared and settled. In practice this will involve the participant assuming a degree of counterparty risk in relation to a direct market access client, and the suppliers of clearing and settlement services will wish to understand that risk fully.

COUNTERPARTY RISK

3.10   From the preceding discussion it is apparent that trading styles engender differing degrees of counterparty risk. Notionally, trading parties take on this risk in relation to each other: if I agree to sell to you, it is, or ought to be, my responsibility to deliver to you; and your responsibility is to pay me the right amount against that delivery. But this is too simplistic. The involvement of clearing and settlement service providers shows that a complex array of differing risk options is the result:

- Where a venue requires that all transactions be cleared through a CCP, unless the market participant is a 'clearing member' of the venue, it will need to hire a GCM to clear for it. The GCM becomes buyer to a selling participant or seller to a buying participant and is therefore involved as counterparty to the trade, assuming counterparty risk on its client (and vice versa). (The role of the GCM is described in **section 2.8**.)

- A market participant may hire a settlement agent who assumes the duty to settle vis-à-vis the participant only, but not in relation to any third party or the operator of the trading venue – this arrangement is sometimes referred to as 'Model A clearing', to distinguish it from Model B arrangements, described in **section 18.26** (even though there is no 'clearing' involved, in the sense used in this book[20]). But, in practice, as **section 18.5** elaborates, even a Model A settlement agent may take on liabilities in carrying out its role.

- A settlement agent may assume the duty of achieving settlement in relation to other participants in the venue and/or the venue operator, effectively underwriting the participant's obligations – this is what is referred to as 'Model B clearing'.

[20] See **section 1.6**

- Trading participants have clients of their own. A client may have its own custodian or preferred GCM and may therefore make its own clearing and settlement arrangements. These may bypass the trading participant altogether.

- Trades may not be carried out on an organised venue but may take place across the books of a broker operating an OTF or as market-maker or systematic internaliser. In such cases the parties will need to make their own arrangements for settlement of the trades; a trade carried out in an OTF could be settled directly between ultimate buyer and ultimate seller without the need for delivery and payment to cross the books of the network provider. These arrangements will not usually involve a CCP.

- An exception to the last-stated proposition is where the transaction involves an OTC derivative for which mandatory clearing has been prescribed under EMIR.[21] Even though the transaction may not have been entered into on an organised trading venue the interposition of a CCP (and, thus, where needed, GCMs) will be added to the requirement of settlement services.

---

21 Regulation (EU) No 648/2012 of the European Parliament and of the Council of 4 July 2012 on OTC derivatives, central counterparties and trade repositories

4 Post-trade support services

INTRODUCTION

4.1   Post-trade services are not limited to clearing and settlement. The difficulty which the European Commission Services had in pinpointing the characteristic activities of clearing and settlement infrastructures[1] is in part attributable to the wide range of associated and ancillary services which may be needed in order to progress from the trade to the successful delivery of securities to a buyer and payment to the seller. In addition to clearing and settlement, there are at least the following: matching and confirmation; data aggregation and distribution; portfolio compression; communications; and data warehousing (trade repositories). Each of these may be a vital component of the post-trade process. The purpose of this chapter is to look at the roles of these services in the post-trade value chain, and legal issues associated with them.

MATCHING AND CONFIRMATION

4.2   Unless you and I both agreed that we have a deal, and what that deal is, there is no trade to clear and settle. Ensuring that there is such an agreement is the role of matching (also known as verification or affirmation).[2] It is essential to capture basic information about transactions in order that clearing and settlement infrastructures know what has been agreed on, so that the bargain can be cleared and settled:

(1) The information that there is indeed a bargain. You may think you sold 100 at a price of 59, but I heard you sell 110 at a price of 59, which was better than the other guy in the market who was offering 110 at a price of 62. Fist-fights broke out on trading floors operating by open outcry when this kind of problem surfaced, and exchanges had to have codes of behaviour as part of their objective of maintaining an orderly market. Now that trading tends to be done by clicking on a mouse, there is less scope for this kind of disagreement, but nevertheless it is there. Matching what you said with what I said guarantees that there is a bargain.[3]

(2) The central elements of the bargain. In a sale transaction, these elements identify who is buyer, who is seller, the price, the thing being sold, and

---

1   European Commission Services, *Draft working document on post-trading* (May 2006), http://ec.europa.eu/internal_market/financial-markets/docs/clearing/draft/draft_en.pdf

2   European Commission Services, *Working document of Definitions of Post-trading Activities* (October   2005),   http://ec.europa.eu/internal_market/financial-markets/docs/cesame/ec-docs/20051027_definitions1_en.pdf

3   See **section 1.3**

the quantity being sold. Some transactions are more complicated, and particularly where OTC derivatives are concerned, there may be more elements. Yet even in a credit derivative transaction there will still be a buyer, a seller, a price, a reference credit (or basket of reference credits), and a notional principal. Additional variability may come in with trigger events, reflecting some optionality in the bargain.

(3) The reference data for the central components and the variable data. Some of the core elements of transaction data are variable, and some are static. The following elements of data ('reference data') are static: the identifiers for the buyer, the seller, and the product. With derivative transactions much energy can be expended on identification of the product, as standardisation is at the heart of straight-through-processing. Obtaining uniformity of standards for recording reference data is surprisingly difficult – it is the twenty-first century's equivalent of agreeing standard screw pitches during the industrial revolution – vital, costly if not done at all, dangerous if done badly, and deeply uninteresting to most business executives focused on the next quarter's profit-and-loss. The other data elements (quantity and price) will be variable; trading platforms aim to minimise the number of different things to be agreed in order to promote liquidity, so will typically impose unitised lot and tick sizes.

4.3   Matching is primarily a matter of capturing inputs, and comparing them. If a transaction is concluded on an exchange or MTF, it should be a simple matter of noting that an offer or bid was accepted; disputes over the existence or fundamentals of the trade should therefore be rare. In an OTC environment the need for a matching service is more acute, because there is no standardised infrastructure on which the offers, counter-offers, acceptances and data elements are recorded. Historically mismatches were picked up at the 'confirmation' stage – that is, when the parties sought to document the particular trade in order to fit it underneath a 'master agreement' governing general aspects of inter-party contractual dealings. Confirmation practices were overhauled before the financial crisis:

> 'Early in 2005 prudential supervisors began to express increasing concern about the size and rapid growth of confirmation backlogs for credit derivatives. ... The [Counterparty Risk Management Policy Group II] report, entitled *Toward greater financial stability: a private sector perspective*, which was released in July 2005, highlighted the serious and growing backlogs in the credit derivatives markets and called for an industry roundtable to be convened to address them. In September 2005, prudential supervisors took the lead and called 14 leading credit derivatives dealers to the Federal Reserve Bank of New York, where the supervisors collectively made clear their concerns about the risks created by the backlogs... By September 2006 these firms had made very substantial progress in reducing existing backlogs and in preventing new backlogs from arising by moving towards an automated processing environment and dedicating appropriate resources to the back office. The total number of confirmations outstanding had been reduced by 70%. The percentage of trades confirmed electronically had doubled, exceeding 80% of total trade volume.'[4]

---

4   Bank for International Settlements Committee on Payment and Settlement Systems, *New developments in clearing and settlement arrangements for OTC derivatives* (March 2007), http://www.bis.org/publ/cpss77.pdf, p 2

4.4   *Post-trade support services*

Automated data capture and upload to a service provider at the moment of trade is the start of the process; then the matching engine can check that both parties have reached agreement, and reject the trade if there is a mismatch. Confirmation and matching services 'increase efficiency and mitigate credit and counterparty risk.'[5]

The matching service provider will, by virtue of these activities, be equipped with a useful database of transaction information, which can then be used to feed into clearing and settlement systems or trade repositories.

4.4   There is a tendency for a 'network externality' to develop in respect of matching services, as indeed there is for most post-trade services.[6] In this context it may be noted that MarkitWire serves as the data capture and matching system for both the SwapClear and ICE Clear Europe clearing platforms in respect of OTC credit derivatives transactions.

4.5   Finally, it may be noted that the problem of matching is not confined to derivatives markets. Securities may also be traded over-the-counter, and national differences in matching practices were noted to cause increased costs and risk. Harmonised processes were agreed between the industry and the CSDs in 2006;[7] in due course the use of the Target2-Securities settlement platform is expected to lead to still further harmonisation.

DATA AGGREGATION AND DISTRIBUTION

4.6   Transaction data are an essential commodity for providers of clearing and settlement services. The slow dissolution of national models for trading, clearing and settlement and the opening of Europe as a single financial market have spawned a secondary market for data about trades. It is no longer appropriate to imagine that transaction data can be put into a pipe by the stock exchange, down which it will flow to the CCP and CSD so as to achieve a seamless process from trade to settlement. Rather, there are multiple services providers at many stages. First, and most importantly, there are many venues on which a transaction in a single type of security may be carried out. Different venues may prescribe the use of different CCPs, or there may be competing interoperable CCPs serving a single venue; or the trade may not require to be cleared at all, for example if it is an over-the-counter trade. The CCPs and associated GCMs will need details of the trade in order to take on their primary role of managing risk, collecting margin and netting. Then there is the settlement stage to organise. While competing settlement venues are still an idea for the future, settlement agents compete for the business of providing access to CSDs and payment systems, and they too need to know what their obligations will be.

---

5   European Central Bank, *OTC Derivatives and Post-trading Structures* (September 2009), http://www.ecb.eu/pub/pdf/other/overthecounterderivatives200909en.pdf, p 19
6   See **section 7.24(2)**
7   European Securities Forum and European Central Securities Depositories Association, *Proposals to harmonise and standardise pre-settlement date matching processes throughout Europe* (October 2006), http://ec.europa.eu/internal_market/financial-markets/docs/cesame/ giovannini/20061023-esf-ecsda-matching_en.pdf

So a new type of service has been able to emerge: the data aggregator and distributor. However, the primary role of this service-provider has not been the facilitation of clearing and settlement. The implementation of the Markets in Financial Instruments Directive (MiFID)[8] imposed a collection of reporting obligations on investment firms with regard to transactions in financial instruments admitted to trading on a regulated market, and introduced a requirement for regulated markets, MTFs and investment firms to make public volume and price data about transactions in shares.[9] It is these obligations which created the market for data vendors. First, that market will be reviewed; and then the implications for clearing and settlement will be considered.

MiFID

4.7   The MiFID obligations were partly to facilitate the policing of market abuse, and partly to enable transparency of pricing, which is an essential requirement if trading firms are to select trading venues by reference to the 'best execution' they can achieve for their clients.[10] A distinction may thus be drawn between 'trade reporting' obligations, directed towards market transparency; and 'transaction reporting', directed towards edification of the regulator. The reporting obligations include a duty for firms to report data relating to transactions to the competent authority as quickly as possible;[11] a duty for 'systematic internalisers' to publish quotes relating to shares;[12] a duty for firms, MTFs and regulated markets to publish the volume, price and timing of transactions in shares;[13] and a duty for MTFs and regulated markets to publish bid and offer prices and the depth of trading interests in respect of shares.[14] These obligations are to be broadened under the Markets in Financial Instruments Regulation (MiFIR) proposed as part of the revision of MiFID, so that they will apply to OTFs and to the entire range of MiFID financial instruments.[15]

4.8   MiFID also provided for reporting to be made on behalf of firms by trade-matching or reporting systems approved by competent authorities, by regulated markets, or by MTFs.[16] Regulated markets were permitted by MiFID, but not obliged, to give access to their publication arrangements to investment firms to facilitate compliance with their transparency obligations.[17] Furthermore, subordinate legislation under MiFID provided specifications for the content of trade and transaction reports.[18]

---

8   Directive 2004/39/EC of the European Parliament and of the Council of 21 April 2004 on markets in financial instruments, etc

9   MiFID art 28 (investment firms); art 30 (MTFs); art 45 (regulated markets)

10 See MiFID, recital (44) in particular

11 MiFID, art 25(3)

12 MiFID, art 27(1)

13 MiFID, arts 28(1), 30(1), 45(1)

14 MiFID, arts 29(1), 44(1)

15 European Commission, *Proposal for a Regulation of the European Parliament and of the Council on markets in financial instruments* (October 2011), COM(2011) 652 final, http://eur-lex.europa.eu/LexUriServ/LexUriServ.do?uri=COM:2011:0652:FIN:EN:PDF, Title II

16 MiFID, art 25(5)

17 MiFID, art 44(1), 45(1)

18 Commission Regulation 1287/2006/EC of 10 August 2006 implementing Directive 2004/39/EC of the European Parliament and of the Council as regards record-keeping obligations for investment firms, transaction reporting, market transparency, etc

4.9   Post-trade support services

In respect of transaction reporting, the FSA allows for reports to be made to it via 'Approved Reporting Mechanisms'; an applicant for that status will be expected to comply with technical requirements laid down by the FSA.[19] The technical criteria are not publicly available, presumably because of the risk to integrity of the FSA's own security.

In respect of trade reporting, regulated firms may choose either to use an FSA-approved 'trade data monitor' (TDM) or some other system which ensures that the firm complies fully with its MiFID obligations. The FSA has issued Guidelines for firms using TDMs, which includes an official list of the TDMs recognised by the FSA to satisfy its requirements.[20] There is also a set of standards required to be met by TDMs wishing to be included in the FSA's official list. These are set out in an FSA Policy Statement,[21] and cover security, timeliness of dissemination, identification and correction of errors, and transparency of pricing, as well as various operational requirements resembling those imposed on regulated firms.

4.9   The European Commission's proposal for a revised Directive on markets in financial instruments (MiFID2)[22] will introduce a uniform European regulatory regime for data reporting service providers. Three types of data reporting service are identified, each of which will require a licence: an approved publication arrangement (the service of publishing trade reports), providing a consolidated tape (the service of collecting trade reports and consolidating them into a continuous electronic live data stream providing real-time price and volume data), and an approved reporting mechanism (the service of reporting details of transactions to regulators). The regulatory regime will require the management of a data reporting service provider to be of good repute and have sufficient knowledge, skills and experience, and commit sufficient time, to perform their duties. The provider has to be managed in a sound and prudent way and a manner which promotes the integrity of the market and the interests of its clients.[23] Finally, market operators can operate these services without the need for a supplementary licence.[24]

4.10   Stock exchanges are ideally positioned to act as data aggregators and distributors, for various reasons. First, as incumbent 'regulated markets' under MiFID, they are likely to be the 'most relevant market in terms of liquidity.'[25] (The significance of this is that the competent authority of such a market must assess for each traded share the standard market size, which affects the obligations of systematic internalisers to publish quotes.[26]) If the exchange is the most liquid market then there will be network effects, attracting more

---

19   Financial Services Authority, *Approved Reporting Mechanisms* (February 2011), http://www. fsa.gov.uk/Pages/Doing/Regulated/Returns/mtr/arms/index.shtml

20   Financial Services Authority, *Guidelines for investment firms using TDMs* (July 2009), http:// www.fsa.gov.uk/pubs/international/guidelines_tdm.pdf

21   Financial Services Authority, *Implementing the Markets in Financial Instruments Directive* (January 2007), Policy Statement PS07/2, pp 60–63

22   European Commission, *Proposal for a Directive of the European Parliament and of the Council on markets in financial instruments etc* (October 2011), COM(2011) 656 final, http:// eur-lex.europa.eu/LexUriServ/LexUriServ.do?uri=COM:2011:0656:FIN:EN:PDF

23   MiFID2 Proposal, art 65

24   MiFID2 Proposal, art 61(2)

25   Commission Regulation 1287/2006/EC of 10 August 2006 implementing Directive 2004/39/ EC as regards market transparency, etc, art 9

26   MiFID, art 27

trading, and (as far as the present context is concerned) attracting more buyers for the market data, since a deeper market implies superior accuracy as regards the price of the share. Furthermore, a market participant's obligation to report transactions to its regulator can be waived if the exchange reports the transactions directly.[27] These features may tend to encourage participants to trade on the incumbent exchange and to rely on it both as a data aggregator and a data distributor.

Notwithstanding the importance of control of data and its exploitation in this context, there have been few studies of the effect which the controllers of data may have on the post-trading environment, as contrasted with the *costs* of trading, clearing and settlement,[28] or the *content* of data in respect of which transparency is required.[29] A notable exception is a study by Dr Karel Lannoo,[30] who noted at the inception of MiFID that data consolidation is essential to enable multi-venue trading in a single market; that distribution of financial market data was a big business and that MiFID acknowledged that market data can be commercialised, and that an unregulated market-led approach to post-trade data consolidation might not deliver transparency owing to lack of standardisation and data quality.

Transaction data feeds for clearing and settlement

4.11   The purposes of MiFID's requirements are thus to enhance the process of price discovery, to ensure firms to deliver best execution to their clients, and to enable regulators to police the markets. MiFID's rules on transaction data were not intended to improve the flow to other service providers, or to potential competitors, in the clearing and settlement space. Since clearing and settlement service providers cannot perform their functions without the flow of trade data, it may be asked who owns the data on which the post-trade services depend? This area is troublesome not only in that ownership is difficult to establish, but also because exploitation of data is potentially lucrative in a post-MiFID world. The London Stock Exchange Group derived £102 million from cash equities trading in the UK but £104 million from selling real time data in its financial year ending March 2010.[31] In order to exploit data relating to the markets, the exchange must own the information. It is unclear that a trader or investor owns information relating to its trading activity, or an issuer owns information about the price of its stock; it would therefore be difficult to say that an exchange which uses the information it is able to gather, process and disseminate from the trading activity carried out on its systems is anything other than legitimate.

---

27 MiFID, art 25(5)
28 Cf European Commission Competition DG, *Competition in EU Securities trading and post-trading* (May 2006), Issues Paper, http://ec.europa.eu/competition/sectors/financial_services/securities_trading.pdf
29 Cf Committee of European Securities Regulators, *CESR Technical Advice to the European Commission in the Context of the MiFID Review – Equity Markets – Post-trade Transparency Standards* (October 2010), http://www.esma.europa.eu/popup2.php?id=7282
30 Lannoo, K, *Financial Market Data and MiFID* (March 2007), ECMI Policy Brief No 6, http://www.ceps.eu/book/financial-market-data-and-mifid
31 London Stock Exchange Group, *Annual Report 2010* (March 2010), http://www.londonstockexchangegroup.com/investor-relations/financial-performance/financial-key-documents/annual-report-2010.pdf

4.12   Competition law concerns may arise. The European Commission initiated an investigation into the handling of price and other information in the credit default swaps (CDS) market. This information is of great relevance given that CDS transactions are OTC derivatives for which CCPs provide clearing services and that CCPs have a statutory right of access to pricing sources.[32]

> 'The Commission has indications that the 16 banks that act as dealers in the CDS market give most of the pricing, indices and other essential daily data only to Markit, the leading financial information company in the market concerned. This could be the consequence of collusion between them or an abuse of a possible collective dominance and may have the effect of foreclosing the access to the valuable raw data by other information service providers. ... The probe will also examine the behaviour of Markit, a UK-based company created originally to enhance transparency in the CDS market. The Commission is now concerned certain clauses in Markit's licence and distribution agreements could be abusive and impede the development of competition in the market for the provision of CDS information. ... The lack of transparency about the trading of derivatives and financial instruments traded Over the Counter (OTC) became apparent during the recent financial crisis. Given the importance of financial markets for the real economy, the Commission has been working to improve the regulation of CDS and other derivatives ... The Commission's antitrust tools are complementary to these regulatory measures, which together seek to ensure safe, sound and efficient financial markets.'[33]

4.13   It may also be asked what regulatory or other controls exist to ensure that post-trade infrastructures and service providers are given access to the data, and to regulate the price payable for the data. The following observations may be made.

(1) Pricing may be a real concern: in the United States, where Regulation NMS was implemented at approximately the same time as MiFID, raising similar issues, a study was commissioned by the Securities Industry and Financial Markets Association,[34] which found that two exchanges had dominant positions with the opportunity to exert monopoly pricing power. In Europe, monopolistic behaviour and its attendant abuses tend, as just observed, to be dealt with by ex-post regulatory intervention, rather than through up-front legislative rules.[35] Until the post-crisis spate of legislation, that was the position in Europe.

(2) In relation to OTC derivatives traded on a venue of execution, that venue will be obliged under article 8 of EMIR[36] to provide trade feeds on a non-discriminatory and transparent basis to any CCP that has been authorised to clear those contracts.

---

32   Regulation (EU) No 648/2012 of the European Parliament and of the Council of 4 July 2012 on OTC derivatives, central counterparties and trade repositories, arts 8, 40

33   European Commission, *Antitrust: Commission probes Credit Default Swaps market* (April 2011), Press Release IP/11/509

34   Securities Litigation & Consulting Group, Inc., *An Economic Study of Securities Market Data Pricing by the Exchanges* (July 2008), https://www.sifma.org/workarea/downloadasset. aspx?id=22962

35   See **Chapter 7**

36   Regulation (EU) No 648/2012 of the European Parliament and of the Council of 4 July 2012 on OTC derivatives, central counterparties and trade repositories

(3) Furthermore, article 40 of EMIR will give CCPs a statutory right to have access on a non-discriminatory basis to pricing sources to effectively measure its exposures, and in interoperability arrangements a CCP will have a right under article 51 to non-discriminatory access to the data needed for the performance of its functions from a venue of execution for which it provides services. These additional rights apply regardless of the product cleared.

(4) Under article 29 of the proposed MiFIR, a trading venue will be obliged to provide trade feeds on a non-discriminatory and transparent basis, including as regards fees related to access, on request to any authorised or recognised CCP that wishes to clear 'financial transactions' executed on that venue.

(5) Finally, under article 51 of the proposed Regulation on CSDs,[37] trading venues will be obliged to 'provide transaction feeds on a non-discriminatory and transparent basis to a CSD upon request by the CSD and may charge a fee for such transaction feeds to the requesting CSD on a cost-plus basis.' This is all very well, but the home state CSD is already in a good bargaining position: the trades cannot settle unless that CSD gets a feed, so a venue which denied a feed to CSDs in which their traded securities settle would rapidly go out of business. What this provision is trying to do is to ensure that feeds are not given exclusively to a single CSD; it is not going to help CCPs, GCMs, or settlement agents.

PORTFOLIO COMPRESSION SERVICES

4.14 The essence of a portfolio compression service is to take a market participant's portfolio of trades, and to squash it down so as to end up with a significantly smaller number of trades with fewer counterparties. At its simplest, two counterparties dealing with each other may have countervailing trades in the same product, such as a US dollar interest rate swap. While these might not net off exactly, it would be possible to tear them both up and replace them with a net swap product which replicates their economic position exactly, possibly involving a balancing payment or delivery of collateral to re-base the new transaction. In practice portfolio compression will be multilateral and to some extent cover a range of transaction types. That can lead to a compression whereby party A's trades with B, C and D are all cancelled, its trades with E and F are reduced in size, and party A receives a balancing payment from G (with whom it happened to have no trades at all).[38]

4.15 It will immediately be apparent that this type of arrangement is a multilateral netting scheme. The operator of the scheme will not act as central counterparty, so *British Eagle* risk will arise.[39] It should be noted that the *British Eagle* problem does not materialise unless one of the participants in the scheme becomes insolvent, so as an everyday device for risk reduction the

---

37 European Commission, *Proposal for a Regulation of the European Parliament and of the Council on improving securities settlement in the European Union and on central securities depositories etc* (March 2012), COM(2012) 73 final, http://eur-lex.europa.eu/LexUriServ/ LexUriServ.do?uri=CELEX:52012PC0073:EN:PDF

38 See European Central Bank, *OTC Derivatives and Post-trading Structures* (September 2009), http://www.ecb.eu/pub/pdf/other/overthecounterderivatives200909en.pdf, p 20

39 See **box 2.1**

possibility of an unwind of a post-insolvency compression does not invalidate the general desirability of the scheme. Indeed, the Committee on Payment and Settlement Systems (CPSS) has urged that 'market participants should routinely identify trades that could be voluntarily terminated, so as to reduce to the extent possible the positions that would need to be replaced following a default. To that end, they should expand their use of new services that facilitate multilateral voluntary termination of trades.'[40]

4.16 It could also be noted that portfolio compression will be unnecessary where there is a CCP in place, since reliable multilateral netting will already operate. With the drive toward clearing of standardised OTC derivatives transactions – that is, the type of transaction which is most readily amenable to compression – the future demand for portfolio compression is unclear.

COMMUNICATIONS NETWORK PROVIDERS

4.17 Communication links between infrastructures are vital to allow transaction information to flow to where it is needed: from traders to matching agencies; from trading platforms and matching agencies to clearing systems; from platforms or clearing systems to settlement and payment systems. Arguably the most important provider of communications services is SWIFT – the Society for Worldwide Interbank Financial Telecommunication. SWIFT is a member-owned cooperative based in Belgium.[41]

4.18 SWIFT is ignored by the FMI Principles,[42] and has no formal regulated status. Despite this, SWIFT is not ignored by the regulatory system. SWIFT is subject to extra-statutory oversight by the National Bank of Belgium (NBB), which has memoranda of understanding with other interested regulators.[43]

The starting point is a set of 'cooperative oversight principles' which are applied by the National Bank of Belgium to the cases of Euroclear and SWIFT. [44] These principles are: notification among central banks of cross-border systems; subjecting systems to oversight, specifically by the home state central bank; oversight of the system as a whole; assessment of the adequacy of the system's settlement and failure-to-settle procedures; and discouragement of the use of unsound systems. These principles seem to have weak, if any, relevance to SWIFT, though the NBB points out in its paper that the principles need to be 'reinterpreted to suit the specificities of a services provider in which the major sources of risk are almost exclusively of an operational nature.'[45] Under this framework the NBB has established various oversight groups composed of

---

40 CPSS, *New developments in clearing and settlement arrangements for OTC derivatives* (March 2007), http://www.bis.org/publ/cpss77.pdf, p 5

41 See http://www.swift.com/

42 Bank for International Settlements Committee on Payment and Settlement Systems and Technical Committee of the International Organization of Securities Commissions, *Principles for Financial Market Infrastructures* (April 2012), http://www.bis.org/publ/cpss101a.pdf; see **section 6.41(2)**

43 Kokkola, T, (ed), *The Payment System* (European Central Bank, September 2010), ISBN 978-928990632-6, http://www.ecb.eu/pub/pdf/other/paymentsystem200909en.pdf, p 289

44 National Bank of Belgium, 'High level expectation for the oversight of SWIFT' (June 2007) Financial Stability Review 2007, http://www.nbb.be/doc/ts/Publications/FSR/FSR_2007EN.pdf, pp 85–101

45 NBB, Financial Stability Review 2007, p 93

G10 central banks, the European Central Bank and the CPSS. The 'cup of tea' technique is used for supervision.[46]

SWIFT's regulatory obligations are set out in five High Level Expectations, viz:[47]

(1) Risk identification and management: SWIFT is expected to identify and manage relevant operational and financial risks to its critical services and ensure that its risk management processes are effective.

(2) Information security: SWIFT is expected to implement appropriate policies and procedures, and devote sufficient resources, to ensure the confidentiality and integrity of information, and the availability of its critical services.

(3) Reliability and resilience: Commensurate with its role in the global financial system, SWIFT is expected to implement appropriate policies and procedures, and devote sufficient resources, to ensure that its critical services are available, reliable and resilient and that business continuity management and disaster recovery plans support the timely resumption of its critical services in the event of an outage.

(4) Technology planning: SWIFT is expected to have in place robust methods to plan for the entire lifecycle of the use of technologies and the selection of technological standards.

(5) Communication with users: SWIFT is expected to be transparent to its users and provide them information that is sufficient to enable users to understand well their role and responsibilities in managing risks related to their use of SWIFT.

Assessment methodologies are provided in respect of each of these expectations.

TRADE REPOSITORIES

4.19 Trade repositories are an emerging class of infrastructure. Until the financial crisis of 2008, it would hardly have been imagined that trade repositories would be considered a vital part of the financial system. But the consensus among policy-makers, following the financial crisis of 2008, was that opacity was partly to blame. In particular, lack of transparency as regards the extent of key market participants' exposure to each other under OTC derivatives transactions was perceived to have led to reduced willingness to incur exposure, increases in collateral demands, and other self-protective behaviours which collectively worked to reduce liquidity, increase spreads, and deepen and lengthen the economic recession which ensued. Consequently, greater transparency in relation to OTC derivatives has been seen as a useful tool in order to prevent a similar problem in the future.[48]

A trade repository 'is a centralised registry that maintains an electronic database of the records of open OTC derivatives transactions. The primary public policy

---

46 NBB, Financial Stability Review 2007, p 92; see **section 6.14**
47 NBB, Financial Stability Review 2007, pp 96–101
48 Cf De Larosière, J, *The High-Level Group on Financial Supervision in the EU, Report* (February 2009), http://ec.europa.eu/economy_finance/publications/publication14527_en.pdf, paras 15, 27, 36, 93

benefit of a TR steps from the improved market transparency facilitated by its record keeping function, the integrity of information it maintains and effective access to this information by relevant authorities and the public in line with their respective information needs.'[49] 'A central data repository collects data ... with the purpose of increasing transparency and knowledge. This not only contributes to transparency, but also improves the operational efficiency of the market.'[50]

A trade repository will, often in conjunction with a matching service provider, capture transaction data from OTC traders, store it, and make it available to certain persons. The Depository Trust & Clearing Corporation (DTCC) set up its Trade Information Warehouse in the United States in November 2006. 'The Warehouse centralises OTC credit derivatives contracts and eliminates the risks, inefficiencies, and uncertainties that arise from incomplete documentation. This comprehensive database serves as the repository for all legally binding OTC credit derivatives contracts. The Warehouse services the contracts in its database ... provides payment services for these contracts, including calculation of payment amounts, netting of offsetting payment obligations ... and, in partnership with CLS Bank International, central settlement of these obligations in multiple currencies.'[51]

The scope of the data collected is likely to be mainly a matter of commercial need, but the CPSS and the International Organization of Securities Commissions (IOSCO) have issued recommendations on content: functional data categories for OTC derivatives could include operational data such as transaction numbering, product information, material transaction terms, valuation data such as pricing sources, counterparty information, information about underlying products or reference entities, and time-stamped event data.[52]

It may be noted that market participants may see benefits in participating in a trade repository even without being legally compelled to do so. The benefits are likely to be unconnected to the idea that the regulator has full information about their activities: rather the trade repository is likely to offer ancillary services, such as managing 'life-cycle events' arising in the course of a long-term transaction, such as payments and collateral transfers, portfolio reconciliation, and multilateral tear-up of redundant transactions.[53] Perhaps it is worth a note on what trade repositories may not be willing to do: they are not valuation agencies which calculate the mark-to-market position on the registered trades; they are not collateral monitoring agencies which determine what collateral has been posted by one counterparty to another or issue collateral calls; and they are not responsible for interpreting the data in their charge, or interrogating the data they have in order to find answers to questions which might be derived from the data.

---

49 CPSS, *Considerations for trade repositories in OTC derivatives markets* (May 2010), consultative report, http://www.bis.org/publ/cpss90.pdf, s 1

50 European Commission, *Ensuring efficient, safe and sound derivatives markets* (July 2009), Communication COM(2009) 332 final, http://eur-lex.europa.eu/LexUriServ/LexUriServ.do?uri=COM:2009:0332:FIN:EN:PDF, para 5.2

51 Morris, V, and Goldstein, S, *Guide to Clearance and Settlement* (Lightbulb Press, 2009), ISBN 978-1933569-98-7

52 CPSS and Technical Committee of IOSCO, *Report on OTC derivatives data reporting and aggregation requirements* (January 2012), http://www.bis.org/publ/cpss100.pdf

53 Ledrut, E, and Upper, C, 'Changing post-trading arrangements for OTC derivatives' (December 2007) BIS Quarterly Review, http://www.bis.org/publ/qtrpdf/r_qt0712i.pdf

4.20 The enthusiasm for trade repositories may also be partly a result of the success which the DTCC had in handling the default of Lehman Brothers in 2008. In relation to the Lehman default, the DTCC reported:

'DTCC also acted to minimize risk for its OTC derivatives customers from the Lehman bankruptcy. The actions included stopping the automated central settlement of credit default swap (CDS) payment obligations on Sept. 15 that were maintained in DTCC's Trade Information Warehouse (Warehouse) for counterparties of Lehman Brothers International (Europe) and Lehman Brothers Special Financing, Inc. On Oct. 21, DTCC also completed, without incident, the automated credit event processing of Lehman Brothers Holdings Inc. (LBHI) involving $72 billion of credit default swaps. DTCC calculated and bilaterally netted all amounts due on credit default swaps written on LBHI. This resulted in approximately US$5.2 billion owed from net sellers of protection on LBHI to net buyers of protection. The portion of this net funds settlement allocable to trades between major dealers was handled through the normal settlement procedures of CLS Bank International.'[54]

Issues faced by trade repositories

4.21 If trade repositories are to carry out these roles effectively, they will need to be mindful of the following matters which have a bearing on their work.

(1) *Standardisation.* In order to capture quickly and efficiently the trades entered into by a market participant, it is vital that the trade repository can establish a standardised modality for capture of data pertaining to transactions within the trading firms themselves. It follows that the pre-requisites for a matching service are also needed by a trade repository, since if the details of a purported trade provided by different counterparties do not match, there is no trade, and to report it as such would be misleading. The requirement for standardisation leads also to the conclusion that trade repositories will have limited scope, since the more tailored or uncommon the transaction is, the less likely the trade repository will have designed functionality to capture the essential elements of the transaction. Trade repositories thus walk in the same ground as organised trading platforms and CCPs; they cannot be relied on to 'plug a gap' in transparency left by these alternative transparency-enhancing solutions. Hence, under EMIR, a fall-back option is left to firms to enable them to report to ESMA any transaction which can neither be cleared nor reported to a trade repository.[55]

(2) *Communications.* Likewise, the accuracy of a trade repository's records depends on the integrity of the communications systems under which firms report transactions. The communications network needs to be secure and fast.

(3) *Data storage, correction and backup.* A trade repository is both a data processor and a data storage facility. Numerous legal and regulatory obligations are associated with these functions, which may oblige the trade repository to comply with data protection registration requirements, business continuity and disaster recovery standards, anti-terrorism and anti-money-laundering laws and similar legislation imposed on organisations handling financial data, and bank secrecy and confidentiality restrictions.

---

54 DTCC, *DTCC Successfully closes out Lehman Brothers bankruptcy* (October 2008), Press release, http://www.dtcc.com/news/press/releases/2008/dtcc_closes_lehman_cds.php
55 Article 9(3)

In some cases the legislation will not apply directly to the trade repository but will apply indirectly, because its participating firms have no choice but to transfer their own requirements to the repository, either because the legislation so requires or because the firm is subject to regulatory outsourcing rules which have the same effect.

(4) *Disclosure.* If a central role of a trade repository is to share the information it gathers with relevant authorities 'and the public', it will need clear legal powers to enable it to do so. There is a balance to be struck between public and private disclosure of a market participant's book. Complete transparency may provide a greater degree of general reassurance in moments of stress, but a trading strategy is a highly secret matter and a policy of general disclosure could threaten the viability of markets.[56] Even where disclosure to the regulator is concerned, the existence of a power to disclose is not self-evident, especially where confidential information about a firm's trading positions, its strategy and its financial robustness – all information vital to the raison d'être of gathering the information in the first place, but from the firm's viewpoint highly secret – is concerned. The DTCC has reversed its policy of not providing specific counterparty information, and has publicly indicated that 'regulators and other governmental entities can expect that ... counterparty names will be included in both aggregate and trade-level information provided by the [Trade Information] Warehouse if the requesting regulator or other governmental entity affirms that it has a material interest in that information in furtherance of its regulatory or governmental responsibilities.'[57] As policy this is unobjectionable. It is more difficult to be confident that the policy is allowable under all relevant legal systems. The subject is discussed further in the CPSS-IOSCO report.[58]

Regulation of trade repositories

4.22   The regulatory approach to trade repositories is recommended by the FMI Principles[59] and implemented in Europe through Title VII of EMIR. The FMI Principles state that a trade repository 'should provide timely and accurate data to relevant authorities and the public in line with their respective needs.'[60] The principal risks which were identified by the CPSS[61] are twofold:

- Operational reliability – the need for the trade repository to maintain functionality continuously and accurately, including when there is a threat to business continuity.
- Safeguarding of data – the need for the trade repository to ensure the integrity of the information which it collects and stores, and to avoid loss, leakage, unauthorised access and mis-processing.

Trade repositories are also expected to obey a swathe of other FMI Principles which were originally designed for infrastructures which handle investors' assets

---

56 Cf Acharya, V, *A transparency standard for derivatives* (November 2010), http://pages.stern. nyu.edu/~sternfin/vacharya/public_html/Acharya_Proposal_Disclosure_Standard_v3.pdf
57 Depository Trust & Clearing Corporation, *DTCC Policy for Releasing CDS Data to Global Regulators* (March 2010), Media Statement, http://www.dtcc.com/news/press/releases/2010/ data_release_policy.php
58 CPSS 100, http://www.bis.org/publ/cpss100.pdf
59 Principles 23 and 24
60 FMI Principle 24
61 CPSS May 2010 consultative report

and entitlements: Principles 1 (sound legal basis in all relevant jurisdictions), 2 (governance), 3 (risk management framework), 15 (general business risk controls), 17 (operational risk), 20 (links to other infrastructures), 21 (efficiency and effectiveness), 22 (communication procedures and standards) and 23 (disclosure of rules) are all applied to trade repositories notwithstanding that their role is wholly ancillary to the smooth everyday functioning of financial markets. This might be thought heavy-handed. On the other hand, some rules such as Principles 13 (default rules), 18 (access conditions) or 19 (tiering) might be thought useful, but are not applied. Unfortunately, regulation is a one-way ratchet, so once rules of doubtful utility are in place, they are unlikely to be repealed.

Oddly, though, there is a regulatory gap in the FMI Principles. If disclosure to the public and to regulators of information on registered transactions is a core regulated activity for trade repositories, it seems odd that CCPs might be exempt from equivalent obligations. After all, the role of CCPs in this process has been acknowledged, by the European Commission in particular.[62] EMIR, on the other hand, does oblige CCPs to make reports to trade repositories of derivative contracts they enter into which fall within paragraphs (4) to (10) of Section C of the Annex to MiFID, either directly or via a reporting service.[63]

4.23   EMIR sets out the European regulatory regime. Trade repositories will require to be authorised by ESMA and will be entitled to passport into all Member States.[64] Third-country trade repositories may be recognised by ESMA and then provide services to entities established in the EU.[65]

EMIR sets out the compliance obligations of trade repositories as follows. A trade repository is to have: robust governance arrangements, including internal reporting lines and internal controls;[66] non-discriminatory conditions for access;[67] price transparency;[68] and operational risk management systems, including business continuity and disaster recovery plans.[69] A plan to implement FMI Principle 22 on communications procedures conforming to open industry standards did not make it to the final text of EMIR. On the other hand, EMIR goes further than the FMI Principles by requiring trade repositories to keep their trade repository function operationally separate from other services provided by the same body, such as matching and portfolio compression.[70] The central functions of a trade repository are addressed as follows:

- Trade repositories must calculate the positions in respect of each reporting entity by class of derivative.[71] They must publish aggregate positions by class of derivative.[72]
- Trade repositories must make 'the necessary information' available to various bodies, including ESMA, the ESRB, the regulator of the reporting party, regulators of CCPs, and others.[73]

---

62   For example European Commission Communication COM(2009) 332 final, pp 2, 7, 9, 10 etc
63   Article 9
64   EMIR, art 55
65   EMIR, art 77
66   EMIR, art 78(1)–(4)
67   EMIR, art 78(7)
68   EMIR, art 78(8)
69   EMIR, art 79
70   EMIR, art 78(5)
71   EMIR, art 80(4)
72   EMIR, art 81(1)
73   EMIR, art 81

- Confidentiality and integrity of the information received are otherwise to be ensured. Use of data received for commercial purposes is prohibited. Records must be kept for ten years, and must be updated as necessary. Parties to a contract must be allowed to access and correct the information held about that contract.[74]

ESMA is given disciplinary powers, including a power to fine a trade repository which fails to comply with these requirements.[75]

REGULATION OF POST-TRADE SERVICES IN THE UNITED KINGDOM

4.24 The discussion of the status of particular classes of post-trade service provider shows two things: first, that it is by no means clear that all post-trade services are subject to regulation at all at European level; secondly, that regulatory reach is widening, bringing more providers within its grip. Within the United Kingdom, by contrast, there has for many years been a broad requirement for post-trade service providers to seek a regulatory licence. Furthermore, the scope of regulation is also continuing to expand.

4.25 Article 25(2) of the Financial Services and Markets Act 2000 (Regulated Activities) Order 2001 (RAO)[76] lists the following as a 'specified kind of activity', thereby rendering such activity a criminal offence if carried on in the United Kingdom without authorisation: 'making arrangements with a view to a person who participates in the arrangements buying, selling, subscribing for or underwriting [securities, options, futures, contracts for differences and certain other types of investment] (whether as principal or agent).' Furthermore, 'agreeing to carry on an activity of the kind specified by [article 25(2)]' is also a specified kind of activity.[77] Interpreting these provisions is not easy. If I establish a coffee-shop in the City of London, with a view to City folk carrying out investment transactions while they enjoy my coffee, this would on the face of the legislation require me to obtain a financial services licence. Moreover, a coffee company entering into a franchise arrangement with a shop-owner in the City would also apparently be caught. Case law on article 25(2) is sparse and appears to focus on pre-trade activities.[78] However, the language is wide enough, in theory, to cover post-trade services as well. The FSA has this to say about article 25(2):

> 'It is also the FSA's view that certain arrangements may come within the activity even though the parties may have already committed to the transaction using other arrangements. This would typically apply to a clearing house whose clearing and settlement facilities may be seen to be made with a view to the members of the clearing house, as participants in its arrangements, entering into transactions (usually through an investment exchange) which must be cleared through the clearing house to be completed. The clearing house is providing an essential part of the market infrastructure

---

74 EMIR, art 80
75 EMIR, art 73
76 2001 SI No 516
77 RAO, art 64
78 *Re Inertia Partnership LLP* [2007] 1 BCLC 739 ; *Watersheds v da Costa and Gentleman* [2009] EWHC 1299 (QB)

that is necessary to support trading activities. The same principle applies outside the markets context. So for example if a company that wishes to raise capital from private investors tells the potential investors, in order to increase their confidence, that all aspects of paying for and issuing shares will be handled by a particular firm, that firm may come within article 25(2) when it provides those services.'[79]

Evidently all providers of matching, data collection and publication, portfolio compression, communications networks, and trade repositories – not to mention clearing and settlement systems – would prima facie fall within these legislative provisions.

4.26 Various exceptions cut back the scope of article 25(2). Most significantly, article 27 of the RAO states that a person does not carry on the activity specified by article 25(2) 'merely by providing means by which one party to a transaction (or potential transaction) is able to communicate with other such parties.' However, the conclusion is that other types of post-trade service providers may well find themselves caught by the RAO.

The Service Company Regime

4.27 The FSA has developed a 'service company regime' of light-touch regulation specifically for the providers of services so caught. This regime does not require a person with authorisation to comply with the full gamut of regulation: in particular, the provisions of the FSA's Handbook of Rules and Guidance which relate to senior management, systems and controls apply, but the prudential sourcebooks (applying capital requirements) are disapplied and only limited parts of the conduct of business sourcebooks apply. The outcome is to give the FSA formal regulatory oversight over service companies without imposing irrelevant regulatory standards. The rules applicable to service companies are set out in a special 'Handbook Guide'[80] and further explanation of the regime is set out in an old consultation document.[81]

Service providers to payment systems

4.28 Although this chapter focuses on services more likely to be associated with clearing and securities settlement, it is possible for service providers to support the payment sector as well. Typically such services will take the form of software or other facilities enabling a payment system to discharge its functions. Under section 206A of the Banking Act 2009, it is open to the Treasury to draw a service provider into the ambit of payment systems regulation. 'Telecommunication or information technology services are examples of the kind of services that may fall within [the power].'[82] As to the implications, see **sections 11.3ff**.

79 Financial Services Authority, *The Perimeter Guidance Manual* (August 2009), PERG 2.7.7BB
80 Financial Services Authority, Handbook of Rules and Guidance, *Handbook requirements for service companies* (February 2004, August 2010), SERV
81 Financial Services Authority, *The Service Company Regime* (June 2000), CP 55, http://www. fsa.gov.uk/library/policy/cp/2000/55.shtml
82 Section 206A(3)

Table 4.1   Regulation of Selected Post-trade Service Providers

Service Provider	Principal Services	Regulatory arrangements
SWIFT (Society for Worldwide Interbank Financial Telecommunication)	Interbank communications including payment, securities settlement and corporate actions messages	National Bank of Belgium leads a group of 12 central banks formed into an oversight group.[83] Regulatory standards are set out in specifically-created 'High Level Expectations' which have no statutory basis[84]
Omgeo	Automated trade allocation, confirmation, settlement notification	In the United Kingdom Omgeo Limited is authorised and regulated under the Service Company regime[85]
MarkitSERV	Matching of OTC derivatives trades for feeding to CCPs	In the United Kingdom MarkitSERV Limited is authorised and regulated under the Service Company regime[86]

STANDARDISATION

4.29   In order to achieve efficiency in post-trade services, unless all services are to be provided within a single organisation it is essential that the various service providers can interoperate smoothly. This type of interoperation – between complementary, rather than competing, services – demands not only effective communication but also, in order to allow competition between alternative service providers to flourish, standardisation. Unfortunately achieving standardisation has been difficult. The difficulties can be classified as follows.

4.30   In the first place, it has been difficult to obtain recognition among both regulated firms and the regulators who supervise them that standardised data and reporting methodologies relating to transactions is desirable. Data is the poor relation of the middle and back office, which itself is frequently not a 'profit centre' and therefore the recipient of little management attention unless things go wrong.

4.31   Secondly, it has been difficult to get regulators to agree that standardisation of data formats and related issues is desirable, let alone agree on what standard approaches should be adopted. Europe has a plethora of regulators, whose attention has been elsewhere; and while the desire to convert

83 Bank of England, *Payment Systems Oversight Report 2010* (March 2011), http://www.bankofengland.co.uk/publications/psor/psor2010.pdf, p 7
84 National Bank of Belgium, 'High level expectations for the oversight of SWIFT' (June 2007) Financial Stability Review, http://www.nbb.be/doc/ts/enterprise/activities/oversight/FSR_2007EN_oversight%20of%20SWIFT_article%20HLEs.pdf, pp 95–101
85 FSA Register (March 2011), http://www.fsa.gov.uk/register/firmBasicDetails.do?sid=77015; http://www.omgeo.com/regulation
86 FSA Register (March 2011), http://www.fsa.gov.uk/register/firmPermissions.do?sid=80437

from a collection of national markets to a single European financial services market is enthusiastically embraced, completion of the single market is rarely perceived as a matter of standardisation. So, regulators make little effort to agree common standards for regulatory reporting purposes. Establishing a single market in financial services, being 'services' rather than goods, has been perceived to be a matter of removing national barriers impeding foreign service providers, which can be achieved through mutual recognition as much as by establishing pan-European rules. Since the 2008 financial crisis, a more centralised approach to regulation may lead to a re-think of this approach, but there is as little voting power in data formats as there is senior management excitement.

4.32   Thirdly, and most significantly, the European Commission has an embedded philosophical distaste for uniformity. Uniformity, especially when requested by an industry, and certainly when requested by the financial sector, arouses suspicions of collusion and anti-competitive behaviour. Scrutiny is needed to ensure that what is demanded as a 'standard' is in fact an essential requirement enabling customers to switch from one provider or product to another, and not an excuse for behaviour which forecloses a market to competitors. The Commission's own policy is set forth in an official Communication.[87] The Communication notes the opposing forces in standard-setting. On the one hand, standardisation can promote economic interpenetration, encourage development of new and improved products, and can improve supply conditions: 'standards thus normally increase competition.'[88] On the other hand, standardisation can be restrictive, through reduced price competition, foreclosure of innovative technologies and discrimination by preventing effective access to the standard.[89] To achieve balance between these forces, the Commission sets out four conditions under which standardisation would be unchallenged under article 101 of the Treaty.[90] These can be broadly summarised as follows:[91]

(1) Participation in standard-setting should be unrestricted. The ideal is that all competitors affected by the standard can participate in the process leading to the selection of the standard.

(2) The procedure for adopting the standard should be transparent. Stakeholders should be able to inform themselves of upcoming, on-going and finalised standardisation work in good time.

(3) There should be no obligation to comply with the standard. Moreover, the Communication indicates that whether a standardisation agreement has restrictive effects on competition may depend on whether members of the standard-setting organisation remain free to develop alternatives.[92]

(4) Access to the standard should be provided on 'FRAND' terms. FRAND stands for 'fair, reasonable and non-discriminatory'. The chief difficulty here is that the developers of the standard have typically invested in its

---

87 European Commission, *Guidelines on the applicability of Article 101 of the Treaty on the Functioning of the European Union to horizontal co-operation agreements* (January 2011), Communication 2011/C11/01, OJ(C)11/1
88 Communication, para 263
89 Communication, para 264
90 See **sections 7.2** and **7.28**
91 Communication, paras 280–286
92 Communication, para 293

development and may wish to recover their outlay through retention of, and licensing of access to, the intellectual property rights in the standard.

DATA PRIVACY

4.33   Privacy, on the other hand, attracts a good deal of attention. There is a collection of legal issues relating to information about trades, which include confidentiality, data protection and bank secrecy. While it may be relatively uncontroversial that a regulator should be entitled to a feed of information about the prices and volumes of securities transactions, debate becomes more animated when it is proposed that the information to be given should include data on the persons involved in the trade, to be precise the end-investors. Customers of banks (and, by implication, brokers) are entitled under English law to have their affairs kept confidential;[93] exceptions include where they have agreed to the disclosure or there is a supervening legal obligation on the part of the banker to disclose. This common-law obligation is buttressed by the Data Protection Act 1998.

4.34   Persons handling transaction information will need to be careful, therefore, whenever that information relates back to a person whose confidence or personal data are being used. In a MiFID transparency context, there should be no danger, because the trade and transaction reporting obligations imposed by MiFID do not require disclosure of this type of information. However, the requirement in EMIR for trade repositories to be informed who is a party to, and who is behind, each reportable transaction[94] has made the issue newly prominent.

4.35   Finally, mention should be made of the dangers of misuse of information. Under the Market Abuse Directive,[95] market manipulation is prohibited.[96] This concept includes 'dissemination of information ... which gives, or is likely to give, false or misleading signals as to financial instruments, ... where the person who made the dissemination knew, or ought to have known, that the information was false or misleading.'[97] While this would not ordinarily give rise to difficulty, it imposes a burden of accuracy on data distributors going beyond a mere civil duty to take reasonable care.

---

93 *Tournier v National Provincial and Union Bank of England* [1924] 1 KB 461
94 EMIR, art 9(5)(a)
95 Directive 2003/6/EC of the European Parliament and of the Council of 28 January 2003 on insider dealing and market manipulation
96 Market Abuse Directive, art 5
97 Market Abuse Directive, art 1(2)(c)

5   Clearing of OTC Derivatives

BACKGROUND

5.1   In September 2009, the G20 met in Pittsburgh, and resolved that 'all standardised OTC derivative contracts should be traded on exchanges or electronic trading platforms, where appropriate, and cleared through central counterparties by end-2012 at the latest. OTC derivative contracts should be reported to trade repositories. Non-centrally cleared contracts should be subject to higher capital requirements.'[1] Since then, a huge effort has been made in the European Union and elsewhere to introduce clearing obligations for OTC derivatives, culminating in the EU Regulation on OTC derivative transactions, central counterparties and trade repositories (more familiarly known as EMIR, an acronym reflecting an earlier name – 'European market infrastructure legislation' – for the proposed legislation).[2] Since then, also, a huge amount of literature has been spawned on the subject of clearing.

It is the purpose of this chapter to consider critically the policy decision to force the OTC derivatives market into clearing, and to describe the clearing obligation as implemented under EMIR.

MERITS OF CLEARING OTC DERIVATIVES

5.2   Central counterparties have been clearing derivative products for a very long time.[3] Central counterparties were perceived to have performed resiliently during the 2008 financial crisis. And for a variety of reasons, policymakers concluded that greater take-up of clearing would have limited the severity of the crisis, if not avoiding it altogether. The following advantages of clearing have been claimed:

(1) *Reduction of counterparty risk.* Using a CCP reduces counterparty risk because it allows for multilateral netting, because CCPs select only high-quality participants, because CCPs insist on taking collateral, and because CCPs have a default fund – effectively a credit insurance fund – against participant default. Although there is evidence that multilateral netting

---

1   G20 Leaders Statement: *The Pittsburgh Summit* (September 2009), http://www.g20.utoronto. ca/2009/2009communique0925.html, para 13

2   Regulation (EU) No 648/2012 of the European Parliament and of the Council of 4 July 2012 on OTC derivatives, central counterparties and trade repositories

3   Kroszner, R, 'Central Counterparty Clearing: History, Innovation and Regulation' in *The Role of Central Counterparties* (European Central Bank/Federal Reserve Bank of Chicago, July 2007), http://www.ecb.eu/pub/pdf/other/rolecentralcounterparties200707en.pdf, pp 30–35

of credit default swaps reduces gross notional exposures by 90 per cent,[4] Professor Darrell Duffie and Dr Haoxiang Zhu have questioned the central premise that introducing clearing will in fact have this result, at least across multiple asset classes.[5] CCPs' membership criteria for OTC derivatives clearing are also a source of controversy, and this subject is also considered below. Margining and default backing are less contentious: whether collateral is delivered to cover post-default replacement costs in the uncleared derivatives markets has been dependent on the identity of the transaction counterparty.[6] CCPs do not grant favours and take initial margin from all participants indiscriminately. Default backing is not available in the derivatives markets except where provided by infrastructures such as CCPs, because the Investor Compensation Schemes Directive[7] does not apply to losses on OTC derivative instruments. It must also be borne in mind that clearing does not *eliminate* counterparty risk: despite all the precautions taken by CCPs, the essence of clearing is the substitution of the CCP for the participant's original counterparty, so that the participant assumes risk on the CCP. CCPs are not risk-free creatures.

(2) *Risk mutualisation.* Because a CCP has a default fund, exceptional costs of default (that is, those not satisfied by the defaulter's own margin and default fund contributions) are borne by the defaulter's co-participants. The advantage of this structure over the uncleared marketplace is the spreading of risk: a CCP distributes the costs of a CCP participant's failure fairly among the survivors.[8] A closed-out OTC master agreement may leave the non-defaulting party with a large receivable item due from the defaulter, for which there is little prospect of payment in full and no prospect whatever of timely payment. The non-defaulting party may be destabilised by this result, and will have no mutual support scheme to fall back on. CCPs are designed to be loss-absorbers.[9] Reduction of 'interconnectedness' is thus cited as one of the advantages of clearing: 'The framers of the Dodd-Frank Act observe that the clearing of swap contracts constitutes a key means for managing systemic risk, because clearing removes the type of interconnectedness between financial institutions that contributed to the financial crisis resulting from the failure and bankruptcy of firms such as Bear Stearns, Lehman Brothers, and

---

4   Cecchetti, S, Gyntelberg, J and Hollanders, M, 'Central counterparties for over-the-counter derivatives' (September 2009) Bank for International Settlements Quarterly Review, http://www.bis.org/publ/qtrpdf/r_qt0909f.pdf, pp 45–58

5   Duffie, D, and Zhu, H, *Does a Central Clearing Counterparty Reduce Counterparty Risk?* (May 2009) Rock Center for Corporate Governance Working Paper No 46, http://ssrn.com/abstract=1348343

6   Cf Singh, M, 'Under-collateralisation and rehypothecation in the OTC derivatives markets' (July 2010) Banque de France Financial Stability Review, http://www.banque-france.fr/fileadmin/user_upload/banque_de_france/publications/Revue_de_la_stabilite_financiere/etude13_rsf_1007.pdf, No 14 (English version) pp 113–119

7   Directive 97/9/EC of the European Parliament and of the Council of 3 March 1997 on investor-compensation schemes

8   Hills, B, Rule, D, and Parkinson, S, 'Central counterparty clearing houses and financial stability' (June 1999) Bank of England Financial Stability Review, p 122

9   Bliss, R, and Papathanassiou, C, *Derivatives clearing, central counterparties and novation: The economic implications* (March 2006), http://www.ecb.int/events/pdf/conferences/ccp/BlissPapathanassiou_final.pdf

AIG.'[10] 'To lower risk further, standard OTC derivatives should be brought to clearing houses. ... With their use, transactions with counterparties can be moved off the books of financial institutions that may have become "too big to fail" and "too interconnected to fail."'[11] Professor Craig Pirrong disputes the correctness of these assertions, on the incontrovertible ground that a CCP is an interconnection between financial firms: 'creation of CCPs changes the topology of the network of interconnections among firms, but it does not eliminate these connections.'[12]

(3) *Orderly default management.* In the OTC markets, users of the International Swaps and Derivatives Association (ISDA) master agreements will have the ability to close out their derivatives transactions with a defaulting counterparty, which will involve a process of ascribing a value to the terminated transactions and calculating a net sum due to or from the counterparty. Some versions of the ISDA documentation rely on a process of seeking quotations from other dealers in order to complete the valuation process. In times of reduced liquidity, such as that which prevailed in the immediate aftermath of the collapse of Lehman Brothers, obtaining reliable quotations may be impeded or even impossible. CCPs are expected to have more robust default-handling procedures. 'The main problematic feature of bilateral markets is that the uncoordinated efforts of market participants to replace the positions lost due to a default can be destabilising. In contrast, cleared markets can engage in a coordinated response that places less stress on the pricing mechanism.'[13]

(4) *Systemic risk reduction.* 'Owing to a lack of information about where risks related to OTC derivatives arise and are distributed throughout the financial system, the large size of OTC derivatives markets and their close linkages with cash markets, OTC derivatives markets seem to have acted as a contagion channel during the financial market turbulence.'[14] The policy responses to this observation are that OTC derivatives transactions should be traded on organised platforms, cleared through CCPs, and be subject to centralised reporting at trade repositories. 'The primary advantage of a CCP is its ability to reduce systemic risk through multilateral netting of exposures, the enforcement of robust risk management standards, and mutualisation of losses resulting from clearing member failures.'[15]

(5) *Increased transparency.* Transparency is a complex subject. The starting-point for the transparency debate in the context of clearing is that opacity

10 Commodity Futures Trading Commission, 'Requirements for Derivatives Clearing Organizations, Designated Contract Markets, and Swap Execution Facilities Regarding the Mitigation of Conflicts of Interest' (October 2010), Proposed rulemaking under Dodd-Frank Act, 75 Federal Register 63732, https://www.federalregister.gov/articles/2010/10/18/2010-26220/requirements-for-derivatives-clearing-organizations-designated-contract-markets-and-swap-execution#p-79, p 63736

11 Gensler, G, Chairman of the Commodity Futures Trading Commission, *OTC Derivatives Reform* (March 2010), Speech, http://www.cftc.gov/PressRoom/SpeechesTestimony/opagensler-32

12 Pirrong, C, *The Inefficiency of Clearing Mandates* (July 2010), Cato Institute Policy Analysis No 665, http://www.cato.org/pubs/pas/PA665.pdf, pp 24, 28

13 Pirrong, Cato Institute paper, p 4

14 European Central Bank, *OTC derivatives and post-trading infrastructures* (September 2009), http://www.ecb.eu/pub/pdf/other/overthecounterderivatives200909en.pdf, p 7

15 Kiff, J, et al, 'Making Over-the-Counter Derivatives Safer: The Role of Central Counterparties' (April 2010) IMF Global Financial Stability Report, http://www.imf.org/external/pubs/ft/gfsr/2010/01/index.htm, ch III

is blamed as one reason for the severity of the 2008 financial crisis.[16] When dealers have inadequate information about each other's exposures they adopt self-protective, but collectively dangerous, behaviour, such as exercising discretionary powers to call for additional collateral.

> 'Introducing CCPs would improve transparency by allowing for easy collection of high-frequency market-wide information on market activity, transaction prices and counterparty exposures for market participants who rely on them. The centralisation of information in a CCP makes it possible to provide market participants, policymakers and researchers with the information to better gauge developments in various markets on the position of individual market participants.'[17]

A related, but perhaps more convincing argument is that a CCP reduces disruption due to informational asymmetries following a default. 'CCPs also solve a potentially disruptive information problem. When a major player in bilaterally-cleared derivatives markets fails, it is not immediately apparent to the remaining market participants: who is absorbing the losses, how big the losses are, and whether the failed firm's counterparties are themselves threatened by the failure. This uncertainty is mitigated when there is a single counterparty with an effective (and perceived to be fair) means of allocating losses across the whole market. ... [The CCP's] perceived neutrality and ability to disperse losses widely may be expected to do much to mitigate the information concerns that can infect bilaterally-cleared markets in times of market stress.'[18] On the other hand, it would be wrong to ascribe too much benefit to the all-seeing nature of the CCP. First, it is not self-evident that a CCP, whose job is to manage counterparty risk, will regard itself as obliged to carry out this possibly valuable, but ancillary, function of gathering market-wide information – indeed EMIR acknowledges that the CCP will need to involve a trade repository in the process.[19] Secondly, the CCP may actually be a victim of information asymmetry.[20]

(6) *Liquidity improvement.* It has been argued that multilateral netting potentially increases liquidity in the OTC derivatives markets.[21] This is because reduction of counterparty risk frees up capital, capacity and credit lines to enable greater volumes of trading to be done for the same balance sheet impact. A further point on liquidity concerns the management of defaults. The CCP's default management mechanism, backed by the available funds contributed through margin and default funding, ensures a degree of liquidity in the post-default marketplace, improves confidence, and should mitigate the tendency of market participants to disengage due to

---

16 See **section 4.19**
17 Cecchetti et al, BIS QR article, p 51
18 Bliss and Papathanassiou, p 4; see also Gibson, R, and Murawski, C, *The Price of Protection: Derivatives, Default Risk and Margining* (January 2007), https://www.fdic.gov/bank/analytical/cfr/2007/apr/murawski_priceofprotection.pdf, p 49
19 EMIR, art 9
20 Pirrong, C, *The Economics of Clearing in Derivatives Markets: Netting, Asymmetric Information, and the Sharing of Default Risks Through a Central Counterparty* (January 2009), Working Paper, http://papers.ssrn.com/sol3/papers.cfm?abstract_id=1340660, pp 34–41; see also **section 5.6(1)**
21 Bliss and Papathanassiou, p 3; Schröder, M, et al, *Assessment of the cumulative impact of various regulatory initiatives on the European Banking Sector* (August 2011), Study for the European Parliament, IP/A/ECON/ST/2010-21, para 2.2.3

fear of further failures.[22] On the other hand, large-scale margin calls from futures CCPs were considered to have drained liquidity from the system during the 1987 stock market crash.[23]

(7) *Cost reduction.* Transaction costs should be reduced and operational efficiency and liquidity improved by virtue of the concentration effect of multilateral netting. The more participants a CCP attracts, the greater the benefit, and in this way the cost of managing risk (in terms of cost of collateral, and over a longer time horizon, in terms of reduced losses attributable to counterparty defaults) also comes down. This has been demonstrated quantitatively using economic modelling by staffers at the Bank of England.[24] Margin offsets may be achievable if the CCP can identify a risk reduction where a participant takes a long position in the cash markets which temporarily offsets a short position in a related derivative product, and the CCP clears both positions: thus there may be a mitigant to the negative impact on costs of the overall reduction of netting foreseen by Duffie and Zhu. Furthermore, the regulatory capital requirement will be lower in respect of an exposure to a CCP than for an exposure to another non-CCP financial institution.[25]

(8) *Optimal position management.* Exiting from an OTC position is easier if it is cleared. To tear up an OTC transaction so that both market and counterparty risk are eliminated requires a party to enter into an equal and opposite trade with its original counterparty, which may not be achievable at a reasonable price. An opposite trade with a different counterparty eliminates the market risk only, unless it is put into a portfolio compression service.[26] An alternative is for the trades in the product to be cleared, in which case the CCP substitutes for the original counterparties to both trades and the exposure is completely erased.

(9) *Improved collateral practices.* OTC counterparties depend on their own 'risk engine' and operational efficiency. Each firm will have slightly different approaches to risk assessment, otherwise disputes over valuation and collateral calls would never arise. Disputes cause delay in collateral postings and exacerbate exposures. In the bilateral world, daily marking-to-market and daily posting of collateral may be the ideal but may not be the practice. Where securities collateral is involved, there will also be delays between calling the collateral and its arrival. Collateral calls vary with the credit of the counterparty; and firms may rely on credit ratings to set collateral levels. Some counterparties may be exempted by their trading partners from posting collateral at all, sometimes based on business reasons unrelated to credit. Rating practices came under fire during the financial crisis. And credit ratings may change, triggering collateral calls, and deepening liquidity problems for the down-rated firm. CCPs' margin practices avoid all these difficulties.[27]

---

22 Valiante, D, *Shaping Reforms and Business Models for the OTC Derivatives Market – Quo vadis?* (April 2010), ECMI Research Report No 5, http://www.ceps.eu/ceps/download/3093
23 Bernanke, B, 'Clearing and Settlement during the Crash' (January 1990) Review of Financial Studies Vol 3, pp 133–151
24 Jackson, J, and Manning, M, *Comparing the pre-settlement risk implications of alternative clearing arrangements* (April 2007), Bank of England Working Paper no. 321
25 See **section 19.11(1)**
26 See **section 4.14**
27 Cf Pirrong, Cato Institute paper, p 17

> '[T]he fact that each exposure may be covered by collateral
> requirements, which in turn reflect the creditworthiness of the
> counterparties, creates a danger that changes in counterparty credit
> rating can produce disruptive procyclical effects e.g. threatened
> downgrades of AIG's credit rating in September 2008 would have
> required it to post significant collateral to cover its exposure as a
> counterparty in CDS contracts, resulting in severe cash flow strains
> within AIG.'[28]

CLEARED AND UNCLEARED OTC TRANSACTIONS COMPARED

5.3   It may also be mentioned that, by comparison with uncleared OTC
derivative transactions (sometimes confusingly called 'bilaterally cleared'
transactions), a number of additional differences emerge, some of which might
also support arguments in favour of clearing:

(1) *Initial margin.*[29] Annual margin surveys conducted by ISDA[30] indicate that
    (a) the practice of taking collateral from a counterparty in the uncleared
    OTC markets is not universal, and (b) there is even more variability in
    taking 'independent amounts' of collateral – that is collateral which is
    intended, broadly, to fulfil the same function as initial margin in relation to
    cleared transactions.[31] By contrast, CCPs invariably take initial margin. It
    has been pointed out that the requirement to provide collateral as products
    shift into mandatory clearing will involve significant cost for financial
    market participants.[32] Further, as noted above, CCPs do not adjust their
    margin demands according to the credit-worthiness of their participants:
    the amount of margin is determined by the product alone. A final point
    is that a cleared 'client' trade will require two amounts of initial margin:
    margin to support the 'client account' leg of the trade, and margin to
    support the 'house account' leg of the trade.[33]

(2) *Variation margin.*[34] Demands by CCPs for variation margin may differ in
    amount, be more restrictive in terms of acceptability of collateral, and be
    made more frequently than in a purely bilateral (uncleared) relationship. In
    particular, a CCP may treat variation margin as a 'daily settlement' of sums
    owed, which must be paid up in cash. Variation margin requirements may
    impose liquidity burdens on CCP participants.

---

28 Financial Services Authority, *The Turner Review – a regulatory response to the global banking crisis* (March 2009), http://www.fsa.gov.uk/pubs/other/turner_review.pdf, p 82
29 See **sections 14.23ff**
30 Available from http://www2.isda.org/functional-areas/research/surveys/margin-surveys
31 ISDA, Managed Funds Association, and Securities Industry and Financial Markets Association, *Independent Amounts* (March 2010), White Paper, http://www2.isda.org/attachment/ MTY3MA==/Independent-Amount-WhitePaper-Final.pdf
32 Singh, M, 'Under-collateralisation and rehypothecation in the OTC derivatives markets' (July 2010) Banque de France Financial Stability Review, http://www.banque-france.fr/fileadmin/ user_upload/banque_de_france/publications/Revue_de_la_stabilite_financiere/etude13_ rsf_1007.pdf , pp 113–119
33 See **section 2.15**
34 See **section 14.24**

(3) *Client position transfer.*[35] CCPs should have – indeed EMIR imposes an obligation for them to have[36] – machinery to enable the client of a failed clearing member to transfer its portfolio of transactions and margin deposits to a replacement clearing member. Such arrangements will provide a form of counterparty-risk protection unavailable in uncleared OTC markets.

(4) *Regulatory capital.* Although credit exposures to CCPs are no longer zero-weighted for regulatory capital purposes, the cost in terms of capital required to support sums receivable under cleared transactions remains significantly lower than the amount required for the same transaction exposure on an uncleared transaction.[37]

(5) *Insolvency protection.* Various defences are available against attack on close-out and default management processes which would otherwise be available to insolvency officers, as discussed in **section 8.8**. The defences available to non-infrastructure counterparties tend to be more limited, since special statutory protection is given to CCPs, notably under the Settlement Finality Directive.[38] Such protection enables a CCP to proceed robustly to close out, set off, receive and apply collateral, and allocate losses to a defaulter's account, without fear of challenge. In the uncleared OTC marketplace the default management mechanisms of close-out, set-off and application of collateral have been tried and tested over many years, but even standard market documentation is not immune from examination by the courts, and the uncertainties[39] surrounding the immunity granted under the Financial Collateral Directive[40] may limit the range of protection and the action which can be taken in relation to uncleared transactions.

(6) *Matching and trade capture.* In order to bring transactions into clearing, it is necessary to have some system which identifies clearable transactions entered into by market counterparties, checks for absence of discrepancies, and then notifies the transactions to the CCP for registration.[41] In the uncleared marketplace, such systems may be used but are not mandated.

(7) *Collateral velocity.* Dr Manmohan Singh has explained that, like money, securities collateral is recyclable through rehypothecation, and therefore has a 'velocity', in the sense that money recycled through the financial system is said to have velocity.[42] Collateral supporting an uncleared OTC transaction may be transferred outright[43] or subject to rights of rehypothecation, and can therefore be re-used by the transferee. Collateral transferred to a CCP is less likely to be re-used: CCPs do no or little own-account trading and may have sufficient market power (high credit standing) to avoid posting any collateral themselves. CCPs may, but are not encouraged to, enter into

---

35 See **sections 14.47ff**
36 Article 48
37 See **section 19.11**
38 Directive 98/26/EC of the European Parliament and of the Council of 19 May 1998 on settlement finality in payment and securities settlement systems
39 See **section 8.28**
40 Directive 2002/47/EC of the European Parliament and of the Council of 6 June 2002 on financial collateral arrangements
41 See **section 4.2**
42 Singh, M, *Velocity of Pledged Collateral: Analysis and Implications* (November 2011), IMF Working Paper WP/11/256, http://www.imf.org/external/pubs/ft/wp/2011/wp11256.pdf
43 See **section 10.10(2)**

repo transactions with the collateral they receive.[44] Accordingly, securities collateral posted to support cleared transactions is likely to have lower velocity.

DERIVATIVES AND CASH MARKET TRANSACTIONS COMPARED

5.4   There are also differences between an OTC derivative transaction and an OTC cash market transaction, which may mean that the subject of OTC derivatives clearing needs to be approached with caution.[45] The following may be mentioned:

(1) *Lifespan of contracts.* Derivative trades tend to have a longer duration to maturity than cash market trades. The tenor of derivatives trades creates a number of risk features which CCPs may struggle to manage.[46] 'Derivative clearing facilities need special risk management systems because these contracts have long lifespans as compared with cash and securities.'[47] Futures markets, which share the problem of long-term contracts with OTC derivatives markets, developed CCPs long before equities exchanges, however. The transfer of counterparty risk to the CCP provided strength and enhanced liquidity for the futures markets; but OTC derivatives are different from futures in that there is no reasonably well-assured source of liquidity for a CCP to trade out of a position following a default.

(2) *Default management obligations.* Close-out of an uncleared transaction can be achieved by 'termination and liquidation': that is, the non-defaulting party exercises a contractual right to terminate the transaction, thereby bringing to an end the obligations of both parties under the transaction; the replacement cost (or loss) to the non-defaulting party is evaluated, for example by seeking quotes from market participants, and this amount is due from the defaulting party (or, if negative, due to the defaulting party) as a cash debt. That mechanism is, however, of limited use to a CCP. The CCP *must* replace the transactions it had with the defaulter, whether or not it carries out a process of termination and liquidation: otherwise the CCP would be operating an unmatched book, and take unhedged market risk on the equivalent transaction it has with its non-defaulting participant which was the original counterparty to transaction with the defaulter. The imperative to replace requires the CCP to have a portfolio disposal mechanism which can be operated following a default. The details are considered in **Chapter 14**, but the likelihood is that surviving participants will be required to take over some share of the defaulter's portfolio. This

---

44 EMIR arts 39(8), 47; Bank for International Settlements Committee on Payment and Settlement Systems and Technical Committee of the International Organization of Securities Commissions, *Principles for Financial Market Infrastructures* (April 2012), http://www.bis.org/publ/cpss101a.pdf, Principle 16

45 Cf Bank for International Settlements Committee on Payment and Settlement Systems and Technical Committee of the International Organization of Securities Commissions, *Guidance on the application of the 2004 CPSS-IOSCO Recommendations for Central Counterparties to OTC derivatives CCPs* (May 2010), Consultative Report, http://www.bis.org/publ/cpss89.pdf

46 Bliss, R, and Steigerwald, R, 'Derivatives clearing and settlement: A comparison of central counterparties and alternative structures' (December 2006) Federal Reserve Bank of Chicago Economic Perspectives, p 22

47 Kiff et al, fn 3, p 4

process may encounter difficulties.[48] Traders participating in a CCP may thus face a range of contingent hazards associated with the CCP default management process, which may have very different outcomes from close-out of master agreements, particularly in times of market turmoil.

(3) *Pricing sources.* Cash market or futures transactions emanating from organised markets have available and transparent pricing sources. These sources underpin the risk modelling of the CCP, enabling it to decide with reasonable confidence the likely behaviour of prices following a default, and thereby to set the level of initial margin needed for a given portfolio. 'While listed markets generally provide prices based on a centralised order book, OTC derivatives markets are quote-driven and therefore require separate services that aggregate quoted prices from multiple market participants (eg major dealers) and calculate composite consensus prices.'[49] The Committee on Payment and Settlement Systems and the International Organization of Securities Commissions point out that a CCP clearing OTC products is likely to be especially dependent on information sources and service providers,[50] for example in order to ensure that its determination of prices is sound. There may be disputes about the valuation of transactions: for example the pricing of credit default swaps in 2007–2008.[51] In the absence of an organised market there is thus a question for the CCP as to how the value of a portfolio – the cost of operating the default management mechanism just discussed – can be reliably determined. OTC markets may be vulnerable to illiquidity or extreme volatility following a default.

DISADVANTAGES OF MANDATORY CLEARING

5.5 Unfortunately for the policy-makers, there are abundant reasons why clearing is not a panacea. Perhaps the most obvious is that a CCP does not take away counterparty risk, but it concentrates it. Consequently, if belatedly, regulators and policymakers have given attention to the need to have safety standards for CCPs, and even to open a debate on the unthinkable, namely what to do if the risk management of a CCP fails and the CCP itself has inadequate financial resources.[52]

5.6 In addition to concentration risk, the following matters might argue against a policy of requiring all OTC transactions to be cleared:

(1) *Moral Hazard.* 'Risk sharing through a clearinghouse makes the balance sheets of the clearinghouse members public goods, and encourages excessive risk taking. That is, the clearing mechanism is vulnerable to moral hazard.'[53] Clearing has the effect of mutualising losses among the CCP's participants; it also takes away wealth from the general body of creditors of a defaulter owing to the *British Eagle* effect.[54] Further, the risk associated

---

48 See **sections 14.40ff**
49 CPSS-IOSCO Consultative Report, para 3(d)
50 CPSS-IOSCO Consultative Report, Recommendation 8 and paras 3(d), (e), (h)
51 Cf Culp, C, 'OTC-Cleared Derivatives: Benefits, Costs, and Implications of the "Dodd-Frank Wall Street Reform and Consumer Protection Act"' (2010) Journal of Applied Finance, Issue 2, http://www.rmcsinc.com/articles/OTCCleared.pdf, pp 1–27
52 See **sections 17.12ff**
53 Pirrong, Cato Institute paper, p 3; see also pp 12ff
54 See **section 2.6**; also Pirrong, 2009 Working Paper, pp 29–32

with a cleared transaction does not depend on the credit-worthiness of the original counterparty, because these risks are absorbed by the CCP and the counterparty's GCM. In other words, moral hazard is the flip side of the liquidity enhancement noted by some champions of clearing. And moreover, the risk is worsened according to the judgment reached by the CCP on margin levels: if the risk is 'under-margined', that makes the transaction type in question economically attractive, but deepens the risk of losses on default. Professor Craig Pirrong argues that the quality of the information available to the CCP is crucial to the setting of suitable margin levels, but that dealers will (because they are dealers) have far better information and can evaluate and price risks more effectively than any CCP.[55]

(2) *Crisis exacerbation*. Clearing can deepen crises in various ways:

    (a) Contagion. Clearing obliges CCP participants to take on risk in the form of default fund obligations and default management commitments, both of which expose the participants to a risk of contagion – the risk that the insolvency of one market participant causes the demise of another – which is absent in uncleared markets.

    (b) Increased risk for participants. CCPs react to spikes in prices by making intra-day margin calls.[56] 'The very mechanism that is commonly asserted as the way that clearing reduces systemic risk – rigid and frequent collateralization in cash – can be the mechanism that creates systemic risk.'[57] If the objective of mandatory clearing is to reduce demands on financial firms in times of stress, the combination of reduced netting and compulsory margin calls may not achieve it.

    (c) Wrong way risk. CCPs are particularly vulnerable to wrong-way risk[58] – which occurs when the risk to which one is exposed on a default *increases* alongside increases in the probability of default. Wrong-way risk is observed when a credit insurer (which is one way of looking at the activities of a CCP) experiences a high rate of claims: the viability of the insurer is called into question precisely because there are many claims, namely at exactly the moment when the insurer's viability is most needed. An example of this observation is the near-default of AIG in 2008.[59] The same problem besets CCPs: 'A big financial shock that is sufficient to cause movements in derivatives prices big enough to breach margin levels, and/or which damages a CCP member's balance sheet (or multiple members' balance sheets) severely enough to force it (them) into default is likely to be associated with severe financial difficulties at other CCP member firms. ... Thus, in crisis periods, dependencies between the value of the backers of CCPs – the member firms (often banks) – and the exposures that CCPs are effectively writing protection against are highly likely to be of the wrong way variety. This means that CCPs offer dubious protection against systemic risk. ... Even if a CCP does not fail during a crisis, the wrong way risk problem means that the financial institutions that backstop it will have to make payouts at precisely the times that they are under strain. That is, CCPs load risk onto big financial institutions precisely

---

55 Pirrong, Cato Institute paper, p 16
56 FMI Principle 6, key consideration 4
57 Pirrong, Cato Institute paper, p 28
58 Cf **section 14.17**
59 Cf Kiff et al, box 3.3, p 9

during crises that are already stressing them. ... CCPs themselves are most vulnerable to default precisely at the time that their advocates look to them to be the breaks that contain financial firestorms.'[60]

(3) *Systemic oligopoly.* The criteria for becoming a participant in an OTC derivatives CCP are onerous. 'Broad access to central clearing from all trading and qualified clearing firms is essential to realise its systemic benefits and the goals of global regulators. Limited access to central clearing compromises liquidity, distorts prices, concentrates risk and reduces competition and customer choice. Systemic risk is most effectively diffused among a large number of non-correlated market participants employing central clearing in their risk management framework – not among just a handful of global dealer banks. Artificial barriers to clearing house membership intended principally to maintain the status quo must be avoided.'[61] One example of a barrier to entry complained of[62] is the requirement of LCH.Clearnet Limited that a candidate for participation on its SwapClear platform have a portfolio of swaps of a size of $1 trillion.[63] Whether this barrier is 'artificial' might, however, be disputed: presumably LCH.Clearnet has in mind that its default management auctions will be successful only if the participants in the auction have adequate capacity to absorb the (potentially damaging) portfolio of a defaulter, and requiring a minimum size of business is a valid criterion to check for that. (On the other hand, the participant eligibility rules for American CCPs would prohibit such a restrictive rule.[64]) But the implication of CCPs having size or similar criteria, which may be excessively conservative,[65] is that participation will be restricted to a small group of systemically-significant market participants. This conclusion worries policy-makers.[66] Commentators are also concerned that 'the largest global dealers may have significant influence over the access rules at some CCPs as they dominate their risk committees. Given their exposure to risks from the CCP, these dealers are justified in seeking strong risk management practices. But it is difficult to differentiate risk management motives from other motives in the configuration of access controls.'[67] It might also be observed that there is concentration risk in confining the default auction process to a small group of market participants: the defaulter's book has to be absorbed among the survivors, which might endanger the survivors themselves.

(4) *Indirect access.* Limiting participation to a small group of large players forces smaller players to clear 'indirectly', that is by becoming clients of

---

60 Pirrong, C, *Wrongway Peachfuzz Returns to Wall Street?* (January 2011) Streetwise Professor blog, http://streetwiseprofessor.com/?p=4683

61 Swaps and Derivatives Market Association, *The 10 Principles of the SDMA* (2010), http://www.thesdma.org/10principles.htm#3, Principle 3

62 Litan, R, *The Derivatives Dealers' Club and Derivatives Markets Reform: A Guide for Policy Makers, Citizens and Other Interested Parties* (April 2010), http://www.thesdma.org/pdf/brookings.pdf, p 24

63 LCH.Clearnet Limited, *Clearing House Procedures*, s 1.2.3(b)

64 Commodity Futures Trading Commission, *Final Rules for derivatives clearing organizations* (November 2011), 76 FR 69334, §39.12 (a)(1)(iv) and (v)

65 Cf Valiante, ECMI Research Report No 5, pp 24–25

66 Bank for International Settlements Committee on the Global Financial System, *The macrofinancial implications of alternative configurations for access to central counterparties on OTC derivatives markets* (November 2011), CGFS Paper No 46, http://www.bis.org/publ/cgfs46.pdf

67 CGFS Paper No 46, fn 8, p 10

GCMs. Several unwelcome consequences follow: indirect clearers typically take some degree of credit risk on their GCM, owing to the uncertainties of 'portability' of client transactions on a GCM default,[68] and the GCM may be a weaker credit than the indirect clearer wishes to tolerate; the indirect clearer may be subject to its GCM's discretion (as opposed to the CCP's) on the amount of margin needed, which may be burdensome owing to lack of price transparency in OTC markets; GCMs may be competitors of indirect clearers, and having to depend on your competitors for services is awkward; and no fewer than eight technical issues associated with provision of indirect access were identified by the group of dealers and buy-side firms entering into formal commitments with the United States regulators in 2011.[69] (These, in summary, relate to documentation, onboarding, collateral, netting, uncleared trades, operational differences between CCPs, switching, and transparency.)

(5) *Narrow-range CCPs and netting.* CCPs which offer a clearing service for OTC products are unlikely to provide the service across a multitude of asset classes. CCPs clearing futures markets have traditionally offered clearing services for off-market (OTC) transactions which are similar enough to the exchange-traded contracts to be risk-managed alongside them; but where there is no futures exchange, the CCP will have to evaluate the risk profile (with all that implies as to pricing risk) for each cleared product. Accordingly, the pattern is for CCPs to choose a narrow range of products. A pair of OTC market dealers who, before mandatory clearing was introduced, had a multi-product bilateral master netting agreement covering all products, will have to divide up their derivatives transactions between various CCPs, according to the products accepted by them for clearing. Trades registered with different CCPs are not netted, and will therefore require separate margining and capital allocations. Furthermore, if more than one CCP is introduced for a particular asset class, the amount of netting achievable is reduced still further.[70] Netting sets will be split up yet more as clients of GCMs opt in to 'portable' client clearing solutions which require individual accounts.[71] As if all this were not bad enough, EMIR does not require OTC derivatives CCPs to interoperate,[72] so OTC derivatives trading firms may need to participate in several CCPs in order to be sure of the ability to clear transactions done with the broadest range of counterparties.

(6) *Cost of collateral.* While the need to collateralise derivatives transactions may be apparent to policy-makers, it is less self-evident across the market. A corporate user of derivatives products may be a stronger credit than the financial institution on which it depends as counterparty. The obligation to clear will demand that the corporate user post collateral to its GCM unless the GCM is willing to bear the costs and risks associated with forgoing collection of (or, to express it differently, lending) the collateral which the GCM must itself post to the CCP. In some cases the GCM may be obliged

---

68 See **sections 14.51ff**
69 AllianceBernstein et al, Commitment Letter to William C. Dudley, President of the Federal Reserve Bank of New York (March 2011), http://www.newyorkfed.org/newsevents/news/markets/2011/an110405.html, Annex A, p 15
70 Duffie and Zhu, Rock Center Working Paper No 46
71 See **section 14.52**
72 EMIR, art 1(3)

by CCP rules not to lend collateral.[73] Collateral may be in short supply – Professor Pirrong cites figures of $75 billion of extra collateral required to support mandatory clearing of credit default swaps and $570 billion for interest rate swaps[74], and the dampening effect of mandatory clearing on collateral 'velocity' has already been noted – and thus collateral is likely to be expensive for the user, which may influence the user not to enter into the transaction in the first place, leaving itself unhedged.[75] The potential for macroeconomic effects of compulsory clearing and the associated margining practices was the subject of a warning from the European Systemic Risk Board when it commented on EMIR.[76]

Table 5.1 OTC Clearing services offered by selected European CCPs in 2012

CCP	Country of main operations	OTC products cleared
Eurex Clearing AG	Germany	Credit default swaps Equity derivatives* Interest rate swaps
ICE Clear Europe Ltd	United Kingdom	Credit default swaps Energy derivatives* Freight swaps Iron ore swaps
LCH.Clearnet Ltd	United Kingdom	Equity derivatives* Emissions products Fertiliser swaps Forward freight agreements Interest rate swaps Iron ore swaps
LCH.Clearnet SA	France	Credit default swaps
Nasdaq OMX Clearing	Sweden	Electricity derivatives* Emissions products*
OMI Clear	Portugal	Electricity derivatives*

*The CCP also clears for a futures or cash market on which related products are traded

(7) *Product selection.* In order to clear a product, the CCP must be confident that it can risk-manage it. That implies that the CCP has confidence in the post-default depth of the market, which in turn demands a certain degree of fungibility of the cleared product with what is ordinarily traded in the market-place; or, in other words, cleared products will tend to be standardised. Users may prefer bespoke products to hedge risks which are

---

73 Cf FMI Principles, para 3.19.4

74 Pirrong, Cato Institute paper, p 21

75 European Association of Corporate Treasurers, *Comments in response to Consultation document: Possible initiatives to enhance the resilience of OTC derivatives markets* (July 2009), https://circabc.europa.eu/d/d/workspace/SpacesStore/31201fef-3476-44a9-96b9-a20538722dbd/eact_en.pdf

76 European Systemic Risk Board, *Macro-prudential comments by the ESRB on margin and haircut requirements in EMIR* (December 2011), http://register.consilium.europa.eu/pdf/en/11/st18/st18604.en11.pdf

peculiar to their businesses. Bespoke products are less likely to be accepted for clearing. Uncleared products, at least when entered into by a user who is personally subject to the clearing obligation,[77] are subject to financial disincentives,[78] which may again discourage the user from hedging.

(8) *Monopoly.* 'With respect to competitive evolution, scale and scope economies will tend to result in the survival of a small number of large CCPs. CCPs have strong natural monopoly characteristics. It is therefore likely that CCPs will raise anti-trust concerns.'[79] To amplify: mandating clearing for OTC derivative products demands that CCPs offer clearing services for OTC derivative products. Where only one CCP offers clearing for a particular product, all market participants are obliged to use that CCP. Incumbents have an overwhelming advantage over newcomers owing to the cost of switching. The failure to mandate interoperability between OTC derivatives CCPs exacerbates this problem.

5.7   Having digested the points made on all sides of the debate, the following conclusions might be drawn. First, compulsory clearing is likely to cause more attention to be paid to the risk management systems of CCPs generally, and derivatives CCPs in particular. CCPs may come under political and regulatory pressure to clear more asset classes, with the consequence that affected CCPs adopt highly conservative risk-management measures; which, in turn, may drive products back into the uncleared market-place – if needs be to jurisdictions where the activity is more freely tolerated – or lead treasurers to conclude that the costs of hedging exceed the benefits, leaving corporates in the 'real economy' exposed to risks which could have been managed. Secondly, a squeeze on eligible collateral may occur, with similar results. Thirdly, the absence of interoperability between OTC-derivatives CCPs is likely to lead over a period of time (potentially a very long time) to consolidation between CCPs clearing similar products, with the emergence of product monopolies. Finally, the absence of agreed standards for resolution of failed CCPs, coupled with the disastrous impact which an uncontrolled CCP insolvency would have on the wider economy, makes it difficult to avoid the conclusion that such monopolies would be too important to fail.

EMIR – THE CLEARING OBLIGATION

5.8   The Regulation on OTC derivative transactions, central counterparties and trade repositories (EMIR) imposes an obligation to clear OTC derivative transactions from the moment when both (a) there is a CCP duly authorised and capable of clearing the transaction and (b) the transaction is of a class declared subject to the clearing obligation. (At the time EMIR came into force, neither of these conditions applied, since no CCPs able to clear OTC derivatives in the European Union had the requisite form of authorisation required by EMIR, and no declarations had been made in relation to the classes of asset to be cleared.) In this section the extent and implications of the clearing obligation are examined.

---

77   See **section 5.9**
78   EMIR, art 11
79   Pirrong, C, *The Economics of Central Clearing: Theory and Practice* (May 2011), ISDA Discussion Paper No 1, http://www2.isda.org/images/file_exts/fileext_pdf.png, p 15

The obligation is set out in article 4 of EMIR, which provides that '(1) Counterparties shall clear all OTC derivative contracts pertaining to a class of OTC derivatives that has been declared subject to the clearing obligation. ... (3) The OTC derivative contracts that are subject to the clearing obligation pursuant to paragraph 1 shall be cleared in a CCP authorised under Article 14 or recognised under Article 25 to clear that class of OTC derivatives. ... ' 'Authorised' CCPs are those which are incorporated in, and licensed by the competent authority of, a Member State; 'recognised' CCPs are third country CCPs which have been recognised by ESMA.

To whom the obligation applies

5.9   The clearing obligation applies if the derivative transaction has been concluded between two 'financial counterparties', and also where one or both of the parties is a non-financial counterparty[80] for whom the 30-day rolling average of its positions exceeds a threshold set by ESMA.[81] 'Financial' counterparties will include credit institutions, investment firms, life and general insurers, reinsurers, funds and pension funds.[82] 'Non-financial counterparties' means everybody else, apart from CCPs themselves[83] and out-of-scope persons. Articles 1(4) and (5) limit the scope of EMIR, so that transactions involving some governmental and international bodies are excluded from the clearing obligation.

Where the trade involves a non-financial counterparty, a comparison must be carried out between the ESMA threshold and to the volume of derivatives business transacted by that counterparty. Whether the threshold is to be based on notional amount of the transactions, or their mark-to-market valuation, is left unclear in the level 1 Regulation.[84] All contracts entered into by all non-financial entities in the group must be included in the calculation, unless they are hedges or needed for treasury financing.[85] What happens when a non-financial counterparty's business wavers around the threshold is addressed as follows. If the rolling 30-day average position rises, so that the threshold is exceeded, the non-financial counterparty must clear all relevant future contracts within four months of becoming subject to the clearing obligation.[86] If the rolling 30-day average position falls below the ESMA threshold, it is no longer subject to the clearing obligation.[87] There seems to be no obligation to back-load old trades when the clearing obligation threshold is reached, but they must be collateralised then if they are not cleared.[88]

5.10   The position of third-country entities is troublesome, because it requires an EEA person who is a financial counterparty or a non-financial counterparty dealing with a third-country entity to assess whether the third country entity would be subject to the clearing obligation if it were established in the European

80   EMIR, art 4(1)
81   EMIR, arts 10(1)(b), 10(4)
82   EMIR, art 2(8)
83   EMIR, art 2(9)
84   EMIR, art 10(4)
85   EMIR, art 10(3)
86   EMIR, art 10(1)(b)
87   EMIR, art 10(2)
88   EMIR, art 11(3)

Union.[89] This may be difficult, because the regulatory classifications of non-EEA countries may not correspond well with the classes of 'financial' counterparty listed in the Regulation. A further challenge with third-country entities is that if *both* parties are third-country entities, the EEA clearing obligation can still apply, if 'the contract has a direct, substantial and foreseeable effect within the Union or where such obligation is necessary or appropriate to prevent the evasion of any provisions of this Regulation.'[90] ESMA is to set out in technical standards specifications intended to elucidate this phrase.

5.11   There are only two noteworthy exemptions:

(1) *Intra-group transactions*. Intra-group transactions are exempt, provided that they meet the definition of intra-group transaction, and provided that the competent authorities of both parties (or the competent authority of the party in the EEA, if only one) agree.[91] The definition[92] of 'intra-group transaction' is an example of tortuous drafting at its most unpleasant, because it differs according to whether the problem is considered from the viewpoint of a financial or a non-financial counterparty – thus raising the possibility that a trade to which both you and I are parties might be an intra-group transaction for me (and therefore exempt from clearing) but not for you (and therefore not actually exempt after all). Broadly, though, both parties have to be included in the same accounting consolidation, share centralised risk evaluation, and (as regards any third-country entity) the third country has been recognised by ESMA as having equivalent requirements to those in the Regulation.[93] Further, the intra-group exemption applies only where the relevant European competent authorities have been notified, and, where both parties are in the European Union, had the opportunity to object.[94]

(2) *Indirect clearing*. Article 4(3) specifies that, in order to satisfy the clearing requirement, 'a counterparty shall become a clearing member, a client, or shall establish indirect clearing arrangements with a clearing member … ' This provision means that it is not necessary for every party to a clearable OTC derivative transaction to be a clearing member of a CCP. A clearing member is an undertaking which participates in a CCP; a client is an undertaking with a contractual relationship with a clearing member which enables it to clear its transactions with that CCP.[95] Indirect clearing – that is, where the party to the transaction is not a clearing member or a client – involves additional steps. The arrangements must not increase counterparty risk, and the assets and positions of the counterparty must benefit from segregation, portability and default-handling protections with equivalent effect to those laid down in the Regulation as regards clearing members and clients. Achieving these additional steps may be difficult in practice, particularly in light of the legal complexity of establishing them, and rendering them insolvency-proof, at the level of clearing members and clients.

---

89 EMIR, art 4(1)(a)(iv)
90 EMIR, art 4(1)(a)(v)
91 EMIR, art 4(2)
92 EMIR, art 3
93 EMIR, art 13(2)
94 EMIR, art 4(2)
95 EMIR, arts 2(14), (15)

Finally, different start dates may apply to different types of entity.[96]

A further obligation is proposed under the European Commission's proposal for a Regulation on markets in financial instruments (MiFIR): this will oblige operators of regulated markets to ensure that all transactions in derivatives declared subject to the EMIR clearing obligation, which are traded on that market, are cleared by a CCP.[97] This provision does not expand the clearing obligation, but imposes a statutory duty on regulated markets to ensure that clearing arrangements are put in place.

Which transactions must be cleared

5.12   EMIR is concerned with the mandatory clearing of OTC derivative contracts.[98] These are defined[99] as derivative contracts whose execution does not take place on a regulated market, or a third country market considered equivalent to a regulated market – thus excluding futures transactions from the clearing obligation (but not, it should be noted, excluding futures CCPs or equities CCPs from the Titles of EMIR which address regulation of CCPs and investor protection). 'Derivative contracts' are those listed in points (4) to (10) of the list of financial instruments in the list of financial instruments in MiFID,[100] namely:

'(4) Options, futures, swaps, forward rate agreements and any other derivative contracts relating to securities, currencies, interest rates or yields, *emission allowances* or other derivatives instruments, financial indices or financial measures which may be settled physically or in cash;

(5) Options, futures, swaps, forward rate agreements and any other derivative contracts relating to commodities that must be settled in cash or may be settled in cash at the option of one of the parties (other[wise] than by reason of a default or other termination event);

(6) Options, futures, swaps, and any other derivative contract relating to commodities that can be physically settled provided that they are traded on a regulated market, *OTF,* [and/]or an MTF;

(7) Options, futures, swaps, forwards and any other derivative contracts relating to commodities, that can be physically settled not otherwise mentioned in C.6 and not being for commercial purposes, which have the characteristics of other derivative financial instruments, having regard to whether, inter alia, they are cleared and settled through recognised clearing houses or are subject to regular margin calls;

(8) Derivative instruments for the transfer of credit risk;

(9) Financial contracts for differences;

---

96   EMIR, art 5(2)(b)
97   European Commission, *Proposal for a Regulation of the European Parliament and of the Council on markets in financial instruments etc* (October 2011), COM(2011) 652 final, http://eur-lex.europa.eu/LexUriServ/LexUriServ.do?uri=COM:2011:0652:FIN:EN:PDF, art 25
98   EMIR, art 1(1)
99   EMIR, art 2(7)
100 Directive 2004/39/EC of the European Parliament and of the Council of 21 April 2004 on markets in financial instruments, etc, Section C, Annex 1

(10) Options, futures, swaps, forward rate agreements and any other derivative contracts relating to climatic variables, freight rates, [emission allowances] or inflation rates or other official economic statistics that must be settled in cash or may be settled in cash at the option of one of the parties (other[wise] than by reason of [a] default or other termination event), as well as any other derivative contracts relating to assets, rights, obligations, indices and measures not otherwise mentioned in this Section, which have the characteristics of other derivative financial instruments, having regard to whether, inter alia, they are traded on a regulated market, *OTF,* or an MTF, are cleared and settled through recognised clearing houses or are subject to regular margin calls.'

(The European Commission proposes to insert the italicised words, and delete the words between square brackets, in its proposal for a revised version of MiFID.[101])

Some of the items in C(4) to C(10) are in that list because they are cleared; so ESMA's clearing obligation rules must be targeted at the remainder.

It does not follow that because a derivative contract is included in the MiFID list that a transaction of this type must inevitably be cleared if entered into by a person subject to the clearing obligation: there is a further assessment to make, of the eligibility of the contract for clearing. Only those contracts which are of a class 'declared subject to the clearing obligation' must be cleared.[102] The responsibility for making the relevant declaration is given to ESMA.[103]

5.13   The position is even more confusing, because MiFIR will also oblige financial counterparties (and non-financial counterparties who exceed the threshold described at **section 5.9**) to conclude derivatives transactions on a regulated market, MTF, OTF or third country trading venue if (a) those transactions have been subject to a 'trading obligation' set by ESMA and (b) the transaction is not an 'intragroup' transaction, as described at **section 5.11**.[104] ESMA can only subject a transaction to the 'trading' obligation if it is subject to the 'clearing' obligation in EMIR.[105]

If ESMA has ordained that a transaction type shall be executed only on an organised venue, this would have the merit of simplifying the routing of transactions for clearing, since the venue will have matching functionality and be obliged to feed transactions to CCPs.[106]

5.14   In **section 14.16** it is noted that a critical question for risk managers at CCPs is the choice of products for clearing. There is, then, potential for conflict between a general policy to force-feed CCPs with all manner of OTC derivatives, and the prudence of CCPs which will wish to pick their diet more delicately. The choice is between a 'top-down' approach, whereby the market

---

101 European Commission, *Proposal for a Directive of the European Parliament and of the Council on markets in financial instruments etc* (October 2011), COM(2011) 656 final, http://eur-lex.europa.eu/LexUriServ/LexUriServ.do?uri=COM:2011:0656:FIN:EN:PDF
102 EMIR, art 4(1)
103 EMIR, art 5(2)
104 Proposal for MiFIR, art 24
105 Proposal for MiFIR, art 26
106 See **section 4.13**

is told by legislators and regulators what must or should be cleared, with the implication that user-governance will encourage CCPs towards greater appetite, and a 'bottom-up' approach, which allows CCPs to choose which products are suitable for clearing, subject to veto by regulators. EMIR allows for both approaches in Europe. A rather weak set of guidelines was issued by the International Organization of Securities Commissions (IOSCO) to regulators in order to help them avoid the grosser errors in applying either approach to the implementation of mandatory clearing.[107]

ESMA will (a) start with the list of contracts already approved by national regulators for clearing by the CCPs under their local regulatory regimes and the contracts cleared by recognised third-country CCPs, and use this to determine which classes of OTC derivatives should be subject to clearing (bottom-up);[108] and (b) carry out a public consultation, and determine which classes of contract should be so subject but which no CCP is yet authorised to clear (top-down).[109] In carrying out the top-down exercise, ESMA must take three criteria into consideration, namely standardisation, volume and liquidity, and availability of pricing data. These criteria are recited in the IOSCO guidelines, but a consideration of IOSCO's other guidance implies that many other factors ought properly to be considered when determining the appropriateness of a product for clearing.[110]

Uncleared transactions

5.15 Even where the clearing obligation does not apply, EMIR imposes risk-management obligations on parties to OTC derivative transactions. It is perhaps worth noting that clearing remains an option for such parties, assuming that an eligible CCP is willing to clear the transaction. Failing that, a number of obligations will apply to both financial and non-financial counterparties (but not to the out-of-scope governmental entities) unless an intra-group exemption from risk management is available: the obligations include, for financial counterparties, marking-to-market, collateralisation and capital adequacy; and for all party types, having procedures for confirmations and for reconciliation, dispute management, and valuation, and generally being able to manage operational aspects of counterparty risk.[111]

---

107 Technical Committee of the International Organization of Securities Commissions, *Requirements for Mandatory Clearing* (February 2012), OR05/12, http://www.iosco.org/library/pubdocs/pdf/IOSCOPD374.pdf
108 EMIR, art 5(2)
109 EMIR, art 5(3)
110 Cf **section 14.17**
111 EMIR, art 11

6 International regulation

INTRODUCTION – THE DEMISE OF SOFT LAW

6.1　Until the financial crisis which unfolded at the end of the first decade of the 21st century, it was generally accepted that the regulation of financial market infrastructures would be achieved through 'soft law' measures, rather than international legislation. Certainly, individual member states might have their local laws and regulations, but there was no need for mandatory international measures to ensure a uniformity of approach. Rather, the operators of infrastructures could be relied on to comply with guidance and recommendations laid down at supranational level.

6.2　Quasi-legislation of this nature has been abundant:

- The Bank for International Settlements (BIS) produced a report in 1990 on payment systems which contained five 'minimum standards' for systems which relied on netting.[1]

- The BIS Committee on Payment and Settlement Systems (CPSS) produced its Core Principles for Systemically Important Payment Systems in 2001.[2]

- The European Central Bank (ECB) created oversight standards for euro retail payment systems in 2003.[3]

- Working with the International Organisation of Securities Commissions (IOSCO), the CPSS produced recommendations for securities settlement systems in 2001[4] and for CCPs in 2004.[5]

- The ECB and the Committee of European Securities Regulators (CESR) produced its own versions of the CPSS-IOSCO Recommendations, in 2004 (covering securities settlement systems only)[6] and in 2009 (covering both settlement systems and CCPs).[7]

1　BIS, *Report of the Committee on Interbank Netting Schemes of the Central Banks of the Group of Ten countries* (November 1990), http://www.bis.org/publ/cpss04.pdf
2　CPSS, *Core Principles for Systemically Important Payment Systems* (January 2001), http://www.bis.org/publ/cpss43.pdf
3　ECB, *Oversight Standards for Euro Retail Payment Systems* (June 2003), http://www.ecb.eu/pub/pdf/other/retailpsoversightstandardsen.pdf
4　CPSS and Technical Committee of IOSCO, *Recommendations for Securities Settlement Systems* (November 2001), http://www.bis.org/publ/cpss46.pdf
5　CPSS and Technical Committee of IOSCO, Recommendations for Central Counterparties (November 2004), http://www.bis.org/publ/cpss64.pdf
6　CESR and ECB, Standards for Securities Clearing and Settlement in the European Union (September 2004), http://www.ecb.eu/pub/pdf/other/escb-cesr-standardssecurities2004en.pdf
7　CESR and ECB, Recommendations for Securities Settlement Systems and Recommendations for Central Counterparties in the European Union (May 2009), http://www.ecb.eu/pub/pdf/other/pr090623_escb-cesr_recommendationsen.pdf

● The ECB has produced oversight policies for payment systems in 2009[8] and 2011.[9]

6.3   Yet, as noted in **sections 1.26–1.30**, these recommendations and standards did not achieve all policy objectives, even if the post-trade system tended to work as it should. The European Commission devoted a good deal of energy in the early years of the century to study, with a possible view to legislation, of the causes of high cost and inefficiency in the post-trade area relating to securities. During the years 2000–4 there were three Commission consultations, two Giovannini reports and the establishment of an expert group. In its communications, the Commission contemplated a directive to bring about change. But by mid-2006 Commissioner McCreevy, the Commissioner then having responsibility for financial services, had concluded that it would be unwise to press ahead with a clearing and settlement directive:

> 'I am convinced that if the Commission were to propose any kind of a regulatory measure, we could slow down, or even block the restructuring process already underway – possibly even for years. A regulation now would be a distraction to market participants. It could lead to an outcome far less optimal than letting things evolve and then assessing what, if anything, is necessary at EU level.'[10]

All that changed when the demise of Lehman Brothers demonstrated the fragility of the previous regulatory environment. Sweeping legislative measures were agreed at the highest international levels to ensure that such a disaster should never recur. And yet the financial market infrastructure had borne up well during the crisis – better than, say, after the stock market crash of 1987[11] or the terrorist attacks of 11 September 2001.[12]

6.4   As discussed in **Chapter 5**, the new agenda is at least in part driven by the fear of OTC derivatives. Given that the European Union was party to the G-20 pledge to introduce compulsory clearing for OTC derivatives by the end of 2012,[13] the formalisation of regulatory standards for infrastructures in Europe has been led by the creation of EMIR.[14] A uniform standard for regulation of CCPs was not essential, though, in order to introduce compulsory clearing. Nor was it self-evident that a European statute for the regulation of CCPs should be twinned with a European statute for the regulation of CSD. On these issues, the following observations may be made.

---

8   ECB, Eurosystem Oversight Policy Framework (February 2009), http://www.ecb.int/pub/pdf/other/eurosystemoversightpolicyframework2009en.pdf?6f7a2d8dc6dc35374138e76d2be57679

9   ECB, Eurosystem Oversight Policy Framework (July 2011), http://www.ecb.int/pub/pdf/other/eurosystemoversightpolicyframework2011en.pdf?90662f1a6c3f04597b94078271fb7537

10   McCreevy, C, Clearing and settlement: The way forward (July 2006), Speech 06/450, http://europa.eu/rapid/pressReleasesAction.do?reference=SPEECH/06/560&format=PDF&aged=1&language=EN&guiLanguage=en

11   See **section 17.9**

12   Federal Reserve Bank of New York, Domestic Open Market Operations During 2001 (February 2002), http://www.newyorkfed.org/markets/omo/omo2001.pdf, p 21

13   G-20, Progress Report on the Economic and Financial Actions of the London, Washington And Pittsburgh G20 Summits Prepared by the UK Chair of the G20 (November 2009), http://www.g20.org/Documents/20091107_progress_report_standrews.pdf, item 68

14   Regulation (EU) No 648/2012 of the European Parliament and of the Council of 4 July 2012 on OTC derivatives, central counterparties and trade repositories

Rationale for CCPs to be uniformly regulated

6.5   As one might expect, the justification given by the European Commission[15] is that CCPs should be safe, being 'systemically relevant' institutions. With no choice left for trading firms and investors as to whether certain financial products should be cleared, it is clearly important that minimum standards should be established, and that these minima should apply also to non-EEA CCPs plying their trade in the EU in order to capture the mandatory-clearing market.

However, it might also be remarked that in the absence of globally-agreed standards, the creation by the European authorities of their own standards has the potential to exclude non-EEA CCPs from the European marketplace, shielding the European CCPs from competition. Given the trouble which the question where a CCP should be 'located' has already spawned,[16] a consequence of the desire to have robust regulation of CCPs might be to restrict the ability of European investors to trade with non-EEA counterparties or in foreign products.

Furthermore, EMIR is neutral on the important question whether a CCP must be structured as a bank.[17] Prudential and other regulatory standards exist for banks which EMIR does not seek to disapply, thereby perpetuating a lack of uniformity even within Europe.

Rationale for CSDs becoming subject to EU-level regulation

6.6   The European Commission's commentary on the proposed Regulation on Central Securities Depositories (CSDR)[18] explains:

> 'The absence of an efficient single internal market for settlement also raises important concerns. Important barriers to the European post trading market continue to exist, such as for instance the limitation of securities issuers' access to CSDs, different national licensing regimes and rules for CSDs across the EU and limited competition between different national CSDs. These barriers result in a very fragmented market. As a consequence, the cross-border settlement of transactions relies on unnecessarily complex holding 'chains' often involving several CSDs and several other intermediaries. This has a negative impact on the efficiency, but also on the risks associated with cross-border transactions.'[19]

It would therefore appear that competition policy is an important force. However confused the world is on the removal of Giovannini Barrier 9 (National restrictions on the location of securities),[20] the policy objective of the

---

15   European Commission, Proposal for a Regulation of the European Parliament and of the Council on OTC derivatives, central counterparties and trade repositories (September 2010), COM(2010) 484 final, http://eur-lex.europa.eu/LexUriServ/LexUriServ.do?uri=COM:2010:04 84:FIN:EN:PDF, para 4.3.3

16   See **section 12.13**

17   Cf **section 12.9**

18   European Commission, Proposal for a Regulation of the European Parliament and of the Council on improving securities settlement in the European Union and on central securities depositories etc (March 2012), COM(2012) 73 final, http://eur-lex.europa.eu/LexUriServ/ LexUriServ.do?uri=CELEX:52012PC0073:EN:PDF

19   Explanatory memorandum to CSDR, p 3

20   See **sections 10.24–10.25**

CSDR is to provide for competition in the pursuit of lower settlement costs. Enabling one CSD to provide services in another CSD's home market requires that there be a basic minimum set of standards to enable passporting to occur without legitimate objection from the host state regulator. In practice, the issues which are uniformly regulated by the CSDR proposal do not necessarily cover everything which might be regarded as of importance, so the future success of this policy measure remains uncertain.

6.7   There are further questions which might be asked on the subject of a developing legislative framework for regulation of infrastructures in Europe, including the following:

(1) Why did soft law fail?

It might be thought that the development of formal statutes for regulation of CCPs and CSDs indicated that the self-regulatory approach under the Code of Conduct[21] heralded by Commissioner McCreevy in 2006[22] had failed. However, the Code of Conduct had limited objectives, and in retrospect those objectives might have been fulfilled insofar as reasonably achievable.

First, the aims of the Code were to achieve price transparency, to enable access and interoperability, and to unbundle services and account for them separately. Transparency and unbundling have not been regarded as problem areas since the Code came into effect. Interoperability is a major challenge, but there are many reasons for this which cannot be laid at the door of weaknesses in the Code.[23] Secondly, the scope of the Code was limited to post trading in cash equities. The new legislation on CCPs is primarily about clearing of OTC derivative transactions. The new agenda is different from the old one: the old agenda was primarily about competition and the reduction of inefficiency in the post-trade arena, whereas the new focus is on safety in the financial sector.

(2) How are the Giovannini barriers being dismantled?

Unfortunately it might be thought that the Giovannini barriers have been disregarded in the push for new legislation. With derivatives at the forefront of thinking, the cost of equities clearing and settlement has receded from the priority list. The European Commission's Expert Group on Market Infrastructures[24] wants to re-boot Giovannini, or do even better, but their report had not by 2012 achieved the status of a blueprint for legislation or indeed other governmental action.

(3) Why are payment systems treated differently?

It is notable that the drive towards formal legislative regulation of infrastructures has not touched payment systems. Payment *services* have hardly been immune from legislative attention, with no fewer than seven

---

21 Federation of European Securities Exchanges, European Association of Central Counterparty Clearing Houses, and European Central Securities Depositories Association, European Code of Conduct for Clearing and Settlement (November 2006), http://ec.europa.eu/internal_market/financial-markets/docs/code/code_en.pdf; see **section 7.18**

22 McCreevy, Speech 06/450

23 See **Chapter 13**

24 Expert Group on Market Infrastructures, Report (October 2011), http://ec.europa.eu/internal_market/financial-markets/docs/clearing/egmi/101011_report_en.pdf

European legislative measures passed since 1997.[25] This is a higher rate of creation of primary legislation than in banking or investment services. Yet payment infrastructures and payment schemes are not the target of these measures. Payment systems might be expected to raise greater concerns about safety and reliability, given their pivotal role in financial stability. But they are largely left in the realm of soft law.

In part this anomaly can be explained by the creation of the euro. Much of Europe now uses the euro as its currency. The ECB has accordingly established the Target-2 system, and the ECB operates the system under a series of legislative acts.[26] Furthermore, the European System of Central Banks (ESCB) is responsible under the Treaty on the Functioning of the European Union for promoting the smooth operation of payment systems in Europe, even in respect of non-euro countries.[27]

Secondly, however, it may in part be that systemically important payment systems are still largely operated by central banks. Public general legislation is rarely considered by governments to be an optimal way of regulating themselves or their creatures. An example of this reluctance may be seen in the comment of the International Monetary Fund on the United Kingdom's approach to regulating its own payment systems:

> 'CHAPS is a recognized system under the Banking Act 2009, but the [Bank of England's] RTGS system is not. The RTGS system would have the potential to threaten the stability of, or confidence in, the U.K. financial system if there were any deficiencies in its design or if its operation were disrupted. However, the RTGS is not an interbank payment system for the purposes of the Banking Act 2009, since, of itself, it is not considered to constitute arrangements designed to facilitate or control the transfer of money between financial institutions (the BoE considers it is an arrangement to transfer money between financial institutions' accounts at the BoE, not between the institutions themselves). In addition, the BoE's RTGS system is not designated under the Settlement Finality Regulations.'[28]

It may be noted that, perhaps for these reasons, even before the financial crisis the ESCB did not adopt external soft-law standards for wholesale payment systems, although it did so for CSDs and CCPs. The standards adopted for retail payment systems are considered further below.

6.8 A final introductory observation is that soft law persists. There may be new statute law in Europe, but its coverage is limited and its focus is narrow. Payment systems and much that is relevant to the operation of CSDs and CCPs are outside the scope of the new regime. And the fount of soft law, the guidance and recommendations given out by the CPSS and IOSCO, has been overhauled,

25 Directive 97/5/EC; Directive 2000/48/EC; Regulation (EC) No 1781/2006; Directive 2007/64/EC; Regulation (EC) No 924/2009; Directive 2009/110/EC; Regulation (EU) No 260/2012
26 Located at http://www.ecb.eu/ecb/legal/1003/1349/html/index.en.html
27 Consolidated Version of the Treaty on the Functioning of the European Union (TFEU) (May 2008), OJ 2008/C115/01, art 127(2)
28 International Monetary Fund, United Kingdom: Observance by CHAPS of CPSS Core Principles for Systemically Important Payment Systems Detailed Assessment of Observance (July 2011), Country Report No 11/237, http://www.imf.org/external/pubs/ft/scr/2011/cr11237.pdf, p 31

extended in scope, and made more detailed. The new regulatory template is set down in the FMI Principles,[29] which are reviewed in **section 6.39** below.

PAYMENT SYSTEM REGULATION

6.9   The ESCB has a Treaty power to oversee payment systems.[30] Article 22 of the ESCB and ECB Statute states that 'the ECB may make regulations to ensure efficient and sound clearing and payment systems within the Union.'[31] In its 2011 Oversight Policy Framework, the ECB interprets the oversight role as being given to the 'Eurosystem' (that is, the ECB and the national central banks of the euro area) and in respect of euro area systems. However, the power to make formal regulations has never been exercised, and the 2011 Oversight Policy Framework is the ECB's main document on payment systems oversight.[32]

The 2011 Oversight Policy Framework does not contain a set of rules to be followed by payment system operators. Instead it confirms that the CPSS Core Principles,[33] together with the ECB's own 'business continuity oversight expectations'[34] apply in the case of large-value payment systems, and that a different approach, set out in its 'oversight standards for euro retail payment systems,'[35] applies in other cases.[36]

6.10   The CPSS Core Principles have now been subsumed into the FMI Principles. It is to be presumed that the ECB will adopt the FMI Principles in due course: there are gaps, because of the greater breadth of the FMI Principles. Among the gaps are the more detailed approach to management of credit and liquidity risks in payment systems; a requirement for robust Payment-versus-Payment in exchange-of-value systems like CLS; a requirement for default rules; principles for management of general business risk; and the introduction of guidance on tiering. As regards tiering, a relative newcomer in regulatory thinking, the Bank of England has led the way by adopting its own supervisory principles for this, as discussed in **section 11.5**.

6.11   The ECB's business continuity expectations amplify Core Principle VII, and require payment systems to have business continuity plans aimed at resumption of critical functions within the same day, to have a secondary site, to have a crisis management team and communications procedures, and to engage in industry-wide testing. The business continuity expectations are now

29 CPSS and Technical Committee of IOSCO, Principles for Financial Market Infrastructures (April 2012), http://www.bis.org/publ/cpss101a.pdf
30 TFEU, art 127
31 TFEU, Protocol (No 4) on the Statute of the European System of Central Banks and of the European Central Bank
32 2011 Oversight Policy Framework, p 7
33 CPSS, Core Principles for Systemically Important Payment Systems (January 2001), http://www.bis.org/publ/cpss43.pdf
34 ECB, Business Continuity Oversight Expectations for Systemically Important Payment Systems (SIPS) (June 2006), http://www.ecb.int/pub/pdf/other/businesscontinuitysips2006en.pdf?43610eb2b5449d7a640e1319599dd74c
35 ECB, Oversight Standards for Euro Retail Payment Systems (June 2003), http://www.ecb.int/pub/pdf/other/retailpsoversightstandardsen.pdf?2189cab2af1204f4edb42772eac0429c
36 2011 Oversight Policy Framework, p 4

replicated in the key considerations related to FMI Principle 17, with restoration of functions now expected within two hours.[37]

Box 6.1   CPSS Core Principles for Systemically Important Payment Systems

I.   The system should have a well-founded legal basis under all relevant jurisdictions.

II.   The system's rules and procedures should enable participants to have a clear understanding of the system's impact on each of the financial risks they incur through participation in it.

III.   The system should have clearly defined procedures for the management of credit risks and liquidity risks, which specify the respective responsibilities of the system operator and the participants and which provide appropriate incentives to manage and contain those risks.

IV.*   The system should provide prompt final settlement on the day of value, preferably during the day and at a minimum at the end of the day.

V.*   A system in which multilateral netting takes place should, at a minimum, be capable of ensuring the timely completion of daily settlements in the event of an inability to settle by the participant with the largest single settlement obligation.

VI.   Assets used for settlement should preferably be a claim on the central bank; where other assets are used, they should carry little or no credit risk and little or no liquidity risk.

VII.   The system should ensure a high degree of security and operational reliability and should have contingency arrangements for timely completion of daily processing.

VIII.   The system should provide a means of making payments which is practical for its users and efficient for the economy.

IX.   The system should have objective and publicly disclosed criteria for participation, which permit fair and open access.

X.   The system's governance arrangements should be effective, accountable and transparent.

* Systems should seek to exceed the minima included in these two Core Principles.

6.12   'Prominent' retail payment systems are those considered by the ECB not to have systemic implications but which could nonetheless have a severe impact if disrupted. 'A system is likely to be of systemic importance if at least one of the following is true: i) it is the only payment system in a country, or the principal system in terms of the aggregate value of payments; ii) it mainly handles payments of high individual value; or iii) it is used for the settlement of financial market transactions or the settlement of other payment systems.'[38] This statement reflects the view of the CPSS itself.[39] The CPSS Core Principles are applied to all systemic payment systems, and also to retail 'systems that are of prominent importance to the economy,' except that Core Principles III to VI

---

37 FMI Principles, Principle 17, Key consideration 5
38 ECB Oversight Standards for Euro Retail Payment Systems, p 2; cf **section 16.2**
39 CPSS Core Principles, para 6.9

are disapplied for the prominent systems.[40] No rules, other than national rules if any, apply to payment systems which are neither systemic nor prominent.[41] The ECB website lists retail systems which are of 'systemic' and merely 'prominent' importance.[42]

6.13 The conclusion that national supervisors are the first line of defence in ensuring the integrity of a payment system opens the question how supranational systems should be dealt with. There are several important payment systems operating specifically for cross-border services or to serve the euro: TARGET-2, CLS, and the systems operated by EBA Clearing. In these cases the ECB itself is assigned the primary role in oversight, with the exception of CLS, where the leading role is given to the Federal Reserve System.[43] However, the principles applied are no different in these cases. Lest there be concern that the ECB is both supervisor and supervisee in the case of TARGET-2, a separate team within the ECB is responsible for oversight.[44]

6.14 Where the ECB is responsible for supervision of a payment system, an assessment methodology is available to facilitate its judgment on whether the CPSS Core Principles are being observed.[45] While each of the CPSS Core Principles has an 'implementation summary', the ECB's assessment methodology differs from the CPSS by adding significantly more detail to the issues to be considered, and converting them to questions rather than guidance. The relationship between the questions and achieving 'observed' status is less clear than for the Recommendations issued by the ECB and CESR for CSDs and CCPs. It would seem – to select three examples, and with the caveat that the interpretation of the subtext of the questions might be assessed differently – that a compliant system needs to be designated under the Settlement Finality Directive (SFD);[46] if it relies on DNS methodology[47] it should have default backing; and that there should be stakeholder consultation on major decisions. It might also be noted that, although a good deal of attention is given to operational risk management, outsourcings receive scant attention.

The ECB's supervision technique is not founded on a rulebook. The supervisory technique used is known in the United Kingdom as the 'cup of tea' method, from the historical (possibly apocryphal) practice of the Bank of England, in its previous role as banking supervisor, inviting senior managers of recalcitrant banks in for a cup of tea over which misdemeanours might be 'discussed'. The ECB's supervisory tools are described as collection of information, and 'inducing change' through 'moral suasion, public statements, influence

---

40 ECB Oversight Standards for Euro Retail Payment Systems, p 4
41 ECB Oversight Standards for Euro Retail Payment Systems, p 4
42 See http://www.ecb.eu/paym/pol/activ/retail/html/index.en.html
43 2011 Oversight Policy Framework, p 8; Board of Governors of the Federal Reserve System, Protocol for the Cooperative Oversight Arrangement of CLS (November 2008), http://www.federalreserve.gov/paymentsystems/cls_protocol.htm
44 Kokkola, T, (ed), The Payment System (European Central Bank, September 2010), ISBN 978-92-899-0632-6, p 271
45 ECB, Terms of Reference for the Oversight Assessment of Euro Systemically and Prominently Important Payment Systems against the Core Principles, http://www.ecb.int/paym/cons/shared/files/pscc_terms_070514.pdf (adopted November 2007, see http://www.ecb.int/press/pr/date/2007/html/pr071112.en.html)
46 Directive 98/26/EC of the European Parliament and of the Council on settlement finality in payment and securities settlement systems
47 See **section 2.30**

stemming from its participation in systems, cooperation with other authorities, and binding regulations (a tool the Eurosystem has not used thus far).'[48]

6.15 In addition to the CPSS Core Principles and the FMI Principles, there is further soft law of relevance to payment systems. Mention may be made of the PE-ACH/CSM Framework created by the European Payments Council (EPC).[49] The EPC's Single Euro Payments Area (SEPA) payment schemes give rise to euro payments which need to be settled through payment systems, and the systems need to be compatible with those schemes. Accordingly the PE-ACH/CSM Framework establishes requirements for ACHs which wish to be pan-European, or clearing and settlement mechanisms with less extensive reach, for the settlement of euro transactions subject to the schemes. These include compatibility with the time limits, data formats, and other requirements of the scheme rulebooks; compliance with standard European rules on no-deduction of charges from monies in transit; keeping a count of transactions; having non-discriminatory access criteria and inclusive governance rules; and compliance with the ECB's oversight standards for retail payment systems.[50] A PE-ACH must achieve full reachability – that is, the ability to send to any direct or indirect user, and to receive from any direct or indirect user – across SEPA, either by itself, or through arrangements with other ACHs and CSMs.[51]

Designation under the Settlement Finality Directive

6.16 The SFD is not a regulatory instrument. Its purpose is protection of designated payment and settlement systems from attack under insolvency laws.[52] It has one 'regulatory' provision, which says that 'Member States may impose supervision or authorisation requirements on systems which fall under their jurisdiction.'[53] The SFD's approach to regulation of systems can be explained as follows:

> '[D]esignation falls short of "authorising" the system: the arrangement can function without being designated as a system under the Directive. It nevertheless implies that the Member State has a role to play in assessing the risk profile of a system and in imposing measures to reduce risk. Article [10(1)] goes further. It provides that Member States may impose authorisation or supervision requirements on systems governed by their law. It was important to spell this out, as doubts could otherwise have arisen on Member States' further ability to do so. Under the Codified Banking Directive ... [t]he host Member State may not impose any further authorisation or supervisory requirements on a passported institution.'[54]

---

48 Kokkola, p 283
49 European Payments Council, PE-ACH/CSM Framework (June 2008), http://www. europeanpaymentscouncil.eu/knowledge_bank_download.cfm?file=EPC170-05%20v1%20 2%20CSM%20Framework%20approved.pdf
50 PE-ACH/CSM Framework, paras 2.3, 3.5, 3.6
51 PE-ACH/CSM Framework, paras 3.2, 3.3
52 See **sections 8.18ff**
53 Article 10(1), third para
54 Vereecken, M, 'Directive 98/26/EC on the European Union Payment Systems and Securities Settlement Systems', in Vereecken, M, and Nijenhuis, A, (eds), Settlement Finality in the European Union (Kluwer, April 2003), ISBN 90 130 0487 3, p 64

Although the SFD contains no other 'regulatory' provisions, it is plain that the SFD confers a privileged status on designated systems, and that the competent authorities of Member States have a discretion as to whether to award that status. It would be expected, therefore, that there would be some regulatory *quid pro quo* setting out rules which a designated system should obey in order to retain its privileges. The SFD, equally plainly, does not contain those rules, nor, when the SFD was reviewed in 2006, did this seem to be an important omission.[55] The position would seem to be as follows.

(1) Some Member States, such as the United Kingdom, have introduced limited conditions which have to be adhered to in order to maintain designated status.[56]

(2) Others have concluded that ordinary banking supervision is sufficient to ensure adequate oversight of designated systems.[57]

(3) There are eligibility criteria with which any designated system must comply. These are considered in **section 8.19**.

(4) If any further regulatory rules are sought for designated system, it ought to follow that they are set out in the CPSS Core Principles, or the FMI Principles, given that designation is closely linked to the notion of systemic risk management.

EMIR AND CCPs

6.17 The European Market Infrastructure Regulation (formally the Regulation on OTC derivative transactions, CCPs and trade repositories, but generally referred to as EMIR)[58] introduced a European scheme of regulation for CCPs, including CCPs clearing instruments other than OTC derivatives. Its content can be reviewed by reference to five aspects of a CCP's function: regulation; ownership, governance and capital; counterparty risk management; internal organisation; and competition.

Regulation

6.18 The principal regulator of a CCP is the competent authority in the Member State where the CCP is incorporated.[59]

6.19 However, CCPs may have foreign operations. A CCP's services may, in a sense, be provided in countries other than the home Member State: a CCP may provide clearing services for platforms which might be based elsewhere, the participants in a CCP may be based elsewhere; the financial products which the CCP clears may be securities issued in other countries or contractual entitlements governed by foreign legal systems. EMIR acknowledges that a CCP may wish 'to extend its business into a Member State other than where it

---

55 Cf European Commission, Evaluation report on the Settlement Finality Directive 98/26/EC (EU25) (March 2006), COM (2005) 657 final/2, http://ec.europa.eu/internal_market/financial-markets/docs/settlement/evaluation_report_en.pdf

56 See **section 11.7**

57 Cf Haag, H, Peters, M, and Schneider, H, 'Implementation of the Settlement Finality Directive in Germany', in Vereecken and Nijenhuis, p 241

58 Regulation (EU) No 648/2012 of the European Parliament and of the Council of 4 July 2012 on OTC derivatives, central counterparties and trade repositories

59 EMIR, art 14

is established.'[60] What EMIR does not explain, however, is how a host state is to determine whether the CCP is conducting its business in that state. Financial services are essentially non-material, and therefore in the absence of a bricks-and-mortar branch it may be difficult to ascribe to a 'location' to the provision of services. Old guidance from the European Commission on the second Banking Coordination Directive[61] suggested that a 'characteristic performance' test should be applied to determine whether a financial service was being conducted in a particular state: 'In order to determine where an activity was carried on, the place of provision of what may be termed the "characteristic performance" of the service, ie the essential supply for which payment is due must be determined.'[62] In the case of clearing services, what constitutes the 'characteristic' performance might also be debated, but using the definition provided by EMIR itself ('the process of establishing positions, including the calculation of net obligations, and ensuring that financial instruments, cash, or both, are available to secure its exposures arising from those positions')[63] one might conclude that none of the 'foreign operations' of CCPs listed at the start of this paragraph would displace the characteristic activities of clearing away from the place where the risk management is carried out. Contrary arguments might, no doubt, be adduced, based for example on the presence of participants or even end-users or margin assets in other countries; but the simplest approach would be to assume that CCPs are not extending their business into another Member State unless they set up a physical branch.

6.20 If a CCP does extend its business into other Member States, a notification, by the home state regulator to the host state regulator, is required.[64] However, the competent authority of the host state has little involvement in the supervision of the CCP. The supervisory functions of deciding on authorisation, extension of a CCP's activities and services, review of stress-testing, and approval of interoperability arrangements are to be carried out by a college of regulators;[65] and the composition of the college does not automatically ensure that host state regulators are included. The college consists of ESMA, the CCP's home state regulator, the regulators of the three largest participants (measured by default fund contribution), the regulators of trading venues served by the CCP, CSDs linked to the CCP, and interoperating CCPs, and various central banks.[66] The home state regulator, however, has exclusive control over the day-to-day supervision of the CCP.[67]

CCPs based outside the European Economic Area need to be recognised by ESMA in order to provide clearing services to clearing members or venues of execution in the EU.[68] On one reading of article 25(1) of EMIR, EU persons

60 EMIR, art 15(2)
61 Second Council Directive 89/646/EEC of 15 December 1989 on the coordination of laws, Regulations and administrative provisions relating to the taking up and pursuit of the business of credit institutions, etc
62 European Commission, Freedom to provide services and the interest of the general good in the Second Banking Directive (June 1997), Commission Interpretative Communication, SEC(97) 1193 final, http://ec.europa.eu/internal_market/bank/docs/sec-1997-1193/sec-1997-1193_en.pdf, p 6
63 EMIR, art 2(3)
64 EMIR, art 15(2)
65 EMIR, art 18(1)
66 EMIR, art 18(2)
67 EMIR, art 21
68 EMIR, art 25

would also appear to be unable to accept clearing services provided *outside the EU* by an unrecognised CCP.

Legal form of CCPs

6.21   As discussed in **section 12.9**, there is a divergence of views in Europe as to whether CCPs should take the form of banks. EMIR does not take sides on this debate. Article 14 requires a CCP to obtain a clearing services licence (and article 89(3) makes it clear that even CCPs operating before the commencement of EMIR must re-apply for a licence in accordance with EMIR's procedures, including examination by its international college of regulators), but article 14(5) allows Member States to apply super-equivalent regulatory requirements 'including certain requirements for authorisation under Directive 2006/48/EC [the Banking Directive].'

CCPs cannot be authorised unless they are also designated under the SFD.[69]

Ownership and governance

6.22   Who should be allowed to own and run a CCP has proved to be a topic of some controversy: the debate is touched on in **Chapter 12**, in relation to governance, and in **Chapter 17**, in relation to responsibility for restoration of a CCP to financial health following a catastrophic loss. EMIR has resisted the call for ownership to be divorced from clearing members, and contains only a few stipulations on the subject.

First, the regulator must be informed of the identity of the owners of the CCP,[70] changes in the degree of control enjoyed by those with voting rights,[71] and approve the suitability of owners and those with 'close links'.[72] In these respects, EMIR reflects the requirements of the Banking Directive.[73]

Governance arrangements are also in line with the revised, more detailed approach to governance in banks, being introduced under the proposed Credit Institutions Directive.[74] So, CCPs will have to have clear reporting lines, effective systems and controls, independent risk management, sound compensation policies, adequate IT, transparent governance, independent audit, high-quality management including independent directors, and a risk committee.[75] The role of the risk committee is important: it is obliged to advise the board on any arrangements that might impact the risk management of the CCP, including the risk model, default procedures, membership criteria, clearing of new products and outsourcing.[76] The risk committee may only comprise representatives of

---

69   EMIR, art 17(1)

70   EMIR, art 30(1)

71   EMIR, art 31(2)

72   EMIR, art 30(2), (3)

73   Directive 2006/48/EC of the European Parliament and of the Council of 14 June 2006 relating to the taking up and pursuit of the business of credit institutions, arts 12, 19

74   European Commission, Proposal for a Directive of the European Parliament and of the Council on the access to the activity of credit institutions and the prudential supervision of credit institutions and investment firms etc (July 2011), COM(2011) 453 final, http://eur-lex.europa.eu/LexUriServ/LexUriServ.do?uri=COM:2011:0453:FIN:EN:PDF, arts 73ff

75   EMIR, arts 26–28

76   EMIR, art 28(3)

clearing members and clients, and the independent members of the board.[77] Its role is advisory, but the CCP must inform its regulator if it decides not to follow the advice of the risk committee.[78]

Capital of CCPs

6.23   The ownership of a CCP is a subject closely connected to the provision of its capital. The capital of a CCP may be considered to consist of its 'own funds', that is liabilities of the CCP to its owners and subordinated creditors, and its default fund, contributed by the clearing members. As to the former, the EMIR has little to say. A CCP is required to have initial capital of no less than EUR 7.5 million,[79] which is more than a bank;[80] but instead of the tract of legislation spelling out the risk-based capital requirements which applies to banks, EMIR says that:

- capital should be sufficient to ensure an orderly winding-down or restructuring over an appropriate time span and an adequate protection of the CCP against credit, counterparty, market, operational, legal and business risks;[81] and

- rather more vaguely, '[c]apital including retained earnings and reserves of a CCP shall be proportionate to the risk stemming from the activities of the CCP.'[82]

6.24   More detail is left to subordinate legislation to be drafted by the European Banking Authority (EBA). The EBA's proposals, in summary, suggest that the principal function of capital is not to provide resources to cover participant defaults; instead the focus is on the appropriate amount of financial backing to cover an orderly wind-down and operational risks.[83]

The following comments may be made on the capitalisation of a CCP in accordance with the EBA's proposed principles.

(1) The principles proceed from the basis that the CCP's capital is needed to carry out a 'lift out' of the CCP's business. For the reasons given in **sections 17.3–17.7**, this may be a difficult outcome to achieve for this type of infrastructure, and to prescribe a capital requirement with an artificial objective in mind may be imprudent.

(2) The capital of a CCP is needed primarily to buffer creditors against the risk that the CCP cannot manage counterparty risk effectively. Although the circumstances and quantum of this risk are different in the case of a CCP, the risk is qualitatively identical to that being taken by banks and investment firms, so it could be argued that CCPs should be capitalised according to

---

77   EMIR, art 28(1)
78   EMIR, art 28(5)
79   EMIR, art 16(1)
80   Cf Banking Directive, art 9
81   EMIR, art 16(2)
82   EMIR, art 16(2)
83   See European Banking Authority, EBA Discussion Paper on Draft Regulatory Technical Standards on the capital requirements for CCPs under the draft Regulation on OTC derivatives, CCPs and Trade Repositories (March 2012), EBA/DP/2012/1, http://www.eba.europa.eu/cebs/media/aboutus/News%20and%20Communications/EBA-DP-2012-01--Draft-discussion-paper-on-RTS-on-Article-12-3-EMIR-.pdf

the principles set out in the Banking Directive or its replacement. But this allows a favourable treatment to collateralised exposures.[84] So it is likely that a CCP's capital requirement calculated on the same set of measures as a bank calculating a counterparty-risk-related requirement would lead to a low result.

(3) Unfortunately there is no generally accepted principle for determining the appropriate amount of counterparty-risk-related capital when a CCP has exhausted its default fund. Further, as discussed in **sections 14.32–14.35**, it is hard to quantify an economically viable amount of financial backing which can ensure that a CCP always escapes a loss which exhausts the margin, and to try to repeat the exercise for exhaustion of the default fund is probably impossible.

(4) The EBA's proposals for operational-risk-related capital requirements are based on the Basel II approach which, for many banks, uses a multiple of gross income as a proxy for quantification of operational losses.[85] It can be argued that this is not appropriate for CCPs, whose operational risks are likely to be qualitatively different from those of banks.

6.25   Article 43 of EMIR also requires a CCP to maintain sufficient available pre-funded financial resources to cover potential losses that exceed losses covered by margin requirements and the default fund. It is unclear what is meant by this provision: apart from operational risks, losses not covered by margin and default funding will arise out of participant defaults. If the size of default funds is calculated properly, it is difficult to imagine how a CCP or its regulator should assess the appropriate amount of supplementary pre-funded resources required by this article.

As to the size of the default fund, EMIR requires it to be sufficient to enable the CCP to withstand, under extreme but plausible market conditions, the default of the clearing member to which it has the largest exposures (or of the second and third largest clearing members, if larger).[86] Level 2 subordinate legislation is to specify the framework for defining 'extreme but plausible market conditions.'[87] Stress-testing and back-testing are to be carried out to assess the resilience of the default fund and margin requirements.[88]

Relationship between 'capital', the default fund and other loss protection

6.26   The starting-point is that the function of capital is to absorb losses which are sustained by the entity carrying out the loss-making business.[89] The purpose of capital investment is thus to expose the owners of the business to risk associated with failure of that business, as well as its rewards. A default fund is indeed a species of 'capital' – in the sense that it is a liability of the CCP which is loss-absorbing and therefore protective of senior creditors. Indeed, the

---

84   Banking Directive, Annex VIII
85   Bank for International Settlements Basel Committee on Banking Supervision, International Convergence of Capital Measurement and Capital Standards (June 2006), http://www.bis.org/publ/bcbs128.pdf, part V
86   EMIR, art 42(3)
87   EMIR, art 42(5)
88   EMIR, art 49
89   Cf Financial Services Authority, Handbook of Rules and Guidance, General Prudential Sourcebook (December 2010), GENPRU 2.2.9R, GENPRU 2.280R

computations of a CCP's 'hypothetical capital', to be done under the proposed Capital Requirements Regulation[90] for the purposes of enabling participants in the CCP to determine their own regulatory capital requirements in respect of default fund contributions,[91] treat default fund contributions as a component of hypothetical capital. (But it should be noted that the hypothetical capital of a CCP is not used by the EBA as the method of calculation of the risk-based capital of the CCP.)

However, a typically constituted default fund allows a contributor to withdraw its contribution by quitting membership of the CCP, which is not usually a feature of eligible regulatory capital instruments. (Admittedly the continuing participants would be expected to make good the deficit occasioned by departure of a contributor; but that model of replenishment is based on the notion that participation in the CCP is desirable. If there were many departures, as would be the case where the future of the CCP is in doubt, the willingness of an ever-diminishing pool of participants to contribute an ever-greater share of the default fund must also be in doubt, and the demise of the CCP would follow.)

And in no sense do the contributors to the default fund share in the benefits of capital investors. They have influence on policy, through the risk committee, but there is no statutory guarantee that advice from the risk committee as to the balance between own-funds capital, default funding, margin, and other types of financial backing such as insurance would be heeded by the board. The board of a CCP answers to the CCP's shareholders, not the wider constituency of capital providers. Other factors which the board of a CCP might find influential can legitimately include the profitability of the CCP under different models of risk-sharing.

6.27   There is also no obligation for a CCP to build and retain reserves. The absence of any competitors for clearing products which are subject to mandatory clearing might also introduce distortions in solving this equation: EMIR does not introduce safeguards beyond those already existing under the general law of competition.[92]

6.28   It is suggested that the EMIR approach to capital is simplistic and wrong, and that it would have been better to adapt a model which already exists for calculating capital adequacy in risk-taking organisations with low-probability high-impact risk profiles. Catastrophe insurers take on risks which have these characteristics, and European regulators have devised a regulatory capital regime, commonly called the Solvency II Directive,[93] which is being applied to those businesses. In addition to a 'minimum capital requirement', which may be regarded as analogous to the basic requirement of EMIR for CCPs to have capital of at least EUR 7.5 million, insurance companies are required to have a solvency capital requirement designed to maintain their default probability below a certain

---

90 European Commission, Proposal For a Regulation of the European Parliament and of the Council on prudential requirements for credit institutions and investment firms (July 2011), COM(2011) 452 final, http://eur-lex.europa.eu/LexUriServ/LexUriServ.do?uri=COM:2011:0452:FIN:EN:PDF
91 See **section 19.11(2)**
92 See **Chapter 7**
93 Directive 2009/138/EC of the European Parliament and of the Council of 25 November 2009 on the taking-up and pursuit of the business of Insurance and Reinsurance (Solvency II)

level, namely that it would have 99.5% probability of meeting its obligations over the next 12 months, or to put it differently, would only fail to cover a one-in-200-year maximum loss.[94] Furthermore, insurers may mitigate their risks, and to varying degrees their capital requirements, through a variety of instruments such as reinsurance or capital market products such as catastrophe-linked notes.[95] These options do not seem to be contemplated by EMIR.

Counterparty risk management

6.29 EMIR has a selection of rules on the subject of counterparty risk management. These may be summarised as follows:

(1) *Margin.* CCPs must collect margin sufficient to meet two tests. They must 'cover potential exposures that the CCP estimates will occur until the liquidation of the relevant positions,' and they must 'cover losses that result from at least 99% of the exposures movements over an appropriate time horizon'. Margining must take place daily.[96] Although badly expressed, the requirement appears to mean that CCPs have to collect margin to cover losses up to a one-tailed 99% confidence threshold in ordinary, but not stressed, market conditions. This is consistent with, but not as detailed as, the FMI Principles. Further detail is to be set forth in technical standards created by ESMA. Stress- and back-testing of the CCP's models are to be carried out; Level 2 legislation is to set out what is required.[97]

The margin must consist of highly liquid collateral with minimal credit and market risk. CCPs must apply haircuts reflecting the potential decline in value of the collateral before it is liquidated.[98] In theory, bank guarantees might be accepted from participants which are non-financial counterparties. Level 2 legislation is to add detail to these basic rules.[99]

CCPs are permitted to re-use margin posted by way of security, without restriction except that they must publicly disclose the fact.[100] The exercise of a right of use would have to be reconciled with the duties (a) to invest only in cash or highly liquid financial instruments with minimal market and credit risk,[101] and (b) to place financial instruments provided as margin in 'highly secure arrangements.'[102]

(2) *Liquidity.* CCPs are required to have access to adequate liquidity to perform their functions. There is a 25% limit on the dependency of the CCP for liquidity on any single clearing member and its affiliates – although the FMI Principles do not specify a limit at all, the 25% level seems very generous. The detail of liquidity risk management is left to Level 2 legislation.[103]

---

94 Solvency II, art 101(3)
95 Cf Klein, R, and Wang, S, 'Catastrophe Risk Financing in the United States and the European Union: A Comparative Analysis of Alternative Regulatory Approaches' (September 2009) Journal of Risk and Insurance Vol 76, pp 607–637
96 EMIR, art 41(1)
97 EMIR, art 49
98 EMIR, art 46(1)
99 EMIR, art 46(3)
100 EMIR, art 39(8)
101 EMIR, art 47(1)
102 EMIR, art 47(3)
103 EMIR, art 44

Additional rules pertaining to counterparty risk and to clients reflect the attention newly paid to 'tiering' in the FMI Principles.[104] In the first place, EMIR imposes requirements for CCPs to facilitate segregation of client collateral.[105] EMIR also requires CCPs and clearing members to provide a segregated clearing service, but it allows them to offer an 'omnibus account' option for net margining and cheaper clearing,[106] as an alternative to 'individual client segregation'. Secondly, EMIR requires clearing members who clear client transactions to have sufficient financial resources and operational capacity for this service, and to inform the CCP on request about their criteria for providing access services.[107]

(3) *Default procedures*. CCPs are required to have default procedures; they must take prompt action to contain losses and liquidity pressures resulting from defaults, and ensure that close-out action does not disrupt operations or expose the non-defaulting clearing members to unexpected or uncontrollable losses.[108] This approach can be contrasted with the United Kingdom's requirements for default rules, which oblige a recognised clearing house to close out open positions;[109] similarly, the FMI Principles envisage prompt close-out.[110] EMIR seems to envisage that it may be prudent to keep positions open indefinitely, provided that losses and liquidity are kept under control. CCPs are expected to ensure that their default arrangements are legally enforceable;[111] again this contrasts with the United Kingdom approach, which takes nothing for granted where insolvency is concerned, and provides for statutory supremacy of a recognised clearing house's default procedures over the general law of insolvency.[112] It may be commented here that this is a drawback of European legislation taking the form of a Regulation: this part of EMIR is directed at the CCP, which is powerless to deliver the desired result, whereas a directive would impose obligations on Member States to bring it about.

Client positions are to be made portable on the default of a clearing member.[113] Where a client requests that its positions and assets are transferred, and another (transferee) clearing member agrees, the CCP must trigger its transfer arrangements. Clients' segregated collateral cannot be used to cover anything other than the positions held for their account.[114] The segregation rules set out in article 39 underpin these provisions. Whether segregation and portability of client positions is invariably the right solution is, however, disputed:[115] full portability eliminates the option of net margining and thereby ties up liquidity; it may not be achievable

---

104 FMI Principle 19
105 EMIR, art 39
106 EMIR, art 39(5); cf **sections 10.16** and **14.30**
107 EMIR, art 37(3)
108 EMIR, art 48(1), (2)
109 Financial Services and Markets Act 2000 (Recognition Requirements for Investment Exchanges and Clearing Houses) Regulations 2001, SI 2001 No 995, Schedule, para 25(1)(a)
110 FMI Principles, para 3.13.4
111 EMIR, art 48(4)
112 See **section 8.12**
113 EMIR, art 48(5) and (6)
114 EMIR, art 48(7)
115 Cf Institute of International Finance, IIF Response to CPSS-IOSCO Consultative Report on Principles for financial market infrastructures (July 2011), http://www.bis.org/publ/cpss94/cacomments/ioif.pdf, p 7

fully or in all circumstances; and to suggest that portability is available may lure investors into a false sense of security.[116]

Article 45 sets out a priority waterfall which CCPs must follow in covering default-related losses from their resources. The order is: defaulter's margin; defaulter's default fund contribution; the CCP's dedicated own resources; other pre-funded financial resources provided under article 43 and/or non-defaulters' default fund contributions. No express provision is made for the order of recourse to unfunded backing such as insurance, guarantees or their equivalent. No rules are specified for the sharing of losses among default fund contributors or for passing round the hat to replenish the default fund after it has been utilised. A further criticism which might be made is that any waterfall which requires the CCP to exhaust its own funds before the default fund implies that the CCP may not be able to survive a default which requires the default fund to be utilised: owing to the existence of future and contingent liabilities, connected with the general operation of the CCP and unrelated to the counterparty risk associated with cleared positions, the CCP will be technically insolvent at this point, unless it has an arrangement with its backers for emergency recapitalisation.

Internal organisation

6.30   As regards the way in which a CCP should manage its internal affairs, and in particular operational risks, the precedent followed by EMIR is more like the Markets in Financial Instruments Directive (MiFID)[117] than the Banking Directive. Article 18 of MiFID sets out, for investment firms, requirements for staff to comply with the directive, for avoidance of conflicts of interest, for business continuity, for outsourcing to be done in a way which avoids undue operational risk, for high-quality IT systems, for record-keeping, and for safeguarding of clients' assets. Each of these is reflected in EMIR.[118]

Particular mention might be made of the outsourcing rules. These follow the pattern set by the MiFID implementing directive[119], though with a number of omissions, and perhaps importantly, some additions. The additions are that the outsourcing arrangement must not impair the CCP's systems and controls for risk management,[120] and that the supplier must comply with data protection legislation.[121] This degree of detail is higher than that applicable to other types of market infrastructure, but in view of the risks, it is perhaps more surprising that other infrastructures are subject to more limited regulation in this regard, rather than that CCPs have to comply with detailed outsourcing requirements.

Competition

6.31   Access to CCPs is covered by article 37 of EMIR. As expected, the requirement is for membership criteria to be non-discriminatory, transparent

---

116   See **sections 14.47–14.58**
117   Directive 2004/39 of the European Parliament and of the Council of 21 April 2004 on markets in financial instruments, etc
118   Respectively, arts 26(2); 33; 26(3) and 34; 35; 26(6); 29; and 39
119   Commission Directive 2006/73/EC of 10 August 2006 implementing MiFID as regards organisational requirements etc, art 14
120   EMIR, art 35(1)(e)
121   EMIR, art 35(1)(j)

and objective,[122] while also demanding that the criteria ensure that clearing members have sufficient financial resources and operational capacity to meet their obligations. CCPs are required to measure their participants against the criteria at least annually. CCPs are allowed to make participation in default auctions[123] a membership criterion; but any obligation imposed must be applied in such a way as to restrict participation to limited categories of would-be participants.

As if to indicate that the Code of Conduct is now superseded, EMIR also sets out a statutory framework addressing each of the topics which are addressed by the Code. EMIR, of course, has broader reach than the Code, because it is not limited to cash equities clearing. Transparency of pricing is now given a legislative foundation in article 38 of EMIR. Accounting separation, however, and the associated subject of unbundling, is only tackled perfunctorily.[124] The more detailed provisions of the Code should therefore continue to govern the behaviour of CCPs, as well as CSDs, notwithstanding the implementation of EMIR.

Interoperability is the third subject covered by the Code, and this merits an entire Title to itself in EMIR.[125] But the interoperability rules apply only to CCPs in relation to 'transferable securities and money-market instruments.'[126] The interoperability provisions of EMIR are summarised in **section 13.8(2)**.

Regulation of CCPs – besides EMIR

6.32　Although EMIR is the primary legislative instrument affecting CCPs, it is not the only one. Mention might be made of the following:

(1)　MiFID contains provisions on access to CCPs, limiting rules which prohibit use of an overseas CCP.[127]

(2)　The legislation proposed to replace MiFID includes a Regulation:

> 'In addition to requirements in Directive 2004/39/EC that prevent Member States from unduly restricting access to post trade infrastructure such as central counterparty (CCP) and settlement arrangements, it is necessary that this Regulation removes various other commercial barriers that can be used to prevent competition in the clearing of financial instruments. Barriers may arise from central counterparties not providing clearing services to certain trading venues, trading venues not providing data streams to potential new clearers or information about benchmarks or indices not being provided to clearers or trading venues.'[128]

Accordingly the proposed Regulation is to contain articles requiring CCPs to accept financial instruments on a non-discriminatory basis, regardless of

---

122　Cf **section 7.11**
123　See **sections 14.44** and **14.45**
124　EMIR, art 38(1)
125　Title V
126　EMIR, art 1(3)
127　MiFID, arts 34, 35, 46; see **section 7.21**
128　European Commission, Proposal for a Regulation of the European Parliament and of the Council on markets in financial instruments etc (October 2011), COM(2011) 652 final, http://eur-lex.europa.eu/LexUriServ/LexUriServ.do?uri=COM:2011:0652:FIN:EN:PDF, para 3.4.9

the trading venue of execution;[129] requiring trading venues to provide trade feeds on a non-discriminatory basis to any CCP;[130] and requiring owners of benchmarks to give non-discriminatory access to CCPs (and trading venues) to price and data feeds, as well as methodology information and licences.[131]

(3) The SFD has, since it was modified in 2009,[132] expressly contemplated that a designated system includes a CCP:

> "'system" shall mean a formal arrangement ... with common rules and standardised arrangements for the clearing, whether or not through a central counterparty, or execution of transfer orders between the participants ... '[133]

Consequently, a CCP which is designated (or aspires to designation in order to obtain protection against insolvency laws interfering with its default procedures) will need to comply with the handful of obligations as to the content of the 'system's' rules, the law which governs the rules, and the eligibility criteria for participation.[134]

(4) The proposed Capital Requirements Regulation[135] introduces rules on computation of regulatory capital requirements for clearing members and their clients in relation to default fund contributions to CCPs,[136] also imposes obligations on CCPs. CCPs are to calculate their hypothetical capital and various other items of information, and notify these items of data to participants, so that each participant can in turn perform its own necessary calculations.[137]

(5) The Code of Conduct has not been disapplied, and will continue to govern equities CCPs as regards transparency, unbundling, and interoperability.

(6) The ECB-CESR Recommendations[138] on CCPs, like the FMI Principles, go further than EMIR in some respects. The 15 Recommendations are similar in content to the FMI Principles, and also contain an assessment methodology. A critique by the Dutch regulators[139] of the European Commission's original proposal for legislation noted the gaps between the proposal and the Recommendations, and suggested that EMIR should address the use of commercial settlement agents by CCPs, set out common access criteria to CCPs, and provide for a central technical risk management validation entity. As to the last point, while ESMA will carry out a function of this type, it may be asked whether ESMA will have the necessary resources or highly specialised expertise to discharge it effectively.

---

129 Proposed art 28
130 Proposed art 29
131 Proposed art 30; see also **section 4.13**
132 By Directive 2009/44/EC of the European Parliament and of the Council of 6 May 2009 amending the SFD, etc
133 SFD, art 2(a)
134 See **sections 6.16** and **11.7**
135 Capital Requirements Regulation as proposed, Part Three, Title II, ch 6, s 9
136 See section 19.11(2)
137 Capital Requirements Regulation as proposed, art 299(4)
138 CESR and ECB, Recommendations for Securities Settlement Systems and Recommendations For Central Counterparties in the European Union (May 2009), http://www.ecb.eu/pub/pdf/other/pr090623_escb-cesr_recommendationsen.pdf
139 Autoriteit Financiële Markten and De Nederlandsche Bank, Evaluation of the effects of the MiFID and Code of Conduct on the European securities clearing landscape (January 2010), Position paper, http://www.dnb.nl/en/binaries/DNB%20AFM%20Position%20paper%20sec%20clearing%20Jan%202010_tcm47-235574.pdf

PROPOSED REGULATION ON CENTRAL SECURITIES DEPOSITORIES

6.33 The proposed Regulation on Common Securities Depositories (CSDR) will introduce a regulatory regime, including business restrictions, on entities carrying out the activities of a CSD. At the outset there is a question how a 'CSD' should be defined. The legislative proposal identifies a CSD as a person who carries out the third, and one other of the three 'core services' listed in Section A of the Annex to the CSDR, which are '1. Initial recording of securities in a book-entry system ("notary service"); 2. Maintaining securities accounts at the top tier level ("central maintenance service"); 3. Operating a securities settlement system ("settlement service").' As to this, some initial comments are in order:

(1) It is unclear what these core services are; in particular, how the 'notary service' differs from the 'central maintenance service'. The three core services are also open to criticism as inadequate to describe the main characteristics of a CSD.[140]

(2) The scope of the terms 'securities settlement system' is unexpectedly broad. This is defined by reference to the SFD[141] which says that 'securities' are all instruments referred to in Section C of Annex 1 to MiFID, which includes derivatives and fund units as well as what are thought of as securities in ordinary speech.

6.34 CSDs will not be permitted to carry on activities other than providing the core services, the services set out in Section B of the Annex,[142] and, where permitted by their regulator, banking services set out in Section C of the Annex. The Section B services are those that 'contribute to enhancing the safety, efficiency and transparency of the securities markets,' and a non-exhaustive list is given which includes arranging securities lending, collateral management, matching, corporate actions processing, allocation of ISINs, order routing, and regulatory reporting.

'Banking services' for these purposes mean providing cash accounts, accepting deposits, providing credit, securities lending, and pre-financing of income, redemption proceeds and tax reclaims. In order to carry out banking services the CSD must be authorised as a credit institution under the Banking Directive.[143] Difficult questions arise as to whether a CSD with a banking licence can compete unfairly with agent banks.[144]

Where a banking authorisation is granted, a detailed set of rules, which supplement those in the Banking Directive, will regulate the CSD's management of credit and liquidity risk.[145]

---

140 See **section 2.16**
141 CSDR, art 2(1)(3)
142 CSDR, arts 14(2) and 16, Recital (20)
143 CSDR, art 52(2)
144 Cf Fair & Clear, Contribution to the Communication on Clearing and Settlement in the European Union – the way forward (September 2004), http://ec.europa.eu/internal_market/financial-markets/docs/clearing/2004-consultation/fairandclear_en.pdf, p 12; see also **section 7.17**
145 CSDR, art 57

6.35 The regulatory framework for CSDs will follow much the same path as that laid down in EMIR for CCPs. The CSD's regulator will be that of its Member State of incorporation;[146] the CSD will be allowed to passport its activities into other Member States;[147] and third-country CSDs may provide services in the EU if approved by ESMA.[148] By and large, the regulatory requirements imposed on CSDs follow the FMI Principles – see **table 6.1** – rather more closely than those applicable to other types of European post-trade infrastructure.

Ownership, governance and capital

6.36 Unlike a CCP, the question of capitalisation of a CSD is less problematic, and raises fewer difficulties about ownership and governance of a CSD. The CSDR requires that capital (together with retained earnings and reserves) should be proportional to its risks, and be sufficient to cover an orderly winding-down of the business.[149] If a CSD is providing ancillary banking services, it will also need to comply with the Banking Directive (and in due course the proposed Capital Requirements Regulation), by virtue of its status as a credit institution.

The CSDR imposes requirements on the composition of the board, including the need for independent members.[150] There must also be a User Committee, which has only an advisory role.[151] By contrast with CCPs, there are no requirements about owners or controllers of CSDs, though it should be noted that (a) CSDs are not permitted to own or have a participation in any legal person other than one whose activities are limited to the provision of the services in Section A or Section B of the Annex;[152] and (b) a CSD which has a banking licence will be subject to the change of control regime of the Banking Directive.[153]

Like EMIR, the CSDR regulates outsourcing by CSDs, but EMIR's specific articles relating to conflicts of interest and business continuity are not replicated in the CSDR. There is no obvious reason in principle for the distinction.

Again, following EMIR, there are provisions designed to underpin competition policy in the post-trade arena. These include requirements for transparent, objective, risk-based and non-discriminatory access criteria for participants;[154] for price transparency and unbundling of pricing of different services;[155] for inter-CCP interoperability; [156]and for vertical interoperability with CCPs and trading venues.[157]

---

146 CSDR, art 14(1)
147 CSDR, art 21
148 CSDR, art 23
149 CSDR, art 44; see also **sections 17.3ff**
150 CSDR, art 25
151 CSDR, art 26
152 CSDR, art 16(4)
153 Banking Directive, arts 19–21
154 CSDR, art 30
155 CSDR, art 31
156 CSDR, arts 45, 48–50
157 CSDR, art 51

Core business

6.37   As regards the core business of a CSD, there are rules requiring a CSD to protect the integrity of the issue.[158] The CSD is required to carry out reconciliation intra-day to ensure that the number of securities making up the issue is equal to the sum of securities recorded to the credit of participants' accounts. Securities overdrafts are forbidden. On this topic, the European Commission noted in its impact assessment that:

> 'During the critical winding up of Bear Stearns on 14 March 2008, an excess of 28% of shares in the company compared to the total actually issued was encountered. This obliged the Securities Investment Protection Corporation (SIPC) to reimburse all the investors at the nominal value of the securities.
> 'The causes of this excess are not clear. It may have been either: the result of naked short selling positions; multiple re-use of securities; or a fault of the US system of ownership that provides for a "beneficial ownership" right and a "securities entitlement" at every level in the holding chain. Some confusion is often reported in this context.
> 'Fortunately, Bear Stearns was rescued through a takeover by JP Morgan which bailed out the excess of securities.'[159]

The action to be taken by a CSD to correct a failing under this rule is not specified.

6.38   There are also rules regarding the protection of participants' securities – that is, addressing custody risk.[160] These rules can be compared with those in the MiFID implementing Directive:[161] the obligations to keep records which 'distinguish in the accounts with the CSD the securities of a participant from the securities of any other participant, and if applicable, from the CSD's own assets,' and not to use securities of a participant for any purpose without the participant's express consent, are very similar to the obligations on investment firms holding their clients' financial instruments. The European Central Bank considers that CSDs ought to adhere to at least the standards for custody imposed on banks.[162]

However, a CSD would be expected to have an absolute duty to ensure that each participant's record of entitlement as recorded on the CSD's books equates to an actual entitlement to the securities so recorded. Such an obligation is not there; instead there is the rather odd provision that requires CSDs to disclose the level of protection and costs associated with different levels of segregation it provides. This implies that in some circumstances a CSD could render something less than one hundred per cent protection; that is a surprising proposition which deserves some analysis.

---

158 CSDR, art 34

159 European Commission, Impact Assessment accompanying the document Proposal for a Regulation of the European Parliament and of the Council on improving securities settlement in the European Union and on Central Securities Depositories (March 2012), SWD(2012) 22 final, http://ec.europa.eu/internal_market/financial-markets/docs/SWD_2012_22_en.pdf, p 69

160 CSDR, art 35

161 Commission Directive 2006/73/EC of 10 August 2006 implementing MiFID as regards organisational requirements and operating conditions for investment firms, etc, arts 16, 19

162 Russo, D, et al, Prudential and Oversight Requirements for Securities Settlement (December 2007), ECB Occasional Paper No 76, http://www.ecb.eu/pub/pdf/scpops/ecbocp76.pdf, p 10

(1) An entitlement recorded on the books of the CSD itself ought, where the CSD is 'maintaining securities accounts at the top tier level,' to constitute the root of title, that is an *absolute* entitlement in favour of the participant. The only qualification to that absolute entitlement should arise (where the participant is acting as intermediary) from arrangements agreed between the participant and its own account-holders.

(2) Participants may offer their clients the choice of collective ownership through an omnibus account.[163] An omnibus account does not imply that 'different levels of segregation' could apply at the CSD level: *participants may offer different levels of segregation*, in that they might offer their clients a choice between an individually segregated account at the CSD – akin to the individual account in beneficial owner markets,[164] with the difference that the account name seen on the CSD's books would be that of the participant, rather than the investor – or a tenancy in common in an omnibus account. But CSDs ought, in principle, not to be capable of offering such things.

(3) The confusion in the CSDR almost certainly stems from the dual role of CSDs contemplated through interoperability. As explained in **section 13.46** interoperability of CSDs will involve one CSD becoming a participant – an account-holder – in another CSD. Once that is accepted, it is evident that the participant-CSD (the 'investor CSD' in the jargon) is functionally in no different a position from any other intermediary such as a stockbroker or agent bank. These intermediaries are precisely those persons who may offer different levels of segregation and who are subject to the safeguarding rules for client assets under the MiFID implementing Directive. There is no reason why CSDs, when acting as intermediaries in this way, should not offer a range of segregation options. But the CSDR ought to distinguish more clearly between the obligations of CSDs when they are 'investor CSDs' – segregation options allowed – and the obligations of CSDs acting as 'issuer CSDs' – for whom the absolute duty to confer complete, unconditional entitlement should apply.

6.39   The following additional legal issues may also be mentioned.

(1) The CSDR does not make any special provision for 'beneficial owner' markets. In 'beneficial owner' markets such as those in Denmark, Finland, Norway and Sweden, each investor holds an individual account at the CSD, which is operated on her or his behalf by an 'account operator'.[165] There may be a risk in such markets that the ownership rights of an indirect holder of the securities are not clear. The proposed Securities Law Directive[166] is intended to clarify the entitlement that an investor has when her only record of entitlement exists on the books of an account-provider who is not a CSD.

(2) Article 46 of the CSDR introduces a conflicts of laws rule stating that 'any question with respect to proprietary aspects in relation to financial instruments held by a CSD shall be governed by the law of the country

---

163   See **section 10.16**
164   See **section 6.39(1)**
165   Wallin-Norman, K, Legal survey over the Nordic securities holding systems, http://ec.europa. eu/internal_market/financial-markets/docs/certainty/background/21_4_5_wallion-norman_ en.pdf (April 2005)
166   See **section 10.8**

where the account is maintained'. There is much to be complained about in the drafting of this proposed rule. Further discussion about conflicts of laws, and in particular the question which law should apply to questions of ownership of securities existing only as book entries, is set out in **section 10.6**.

(3) Article 47 of the CSDR is intended to facilitate full cross-border competition between CSDs by granting to issuers of securities a statutory right to choose into which CSD to issue their securities for central maintenance. As discussed in **section 10.24** fulfilment of this promise is likely to be challenging.

(4) Article 37 of the CSDR obliges CSDs to settle the cash payments of securities settlements through accounts at a central bank, unless this is 'not practical and available'. Further discussion of the merits of central bank money is given in **sections 9.14** and **15.4**. Where the CSD has concluded that commercial bank money is to be used, it could provide the cash accounts itself, if it has the requisite authorisation to provide ancillary banking services, or it may designate another authorised credit institution. Regulators may insist that more than one such designated authorised credit institution is offered, if the concentration of risk is not adequately mitigated.[167]

Soft law

6.40 As explained above, the CSDR implements the fundamental recommendations of the FMI Principles, leaving little scope for soft law in relation to this type of infrastructure. Mention may, nevertheless, be made of the four Recommendations for Securities Settlement Systems[168] which were not adopted as part of the FMI Principles, but which remain in force.[169] These are, in outline:

- that trade confirmation should occur as soon as possible after execution, and no later than trade date. This recommendation has not been adopted in European legislation, though in practice the obligations to report transactions in financial instruments no later than T+1, imposed by the proposed Markets in Financial Instruments Regulation, will achieve essentially the same end.[170]

- that settlement cycles should be no longer than T+3. This recommendation is to be overreached, as the CSDR will oblige regulated markets, MTFs and OTFs to move to a T+2 cycle.[171]

- that use of CCPs should be evaluated. This recommendation has not been adopted in European legislation except for derivative products.

- that securities lending should be encouraged for expediting settlement of securities transactions. This recommendation is addressed through the

---

167 CSDR, art 52(3)
168 CPSS and Technical Committee of IOSCO, Recommendations for securities settlement systems, http://www.bis.org/publ/cpss46.pdf (November 2001)
169 FMI Principles, Annex C
170 European Commission, Proposal for a Regulation of the European Parliament and of the Council on markets in financial instruments etc (October 2011), COM(2011) 652 final, http://eur-lex.europa.eu/LexUriServ/LexUriServ.do?uri=COM:2011:0652:FIN:EN:PDF, art 23
171 CSDR, art 5(2)

provisions of the CSDR on settlement fails,[172] which do not specifically prescribe securities lending as the remedy, but which together with the powers given to CSDs to facilitate securities lending will achieve what is recommended.

THE FMI PRINCIPLES

6.41 In April 2012 the CPSS and IOSCO issued a remodelled set of Principles for Financial Market Infrastructures, which superseded the Core Principles and the two sets of Recommendations for Securities Settlement Systems and for CCPs. The FMI Principles are more extensive and detailed than any of their predecessors. New content includes completely new principles addressing General business risk (which also requires infrastructures to have enough capital)[173] and Tiered participation arrangements.[174] The FMI Principles are now addressed to a newly recognised class of infrastructures, namely Trade Repositories, to whom a special Principle on Disclosure of data is addressed.[175]

The following comments might be made about the FMI Principles.

(1) *One size fits all FMIs.* Many of the FMI Principles are applied generally to all types of infrastructure, without differentiating between their functions or differing risk profiles. Several critics of the draft FMI Principles mentioned this in their comments on the consultation version.[176] The general across-the-board application of the FMI Principles leads to some anomalies. As regards payment systems, the FMI Principles specify requirements about collateral: collateral may be used in some payment systems but it is by no means common, and certainly not universal. An ACH which merely operates a multilateral netting system should not be expected to require collateral, if the system operator undertakes no credit risk from its participants. When coupled with the rules concerning management of credit risk, the rules relating to collateral could encourage payment systems which take on no credit risk themselves to introduce rules requiring their participants to take collateral from each other. A second anomaly for payment systems springs from the introduction of a rule on custody risk. For FMIs which accept participants' assets, or which are liable to their participants for delivery up of cash or securities, rules like these are wholly understandable; for payment systems which accept no deposits they appear to be overkill. As regards CCPs, it seems curious that the FMI Principles regard CCPs as 'exchange of value' settlement systems, expecting them to ensure DvP. This is outside the control of most CCPs, which rely on separate settlement arrangements at CSDs and payment systems for this feature. Other examples could be given, but to set out an exhaustive list would be tedious as well as tendentious.

(2) *Scope.* The FMI Principles cover payments systems, CSDs, and CCPs, but not other types of market infrastructure which might be considered every bit as systemically essential to the functioning of the financial markets and deserving of international regulatory standards, with the exception

---

172 CSDR, art 7
173 FMI Principle 15
174 FMI Principle 19
175 FMI Principle 24
176 Available at http://www.bis.org/publ/cpss94/cacomments.htm

of trade repositories which, alone among the possible candidates, have been singled out. That choice seems arbitrary, given that trade repositories have no responsibility for handling of investors' money or other assets, and their failure would be unlikely to have any major market detriment. That last point cannot be said of other infrastructures, for example those providing essential communications architecture. Specific comments on the regulatory standards applied to trade repositories are considered in **section 4.23** in relation to their European transposition in EMIR.

(3) *Addressees.* Some standards apply to infrastructures, and some to their participants. Sometimes, in consequence, it is difficult to know if the standard is to be observed by the infrastructure operator itself or by its participants. Examples are the rules on credit and liquidity risk management, which could apply to an infrastructure itself (such as a CCP), or to the design of the infrastructure's rules insofar as they affect the risks assumed by the participants (as with a payment system or CSD).

(4) *Ownership.* The FMI Principles are directed to both public-sector infrastructures (such as those operated by central banks) and privately-owned or -operated systems. This is appropriate, given the global reality that a mixture of ownership and profit models exists. But the FMI Principles do not attempt to address how a for-profit model could engender risks in a system which would be absent in a non-profit entity. Such risks could include, for example, a race to the bottom;[177] inadequate capital; governance less attuned to risk control; and undiversified or inappropriate market structure, which might be possible where the infrastructures are configured as a vertical silo.[178]

(5) *Capital adequacy.* The rules of prudential regulation for infrastructures do not adhere to the prudential principles applied to banks. No doubt this is in part because some infrastructures do not take on risks akin to those shouldered by banks. But some infrastructures do: payment systems may take deposits and make loans; CSDs are engaged on a macro level in custody, which the Banking Directive considers to be a badge of a banking business;[179] and CCPs assume counterparty risk in relation to transactions in financial instruments, while taking cash and securities as margin, which is enough in some EU countries to require them to be configured as banks.[180] It may therefore be questioned whether infrastructures should in general be permitted to have lower standards of prudential regulation than the agent banks and user communities they are designed to serve. The FMI Principles apply a single and, as applied to CCPs, inappropriate, measure of capital adequacy:

> 'An FMI should hold sufficient liquid net assets funded by equity … so that it can continue providing services as a going concern if it incurs general business losses. … At a minimum … an FMI should hold liquid net assets funded by equity equal to at least six months of current operating expenses.'[181]

---

177 See **section 13.19**
178 See **section 7.20**
179 Directive 2006/48/EC of the European Parliament and of the Council of 14 June 2006 relating to the taking up and pursuit of the business of credit institutions (recast), Item 12, Annex 1,
180 See **section 12.9**
181 FMI Principles, para 3.15.5

A CCP should have to comply with robust capital adequacy rules which adequately protect its senior creditors against loss. This rule fails to do that. Further, the amount of protection needed depends on the liability profile of the infrastructure: infrastructures take on differing degrees of legal responsibility, even when they are not exposed to counterparty risk, and they should be financially able to withstand claims, whether or not they are in run-off.

(6) *Operational risk.* The FMI Principles cite a typical range of operational risks which may be encountered by infrastructures: inadequate understanding of risk and poor controls, inadequate personnel, inadequate management, failure of critical service providers, and natural and man-made disasters.[182] Infrastructures should not only consider the general range of operational risks which are faced by any financial institution, but should particularly bear in mind those which relate to its systemically important activities. It may be suggested, therefore, that the FMI Principles ought to have given weight, and more intensive discussion, to the following:

- *Disaster recovery and business continuity.* The FMI Principles state that an infrastructure should set itself targets for operational reliability, and have procedures for incident management. They should have objectives and procedures for 'rapid' recovery and 'timely' resumption of critical operations following a disruption to service.[183] But these statements could leave it open to infrastructures to choose unambitious service levels and attain standards which underperform the market. This subject is considered further in **section 16.20**.

- *Systems security.* All financial institutions need to consider the risk of fraud and compromise of their firewalls, looking at the risk of internal security breaches as well as external. Infrastructures are no exception, but CSDs may need to be particularly vigilant as the quality of their records affects not just transactions entered into by investors but their title to property.

- *Dependency on other infrastructures.* The FMI Principles mention the importance of links. Although Principle 20 (FMI links) ostensibly covers links between different types of infrastructure as well as horizontal links,[184] the explanatory note focuses almost exclusively on interoperability of the horizontal type. Principle 9 (cash settlements to be in central bank money) is said[185] to address the issues relevant to linkage between infrastructures and payment systems, but there is little of an operational nature in the relevant explanatory note. As to links between CSDs and CCPs, the discussion treats other infrastructures for the purposes of operational risk management in the same way as participants or service providers.[186] However, that may not be appropriate, given that infrastructures may be grouped together in vertical silos, and that infrastructures may be in a position to assert

---

182 FMI Principles, para 3.17.2
183 FMI Principles, para 3.17.13
184 FMI Principles, para 3.20.1
185 FMI Principles, footnote 156
186 FMI Principles, paras 3.17.18–3.17.22

commercial pressure on other infrastructures which depend on them for data feeds or other essential matters.[187]

- *Outsourcing.* Annex F to the FMI Principles sets out some additional considerations which apply to 'critical service providers.' It seems curious that the risk issues associated with outsourcing have not merited a full Principle. Infrastructures are particularly vulnerable to service failure, as they are likely to be highly dependent on IT service providers, and in some cases on other services, to ensure that their systemically important functions are fulfilled. It might also be noted that the issues singled out by the CPSS and IOSCO are by no means a comprehensive recital of the outsourcing risks and mitigants which regulatory bodies commonly expect.[188]

(7) *Tiering.* The subject of indirect participation is considered further in relation to payment systems at **section 11.5**, but it may be mentioned here that the one-size-fits-all approach requires both CCPs and CSDs to consider it too. For CSDs the issues may be elusive: except for 'beneficial owner markets',[189] the concept of tiering is inherent in the service provided. For CCPs, much focus has been given since the 2008 financial crisis to the problem of transferring a client's positions when its clearing member fails – this subject is considered in **sections 14.47–14.58**. For all types of infrastructure, though, some market participants do not have the option of becoming direct participants, and for those that do, the decision whether to do so is likely to be influenced by factors such as the (substantial) costs of direct participation and the likely volume of business.[190] How the CCP itself is supposed to handle the issues which are primarily commercial questions for its participants is not clarified by the FMI Principles.

The status of European legislation and soft law is measured against the standards set by the FMI Principles in **table 6.1**.

---

187 Cf **sections 7.20** and **4.11ff**
188 Cf **sections 14.5** and **15.18**
189 See **section 6.39(1)**
190 Cf Bank for International Settlements Committee on the Global Financial System, The macrofinancial implications of alternative configurations for access to central counterparties in OTC derivatives markets (November 2011), CGFS Paper No 46, http://www.bis.org/publ/cgfs46.htm, p 10

Table 6.1   Principles for financial market infrastructures [191]

Comparison with European regulatory measures

FMI Principles	European Approach				
	Payment systems	CSDs[191]	CCPs	Trade repositories	
Principle 1: Legal basis An FMI should have a well-founded, clear, transparent, and enforceable legal basis for each material aspect of its activities in all relevant jurisdictions.	CPSS Core Principle I	CSDR art 40	[not covered]	[not covered]	
Principle 2: Governance An FMI should have governance arrangements that are clear and transparent, promote the safety and efficiency of the FMI, and support the stability of the broader financial system, other relevant public interest considerations, and the objectives of relevant stakeholders.	CPSS Core Principle X	CSDR arts 24–26	EMIR arts 26–28	EMIR art 78	
Principle 3: Framework for the comprehensive management of risks An FMI should have a sound risk-management framework for comprehensively managing legal, credit, liquidity, operational, and other risks.	CPSS Core Principle III but CP III is disapplied for 'retail' payment systems, and the Core Principles do not specifically address operational 'risk' (as opposed to operational 'reliability', covered in CP VII)	CSDR arts 24(1), 39–43, 57	EMIR arts 26(1), 28	EMIR art 79, as to operational risks	

Shading convention:

not applicable	not or only partially implemented	broadly compliant

191 The FMI Principles treat 'CSDs' as a species different from 'Securities Settlement Systems' (SSSs), which is not the convention used in this book. This column combines the Principles applicable to 'CSDs' in the narrower sense used by the FMI Principles together with those applicable to SSSs.

FMI Principles	European Approach			
	Payment systems	CSDs[191]	CCPs	Trade repositories
Principle 4: Credit risk An FMI should effectively measure, monitor, and manage its credit exposures to participants and those arising from its payment, clearing, and settlement processes. An FMI should maintain sufficient financial resources to cover its credit exposure to each participant fully with a high degree of confidence. In addition, a CCP that is involved in activities with a more complex risk-profile or that is systemically important in multiple jurisdictions should maintain additional financial resources sufficient to cover a wide range of potential stress scenarios that should include, but not be limited to, the default of the participants and their affiliates that would potentially cause the largest aggregate credit exposure to the CCP in extreme but plausible market conditions. All other CCPs should maintain additional financial resources sufficient to cover a wide range of potential stress scenarios that should include, but not be limited to, the default of the participant and its affiliates that would potentially cause the largest aggregate credit exposure to the CCP in extreme but plausible market conditions.	CPSS Core Principle V but only as regards effectiveness of multilateral netting, and in any case CP V is disapplied for 'retail' payment systems	CSDR Title IV, as regards credit activities art 43(4), as regards investment decisions	EMIR Title IV, chapter 3	[not applicable]
Principle 5: Collateral An FMI that requires collateral to manage its or its participants' credit exposure should accept collateral with low credit, liquidity, and market risks. An FMI should also set and enforce appropriately conservative haircuts and concentration limits.	[not covered; see text]	CSDR art 57(3)	EMIR art 46	[not applicable]

FMI Principles	European Approach			
	Payment systems	CSDs[191]	CCPs	Trade repositories
Principle 6: Margin A CCP should cover its credit exposures to its participants for all products through an effective margin system that is risk-based and regularly reviewed.	[not applicable]	[not applicable]	EMIR art 41	[not applicable]
Principle 7: Liquidity risk An FMI should effectively measure, monitor, and manage its liquidity risk. An FMI should maintain sufficient liquid resources in all relevant currencies to effect same-day and, where appropriate, intraday and multiday settlement of payment obligations with a high degree of confidence under a wide range of potential stress scenarios that should include, but not be limited to, the default of the participant and its affiliates that would generate the largest aggregate liquidity obligation for the FMI in extreme but plausible market conditions.	CPSS Core Principle III but CP III is disapplied for 'retail' payment systems	CSDR art 57(4) but only as regards the CSD's own banking activities, not the obligations of participants	EMIR art 44	[not applicable]
Principle 8: Settlement finality An FMI should provide clear and certain final settlement, at a minimum, by the end of the value date. Where necessary or preferable, an FMI should provide final settlement intraday or in real time.	CPSS Core Principle IV but CPIV is disapplied for 'retail' payment systems Settlement Finality Directive, where system is designated	CSDR art 36 Settlement Finality Directive, where CSD is designated	Settlement Finality Directive, where CCP is designated	[not applicable]
Principle 9: Money settlements An FMI should conduct its money settlements in central bank money where practical and available. If central bank money is not used, an FMI should minimise and strictly control the credit and liquidity risk arising from the use of commercial bank money.	CPSS Core Principle VI but CP VI is disapplied for 'retail' payment systems	CSDR art 37	EMIR art 47	[not applicable]

FMI Principles

FMI Principles	European Approach			
	Payment systems	CSDs[191]	CCPs	Trade repositories
Principle 10: Physical deliveries An FMI should clearly state its obligations with respect to the delivery of physical instruments or commodities and should identify, monitor, and manage the risks associated with such physical deliveries.	[not applicable]	CSDR art 3 will abolish physical deliveries	[not covered]	[not applicable]
Principle 11: Central securities depositories A CSD should have appropriate rules and procedures to help ensure the integrity of securities issues and minimise and manage the risks associated with the safekeeping and transfer of securities. A CSD should maintain securities in an immobilised or dematerialised form for their transfer by book entry.	[not applicable]	CSDR arts 3, 34	[not applicable]	[not applicable]
Principle 12: Exchange-of-value settlement systems If an FMI settles transactions that involve the settlement of two linked obligations (for example, securities or foreign exchange transactions), it should eliminate principal risk by conditioning the final settlement of one obligation upon the final settlement of the other.	[not covered]	CSDR art 36(8)	[not covered; see text]	[not applicable]
Principle 13: Participant-default rules and procedures An FMI should have effective and clearly defined rules and procedures to manage a participant default. These rules and procedures should be designed to ensure that the FMI can take timely action to contain losses and liquidity pressures, and continue to meet its obligations.	[not covered]	CSDR art 38	EMIR arts 45, 48	[not applicable]

FMI Principles	European Approach			
	Payment systems	CSDs[191]	CCPs	Trade repositories
Principle 14: Segregation and portability A CCP should have rules and procedures that enable the segregation and portability of positions of a participant's customers and the collateral provided to the CCP with respect to those positions.	[not applicable]	[not applicable]	EMIR arts 39, 48	[not applicable]
Principle 15: General business risk An FMI should identify, monitor, and manage its general business risk and hold sufficient liquid net assets funded by equity to cover potential general business losses so that it can continue operations and services as a going concern if those losses materialise. Further, liquid net assets should at all times be sufficient to ensure a recovery or orderly wind-down of critical operations and services.	[not covered]	CSDR arts 42, 44	[not covered, but addressable in subordinate legislation]	[not covered]
Principle 16: Custody and investment risks An FMI should safeguard its own and its participants' assets and minimise the risk of loss on and delay in access to these assets. An FMI's investments should be in instruments with minimal credit, market, and liquidity risks.	[not covered; see text]	CSDR arts 35, 43	EMIR art 47	[not applicable]
Principle 17: Operational risk An FMI should identify the plausible sources of operational risk, both internal and external, and mitigate their impact through the use of appropriate systems, policies, procedures, and controls. Systems should be designed to ensure a high degree of security and operational reliability and should have adequate, scalable capacity. Business continuity management should aim for timely recovery of operations and fulfilment of the FMI's obligations, including in the event of a wide-scale or major disruption.	CPSS Core Principle VII plus ECB's Business Continuity Oversight Expectations for Systemically Important Payment Systems (but requiring restoration of critical systems same-day rather than within two hours)	CSDR art 42	EMIR arts 26, 34, 35	EMIR art 79

FMI Principles

FMI Principles	European Approach			
	Payment systems	CSDs[191]	CCPs	Trade repositories
Principle 18: Access and participation requirements An FMI should have objective, risk-based, and publicly disclosed criteria for participation, which permit fair and open access.	CPSS Core Principle IX	CSDR art 30	EMIR art 37	EMIR art 78(7)
Principle 19: Tiered participation arrangements An FMI should identify, monitor, and manage the material risks to the FMI arising from tiered participation arrangements.	[not covered]	[not covered]	EMIR arts 37(3), 39	[not covered]
Principle 20: FMI links An FMI that establishes a link with one or more FMIs should identify, monitor, and manage link-related risks.	[not applicable]	CSDR arts 45, 51	EMIR Title V, as regards in-scope links only	[not covered]
Principle 21: Efficiency and effectiveness An FMI should be efficient and effective in meeting the requirements of its participants and the markets it serves.	CPSS Core Principle VIII	CSDR art 29(1)	[not covered]	[not covered]
Principle 22: Communication procedures and standards An FMI should use, or at a minimum accommodate, relevant internationally accepted communication procedures and standards in order to facilitate efficient payment, clearing, settlement, and recording.	[not covered]	CSDR art 32	[not covered]	[not covered]

FMI Principles

		European Approach		
	Payment systems	CSDs[191]	CCPs	Trade repositories
Principle 23: Disclosure of rules, key procedures, and market data An FMI should have clear and comprehensive rules and procedures and should provide sufficient information to enable participants to have an accurate understanding of the risks, fees, and other material costs they incur by participating in the FMI. All relevant rules and key procedures should be publicly disclosed.	CPSS Core Principle II	CSDR arts 29(2), as regards complaints; 30(1), as regards participation criteria; 31, as regards prices but no express requirement to have or disclose clear and comprehensive rules and procedures	EMIR arts 36(2), as regards complaints; 38, as regards participation criteria; 38(2) as regards risks but no express requirement to have or disclose clear and comprehensive rules and procedures	EMIR art 78, as regards participation criteria and fees only but no express requirement to have or disclose clear and comprehensive rules and procedures
Principle 24: Disclosure of market data by trade repositories A TR should provide timely and accurate data to relevant authorities and the public in line with their respective needs.	[not applicable]	[not applicable]	[not applicable]	EMIR art 81

Shading convention:

not applicable	not or only partially implemented	broadly compliant

7 Competition Law

THE ROLE OF COMPETITION LAW IN CLEARING AND SETTLEMENT

7.1 Competition law plays a fundamental part in directing European policy with regard to clearing and settlement. At the heart of it is a tension between the principle that competition between service providers drives down cost, encourages innovation, and improves customer service, and the simple fact that infrastructures are single, centralised organisations designed and built to serve the whole market. How can competition policy apply in a marketplace where there is, and ought to be, only one provider? Europe, unlike other parts of the world, believes that competition law not only should apply but will, almost whatever the cost, be made to apply. In part this is dogma; in part this is the legacy of forming a union from 30 states with different languages, cultures and national infrastructures.

The historical diversity is, in fact, the problem. In each country there is a distinct legal and fiscal system, which allowed different technical standards and structures to develop, as shown by the Giovannini reports.[1] This means that Europe has a very high number of providers of central clearing and settlement services, each of which can levy whatever charges it prefers, innovate (or not) at whatever rate it prefers, and impose whatever conditions it prefers, without the threat of its business being sucked away by a competitor. Given that background, it is encouraging that there has been no significant restriction of services to local participants[2] and that cross-border consolidation has, to a degree, been attempted. The European Commission's Directorate General for Competition (DG Comp) – the European competition authority – has, however, been keeping a close eye on the industry, and has intervened periodically.

The intervention of competition doctrine does not imply that the industry is inherently evil. The theory of competition begins with an analysis of the 'market' in which competitors should be free to act, and notions of what constitutes the 'market' evolve over time. With regard to clearing and settlement, the idea that there was any market at all would have been challenged as ridiculous as recently as 1970. CCPs' activities were confined to, and often regarded as part of, derivatives exchanges; securities settlement functions were carried out by the issuers of the securities, or their agents, rather than a central depository; and settlement of payment obligations was carried out by banks. Insofar as post-trade activities were acknowledged to exist at all, they would have been regarded as inextricably bound up with trading itself. But markets

---

1 See **section 1.26**
2 See **section 22.1** for an exception

grow and evolve, and what was yesterday a single service can today be seen as a combination of services (or, to use competition phraseology, adjacent markets); and if restrictions apply, for historical reasons, to deny or discourage alternatives to some of the services, the incumbent provider may find itself under challenge for abuse of a dominant position.

Europe's clearing and settlement infrastructure is not so perfect that traditional free-market solutions have no place. Cost is high.[3] Infrastructures are combined in ways which do not conduce to efficiency, innovation and service; in some cases there are restrictions on access. Competition policy has, evidently, a right to be heard. DG Comp has set this out fully in an issues paper[4] submitted for public consultation. In reporting on its findings, the EU Commissioner Neelie Kroes said:[5]

> 'At the trading level, we certainly want to see more competition amongst exchanges, but also between exchanges and alternative trading platforms. Such competition relies on access to clearing and settlement. Whether within or outside a vertical silo structure, it is all too easy for exchanges to block such access today. Competition also relies on rules that are the same for all. It is not logical that the incumbent exchange can impose rules on its members which limit their effective choice of trading platform. If such rules are required, this must be a matter for regulators, not for the incumbent to decide. ...

> 'Clearing is not only a precondition of effective competition in trading; it should also be looked at as a market in its own right. ...

> 'In the area of settlement, I think no-one argues that competition policy alone could solve the many inefficiencies that exist in cross-border operations. This is why the primary focus must remain the removal of the so-called "Giovannini barriers" so as to allow cross border competition on both price of the services and innovation in service provision.'

Since Mrs Kroes's speech, there have been several important developments. First, the Markets in Financial Instruments Directive[6] (MiFID) exposed national stock exchanges in the EEA to competition from multilateral trading facilities and other types of trading platform. Secondly, the financial crisis of 2008 has spawned a set of EU legislation, summarised in **Chapter 6**, which, among other things, is imposing uniform European regulatory standards on CCPs and requiring Member States to facilitate issuance of securities into foreign CSDs. Thirdly, the European Central Bank is establishing a single platform for securities settlements in the form of Target2-Securities.[7] These developments have all had a significant effect on the competition agenda in relation to clearing and settlement infrastructures.

---

3 See **sections 1.28–1.29**
4 European Commission services, Competition in EU securities trading and post-trading (May 2006), Issues Paper, http://ec.europa.eu/competition/sectors/financial_services/securities_ trading.pdf
5 Kroes, N, Competition aspects of EU securities trading and post trading (July 2006), remarks at ECON meeting, http://ec.europa.eu/competition/sectors/financial_services/speech11072006. pdf
6 Directive of the European Parliament and of the Council of 21 April 2004 on markets in financial instruments etc (April 2004), 2004/39/EC
7 See **section 2.22**

THE TREATY

7.2   Competition law starts from the basic provisions of the EU Treaty.[8] Article 101 prohibits agreements between undertakings which have as their object or effect the prevention, restriction or distortion of competition within the internal market, unless the arrangement contributes to improving the production or distribution of goods or to promoting technical or economic progress, and (a) it does not impose on the undertakings concerned restrictions which are not indispensable to the attainment of these objectives and (b) it does not afford the undertakings the possibility of eliminating competition in respect of a substantial part of the products in question. Operators of infrastructures may fall foul of this rule by attempting to integrate provision of a combination of centralised trading, clearing or settlement activities formerly carried on by different undertakings.

Also, article 102 of the Treaty prohibits abuse by undertakings of a dominant position within the internal market. This article in particular is likely to apply to centralised providers of clearing and settlement infrastructure. Again, operators of infrastructures may be open to challenge under this rule, by imposing pricing, access or other conditions which appear to be abusive, given their centralised (and thus prima facie dominant) status.

7.3   Accordingly, various practices observed among providers of infrastructure services may be questioned:

(1) *Monopolies.* Because of the prevalence of idiosyncratic national technical standards, laws and taxation systems, there have typically been single central providers of clearing and settlement services. Although the Treaty does not prohibit monopolies or having a dominant position in a particular market, a person who is in a dominant position will be at risk of challenge under article 102.

(2) *Conditions of access.* Very few cases can be found where a monopolistic provider of clearing or settlement services has improperly imposed excessive conditions on access to its services. But a few such cases can, unfortunately, be found. And, for reasons of operational convenience, rooted in different technical standards, laws and regulations, national market practices still constrain users to favour incumbent local providers of clearing and settlement facilities even though there may be no formal requirement to do so.

(3) *Adjacent markets.* Infrastructures are not typically required by their constitutions to confine their activities to clearing, settlement, or the provision of payment schemes. Crossing into neighbouring territory might be criticised, however; for example, where there is confusion between roles of CSDs (or ICSDs) and custodians, and other arrangements whereby services now perceived to belong in different 'markets' are bundled together.

(4) *Vertical linkages.* The existence of 'vertical silos' in some countries, combining trading, clearing and settlement functions into a single corporate group or even a single corporate entity, has been criticised as potentially foreclosing competition in the post-trade sector.

---

8   Treaty on the Functioning of the European Union, as recast and renumbered (May 2008), OJ C115 vol 51, p 47

(5) *Horizontal consolidation.* Cross-border consolidation between CCPs, CSDs and payment systems has been a feature of the evolving post-trade environment in Europe. But consolidation might exacerbate any monopolistic tendency which a single-country infrastructure already enjoyed.

(6) *Development of standards.* Cooperation among providers of clearing and settlement services in order to make markets more efficient may be at risk of challenge under article 101. The European Commission has guidelines on the creation of standards, which may be difficult to comply with.[9]

These issues will be examined in subsequent sections of this chapter. It may also be noted that DG Comp is active in policing other parts of the post-trade space than those occupied by infrastructures. In particular, there have been anti-trust investigations into how information is shared[10] and access to standard-setting by banks.[11]

MONOPOLIES

7.4   It is axiomatic that monopolies are anti-competitive, but it may be counter-intuitive for the non-specialist that monopolies are not outlawed by the Treaty. It is also, perhaps, counter-intuitive that clearing and settlement infrastructures do not have to be structured as monopolies:

'It has long been assumed that the various levels of the trading infrastructure enjoyed some kind of "natural monopoly." In recent years, however, there has been evidence to challenge this view. Experience has shown that virtually all instances of competition between trading venues have led in practice to decreased trading spreads and therefore more efficient markets. In any case, even if the market were eventually to tend towards monopoly provision, there would still be significant scope for competition amongst legacy national providers during a possibly lengthy transitional phase, and with providers from third countries, due to the potentially low marginal costs of entry. The notion of "natural monopoly" fails to capture this reality.'[12]

Yet the infrastructures were established monopolies, or near-monopolies, even if that was not a 'natural' state of things. Numerous commentators have noted that nationally-developed clearing and settlement systems created a patchwork of mutually incompatible infrastructures each enjoying a local monopoly.[13] While everyone – everyone except the incumbents, that is – agreed that this was bad,

---

9   European Commission, Guidelines on the applicability of Article 101 of the Treaty on the Functioning of the European Union to horizontal co-operation agreements (January 2011), Communication 2011/C11/01, OJ(C)11/1
10   See **section 4.12**
11   See **section 7.28**
12   European Commission services, Competition in EU Securities trading and post-trading (May 2006), Issues Paper, http://ec.europa.eu/competition/sectors/financial_services/securities_trading.pdf, paras 11–12
13   See, for example, Niels, G, Barnes, F, and van Dijk, R, 'Unclear and Unsettled: the Debate on Competition in the Clearing and Settlement of Securities Trades' (December 2003) ECLR 634; Tapking, J, and Yang, J, Horizontal and Vertical Integration in Securities Trading and Settlement (August 2004), European Central Bank Working Paper No 387; van Cayseele, P, and Wuyts, C, Cost Efficiency in the European Securities Settlement and Safekeeping Industry (April 2005), http://papers.ssrn.com/sol3/papers.cfm?abstract_id=808824; Baur, D, Integration and Competition in Securities Trading, Clearing and Settlement (March 2006), http://papers.ssrn.com/sol3/papers.cfm?abstract_id=891223

there has been no consensus as to whether consolidation or competition was the solution. Vertical and horizontal consolidation are considered in **sections 7.20–7.22** and **7.23–7.27** respectively. DG Comp is clear that competition is the right answer.

So the question then is: how can a clearing or settlement system *not* operate as a monopoly?

Competition among CCPs

7.5   Starting with CCPs: it has been obvious, since the advent of MiFID, that there is a role for new CCPs. CCPs without any vertical link to an existing stock exchange have sprung up and offered their services for a variety of markets. No doubt this phenomenon was triggered by the creation of new trading platforms which compete with the stock exchanges as the primary trading venues for European equities. But this is not the full story. Encouraged by DG Comp and the European Code of Conduct,[14] various CCPs have aimed to clear for users of stock exchanges notwithstanding the existence of an established incumbent. The ability of entrant CCPs to operate in parallel to an incumbent is not unknown (x-clear co-cleared for the London Stock Exchange with LCH. Clearnet Ltd from December 2008). The existence of these cases, even if they are rare, demonstrates that monopolistic behaviour by CCPs is not inevitable.

Co-clearing does, however, require a link between the CCPs which are inter-operating: the reasons for this, and the complexities which interoperability throws out, are explored in **Chapter 13**. Here it may be noted that:

● Competition among CCPs raises fears of a 'race to the bottom', which means a competition to reduce costs through easier-to-meet risk-protection standards.[15]

● It is not self-evident that competition reduces costs: in the absence of standardisation and interoperability, it might mean that market participants need to invest in connectivity several times over. The optimal number of CCPs to provide resilience in crises is also open to debate.[16]

● Market participants nevertheless argue that 'the commercial benefits of the user choice model are multiple and manifest,'[17] citing reductions in clearing fees, and several benefits from consolidation of flow into a single CCP chosen by the user rather than (the plethora of) CCPs chosen by venues.

Competition between CSDs?

7.6   The story is more complex for CSDs than for CCPs.[18] The role of a CSD is intertwined with assuring the integrity of the 'root of title' to

---

14 See **section 7.18**

15 See **section 13.19**

16 Renault, F, 'Concentration risk and the optimal number of central counterparties for a single asset' (July 2010) Banque de France Financial Stability Review, http://www.banque-france. fr/fileadmin/user_upload/banque_de_france/publications/Revue_de_la_stabilite_financiere/ etude20_rsf_1007.pdf, No 14 (English version) pp 169–176

17 Barnes, R, Counterparty clearing house user choice: an evolving European landscape, (March 2010) Oxera Agenda, http://www.oxera.com/cmsDocuments/Agenda_March%2010/ Counterparty%20clearing%20house%20user%20choice.pdf

18 See **section 13.46**

securities, and for that reason the ability to act as CSD may be reserved to a person who has a particular regulatory status – such as an 'Operator' under the United Kingdom's Uncertificated Securities Regulations 2001 (USRs)[19] or a *Wertpapiersammelbank* under the German Securities Deposit Act.[20] It may be possible for more than one CSD to exist in a single country (Clearstream Banking AG Frankfurt, formerly called the *Deutsche Kassenverein*, is the product of a merger of several regional CSDs), but for more than one CSD to hold the key to title of a single issue of securities is highly unusual. Yet, again, there are examples of this. Perhaps the most obvious is that of Eurobonds, which can be settled centrally at both the ICSDs Euroclear Bank and Clearstream International SA Luxembourg. This is achieved by the ICSDs appointing a common depository – that is, by splitting off the 'depository' role of the CSD from the 'settlement system' role.[21] It can be argued that pushing the function of acting as common depository into a third party's hands merely displaces the monopoly problem to a different level, but there is hot competition, at least in relation to Eurobonds, among depository banks for the role of common depository. Evidently, one solution to breaking a monopoly at the level of CSDs would be to replicate the ICSD approach. This is what underlies the provisions of the proposed Regulation on CSDs which will allow issuers to choose a CSD established in any Member State.[22]

An alternative might be to replicate the interoperability model for CCPs – that is, mutual membership. That has been a guiding principle underlying Target2-Securities.[23] As with links between CCPs, however, links between CSDs also introduce risk and cost, and again a cost-benefit study of the various models of full consolidation, ICSD-style competition, and links between competitors, would be needed to prove which is most effective.

Competition between payment systems?

7.7   Payment systems have been, at least so far, immune from challenge. To take on the European Central Bank (ECB) by alleging that it operates a monopoly in the form of its TARGET-2 settlement system might seem presumptuous. But it is also instructive to compare the characteristics of TARGET-2, which operates as a network of interoperating national central banks, with other infrastructures. The national central banks (NCBs) have, in relation to payments, roles similar to that of CSDs in relation to securities settlement: they hold the root of title to money (central bank money), and historically they had settlement systems which transferred balances between the accounts of their participants. TARGET did not change any of that, but since the migration to TARGET-2, NCBs have been required to use the ECB's central settlement platform as the technical system which determines what is

---

19   SI 2001 No 3755, reg 4
20   Gesetz über die Verwahrung und Anschaffung von Wertpapieren of 4 February 1937, art 5
21   Cf **section 2.24**
22   European Commission, Proposal for a Regulation of the European Parliament and of the Council on improving securities settlement in the European Union and on central securities depositories etc (March 2012), COM(2012) 73 final, http://eur-lex.europa.eu/LexUriServ/LexUriServ.do?uri=CELEX:52012PC0073:EN:PDF, art 47
23   See **section 13.48**

paid and when and by whom.[24] In this can be seen the precursor of the structure constituting Target2-Securities, and the comments made below in relation to that arrangement could be applied here.

However, it can also be argued that the TARGET-2 system is not monopolistic. In the first place, there is competition from other payment systems. The components of a payment system may include one or more ACHs as well as the bank – typically the central bank – across whose books the ultimate settlement of inter-bank payment obligations will occur.[25] ACHs may be in competition for the clearing business of banks in different countries, particularly following the introduction of a single currency in the eurozone. Secondly, TARGET-2 is not really a system;[26] it is the platform on which interbank obligations can be settled when the banks' home central banks are situated in different countries. Certainly, the ECB is the only platform provider; but then in single-country currencies, the national central bank is the only place where ultimately there is certainty that payment obligations can be settled without recourse to physical cash or taking risk on a commercial bank. The logic is the same as that with a CSD: the central bank is the root of title to money, so the 'monopoly' is finally inherent in the service provided by a central bank. The ECB is not far different in this regard where the euro is concerned. Thirdly, settlement of payment obligations does not always require involvement of a settlement system. Correspondent banking allows payments to be settled without recourse to a formal multi-party system. All that is required is for a bank to open an account with a correspondent which can settle on the bank's behalf. Correspondent banking involves the assumption of credit risk on other banks – the absence of 'root of title' inherent in central bank money – but may be cheap and effective; in cross-currency payments it is also the norm. Use of correspondent banks can be seen as analogous, in the mirror world of securities settlement, as using agent or custodian banks: in securities, you take custody risk if you use an agent; in payments, you take credit risk if you use a correspondent.

So, nothing requires banks to use TARGET-2 to settle their payments. But the central banks which control the gateways to TARGET-2 provide an essential and unique service, in addition to the gold standard of central bank money which cannot, unlike commercial bank money, become valueless due to bank insolvency. That unique service is the provision of liquidity as part of the Eurosystem's monetary operations: the ultimate outlet through which banks obtain their funding and, in a crisis, can draw funds from the 'lender of last resort'. The position of central banks is monopolistic in this sense: every government wants the banks which are under its supervisory oversight, and therefore the constituency of banks which it would have to bail out in the event of a banking crisis, to be firmly under the control of the central bank in its own territory. The monopolistic features of central banking are thus unavoidable, and in a multi-state Europe an oligarchy of central banks constituting the Eurosystem is a settled feature. And no challenge from competition authorities is going to succeed, or, probably, even be contemplated, owing to the critical role played by the NCBs in the day-to-day running of the economy and in crisis management.

---

24 European Central Bank, Information Guide for TARGET2 Users (October 2009), http://www.ecb.int/paym/t2/shared/pdf/infoguide_V3_1_0.pdf
25 See **sections 1.18 and 2.27**
26 See **section 2.35**

Essential facilities

7.8   If operating a monopoly or near-monopoly is not illegal, it can, nonetheless, be a problem. As will be apparent from article 102 of the Treaty, abuse of a dominant position is outlawed: some of the consequences of that include commercially-driven access rights and criticism of the vertical silo model, both of which are discussed below. More subtly, an occupant of a dominant position has implicit duties if it can be shown to be providing an 'essential facility'. It is of no consequence if I have just invented a new device, and therefore have the pleasure of being the monopoly supplier of the device. I will only court trouble with the competition authorities if I abuse my position; and this is only likely if my device becomes so successful that everybody has to have one. Sooner or later, my device may become essential for normal civilised existence, like railways in the 19th century or telephones in the 20th. Clearing and settlement systems are obvious candidates to be treated as essential facilities.[27]

The doctrine of 'essential facilities' was developed in American anti-trust law and imported into Europe. The principle is as stated as follows. 'Under this doctrine, a single firm, or group of firms, controlling an input at an upstream level of production that is essential for competitors on a downstream market may be obliged to deal with third parties where a refusal to do so would eliminate competition on the relevant downstream market.'[28]

The doctrine is relevant to vertical silos and other situations where a clearing or settlement infrastructure is exploiting its dominant position to obtain an advantage in a 'downstream' market where a multiplicity of parties may operate and compete. The leading case is *Oscar Bronner v Mediaprint.*[29] This case has nothing to do with clearing and settlement, but establishes important principles about abuse of a dominant position. Oscar Bronner wanted to use a domestic daily-newspaper distribution service developed and used exclusively by Mediaprint. Ultimately, Oscar Bronner lost, because there were other channels available to enable it to distribute its products, notwithstanding that Mediaprint's service occupied a dominant position. The European Court of Justice held that, in order to establish abuse of a dominant position, refusal of the service must be shown to be both (i) likely to eliminate all competition in the market on the part of the person requesting the service and (ii) incapable of being objectively justified; and the service must be shown to be indispensable to carrying on the person's business, inasmuch as there is no actual or potential substitute for that service.

Advocate-General Jacobs's opinion, which was followed by the court, stated:

'The US essential facilities doctrine has developed to require a company with monopoly power to contract with a competitor where five conditions are met. First, an essential facility is controlled by a monopolist. A facility will be regarded as essential when access to it is indispensable in order to compete on the market with the company that controls it. The following have

---

27 Cf Lee, R, *Running the World's Markets: The Governance of Financial Infrastructure* (Princeton University Press, 2011), ISBN 978-0-691-13353-9, pp 13–15

28 O'Donoghue, R, and Padilla, AJ, *The Law and Economics of Article 82 EC* (Hart Publishing, March 2006), p 408

29 Oscar Bronner GmbH & Co KG v Mediaprint Zeitungs- und Zeitschriftenverlag GmbH & Co KG and others Case C-7/1997, [1998] ECR I-07791

for example been held to be essential facilities: railroad bridges serving the town of St Louis; a local telecommunications network; a local electricity network. Secondly, a competitor is unable practically or reasonably to duplicate the essential facility. It is not sufficient that duplication would be difficult or expensive, but absolute impossibility is not required. Thirdly, the use of the facility is denied to a competitor. That condition would appear to include the refusal to contract on reasonable terms. Fourthly, it is feasible for the facility to be provided. Fifthly, there is no legitimate business reason for refusing access to the facility. A company in a dominant position which controls an essential facility can justify the refusal to enter a contract for legitimate technical or commercial reasons. It may also be possible to justify a refusal to contract on grounds of efficiency.'

The case shows that if a service *is* shown to be indispensable, access to that service may have to be made available, even to a competitor. Deconstructing the facts further, an *Oscar Bronner* challenge depends on an organisation carrying on two activities, one of which is in competition with the challenger – Mediaprint competed with Oscar Bronner in producing newspapers – and the other where the organisation being challenged is in a dominant position – Mediaprint was the sole doorstep distributor. Oscar Bronner failed because they could not show that the distribution service was indispensable or that failure to provide it would wipe out Oscar Bronner's ability to compete in providing daily news to readers. But a provider of (say) settlement infrastructure, who would be in a position analogous to Mediaprint as sole service provider, would have to be careful in providing services in an adjacent competitive marketplace, such as (for instance) a clearing system, in case a competing CCP were to argue that settlement is indispensable and that failure to provide access wipes out the competitor CCP's ability to compete in providing clearing services to brokers and investors.

The upshot of the *Oscar Bronner* principle is that a market infrastructure may be compelled to deal with persons it would not ordinarily wish to deal with, notwithstanding the general principle of law that one is free to choose one's contractual counterparties. This has implications for the admission of applicants to membership of infrastructures and payment schemes, which are explored in the next section.

In its Notice on the application of competition rules to cross-border credit transfers,[30] the European Commission helpfully and simply defined an essential facility as 'a facility or infrastructure without access to which competitors cannot provide services to their customers.' The Notice, discussed below, applies the essential facilities doctrine to access criteria applied by payments infrastructures, stating 'A cross-border credit transfer system will be an essential facility when participation in it is necessary for banks to compete on the relevant market. In other words, lack of access to the system amounts to a significant barrier to entry for a new competitor. This would be the case if a new competitor could not feasibly gain access to another system or create its own system in order to compete on the relevant market.' Access criteria constitute one potential area in which infrastructures may be tempted to misuse their market power, and so this is the next subject for discussion.

---

30 (September 1995) Official Journal of the European Communities, C251, pp 3–10, para 25

ACCESS TO INFRASTRUCTURES

7.9 Rights of access to financial market infrastructure have given rise to two main items of case-law at the European level. The case of SWIFT[31] provides an example of what can happen in the post-trade space where an organisation is providing an essential facility. SWIFT is the network and messaging service provider for the financial industry.[32] In 1997 action was taken by the European Commission because SWIFT had refused La Poste, the French post office, access to its network. The Commission argued that SWIFT was an essential facility, because it had a monopolistic dominant position, being the only international network to transmit payment messages providing connections to banks anywhere in the world. It was claimed that SWIFT had abused its dominant position by imposing unjustified admission criteria. The case was ultimately settled after SWIFT had given a formal undertaking to grant full access to all entities fulfilling criteria set by the European Monetary Institute (the forerunner of the European Central Bank) for admission to domestic payment systems.

More troublesome was the case of Clearstream.[33] Clearstream Banking AG Frankfurt provides the settlement system (CSD) for German equities via a platform called CASCADE. Most German equities are in 'registered' form, for which a sub-system called CASCADE-RS exists. Euroclear applied to Clearstream, for access to CASCADE-RS. (Euroclear happens to be the major, if not the only, competitor of Clearstream's parent company, Clearstream International, as ICSD, though this was not formally relevant to the case, as neither Clearstream nor Euroclear was carrying out ICSD activities in relation to access to CASCADE-RS.) Euroclear was acting more as an agent bank; Clearstream as CSD for German equities. Although Clearstream admitted various applicants to participate in CASCADE-RS, Euroclear's application was for a period of two years deferred, questioned and obstructed by Clearstream, although eventually allowed, but on price terms which were 20% above the rate charged to national CSDs. Clearstream's behaviour was found to be a violation of article 102[34] of the Treaty. However, in light of this being the 'first decision in a complex sector', that the infringement had come to an end, and that 'cross-border clearing and settlement in the EU is an evolving sector ... different institutions are presently debating issues related to the functions of service providers' imposing a fine did not appear appropriate.

Denying access to Euroclear for such a long period without justification was clearly wrong. Applying different pricing to different clients may not be wrong, but the decision on this point shows how care needs to be applied in relation to a service constituting an essential facility. The problem, though, was that Clearstream appears to have been motivated by its parent company's rivalry with Euroclear – differently stated, the problem was that the Clearstream group was operating in adjacent markets, namely being an ICSD and also a CSD.

---

31 Case No IV/36.120 – La Poste/SWIFT + GUF, Notice 97/C335/03 (November 1997), OJ C335, p 3
32 See **sections 4.17–4.18**
33 Case COMP/38.096 – Clearstream (Clearing and Settlement), Commission Decision C (2004) 1958 final http://ec.europa.eu/competition/antitrust/cases/decisions/38096/en.pdf (June 2004); for a summary see Official Journal of the European Union, C165, p 7 (July 2009)
34 Article 82 as the Treaty was then numbered

7.10 From these cases it can readily be concluded that infrastructure providers cannot exclude competitors, either by designing restrictive admission criteria or by dragging their feet when an unwanted applicant knocks on the door. That conclusion demands a critical reaction: why, then, have CCPs and CSDs not insisted on links so they can clear and settle in new markets? The answers are not that competition law has failed, but that there are legal and practical obstacles to establishing interoperability links, as discussed in **Chapter 13**. In a report commissioned by DG Comp, some reasons were given:

> '1. In some cases, there exists a legal requirement to use a certain clearing and/or settlement infrastructure.
> 2. In other cases, the trading or clearing membership rules are prescriptive in terms of which clearing or settlement service provider is to be sued and only one service provider is prescribed.
> 3. In some other cases, the trading or clearing membership rules are prescriptive in terms of which clearing and settlement service providers can be used, but offer some choice. Thus, in this case members have theoretically the flexibility of using clearing and settlement service providers of their choice. But, in practice they do not because, at the present time, only one such service provider exists in the country.
> 4. In a few cases, the trading and clearing membership rules are not prescriptive, and membership is simply conditional on having proper clearing and settlement arrangements in place.'[35]

Competition requires the door to be opened, but it cannot deal with all the practical problems of getting over the threshold.

Acceptable membership criteria

7.11 What competition law has managed to achieve is a reasonably clear set of rules on what are, and what are not, acceptable membership criteria for market infrastructures to adopt. Article 102(c) states that abuse of a dominant position may, in particular, consist in 'applying dissimilar conditions to equivalent transactions with other trading parties, thereby placing them at a competitive disadvantage.' In principle, it is likely to be an abuse of a dominant position to have membership or access criteria which are not transparent, non-discriminatory, and justifiable.

(1) In the first place, the provider of a clearing or settlement infrastructure or payment scheme is likely to be in a dominant position. If not, there is no compulsion from competition law. It may even be the case that a duty to deal with applicants in accordance with article 102 only applies to 'essential facilities'.[36]

(2) But it will be prima facie abusive to discriminate between applicants for membership if their applications are equivalent. This implies that applicants should be treated equally.

(3) Having said that, it may be possible to justify different treatment on a variety of grounds. The most obvious is risk: where an infrastructure is exposed to

---

35 London Economics, Securities trading, clearing, central counterparties and settlement in EU25 – an overview of current arrangements (June 2005)
36 O'Donoghue and Padilla, pp 466–7

the credit quality of its members it should be entitled to reject an application from a weak applicant whose participation may jeopardise the integrity or viability of the system and its other members. More difficult is the question of 'free riders': those who seek to join late, having avoided the expense and risk of setting up the infrastructure in the first place, but demand access on equal terms to those who made a full up-front contribution. Here it appears that differential pricing may legitimately be applied.

(4) If membership criteria are kept confidential it seems unlikely that their objectivity would be easy to establish.

These principles are apparent from the European Commission's Notice on the application of the EC competition rules to cross-border credit transfers, which is discussed further in **section 7.14**.

7.12   Until the Financial Services Act 2012 comes into force, a peculiar competition regime will have been in existence for some market infrastructures in the United Kingdom. This historical regime disapplied section 18 of the Competition Act 1998 (which copies out article 102 verbatim) in relation to '(a) practices of a recognised body; (b) the adoption or enforcement of such a body's regulatory provisions; (c) any conduct which is engaged in by such a body or by a person who is subject to the rules of such a body to the extent to which it is encouraged or required by the regulatory provisions of the body.' However, the United Kingdom Treasury considered that the regime 'is now considered to be redundant, particularly as a result of the coming into force of section 290A.'[37] Accordingly, under section 31 of the 2012 Act[38] the special regime is to be repealed.

The reference by the Treasury to section 290A is to a section inserted into the Financial Services and Markets Act 2000 (FSMA) by section 4 of the Investment Exchanges and Clearing Houses Act 2006. This allows the appropriate regulator (to be the Bank of England in respect of a 'recognised clearing house'[39]) to deny recognised status – in effect to withhold a regulatory licence – if a clearing house has a regulatory provision which imposes an 'excessive requirement'. For these purposes an 'excessive requirement' means any obligation or burden which is not required by law and either is not justified as pursuing a reasonable regulatory objective or is disproportionate to the end to be achieved.[40] The meaning of 'regulatory provision' is explored in **section 11.13**.

'Recognised bodies' will include CCPs and CSDs, insofar as they are treated as recognised clearing houses under Part XVIII of FSMA. This is the case in respect of the CCPs and the CSD operating in the United Kingdom, but not payment systems, which are covered by different regulatory arrangements.[41]

7.13   For United Kingdom CSDs – which is to say any Operator regulated under the USRs – there is also a special competition regime, which may survive the Financial Services Act 2012, notwithstanding that CREST is a recognised

---

37 HM Treasury, Financial Services Bill Explanatory Notes (January 2012), http://www. publications.parliament.uk/pa/bills/cbill/2010-2012/0278/en/2012278en.pdf, para 368
38 Based on clause 31 of the Financial Services Bill as introduced to the House of Lords in May 2012
39 FSMA, s 285A(2), as amended by the 2012 Act
40 FSMA, s 300A
41 See **Chapter 11**

clearing house. Schedule 2 to the USRs is entitled 'Prevention of Restrictive Practices', and includes provisions with the following effects:

(1) The Treasury may not approve a person as an Operator (that is to say, the provider of CSD services for transfer of dematerialised shares in the United Kingdom[42]) unless the rules of its system do not have the effect of restricting, distorting or preventing competition.[43] The Treasury has to send to the Office of Fair Trading (OFT) a set of the rules of an applicant for the position of Operator, and the OFT must report whether the rules will have that effect.[44] The OFT is also given investigatory powers,[45] and the Treasury has to have regard to the OFT's report.[46]

(2) The prohibition imposed by section 2(1) of the Competition Act 1998 ('agreements between undertakings, decisions by associations of undertakings or concerted practices which (a) may affect trade within the United Kingdom, and (b) have as their object or effect the prevention, restriction or distortion of competition within the United Kingdom, are prohibited') is disapplied in respect of an agreement for the constitution of an Operator or an applicant for that role.[47]

These provisions are in substance among those which are repealed, in respect of recognised clearing houses, by the Financial Services Act 2012. While the USRs do not include a provision equivalent to section 290A of FSMA, and so the rationale for the repeal applied to recognised clearing houses does not apply in theory, the distinction is in fact specious. This is because CREST is a recognised clearing house as well as an Operator.[48] There is no reason in principle to retain a special competition regime for Operators when it cannot have any substantive effect once the standard regime is applied to the same persons.

It can also be asserted that the Treasury's stated rationale for the repeal in respect of recognised clearing houses appears to be shaky, since the ability of regulators to deal with excessive regulatory provisions hardly travels across ground similar to exemptions from ordinary competition law. But the policy point which the Treasury were making is, presumably, that the time for special treatment for infrastructures is past. Repeal of the exemption in the USRs is likely to follow, therefore.

Payment systems

7.14   In the European Commission's Notice relating to credit transfers, [49] membership criteria for payment systems is discussed and ruled on at some length. The Notice applies to cross-border credit transfer systems, defined as 'system[s] through which payment instructions and the funds described therein may be transmitted for the purpose of effecting credit transfers.' This would encompass many payment 'schemes' as the term is used in this book,

---

42   See **sections 11.21ff**
43   USRs, Sch 2, para 1
44   USRs, Sch 2, para 3
45   USRs, Sch 2, paras 4–4B
46   USRs, Sch 2, para 3(2)
47   USRs, Sch 2, para 6
48   See **section 11.15**
49   Notice on the application of the EC competition rules to cross-border credit transfers (September 1995), OJ C251, pp 3–10, paras 23–29

as well as payments systems properly so called; but the broader point is that what the Commission says ought to be of general application to any market infrastructure. The Notice lays down the following:

(1) Where a system constitutes an essential facility it must be open for further membership (as distinct from ownership) provided that candidates meet appropriate criteria.

(2) A system which is an essential facility may apply membership criteria provided that these are objectively justified.

(3) Membership criteria for direct and indirect members may differ in relation to differences in the nature of their responsibilities.

(4) Membership criteria should be written, accessible, and non-discriminatory. They may cover financial standing, technical or management capacities, and creditworthiness.

(5) The payment of an entry fee may be required, but must not be set so high that it becomes a barrier to entry, and must not exceed a fair share of the real cost of past investments in the system.

(6) Membership criteria may not make membership conditional on acceptance of other, unrelated, services.

(7) Wherever possible, low-volume participants should be admitted to membership, for example through indirect participation; if this option is not available, a requirement for minimum volume must be objectively justified.

(8) Rejection of an application or exclusion should be accompanied by a written justification of the reasons and should be subject to an independent review procedure.

7.15 The right of access to payments infrastructure has subsequently been entrenched in statute law. Article 28 of the Payment Services Directive (PSD)[50] requires member states to ensure that the rules of access to payment systems are 'objective, non-discriminatory and proportionate, and that those rules do not inhibit access more than is necessary to safeguard against specific risks such as settlement risk, operational risk and business risk and to protect the financial and operational stability of the payment system.' In particular, payment systems are not permitted to have: exclusivity rules which preclude their participants from participating in other systems; rules which discriminate between 'authorised' payment service providers such as payment institutions and banks, on the one hand, and 'registered' payment service providers[51] on the other; or restrictions on the basis of institutional status. These rules appear at first blush to codify general principles of competition law; but a closer look at the scope of application of article 28 gives some clue as to an extension of scope.

It is noteworthy that for article 28 to apply there is no requirement for the payment scheme in question to be 'dominant', so article 28 goes some way further than competition law. In fact, it appears that its purpose is to capture precisely those payment systems which *not* dominant. While a 'payment system' means a funds transfer system with formal and standardised arrangements and common rules for the processing, clearing and/or settlement of payment transactions, and thus appears to capture those arrangements which

---

50 Directive 2007/64/EC of the European Parliament and of the Council of 13 November 2007 on payment services in the internal market etc
51 Cf PSD, art 26

in this book are called 'payment schemes'[52] as well as organisations for the netting and settlement of payment obligations, the scope of article 28 is cut right back by an exclusionary provision in article 28(2). Article 28(2) excludes, first of all, payment systems designated under the Settlement Finality Directive (SFD).[53] That will confine article 28's ambit to minor payment systems which are not posing systemic risk, since any payment system which admits only credit institutions and faces some threat from the risk of insolvency of its members will have wanted to avail itself of the protections given by SFD designation. Article 28(2) also excludes intra-group payment systems; and, significantly, it excludes systems where a sole payment service provider acts for both payer and payee, is exclusively responsible for management of the system, and licenses other payment service providers to participate in the system without giving them the right to negotiate fees among themselves. This third exclusion gives the clue to what is going on, although it is on any measure extremely complex to fathom out. Recital (16) of the PSD says that payment systems typically include the four-party card schemes as well as major systems processing credit transfers and direct debits: card schemes are thus the primary target of article 28. The third exclusion (sole provider acting for both payer and payee) is thus intended to exempt three-party card schemes from the open access rule.[54] One might conclude that a judgment had been made that four-party card schemes were deemed to be dominant, and thus to have to apply competition rules as to their access and membership criteria, whereas for three-party schemes the dominance test of article 102 of the Treaty continues to apply.

However, article 28 of the PSD is not confined to card schemes, as the Recital shows. Any scheme or system for processing, clearing or settlement of payments is liable to be caught by article 28 unless there is only one payment service provider (operating as a single entity or a group) serving both payer and payee. There is no test of size or dominance. Article 28 thus has the potential to impose competition constraints even on new market entrants, unlike the Treaty.

ADJACENT MARKETS

7.16   One difficult area for providers of clearing and settlement infrastructures concerns activities they wish to pursue in neighbouring areas of endeavour. At least part of the complication stems from changing perceptions of what it is that constitutes the central activity of an infrastructure – is it record-keeping, safekeeping of assets, transferring title, netting obligations, management of risk, or achieving standardisation? Which of these is a 'market' in which there is cut-and-thrust competition, and which is a monopolistic endeavour or essential facility? What was safely monopolistic yesterday may be challenged by a new business model and become a contested market tomorrow; fees may be at risk and litigation may be threatened.

7.17   A case-study in overlapping market territories is that of the ICSDs. The following introductory points may be helpful by way of orientation:

---

52 See **section 1.15**
53 Directive 98/26/EC of the European Parliament and of the Council of 19 May 1998 on settlement finality in payment and securities settlement systems
54 See also recital (17)

- The term 'ICSD' is a misnomer. ICSDs are not depositories, they are settlement systems for Eurobonds.[55] They are 'central', but there are two of them, in competition.
- ICSDs are operated by banking entities which provide credit facilities for their participants in order to facilitate settlement.
- ICSDs also provide securities accounts for their participants, to which the securities are credited or from which they are debited when transactions settle.
- There is no fundamental legal reason why the securities credited to the accounts provided by ICSDs have to be restricted to Eurobonds.
- All these features make ICSDs sound very similar to custodian banks.

But ICSDs are special. They have special legislation[56] which enables their participants to have a higher degree of legal certainty about the ownership of assets credited to an account provided for them. The reason for this is that the ICSDs are, notwithstanding that they are competitors, providing the central settlement infrastructure for Eurobonds – there is nowhere else to go to get a better title to a Eurobond.

The tension between the infrastructure role of ICSDs and their ability to act like custodians has caused some friction.[57] The main concern of the custodians was that the ICSDs could exploit their special position in the marketplace for custodial services. The risk would manifest itself in bundled packages of services offered by the ICSDs for an integrated price. One bank said 'While the Euroclear Group claims to be operating as a CSD in relation to the securities settlement services it provides, it in fact provides services similar to those of an intermediary rather than a CSD. The implementation of its [single settlement engine] will lead to the exclusion of the other intermediaries from the system by internalising of the settlement of transactions where it owns the relevant CSD in the books of Euroclear Bank.'[58] Euroclear would thus, it was feared, use its common brand to offer 'internalised settlement' on the books of the ICSD operator (Euroclear Bank), bypassing the CSDs it owned, presumably without attracting complaint from those CSDs.[59]

A handful of custodian banks marshalled under a banner nattily tagged 'Fair and Clear', and invited the European Commission, in various responses to its consultations on the post-trade space, to consider legislative or regulatory measures to treat CSDs as utilities and impose restrictions on bundling. The Commission's Second Communication on Clearing and Settlement[60] broadly agreed, proposing that CCPs and 'Securities Settlement Systems' keep segregated accounts of, and provide for the unbundling of, services they offer in their intermediary capacity. In particular, the Second Communication mentioned the provision of 'banking' services – lending of cash and securities

---

55 See **section 2.24**
56 Belgian Royal Decree no 62 of 10 November 1967 facilitating the circulation of securities; Grand-Ducal Decree of Luxembourg dated 17 February 1971 on the Circulation of Securities
57 See, for example, European Financial Services Round Table, Securities clearing and settlement in Europe (December 2003); Citigroup, Creating a Safe and Level Playing Field (July 2003), White Paper
58 Citigroup, Creating a Safe and Level Playing Field, p 22
59 Cf **section 2.21**
60 European Commission, Clearing and Settlement in the European Union – The way forward (April 2004), http://eur-lex.europa.eu/LexUriServ/LexUriServ. do?uri=COM:2004:0312:FIN:EN:PDF

specifically to facilitate settlement, which is within the capabilities of both ICSDs although out of reach for most CSDs. Now the proposed Regulation on CSDs will make special regulatory arrangements for CSDs which wish to provide banking services.[61]

The Code of Conduct

7.18   The Commission's plan to wrap this into a clearing and settlement directive evolved into the Code of Conduct, which dealt with the subject in the following way:

> '*Unbundling of prices.* Unbundling means that: (a) the Organisations will allow any customer to purchase an unbundled service without compelling that customer to purchase also another unbundled service, and (b) each unbundled service will be available at a price applicable to this service. Unbundling does not preclude Organisations offering special prices for the purchase of several unbundled services together, with each service available at a separate price. And any such special prices shall meet the Price Transparency elements of the Code …

> '*Accounting separation.* Any group that includes one or more trading venue, CCP or CSD shall disclose to the National Regulators the annual non-consolidated accounts separately upon request from the National Regulator. Organisations which offer trading, clearing and/or settlement services in a single corporate structure shall disclose to the National Regulators the costs and revenues of these services separately upon request from the National Regulator. Each Organisation shall disclose to the National Regulators its costs and revenues for each unbundled service … in order to make transparent potential cross-subsidies.'[62]

It may be thought that this falls short of what was being asked for, in particular as regards 'banking services' and public transparency of cross-subsidisation. Cross-subsidy is a very troublesome area, because of the difficulty of allocating the cost of shared functions and services between businesses. But on the other hand the concessions actually made in the Code represented a big change for organisations which had until then been able to maintain complete privacy over their internal affairs.[63]

7.19   However, it can be argued that it is open to custodian banks to 'internalise' settlement. What this means, in effect, is that the internaliser effectuates a settlement between a buyer client and a seller client by book transfer on its own books (also described as an 'on-us settlement'[64]). On-us settlement is routine in relation to settlement of payment obligations but is rarer in securities settlements. This is because in securities settlement there is no equivalent to 'commercial bank money'. Settlement of a payment always

---

61 See **section 6.34**
62 FESE, EACH and ECSDA, European Code of Conduct for Clearing and Settlement (November 2006), http://ec.europa.eu/internal_market/financial-markets/docs/code/code_en.pdf, paras 40–43
63 Lannoo, K, and Valiante, D, 'Integrating Europe's Back Office – 10 years of turning in circles', in Engelen, P-J, and Lannoo, K, (eds), Facing New Regulatory Frameworks in Securities Trading in Europe (Intersentia 2010), ISBN 978-90-5095-973-5, p 173
64 Cf **sections 2.21** and **18.33**

requires acceptance of a commercial bank's obligation to pay unless settlement is across the books of a central bank. But settlement of a securities transaction requires a transfer of title, something which is out of the control of a commercial bank unless the bank happens to hold securities of the relevant type in its own inventory. For this reason it is not correct, as some eminent commentators have suggested,[65] that settlement is inseparable from custody. Rather, custody provides access to settlement. 'Internalised' settlement is a theoretical possibility for a custodian who has sufficient custody of own-inventory assets to allow a buyer to acquire title to securities even if the custodian does not act for the seller, or if the custodian acts for seller as well as buyer; but not otherwise. The fear that the custodian banks in the Fair and Clear grouping had was that, as ICSD, Euroclear Bank might be able to assert such a dominant position in custody services that it could internalise settlement to a significant degree. But the linkage to Euroclear Bank's ownership of CSDs was only indirectly advantageous: the single settlement engine it was developing would assist all custodians, not just Euroclear Bank. Moreover, many settlement instructions for securities transfers originate from trading platforms or CCPs and are straight-through-processed to the CSD, so the custodian does not have the opportunity to intervene and demand internalised settlement.

Whatever the validity of the arguments concerning 'internalised settlement', there are certainly ways in which all infrastructures in the clearing and settlement space may seek to encroach on competitive activities of service providers which do not operate infrastructures.

- *CSDs* may seek to provide service to issuers of securities such as transfer of information, enhanced corporate action management, voting administration, and other services more commonly associated with custody. They may also venture into 'banking' (provision of cash liquidity) as described in **section 7.17**.
- *CCPs* may seek to provide trading information, including valuable transaction pricing data, and collateral administration and management services more commonly associated with data repositories and banks.
- *Payment systems* may seek to provide liquidity and to establish or control payment schemes.
- Another area in which infrastructures may seek to extend their activities is by encroaching on each other's natural space. The most obvious example of this activity is the 'vertical silo', under which an exchange, a CCP and a CSD are grouped together, which is the next subject for consideration.

VERTICAL SILO ARRANGEMENTS

7.20   It has been traditional, at least in the United States, for futures exchanges to own a 'captive' CCP.[66] This connection is likely to be attributable not just to the revenues which flow to the owners from providing clearing services, but due to economies of scope: greater operational efficiency can be achieved by straight-through processing, which is bound to be easier if the post-trade

---

65 See Friess, B, and Greenaway, S, 'Competition in EU Trading and Post-Trading Service Markets' (Spring 2006) Competition Policy International, vol 2, p 166

66 Kroszner, R, 'Can the Financial Markets Privately Regulate Risk? The Development of Derivatives Clearing Houses and Recent Over-the-Counter Innovations' (August 1999) Journal of Money, Credit, and Banking, vol 31, p 569

services are provided by the same organisation. (Economies of scope can be defined as efficiencies associated with providing additional types of products or services.) Similarly, stock exchanges have close operational links with securities settlement systems, and can be found in common ownership with them.

A 'vertical silo', which comprises an exchange, a CCP, and a CSD, in common ownership and typically under control of a single management structure, would appear to be vulnerable to challenge under both articles 101 and 102 of the Treaty. Article 101 prohibits price-fixing agreements, which could expose to challenge an arrangement between different legal entities providing unified bundled pricing, or under which the pricing of one part of the chain is determined by agreement with the provider of an infrastructure in another part of the chain. However, a successful article 101 challenge requires proof that the practices complained of 'affect trade between Member States'; vertical silos have historically existed as single-country arrangements and may therefore be safe from attack, at least from the European Commission. Given that trading in securities (and thus the demand for post-trading services) is fully internationalised, it can however be argued that trade in securities between member states is indeed affected, and so the risk of challenge to vertical silos at European level should not be ruled out, even if the silo is confined to a single country in its operations. As to article 102, there may be a risk of challenge on the grounds that one or other of the infrastructures in the chain is abusing a dominant position, particularly if there is a request from a competitor to access another part of the value-chain. In practice, a challenge can only be made by a CCP: there are likely to be many platforms competing for trading activity; CSDs occupy an uncontestable space in the value chain and are therefore immune from competition; but, as explained below, CCPs are hired by trading platforms, and are dependent on cooperation from the exchange in order to offer an alternative to the incumbent CCP. So, only a clearing service can be foreclosed by a vertical silo – but such foreclosure could constitute abuse of a dominant position.

The examples of vertical consolidation cited above were built in an era when, for most investment products, there was a single trading venue which needed to be connected to a single CSD, or a single CCP, or both. That assumption may no longer be valid in Europe. Following the adoption of MiFID, it has not been open to member states of the European Union to insist that all transactions in equities be traded exclusively on a single regulated market,[67] and it has been possible for an investment firm to establish a 'multilateral trading facility' offering an alternative execution venue for trading in equities. One consequence of MiFID has thus been to introduce competition between trading venues. Each venue needs to be able to offer its participants access to clearing and settlement facilities, thus challenging the exclusivity of vertical consolidation models.

7.21   Article 34 of MiFID allows investment firms rights of access to regulated markets, CCPs, and clearing and settlement systems of their choice (subject to satisfying the admission criteria), and requires regulated markets to allow their participants to designate a settlement system of their choice. Articles 35 and 46 allow multilateral trading facilities (MTFs) and regulated markets respectively

---

67   MiFID, art 40(5)

to use foreign CCPs and clearing and settlement systems.[68] So far, so good; but what MiFID leaves out is as important as what it says:

- MiFID does not give a CCP a right of access to the trade flow from an MTF or a regulated market. This omission will be corrected when the proposed Regulation on markets in financial instruments (MiFIR) takes effect.[69] Venues should therefore be obliged to establish multiple clearing links if so requested by CCPs.

- MiFID does not allow participants in an MTF or regulated market to designate a CCP of their choice. It is wrong to suppose that the right given to investment firms to have *access* to a CCP gives them a right to choose which CCP clears their trades. This will be partly tackled by MiFIR, which (as well as giving CCPs a right to a trade feed from trading venues) will deny CCPs the ability to discriminate unfairly between trading venues,[70] but the provision assumes that CCPs dictate the arrangements, which (as discussed below) is rarely the case. In the past, the markets cleared by a CCP were chosen not by the CCP's participants, but the venue, in a process in which the investment firms affected may have had little influence, or where the majority of firms affected provide services for a domestic investor base only and for whom international issues such as access to foreign venues are little more than a distraction.

- MiFID does not require member states to allow issuers to designate a CSD of their choice. The MiFID provisions allowing firms and trading systems to designate a CSD of their choice flew in the face of the reality, which is that national legal systems are not designed to enable an issuer to select a foreign CSD as the place for settlement of transactions in their securities. Certainly a link between CSDs could enable such a selection to be made, but links between CSDs introduce cost, as explained in **section 13.42**, so it is difficult to see what could be achieved by the rights apparently created by MiFID. This omission will be partially corrected by the proposed Regulation on CSDs.[71]

Nevertheless, in some countries, vertical consolidation persists or has even been created. In Italy, the national stock exchange Borsa Italiana, the CCP CC&G, and the CSD Monte Titoli are all in common ownership, along with the London Stock Exchange and various other organisations active in post-trade services. In Germany, Clearstream Banking AG Frankfurt provides the CSD function, and Eurex Clearing AG the CCP function, and these are linked in a vertical arrangement with Deutsche Börse AG.[72] In Hungary, KELER operates the CCP as well as the CSD (albeit in different legal entities, having separated them in 2008[73]). The persistence of these arrangements needs to be examined.

---

68 Renumbered, in the proposal for a replacement Directive on markets in financial instruments (http://eur-lex.europa.eu/LexUriServ/LexUriServ.do?uri=COM:2011:0656:FIN:EN:PDF), arts 39, 40 and 57 respectively

69 European Commission, Proposal for a Regulation of the European Parliament and of the Council on markets in financial instruments etc (October 2011), COM(2011) 652 final, http://eur-lex.europa.eu/LexUriServ/LexUriServ.do?uri=COM:2011:0652:FIN:EN:PDF, art 29

70 MiFIR proposal, art 28

71 See **sections 10.24–10.25**

72 European Central Bank, Payment and Securities Settlement Systems in the European Union (the Blue Book) (August 2007), http://www.ecb.int/pub/pdf/other/ecbbluebookea200708en.pdf

73 http://www.keler.hu/keler/keler_angol.head.page?nodeid=137

Reasons for persistence of vertical silos

7.22   In the first place, it may be observed that a CSD's income is at risk of being adversely affected by the introduction of a CCP. As noted in **section 2.5**, clearing has the effect that the number of trades requiring settlement is reduced, and if a CSD charges so many cents per side or per security for settlement, its revenue will fall when a CCP is introduced to the marketplace. Controlling the CCP so that the loss of settlement revenue can be recouped from CCP fees would be a logical, if anti-competitive, response. However, the evidence available suggests that CSDs' revenue is no worse in cleared compared with uncleared markets.[74] The reasons for this might be that CCPs levy fees according to the number of transactions, as opposed to the number of post-netting settlements. Or, again, it might just be that CSDs are monopolists which can just decide on their pricing and let the market like it or lump it. What one can safely conclude from this evidence is that CSDs have not historically been threatened by the possibility of introducing a CCP or, indeed, by the spectre of internalised settlement.

Costs for users would not be expected to be lower, then, if the post-trade infrastructure is arranged as a vertical silo, by comparison with independently organised post-trade arrangements. There appears to be evidence to support this view,[75] notwithstanding the comments of Deutsche Börse Group,[76] who criticise cost-analysis which ignores 'indirect costs' such as bid-ask spreads and other premiums attributable to trading methodologies. Nevertheless Deutsche Börse did not directly answer the question whether the clearing function should be opened to competition in Germany. More recently, when the proposed merger between Deutsche Börse and NYSE was being discussed, the CCP service provided by Eurex was going to become 'vertical but open', apparently meaning that other trading venues and CSDs would be given access. The ability to test this in practice went away when the merger was prohibited by DG Comp.[77]

Persistence of silos is closely connected to the bargaining power of exchanges. Traders always need to settle their trades, and for so long as there was only one exchange and one CSD able to take the settlement business, there was no choice if the exchange decided to appoint a CCP. Introduction of choice between trading venues did not significantly alter the bargaining power. Trading platforms hire CCPs, not the other way round: the trade is the starting-point, from which all post-trade services flow; without trading, there is no clearing, and trading can survive quite happily without clearing. So, CCPs have had to participate in auctions to be accepted by exchanges, and may be expected to pay fees to the exchanges they serve.[78] Moreover, a CCP challenging an incumbent CCP needs to establish interoperability

---

74   74 Friess, B, and Greenaway, S, 'Competition in EU Trading and Post-Trading Service Markets' (Spring 2006) Competition Policy International Vol 2, pp 157–185

75   Baur, D, Integration and Competition in Securities Trading, Clearing and Settlement (March 2009), http://ssrn.com/abstract=891223

76   Deutsche Börse AG, Observations on the Commission's Issues Paper 'Competition in EU Securities Trading and Post-Trading' (June 2006)

77   European Commission, Mergers: Commission blocks proposed merger between Deutsche Börse and NYSE Euronext (February 2012), Press Release IP/12/94, http://europa.eu/rapid/pressReleasesAction.do?reference=IP/12/94

78   Friess and Greenaway paper

arrangements with the incumbent – no mean feat, as explained in **Chapter 13** – and, on top of that, establish a reliable trade-data flow from the trading platform. Vertical silos will find all sorts of technical and economic obstacles which make it easier to avoid these burdens. It is difficult to avoid DG Comp's conclusion that 'under current arrangements CCPs in vertical silos would not be subject to competition either for, or in, their home market. Consequently competition appears to be foreclosed in this case.'[79]

In addition to these powerful commercial reasons for maintaining the status quo in markets served by vertical silos, the regulatory influences should not be ignored. Regulation of clearing and settlement systems has historically been organised according to the home country principle.[80] A regulator responsible not only for the orderly conduct of markets in its jurisdiction but also for the end-to-end protection of investors will wish to have oversight of the whole value chain. This fragmented system of supervision does not sit comfortably with the competition-policy ideal of a single European market in which foreign entities ply their services without hindrance in target markets. Until EMIR and the proposed Regulation on CSDs, widely differing requirements and standards have been applied in the supervision of post-trade services across Europe, with publicly-known deficiencies.[81] Even with the improvements which followed the financial crisis of 2008, these differences will persist even if they become less acute. Vertical silos provide for regulatory convenience, and a powerful argument can be made that safety in infrastructures requires tight, risk-free regulation which would not be achievable under Europe's patchwork approach to cross-border cooperation among regulators.

One final observation may be made. Competition theory is not universally applauded, but vertical silos have been criticised by the financial services industry's trade associations. Vertical silos have been accused of allowing distortion of competition through abuse of a dominant position in one part of the value chain, restricting access, bundling and cross-subsidy, and opacity in pricing. But perhaps the most serious objection is that silos prevent horizontal consolidation of clearing and settlement.[82] This must therefore be the next subject for discussion.

HORIZONTAL CONSOLIDATION

7.23 Horizontal consolidation raises many of the same objections from competition theorists as vertical consolidation. If a single-country monopoly provider of clearing or settlement infrastructure has a dominant position, how much worse would the effects of any abusive behaviour be if that infrastructure served several countries or even the whole of Europe? Nevertheless there was

---

79 European Commission services, Competition in EUC securities trading and post-trading (May 2006), Issues Paper http://ec.europa.eu/competition/sectors/financial_services/securities_trading.pdf
80 Kazarian, E, Integration of the Securities Market Infrastructure in the European Union: Policy and Regulatory Issues (October 2006), IMF Working Paper WP/06/241
81 Kazarian paper
82 AFEI et al, Post-trading in Europe: calls for consolidation (February 2006), http://www.liba.org.uk/publications/2006/Post-trading%2020Feb06Final%20AFEI%20FBF%20LIBA%20Final%20Version.pdf

in the past a chorus of voices urging those responsible for the government of Europe to bring about a single CCP and a single CSD for Europe.[83]

Arguments in favour of consolidation have included improved collateral management for participants, reduction in the number of trades to be settled, reduced unit cost, reduced operational cost and risk, and the danger of competition starting a 'race to the bottom'.[84] From a practical viewpoint, CCPs should be easier to integrate than CSDs. The following comments illustrate the issues:

> 'In particular, an uncontrolled proliferation of clearing infrastructures could create inefficiencies. For instance, the existence of a fragmented infrastructure would oblige banks and investment firms to participate in more than one central counterparty clearing house, and therefore to maintain several interfaces and to cope with different standards, market practices and clearing rules. Service providers may also face inefficiencies in terms of multiple investments used to maintain, enhance and develop central counterparty technology.
>
> 'Competition between central counterparties entails the risk that these service providers may try to improve competitiveness by applying more lenient risk management standards.'[85]

Horizontal consolidation of CCPs should in theory reduce costs for users because of greater netting. One role of the CCP is to reduce a large number of trades to a small number of transactions which proceed all the way to settlement. The creation of the consolidated CCP Clearnet SA out of the national CCPs in France and the Netherlands would not be a good model to demonstrate the netting effect of consolidation, because the parent CCPs were clearing transactions in completely different securities, which cannot be netted against each other for the purposes of settlement. But, with the opening up of trading engineered through MiFID, and the possibility to trade highly-liquid stocks in many marketplaces using different CCPs, efficiency gains through consolidation subsequently became a real possibility.

Reading these remarks, one would assume that the logical outcome would be to foster the development of a single CCP for Europe, and perhaps to seek to challenge the monopolies of CSDs in their respective home countries. However, as explained in **sections 7.20** and **7.21**, the market for CCP services is more readily contestable, and the outcome is the reverse: there is active competition among CCPs, and a single, monolithic (if not monopolistic) organisation is providing settlement services at CSD level. These phenomena require further examination.

---

83 European Securities Forum, EuroCCP – ESF's Blueprint for a Single Pan-European Central Counterparty (December 2000); European Central Bank, 'Consolidation in central counterparty clearing in the euro area' (August 2001), Monthly bulletin, p 69; European Financial Services Round Table, Securities clearing and settlement in Europe (December 2003); Bourse Consult, The Future of Clearing and Settlement in Europe (December 2005), Corporation of London City Research Series No.7; French Association of Investment Firms et al, Post-trading in Europe: Calls for Consolidation (February 2006); European Parliament, Clearing and Settlement in the EU (August 2009), IP/A/ECON/ST/2008-31 PE 416.242

84 See **section 13.19**

85 European Central Bank, 'Consolidation in central counterparty clearing in the euro area' (August 2001), Monthly bulletin, pp 73, 77

CCPs

7.24 In relation to CCPs, various factors are at work, in addition to contestability of the marketplace, which have helped to shape this outcome.

(1) In the first place, mergers are extremely difficult to do, which places a formidable obstacle in the way of consolidation. In practice cross-border regulatory requirements inhibit horizontal consolidation of CCPs. Consider the example of LCH.Clearnet: during the 1980s, the London Clearing House (LCH.Clearnet) built an effective model acting as CCP for a number of futures markets in London, enabling members to share efficiency gains inherent in a single set of processes and partially-offsetting margining arrangements. These markets enjoyed a common regulatory and legal system as well as a significantly overlapping membership, which encouraged that integrated structure. But when LCH came into common ownership with Clearnet, its equivalent in France, the legal and regulatory obstacles effectively precluded a full merger at an international level. This might be contrasted with the international acceptability of Clearnet's own service offering, as CCP to the Belgian, Dutch and Portuguese equities exchanges operated by Euronext, as well as the French exchange. More examples can be given of other CCPs successfully accessing several national markets since MiFID.

Schmiedel and Schönenberger[86] studied consolidation among market infrastructures in the eurozone between 1999 and 2005. They found that the number of CCPs had decreased from 14 to 8, but that 'most of the mergers and consolidation initiatives at the European level have been purely legal mergers, ie the systems are still operating separate technical platforms.' Concentration of ownership does not lead to efficiency improvements unless operational integration follows, and legal and regulatory obstacles impede that process. Tax issues and vested interests of users and owners have also been blamed.

(2) Secondly, a feature which some natural monopolies have is that they enjoy a 'network effect' – that is, the value of the service is increased according to the number of people that use it.[87] So, the more participants in a CCP, the greater the netting benefit and, on the whole, the greater the other advantages of using that CCP. Network effects may also include the tendency of an established CCP to add more products to its range and the potential for cross-margining, thus strengthening the effect.[88] CCP participation may be subject to a 'tipping' effect – a point beyond which there are already so many participants in the CCP that it is pointless to join a competitor and impossible for a challenger to try and compete with the incumbent.

(3) Thirdly, the Client of a CCP is not its users but the trading platform which hires it. The incentives for a platform to allow consolidation may not be there: there would be loss of fees or loss of control; the regulator of the

---

86 Schmiedel, H, and Schönenberger, A, 'Integration, regulation, and policy of securities market infrastructures in the euro area' (2006), Journal of Financial Regulation and Compliance Vol 14, No 4, p 328

87 See also Lee, Running the World's Markets, pp 15–18

88 Hasenpusch, T, 'Network Economics with Application to Clearing Services and their Impact on the Organisation of the European Clearing Industry', in Engelen, P-J, and Lannoo, K, (eds), Facing New Regulatory Frameworks in Securities Trading in Europe (Intersentia, 2010), ISBN 978-90-5095-973-5

exchange may object; there will be technical difficulties in connecting the market to a foreign CCP and enabling data to flow. These problems are the same obstacles which obstruct the breaking up of vertical silos.

Without the force of legislation, these three difficulties are likely to overwhelm an attempt to consolidate.

Furthermore, competition among CCPs also reduces cost. Where new CCPs have been competing actively for trade-flow since the implementation of MiFID, there is some evidence of cost reduction. The London Stock Exchange stated in 2008 that since the announcement of competitive clearing for its marketplace in May 2006, CCP clearing fees had declined by about 60% on average and up to about 75% for the largest customers.[89] And a report commissioned by the European Commission stated in 2009 that the average CCP cost per transaction incurred by market participants in 2008 was 'significantly lower' than that in 2006.[90]

However, the decision whether to require competition or to facilitate or even force consolidation remains contentious. The present arrangement is to let the competing CCPs fight for market share or market segments. Some will fail. Others may emerge as dominant pan-European players. But it is illusory to imagine that this is a perfect marketplace in which only economic forces are at work.

CSDs

7.25 In relation to CSDs, the forces at work are rather different. In the first place, there is the fundamental, unsolved, legal problem of root of title: only a CSD is legally capable of providing the equivalent quality of title to securities that a central bank provides in relation to cash. In close second, there is the concern of central banks over the integrity of systems for settlement of securities transactions taking place in connection with their monetary and liquidity operations.[91] Concerns for safety will dominate more in relation to settlement than in relation to clearing; and safety fears tend to encourage regulators to preserve the status quo – that is, a locally-controllable national settlement system – notwithstanding that this might be inimical to the broader European agenda of a single market for investment services. The regulatory patchwork, rather than the impact of competition policy, may therefore inhibit consolidation. The technical obstacles are also formidable, which make the task of building a business case for operational consolidation challenging: the Giovannini barriers are the main difficulties, in particular differences between one market and another in settlement periods, corporate actions, issuance practices and tax rules.

Schmiedel and Schönenberger also noted that the number of CSDs had decreased from 23 to 18 in the eurozone between 1999 and 2005. That decrease indicates that consolidation is possible, but the statistic conceals some of the detail. Most of the consolidations had taken place within single countries – ie,

---

89 London Stock Exchange, Netting – Consultation Document (January 2008)
90 Oxera, Monitoring prices, costs and volumes of trading and post-trading services (July 2009), http://ec.europa.eu/internal_market/financial-markets/docs/clearing/2009_07_ec_report_ oxera_en.pdf
91 Kazarian paper

where the legal problem does not arise – and across borders, consolidation of ownership had happened without necessarily implying consolidation of operational arrangements. In other words, the pattern observed for CCPs had repeated itself, albeit to a lesser degree.

The difficulties just cited are obstacles to competition between CSDs as much as obstacles to international consolidation of CSDs. To cure them, it would appear that legal change, in particular to allow a foreign CSD to act as root of title for an issuer of securities, regulatory consolidation, and technical equivalence are all required.

Various recipes for the technical equivalence problem have been available, in the absence of a legislative solution. The traditional one is to hire an agent bank, which will take care of the diversity of standards and requirements across several jurisdictions, if necessary relying on a network of subcustodians. In truth this is not achieving technical equivalence; it is just a means of making the existing system work, with all that entails in terms of cost and complexity. Similar objections can be made to the next solution, Link up Markets[92], which can be viewed as a 'black box' which processes and adapts settlement instructions so as to achieve international compatibility. Link up Markets is not achieving technical equivalence; it is rather a modified version of the agent bank solution under which the user's CSD has taken the role of the agent bank. Accordingly, CSDs participating in the Link Up Markets structure could risk competition scrutiny on the basis that they have strayed outside the natural area of operations for an essential facility, and that their operations in the marketplace usually occupied by agent banks could be challenged if they do not comply strictly with the principles discussed earlier in relation to essential facilities, unbundling, and operating in adjacent markets.

7.26 Another, and more radical, solution to the problem of technical equivalence has taken the form of the Target2-Securities (T2S) platform developed by the European Central Bank (ECB). Although this has been described as a monopoly,[93] it is probably more accurately described as an exercise in standardisation, though this may depend on the observer's opinion about the primary function of a CSD – viz, as a settlement system for transferring title or as a recording system for guaranteeing title. All CSDs participating in T2S retain their 'root of title' function, but are required to outsource the provision of settlement (between-accounts transfer functionality) to the T2S platform – just as the national central banks outsource the equivalent functionality in relation to euro transfers to the TARGET 2 platform. As to whether this constitutes a monopoly, the ECB has said this:

> 'The underlying assumption is that by merging CSDs' settlement platforms into a single one, we will create a monopoly and therefore eliminate competition. … In reality, even if there are many CSDs in Europe today, competition between them is very limited. The multiplicity of actors is a necessary condition for competition. But it is not a sufficient condition. CSDs in the euro area are, to a large extent, small local monopolies. By merging their settlement function in to a single system, the marked will benefit from economies of scale, without any meaningful reduction of competition. In fact, competition in the settlement business does exist, not between CSDs,

---

92 See **section 13.44**
93 Lannoo and Valiante, p 161

but between settlement in central bank money and settlement in commercial bank money.'[94]

What, then, is the competition problem with T2S? In order to answer this, it is necessary to examine the legal obstacle in the way of competition between CSDs. The principal legal problem is that CSDs have one entrenched advantage over any challenger: they alone can offer the 'root of title' – the ultimate book-entry record which establishes ownership of securities in the eye of the issuer.[95] Assuming that the proposed Regulation on CSDs will actually allow the issuer of securities to use a foreign CSD, and that such a practice catches on, then it would become practically possible for CSDs to compete for root-of-title services and for a real market to develop.

But even if the proposed Regulation does not achieve this objective, CSDs participating in T2S must offer accounts to each other,[96] and hence must overcome any reluctance to interoperation. In **Chapter 13**, the question whether interoperation between CSDs achieves true equivalence is examined; but the theory, for the purposes of T2S, is that a user could participate indirectly in T2S via a single chosen CSD as point of entry, with that CSD providing settlement services for many jurisdictions and the whole range of eligible securities, albeit that the chosen CSD would be providing root of title only for securities for which it is the national, or issuer-selected, CSD. Stripped of the ability to compete on quality of their settlement systems, CSDs will have businesses much closer to those of agent banks and will compete with each other on the quality of their ancillary services. But it would be impossible for any participating CSD to fail, as no person (other than a replacement national CSD) could provide the root of title function. National interests, particularly where title and ownership questions are concerned, are likely to ensure the long-term persistence of local providers of the root-of-title function much in the same way that national central banks have survived the introduction of the Eurosystem.

Investors have not historically 'selected' CSDs, and certainly not on the basis of competing efficiency between settlement engines. In this regard T2S is competitively neutral. Nevertheless, the establishment of T2S leaves open the question whether T2S operates a monopolistic service to which CSDs have, without much choice, to subscribe, owing to network effects and aggressive pricing.[97]

The final obstacle to consolidation and competition among CSDs is the regulatory patchwork. As to this, it has been noted: 'in the face of increased consolidation across borders, it is unclear whether the variations and disparities among the current national regulations in the member states necessarily guarantee public interest in equivalent and fair market conditions to the greatest extent possible.'[98]

---

94 Godeffroy, J-M, Ten frequently asked questions about TARGET2-Securities, Speech to the British Bankers Association, http://www.ecb.int/paym/t2s/defining/outgoing/html/10faq. en.html (September 2006)
95 See **section 2.17**
96 Article 15(1)(d), Guideline of the European Central Bank of 21 April 2010 on TARGET2-Securities (April 2010), ECB 2010/2, OJ L118, p 65
97 Lannoo and Valiante, pp 161, 163
98 Schmiedel and Schönenberger paper

Fully free competition among CSDs is unlikely to thrive just yet. Nonetheless, DG Comp is no more likely to take on the ECB in relation to securities settlement than it is in relation to cash transfers, so the question whether the ECB is in a dominant position or providing an essential facility, and even if it is whether it is abusing its position, is set to remain a question for academic enquiry only.

Payment systems

7.27 Payment systems and ACHs are subject to quite different pressures by comparison to CSDs and CCPs. In the first place, systems serving a non-euro national currency may not have any significant pressure to consolidate. In the euro area, such systems did not exist before the creation of the euro, with the exception of EBA Clearing, which grew out of the Ecu Banking Association. So, consolidation is not the agenda among payment systems and payment schemes – rather there is a need to develop new arrangements if competition is to be fostered.

DEVELOPMENT OF STANDARDS

7.28 A further example of horizontal arrangements arises when market participants come together to agree standardised protocols for clearing and settlement. Such an exercise can cause difficulty if there is a suggestion that the purpose of the standard-setting is to foreclose the market to participants. For example, standards could be created in such a way as to exclude legitimate contestants. There is also a philosophical battle between the creation of standards, which ought in principle to be pro-competitive, as it facilitates switching between service providers, and the entrenched nature of standards, which precludes the development of alternative and innovative technologies. To try to cut a way through this maze, chapter 7 of the European Commission's Horizontal Guidelines has 71 paragraphs of guidance on standard-setting.[99]

The Horizontal Guidelines may be summarised, insofar as relevant, as follows:

(1) Standard-setting can give rise to restrictive effects on competition by potentially restricting price competition and limiting or controlling production, markets, innovation or technical development. Once one standard has been set, competing technologies or approaches are potentially excluded from the market.[100]

(2) Restrictive effects on competition can arise because the process for selection of technologies or approaches is controlled by one or more types of stakeholder and biased towards certain types of participants.[101]

(3) Freedom to develop alternatives is a positive indicator that restrictive effects are not present.[102] So is the provision of access to any intellectual property

---

99 European Commission, Guidelines on the applicability of Article 101 of the Treaty on the Functioning of the European Union to horizontal co-operation agreements (January 2011), Communication 2011/C11/01, OJ(C)11/1; see also **section 4.32**
100 Horizontal Guidelines, paras 259, 260
101 Horizontal Guidelines, para 261
102 Horizontal Guidelines, para 269

rights in the standards developed on terms which are fair, reasonable and non-discriminatory.[103]

(4) All actors should be guaranteed the ability to participate in the process leading to the selection of a standard.[104] This requires a transparent process allowing stakeholders to keep informed of upcoming work.[105]

The following observations might be made in this context. Agent banks and market infrastructures occupy a different space from providers of IT and other support services: they have to have financial services licences. It is therefore likely that standard-setting is done among the licensed community, who may have different needs and responsibilities from the providers of other services. Inevitably there is overlap between the providers of core clearing and settlement services and those who wish to provide other post-trade support services of the descriptions reviewed in **Chapter 4**. Standard-setting in this overlap area can be fraught with difficulty.[106] However, the setting of standards in order to dismantle Giovannini Barrier 1[107] has apparently not been challenged in this way.[108]

---

103 Horizontal Guidelines, para 282
104 Horizontal Guidelines, para 278
105 Horizontal Guidelines, para 279
106 Cf European Commission, Antitrust: Commission opens investigation in e-payment market (September 2011), Press Release IP/11/1076, http://europa.eu/rapid/pressReleasesAction.do?reference=IP/11/1076&format=HTML&aged=0&language=EN&guiLanguage=en
107 See **section 1.26**
108 European Commission, Minutes of the 5th CESAME2 meeting (April 2010), http://ec.europa.eu/internal_market/financial-markets/docs/cesame2/meetings/20100408-minutes.pdf

8 Insolvency

INSOLVENCY LAW AT THE HEART OF RISK MANAGEMENT

8.1   Trading is about striking bargains; clearing and settlement is about ensuring that the parties' obligations are duly performed. Ensuring traders stick to their bargains can be achieved through regulatory standards, such as disciplinary action taken by exchanges and regulators, or through ordinary judicial processes dependent on there being a legally binding and enforceable contract between them. These processes will be effective to deal with everyday problems such as reconciliation errors or negligent failure to comply; they may even be up to the challenge of fraudulent and dishonest behaviour. However, in insolvency these processes will fail. In the first place, there are insufficient assets to pay creditors and perform non-monetary obligations, which means that even if satisfaction could be obtained in the form of a court judgment or regulatory or arbitral award, there is only a limited prospect that the insolvent party will ever pay or perform. Secondly, legal proceedings against insolvent entities are often curtailed by law, and the law of insolvency gives special rights to an insolvent company to defend itself and even to attack its potential challengers. Thirdly, insolvency brings with it whole-business failure, the ejection of management, the cancellation of contracts, and a reversal of the ordinary precepts of doing business.

Risk management in the post-trade space is thus not solely focused on operational efficiency: clearing and settlement must face up to the prospect that market participants will fail and become subject to insolvency proceedings. This chapter first considers the basic types of insolvency procedure to which financial institutions may become subject, and the risks which they pose to the integrity of clearing and settlement processes. Owing to these risks, special defences are available to protect the processes of clearing and settlement against those risks, which are examined in detail. Finally the chapter considers issues deriving from insolvency procedures initiated in other jurisdictions.

NATURE OF INSOLVENCY PROCEEDINGS

8.2   The English law of insolvency is extremely confusing. By 2012 it had become possible for a company incorporated as a bank in England to be subject to no fewer than eleven different types of formal insolvency procedure: creditors' voluntary liquidation, members' voluntary liquidation, compulsory liquidation (also known as winding-up by the court), bank insolvency, special administration (bank insolvency), administration, bank administration, special administration (bank administration), receivership, administrative receivership, and company voluntary arrangement. A creditors' scheme of arrangement under section 895 of the Companies Act 2006 may also be added to the list, as could the special resolution regimes under the Banking Act 2009 (which are invoked in relation to failed banks but are not technically 'insolvency' procedures). Other financial institutions have different arrays of procedures available. To go through each possibility would be tedious: a thematic approach is called for.

Insolvency proceedings can broadly be divided into two classes, namely rehabilitation procedures and winding-up procedures. English law, in its confused approach to insolvency policy, has muddled the distinction, so that 'administration', which is the second most common form of insolvency procedure in the United Kingdom,[1] can be used for either or both of these purposes. Caution and further investigation is usually needed in order to gain a full understanding of the type of insolvency in which a failed financial institution finds itself.

Administration

8.3   Rehabilitation regimes are designed to give a breathing-space to a company in financial difficulties so that it can re-establish itself. The central feature of a rehabilitation regime is that a moratorium, or stay, comes into effect immediately so that no creditor can initiate legal proceedings or petition to wind up the company. Enforcement of security is typically forbidden and the exercise of other contractual rights may be stayed. Furthermore, the process may be accompanied by the appointment of insolvency officers with special powers.

Administration is the main rehabilitation regime in English insolvency law. The law is set out in Schedule B1 of the Insolvency Act 1986 and chapter 2 of the Insolvency Rules 1986.[2] The administration must be conducted with the objective of (a) rescuing the company as a going concern; or, failing that, (b) achieving a better result for the company's creditors 'as a whole' than if the company were wound up. As a last resort the administration may be conducted with the objective of realising property in order to make a distribution to secured or preferential creditors.[3] Meanwhile, there is a moratorium on legal proceedings and security enforcement,[4] though this does not prevent the exercise of contractual rights[5] or the enforcement of a security financial collateral arrangement.[6] Administrators have extensive powers to manage the company[7] as well as to liquidate[8] and distribute its property,[9] to challenge past transactions, to investigate the company's affairs, and to insist on the continuation of essential services.[10] These make administration a very flexible and useful regime for dealing with an insolvent financial firm. The slide from objective (a) to objective (b) may in practice be imperceptible, but the administrator may,

1   The Insolvency Service, *Insolvency Statistics,* http://www.insolvency.gov.uk/otherinformation/ statistics/insolv.htm (quarterly)
2   SI 1986 No 1925
3   Insolvency Act 1986, Sch B1, para 3(1)
4   Sch B1, para 43
5   *Re Olympia and York (Canary Wharf) Ltd* [1993] BCLC 453
6   Financial Collateral Arrangements (No.2) Regulations 2003, SI 2003 No. 3226, reg 8(1),
7   Insolvency Act 1986, Sch B1, para 60, and Sch 1
8   Insolvency Act 1986, Sch 1, para 1
9   Insolvency Act 1986, Sch B1, para 65
10   Insolvency Act 1986, s 233–241

with permission of the court, make distributions to unsecured non-preferential creditors; and he must then signal his intention to make a distribution by issuing a notice under Rule 2.95 of the Insolvency Rules 1986.

There is a paradox here – a failing financial institution will lose its credibility overnight if it fails to meet margin calls or to perform any other type of financial obligation. For a financial firm to seek a moratorium is a way for the firm to write its own death-warrant. Yet administration, with the moratorium, is apparently the insolvency procedure of choice for financial institutions in the United Kingdom: well-known examples include Lehman Brothers[11] and Baring Brothers.[12] The explanation is that, for the incoming insolvency practitioner, the moratorium is vitally needed to salvage whatever valuable businesses remain within the insolvent company, through an immediate sale to a third party (which is what happened in both the cited cases).

Yet administration in this form has been open to criticism. The experience of clients of Lehman Brothers, who had legitimate expectations that the client money and client asset segregation rules of the FSA[13] would operate so as to keep their money and non-cash assets outside the scope of the administration, was unfortunately that both cash and securities became trapped in the insolvency process for many months. Furthermore, the administration led CREST to freeze (and ultimately compel cancellation) of settlement instructions for securities transfers pursuant to OTC trades in the CREST system.[14] These and other concerns caused the Treasury to implement through the Investment Bank Special Administration Regulations (IBSARs)[15] an enhancement of the administration regime as applied to 'investment banks', with new powers facilitating the distribution of client assets.

And finally, the notion that a large, systemically-important financial firm such as Lehmans was put into a terminal proceeding such as administration, with consequences for the global economy that do not need to be repeated here, raises a much larger question as to the suitability for financial sector firms of insolvency procedures designed for manufacturing and trading companies. Other rehabilitative regimes may be more appropriate.

Banking Act rehabilitation

8.4   For banks, the best means of achieving rehabilitation is to avoid a formal insolvency procedure altogether. This concept was recognised by the United Kingdom authorities when the painful throes of Northern Rock (which sought emergency liquidity from the Bank of England, suffered the first run on a British bank for 150 years, and was nationalised after months of negotiation intended to keep the bank in the private sector) revealed the need for a more

---

11 PricewaterhouseCoopers, *Companies in Administration* (July 2010), http://www.pwc.co.uk/eng/issues/lehmans_stakeholder_companies_in_administration.html

12 Bank of England, *Report of the Board of Banking Supervision Inquiry into the Circumstances of the Collapse of Barings* (HMSO, July 1995), ISBN 0-10-270195-4

13 Financial Services Authority, *Handbook of Rules and Guidance,* Client Assets (CASS); see also **sections 9.7ff** (client money) and **10.19ff** (client assets)

14 PricewaterhouseCoopers, *Lehman Brothers International (Europe) (in administration) – Unsettled OTC trades – Update* http://www.pwc.co.uk/eng/issues/lehman_otctrades_update_081008.html

15 2011 SI No 245

modern toolkit to deal with failing banks.[16] By virtue of the Banking Act 2009, there are now additional tools, called the 'Special Resolution Regime', available to the authorities which are designed to enable early intervention, before the implementation of formal insolvency proceedings.[17] The Treasury, or as the case may be the Bank of England, may make an order for the sale of all or part of the bank's business to a private sector purchaser,[18] the transfer of all or part of the bank's business to a 'bridge bank' owned by the Bank of England,[19] or temporary nationalisation.[20] Equivalent measures, being introduced at a European level, are briefly outlined at **section 8.33**.

To deal with the residue of the business of a failed bank, a special variant of administration, called 'bank administration', and a special variant of winding-up, called 'bank insolvency', were created.[21] The primary duty of a bank administrator is to support a commercial purchaser or bridge bank, and then to apply the objectives of 'normal' administration;[22] the thinking is that some contracts or essential facilities might not be capable of being transferred on day one to the rescuing entities, and the continuation of these contracts and facilities must be mandated in order to permit the rescuers to carry out their plans.

The insolvency of the Dunfermline Building Society showed how in practice these new powers might be exercised: part of the business was transferred to the Nationwide Building Society (a private sector buyer), part transferred to a bridge bank, and part left behind in a rump of the old building society which was placed into a hastily-created building society administration regime.[23] The assets of the bridge bank were auctioned and, after repayment of funding, fees and tax, the proceeds of sale were transferred to the Dunfermline Resolution Fund,[24] for eventual payment back to Dunfermline for the benefit of its creditors and other interested parties.[25]

The Special Resolution Regime, like administration, includes certain legal rules which deviate from the freedom of contract ordinarily applicable to a solvent company. These rules include restrictions on termination of contracts,[26] powers to change the parties to contracts and override restrictive clauses,[27] alteration

16   H M Treasury, *Financial stability and depositor protection: further consultation* (July 2008), http://webarchive.nationalarchives.gov.uk/20100407010852/http://www.hm-treasury.gov.uk/d/consult_depositorprotection010708.pdf , paras 1.12ff
17   See H M Treasury, *Financial stability and depositor protection: special resolution regime* (July 2008), http://www.bankofengland.co.uk/publications/other/financialstability/financialstabilitydepositorprotection080722.pdf
18   Banking Act 2009, s 11
19   Banking Act 2009, s 12
20   Banking Act 2009, s 13
21   Parts 3 and 2 respectively of the Banking Act 2009
22   Banking Act 2009, s 137
23   Bank of England, Dunfermline Building Society Property Transfer Instrument 2009, http://www.bankofengland.co.uk/financialstability/role/risk_reduction/srr/resolutions/DunfermlineCombinedTransferInstrument.pdf; Building Society Special Administration (Scotland) Rules 2009 (SI 2009 No. 806), which came into force 53 minutes after it was made (March 2009)
24   Bank of England, *Report under Section 80(1) of the Banking Act 2009 on the Dunfermline Building Society (DBS) Bridge Bank* (July 2010), http://www.bankofengland.co.uk/financialstability/role/risk_reduction/srr/resolutions/DBSreport.pdf
25   Dunfermline Building Society Compensation Scheme, Resolution Fund and Third Party Compensation Scheme Order 2009, SI 2009 No 1800
26   Banking Act 2009, ss 22, 38; IBSARs, reg 14
27   Banking Act 2009, ss 17, 18, 34, 36

of trusts,[28] and the constitutionally alarming power to 'amend the law for the purpose of enabling the powers under this Part to be used effectively.'[29] These rules facilitate the dismantling of a failed bank and the transfer of part, rather than the whole, of its business to a successor entity; the risk that entails for clearing and settlement is that parts which ought to be transferred together become detached – for example collateral becoming detached from its secured obligation, or countervailing claims intended to be set off being left with different entities. The majority of the risks associated with partial dismemberment have been addressed under the Banking Act 2009 (Restriction of Partial Property Transfers) Order 2009,[30] which protects set-off and netting, security arrangements, and, importantly in this context, the special protections granted by the Settlement Finality Directive (SFD)[31] and Part VII of the Companies Act 1989, discussed later in this chapter.

8.5   Where the bank is an 'investment bank', that is an institution incorporated or formed in the United Kingdom with permission to deal in or safeguard investments, and which holds client assets (a term which includes money),[32] it is possible for a 'special administration' regime to apply. In special administration the administrators' priorities are further varied, with the primary objective being to ensure the return of client assets as soon as is reasonably practicable, and to ensure timely engagement with market infrastructure bodies and certain authorities.[33] Special administration can also be applied to an investment bank which takes deposits, hence the creation of the sub-species 'special administration (bank administration)' and 'special administration (bank insolvency)'.[34] These powers were put to use when MF Global failed.[35]

Resolution and Recovery Plans

8.6   Finally, it should be mentioned that systemically important banks will be expected to put in place 'living wills', or more properly, recovery and resolution plans (RRPs). In outline, the requirements are to have a plan to re-establish solvency, for example through conversion of debt to equity, in times of crisis, and to pre-prepare the bank for implementation of a resolution plan, which might involve a combination of formal insolvency procedures or measures such as a local variant of the special resolution regime.[36] To this end, systemically important financial institutions are thus expected to be able to separate their businesses into components which can be disposed of independently, minimising disruption to clients and other outsiders who may

---

28 Banking Act 2009, s 34(7)
29 Banking Act 2009, s 75
30 SI 2009 No 322
31 Directive 98/26/EC of the European Parliament and of the Council of 19 May 1998 on settlement finality in payment and securities settlement systems
32 Banking Act 2009, s 232
33 IBSARs, reg 10
34 IBSARs, Sch 1 and 2
35 KPMG, MF *Global UK special administration* (October 2011 onwards), webpage, http://www.kpmg.com/UK/en/IssuesAndInsights/ArticlesPublications/Pages/mfglobaluk.aspx
36 Financial Stability Board, *Policy Measures to Address Systemically Important Financial Institutions* (November 2011), http://www.financialstabilityboard.org/publications/r_111104bb.pdf

be dependent on the continuation of certain services.[37] At a European level, the requirement for RRPs will be implemented through the proposed Recovery and Resolution Directive,[38] outlined in **section 8.33**.

8.7   In this context, the question arises how clearing, payment and settlement services should be arranged as part of an agent bank's RRP.[39] Payment services in particular are regarded as having a crucial role in relation to systemic risk management. The following observations might be made:

(1) The Financial Stability Board (FSB) says that 'An effective resolution regime (interacting with applicable schemes and arrangements for the protection of depositors, insurance policy holders and retail investors) should: (i) ensure continuity of systemically important financial services, and payment, clearing and settlement functions.'[40] The FSB also says 'All financial institutions should be resolvable in an orderly manner and without taxpayers' solvency support under the applicable resolution regimes in the jurisdictions in which they operate. ... Where a [systemically important financial institution] has multiple significant legal entities, it should ... ensure that significant global payment and settlement services are legally separable and continued operability is ensured.'[41] It is therefore apparent that payment, settlement and clearing services have to be treated in a special way: continuity and separability are the objectives.

(2) To some degree, the means of achieving continuity are the same as those for achieving separability. The Basel Committee on Banking Supervision recommends that 'National authorities should have appropriate tools to deal with all types of financial institutions in difficulties. ... Such frameworks should ... promote the continuity of systemically important functions. Examples ... are ... to create bridge financial institutions, transfer assets, liabilities, and business operations to other institutions, and resolve claims.'[42] However, continuity cannot be guaranteed simply by virtue of the existence of a power to carry out an emergency transfer of business from the failed institution. Of course, transfer of liabilities requires a particular legal power, but such a power is not sufficient. Continuity of contractual relationships assumes that the counterparty has no right to terminate the contract and can be compelled to continue to perform, even if the failed bank is in breach. 'Firms should be required to ensure that key Service Level Agreements can be maintained in crisis situations and in

---

37 Financial Stability Board, *Reducing the moral hazard posed by systemically important financial institutions* (October 2010), http://www.financialstabilityboard.org/publications/r_101111a. pdf, para 20

38 European Commission, *Proposal for a Directive of the European Parliament and of the Council establishing a framework for the recovery and resolution of credit institutions and investment firms, etc* (June 2012), COM(2012) 280 final, http://eur-lex.europa.eu/LexUriServ/ LexUriServ.do?uri=COM:2012:0280:FIN:EN:PDF; Inter-institutional file 2012/0150 (COD)

39 Financial Services Authority, *Recovery and Resolution Plans* (August 2011), CP 11/16, http:// www.fsa.gov.uk/pubs/cp/cp11_16.pdf, para 2.5

40 Financial Stability Board, *Key Attributes of Effective Resolution Regimes for Financial Institutions* (October 2011), http://www.financialstabilityboard.org/publications/r_111104cc. pdf, p 3

41 Financial Stability Board, *Reducing the moral hazard* paper, paras 17, 20

42 Bank for International Settlements, Basel Committee on Banking Supervision Cross-border Bank Resolution Group, *Report and Recommendations of the Cross-border Bank Resolution Group* (March 2010), http://www.bis.org/publ/bcbs169.pdf, Recommendation 1

resolution, and that the underlying contracts include provisions that prevent termination triggered by recovery or resolution events and facilitate transfer of the contract to a bridge institution or a third party acquirer.'[43] The FSB draws attention to the risk that the failed bank may lose its membership of financial market infrastructures; that its cleared financial contracts might not be transferable to a bridge bank or third party purchaser; and that its indirect participant clients will need to switch to a replacement service provider. [44] With reference to the transferability of payment operations, the FSB recommends that there should be:

'(i) a centralised repository for all their [financial market infrastructure] membership agreements;

(ii) standardised documentation for payment services, covering issues including notice periods, termination provisions and continuing obligations, to facilitate orderly exit;

(iii) a draft Transitional Services Agreement as part of RRPs that, if needed, will allow the firm to continue to provide uninterrupted payment services (including access to [financial market infrastructures]) on behalf of the new purchaser, by using existing staff and infrastructure; and

(iv) a "purchaser's pack" that includes key information on the payment operations and credit exposures, and lists of key staff, to facilitate transfers of payment operations to a surviving entity, bridge institution or purchaser.'[45]

(3) Further, where a failed bank has been broken up and its functions shared among various successor entities, the new entities must be obliged to perform obligations to each other. So, to achieve the continuity objective, additional legal rules, such as those in sections 38 and 63 of the Banking Act 2009 preventing the operation of termination clauses and requiring failed entities and their affiliates to provide services to bridge banks and other transferees, will be needed to buttress the use of transfer powers. By modifying rights which were privately agreed to, the existence of continuity powers raises questions as to the need for safeguards for counterparties. In this context it may be remarked that the proposals for the European Recovery and Resolution Directive may go further than the Banking Act in the potential for restriction of termination rights.[46]

(4) Separability may not be so simple, either. Payment and settlement services may be provided by a bank through a network of subsidiaries, foreign branches, and agents. Although efforts persist directed towards resolution of failed banks as global, multi-entity creatures, in practice that goal is difficult to achieve. The idea of putting a 'payment service' into a box ready-packed like a Christmas parcel for transfer to a bridge bank is aspirational in the case of a bank providing a network-based service.

---

43 Financial Stability Board, *Key Attributes* paper, para 11.7
44 Financial Stability Board, *Key Attributes* paper, paras 4.7, 4.8, 4.10
45 Financial Stability Board, *Key Attributes* paper, para 4.9
46 See **section 8.33(2)**

Table 8.1   Difficulties in resolution: participation in payment, clearing and settlement systems[47]

Issue	Payments	Clearing	Settlement
Failed firm is a direct participant	Membership will cease	Default rules will come into operation	Accounts will be frozen
Failed firm accesses infrastructure indirectly	Service provider may terminate service contract Network access may be withdrawn	GCM may close out position Matching system participation may be terminated	Cash settlement bank may terminate credit Custodian may terminate services
Obstacles to continuity	Transfer of sort codes to bridge bank or purchaser	Transferability of client positions	Termination of transactions
Assuring continuity: access to infrastructure	S 191, Banking Act 2009: Bank of England can direct system to take specified action (or prohibit action)	EMIR, art 48: duty of CCPs to implement client portability procedures	Reg 14, Investment Bank Special Administration Regulations 2011: obligation to continue to provide access to CREST (but not other systems)
Assuring continuity: use of network	Ss 191 and 206A, Banking Act 2009: Bank of England can direct service provider to take specified action (or prohibit action)		Reg 14, Investment Bank Special Administration Regulations 2011: obligation to continue to provide network for access to CREST (but not other systems)

(5)   There is a tension between the need to ensure continuity of payment, settlement and clearing services and the protection of payment, settlement and clearing systems. One policy objective is to ensure continuity, the other is to close off the risk introduced by a failed participant. The SFD regime may be regarded by some as beatified, and therefore immutable. Under the proposed European crisis management regime 'where: (a) a resolution authority transfers some but not all of the property, rights or liabilities of a bank to another entity … or (b) a resolution authority uses ancillary powers to cancel or modify the terms of a contract to which the credit institution under resolution is a party or to substitute a transferee as a party; that transfer, cancellation or modification should not affect the operation of systems and rules of systems covered by the Settlement Finality Directive.'[48]

---

47   Based on Financial Services Authority, *Recovery and Resolution Plans* (August 2011), CP 11/16, http://www.fsa.gov.uk/pubs/cp/cp11_16.pdf, Annex 7
48   European Commission Services, *Technical Details of a Possible EU Framework for Bank Recovery and Resolution* (January 2011), DG Internal Market And Services working document, http://ec.europa.eu/internal_market/consultations/docs/2011/crisis_management/consultation_paper_en.pdf, section H5

Notwithstanding that assertion public comment on resolution of the conflict between these policy objectives has been limited.[49] The FSA has noted various difficulties of unravelling participation in payment, clearing and settlement systems, summarised in **table 8.1**.

(6) The United Kingdom has initiated a policy programme intended to provide more stability, and less taxpayer-dependency, for the financial sector. Part of this programme involves the separation between retail and investment banking. Payment, settlement and clearing services are assigned to the retail sub-sphere. Frequent mention is made of 'payment services' in this context – but these references are usually to payment services in the sense used in the Payment Services Directive,[50] such as allowing credits and debits to payment accounts, rather than wholesale services such as access to payments infrastructures. Needless to say, it is essential for users of banks to continue to have access to payment services in order to avoid defaulting on their obligations; keeping the providers of such services inside the more restricted 'retail banking' sub-sector makes policy sense. But, even if loosely related, this is a different question from how to separate the payment, settlement and clearing functions of a bank from the failed whole of a complex multi-entity financial institution.

Winding-up

8.8   The purpose of winding-up is to enable the assets of an insolvent company to be liquidated, and a distribution made to the creditors. The legal regime is designed to protect the estate and empower the liquidator to maximise its value. Accordingly, the powers given to a liquidator are in many cases identical to those given to an administrator: powers to carry on the business of the company,[51] to liquidate[52] and distribute its property,[53] to challenge past transactions, to investigate the company's affairs, and to insist on the continuation of essential services.[54] The main distinctions from an administration are: there is no stay on enforcement of security; dispositions of the company's property after the presentation of a winding-up petition are void unless the sanction of the court is obtained;[55] and the liquidator has much simpler duties than an administrator, in that he is not required to strive to save anything.

---

49 European Commission Services, *Overview of the results of the public consultation on technical details of a possible EU framework for bank resolution and recovery* (May 2011), http://ec.europa.eu/internal_market/consultations/docs/2011/crisis_management/ consultation_overview_en.pdf; responses can be found at https://circabc.europa.eu/ faces/jsp/extension/wai/navigation/container.jsp?FormPrincipal:_idcl=FormPrincipal:_ id3&FormPrincipal_SUBMIT=1&id=3e98fc27-19f5-424f-8a8c-feff3a8a148b&javax. faces. ViewState=rO0ABXVyABNbTGphdmEubGFuZy5PYmplY3Q7kM5YnxBzKWw CAAB4c AAAAAN0AAExcHQAKy9qc3AvZXh0ZW5zaW9uL3dhaS9uYXZpZZ2F0aW9uL2Nvbn RhaW5lci5qc3A=

50 Directive 2007/64/EC of the European Parliament and of the Council of 13 November 2007 on payment services in the internal market, etc

51 Insolvency Act 1986, Sch 4, para 5

52 Sch 4, para 6

53 Sch 4, para 1

54 Insolvency Act 1986, ss 233–241

55 Insolvency Act 1986, s 127

The 'bank insolvency' regime under the Banking Act 2009[56] provides for a modified form of winding-up of the rump of a bank which has been dealt with under the Special Resolution Regime. The liquidator of the insolvent rump's principal objective is to work with the Financial Services Compensation Scheme (FSCS) to ensure that each depositor eligible for compensation has his account transferred to another financial institution or receives a compensation payment from the FSCS.[57] If the bank is in 'special administration (bank insolvency)', the insolvency officer is confusingly called an 'administrator', and his FSCS-related objective prevails over the other objectives of special administration.[58]

INSOLVENCY RISKS

8.9   Why should insolvency be so fearsome? Operational failure such as computer-system meltdown can have a devastating impact on investors' rights, and may therefore be regarded as a potent source of problems needing proactive management. But operational risks have a single, but overwhelming, difference from insolvency risks: a company which experiences an operational failure but which is solvent can repair the damage. Repair may be costly and time-consuming, but in the meantime anyone who has suffered loss can, through the usual mechanisms of legal redress, obtain compensation for that loss. Operational risks can thus, with a degree of safety, be assumed to be ones which the perpetrator will be called upon to rectify – they do not (absent specific regulatory requirements) require third parties to take ownership of the prevention and management of operational risk events.

Insolvency risk events, by contrast, require management by counterparties. There is no prospect of the insolvent firm giving redress for the consequences of its failure. Moreover, insolvency officers are given peculiar powers which significantly alter the balance of power in favour of the insolvent firm once formal insolvency proceedings begin. The following summary examines the main kinds of challenge which may confront solvent counterparties upon the rehabilitation or liquidation of a financial sector firm.

Normal operations will be interfered with

(1) *Inaction*. The insolvency officer's most troublesome weapon is his ability to do absolutely nothing with impunity. Mostly, the problem with insolvency is that the insolvent firm is not paying or not performing its other obligations. And, unfortunately, there is very little the solvent counterparty can do about that. Even if insolvency law allows legal action to be taken against the insolvent firm, it is unlikely that the insolvency officer would trouble to defend the proceedings: judgment entered against the insolvent firm will rank as an unsecured claim, along with all other unpaid debts. There is in practice little point in suing for an unpaid debt, because the insolvency process will in any event provide a mechanism for collection and evaluation of creditors' claims so that any distribution of assets is fair. Furthermore, the courts in England have shown a desire to assist insolvency officers by allowing them to get on with the job, without being

---

56 Banking Act 2009, Part 2
57 Banking Act 2009, s 99
58 IBSARs, Sch 1, para 4

hurried by creditors and other types of claimant. In one of the cases relating to Lehman Brothers,[59] various claimants asserted that their assets were trapped in the administration of Lehman Brothers International (Europe), and applied to the court for relief, claiming that the administrators were delaying in dealing with their case, which was causing them loss. The court ruled that the claimants had to wait until the administrators had sorted out who was entitled to what.

(2) *Segregation risk.* The problem of assets believed to be in the continuing ownership of a solvent claimant, but nonetheless becoming trapped in the insolvency, is a difficult but frequently encountered one. It demonstrates that retaining proprietary rights in an asset the possession of which is with an insolvent firm is of less value than might be expected. One example of this type of danger are where collateral has been transferred to an insolvent firm, using a security interest rather than a title-transfer technique in order to avoid credit risk, but it is unclear to the insolvency officer whether the assets comprising the collateral which are held by the insolvent firm belong to the firm or to the collateral providers. The problem is in the act of transfer: with regard to securities collateral the distinction between possession and ownership is fuzzy.[60] This makes securities rather like chattels: possession is the ostensible characteristic of ownership, but it is not determinative. The classic case where the distinction made a real difference was *Re Goldcorp Exchange Ltd*,[61] where investors had invested in gold bullion, ostensibly purchased for them and transferred into their ownership, but not to their possession, by a firm which subsequently went into receivership. Unfortunately for the investors, particularly those who had received reassurance as to their ownership rights in the form of ownership certificates confirming segregation of their own bullion, where the firm had not segregated the investors' assets from its own, or a general mass of unallocated assets, the inability to identify separate assets 'belonging' to clients was fatal to those clients' ownership claims. The Lehman Brothers insolvency demonstrated how complex the question of segregation can become, when clients empower their broker to rehypothecate their segregated holdings.[62] The conclusions which can be drawn are twofold. First, when possession of securities has been transferred to another person, the control of ownership of the asset is wholly transferred to that other person – where the recipient of the assets has failed to keep adequate records, the transferor loses his entitlement just as surely as if he had transferred title, not just possession, of the assets. Secondly, inadequate record-keeping can be rectified when the transferee is solvent; reconciliation problems can be resolved without fuss by buying in any missing securities.

(3) *British Eagle risk.* Of particular importance in the world of clearing and settlement is the ability of a person carrying out a central role on behalf of numerous market participants (such as an ACH, a CCP or a GCM[63]) to carry out multilateral netting, that is to maximise efficiency of settlements by establishing a clearing arrangement. Clearing recognises that each participant has both bought and sold, and allows each participant to net

---

59 *Four Private Investment Funds v Lomas and ors* [2008] All ER (D) 237
60 See **sections 8.29(2), 10.10(4)** and **10.11**
61 [1995] 1 AC 74 (Privy Council)
62 Financial Services Authority, *Enhancing the Client Assets Sourcebook* (March 2010), Consultation Paper CP10/9, http://www.fsa.gov.uk/pubs/cp/cp10_09.pdf , paras 2.9 ff
63 See **Chapter 2** for explanations of these terms and roles

down its delivery obligations and receipt entitlements notwithstanding that the counterparties to the buy and sell trades were different. Unfortunately, clearing arrangements are disallowed under general principles of insolvency law, as confirmed by the House of Lords in *British Eagle International Air Lines v Compagnie Nationale Air France.*[64] The reason is that the surviving participants in the clearing scheme receive a better outcome than they would if they had dealt bilaterally with the failed participant: and that is a result which is detrimental to the general body of creditors. The conclusion which might be drawn from this is that clearing systems will cease to function if one of their participants fails. Indeed, that conclusion would be justified if the rules of the system are not structured well and there are no statutory protections available. However, under English law it is common to address *British Eagle* risk by providing that all participants in a clearing system deal with the central clearing system provider as principal, so that the clearing system provider is always in a bilateral relationship with each participant. This device converts multilateral netting into bilateral netting, which is not only permitted but actually mandatory under English insolvency law.[65] Common, but not invariable: some settlement systems would not describe themselves as operating multilateral clearing arrangements, but their processing techniques, such as 'circles processing', rely on embedded multilateral netting.[66] Care in systems design, and where appropriate, statutory protection from *British Eagle* challenge, may be needed.

(4) *Authority cancelled.* Some (but not all) types of insolvency procedure terminate, automatically by operation of law alone, and without notice, agency relationships. This is the effect of a winding-up in England, but not an administration.[67] Many clearing and settlement arrangements rely on the agency of others, such as direct participants in payment systems, GCMs in CCPs, and agent banks in securities settlement systems, which may be affected by this effect of insolvency proceedings. The unfortunate consequences of terminated agency include the deemed unlawfulness of continuing to process the insolvent client's instructions, even though these are irretrievably buried in a straight-through-processing technical environment – to act notwithstanding cancellation of agency can in theory expose the agent to 'gross risk', as described in **sections 18.15** and **18.23**. Some techniques to avoid termination of agency include dealing with a client as principal, rather than agent, and creating agency coupled with an interest.[68]

(5) *Different legal persona.* When a company goes into liquidation, it may change its legal personality. It is well-established in English law that the assets in the estate of a company in liquidation are held on trust for the creditors,[69] similar to the position in a bankruptcy. This has a variety of consequences, including that dealings with the company before the liquidation began are treated as separate from those after it. Examples are that the remedies for breach by the company of its obligations after

---

64 [1975] 1 WLR 758; see box 2.1
65 *National Westminster Bank v Halesowen Presswork and Assemblies* [1972] AC 785
66 See **section 16.15**
67 *Pacific and General Insurance Co Ltd v Hazell* [1997] BCC 400, CA
68 Powers of Attorney Act 1971, s 4; Clerk v Laurie (1857) 2 H & N 199
69 *Ayerst (Inspector of Taxes) v C&K (Construction)Ltd* [1976] AC 167, HL

the liquidation began will be different (claims against a liquidator will ordinarily rank as an expense of the liquidation and are payable out of floating charge realisations);[70] there is no right of set-off in respect of pre-against post-liquidation debts;[71] and claims such as interest which accrue over time will be apportioned.[72] For suppliers who provide, and under rules designed to protect against systemic risk events are required to continue to provide,[73] services to failed financial sector firms notwithstanding the occurrence of an insolvency event, these rules complicate the business of risk management.

(6) *Service provider behaviour.* The bankers, settlement agents and other service providers to an insolvent financial firm will have their own interests to protect; it is likely that they have extended credit to their client, and will be aiming to minimise their exposure. Their instinct of self-preservation will have the effect that they will seek to exercise rights of set-off or collateral enforcement, wherever possible, and it cannot be assured that assets or cash transferred into the hands of a service provider will be processed as it would have been before the insolvency event. The problem is exacerbated if the insolvent firm was acting as a conduit for payment or delivery of assets to its own clients. For example, if the assets or cash transferred to the insolvent firm's account at its bank or custodian were intended for the account of a client the insolvent firm, the bank or custodian may nevertheless be entitled to regard them as transferred for the exclusive benefit of the insolvent firm, if it had not effectively been given notice of the third party's entitlement:[74] the transferor may thus be in a very unfortunate position of having failed to discharge an obligation to a third party and having unwittingly mitigated the credit exposure of a completely unrelated party.

(7) *Zero hour risk.* In some legal systems, an insolvency proceeding is deemed to have begun at the beginning of the day on which the judgment or order for the insolvency is issued. This legal fiction is self-evidently of retrospective effect: an action taken in full knowledge that a client is solvent and in business at 12 noon can be invalidated because of a judgment granted at 3 p.m. Where the opening of insolvency proceedings has the effect of terminating authority or introduces other legal changes to the counterparty relationship, the solvent party is at risk of being taken by surprise and discovering it has done things which were either unlawful or imprudent. It is widely, but incorrectly, thought that the SFD required Member States to repeal zero hour laws; while some have done so, the Directive merely required that 'insolvency proceedings shall not have retroactive effects on the rights and obligations of a participant arising from, or in connection with, its participation in a system from earlier than the moment of opening of such proceedings.'[75] Thus, unless Member States have gone further than strictly required by the SFD, if an insolvent firm is not a participant (or not acting as such in its dealings with a solvent person), there is still a danger that a zero hour law will continue to apply. Moreover, even in countries

---

70 Insolvency Act 1986, s 176ZA
71 Insolvency Rules 1986, r 4.90(1)
72 Insolvency Rules 1986, rr 4.92 and 4.93
73 For example, under the Banking Act 2009, s 191, or IBSARs, reg 14
74 *BCCI v Al-Saud* [1997] 1 BCLC 457; *Thomson v Clydesdale Bank* [1893] AC 282
75 Article 7, SFD

or circumstances where a zero hour law does not apply, there may be similar effects because insolvency proceedings may have immediate effect regardless of whether counterparties have notice of their inception.

Protective action will be blocked

(8) *Pull the plug risk.* A person providing clearing or settlement services to a client who becomes subject to an insolvency event will wish, at least, to consider the possibility of terminating the services. There is, as a matter of general principle, no objection to contract termination in either liquidation or administration under English law.[76] However, there are some exceptions. Other systems of insolvency law have a concept of improper contract termination or *rupture abusive*. (For example, under the French banking law a credit agreement with no fixed termination date cannot be terminated immediately without risk of liability for the bank.)[77] English law requires the continuation of certain essential supplies to an insolvent entity: water, gas, electricity and telephone services are assured under section 233 of the Insolvency Act 1986. In the case of an investment bank in special administration, the IBSARs prohibit the termination of a 'supply' – which means supply of various IT services and equipment, financial data, and access to CREST – but allow the ongoing cost of the supply (but not outstanding charges) to be an expense of the special administration.[78] If the service provider is regulated, the regulator may seek to encourage the service provider not to exercise termination rights if this is in the wider interests of the financial system – it is an obligation for FSA-regulated firms to 'observe proper standards of market conduct,'[79] a principle which could be relied on to justify regulatory pressure. In relation to operators of 'recognised inter-bank payment systems', and their service providers, the Bank of England has an express statutory power to direct the operator not terminate a participant's access to the system.[80] What is more, if the insolvent firm is a bank which has become subject to the special resolution regime, the contract which the service provider had with the client may be transferred by means of a property transfer instrument to a completely different person, and any contract term which purports to allow the service provider to terminate the contract on the grounds of change of party may be rendered ineffective.[81]

(9) *Not pulling the plug risk.* Playing Charybdis to the Scylla of *rupture abusive* is *soutien abusif*. Under English law there is no danger in continuing to provide services, or more particularly credit, to an insolvent company. It is not so simple in other legal systems. Again, to take France, there is a case-law doctrine relating to the provision of finance to a non-viable business which is likely to give a false appearance of wealth and which sustains the business artificially.[82]

---

76 *Re Olympia and York (Canary Wharf) Ltd* [1993] BCLC 453
77 Loi No 84-46 of 24 January 1984 relative à l'activité et au contrôle des établissements de crédit, art 60
78 Regulation 14
79 Financial Services Authority, *Handbook of Rules and Guidance, Principles for Businesses,* PRIN 2.1.1R Principle 3
80 Banking Act 2009, ss 191(2), 206A
81 Banking Act 2009, ss 36, 38
82 Neuville, S, *Droit de la banque et des marchés financiers* (August 2005), Presses Universitaires de France, ISBN 978-2130519577, p 300

(10) *Stay of enforcement.* If the insolvent party is subject to an administration application or has entered administration (or, if it is a 'small company',[83] has become subject to a moratorium under Schedule A1 to the Insolvency Act 1986), taking any step to enforce security will be barred unless the consent of the administrator (where appointed) or leave of the court has been obtained.[84] This rule clearly prohibits a collateral-taker from enforcing a security interest; it might apparently prohibit a custodian retaining possession under a lien, by analogy with the outcome in *Bristol Airport v Powdrill*,[85] where an airport authority's action in detaining an aircraft for non-payment of fees was held unlawful in administration. It is very difficult to predict whether leave of the court will be obtained; the leading authority is *Re Atlantic Computer Systems*;[86] the following ideas may be deduced from that case and subsequent jurisprudence.

- The primary task of the court is to consider the purpose for which the administration order has been made. In the case of a financial institution, the 'statutory' purpose is less likely to be influential than the 'commercial' purpose: an administrator is likely to be trying to maximise value for the estate by selling, very rapidly, the viable parts of the business, then entering a long phase of understanding the composition of the estate and preparing the way for a distribution.

- Leave will not be granted if it impedes the administrator in carrying out his duties, as he sees them; the court is likely to be unsympathetic to a creditor who claims to have a better view of the situation than the administrator.

- The enforcement of security over collateral might be thought not to interfere with the administrator's functions, but if the books of the insolvent firm are in disarray, or the collateral-taker's rights are in any degree unclear, some period of reconciliation and validation of the collateral-taker's rights is likely to be insisted upon by the administrator.

- Volatile or depreciating assets can be sold by agreement with the administrator and the creation of escrow arrangements relating to the proceeds: leave of the court for non-consensual enforcement is unlikely to be a normal course of action in such cases.

- Administrators may wish to preserve their rights to challenge pre-insolvency dealings and to apply the proceeds of floating charge realisation to meet administration expenses and priority creditors' claims.

- In light of all these factors, leave to enforce is likely to be a rarity.

Risk-free enforcement of collateral arrangements which constitute 'security'[87] thus requires specific statutory protection. Some other activities are also stayed in an administration, in particular making of a winding-up order,[88] repossession of goods, forfeiture of a lease of premises, institution of legal process, and appointment of an administrative receiver.[89] But the administration stay does not prohibit the exercise of set-off rights against cash balances or implementation of the enforcement mechanism of

---

83 Defined in Companies Act 2006, s 382(3)
84 Insolvency Act 1986, Sch B1, paras 43(1), 44(5); Insolvency Act 1986, Sch A1, para 12(g)
85 [1990] Ch 744, CA
86 [1992] Ch 505, CA
87 Defined in Insolvency Act 1986, s 248
88 Insolvency Act 1986, Sch B1, para 42(3)
89 Sch B1, paras 43(3), (4), (6), (6A) respectively

title transfer collateral arrangements.[90] In liquidation, there is no stay on enforcement of security, but proceedings can be stayed on application.[91]

(11) *Set-off blocked.* In some legal systems,[92] the exercise of set-off rights is considered to be detrimental to the general body of creditors, and generally prohibited once insolvency proceedings have been initiated. Under English law, by contrast, set-off of bilateral mutual debts is mandatory in liquidation[93] and, if the administrator has given notice that he intends to make a distribution to creditors, in administration.[94] Unfortunately, complex lists of exceptions may be found to the general English law principle as well. The main cases where set-off is disallowed in an English insolvency are as follows.

- Triangular or multilateral set-off rights are not mutual and will not be allowed after the mandatory insolvency set-off regime has come into effect.
- Where one party's claim is held for the benefit of another, for example there is a trust or agency relationship or a security interest is involved, again there will be a mutuality defect.
- Claims which arise or are transferred after the cut-off times specified in the Insolvency Rules 1986[95] will be rendered ineligible for set-off.
- Claims which are not provable (such as counter-indemnity rights)[96] or not expressed in monetary terms (such as an obligation to deliver up property held)[97] cannot be set off.

(12) *Loss of priority.* Secured creditors may not rank ahead of all other claimants in relation to the proceeds of successful enforcement of their security. In an English insolvency, this risk applies primarily to the holder of a 'floating charge', who ranks behind the following: (i) expenses of an administration;[98] (ii) expenses of liquidation;[99] (iii) preferential creditors;[100] and (iv) the prescribed part of the company's assets required to be set aside for unsecured creditors.[101] In other jurisdictions, similar rules may apply.

(13) *Transfers denied.* It may be desirable to transfer a customer's portfolio of assets, contracts, margin deposits and so forth to a new GCM if his existing GCM has suffered an insolvency event. A variety of legal obstacles may stand in the way of such action if the insolvent GCM has dealt with the relevant CCP and the customer on a principal-to-principal basis and/or the customer's entitlements are pooled in an omnibus account. These obstacles are discussed in **sections 14.51ff**.

(14) *Deprivation clauses.* Although this might seem a try-on, and self-evidently open to attack, a clause in a contract which provides that the property of an insolvent person is automatically transferred into the ownership of a

---

90 For the rationale, see Turing, D, 'Set-off' in Marks, D (ed), *Tolleys Insolvency Law* (looseleaf, December 2010), para S6027/2
91 Insolvency Act 1986, s 126
92 Wood, P, *Principles of International Insolvency* (2nd ed, Sweet & Maxwell, May 2007), ISBN 978 184 703 2102, para 4-002
93 Insolvency Rules 1986, r 4.90
94 Insolvency Rules 1986, r 2.85
95 Insolvency Rules 1986, rr 2.85(2) and 4.90(2)
96 *Re Fenton* [1931] 1 Ch 85
97 *Eberle's Hotels v E Jonas & Bros* (1887) 18 QBD 459
98 Insolvency Act 1986, Sch B1, para 99(3)
99 Insolvency Act 1986, s 176ZA,
100 Insolvency Act 1986, ss 40, 176, 386 and Sch 6, and Companies Act 2006, s 754
101 Insolvency Act 1986, s 176A, and Insolvency Act 1986 (Prescribed Part) Order 2003, SI 2003 No 2097

solvent person upon bankruptcy is void.[102] In practice the principle is less straightforward. Some things like security, set-off, and forfeiture of leases, would apparently violate the principle if expressed in those bald terms, so a more nuanced formulation is needed, and significant English case-law has been devoted to delineation of the boundary between what is acceptable and what is not.[103]

Past actions will be attacked

(15) *Void dispositions.* One of many tools available to an insolvency officer to protect the estate for creditors is the power to challenge transfers of the insolvent company's property which were carried out after the deemed commencement of the insolvency proceeding. In the case of a winding-up by the court, the 'commencement' is deemed to take place upon the presentation of the winding-up petition,[104] notwithstanding that the company will not formally 'go into liquidation' until the winding-up order is made, usually some weeks later.[105] So, any dispositions of a company's property after the commencement of winding-up are void, unless the sanction of the court is obtained, by virtue of section 127 of the Insolvency Act 1986. The void dispositions rule has many complex consequences for clearing and settlement, and is a more potent risk than the other, perhaps better-known, challenges available under the insolvency legislation. Under older judicial authority, *In re Gray's Inn Construction Co Ltd*,[106] it was considered that any transfer after commencement into or out of a cash account, whether or not in credit at the time, is void unless sanctioned. However, current authority from the Court of Appeal indicates that movements out of an account (whether or not overdrawn) ought not to expose the bank (as opposed to the payee) to a challenge under section 127.[107] New contracts entered into by the insolvent company should not *per se* amount to void dispositions, unless they create specifically enforceable property rights in favour of the counterparty;[108] this would be unusual in financial market transactions. The void dispositions rule is thus most likely to cause problems where cash or securities are to be delivered automatically after the petition under pre-instructed mechanisms. It may also be doubtful whether a bank can safely post a credit to an overdrawn account after notice of a winding-up petition, both on the authority of *Gray's Inn* and because the exclusion period for set-offs[109] would have begun. None of these problems arise in administrations, where section 127 does not apply.

(16) *Preference.* Section 239 of the Insolvency Act 1986 allows an administrator or liquidator to apply to the court for an order declaring a pre-insolvency transaction void on the ground that it has put the solvent counterparty in a better position than the counterparty would have had in the event of an

---

102 *Re Jeavons, ex p Mackay* (1872–3) LR 8 Ch App 643
103 *Money Markets International Stockbrokers Ltd v London Stock Exchange Ltd* [2002] 1 WLR 1150; *Belmont Park Investments PTY Limited v BNY Corporate Trustee Services Limited and Lehman Brothers Special Financing Inc* [2011] UKSC 38
104 Insolvency Act 1986, s 129
105 Insolvency Act 1986, s 247(2)
106 [1980] 1 WLR 711, CA
107 *Hollicourt (Contracts) Ltd v Bank of Ireland* [2001] Ch 555, CA
108 *Re French's Wine Bar Ltd* (1987) 3 BCC 173; *Sowman v David Samuel Trust Ltd* [1978] 1 WLR 22
109 See **section 8.9(11)**

insolvent liquidation. This type of provision is common to all developed systems of insolvency law, and is designed to enable insolvency officers to recoup prematurely-made payments by a firm approaching insolvency, as well as the creation of security or other arrangements which unfairly place one creditor in a superior position to others. Under most legal systems it is necessary to establish that the unfair transaction was actuated by an improper motive on the part of the insolvent company (as opposed to legitimate commercial need), or that the insolvent company was unable to pay its debts at the time, or both. Preference laws may be used to challenge not just payments, deliveries of property, and creation of security, but also set-off rights where the system of insolvency law does not favour such rights.

(17) *Undervalue.* Section 238 of the Insolvency Act 1986 allows an administrator or liquidator to apply to the court for an order declaring a pre-insolvency transaction void on the ground that it was 'at an undervalue', that is that the insolvent company received significantly less value than it gave. Again, this type of provision, prohibiting gratuitous transactions at a time when the company's assets ought properly to be saved for the collective benefit of the creditors, is common to all developed systems of insolvency law, and usually requires the insolvency officer to show that there was an improper motive, or insolvency at the time, or both. Gratuitous transaction challenges may apply to credit support arrangements such as guarantees or third-party security arrangements, where it is not obvious why the guarantor or surety would benefit from the arrangement, but the power may also allow any new contract to be scrutinised.

(18) *Disclaimer.* English liquidators and special administrators have a statutory power to apply to disclaim onerous property, including unprofitable contracts.[110] The historical reason for this draconian power is to deal with the English law real property rule which provided trustees in bankruptcy with no mechanism to escape personal liability for burdensome covenants attached to land which had vested in them personally by virtue of their office. The power extends much more widely than land, and contracts pertaining to land, although the preponderance of uses of the power and associated case-law continues to relate to leases with repairing covenants. Much difficulty is caused by the concept of an 'unprofitable contract', as this could (if widely interpreted) include agreements which do not qualify for challenge as transactions at an undervalue, simply on the ground that the circumstances had not worked out to the favour of the now-insolvent party. Yet this type of 'unfortunate bargain' challenge is not permitted.[111] The reasons why liquidators rarely need to resort to the power are threefold: first, a contract is unprofitable only if, in addition to lack of reciprocal benefit, it gives rise to prospective liabilities and/or will delay the winding-up or incur irrecoverable expense;[112] secondly, the counterparty against whom a disclaimer is exercised is given a statutory right to claim in the liquidation for damages for his loss,[113] which means that the burden on the estate may not be lifted after all; and thirdly, the liquidator can probably achieve the same ends by using the power first described above, that is, by doing nothing at all.

---

110   Insolvency Act 1986, s 178; IBSARs, reg 15(4) and Table 2
111   *Squires v AIG Europe (UK) Ltd* [2006] EWCA Civ 7
112   *Squires v AIG Europe (UK) Ltd*; see also *Transmetro Corporation v Real Investments Pty Ltd* (1999) 17 ACLC 1314
113   Insolvency Act 1986, s 178(6)

(19) *Unregistered security interest.* Under section 874 of the Companies Act 2006, if section 860 of that Act applies to a charge, that charge is void against a liquidator, administrator or creditor of the company unless the charge has been registered at Companies House. Certain exemptions to the requirement for registration apply: notably, charges created by foreign companies[114] and cases where the Financial Collateral Arrangements Regulations apply.[115]

The notion that a blanket requirement to register charges might be too harsh, and needs specific statutory disapplication in relation to financial markets activity, introduces the next section, which describes the various entrenchments and counter-measures which are available to providers of clearing and settlement services against this rather formidable arsenal.

The fear of adverse action by insolvency officers may destabilise clearing and settlement arrangements. The powers described above may, in theory, be available to disrupt the traditional tools of counterparty risk management, in particular the taking and application of collateral, the exercise of set-off rights, multilateral netting arrangements, and the termination of services. Consequently the law may allow for a protective shield against insolvency challenge to be deployed by a market infrastructure.

DEFENCES – PART VII

8.10 Part VII of the Companies Act 1989 is the prototype for protective legislation in the United Kingdom, designed to neutralise the principal threats caused by an insolvency procedure in relation to a person who is party to a 'market contract'. Although Part VII operates by disapplying various insolvency rules which may threaten the handling of default scenarios by infrastructures, it is built upon a somewhat narrow foundation: an understanding of the limits of Part VII thus requires a structural outline.

To whom Part VII applies

8.11 To begin with, the objective of Part VII is to protect 'recognised investment exchanges' and 'recognised clearing houses'. The focus is perhaps old-fashioned: thinking of *trading* infrastructures as the centre of risk management, rather than *post-trade* bodies. Managing market risk remains important, but high-profile market participant failures can induce counterparty- and credit-risk-related disruption to the financial system, as demonstrated by the 2008 failure of Lehman Brothers. Post-trade risk management, which looks to the operational, credit, and counterparty risk elements of a transaction, is vital. Recognised investment exchanges may be involved in both the market risk and post-trade risk factors in this equation, because in some cases they may take care of post-trade processing. But, in relation to insolvency-risk defence, the 'recognised clearing house' is far more important. This is because a recognised clearing house may be a CCP or a securities settlement system operator.

---

114 Overseas Companies (Execution of Documents and Registration of Charges) (Amendment) Regulations 2011, SI 2011 No 2194, reg 2(3), repealing the material parts of the Overseas Companies (Execution of Documents and Registration of Charges) Regulations 2009, SI 2009 No 1917
115 Financial Collateral Arrangements (No 2) Regulations 2003, SI 2003 No 3226; **see section 8.27**

It may be noted that a clearing house may be 'recognised' even if it is incorporated or formed in another jurisdiction. Furthermore, Part VII can be applied by regulations to overseas CCPs which have not obtained recognised overseas clearing house status at all,[116] which may be useful to protect such a CCP in relation to participation by United Kingdom participants; but it would appear that no regulations have yet been made for this purpose.

Part VII applies to 'market contracts'. These are defined in section 155 of the Companies Act 1989. As far as recognised clearing houses are concerned, market contracts are: '(a) contracts entered into by the clearing house, in its capacity as such, with a member of the clearing house … for the purpose of enabling the rights and liabilities of that member … under a transaction to be settled; and (b) contracts entered into by the clearing house with a member of the clearing house … for the purpose of providing central counterparty clearing services to that member … ' 'Central counterparty clearing services' is defined as services provided 'to the parties to a transaction in connection with contracts between each of the parties and … the clearing house (in place of, or as an alternative to, a contract directly between the parties).' Section 155 makes similar provisions for recognised investment exchanges, and also envisages that recognised clearing houses may have contracts with recognised investment exchanges or other recognised clearing houses, and treats those as market contracts as well.

At the centre of Part VII, therefore, is the 'recognised clearing house' and the 'recognised investment exchange'. A contract cannot (subject to the section 301 exception for listed contracts described in **section 8.17**) be protected by Part VII from the depredations of insolvency officers unless it is entered into with or on a recognised clearing house or recognised investment exchange. These 'recognised bodies' encompass much, but not all, of the trading, clearing and settlement infrastructure. The function of a recognised investment exchange is reasonably easy to discern from the label: it is, essentially, a 'regulated market' within the meaning of MiFID[117] – notwithstanding that perhaps officially recognised exchanges are somewhat anomalous creatures since MiFID eroded many of the qualities which made national or regional stock exchanges special.[118] The function of a recognised clearing house is rather more diffuse, as the term encompasses both CCPs and CSDs.[119] However, multilateral trading facilities under MiFID are not recognised bodies, nor are payment systems.

Default rules and protection of default action

8.12 Both types of recognised body must comply with the Financial Services and Markets Act 2000 (Recognition Requirements for Investment Exchanges and Clearing Houses) Regulations 2001 (RRRs).[120] Part II (for

---

116 Companies Act 1989, s 170
117 Directive 2004/39/EC of the European Parliament and of the Council of 21 April 2004 on markets in financial instruments, etc
118 See, for example, Gomber, P, et al, 'Regulation and Technology in Equity Trading – The Impact of Regulatory and Technological Changes on Order Execution and the Trading Venue Landscape in Europe', in Engelen, P-J, and Lannoo, K (eds), *Facing New Regulatory Frameworks in Securities Trading in Europe* (Intersentia, March 2010), ISBN 978-90-5095-973-5, pp 44ff
119 See **section 11.15**
120 2001 SI No 995

exchanges) and Part IV (for clearing houses) of the Schedule to the RRRs require that the recognised body must have *default rules* making provision for the following:

- Action to be taken (specifically, in the case of a clearing house, close-out) in respect of unsettled market contracts to which a member who is, or may be, unable to meet his obligations, is a party;
- The discharge of all the rights and obligations of the defaulter in respect of unsettled market contracts (a *defaulter* being a person against whom a recognised body has taken action under its default rules[121]); and
- The calculation of a net sum due to or from the defaulter in respect of those market contracts.

The scheme of Part VII is to protect this process, of close-out, discharge and reaching of a net sum, from attack by insolvency officers who have taken control of the defaulter. This objective is achieved by section 158(1) of the Companies Act 1989, which states: 'The general law of insolvency has effect in relation to market contracts, and action taken under the rules of a recognised investment exchange or recognised clearing house with respect to such contracts, subject to the provisions of sections 159 to 165.' The language used is curious, but if read with the emphasis on *subject to the provisions of sections 159 to 165* its sense becomes clear: the general law of insolvency must give way to what is set out in the following sections.

Accordingly, once the recognised body initiates default action, section 159 of the Companies Act 1989 provides a general and almost comprehensive immunity from insolvency attack. Section 159 says:

'None of the following shall be regarded as to any extent invalid at law on the ground of inconsistency with the law relating to the distribution of the assets of a person on bankruptcy, winding up or sequestration or in the administration of a company or other body or in the administration of an insolvent estate –

(a) a market contract,
(b) the default rules of a recognised investment exchange or recognised clearing house,
(c) the rules of a recognised investment exchange or recognised clearing house as to the settlement of market contracts not dealt with under its default rules.'

Default rules are accorded a quasi-legislative status, and thus the default rules cannot be changed without prior notification to the regulator.[122]

Margin

8.13   Furthermore, additional protections are given in respect of margin, where it is provided under a 'market charge'. A market charge in favour of a recognised clearing house is a charge for the purpose of securing debts or liabilities arising in connection with ensuring the performance of market contracts.[123] In similar fashion to the protection given to market contracts, market charges are rendered immune from insolvency challenge by sections

---

121 Companies Act 1989, s 188(2)
122 Companies Act 1989, s 157
123 Companies Act 1989, s 173

174 and 175 of the Companies Act 1989: 'The general law of insolvency has effect in relation to market charges and action taken in enforcing them subject to the provisions of section 175.' Section 175 sets out a collection of specific disapplications of the Insolvency Act 1986.

Finally, in respect of 'margin', as distinct from market charges, section 177 of the Companies Act 1989 provides a degree of protection to a recognised clearing house against unknown third party interests in the property provided as margin. As regards property provided as margin or a default fund contribution, prior equitable interests (including rights and remedies arising from breach of fiduciary duty) of which the CCP has no notice do not bind the CCP.[124] Market charges which are floating charges also take priority over subsequent fixed charges and vendors' liens, and property delivered under market contracts, subject to market charges or contributed to a default fund cannot be attached in execution of judgments.[125]

The following supplementary points of interpretation may arise in relation to margin and market charges:

(1)   'Margin' is not helpfully defined: section 190(3) of the Companies Act 1989 says merely that margin and cover for margin have the same meaning. It may be argued that historically 'margin' meant the difference between one price and another, and 'cover' meant the collateral posted to bridge that difference. The rules of LCH.Clearnet Ltd use the word 'cover' to mean margin.[126]

(2)   It is not clear why the draftsman deals with margin and market charges as if they were separate concepts. Presumably 'margin' is wider, in that cash margin which is not in the ownership of the defaulter, is included in that concept, and charged property in which the defaulter retains an interest could be open to different challenges, requiring additional specific protections to be provided in section 175.

(3)   There are some vestigial provisions in the legislation dealing with market charges, which can be ignored: those relating to 'short term certificates' on the London Stock Exchange would no longer appear to be relevant since the TALISMAN settlement system was withdrawn in 1997, and are not summarised here; likewise provisions referring to liabilities relating to settlement of gilts in the Central Gilts Office, a function transferred to CREST in 2000.

Review of Part VII

8.14   In case the general principle were not clear enough, various statutory provisions of the Insolvency Act[127] are then specifically disapplied in relation to default action and market charges. When the protections afforded by Part VII are tested against the range of challenges potentially available to insolvency officers, the broad conclusion is that the shield is good, but not perfect. One further defect is that the immunity granted against foreign insolvency officers is weaker than it should be: the draftsman seems not to have imagined that foreign insolvency officers might have powers going wider than those of an English insolvency office-holder.

---

124   Companies Act 1989, s 177
125   Companies Act 1989, ss 178–180
126   LCH.Clearnet, *General Regulations* (May 2012), Definitions
127   Sections 43, 127, 284; Sch B1 paras 41(2), 43(2) and (3), 70–72

8.15 So, to summarise: the default rules, market charges, and action taken under default rules by a recognised body in relation to market contracts are generally protected. Many clearing and settlement activities might, however, not fall within the scope of those protections. The following is a non-exhaustive list:

(1) *Payments*. Payment systems such as ACHs are not 'recognised clearing houses' under the Financial Services and Markets Act 2000 (FSMA). Protection for these entities has to be sought elsewhere, typically through the settlement finality legislation considered below. Payments made to or by a recognised clearing house can, however, receive protection under Part VII. Furthermore, there is the possibility of protection under section 301 of FSMA, or section 172 of the Companies Act 1989, though these options appear to be in desuetude.[128]

(2) *OTC and platform-based trading*. After the collapse of Lehman Brothers, it became a matter of contention that transactions carried out outside organised market-places and not cleared through a CCP had no orderly mechanism for their close-out or settlement.[129] While a settlement system might (as in the case of CREST) be a recognised clearing house, its rules do not apply to the pre-settlement phase of transaction's life-cycle. Netting agreements to achieve certainty of outcome in the event of a counterparty's default, in the off-exchange cash equities trading world such agreements were formerly uncommon, though an optional close-out protocol is now in place.[130] Trading platforms which are neither recognised investment exchanges nor cleared through a CCP (which may include some MTFs and OTFs) may have the same problem. Even if a netting agreement is used, some of the attacks against which Part VII would provide a defence may be viable.

(3) *Non-clearing members' and end-investors' positions*. Not everyone is protected even if Part VII does, *prima facie*, apply. The protections described above start with the market contract – that is, the contract involving a *member* of the clearing house or investment exchange. Where the protection is sought by virtue of membership of a clearing house, the clearing house must be a party to the contract; where it is sought by virtue of membership of an exchange, the contract must have been entered into on the exchange or under the rules of the exchange, or the exchange must be a party. Clients of the members may be left outside the circle of protection if their broker or clearer fails, because their contracts may not be 'market' contracts.

(4) *Transactions settled outside the United Kingdom*. The protection afforded by Part VII may operate outside the United Kingdom, by virtue of the EU Insolvency Regulation or Winding-up Directives.[131] This will be helpful particularly in the case of default by an overseas participant in a British clearing or settlement system. However, it is less probable that a foreign CSD would be a recognised (overseas) clearing house. The consequence will be that the participation by British market participants in an overseas settlement system will not be protected by Part VII, although there may be local equivalent protection.

---

128 See section 8.17
129 Investment Management Association, *Problems Revealed by the Lehman Collapse* (December 2008), http://www.investmentuk.org/assets/files/press/2008/20081205-01.pdf
130 Association for Financial Markets in Europe, *OTC Cash Equity Trades – Default Protocol* (September 2010), http://www.afme.eu/WorkArea//DownloadAsset.aspx?id=239
131 See **section 8.31**

Table 8.2   Protection against insolvency challenges

Scope / Challenges	Part VII Companies Act 1989[128]	Settlement Finality Regulations[129]	Financial Collateral Regulations[130]	Comment
	Market contracts Margin Market charges	Transfer orders Collateral security charges	Financial collateral arrangements	
Set-off disallowed for obligations entered into at time of insolvency	Protected, subject to handover of the value of any profit from market contract entered into after notice of proceedings[131]	Protected, subject to general proviso that transfer order is carried out on the same day and without notice of insolvency proceedings[132]	Protected if unaware of insolvency proceedings[133]	Despite updating amendments, FCRs unfortunately still cross-refer to out-of-date sub-rules 2.85(4) and 4.90(3) of the Insolvency Rules 1986
Void disposition rule	Protected, subject to handover of profit if market contract entered into or margin accepted after notice of proceedings[134]	Protected, subject to general proviso as regards same-day execution of transfer orders[135]	Full protection[136]	All protections apply to deliveries of collateral; also Part VII applies to market contracts and SFRs apply to transfer orders

132   See sections 8.10–8.16
133   See sections 8.18 – 8.24
134   See sections 8.25 – 8.29
135   Section 163(4)
136   Regulations 12, 20
137   Regulation 12
138   Sections 164, 175
139   Regulations 16, 19
140   Regulation 10
141   Section 175
142   Regulation 19
143   Regulation 8

	Part VII Companies Act 1989[128]	Settlement Finality Regulations[129]	Financial Collateral Regulations[130]	
Moratorium on security enforcement	Protected, subject to rights of prior or equal charge[137]	Protected, subject to rights of prior or equal chargee[138]	Full protection[139]	Protections also apply to insolvency officers' powers to sell charged property
Loss of priority to insolvency expenses, preferential creditors etc	No protection	Protected[140]	Protected[141]	FCRs do not protect against liquidation expenses taking priority in some cases
Preference and undervalue	Full protection[142]	Protected, subject to general proviso as regards same-day execution of transfer orders[143]	No protection	Part VII protects 'margin' but not 'market charges' from these challenges
Voidable floating charges	No protection	Protected[144]	Full protection[145]	
Disclaimer and rescission of property and contracts	Full protection[146]	Protected, subject to general proviso as regards same-day execution of transfer orders[147]	Protected against disclaimer[148] but not rescission	

144 Regulation 14
145 Regulations 8, 10
146 Section 165
147 Regulation 17
148 Regulation 16
149 Regulation 10
150 Section 164
151 Regulation 16
152 Regulation 10

(5) *Insolvency of the CCP itself.* While Part VII has since 2009[153] been modified so as to enable the protections of Part VII to apply in the event of insolvency of a recognised clearing house, the principal manner in which the protections work – namely, to immunise the operation of the default rules of the CCP from insolvency attack – is irrelevant to the insolvency of the clearing house unless its default rules cater for its own insolvency, which is not commonly, indeed if ever, the case.

8.16 In addition, the following technical insolvency issues are not provided for by dint of protection of market contracts *per se*:

(1) *Special Resolution Regimes.* The special resolution regime for banks under the Banking Act 2009 is designed to come into play before a formal insolvency proceeding starts. Part VII contains no protection against the powers given to the authorities under the special resolution regimes. The special resolution regimes are limited in that a 'partial property transfer order' may not have the effect of modifying or rendering unenforceable a market contract, the default rules of a recognised body, or other rules of a recognised body as to the settlement of market contracts;[154] but partial property transfers are not the only possible threat to the integrity of clearing and settlement posed by the regimes.

(2) *Foreign insolvency attack.* As mentioned above, the protections granted by Part VII do not cater for foreign insolvency officers' powers very thoroughly. Part VII does contain a useful provision, section 183 of the Companies Act 1989, which prevents a United Kingdom court from recognising or giving effect to an 'act [which] would be prohibited in the case of … a relevant office-holder by provisions made by or under this Part.'[155] This wording invites the question whether foreign insolvency officers seeking to assert powers which are not explicitly disapplied by Part VII can be blocked, a question considered further at **section 8.32(5)**.

(3) *Transfer of positions and collateral.* Finally, the difficulties with transfer of positions and collateral should not be under-estimated. These are studied further in **sections 14.51ff**.

Section 301 – Listed Contracts

8.17 Under section 301 of FSMA, Part VII may be extended by regulations to apply to 'relevant contracts', that is to say 'contracts of a prescribed description in relation to which the settlement arrangements are provided by a person for the time being included in a list maintained by the Bank of England.'[156] There are currently no such regulations or list in force, but the section (in its previous incarnation as section 171 of the Companies Act 1989) had a brief burst of glory in the 1990s, described below. Section 172 of the Companies Act 1989, which allows extension of Part VII to 'contracts of a specified description in relation to which settlement arrangements are provided by the Bank of England,' has not been used.

---

153 Financial Markets and Insolvency Regulations 2009, SI 2009 No 853
154 Banking Act (Restriction of Partial Property Transfers) Order 2009, SI 2009 No 322, art 7
155 Companies Act 1989, s 183(2)
156 FSMA, s 301(2), as modified by the Financial Services Act 2012, s 32 and Sch 8, para 22

Section 171/section 301 was used to provide a protective regime for a CCP established for the purposes of managing counterparty risk arising in relation to foreign exchange contracts. The CCP was called Exchange Clearing House Limited (ECHO). Under the Financial Markets and Insolvency (Money Market) Regulations 1995,[157] 'money market contracts', being contracts for the acquisition or disposal of currency of the United Kingdom or of any other country or territory or the Ecu,[158] became relevant contracts for the purposes of section 171. The regulations provided for listed persons to be regulated by the Bank of England, under a regime which broadly followed the RRRs. Protection was given to action taken under default rules of a listed person, and 'money market charges' were also protected from attack in the same way as market charges under Part VII. Notwithstanding that ECHO was a CCP, the emphasis, as with Part VII, was on action taken to 'settle' money market contracts. The preamble to the regulations states: 'Whereas the Treasury and the Secretary of State are satisfied that, having regard to the extent to which the contracts described in these Regulations as "money market contracts" are of a kind dealt in by persons supervised by the Bank of England, it is appropriate that settlement arrangements in relation to those contracts should be subject to the supervision of the Bank of England...'

ECHO was removed from the FSA's list on 13 May 1999 at its own request, having been acquired by CLS Services Limited and wound down its operations.[159] The closure of a system intended to reduce pre-settlement counterparty risk as a result of introducing a new system designed to reduce settlement risk is of questionable logic, but may be explained as a result of regulatory policy having been directed for many years at settlement risk in particular in the FX market;[160] ECHO may, in that context, be seen as a netting mechanism designed to reduce exposure size rather than (as with other CCPs) a device for management of pre-settlement risk. Since the 1990s, the importance of CCPs as managers of pre-settlement risk has been recognised, yet protection of 'settlement' continues to be the mantra which CCPs have to call upon to obtain the shield they need.

DEFENCES – SETTLEMENT FINALITY

8.18   It may be thought curious that CREST, the United Kingdom's securities settlement system, is regulated and receives insolvency protection under Part VII as a 'recognised clearing house', an appellation more suited to a CCP or an ACH (of which CREST is neither). The principal European-law-based source of insolvency protection, is, by contrast to Part VII, designed to protect payment and securities settlement systems rather than CCPs and recognised investment

---

157 1995 SI No 2049 (revoked under the Financial Services and Markets Act 2000 (Consequential Amendments and Repeals) Order 2001, SI 2001 No 3649)
158 See the Financial Markets and Insolvency (Ecu Contracts) Regulations 1998, SI 1998 No 27
159 Financial Services Authority, Press Release FSA/PN/046/1999 (May 1999), http://www.fsa. gov.uk/Pages/Library/Communication?PR?1999/046.shtml
160 See Bank for International Payments Committee on Payment and Settlement Systems, *Settlement Risk in Foreign Exchange Transactions* (the Allsopp Report) (March 1996), http://www.bis.org/publ/cpss17.pdf

exchanges. This is the Settlement Finality Directive (SFD),[161] and it at least equals Part VII in its eccentricity of application.

This is because the 'principal objectives' of the SFD, as originally stated, were:

> 'to reduce legal risks associated with participation in payment systems … in particular as regards the legal validity of netting agreements and the enforceability of collateral security; to ensure that in the Internal Market payments may be made free of impediments … by taking into account collateral constituted for monetary policy purposes, to contribute to developing the necessary legal framework in which the future European Central Bank may develop its monetary policy.'[162]

During its legislative passage, the draft SFD was expanded so as to cover participation in securities settlement systems as well as payment systems, and after it was transposed into member state law, the seekers of status of 'designated system' have included not only payment and settlement systems but also CCPs. In the United Kingdom, LCH.Clearnet Ltd, ICE Clear Europe and EuroCCP are both designated as 'systems', as for example are LCH.Clearnet SA in France and EMCF in the Netherlands, with a similar pattern all across Europe.[163] The reason for this curious expansion of scope is that the SFD is the main provider at European level of protection for infrastructures against insolvency risk. The expansion was recognised in modifications made to the SFD in 2009, which explicitly recognise that CCPs may be system operators.[164]

Given that background, it may be appropriate both to examine the substance of the SFD's protection and its transposition, but also to examine whether indeed the SFD is capable of providing adequate protection to the unexpectedly wide range of infrastructures claiming to be 'systems'.

To whom the SFD applies

8.19   The starting-point in an assessment of the SFD is that it applies to 'designated systems', their participants, and collateral security provided in connection with participation in a system or the operations of central banks and the ECB.[165] Central to the SFD, therefore, is the question who is a designated system; the scattered definitions in article 2 of the SFD set out the parameters.

- A system must have at least three (or, if warranted on systemic risk grounds, two) participants, not counting the system operator itself.

- The system must have common rules and standardised arrangements for clearing or execution of 'transfer orders' between participants.

- The system must be governed by the law of a member state in which at least one participant's head office is located.

---

161 Directive 98/26/EC of the European Parliament and of the Council of 19 May 1998 on settlement finality in payment and securities settlement systems

162 European Commission, *Proposal for a European Parliament and Council Directive on Settlement Finality and Collateral Security* (May 1996), http://eur-lex.europa.eu/LexUriServ/LexUriServ.do?uri=COM:1996:0193:FIN:EN:PDF, COM(96) 193 final

163 See the European Commission list at http://ec.europa.eu/internal_market/financial-markets/settlement/dir-98-26-art10-national_en.htm

164 Directive 2009/44/EC of the European Parliament and of the Council of 6 May 2009 amending Directive 98/26/EC on settlement finality, etc

165 SFD, art 1

- If warranted on systemic risk grounds, securities settlement systems may to a limited extent execute orders relating to other financial instruments.

However, this is not quite it: a system only qualifies for designation if it is for clearing or execution of transfer orders between participants: clearing and settlement of things other than 'transfer orders', and membership of persons who do not qualify as 'participants', would be fatal to the system's eligibility for designation, and thus to obtaining insolvency protections. Transfer orders are defined in article 2(i) as:

> 'any instruction by a participant to place at the disposal of a recipient an amount of money by means of a book entry on the accounts of a credit institution, a central bank, a central counterparty or a settlement agent, or any instruction which results in the assumption or discharge of a payment obligation as defined by the rules of the system, or an instruction by a participant to transfer the title to, or interest in, a security or securities by means of a book entry on a register, or otherwise.'

Evidently transfer orders are payment or securities settlement instructions; but in the United Kingdom a more expansive interpretation has been adopted, which includes a transaction creating obligations to transfer securities or cash as well as instructions intended to bring about the discharge of such obligations.[166] As to 'participants', these are limited to credit institutions, investment firms, public authorities and publicly guaranteed undertakings, non-EEA undertakings corresponding to credit institutions and investment firms, CCPs, settlement agents, clearing houses and system operators.[167] Indirect participants (any of the foregoing, which has a contractual relationship with a participant in a system which allows the indirect participant to pass transfer orders through the system)[168] may be considered participants if justified on the grounds of systemic risk.[169] So, designation would not be open to a system which admitted non-financial firms, payment institutions or insurers into its membership. (This makes the position of CREST and CSDs in beneficial owner markets[170] confusing: these securities settlement systems provide accounts for ordinary investors who do not fall into these special regulatory categories. Presumably a distinction is to be drawn between the account-operators, who do need regulatory licences in order to carry out movements on the accounts and thus to participate in the *settlement* system, and the account-holders, who do not need licences in order to participate in the *holding* system. Were it otherwise, CREST and beneficial owner market CSDs could not obtain SFD designation.)

8.20 Member states are responsible for designation of systems. Once designated, the insolvency protections described below will apply to the system and its participants:

- Transfer orders and netting will be enforceable and binding on third parties, even in the event of insolvency proceedings against a participant, subject to

---

166 See Turing, D, 'Implementation of the Settlement Finality Directive in England' in Vereecken, M, and Nijenhuis, A, eds, *Settlement Finality in the European Union* (Kluwer, April 2003), ISBN 90 130 048 73, pp 120–121
167 SFD, art 2(f)
168 SFD, art 2(g)
169 SFD, art 2(f)
170 See **section 6.39(1)**

provisos concerning transfer orders not entered into the system before the moment of opening of the insolvency proceedings.[171]

- Funds or securities on a participant's account can be used to settle obligations of the participant on the day of opening of insolvency proceedings.[172]

- Transfer orders cannot be revoked by a participant or a third party after the moment defined by the rules of the system.[173]

- Insolvency proceedings may not have retroactive effects on the rights and obligations of participants before the moment of opening of insolvency proceedings.[174]

- The rights of a participant (a term which includes the system operator) to collateral security are not to be affected by insolvency proceedings.[175]

8.21 Some comments may usefully be made at this point:

(1) These protections are not comprehensive, even for payment and securities settlement systems, against the range of insolvency attacks listed above. That said, the principal risks confronted by a settlement system in the insolvency of a participant (voidness of settlement instructions or of transfers of securities or cash, *British Eagle* risk, and a stay on enforcement of collateral) are largely addressed by the SFD. The weaknesses as regards systems which are CCPs are discussed in more detail below.

(2) Where transfer orders result from securities trades which have a T+2 or longer settlement cycle, the ability to use funds or securities on an account for one day is of limited value.

(3) The prohibition against 'revocation' of transfer orders is a false friend. Finality, in the sense that no risk of being asked to give back what I think I have received can arise, may be jeopardised by a number of issues: revocation, conditionality, reversal under the rules of the system, and insolvency challenge.[176]

(4) Settlement finality does not guarantee that settlement will occur. The distinction between *finality* of settlement and *certainty* of settlement cannot be sufficiently emphasised. Finality occurs when there is no danger of reversal of the settlement; certainty is that the trade will, come what may, actually settle so that my securities are replaced with your cash (or vice versa). Delivery-versus-payment (DvP) techniques[177] are designed to eliminate settlement risk: that is, to ensure you are never left having parted with your securities without having received your cash (or vice versa). But DvP does not guarantee that the transaction will settle. As the Lehman insolvency revealed – with 142,000 failed trades globally relating to Lehman Brothers International (Europe)[178] – an unsettled transaction can leave trading

---

171 SFD, art 3
172 SFD, art 4
173 SFD, art 5
174 SFD, art 7
175 SFD, art 9(1)
176 See Turing, D, and Cramb, E, *Managing Risk in Financial Firms* (Tottel, March 2009), ISBN 978-1-84766-3030-0, pp 221–223
177 See **section 15.3**
178 PricewaterhouseCoopers, *Lehman Brothers International (Europe) (in administration) ('LBIE'), Unsettled Trades – Market Update* (November 2008), http://www.pwc.co.uk/pdf/LBIE_Failed_trades_Update_7_Nov_2008.pdf

parties in almost as perilous a position as if DvP does not work.[179] The SFD prevents unwinding of settlements which do occur. But they do not force operators of settlement systems to ensure that settlements will take place, even if both trading parties are able to settle, let alone when one is insolvent. The SFD is therefore of no help in assuring certainty of settlement. Certainty of settlement appears to be an objective of the RRRs, but one which is not carried into practice, as demonstrated by the case of Lehman Brothers. The CREST system is a recognised clearing house; yet, notwithstanding the RRRs, it took several weeks to deal with unsettled OTC market contracts, and then they were deleted from the CREST system rather than settled.[180]

(5) The SFD provides no protection in respect of anything other than 'transfer orders' and 'collateral security' (which secures obligations arising in connection with a 'system', which is defined by reference to transfer orders, and obligations owed to central banks). Since transfer orders are only payment instructions and 'securities' transfer instructions, the handling of other types of obligation is not capable of being protected.[181]

(6) The SFD does not help a participant in relation to the insolvency of its client, unless the client has been accorded the status of 'indirect participant'.[182]

UK implementation of the SFD

8.22 By contrast with the five protections contemplated by the SFD itself, the transposition into United Kingdom law is much more extensive. The Settlement Finality Regulations (SFRs)[183] follow the same logical structure as Part VII. As with the SFD, the starting point is the designated system; a designated system is required to have default arrangements as a condition for becoming designated;[184] the general law of insolvency has effect in relation to transfer orders and collateral security, subject to a list of overrides;[185] and the overrides specify that none of the following shall be regarded as invalid on grounds of inconsistency with insolvency law: a transfer order, the default arrangements of a designated system, the rules of a designated system as to the settlement of transfer orders not dealt with under the default arrangements, or contracts for realising collateral security.[186]

As with Part VII, some enumerated provisions of insolvency law are specifically disapplied as regards transfer orders and collateral security, in some cases subject to provisos. There is a general proviso, that the whole range of protections is disapplied in relation to a transfer order entered into a designated system after an insolvency order has been made, unless the transfer order is

---

179 Investment Management Association, *Problems Revealed by the Lehman Collapse* (December 2008), http://www.investmentuk.org/assets/files/press/2008/20081205-01.pdf

180 PricewaterhouseCoopers, *Lehman Brothers International (Europe) (in administration), Unsettled OTC Trades – Update* (October 2008), http://www.pwc.co.uk/eng/issues/lehman_otctrades_update_081008.html; see **section 15.16**

181 See **section 8.23(1)**

182 See **sections 2.42** and **16.7**

183 Financial Markets and Insolvency (Settlement Finality) Regulations 1999, SI 1999 No 2979

184 SFRs, Schedule, para 6

185 SFRs, reg 13(1)

186 SFRs, reg 14(1)

carried out on the same date as the insolvency event, and the system operator did not have notice of the event at the time of settlement.[187]

For insolvency challenges of foreign origin, regulation 25(2) of the SFRs follows the clumsy formula of section 183 of the Companies Act 1989, precluding acts which 'would be prohibited ... by this Part' in the case of an insolvency office-holder appointed in the United Kingdom. However, as regards attacks which are not known to domestic law, regulation 14(1) expressly states that the protected arrangements (transfer orders, default arrangements, rules, etc) cannot be regarded as invalid on the ground of inconsistency with the law relating to insolvency proceedings of a country or territory outside the United Kingdom.

Evaluation of the SFD protection for CCPs

8.23 The list of specific statutory disapplications is longer in the case of the SFRs than in the case of Part VII. That implies that the protection may be better. There is, however, some difficulty in the application of the SFRs, and indeed the SFD, to CCPs. From a European perspective it should be borne in mind that there is no other protective legislation, like Part VII, of pan-European scope. CCPs across Europe are now expected to rely on the SFD to provide a shield against insolvency attack: indeed article 17(4) of EMIR[188] states that a competent authority of a CCP may not authorise the CCP unless it is designated under the SFD. CCPs may need to exercise the following powers, in the event of a participant's failure: to close out the participant's open contracts; to set off what is due to and from the CCP to the failed participant; to apply cash and securities collateral; and to transfer open positions and margin balances attributable to the failed participant's clients to a replacement participant. Coupled with the Financial Collateral Directive,[189] the SFD may provide a useful, but ultimately incomplete set of protections.[190]

In this regard, one might make the following comments:

(1) A CCP which clears physically-settled commodity transactions may need to make a case to be eligible for designation. To be eligible, a CCP must clear or execute 'transfer orders',[191] which can be either payment orders or securities transfer instructions.[192] For the purposes of the SFD, 'securities' has a very wide definition, embracing all financial instruments in Section C of Annex I to MiFID.[193] This expressly includes 'futures' and cash-settled derivative products. Equities CCPs and CCPs which clear only cash-settled derivative products should thus be eligible for designation. Physically-settled commodity transactions which are not traded on regulated markets or MTFs are not automatically in the MiFID list, but if they are 'not for commercial

187 SFRs, reg 20
188 Regulation (EU) No 648/2012 of the European Parliament and of the Council of 4 July 2012 on OTC derivatives, central counterparties and trade repositories
189 Directive 2002/47/EC of the European Parliament and of the Council of 6 June 2002 on financial collateral arrangements; see **section 8.25**
190 Bliss, R, and Papathanassiou, C, *Derivatives clearing, central counterparties and novation: The economic implications* (March 2006), http://www.ecb.int/events/pdf/conferences/ccp/BlissPapathanassiou_final.pdf, pp 25–28
191 SFD, art 2(a), first indent
192 SFD, art 2(i)
193 SFD, art 2(h)

purposes' and have the characteristics of other derivative instruments they are included; and one of these characteristics is that they are cleared through recognised clearing houses. So, on the whole, CCPs which clear commodity transactions should be eligible. In any event, it is not fatal that the system executes orders relating to 'other' financial instruments, such as out-of-scope commodity transactions, but designation is allowed only if the system (i) executes securities transfer orders; (ii) executes orders relating to the other financial instruments 'to a limited extent'; and (iii) then only if designation is warranted on grounds of systemic risk.[194]

(2) The general proviso, alluded to in **section 8.22**, is problematic. The insolvency protection conferred on transfer orders does not apply in relation to transfer orders entered into the designated system after the opening of insolvency proceedings, unless 'the transfer order is carried out on the same business day of the designated system that the [insolvency] event occurs.'[195] The application of the concept of 'carrying out' transfer orders to a CCP is, to express it mildly, uncertain. With a settlement system proper one can see exactly what is being got at: settlement, in the sense of transferring cash or securities from the transferor's account to the transferee. But a CCP does not do this. The CCP manages *pre-settlement* counterparty risk. Certainly, the CCP wishes to receive cash or securities at the settlement date for each cleared transaction, and insofar as the date of default is the settlement day then this protection will be useful. But if the transaction is not mature yet on the date of the insolvency event, and the CCP is taking close-out action by entering into neutralising transactions for the account of its defaulting participant, it is hard to characterise its action as 'carrying out a transfer order'. Furthermore, the default management process may take much longer than one day.

(3) Insolvency rules may forbid the termination of contracts or the creation of new obligations (ie, booking transactions opposite in sense to existing open positions) for the account of the defaulter. It is not clear that the SFD or SFRs protect these actions against attack. These actions might involve the cancellation of transfer orders or the creation of new ones, neither of which is contemplated by the SFD or SFRs. However, insofar as the insolvency attack is based on void disposition rules, the SFRs are probably sound enough. CCPs in countries which have not taken the blanket approach of regulation 12 of the SFRs, so that any action taken under the default arrangements of a designated system are immune from insolvency attacks of any nature, may have more trouble.

(4) Transfer of client positions which requires consent of a third party, or any interference in rights in rem, will require more explicit statutory treatment than is afforded by the SFD or SFRs.

8.24 Yet perhaps the key point on all these protections is that they are of use principally to the infrastructure operator. Although each participant in a designated system is protected against the worst consequences of a default of another participant, and the same will be true in a CCP (whether or not a designated system) because of the interposition of the CCP as counterparty between other participants, neither statutory scheme for protection addresses

---

194 SFD, art 2(a), penultimate paragraph
195 SFRs, reg 20(2); SFD, art 3(1)

the relationship between a participant and its clients. It was noted above that a member state can decide that an indirect participant may be considered a 'participant' in a designated system where this is justified on grounds of systemic risk. The European Central Bank's 'blue book' does not suggest that the 'indirect participant' option has been taken up by leading ACHs,[196] and a European Commission report on the SFD said that only nine Member States had considered 'indirect participants or other undertakings' as participants in designated systems.[197] It may therefore be concluded that designation of indirect participants is not a feasible route for protection of clearing and settlement service providers such as agent banks. These banks must look elsewhere for protection.

FINANCIAL COLLATERAL ARRANGEMENTS

8.25 The main protective legislation on which service providers may seek to rely derives from the Financial Collateral Directive (FCD).[198] This important legislation simplified the legal rules for taking and enforcing collateral comprising cash or financial instruments, provided that at least one of the parties was a financial institution. The benefits of having a 'financial collateral arrangement' are that the arrangement is enforceable notwithstanding the opening of insolvency proceedings. The financial collateral arrangement can therefore be a powerful tool for protecting a firm.

What is a financial collateral arrangement?

8.26 The FCD envisages two types of financial collateral arrangement – the 'title transfer' collateral arrangement and the 'security' financial collateral arrangement. The differences between these, and the factors which influence collateral takers to choose one over the other,[199] are not peculiar to the world of clearing and settlement. Essentially a title transfer arrangement involves an outright transfer of ownership of collateral, coupled with a promise to convey back equivalent collateral when the debts owed by the collateral provider have been discharged. In the meantime, if the debtor defaults, the obligation to convey back is converted to a monetary obligation and set off against the debt. A security arrangement is the more traditional form of pledge, charge or mortgage, where the collateral provider retains an ownership right in the collateral. Because the FCD is primarily about abolishing formalities, it does not stipulate more than the following requirements for constituting financial collateral arrangements:

(1) Title transfer arrangements require the collateral provider to 'transfer full ownership of, or full entitlement to' the collateral, and the purpose must

---

196 European Central Bank, *Payment and Securities Settlement Systems in the European Union* (August 2007), http://www.ecb.int/pub/pdf/other/ecbbluebookea200708en.pdf
197 European Commission, *Evaluation report on the Settlement Finality Directive 98/26/EC* (EU25) (March 2006), COM (2005) 657 final/2, http://ec.europa.eu/internal_market/financial-markets/docs/settlement/evaluation_report_en.pdf, p 6
198 Directive 2002/47/EC of the European Parliament and of the Council of 6 June 2002 on financial collateral arrangements
199 See Turing, D, and Cramb, E, *Managing Risk in Financial Firms* (Tottel, March 2009), ISBN 978-1-84766-3030-0, pp 204ff

be to secure 'relevant financial obligations'[200] (defined as the obligations secured by a financial collateral arrangement and which give a right to cash settlement and/or delivery of financial instruments).[201]

(2) Security arrangements require the collateral provider to 'provide' the collateral by way of security, where the full or qualified ownership of, or full entitlement to, the collateral remains with the collateral provider. Collateral is 'provided' when it has been delivered, transferred, held, registered or otherwise designated so as to be in the possession or under the control of the collateral taker or of a person acting on the collateral taker's behalf.[202] The concepts of 'possession' and 'control' have given a certain amount of trouble in English law, as discussed below.

(3) In both cases, the financial collateral arrangement must be evidenced in writing or a legally equivalent manner.

(4) The parties to the arrangement must be eligible. The FCD gives a list:[203] public authorities, central banks, credit institutions, investment firms, 'financial institutions' as defined in the Banking Directive,[204] insurance undertakings, UCITS and their management companies, CCPs, settlement agents and clearing houses as defined in the SFD and including similar organisations in relation to the futures markets, and bond trustees or agents. Any arrangement between such persons is deemed to qualify. Arrangements between one such person and an ineligible corporate or partnership also qualify.[205] Member states can exclude the latter type of arrangements from scope,[206] but according to the European Commission only in Austria has this been done (though limitations on such arrangements are also reported to exist in the Czech Republic, France, Germany, Slovenia and Sweden).[207] Indeed, some member states such as the United Kingdom have gone further and consider a financial collateral arrangement to qualify as long as each party is a non-natural person.[208]

(5) The collateral must be eligible: that is, it must consist of financial instruments (which are broadly defined)[209] or cash (meaning money credited to an account or similar claims for repayment of money;[210] in the United Kingdom this definition has been widened to include sums payable under a financial collateral arrangement or a close-out netting provision[211]).

The advantages of having a financial collateral arrangement are most apparent when the collateral provider is subject to insolvency proceedings. The main

---

200 FCD, art 2(1)(b)
201 FCD, art 2(1)(f)
202 FCD, art 2(2)
203 FCD, art 1(2)
204 Directive 2006/48/EC of 14 June 2006 relating to the taking up and pursuit of the business of credit institutions, art 4(5)
205 FCD, art 1(2)(e)
206 FCD, art 1(3)
207 European Commission, *Evaluation report on the Financial Collateral Arrangements Directive* (December 2006), Report from the Commission to the Council and the European Parliament, COM (2006) 833 final, http://ec.europa.eu/internal_market/financial-markets/docs/collateral/fcd_report_en.pdf
208 Financial Collateral Arrangements (No.2) Regulations 2003, SI 2003 No 3226, reg 3, definitions of 'security financial collateral arrangement' and 'title transfer financial collateral arrangement'
209 FCD, art 2(1)(e)
210 FCD, art 2(1)(g)
211 Financial Collateral Arrangements (No.2) Regulations, reg 3

protections given by the FCD are that on the occurrence of an enforcement event, the collateral taker shall be able, notwithstanding any insolvency proceedings, to realize any financial collateral provided under a security financial collateral arrangement, by sale or appropriation, or (in the case of cash) set-off, and any formalities delaying or impeding such actions are abolished;[212] and title transfer financial collateral arrangements and close-out netting provisions, which are at the heart of title transfer collateral enforcement, must take effect in accordance with their terms, again notwithstanding any insolvency proceedings.[213] A supplementary protection addresses void disposition and zero hour rules, by abolishing rules which would invalidate collateral provided (or collateral arrangements created) on the day of opening of insolvency proceedings or before them.[214]

Financial Collateral Arrangements (No 2) Regulations 2003

8.27   The legislation implementing the FCD in the United Kingdom is the Financial Collateral Arrangements (No 2) Regulations 2003[215] (FCRs). Part 3 of the FCRs consists of a list of specific disapplications of provisions of insolvency law, although unlike the SFRs or Part VII the confusing phrase 'the general law of insolvency shall have effect, subject to ... ' is not used. In fact, quite the reverse: regulation 13 states that collateral arrangements 'shall be legally enforceable and binding on third parties,' subject to only one proviso. This is that, when the financial collateral arrangement or relevant financial obligation came into existence, and when the collateral was provided, the collateral taker was not aware, nor should have been aware, of the commencement of winding-up proceedings or reorganisation measures.

Once again, in relation to insolvency challenges of foreign origin, the FCRs use the familiar but unwelcome formula of section 183 of the Companies Act 1989, and preclude[216] acts which 'would be prohibited ... by this Part' in the case of an insolvency office-holder appointed in the United Kingdom, and the FCRs are open to the same criticism as section 183 and Regulation 25(2) of the SFRs. The FCRs can also be criticised for an apparently random choice of disapplications, particularly in relation to preferential debts and other priority claims such as expenses of insolvency proceedings, which may rank ahead of floating charges notwithstanding these protections. Nevertheless, FCRs have the very useful effect that the moratorium preventing immediate enforcement of a charge in administration is disapplied, and that enables a collateral taker to seize and sell charged collateral without delay, and to fight with an administrator afterwards.

8.28   Unfortunately it is the case that various aspects of financial collateral arrangements have given rise to significant legal uncertainty, and various issues should therefore be discussed.

(1) *Fluctuating collateral balances.* In the context of clearing and settlement, collateral balances will only rarely be fixed: the available source of collateral is the cash or securities credited to the account to or from which settlements

---

212   FCD, art 4
213   FCD, arts 6, 7
214   FCD, art 8
215   SI 2003 No.3226
216   FCRs, reg 15A(2)

will be made.[217] Traders do not wish to have their stock-in-trade locked away as collateral. What English lawyers would recognise as floating charges is the norm for collateral arrangements. Unfortunately, various Member States do not recognise floating charges or fluctuating collateral balances to ensure that the collateral has been 'provided' to the collateral-taker for the purposes of article 2(2) of the FCD. If a collateral provider is incorporated in such a state it is unlikely to be possible to construct a financial collateral arrangement without locking the collateral away.

(2) *Meaning of 'possession' and 'control'*. English lawyers are content with the concept of the floating charge, but struggle with the gloss given in article 2(2) that the effect of 'providing' the collateral must be that the collateral-taker has possession or control of the collateral. Academic and jurisprudential debate on the meaning of these words has been extensive. It is regrettable that the direction of this debate has been conservative, and along traditional English law lines, notwithstanding that the FCD is self-evidently a European instrument which should not allow for traditional English meanings to be given to words being used across the entire EEA where, outside England, traditional English meanings would be greeted with astonishment. The issues are discussed at **section 8.29**.

(3) *Identifying the relevant account*. In a cross-border context, knowing which system of law applies is vitally important in order to ensure that the correct steps have been taken to ensure the effectiveness of the security interest which is being taken. The FCD helps in this endeavour by specifying that the applicable law, in relation to certain questions pertaining to property rights in securities recorded in accounts, is the law of the country where the 'relevant account' is maintained.[218] The 'relevant account' is the account in which the book entries are made by which the book entry securities collateral is provided to the collateral taker.[219] If the collateral taker's name (or some symbolic equivalent) appears on more than one set of books, there is a danger of there being more than one 'relevant account'.

(4) *The Securities Law Directive*. The European Commission plans to introduce a Securities Law Directive.[220] Included in this will be new arrangements which limit the available effective techniques for taking a security interest in securities credited to an account. The preliminary indications are that the most secure way of taking a security interest will be to have the securities 'earmarked' in the securities account;[221] but there is no indication of how this new concept will fit together with the requirement for possession or control under the FCD.

Possession and control in English law

8.29 To obtain a security interest which qualifies as a 'financial collateral arrangement', and therefore benefits from the protections of the FCD, one

---

217 See **section 18.15**
218 FCD, art 9
219 FCD, art 1(1)(h)
220 See **section 10.8**
221 European Commission Services, *Legislation on legal certainty of securities holding and dispositions* (November 2010), Consultation Document DG Markt G2 MET/OT/acg D(2010) 768690, http://ec.europa.eu/internal_market/consultations/docs/2010/securities/consultation_paper_en.pdf , Principle 9

must have possession or control of the securities. As Professor Hugh Beale et al say,[222] the meaning of the phrase 'possession or control' is not for member state law to determine, and it should be given an 'autonomous' meaning under European law. Unfortunately, this sound advice has not been followed, and fog and mystery have developed around what ought to be fairly simple, and commentaries even conflate 'possession or control' into a single concept, even referring to the need for a definition of 'possession and control'.[223] The following comments may thus be in order.

(1) Dr Joanna Benjamin has explained that interests in securities are 'incapable of possession at common law,' because the common law distinguished choses in possession from choses in action. [224] Beale and his co-authors go further, stating that 'in English law possession has no meaning in relation to intangible property.' No criticism should be made of these comments; but they have limited relevance to the FCD, which is not an exposition of the common law of England.

(2) 'Possession' is an ordinary word and, in a European context involving account-held securities, means nothing more than having the securities credited to one's account. The amended text of the FCRs affirms this, stating:

> 'For the purposes of these Regulations "possession" of financial collateral in the form of cash or financial instruments includes the case where financial collateral has been credited to an account in the name of the collateral-taker ... provided that any rights the collateral-provider may have in relation to that financial collateral are limited to the right to substitute financial collateral of the same or greater value or to withdraw excess financial collateral.'[225]

The proviso is presumably there to deal with recital (10) of the FCD, which requires some form of *dis*possession of the collateral provider if there is to be a privileged financial collateral arrangement. But the proviso is unhelpful and confusing, because it implies that some degree of control is needed in order to establish the fact of possession. The idea that the collateral-provider is not to have *any* rights to the collateral except the two mentioned, when all that has happened is that *possession* has been transferred, is impossible to reconcile with the FCD. The new definition, surely, is wrong. All the FCD is doing is reminding the reader that a transfer of securities from one account to another may amount to a transfer of who *holds* the securities (a transfer of *possession*) without invariably involving a transfer of ownership.[226]

(3) 'Control' is an alternative way of obtaining the 'dispossession' required by recital (10), and self-evidently applies to the case where the collateral taker did not dispossess the collateral provider by having the securities transferred to its (the collateral taker's) account. The FCRs do not define 'control'. Professor Beale et al consider that 'negative control', that is

---

222 Beale, H, et al, *The Law of Personal Property Security* (OUP, March 2007), ISBN 978-0199283293, s 10.25ff
223 See Law Commission, *Company Security Interests* (August 2005), Law Com No 296, Cm 6654, para 5.59
224 Benjamin, J, *Interests in Securities* (OUP, December 2000), ISBN 0-19-826992-7, section 2.25
225 FCRs, reg 3(2)
226 Cf **Chapter 10** as regards ownership of securities credited to accounts

where the collateral provider is prevented from dealing with the collateral, is an essential feature of control. Notice to the account provider of the collateral taker's interest is sufficient, in their opinion, to achieve negative control. As to 'positive control' – that is, where the collateral taker has 'legal and practical' ability to dispose of the collateral without the consent of the collateral provider, typically via a control agreement – Professor Beale and his colleagues do not say that positive control is essential to obtain 'possession or control' for the purposes of the FCD, but they do say that positive control alone is insufficient.

(4) Control can, therefore, be achieved through 'negative control'. This form of control differs from the highly refined version of control which has troubled the House of Lords in relation to fixed charges over book debts.[227] There is nothing in the FCD to say that collateral subject to a floating charge cannot at the same time be under the control of the collateral taker. An example would be an arrangement under which the collateral taker has agreed with both the account provider and the collateral provider that the securities can be withdrawn by the collateral provider to the extent that the value of the remaining security portfolio immediately after withdrawal is no lower than a certain value: that would be a floating charge, and at the same time it ought to be a valid dispossession compliant with the FCD.

(5) Unfortunately the comments of Professor Beale et al were interpreted in *Gray v G-T-P Group Ltd*[228] in a manner which implies that no financial collateral arrangement can exist in English law unless the collateral taker has a fixed charge, because 'possession' is out of the question, and 'control' requires a fixed charge. It is submitted here that the *Gray* approach to control – which, incidentally, predated the inclusion of the new definition of 'possession' in the FCRs – is wrong. Yet, in the absence of clear legislation or senior court jurisprudence, practitioners may feel constrained to construct financial collateral arrangements through taking possession or fixed charges.

CROSS-BORDER INSOLVENCY

8.30 Business in the financial sector is not confined to country boundaries; unfortunately, there is as yet no single code of bankruptcy law in the European Union, each member state being socially and culturally attached to its own historical system. These systems are highly diverse.[229] The danger, then, is that the rights which a provider of clearing and settlement services may wish to exercise could be affected by the application of a foreign system of insolvency law which has quite different effects from those under the local legal system. This section, accordingly, sets out some basic precepts of international insolvencies, before considering some more detailed issues.

8.31 The basic precepts are as follows.

(1) Companies are normally subject to 'home state' insolvency law. When a company is insolvent, the presumption is that the corporate law – that

---

227 *National Westminster Bank plc v Spectrum Plus Limited* [2005] UKHL 41
228 [2010] All ER (D) 80
229 Wood, P, *Principles of International Insolvency* (Sweet and Maxwell, May 2007), ISBN 978-184-703-2102, para 1-037

is, the *lex societatis* – will determine its death as well as its formation. Assets and creditors in foreign states may be dealt with according to the insolvency law of the company's country, not the place where the asset or the creditor is located.

(2) Some courts assert insolvency jurisdiction over foreign companies. Some countries, notably the United Kingdom, have traditionally arrogated to themselves the right to put foreign companies into local insolvency proceedings. English court jurisdiction may be founded on the existence of assets or creditors, even if there is no branch, within its territory.[230]

(3) For banks, insurers and 'non-financial' companies headquartered in the European Union, European law allocates jurisdiction. This is because the Winding-up Directives (WUDs) for credit institutions[231] and insurers[232] restrict the opening of winding up proceedings and reorganisation measures to the home member state; and under the EU Insolvency Regulation (EUIR)[233] a similar restriction applies. The EUIR applies to all corporate entities which are not insurance undertakings, credit institutions, investment undertakings which provide services involving the holding of funds or securities for third parties, or collective investment schemes.[234] It also has three important curiosities: its home-state scheme is slightly modified in that it uses the concept of the place where the 'centre of main interests' is located, which might differ from the place of incorporation;[235] it allows for secondary or territorial proceedings in countries where the company has an 'establishment' (essentially, a branch);[236] and it does not apply to Denmark.[237]

8.32 Thus, in order to work out what insolvency laws will apply, it is first necessary to classify the type of entity one is dealing with, and then to work out where its home state is. That will not identify a complete code of insolvency law which applies, but it will establish the basic framework. The following more detailed issues can be explored:

(1) *Some proceedings are out of scope.* The scope of the EUIR in terms of the insolvency proceedings covered is specified by a list set out in Annex A to the EUIR; in the WUDs the scope is defined conceptually. This can leave questions as to whether procedures such as regulatory interventions (which might have almost identical effects to a judicially-administered proceeding) are covered. For example, there is some doubt as to whether the 'special resolution regimes' applicable to United Kingdom banks under the Banking Act 2009 constitute 'reorganisation measures' under the WUD and thereby qualify for international recognition.

(2) *The basic precepts can have unexpected results.* Infrastructures are not addressed uniformly under the WUDs or the EUIR. CCPs and the CSD incorporated in the United Kingdom are not banks or investment firms,

---

230 *Paramount Airways* (No 2) [1992] BCC 416
231 Directive 2001/24/EC of the European Parliament and of the Council of 4 April 2001 on the reorganisation and winding up of credit institutions
232 Directive 2001/17/EC of the European Parliament and of the Council of 19 March 2001 on the reorganisation and winding up of insurance undertakings
233 Council Regulation (EC) No 1346/2000 of 29 May 2000 on insolvency proceedings
234 EUIR, art 1(2)
235 EUIR, recital (13)
236 EUIR, art 3
237 EUIR, recital 33

and so fall within the EUIR. In other countries they are banks, so will be dealt with under the WUD for credit institutions. Likewise ACHs may be banks, or they may not, and so they might be dealt with under the WUD or the EUIR. Investment firms and banks may sit alongside each other as participants in these infrastructures; but typically investment firms will be outside the scope of both WUDs and also outside the EUIR, allowing member states to apply national approaches to cross-border insolvency.

(3) *The principle of universality is modified.* Even where the relatively simple home-state-only regime applies, as with credit institutions for example, there is a set of exceptions which apply other legal systems to avoid unexpected outcomes. These are, insofar as important to clearing and settlement, as follows. Their effect is to add another layer of protection against insolvency laws.

- Property rights ('rights in rem') in respect of assets situated in another member state are not affected by insolvency proceedings.[238]

- Set-off rights permitted under the law governing the *debt owed to the insolvent person* are not affected by insolvency proceedings.[239]

- The rights and obligations of EUIR entities which are parties to payment and settlement systems and financial markets are governed solely by the law of the member state applicable to the system or market.[240] For credit institutions and insurers, the exception is narrower: it is restricted to regulated markets only, rather than the post-trade space, although for credit institutions the phrase used is 'transactions carried out in the context of a regulated market,' which might be capable of a wider meaning.[241]

- Challenges to transactions based on rules such as preferences or fraud on creditors (rules relating to the voidness, voidability or unenforceability of legal acts detrimental to all the creditors) are precluded in some cases where the act is subject to the law of another member state.[242]

- Repo and netting agreements are, in the case of credit institutions only, to be governed solely by the [insolvency] law of the legal system which governs the agreement.[243]

(4) *Additional cross-border insolvency laws apply in the United Kingdom.* The United Kingdom has signed up to the UNCITRAL Model Law on Cross-border Insolvency.[244] Accordingly, under the Cross-Border Insolvency Regulations 2006,[245] foreign insolvency proceedings will be recognised and foreign insolvency practitioners ('foreign representatives') will be granted relief in the courts of England and Scotland. Schedule 1 to the Regulations sets out a modified version of the UNCITRAL Model Law, the scheme of which is broadly that an application for recognition may be made to the British court, and upon recognition (or, in an emergency, before a

---

238 EUIR, art 5; WUD (credit institutions), art 21; WUD (insurers), art 20
239 EUIR, art 6; WUD (credit institutions), art 23; WUD (insurers), art 22
240 EUIR, art 9
241 WUD (credit institutions), art 27; WUD (insurers), art 23
242 EUIR, art 13; WUD (credit institutions), art 30; WUD (insurers), art 24
243 WUD (credit institutions), arts 25, 26
244 United Nations Commission on International Trade Law, *UNCITRAL Model Law on Cross-Border Insolvency with Guide to Enactment* (May 1997), http://www.uncitral.org/pdf/english/texts/insolven/insolvency-e.pdf
245 SI 2006 No 1030

decision on recognition) a stay is imposed, the assets of the debtor cannot be transferred, and various powers granted to United Kingdom office-holders are made available to the foreign representative.[246] The following observations relating to the Cross-Border Insolvency Regulations may be made:

- Article 1(2) of Schedule 1 to the Regulations restricts the cases in which recognition orders can be made. Significantly, the Regulations do not apply to credit institutions or insurers.[247] Other types of financial institution, in particular investment firms, collective investment undertakings, and market infrastructures which are not constituted as credit institutions, can be made subject to recognition orders.

- Article 20(3) provides that the stay which comes into effect on recognition does not affect any right to take steps to enforce security over the debtor's property, any right exercisable under Part VII, the protective provisions of the SFRs or the FCRs, or a right of set-off, if the right would have been exercisable in the event of a winding-up order under the Insolvency Act 1986.

- The Regulations do not import foreign law into Britain. Apart from the automatic (but limited) stay and the prohibition on transfer of assets, the effect of the Regulations is principally to allow a foreign representative, having applied to the court, to exercise typical Insolvency Act powers. Recognition does not imply unfettered application of all the foreign representative's home state powers in Britain.

In addition, where requested by a court in one of a limited list of Commonwealth and other countries with historical links to the United Kingdom,[248] the courts of the United Kingdom will be obliged to assist the requesting court.[249] This can mean that an administration can take effect in the United Kingdom where it would not otherwise be an available procedure;[250] and unlike the Cross-Border Insolvency Regulations, foreign law can apply directly in the United Kingdom, subject to limitations imposed by the court.[251]

(5) *The effect of overseas insolvency laws is largely blocked where protective legislation applies.* It was noted above that section 183 of the Companies Act 1989 blocks the ability of a court to recognise or give effect to an order of a foreign court or an act of an insolvency officer insofar as the making of the order, or the doing of the act, would be prohibited in the case of a court in the United Kingdom or a relevant United Kingdom insolvency office-holder by provisions made under Part VII. Similar provisions are found in the SFRs and FCRs. Various comments may be made about the blocking provisions.

---

246 Cross-Border Insolvency Regulations, Sch 1, arts 19–23
247 Paragraphs (g)–(l)
248 Anguilla, Australia, the Bahamas, Bermuda, Botswana, Brunei, Canada, Cayman Islands, Falkland Islands, Gibraltar, Hong Kong, Ireland, Malaysia, Montserrat, New Zealand, St Helena, South Africa, Turks and Caicos Islands, Tuvalu, and the Virgin Islands: Cooperation of Insolvency Courts (Designation of Relevant Countries and Territories) Orders 1986, 1996 and 1998, SI 1986 No 2123, SI 1996 No 253 and SI 1998 No 2766
249 Insolvency Act 1986, s 426
250 *Re Dallhold Estates (UK) Pty Ltd* [1992] BCC 394
251 *Hughes v Hannover Ruckversicherungs-Aktiengesellschaft* [1997] 1 BCLC 497, CA

- If the United Kingdom office-holder does not have a power which a foreign insolvency officer seeks to exercise, the protective legislation (Part VII and the SFRs) may not 'prohibit' the officer carrying out that act. It can be argued that foreign insolvency officers may thereby still be able to open attacks on participants in infrastructures which would be denied to UK office-holders because they are not available under the general domestic law of insolvency in the United Kingdom. But Part VII and the SFRs contain general prohibitions on acts which are contrary to the rules of the recognised body or designated system; which reduces the risk, at least as far as the infrastructure itself is concerned. Participants in the infrastructure are more weakly protected by the protective legislation in any event, as previously noted.

- Coupled with the protection found in article 9 of the EUIR and article 8 of the SFD, each of which restricts the application of foreign laws to the treatment of defaulting participants in payment and settlement systems, these provisions allow little scope for foreign insolvency officers to assert rights which might disrupt the system. The gaps arise where the insolvency officer is not based in the EEA (and so is not subject to the EUIR or SFD law in his home country) and has powers which were not imagined by the draftsman of the blocking legislation.

- Furthermore, nothing in the blocking legislation can prevent action being taken in another country by an overseas insolvency officer, provided he can find some means of enforcing a judgment outside the United Kingdom.

(6) *Groups of companies present an intractable cross-border problem.* While much debate has taken place about insolvent groups of companies,[252] there is no solution to the problem. Briefly stated, one policy objective is to recognise that a group is typically run as a single business enterprise, for a variety of reasons; the legal entities are interconnected, as a result: and it follows that the failure of the business should be centrally resolved for the greater good of all creditors universally. However, that policy objective is in fundamental conflict with another, namely that the entire rationale for separate legal personality is to wall off the assets of one entity from the liabilities of another, and failure to respect the integrity of each corporate entity would erase the ability of corporations to raise funds on the security of their own assets. Inevitably an insolvency proceeding affecting one legal entity will have consequences for others in the same group, either because they are mutually dependent for services (such as treasury or technology) or because the inability of one entity to honour its obligations threatens group members which are themselves creditors or their potential trading partners who fear the consequences of interconnectedness and common management. Added to all that is the potential for conflict between the policy of insolvency law in the country of one insolvent legal entity with that in the country of another. Regulators' responses since the financial crisis have been to encourage separability of legal entities[253] or even businesses within those entities, to enable swifter resolution of a problem within a systemically important financial institution.

---

252 Bank for International Settlements Basel Committee on Banking Supervision, *Report and Recommendations of the Cross-border Bank Resolution Group*, http://www.bis.org/publ/bcbs169.pdf (March 2010); Fonteyne, W, et al, Crisis Management and *Resolution for a European Banking System* (March 2010), IMF Working Paper WP/10/70, pp 36–48
253 Cf ss 18, 22 Banking Act 2009; see **section 8.7**

(7) *Default funds, risk mutualisation, investor compensation and client asset protection are essential.* Insolvency and business failure are inevitable. But when the economy, people's ability to make their payments, and their life-savings are at risk, the consequences must be moderated. Protection from insolvency officers is not the solution here: mechanisms to protect investors and market users from wider losses are. The following devices are widely used:

- Default funds are typically a species of risk mutualisation used by CCPs. The basic idea is that the CCP requires each participant to deposit cash or other collateral into a fund which will be used in the event that margin is insufficient to cover losses in the event of a participant's failure. First, the failed participant's contribution will be treated as supplementary margin; any outstanding losses will be absorbed by the remainder of the fund, that is borne by the other participants. Users of the CCP who did not use the failed participant can gain confidence that their business and wealth should be unaffected by the problem.[254]

- Risk mutualisation is used by other infrastructures such as ACHs,[255] though the mechanism may not require the up-front deposit of collateral but rely on the ability of the infrastructure to demand contributions after the event.

- Clients of the failed participant will not be protected by these devices, but client asset rules may serve to isolate the assets of the clients from the insolvent estate of the participant. These are described in **sections 10.19–10.22**. Where assets have not been segregated, it will be necessary to have a compensation scheme in place to protect at least retail investors and depositors from losses occasioned by insolvency events over which they have little or no control: compensation schemes are mandated in Europe in respect of unavailable deposits[256] and (in the case of an investment firm) money and financial instruments claimed.[257]

EUROPEAN RECOVERY AND RESOLUTION DIRECTIVE

8.33   The European Commission has proposed a new Directive on Recovery and Resolution, [258] which will, once finalised and transposed into the laws of Member States, have significant impact on the risks related to clearing and settlement. It is unlikely to emerge from the EU's legislative process without significant modification, and so only the headlines are mentioned here.

---

254 Cf section 14.36
255 European Central Bank, *Payment and Securities Settlement Systems in the European Union* (August 2007), http://www.ecb.int/pub/pdf/other/ecbbluebookea200708en.pdf
256 Directive 94/19/EC of the European Parliament and of the Council of 30 May 1994 on deposit-guarantee schemes
257 Directive 97/9/EC of the European Parliament and of the Council of 3 March 1997 on investor-compensation schemes
258 European Commission, *Proposal for a Directive of the European Parliament and of the Council establishing a framework for the recovery and resolution of credit institutions and investment firms, etc* (June 2012), COM(2012) 280 final, http://eur-lex.europa.eu/LexUriServ/LexUriServ.do?uri=COM:2012:0280:FIN:EN:PDF; Inter-institutional file 2012/0150 (COD)

(1) *RRPs*. Banks and investment firms ('institutions'), and their groups, will be required to have recovery plans for restoring the institution in question to financial health in the event of significant deterioration. The authorities will also have to draw up resolution plans in case recovery plans fail, so that they can implement a bail-in, a sale of business, a transfer to a bridge bank, or a partial property transfer. These proposals closely mirror the existing regime for ailing United Kingdom banks put forward by the FSA and included in the Banking Act 2009.[259]

(2) *Preservative powers*. Resolution authorities will be given various powers relating to institutions under resolution, including: the ability to require an institution and its affiliates to continue to provide services and facilities to transferees; the power to suspend payment and delivery obligations owed by or to an institution; the power to restrict enforcement of security interests; and the power to suspend termination rights under financial contracts until the end of the following business day.

(3) *Protective safeguards*. Various safeguards for shareholders and creditors are contemplated. These include measures similar to those in place in the United Kingdom in relation to the Banking Act Special Resolution Regime.[260] There is also to be special protection for trading, clearing and settlement systems from the side-effects of partial property transfers: transfers must not affect the operation of systems designated under the SFD or their rules.

(4) *Default management*. Although CCPs will be expressly excluded from the moratorium on enforcement of security interests, and property transfers will take effect subject to the protections in the SFD, there are many ways in which the management of a default will be affected by the proposals. In particular, the suspension of close-out rights and delivery and payment obligations will affect credit and liquidity risk profiles for infrastructures and their participants.

(5) *Application to infrastructures*. The proposed Directive is not designed to deal with ailing or failed infrastructures. But some will be structured as banks[261] and thereby within scope. Furthermore, if a non-bank infrastructure provider can be regarded as a 'financial institution' as defined in article 4(5) of the Banking Directive[262] – a question too difficult to be answered here – then it too may be brought within scope. For reasons explored in **section 17.3** it is unlikely that the toolkit set out in the proposed Directive would be of great value in dealing with the problems of failing infrastructures.

(6) *Winding-up Directive*. It is proposed to bring investment firms within the scope of the WUD for credit institutions,[263] thereby closing a loophole which made cross-border insolvencies of investment firms unduly complex. Further, it is to be made clear that resolution tools under the proposed new Directive are internationally recognisable as 'reorganisation measures' under the WUD.

---

259 See **sections 8.4** and **8.6**
260 See **section 8.4**
261 See **section 12.9**
262 Directive 2006/48/EC of 14 June 2006 relating to the taking up and pursuit of the business of credit institutions
263 See **section 8.31(3)**

9   Cash

OWNERSHIP OF CASH

9.1   The question of what you own, when cash is credited to your account at a bank or other financial institution, ought to be very simple; certainly, much simpler than the equivalent question relating to securities.[1] The law was settled a long time ago in the case of *Foley v Hill*[2] that a banker is a debtor, not a trustee, so that a credit to a bank account will merely be a record of indebtedness.

When deposited with a bank, then, cash is not an 'asset' of the bank. Quite the reverse: it is a liability of the bank. A deposit of securities, which will be credited to an account on the bank's books, has a completely different accounting result: securities in the hands of the bank remain in the ownership of the depositor, and are neither an asset nor a liability of the bank. Much confusion stems from this distinction, with the wording of a directive even suggesting that a bank's books might show its own cash (an asset) in the same way as a deposit (a liability),[3] which is evidently nonsensical. Although cash in the hands of a bank is not an 'asset' of the bank, the credit to a depositor's bank account is not valueless, and the 'asset' which is being sought is the liability looked at from the other direction – a chose in action against the bank, to which the depositor is entitled.

9.2   Despite the simplicity of the analysis of 'ownership' of cash, some secondary issues arise.

In the first place, it is important to understand the moment at which entitlement to the value represented by the credit arises, and thus the moment of receipt. Deposits are no longer placed in the ordinary course of financial services business by the physical handover of notes and coins: deposits are made by means of inter-bank transfer, so the question is whether a depositor becomes entitled at the moment that his bank receives a credit at the central bank or its correspondent bank, or when the bank receives notification of the transfer in the payment system (whether or not the advice is given after the moment of finality of receipt by the bank), or when the bank actually gets round to crediting the depositor's account. On this subject there is guidance from the courts to the effect that the bank becomes liable to the depositor when it decides to credit the account, even if the account entries are made later.[4] The moment of receipt by the bank and the moment of finality in the payment system would appear to be

---

1   See **Chapter 10**
2   (1848) 2 HLC 28
3   Directive 2011/61 of the European Parliament and of the Council of 8 June 2011 on Alternative Investment Fund Managers etc, art 21(7)
4   *Momm v Barclays Bank* [1977] QB 790

irrelevant. The question of timing of finality of payment is examined in **section 9.16**.

The implication of this is that a seller of an asset may be told that the settlement system operates on a delivery-versus-payment (DvP)[5] basis, but insofar as the seller accesses the system through an intermediary, there is bound to be a mismatch between the moment of transfer of title to the asset and the moment at which the seller acquires a credit claim on the service provider, unless the service provider is able to provide simultaneous real-time updating of its cash accounts with finality to reflect the DvP receipt it has itself enjoyed.

9.3   Secondly, there is a question as to which legal system governs questions of entitlement as regards cash accounts. Various approaches to this question may be taken:

(1) The Rome I Regulation[6] contains a variety of provisions which appear to solve the problem. Article 3 allows freedom of choice, within limits, for the governing law of a contract. The chosen legal system governs the performance of the contract and the ways of extinguishing obligations.[7] But it can be debated whether the *property* aspects of a contract – that is the rights in rem arising from the fact that a contractual obligation owed by the counterparty to a contract is a chose in action which can be assigned like other items of property – are subject to the same chosen law. Article 14 addresses voluntary assignment of contractual obligations, and states ambiguously that 'the concept of assignment ... includes outright transfers of claims, transfers of claims by way of security and pledges or other security rights over claims,'[8] but the remaining text of article 14 deals with the *contractual* relationship between assignor and assignee, and the *existence and conditions* for assignability, and it is not apparent that article 14 establishes a conflicts-of-laws rule to identify the legal system to be used to solve property questions such as priority among competing claimants. In consequence it is not surprising that different member states interpret the effects of article 14 differently when it comes to the question of property rights.[9]

(2) One theory is that an intangible asset can be said to have a location – a *situs* – and therefore that the property aspects of the asset fall to be dealt with under the *lex situs*. Under this theory, the *situs* is the place of the 'right of recourse to secure its recovery ... in the courts for the place where the debtor resides.'[10] The EU Insolvency Regulation (EUIR)[11] includes a curious provision stating that '"the Member State in which assets are situated" shall mean, in the case of ... claims, the Member State within the territory of which the third party required to meet them has the centre of his main interests.'[12] There has been

---

5   See **section 15.2**
6   Regulation (EC) No 593/2008 of the European Parliament and of the Council of 17 June 2008 on the law applicable to contractual obligations
7   Rome I Regulation, art 12
8   Rome I Regulation, art 14(3)
9   Møllmann, A, *Security assignment of debts and the conflict of laws,* (May 2011) LMCLQ No 2, pp 262–274
10 Dicey, A, Morris, J, and Collins, L, *The Conflict of Laws* (14th ed, Sweet & Maxwell, June 2006), ISBN 978-0-421-88360-4, para 24–053
11 Council Regulation (EC) No 1346/2000 of 29 May 2000 on insolvency proceedings
12 EUIR, art 2(g)

debate[13] as to whether this provision establishes a *lex situs* rule for claims, but the better view is that its role is confined to allocation of assets among liquidators in the context of a Regulation which allows for several concurrent insolvency proceedings for a single entity. If that view were wrong, the EUIR would lend support to the theory cited in Dicey, Morris and Collins that the law of the place of 'residence' – possibly the head office – of the account-provider governs property questions arising from the account relationship. It should also be noted that the Rome I Regulation also states that, in the absence of an express choice, a contract for services shall be governed by the law of the country where the service provider has his habitual residence,[14] or if it is thought that a cash account contract is not a contract for services, the law of the country where the party required to effect the characteristic performance of the contract (presumably the account-provider) has his habitual residence. Again this test would point to the place of the account-provider's head office, which may be different from the branch where the account is held.

(3) Notwithstanding the contrary views, the better view would appear to be that questions of entitlement ought to be left to freedom of contract, subject to the usual policy test of validity of choice of law.[15] If the parties (realistically, this will mean the bank) have failed to specify a chosen governing law in the banking contract, then the property law aspects of the deposit ought to be governed by the system of law of the jurisdiction where the deposit is repayable. Under English law the place where a deposit is repayable is the branch where the account is held;[16] by contrast a bank incorporated in the United States has been held liable to repay in New York a deposit taken in a foreign jurisdiction.[17] So, in relation to clearing and settlement, the currency or the 'home market' of the asset bought or sold would be irrelevant to questions of entitlement as against the account-provider, security, and finality, and only the deposit contract is relevant; except where the deposit contract is silent or involves an illegitimate choice of law, in which case the law of the place where the account-provider is liable to make repayment will prevail.

9.4   This discussion brings into focus a third question, namely to whom a cash balance as an item of property belongs. The issue came up in a case involving mortgage fraud, in which various accused had obtained cash transfers from building societies by deliberately making false statements. The House of Lords quashed their convictions, stating:

'The crucial question, as I see it, is whether the defendant obtained (or attempted to obtain) property belonging to another. Let it be assumed that the lending institution's bank account is in credit, and that there is

---

13 Virgos, M, and Garcimartín, F, *The European Insolvency Regulation: Law and Practice* (Kluwer Law International, 2004), ISBN 90-411-2089-0, pp 163–168; Moss, G, et al, *The EC Regulation on Insolvency Proceedings – A Commentary and Annotated Guide* (OUP, October 2002), ISBN 0-19-925109-6, ss 4–14, 6–47

14 Rome I Regulation, art 4(1)(b)

15 Rome I Regulation, art 3(3)

16 *Joachimson v Swiss Bank* [1921] 3 KB 110, CA; *Libyan Arab Foreign Bank v Bankers Trust Corporation* [1989] QB 728

17 *Wells Fargo Asia Ltd v Citibank NA* 852 F.2d 657 (July 1988); *Citibank NA v Wells Fargo Asia Ltd* 495 US 660, 110 S.Ct. 2034, 109 L.Ed.2d 677 (May 1990); *Wells Fargo Asia Ltd v Citibank NA* 936 F.2d. 723 (June 1991)

therefore no difficulty in identifying a credit balance standing in the account as representing property, ie a chose in action, belonging to the lending institution. The question remains, however, whether the debiting of the lending institution's bank account, and the corresponding crediting of the bank account of the defendant or his solicitor, constitutes obtaining of that property. The difficulty in the way of that conclusion is simply that, when the bank account of the defendant (or his solicitor) is credited, he does not obtain the lending institution's chose in action. On the contrary, that chose in action is extinguished or reduced pro tanto, and a chose in action is brought into existence representing a debt in an equivalent sum owed by a different bank to the defendant or his solicitor. In these circumstances, it is difficult to see how the defendant thereby obtained property belonging to another, ie to the lending institution.'[18]

This case, *R v Preddy*, is also important in the context of clearing and settlement because it makes it absolutely clear that a cash transfer does not involve a transfer of property. It is therefore distinct from a transfer of securities. Cash and securities have to be considered separately, even though many of the ideas and risks which relate to transfers of both types are similar. In fact, cash transfers are simpler than securities transfers, because they involve the discharge and creation of new obligations every time; securities transfers are more confusing, because the credit and debit entries in a securities account-provider's books have some aspects resembling the legal effects of cash account entries, but others which could relate to property which exists independently of those entries.[19]

9.5   Fourthly, the analysis of ownership of cash needs to be repeated in respect of recipients of cash who are not 'banks'. In these cases the judgment in *Foley v Hill* will be of no assistance. An investment firm may receive cash for the account of its client and make credit entries on its books. In these cases there is no legal presumption that the firm owes the money as debtor, and indeed the presumption in the case of a firm regulated by the FSA is that it would be subject to the client money rules[20] and hold funds received from the client (or due to it) as trustee. An alternative analysis is that the sums in question are held as title-transfer cash collateral.[21] In determining the correct analysis one needs to be mindful that it is a criminal offence to accept deposits by way of business without authorisation under the Financial Services and Markets Act 2000 (FSMA).[22] A 'deposit' is, subject to a variety of exceptions and qualifications, defined in the Financial Services and Markets Act 2000 (Regulated Activities) Order 2001 (RAO)[23] as a sum of money paid on terms under which it will be repaid:[24] this formulation is wide enough to capture much cash-related activity. Persons who are not banks, and who do not hold FSMA permission to accept deposits, will need to rely on one of the exceptions in order to handle cash which they intend to repay to their clients. This may limit the extent to which a

---

18   *R v Preddy* [1996] AC 815, HL, per Lord Goff of Chieveley
19   See **section 10.4**
20   See **section 9.7**
21   See **section 9.15**
22   Financial Services and Markets Act 2000, s 23; Financial Services and Markets Act 2000 (Regulated Activities) Order 2001, SI 2001 No 544, art 5
23   SI 2001 No 544
24   RAO, arts 5–9A

non-bank firm can regard casual cash receipts as 'collateral' and thereby avoid the application of the client money rules.[25]

The organisations which hold cash balances include CCPs. CCPs are of key importance in the clearing and settlement environment, but may not be configured as banks.[26] CCPs are not investment firms, with the consequence that the client money rules do not apply; nor would the exception in the RAO excluding from the definition of 'deposit' a sum received by a firm with permission to carry on typical investment activities, namely dealing in investments as principal or agent, arranging deals in investments, managing investments or operating funds.[27] Furthermore, CCPs may not ordinarily wish to hold money as trustee. Their acceptance of cash will typically rely on a different RAO exception, covering the case where the money is 'paid by way of security for the performance of a contract or by way of security in respect of loss which may result from the non-performance of a contract.'[28] CCPs may, however, decide to make special arrangements to hold cash margin deposited on behalf of individually segregated clients separate from the estate of the CCP.

9.6   The fifth subsidiary issue to be considered is the distinction between 'central bank money' and 'commercial bank money', considered by the FMI Principles[29] to be a vital choice in relation to the 'settlement asset' for payment and securities settlement systems.[30] A credit balance at the central bank implies no credit risk at all, since what defines a central bank is the absolute ability to issue currency to meet its obligations. The obligation of a commercial bank, by contrast, is only as good as its solvency. The FMI Principles state:

> '[A Financial Market Infrastructure] should conduct its money settlements using central bank money, where practical and available. ... If central bank money is not used, an FMI should conduct its money settlements using a settlement asset with little or no credit or liquidity risk. An alternative to the use of central bank money is commercial bank money. When settling in commercial bank money, a payment obligation is typically discharged by providing the FMI or its participants with a direct claim on the relevant commercial bank. ... The use of commercial bank money to settle payment obligations, however, can create additional credit and liquidity risks for the FMI and its participants. For example, if the commercial bank conducting settlement becomes insolvent, the FMI and its participants may not have immediate access to their settlement funds or ultimately receive the full value of their funds.'[31]

It might be noted that it does not follow that all payment systems which provide accounts to their participants are offering central bank money, nor are providers of access to payment systems. Care is needed to investigate the structure and operations of the system in order to ascertain whose payment obligation is being accepted.

---

25 See **section 9.8(3)**
26 See **section 12.9**
27 RAO, art 8
28 RAO, art 5(3)(b)
29 Bank for International Settlements Committee on Payment and Settlement Systems and Technical Committee of the International Organization of Securities Commissions, *Principles for Financial Market Infrastructures* (April 2012), http://www.bis.org/publ/cpss101a.pdf
30 Cf **section 9.14**
31 FMI Principles, paras 3.9.3, 3.9.4

Finally, as this discussion comes full circle, it may be appropriate to contextualise the debate on ownership of cash. The central question about cash is not primarily one about property at all. *R v Preddy* highlights a gap between the everyday perception of deposit-taking ('my money in the bank'), reinforced by old-fashioned statutory language ('acceptance of deposits'), and the reality in a modern financial services environment where cash is represented by credit entries in accounts, arising from instructions given via interbank messaging systems. Similar issues are encountered in relation to securities accounts, where the legal problems are more challenging. But questions relating to cash are mostly questions about obligations: questions of credit risk, not questions of property and ownership. The things that matter are therefore made very simple: who is my debtor, does he dispute that he owes me the debt, and can he pay me.

CLIENT MONEY

9.7 Where a firm is not a deposit-taking bank, the 'client money rules'[32] will govern how the firm deals with cash placed with it by or for the account of the firm's client. Sometimes it is said that the client money rules do not apply to banks – in part, this is true, in that the rules do not apply 'in relation to deposits',[33] but 'the exemption for deposits is not an absolute exemption from the client money rules.'[34] Nevertheless, the key thing is once again the distinction between the deposit-taker as debtor, who merely owes an obligation to repay, and the non-debtor recipient of cash, who may be a trustee.

9.8 At the core of the client money rules is the statutory trust, derived from section 139(1) of the Financial Services and Markets Act 2000, which states that rules made by the FSA 'relating to the handling of money held by an authorised person in specific circumstances ("clients' money") may … make provision which results in that clients' money being held on trust in accordance with the rules.' It may be thought curious that the client money rules defer mention of the all-important statutory trust to their 16th page; this is, however, only a minor, if symbolic, instance of the complexity and opacity of the client money rules. The relevant rule is CASS 7.7.2R which states that a firm receives and holds client money as trustee for the purposes of the client money rules, and then sets out a 'waterfall' of priorities of entitlement to the trust property. Other provisions of the client money rules which are relevant to the constitution of the trust are as follows:

(1) What constitutes 'client money' and is therefore the subject of the statutory trust is defined in the FSA Glossary.[35] As far as securities business is concerned, the firm's activities will be classified as 'MiFID business', with the result that client money is money of any currency that a firm receives or holds for, or on behalf of, a client in the course of, or in connection with, investment business classified as such under the Markets in Financial Instruments Directive (MiFID).[36] The definition of 'money' is unhelpful

---

32 Financial Services Authority, *Handbook of Rules and Guidance, Client Assets Sourcebook*, CASS 7
33 CASS 7.1.8R
34 CASS 7.1.11G
35 Financial Services Authority, *Handbook of Rules and Guidance, Glossary*
36 Directive 2004/39/EC of the European Parliament and of the Council of 21 April 2004 on markets in financial instruments etc

9.8 *Cash*

('any form of money, including cheques and other payable orders'[37]) and hardly reflects modern practice where 'money' or 'cash' is more typically constituted by credits on the accounts of a bank or other third party than any physical instrument. Confusion can follow from this lack of clarity: for example, as to whether a banker accepting funds is somehow impressed with the statutory trust and cannot treat the funds in the same way as other deposits. In order to avoid these conundrums it is necessary to construe 'money' as a credit on a bank account, without somehow assuming that the banker has any corresponding asset to which the 'money' can be traced.

(2) There are some exceptions set forth in CASS, which disapply the client money rules by deeming certain money not to be 'client money'. The first of these, perhaps the most significant from the viewpoint of clearing and settlement, relates to money 'in respect of a delivery versus payment transaction.'[38] For this exception to apply, the transaction must be 'through a commercial settlement system,' and there are time-limits on the handling of the cash associated with the transaction. For sales, payment must be made by the firm within one day after settlement of the client's delivery obligation, but the firm can delay if the firm's own delivery is delayed. For purchases the rule is more obscure, but the upshot is that payment by the client must be not more than three business days before, and not more than one day after, the firm's own payment obligation matures. It appears that clients who pay in advance for securities may find that their funds are outside the limited protection given by the client money rules, and if their firm fails, they may need to have recourse to the Financial Services Compensation Scheme and its arrangements for protection of investors.

(3) Also excepted is the case 'where a client transfers full ownership of money to a firm for the purpose of securing or otherwise covering present or future, actual or contingent or prospective obligations.'[39] Cash collateral structures are examined below. A firm will need to show that any holding of cash treated as collateral has some reasonable relationship to the obligations which are supposedly covered. It may also be noted that title transfer collateral arrangements are outlawed for certain types of retail business.[40]

(4) A third exception of note is where the money is due to the firm.[41]

If none of the exceptions applies, cash credited to the firm's account will ostensibly be 'client money' and must then be handled in accordance with the client money rules. The rules are of two groups: the segregation rules, and the rules about disposal of the money.

The segregation rules stem from the obligation in MiFID that 'a firm must, when holding client money, make adequate arrangements to safeguard the client's rights and prevent the use of client money for its own account.'[42] On receiving any client money, the firm must 'promptly place this money into one or more accounts' with a bank or a qualifying money market fund,[43] and must 'take the necessary steps to ensure that client money deposited in [a bank] is

---

37 FSA Glossary
38 CASS 7.2.8R
39 CASS 7.2.3R, citing recital (27) to MiFID
40 CASS 7.2.3AR
41 CASS 7.2.9R
42 CASS 7.3.1R, repeating article 13(8) of MiFID
43 CASS 7.4.1R

held in an account or accounts identified separately from any accounts used to hold money belonging to the firm.'[44] Although commingling of trust and own property is not fatal to the proper constitution of a trust,[45] the separation of accounting on the books of the bank will assist the task of identifying the trust property. Firms must also notify the bank of the existence of the trust and obtain an acknowledgment that the bank will not exercise set-off rights as between the client money account and the firm's own-money account.[46]

9.9   What is more obscure is what the firm is permitted to do with the money so deposited. The client money rules set out only a few rules on this subject, headed 'discharge of fiduciary duty', which state that money ceases to be client money in a few limited circumstances, namely if it is paid to the client, his representative or his bank account, to a third party on the client's instruction (but not including in pursuance of a transaction), or to the firm itself.[47] The inference is that money remains client money even if it is transferred to a third party in order to effect payment in the course of a transaction entered into on the client's instructions, which is a surprising result. Transfer in the course of transactions is dealt with separately in the client money rules,[48] permitting the firm to transfer client money to an exchange, clearing house or intermediate broker without discharge of the fiduciary duty owed to the client. But there remains an apparent gap in cases which are not DvP transactions and cash is needed to settle the trade. In these cases the firm must use its own money for the settlement, and then reimburse itself under the rules for funds due and payable to the firm.[49]

These rules reflect the relatively loose provisions of the MiFID implementing Directive,[50] which require firms to keep good records, hold client funds in separate accounts from funds belonging to the firm, have adequate organisational arrangements to minimise the loss or diminution of client assets, and place funds received into a bank or qualifying money market fund. However, the minimum set of rules laid down by MiFID does not cater for the timing constraints of cash transfers in a modern straight-through-processing environment. Nor do they recognise the difficulties engendered by allowing client funds to be held in an omnibus account. It will be seen that the latter problem is akin to that arising in relation to holdings of clients' securities in an omnibus account, and the issues discussed below travel along a like path.[51]

The alternative approach

9.10   The first additional complexity overlying the MiFID client money rules is the result of a concession, allowing a degree of flexibility for a firm which operates in a 'multi-product, multi-currency environment for which adopting the normal approach [of paying client money into a client bank account promptly] would be unduly burdensome.' Such firms may opt for an 'alternative approach', which allows firms to handle client money as it were the firm's

---

44   CASS 7.4.11R
45   *Re Lehman Brothers International (Europe)(in administration)* [2012] UKSC 6
46   CASS 7.8.1R
47   CASS 7.2.15R
48   CASS 7.5.2R
49   CASS 7.2.10G
50   Commission Directive 2006/63/EC of 10 August 2006 implementing MiFID as regards organisational requirements, etc
51   See **section 10.16**

money and to carry out a daily reconciliation and adjustments of what should be held for clients in the client bank account.[52]

Practical application of the alternative approach caused difficulty in the collapse of Lehman Brothers. The Supreme Court ruled[53] that monies received by Lehmans were impressed with the statutory trust immediately upon receipt, even though Lehmans were using the alternative approach. Moreover, the fact that monies received were paid into Lehmans' general cash account and thereby commingled with 'house' money did not stop them being trust monies; the trust funds 'sink to the bottom' of the cash account so that they are used last – entailing a cumbersome forensic exercise to ascertain the entitlement to the funds remaining in the cash account.

Client money and clearing

9.11 More complexity stems from the fact that a firm may properly pass client money to a CCP, albeit without relieving the firm of its fiduciary duty. Margin calls may thus be settled by direct debit from the GCM's client money account at the GCM's bank, provided always that the GCM has established separate 'client' and 'house' accounts at the level of the CCP.[54] Practicality intrudes at this point, as the CCP knows first what the amount of the margin call is going to be; while the GCM may know at approximately the same point, it may be much harder for the GCM to obtain cash from the clients whose trades led to the margin call, at least within the timescale needed. The reality is that these clients may pay late. In the meantime, if the GCM's client bank account is an omnibus account, cash belonging to other clients has been drawn by the CCP. This reality has various consequences:

(1) In the first place, the client money rules contain complex reconciliation rules relating to the amount of client money which is supposed to be credited to the client money bank account.[55] These rules are designed to ensure that the client bank account balance is topped up by the firm (the GCM) to enable there to be enough funds to meet all the client entitlements in the event of the firm's failure.

(2) But this structure shows its fundamental flaw: it depends on the firm's solvency to ensure that there is sufficient client money to meet all those entitlements. If a large margin call is made, it may be impossible for the firm to top up the client bank account without jeopardising its own solvency. This situation arose in the case of Griffin Trading Company.

(3) In order to avoid shortfalls, the GCM can either insist on pre-funding or it can provide liquidity. Pre-funding is not straightforward, because the GCM can only guess at the amount required and impose contractual limits on the client in an attempt to keep the client's open interest at a level which will be covered by the pre-funded amount. Those controls may, if the client experiences stress or fraud, be unreliable. Thus it appears that part of a GCM's function, by virtue of the client money rules, is to guarantee liquidity in relation to margin. One may then ask whether the CCP might wish to impose a limit on the lending which is implied when a GCM

52 CASS 7.4.14G – 7.4.19G
53 *Re Lehman Brothers International (Europe)(in administration)* [2012] UKSC 6
54 CASS 7.8.2R
55 CASS 7 Annex 1

satisfies the CCP's margin call but the client has yet to pay. Some CCPs prohibit such lending altogether.[56]

Box 9.1   Case study – Griffin Trading Company

One of Griffin's clients had entered into an unauthorised large trade in December 1998 giving rise to margin calls totalling £6.5 million which Griffin was unable to satisfy.[57] Griffin's other clients discovered that there was a shortfall in the client money bank balance, and reports were that 'the liquidator expected 50% of their funds to be returned starting in six to eight weeks.'[58] The then UK regulator, the Securities and Futures Authority, commented, without explaining how a shortfall could arise:

'To ensure that sufficient client money is held in client bank account(s), the firm is required to make a daily calculation comparing the aggregate balance on the firm's client money accounts with the "client money requirement". The requirement is the total of customers' credit balances, plus the total margined transaction required. The client money requirement is compared with the balance according to the firm's own account records. If there is a deficit on the client money as a result of a client failing to pay, then the firm is obliged by SFA Rules to make good the deficit from its own funds. If it cannot and has no likelihood of being able to make good the deficit from its own funds then it is in effect insolvent. From that point onwards payments and trades will be subject to scrutiny under relevant insolvency law.'[59]

---

(4) A further consequence is that there are further rules to compute the entitlement of a client and to ensure a fair distribution of the funds which may be spread among client bank accounts, CCPs and intermediate brokers.[60] Where a firm holding clients' money becomes subject to an insolvency process or certain regulatory events,[61] the firm's client money balances at its approved banks will be pooled, and the trust fund thereby constituted will be distributed pro rata according to the client money entitlements of the clients.[62] The calculation of the client money entitlement is not straightforward, and there is a substantial risk that the pool size is too small to satisfy the totality of entitlements. Clients are unlikely to be aware of this side-effect of the client money protection process. (There are still further rules to address what happens if a bank, intermediate broker, settlement agent or OTC counterparty has failed, also leading to a shortfall albeit for different reasons.[63])

9.12   The simplicity of the idea of client funds being held on trust in order to provide clients with protection against the insolvency of their investment firm

---

56   See for example Eurex Clearing AG, *Clearing Conditions* (April 2012), Part 2, Number 6.3

57   Securities and Futures Authority, *Board Notice 574* (February 2001)

58   Cavaletti, C, *Griffin lessons of trading* (Futures (Cedar Falls, IA), March 1999)

59   Securities and Futures Authority (January 1999), Press Release, http://www.fsa.gov.uk/pubs/additional/sfa001-99.pdf

60   CASS 7A.2.4R–7A.2.10G

61   See CASS 7A.2.2R

62   CASS 7A.2.4R

63   CASS 7A3

has thus become too complex to rely on. The complexity makes it impossible for there to be certainty as to whether the investor will get its funds out of the insolvent firm, or the timescale of any distribution. The problems have confounded because insolvency officers have historically not been authorised to deal with assets outside the insolvent estate and which do not fall to be distributed to creditors, though a revised insolvency procedure, enabling administrators to deal with trust property, was introduced in February 2011.[64] Many inadequacies were exposed in the Lehman case referred to. A general overhaul of the client money regime, in the United Kingdom if not across the entirety of Europe, is certain to follow.[65]

Segregation at the CCP

9.13   Mention should be made of the treatment of the client's funds when passed to a CCP. As CCPs are not investment firms in the United Kingdom,[66] CCPs will not be subject to the client money rules. Cash deposited with a CCP as margin will thus be a debt owed by the CCP to its participant. GCMs take credit risk on CCPs with regard to their margin and default fund contributions.

Under section 187 of the Companies Act 1989, which is confusingly named as if it were a mere interpretation section, a substantive segregation obligation is created for CCPs and other organisations regulated as recognised clearing houses. Section 187 states that 'where a person enters into market contracts in more than one capacity, the provisions of this Part apply ... as if the contracts entered into in each different capacity were entered into by different persons.' In order to understand this section fully, first it must be appreciated that 'this Part' sets forth a code of obligations for handling of defaults by CCPs (and other recognised clearing houses) and gives the clearing house immunity from the effects of insolvency laws otherwise applicable to their participants.[67] If a participant enters into a contract in a manner which constitutes him a trustee in respect of 'client money' passed to the clearing house, the clearing house is obliged to conduct two completely separate sets of default proceedings as if it were dealing with two defaulters: the trustee defaulter, and the own-account defaulter. It follows that the clearing house must operate separate sets of accounts reflecting the different capacities of the participant, to avoid muddling the two sets of default proceedings.

Further segregation at the CCP is achieved by two explicatory measures:

(1) Regulation 16 of the Financial Markets and Insolvency Regulations 1991[68] provides that a member of a recognised clearing house, and the recognised clearing house itself, in effecting 'relevant transactions' are deemed to be acting in a different capacity from other market contracts, for the purposes of section 187 of the 1989 Act. 'Relevant transactions' means market contracts in relation to which the member receives 'clients' money' under the FSA's client money rules.

---

64   Investment Bank Special Administration Regulations 2011, SI 2011 No 245; see also **section 8.5**

65   Financial Services Authority, *Business Plan 2012/13* (March 2012), http://www.fsa.gov.uk/static/pubs/plan/bp2012-13.pdf, p 11

66   See **section 12.5**

67   See **sections 8.10ff**

68   SI 1991 No 880

(2) Paragraph 28 of the Schedule to the Recognition Requirements Regulations 2001[69] formerly provided that margin provided by a defaulter for his own account was not to be applied to meet a shortfall on a client account, but that restriction has now been lifted,[70] with the result that (for example) a default fund contribution classified as margin can be applied to cover a shortfall on a client account. A client account is one to which 'relevant transactions', as defined above, have been booked.

Apart from these provisions, and the limited and weak rule in CASS 6.2.3R requiring use of nominees in relation to custody of client assets, there is no statutory requirement on firms or infrastructures to segregate clients' transactions or securities from the firm's own, nor to subject them to a trust. However, article 39 of EMIR[71] will impose a duty on CCPs to offer separated accounts for individual clients (as well as omnibus client accounts), to which both assets and positions are to be recorded.

CENTRAL AND COMMERCIAL BANK MONEY

9.14   The FMI Principles strongly recommend that infrastructures use central bank money as their settlement asset.[72] In **section 15.4** the question of central bank money for settlement of the cash leg in a CSD is discussed further; it is noted that central bank money may not be available to all market participants, since accounts at the central bank are not made available to all. Here the following comments on central bank money may be made:

(1) Central bank money means nothing different from commercial bank money in terms of the 'asset' which is owned, save that it is a claim on the central bank. Of course, a claim on the central bank is the most robust type of claim there is, because the central bank ought always (barring the insolvency of the state itself) to be able to honour its obligations. But there is no ground for supposing that the central bank is immune from operational errors or asserting defences to claims for repayment of what the account-holder believes to be due. If, however, the depositor is willing to accept the premise that a central bank is incapable of becoming insolvent, then the benefit of central bank money is that no credit risk is entailed, unlike any balance on an account with a commercial bank.

(2) Central bank money might also be subject to different terms from commercial bank money. Central banks are less likely to lend freely, thereby constraining the ability to use a central bank account as a source of liquidity. Commercial banks may thus provide cash services such as 'contractual settlement',[73] and integrated banking facilities, which would be unavailable to account-holders at the central bank. Interest rates are likely to differ, and central banks may impose conditions on withdrawal, for example if the deposit is a reserve deposit.[74]

---

69 Financial Services and Markets Act 2000 (Recognition Requirements for Investment Exchanges and Clearing Houses) Regulations 2001, SI 2001 No 995
70 Financial Markets and Insolvency Regulations 2009, SI 2009 No 853
71 Regulation (EU) No 648/2012 of the European Parliament and of the Council of 4 July 2012 on OTC derivatives, central counterparties and trade repositories
72 FMI Principle 9
73 See **sections 18.30–18.33**
74 Bank of England Act 1998, s 2, Sch 6; Cash Ratio Deposits (Eligible Liabilities) Order 1998, SI 1998 No 1130

(3) Infrastructures are expected to use central bank money owing to the lower degree of risk: '[w]ith the use of central bank money, a payment obligation is typically discharged by providing the FMI or its participants with a direct claim on the central bank, that is, the settlement asset is central bank money. Central banks have the lowest credit risk and are the source of liquidity with regard to their currency of issue.'[75] Be that as it may,[76] there is also an expectation in the case of a CCP that having an account with the central bank makes it more likely that emergency liquidity support would be available to provide stability in the case of a crisis, for example difficulty in liquidating non-cash margin, or even a shortfall in the default fund. The role of a central bank in supporting a CCP in such circumstances has been hotly debated.[77]

CASH AS COLLATERAL

9.15 Cash collateral can be vitally important, as many clearing and settlement activities entail the extension of credit; the cash involved in the payment leg of a transaction may serve as collateral for this credit extension.

There are two principal techniques for taking cash as collateral. The primary method is to acknowledge that cash received constitutes a debt owed by the recipient, and to confer simply a right of set-off on the recipient so that the cash repayment obligation is used to neutralise the client's credit obligation. Set-off rights are subject to various possible challenges in the client's insolvency,[78] and in consequence it is common to find that the set-off right is backed up with a charge over the cash deposit. After a deal of academic wrangling, the House of Lords settled that under English law a charge over a deposit in favour of the deposit-taker is a perfectly acceptable construct, but it is functionally equivalent to a set-off.[79] The conclusion is that, where only two parties are involved, a charge adds nothing to a set-off right.

A firm which has avoided the application of the client money rules by acquiring 'full ownership' of the money – 'full ownership', whenever the client money rules do not apply the statutory trust, meaning nothing more complicated than a credit to the firm's bank account – will ordinarily use this technique.

In a case where the cash is deposited with a person who is not the client's creditor, the second method – a charge – may be the more appropriate technique. This is because a trilateral set-off arrangement will likely fall foul of the requirement for mutuality under the statutory insolvency set-off rule.[80] Accordingly, a deposit placed with a third party, which represents an obligation owed by the third party, can as a chose in action be assigned by way of security or charged to the creditor.

---

75 FMI Principles, para 3.9.3
76 Comotto, R, *The interconnectivity of central and commercial bank money in the clearing and settlement of the European repo market* (September 2011), European repo market report for the International Capital Market Association, http://www.icmagroup.org/assets/documents/Maket-Practice/Regulatory-Policy/Repo-Markets/Central%20and%20commercial%20bank%20money%20-%20ICMA%20report%20September%202011.pdf
77 See **section 14.59**
78 See **section 8.9(11)**
79 *Re Bank of Credit and Commerce International S.A. (No. 8)* [1998] AC 214
80 Insolvency Rules 1986, rr 2.85, 4.90; Bank Insolvency (England and Wales) Rules 2009, r 72; Investment Bank Special Administration (England and Wales) Rules 2011, r 164

In the context of clearing and settlement, this approach to taking collateral may be encountered where the creditor is an investment firm subject to the client money rules, and instead of having taken the client's cash as a deposit (an obligation owed by the firm) has passed it to a deposit-taking bank to be held to the credit of the firm's client money bank account; the cash is thus a debt owed to the client by a third party, and if the firm is to be able to avail itself of the cash as security, it will have to do so by way of charge or assignment.

A third party such as a GCM or settlement agent seeking access to 'client money' by way of security may be unable to achieve its ends. This is because of the difficulties posed by the restrictions on discharge of the fiduciary obligations of the firm handling the client money. Even if the GCM or settlement agent is a third party to whom funds can be passed under CASS 7.5.2R, it will (at least in relation to a 'contingent liability investment') be obliged to waive set-off rights.[81] A possible solution may be to take a springing charge over funds due to the client as they emerge from the statutory trust, taking advantage of the rule which provides for funds paid to a third party at the direction of the client to cease to be 'client money'.[82]

FINALITY OF PAYMENTS

9.16   If one accepts the credit risk issues inherent in a receipt of cash, the main question remaining in the context of clearing and settlement of payments will be when the cash has arrived, and whether it has been received with finality. 'Finality' has been defined by the CPSS in the following terms: 'Final settlement is defined as the *irrevocable* and *unconditional* transfer of an asset or financial instrument, or the *discharge* of an obligation by the [financial market infrastructure] or its participants in accordance with the terms of the underlying contract.'[83] The concept of finality causes confusion of bewildering proportions, so at the outset a glossary of frequently heard terms may be useful.

- *Unconditional.* As a definition of finality, unconditionality is unsatisfactory. Confusion is likely to arise because conditions will often relate to a transfer *obligation*, rather than a transfer viewed as a separate event. However, payment systems do have conditions, and without them being satisfied, there is no likelihood of the payment being made; but equally, fulfillment of conditions does not mean that a transfer has been made, let alone made with finality.

- *Irrevocable.* A transfer might be regarded as final when the payer can no longer revoke it, that is when the settlement process can no longer be stopped by the person obliged to pay. However, irrevocability is not yet a guarantee of finality, since the law or the payment system may allow for the non-completion or even the reversal of transfers in particular circumstances.

- *Discharge.* Discharge occurs on the performance of the transfer obligation. Unfortunately this concept is circular, since an obligation to transfer will be discharged when a transfer is made with finality.

- *Irreversible.* A transfer is final when the credit to the payee's account cannot be reversed. Confusion can still linger, though, since there may be legal grounds for reversal even if the rules of the payment system are clear

---

81   CASS 7.8.2R
82   CASS 7.2.15R(2)
83   FMI Principles, para 3.8.1

that reversal will not occur. The difficulty here is that the rules of payment systems are contractual and may not withstand an attack under insolvency laws. For example, if a transfer is made via a normal correspondent banking relationship, it is a question of contract terms whether a credit entry in the correspondent's books has to be reversed or not. These may be vulnerable to attack by a liquidator under zero-hour laws, or as preferences, or under other insolvency laws.[84]

● *Immune from challenge.* It may be tempting to think of finality as arising when there are no grounds at all on which the payment made to the payee could be reversed. However, that is probably going too far. Fraud and some insolvency risks may be unrelated to the operation of the payment system, and it may be possible for a victim or insolvency officer to challenge the payee in the courts. These dangers should not be seen as a finality problem, since the reversal of the transfer occurs outside the payment system. The irreversibility inherent in a 'final' payment should be seen as irreversibility within the limited world of the payment system.

Perhaps the difference of views on the very definition of finality stems from the different objectives of users of the term. On the one hand there are the regulators and guardians of financial stability, for whom the primary concern is avoidance of systemic risk. On the other is the participant in the financial marketplace, whose concern is that expressed above, namely whether the money has arrived safely so that it can be used for other purposes. The regulatory guidance and legislation is predominantly directed towards the public objective, rather than the simple needs of the end-user. This is made starkly apparent when one considers the scope of the protections afforded by the Settlement Finality Directive.[85] Only designated systems and their participants are granted protection, so that the fundamental question for an end-user, as to whether the money has arrived with sufficient safety that it can be used, is left to private risk management.

It has been observed that the problem of finality arises because of the sheer speed of electronic funds transfer, which causes trouble when parties wish to revoke payments, typically in the event of counterparty or client insolvency.[86] To this, it may be said that finality is precisely what the policy of the law should aim to achieve, notwithstanding the 'very fine arguments ... sometimes addressed to the courts as to precisely when payment is effected under a funds transfer.' Without clear contractual rules between payment service users and their service providers, however, such arguments will persist.

A final word on the subject of finality of payments is simply to note that the same concepts and risks arise in relation to credits of securities to accounts. The settlement finality legislation is the same as for cash, and is directed to the same end. The discussion set out above may thus be applied to questions arising in relation to the transfer of securities. However, the law of transfer and ownership of securities is more complex, and moreover, it enjoys an overlay of legal certainty in that there is now EU legislation which specifies the legal consequences of credits of securities to an account. It is that subject to which the next chapter is devoted.

---

84 See **section 8.9**

85 Directive 98/26/EC of the European Parliament and of the Council of 19 May 1998 on settlement finality in payment and securities settlement systems; see **sections 8.18ff**

86 Brindle, M, and Cox, R, eds, *The Law of Bank Payments* (4th edn, Sweet & Maxwell/Thomson Reuters, November 2010), ISBN 978-1847035516, para 1-020

10 Securities

OWNERSHIP OF SECURITIES

10.1   In order to settle a transaction contemplating the transfer of securities, the legal requirements for obtaining ownership of the securities should be clear. The same logic applies to transfers which stop short of being attempts to acquire complete ownership immediately, such as creation of a security interest. The law of ownership of securities is, accordingly, as important to the subject of clearing and settlement as the law of ownership of money.

It is perhaps surprising, given that introductory remark, and in a context where the values are huge (€ 526 trillion of securities were settled by Euroclear's CSDs in 2010 – that is over 2 trillion each working day)[1], that there should be absence of clarity on the operation of the law in some member states, lack of uniformity across Europe, and downright confusion as to how ownership questions should be answered when a multi-country tiered holding pattern applies. Effort has been made to introduce greater legal certainty, but it is fair to say that the preservation by member states of their differing juridical approaches to ownership of securities will continue to generate questions for which there is no legally simple answer.

The starting-point for this chapter is to consider the problem of ownership of securities under English law and other European legal systems. The solutions offered at an international level, culminating in the Securities Law Directive, will then be reviewed. Legal implications of the legislation will be considered. Finally, the protection given to clients and the operation of the 'client asset' regime will be assessed.

OWNERSHIP OF SECURITIES UNDER ENGLISH LAW

10.2   Starting with the simple case of a share in a registered company incorporated under the Companies Act 2006, the person who owns the share is presumably the person recorded as member of the company in the register of members required to be maintained under section 113 of that Act. Rectification of the register can be ordered by the court under section 125, and on an application for rectification the court 'may decide any question relating to the title of a person ... to have his name entered in or omitted from the register ... and generally may decide any question necessary or expedient to be decided for rectification of the register.'[2]

---

1   Euroclear UK & Ireland, *Corporate News* (February 2011)
2   Companies Act 2006, s 125(3)

These provisions do not, however, say anything about ownership per se: it is implicit in the status of membership, which confers rights of voting and entitlement of distribution of net value on a winding-up, that the status of membership has value proportionate to the size of the shareholding. In that analysis, a shareholding may be regarded as a chose in action constituting a co-ownership interest in a single asset, namely the issuer itself. Professor Roy Goode says 'on a sale or trust of the shares it is not possible to segregate the shares of the subject of the sale or trust from an interest in the remainder of the issuer. In short, such shares are not fungibles at all, they represent co-ownership of a single, identified asset. The same applies to a credit balance in a bank account.'[3] If Professor Goode's analysis were more generally accepted, it would be necessary to analyse the legal aspects of owning shares in the same way as transfer of part of a debt, requiring the assignor to be party to an action by the assignee against the issuer of the shares to establish the assignee's rights.[4]

Ownership and transfer under the Uncertificated Securities Regulations

10.3   Most practitioners, however, take a more pragmatic view of the law, which is to regard each share as a discrete item of property. This is implicit in the Uncertificated Securities Regulations 2001 (USRs),[5] regulation 14 of which provides that 'where [a company] permits ... the transfer of title to [a certain class of] shares by means of a relevant system, title to shares of that class ... may be transferred by means of that relevant system.'

The USRs derive their authority from section 785 of the Companies Act 1989, which allows for regulations enabling title to securities to be evidenced and transferred without a written instrument. Section 785 and regulation 14 of the USRs thus make it unnecessary to comply with the Stock Transfer Act 1963 – which would otherwise require a stock transfer form to be used – where the shares have been accepted for uncertificated transfer within CREST, which is a relevant system for the purposes of the USRs.

Title to a share may thus be transferred via CREST, the 'relevant system' operated by Euroclear UK & Ireland.[6] The USRs address the need for the name of a member of the company – the transferee of shares – to appear on the register of members by providing under regulation 20 that both the issuer of the shares and the Operator of the relevant system maintain registers of members, and that the company must also maintain a copy of the Operator register of members. So, essentially, the issuer keeps a register of certificated shareholders, and a carbon copy of the Operator's definitive record of ownership of uncertificated shares. Detailed provisions regarding maintenance of these registers and records is set out in Schedule 4 of the USRs, including that the company must ensure that the record of uncertificated shares is regularly reconciled with the Operator register of members.

As regards other types of securities than shares, regulation 19 of the USRs makes similar provision to that in regulation 14, so that title to other securities can be transferred by means of a relevant system: CREST is used to settle

---

3   Goode, R, *Legal Problems of Credit and Security* (3rd ed, Sweet & Maxwell, April 2003), ISBN 0-421-47150-6, para 2-06
4   *Re Steel Wing Co Ltd* [1921] 1 Ch 349
5   SI 2001 No 3755
6   See **section 11.21** for the regulation of CREST

'general public sector securities' and 'eligible debt securities' which consist of securities such as UK gilts and certificates of deposit which used to be settled at the Bank of England.[7]

Transfer of securities is provided for under regulation 27 of the USRs: 'upon settlement of a transfer of uncertificated units of a security in accordance with his rules ... an Operator shall register on the relevant Operator register of securities the transfer of title to those units of that security.' Further provisions facilitate the giving of instructions to the Operator to effectuate settlement.[8]

Indirect holdings

10.4   The preceding discussion has been focused on a very simple case, that of 'direct' holding of securities by registration of the owner's name in the register of members of the company. However, investments may not be made in this way, particularly if the investor is located in a different country from the issuer of the securities. In practice a chain of intermediaries (sometimes in Europe called 'account providers') will stand in the chain between the investor and the issuer. This is referred to as an indirect holding of securities, but indirect holdings pose particular problems for the law of ownership in many countries, and England is no exception. It is now generally accepted that a person whose name appears on the register of members but who is not the actual investor acts in the capacity of trustee[9]. English law thus has no fundamental problem with the idea that the trustee is merely a 'legal' owner of the securities and that the investor is the 'beneficial' owner; but there are a number of awkward consequences of a simple trust analysis of indirect holdings:

(1)   A problem which has exercised academics for some time is whether a trust can validly be created in respect of 10 of the 100 shares credited to an account, owing to a doubt as to certainty of subject-matter. This question has been settled by the ruling in *Hunter v Moss*,[10] which (despite its critics[11]) held that 'there is no objection on grounds of uncertainty to a trust of part of a shareholding of the trustee, and has been followed, in this country in *Re Harvard Securities* [1997] 2BCLC 369, in Hong Kong in *Re CA Pacific Finance Limited* [2000] 1BCLC 494, and in Australia in *White v Shortall* [2006] NSW SC 1379.'[12]

(2)   The person acknowledged by the registered member/trustee (A) may not be the actual investor (C), but another account provider (B) acting for the investor. English law does not have a problem with the idea that a mere beneficial entitlement is a piece of property which can be made subject to a trust, so that the intermediate account-provider B actually holds something for the investor C under a sub-trust. But the property which B holds is

---

7   See the Bank of England's webpage *The Future of Money Market Instruments* (papers up to October 2003), https://www.bankofengland.co.uk/markets/money/mmfuture.htm
8   USRs, regs 35, 36
9   Yates, M, and Montagu, G, *The Law of Global Custody* (Tottel, February 2009), ISBN 978-1847661425; Benjamin, J, *Interests in Securities* (Oxford, 2000), ISBN 0-19-826992-7, para 2.36
10   [1994] 1 WLR 452, CA
11   For example, Hayton, D, *Uncertainty of subject-matter of trusts* (July 1994) LQR vol 110, p 335; Birks, P, *Establishing a Proprietary Base (Re Goldcorp)* (September 1999) Restitution Law Review Vol 7, p 83
12   *Re Lehman Brothers International (Europe), Pearson and ors v Lehman Brothers Finance SA and ors,* [2010] EWHC 2914 (Ch), per Briggs J

different from that which A holds. Like it or not, there is risk involved in A's involvement, and there are operational and contractual aspects of the relationship between A and B which mean that C's experience as investor may be different from that of D, who chose a different holding pattern involving E as his immediate service provider, who in turn used F as custodian and directly registered member, not to mention G, who eschewed intermediaries altogether and became a sponsored participant in CREST and direct holder of the securities. So A's, D's and G's investments in the same securities are not quite identical. This is a different result from the holding of a chattel through a series of trusts and sub-trusts. To put it differently, unless an investor's interest is recorded at the ultimate 'root of title' it will be transformed into something slightly different by virtue of the intermediation arrangement.

(3) Without a legal estate, there is a risk to purchasers of securities from those who are mere beneficial owners. A third party can claim superior title: under English law only a bona fide purchaser of a *legal estate* for value without notice can defeat an equitable claimant. This leaves an acquirer open to challenges to his title on the grounds of priority in time. Difficult rules of equity relating to priority include an examination of whether reasonable steps were taken to obtain priority (for example, by giving notice under the rule in *Dearle v Hall*[13]), whether the subsequent acquirer had notice of the competing interest, whether the holder of the prior interest is estopped from relying on its priority through its conduct, and so forth.

(4) Section 126 of the Companies Act 2006 prohibits the entry on the register of members of any notice of a trust. This legal restriction, commonly reflected in companies' articles of association, entrenches the difficulties indirect investors may have in establishing their ability to be regarded as 'shareholders'. This is important as particular rights have been given to 'shareholders' under European law.[14]

(5) Collateral arrangements under which security is taken in accordance with the Financial Collateral Arrangements Regulations (FCRs)[15] are subject to a conflict of laws rule[16] which requires that only the law of the place where the 'relevant account' is maintained is relevant to legal questions relating to ownership and other proprietary interests in the securities. This is incompatible with a strict trust doctrine which would treat such questions as falling to be decided where the 'property' is located, disregarding completely the entries on a trustee's books. Unfortunately, if the strict trust doctrine must apply whenever the FCRs do not, and it is unclear whether the FCRs do apply in any particular case without answering a property law question, the absence of a complete code of law to cover all cases may give rise to irresolvable conflict.

(6) Section 53(1)(c) of the Law of Property Act 1925 requires that 'a disposition of an equitable interest or trust subsisting at the time of the disposition, must be in writing signed by the person disposing of the same,' which could in some situations pose difficulty. Sales and purchases are generally not a problem, either because it can be taken that the Companies Acts and the

---

13 (1828) 3 Russ 1
14 See **section 20.13**
15 Financial Collateral Arrangements (No 2) Regulations 2003, SI 2003 No 3226; see **sections 8.27–8.29**
16 FCRs, reg 19

USRs have abolished the requirement in relation to transfers of uncertificated shares, or because in other cases a written instrument is in any event required by the Stock Transfer Act 1963. Creation of security interests is, however, more troublesome. The FCRs formally abolished the requirements of section 53(1)(c)[17] – but not for all security interests relating to securities, as the abolition applies only to eligible financial collateral arrangements.

(7) Insofar as 'ownership' of an equitable interest in property is to exist, it appears to require the existence of a specifically enforceable contract.[18] Where the securities bought are freely tradeable, the pre-requisites for specific performance may be difficult to establish.[19]

(8) Where a trustee mixes trust property with its own in an account, the rule in *Re Hallett's Estate*[20] will apply. In broad terms, the rule states that any withdrawals from that account are taken to be withdrawals of the trustee's own assets rather than those of the beneficiary; but that any replenishments made by the trustee do not accrue to the beneficiary but to the trustee itself.

(9) Where there is a shortfall in the property held on trust, it is not consistent with trust law principles to distribute the remaining assets on a *pari passu* basis. While English law has provided for shortfalls to be handled in this manner,[21] it has been argued that this is unjustifiable in relation to trust property, because equity requires appropriation of the property in the fund to the first beneficiary of the trust, so that latecomers receive nothing, and where the property over which the trust is created is used improperly, for the beneficiaries to suffer reduction of their entitlements pro rata – in other words, the application of tracing rules.[22] Statutory intervention has been needed to ensure the application of the *pari passu* principle in cases involving distribution of client assets where there is a shortfall.[23] But it will only apply if the account-provider unable to make the shortfall good is an 'investment bank'; in the case of a shortfall at a failed CCP or CSD, neither of which would qualify, the general law of trusts will prevail.

(10) It can be difficult to ascertain whether a person is holding securities as beneficial owner or trustee. The factors which indicate the one rather than the other were examined by Briggs J during the course of the *Lehman Brothers* litigation.[24] The judge ruled (inter alia) that: (a) it is not fatal to a person's beneficial ownership of securities that those securities are co-mingled with the trustee's own securities, that the fund is fluctuating, or that the terms of the trust will decide the identity of the trust property at a future date; (b) 'whether B has a proprietary interest in the property acquired by A for B's account depends upon their mutual intention, to be ascertained by an objective assessment of the terms of the agreement or relationship between A and B with reference to that property;' and (c) the

---

17 FCRs, reg 4(2)
18 *J Sainsbury plc v O'Connor* [1991] 1 WLR 963, CA
19 Micheler, E, *Property in Securities – a Comparative Study* (CUP, August 2006), ISBN 978-0-521-83265-6, section 2.4
20 (1879) 13 Ch D 696, CA
21 *Barlow Clowes International Ltd v Vaughan* [1992] 4 All ER 22, CA
22 See McFarlane, B, and Stevens, R, 'Interests in Securities – Practical Problems and Conceptual Solutions', in Gullifer, L, and Payne, J, eds, *Intermediated Securities – Legal Problems and Practical Issues* (Hart Publishing, November 2009), ISBN 978-1-84946-013-2, pp 40–44
23 Investment Bank Special Administration Regulations 2011, SI 2011 No 245, reg 12(2)
24 *Re Lehman Brothers International (Europe), Pearson and ors v Lehman Brothers Finance SA and ors* [2010] EWHC 2914 (Ch)

fact that A acts as agent or broker for B may suggest the existence of a trust but is not conclusive.

(11) Where the trustee is insolvent, that does not alter the nature of the trust or the duties of the trustee, but the effective management body may have no statutory duty, and possibly no legal power, to deal with the trust assets. Thus, in the Lehman Brothers collapse, the administrators of Lehman Brothers International (Europe) could not be hurried by asset claimants into making an early distribution.[25] English law permits administrators to take over the role of trustee, covering their expenses from the trust assets,[26] but only since the implementation of the Investment Bank Special Administration Regulations has this been a required course of action.[27]

What this discussion illustrates is that, while the practical and operational systems for share ownership and transfer are well understood and for the most part function efficiently, there remains debate at an academic level about how those practical and operational arrangements can be sensibly reconciled with legal rules which were not designed for them. Given the prevalence of settlement fails,[28] contractual settlement,[29] and use of omnibus accounts,[30] it is readily seen that the kind of forensic analysis theoretically required for trustees is unworkable. In practice the issue only gives rise to difficulty for investors if there is a shortfall on the account which the account provider cannot rectify, either because there are no replacement securities to be had, or because the account provider is insolvent – investors are unlikely to complain when they have got their securities and have no idea that for a short period the account balance did not reconcile. So the academic debate is continued in the court-room.

This is an unsatisfactory state of affairs. The European Commission's project for 'legal certainty' is designed to sweep many of these difficulties into oblivion by the expedient of a Securities Law Directive, the possible shape of which is discussed at **section 10.8**.

OWNERSHIP IN OTHER LEGAL SYSTEMS

10.5 The English experience has, to some extent, been reflected in other jurisdictions. While the detailed issues reflect the legal traditions of the countries where they arise, the conclusion is the same: traditional property law is ill-adapted to the concept of the dematerialised security. Dr Christophe Bernasconi has analysed the problem of interests in securities held through indirect holding systems as follows.[31] Traditional principles of civil and common law dictate that property rights are lost when a person's property is fungible and it is commingled with similar property of other persons, such as

25 *Re Lehman Brothers International (Europe), Four Private Investment Funds v Joint Administrators* [2008] EWHC 2869 (Ch)
26 *In re Berkeley Applegate (Investment Consultants) Ltd* [1989] Ch 32
27 Investment Bank Special Administration Regulations 2011, SI 2011 No 245, table 1, modifying the Insolvency Act 1986, Sch B1, para 99
28 See **sections 21.9ff**
29 See **sections 18.30–18.32**
30 See **section 10.16**
31 Bernasconi, C, *The law applicable to dispositions of securities held through indirect holding systems* (November 2000), Hague Conference on Private International Law, Convention No 36, Prel. Doc. No 1, http://www.hcch.net/index_en.php?act=publications. details&pid=2859&dtid=35

the account-provider or other clients of the account-provider. The unpleasant consequence of rigid adherence to traditional principles would be that the client whose securities are combined, at some level in the holding chain, in an omnibus account would see them replaced by a mere contractual right of delivery-up of the securities or possibly by a co-ownership right. Consequently:

- Some legal systems have forbidden commingling. These are the direct holding systems such as those in Scandinavia or Poland.

- Some legal systems recognise only the contractual right of re-delivery, with the consequence that custodians are prohibited from engaging in other activities, to limit the extent to which non-depositor claimants might have any competing rights. This has historically been the situation in the Netherlands.

- Some legal systems provide for co-ownership, allowing a property right in an undivided share of the property held by the account-provider, as in Germany or Spain, or what ought to be held by the account-provider, as in Belgium or Luxembourg. This is also the model, using the device of a trust, historically adopted in England.

- Some legal systems provide for look-through, which allows the ultimate investor to have a property right in the underlying securities, casting the intermediaries as mere administrative agents. This has historically been the situation in France.

- In the United States, the whole debate was done away with in 1994 in article 8 of the Uniform Commercial Code. The idea there is that the investor does not have securities at all, but a 'securities entitlement' conferring certain rights against his account provider, including rights to property belonging to the account provider. The article 8 model has been refined to constitute the basis of the Geneva Securities Convention and, in due course, the proposed Securities Law Directive.

Dr Bernasconi also reported on the difficulties to which the traditional approach gives rise. Quite apart from the complexities which follow from an international holding structure where the issuer, registrar or depositary, custodian, and investor may all be in different countries applying different legal rules to the question of ownership, there are serious practical problems with a look-through approach. These include the absence of records at any level beyond the investor's account-provider suggesting any connection between the investor and the asset, the need for collateral takers to 'perfect' their security in every country where an account provider intermediating between itself and the issuer maintains its accounts, and the impracticality of delivering voting rights or other shareholder entitlements in a uniform manner. In a single European market, a more practical and efficient legal solution is needed. But this is not a straightforward matter, as Professor Alberto Giovannini noted in his first report:

'The third type of barriers reflects the existence of different legal rules defining the effect of the operation of a system, including different legal structures concerning securities themselves. This type of barrier is of a different order to the others. Barriers of market regulation and of tax can generally be changed or abolished without affecting basic legal concepts. However, laws about what securities are and how they may be owned form a basic and intimate part of the legal systems of Member States, and to change them will have many ramifications. Barriers related to legal certainty trouble securities settlement systems, clearing systems, and market intermediaries equally.'[32]

Specifically, Professor Giovannini recommended the removal of two legal barriers relating to questions concerning ownership of securities: Barrier 13, 'The absence of an EU-wide framework for the treatment of interests in securities', and Barrier 15, 'Uneven application of national conflict of law rules.' Each of these topics requires further discussion.

CONFLICTS OF LAWS: PRIMA AND THE HAGUE CONVENTION

10.6 One way of dealing with the problem is to agree a universal set of conflicts of laws rules, which ensures that all countries agree on whose legal system applies to resolve any question arising in respect of property rights. This is the approach of the Hague Convention.[33] The Hague Convention adopts the 'PRIMA' or 'place of the relevant intermediary approach' – that is to say, the law applicable to certain questions of property law are to be answered exclusively by reference to the law of the relevant account. The central proposition of PRIMA is that there is only one relevant relationship in determining entitlement to securities credited to an account, namely that between the account-holder and the account-provider. Each link in a long chain of intermediation is looked at separately.

The Hague Convention also specifies that the 'law of the relevant account' is usually the law governing the account agreement.[34] The Convention thus dispenses entirely with any idea that 'location' or '*lex situs*' are relevant to the choice of law, notwithstanding that the choice affects property rights. It is probably for the latter reason that the European Commission, having proposed in 2003 that the EU should sign the Convention, and in 2006 called upon Member States to sign it, in 2009 withdrew its proposals.[35]

Nevertheless, the PRIMA approach is already embedded in the following European legislation, albeit in a more diluted form than envisaged by the Hague Convention. Each of these pieces of legislation refers to the place of the relevant account:

- The Settlement Finality Directive specifies that where the rights of a person with respect to securities provided as collateral in connection with a payment or securities settlement system, or to a central bank, are recorded on a register, account or centralised deposit system located in a Member State, the determination of the rights shall be governed by the law of that Member State.[36]

---

32 Giovannini, A, *Cross-Border Clearing and Settlement Arrangements in the European Union* (November 2001), http://ec.europa.eu/internal_market/financial-markets/docs/clearing/first_giovannini_report_en.pdf, p 54

33 Hague Conference on Private International Law, *Convention on the law applicable to certain rights in respect of securities held with an intermediary* (July 2006), Convention No 36, http://www.hcch.net/index_en.php?act=conventions.text&cid=72

34 Hague Convention, art 4

35 European Commission, Press Releases IP/03/1725 (December 2003); IP/06/930 (July 2006); OJ C71/17 (March 2009); http://ec.europa.eu/internal_market/financial-markets/hague/index_en.htm

36 Directive of the European Parliament and of the Council of 19 May 1998 on settlement finality in payment and securities settlement systems, 98/26/EC, art 9(2)

- The Financial Collateral Directive (FCD) specifies that any question falling under one of four heads which arises in relation to book entry securities collateral is to be governed by the law of the country in which the relevant account is maintained, disregarding any rule under which reference should be made to the law of another country.[37]

- The proposed Regulation on CSDs specifies that any question with respect to proprietary aspects in relation to financial instruments held by a CSD shall be governed by the law of the country where the account is maintained.[38]

Finally, if a Securities Law Directive is put forward to the European legislature in accordance with the European Commission Services' preliminary suggestions of late 2010, it would provide that any question with respect to any of seven specified matters arising in relation to account-held securities should be governed by the national law of the country where the relevant securities account is maintained by the account provider.[39]

These tests for PRIMA are all open to criticism because it may be extremely hard to pinpoint a single jurisdiction for the place where the account is 'maintained'.[40] In any event, choice of law cannot achieve harmony of substantive rights, without which investors face disparities of treatment in respect of simple questions where, in a single market, one would expect similar investments to be treated identically.

SUBSTANTIVE PROBLEMS OF OWNERSHIP WITH REGARD TO SECURITIES HELD IN AN ACCOUNT

10.7   Accordingly, as a parallel exercise to the Hague Convention, UNIDROIT developed the Geneva Convention on Substantive Rules for Intermediated Securities.[41] This seeks to codify, at international level, the following matters affecting the rights of account-holders and the obligations of account-providers:

(1) *Rights of an account-holder.* The credit of securities to an account confers certain rights on the account-holder. These include the right to receive and exercise certain rights attached to the securities, including dividend and voting rights, the right to effect a disposition, and the right to instruct the account-provider to cause the securities to be held otherwise than through an account, insofar as permitted by applicable law.[42]

---

37 Directive 2002/47/EC of the European Parliament and of the Council of 6 June 2002 on financial collateral arrangements, art 9

38 European Commission, *Proposal for a Regulation of the European Parliament and of the Council on improving securities settlement in the European Union and on central securities depositories, etc* (March 2012), COM(2012) 73 final, http://eur-lex.europa.eu/LexUriServ/ LexUriServ.do?uri=CELEX:52012PC0073:EN:PDF, art 46

39 European Commission Services, *Legislation on legal certainty of securities holding and dispositions* (November 2011), Consultation Document DG Markt G2 MET/OT/acg D(2010) 768690, http://ec.europa.eu/internal_market/consultations/docs/2010/securities/consultation_ paper_en.pdf, Principle 14

40 See for example Bernasconi, C, and Potok, R, 'PRIMA Convention brings certainty to cross-border deals' (January 2003) International Financial Law Review, pp 11–14

41 International Institute for the Unification of Private Law, *Convention on Substantive Rules for Intermediated Securities* (October 2009), http://www.unidroit.org/english/conventions/2009int ermediatedsecurities/main.htm

42 Geneva Convention, art 9

(2) *Obligations of an account-provider.* The account-provider is obliged to take appropriate measures to enable account-holders to exercise those rights, including holding sufficient securities to cover the credits to accounts, steps to isolate the securities held from creditors in the event of its own insolvency, giving effect to the account-holder's instructions, not disposing of the securities without authorisation, passing on information necessary for the exercise of rights, and passing on dividends. The obligations of the account-provider are limited to what is agreed and supervening law.[43]

(3) *Acquisition and disposition.* Acquisition is by credit to an account; disposition is by debit. Lesser interests in securities can be created in three ways only, each requiring an agreement: if the account-provider is the grantee, without further formality; if a 'designating entry' is made on the account in favour of the grantee; and if there is a 'control agreement' in favour of the grantee. Acquisitions and dispositions made in accordance with these rules have effect against third parties. The circumstances in which debits may properly be made are limited.[44]

(4) *Impact of insolvency proceedings.* If the account-holder or the account-provider becomes insolvent, this does not affect the rights and interests which have become effective against third parties.[45]

(5) *Priority rules.* The innocent acquirer (a person in whose favour a credit, designating entry or interest, unless he actually knows or ought to know of another person's interest) takes free of other claimants' interests. Other priority rules rank interests in other circumstances.[46]

(6) *Upper tier attachment.* The ability of a creditor or claimant to 'attach' securities not at the level of the account-provider, but at a more remote level (the 'upper tier') where the account-provider's own interest is recorded, is expressly prohibited.[47]

(7) *Shortfalls.* If an account-provider finds that there are insufficient securities for its account holders and itself, it must replenish them. If the shortfall arises in the insolvency of the account-provider, the account-holders bear the loss rateably to the amounts credited to their accounts.[48]

(8) *Collateral arrangements.* Chapter V of the Geneva Convention, which post-dates the Financial Collateral Directive,[49] contains eight articles on securities collateral arrangements, covering much of the same ground as the FCD.

Certain matters are not, however, addressed by the Geneva Convention, but are left to 'non-Convention law'. Among these are the consequences of unauthorised debiting of accounts, whether debits or credits are invalid or may be conditional, some priority contests, and the relationship of investor with the issuer on matters such as right to attend and vote at meetings.

Securities Law Directive

10.8 Unfortunately the European Union has not adopted the Geneva Convention, despite participating in its development. Instead, building on work

---

43 Geneva Convention, arts 10, 23
44 Geneva Convention, arts 11, 12 15
45 Geneva Convention, arts 14, 21
46 Geneva Convention, arts 18, 19
47 Geneva Convention, art 22
48 Geneva Convention, arts 24, 26
49 See **sections 8.25ff**

done by a group of experts (the 'Legal Certainty Group') established to advise on the need for legislation to lift the Giovannini barriers, the European Commission has been inching its way towards a possible Securities Law Directive (SLD). Detailed commentary on a future proposal for legislation which remains controversial[50] and may be significantly modified before it becomes law (if indeed it gets that far) would be rash. The following points of the proposed SLD, as consulted on in 2010–2011,[51] might, however, be referred to.

(1) *Earmarking and control agreements.* A special method for making a disposition of securities by 'earmarking' the securities in an account, or earmarking the entire account, is added to the more familiar 'control agreement' as well as concluding an agreement in favour of an account provider.[52] These techniques appear to be designed to codify the methods for taking security over securities credited to an account. Earmarking would, if the proposed SLD takes effect, be the most robust technique, as it would have priority over the other forms of disposition barring outright transfer to an account held by the disponee.[53] Earmarking would mean an entry in a securities account which has the effects that the account-provider is not permitted to act on the account-holder's instructions without the disponee's consent, and/or that the account-provider must act on the disponee's instructions. There is much to criticise in both the drafting and the practicality of earmarking as put forward by the proposed SLD.

(2) *Possession, control and ownership.* A good deal of confusion can arise as to whether a credit of securities to an account equates to a transfer of ownership of those securities. Under English law, this is not necessarily the effect of a credit, since English law accepts that legal title and beneficial ownership may be in different hands. An enquiry is needed as to the factual circumstances in order to ascertain whether a person to whose account securities have been credited holds them absolutely or as beneficial owner.[54] Yet there is a question of whether the credit to a third party's account constitutes a transfer of title or merely a transfer of possession. This question is fundamentally unanswered by English law, and has not been at all assisted by the persistence of thinking that possession is not a concept that can be applied to intangible property (a notion which is probably unsustainable in the modern law[55]) or a statutory definition of 'possession' in the context of financial collateral which muddles up possession with the concept of 'control' applicable to fixed charges.[56] As proposed, the SLD would, unfortunately, not give definitions of possession or control; and it might make things worse still, by suggesting that a credit to an account

---

50 Cf European Commission Services, *Legislation on Legal Certainty of Securities Holding and Dispositions – Summary of Responses to the Directorate-General Internal Market and Services' Second Consultation* (September 2011), http://ec.europa.eu/internal_market/consultations/docs/2010/securities/extended_summary_responses_en.pdf

51 European Commission Services, *Legislation on legal certainty of securities holding and dispositions* (November 2010), Consultation Document DG Markt G2 MET/OT/acg D(2010) 768690, http://ec.europa.eu/internal_market/consultations/docs/2010/securities/consultation_paper_en.pdf

52 Proposed SLD, Principle 4, para 5

53 Proposed SLD, Principle 9, para 1

54 *Re Lehman Brothers International (Europe), Pearson and ors v Lehman Brothers Finance SA and ors* [2010] EWHC 2914 (Ch)

55 See discussion at **section 8.29**

56 FCRs, reg 3(2); cf **section 8.29**

invariably gives the account-holder ownership, thereby eliminating a meaning for the word 'possession' altogether.

(3) *Upper tier attachment.*[57] As with the Geneva Convention, attachment at a level other than that of the account provider to the debtor-account-holder is to be prohibited. Dr Bernasconi cites a US case[58] where this was attempted without success, but there seem not to be any cases cited in the leading English law texts or European materials. Despite the paucity of practical difficulties, suggesting that the risk is more mythical than real, upper tier attachment has been generally agreed to be something needing to be addressed.[59]

(4) *Shortfalls.*[60] It would be left to Member States to determine whether to apply rateable distribution of assets in the event of a shortfall. This could lead to inexplicable differences between countries, and to losses being left at unexpected places in a chain of account-providers. Coupled with the no-fault liability provisions of account-providers under the Alternative Investment Fund Managers Directive,[61] the results of errors leading to unrectified shortfalls would be difficult to predict.

(5) *Ultimate account holders.*[62] The proposed SLD would confer rights, over and above those envisaged by the Geneva Convention, directly on an 'ultimate account holder', designed to put the end-investor into the same position as if she were a direct holder whose name appeared on the books of the CSD. How such rights are to be delivered, in practice, given the operational and geographical difficulties involved in a multi-link chain of account-providers,[63] is not addressed by the proposed SLD, and again there is much to criticise in the proposal even if the social objective is meritorious.

SECURITIES AS COLLATERAL

10.9 In the context of clearing and settlement, securities are not just the subject-matter of transactions, but may also constitute a valuable source of collateral. A discussion of issues concerning the ownership of securities must necessarily include coverage of the special considerations which arise when the ownership interest is contingent – that is, the right of a collateral-taker in circumstances typically described as an 'event of default' to take over ownership of the securities, or at least to have a right of sale in respect of the securities.

10.10 There are several techniques for taking securities as collateral.

(1) *Mortgage.* The oldest method of securing a creditor's rights is that of a mortgage, under which title to property is transferred subject to an 'equity

---

57 Proposed SLD, Principle 12
58 *Fidelity Partners Inc v First Trust Co,* 1997 US Dist LEXIS 19287 No 97 Civ.5184
59 Giovannini, A, *Second Report on EUC Clearing and Settlement Arrangements* (April 2003), http://ec.europa.eu/internal_market/financial-markets/docs/clearing/second_giovannini_ report_en.pdf, p 14; European Commission, *Advice of the Legal Certainty Group* (August 2006), http://ec.europa.eu/internal_market/financial-markets/docs/certainty/advice_final_ en.pdf, para 5.5; *Second Advice of the Legal Certainty Group* (August 2008), http://ec.europa. eu/internal_market/financial-markets/docs/certainty/2ndadvice_final_en.pdf, para 11.1
60 Proposed SLD, Principle 10
61 Directive 2011/61 of the European Parliament and of the Council of 8 June 2011 on Alternative Investment Fund Managers etc, art 21
62 Proposed SLD, Principles 16–17
63 See **section 20.12**

of redemption', that is an obligation on the part of the mortgagee to re-convey the property to the mortgagor on repayment of the loan, and in the meantime for the mortgagor to enjoy possession but for the mortgagee to have a power of sale, and potentially a power of foreclosure (a right to appropriate the property for himself) on a failure to repay. A mortgage of securities is possible, if the collateral-taker can get himself registered on the record of ownership as the legal owner of the securities. So, for example, in CREST, if the securities are transferred into the CREST account of the collateral-taker, the collateral-taker may have a mortgage. If an account transfer happens at a different level in the holding chain, it is less clear whether a mortgage has been created. Under English law, the property of the collateral-provider may have been a beneficial interest in securities held for him on trust by a custodian or account-provider – but they may not, because the securities in question are not English securities and the characterisation of the holding pattern under the relevant legal system may not be to confer a property right in the securities themselves upon the collateral-provider, as discussed above. Until the Securities Law Directive has been given effect, it is possible to create a mortgage of the collateral-provider's beneficial interest in the securities, where that is what the collateral-provider has to give.[64] This would ordinarily require a transfer of the 'securities' to the account of the collateral-taker, and the entry into documentation indicating clearly that the arrangement was intended to create a security interest.

(2) *Title transfer collateral.* Mortgages are distinguished from title transfer collateral arrangements. Title transfer collateral involves an outright transfer with no equity of redemption – the collateral-provider completely surrenders its rights to the collateral. This technique is accordingly at risk of challenge in a court exercising equitable jurisdiction, on the grounds that a collateral arrangement of necessity involves an equity of redemption, whether or not the parties recognised that and provided for it in their documentation. This risk is called 'recharacterisation risk'. The accepted way of avoiding recharacterisation risk is to ensure that, at the moment the collateral-provider no longer owes anything to the collateral-taker, or upon an event of default, the collateral-taker is contractually obliged to transfer immediately to the collateral-taker securities equivalent to those originally transferred, or their cash value. If the collateral-provider has defaulted, the cash value of the collateral return obligation can be set off against what the collateral-provider owed, giving the same economic effect as a mortgage.

(3) *Charge.* A charge is an encumbrance on the collateral-provider's property which confers a security interest, that is the right to sell on an event of default and any other rights which have been contractually agreed. It is, in essence, a mortgage without the requirement for a conveyance of legal title to the collateral. Charges typically come in two forms: fixed and floating. The distinction has spawned immense amount of judicial and academic debate, because of the dire consequences of mis-characterisation. A floating charge may be void in insolvency unless registered under section 860 of the Companies Act 2006,[65] the rights of the chargee rank behind various other

---

64 Cf. Benjamin, J, *Interests in Securities* (Oxford, December 2000), ISBN 0-19-826992-7, para 5.07

65 Companies Act 2006, s 874

claims,[66] and additional insolvency challenges are available.[67] To avoid these evils it is necessary for the collateral-taker to obtain 'control' of the collateral, a term which has been much considered in relation to charges over receivables but less intensively in relation to securities. The following specific instances of attempts to create fixed charges may be noted:

- In *Re Spectrum Plus Ltd*,[68] a case concerning receivables, the critical feature of a floating charge was stated to be the 'chargor's ability to control and manage the charged assets and withdraw them from the security.' As usual with receivables cases, the point at issue was whether the chargor's ability to deal with the proceeds of collection. It may be thought, by analogy, that a chargor's ability to deal with the proceeds of sale or redemption of charged securities might similarly be fatal to a fixed charge.

- In *Re Lin Securities Pte*,[69] the chargor charged all shares etc in its custody or possession and stated in a daily certificate given to the chargee, but the chargor was free to select the securities to be included in the daily certificate. This structure was held to constitute a floating charge.

Despite the confusion which the fixed-versus-floating debate engenders, the charge is an extremely useful and flexible technique.

(4) *Lien.* A lien is a possessory right, which allows a person who has possession of another person's property to detain it – that is, to refuse to act on instructions to deliver up or transfer the property – until payment is made. Bankers have taken liens over securities for centuries,[70] notwithstanding that the lien applies only to a scrip component of mere evidential value.[71] A lien may take the form of a specific lien covering the price of the specific asset only (that is, a form of purchase-money security interest) or a general lien covering all monies due in respect of an account or a client relationship. A lien may be coupled with a contractual right of sale. It has been held that a contractual possessory lien – a mere right to detain, not to seize possession – coupled with a right of sale is not a 'floating charge',[72] and thus does not need registration under the Companies Acts. What is more difficult to discern is the extent to which the concept of a lien can be applied to intangible assets such as securities credited to an account. Here it may be noted that the concept of possession of intangible property is not universally accepted by English lawyers.[73] However, assuming that a modern interpretation of 'possession' in this context accommodates the case where securities are credited to an account, a lien should be available over securities credited to an account. (Many banks' modern custody documentation includes a lien; the FCRs[74] contemplate the existence of liens over securities as a form of collateral; and the FSA's rules restrict

---

66 See **section 8.9(12)**
67 Notably under Insolvency Act 1986, s 245
68 [2005] UKHL 41
69 [1988] 2 MLJ 137
70 *Currie v Misa* (1875–76) LR 1 App Cas 554, HL; there are older cases
71 *In re United Service Company* (1870–71) LR 6 Ch App 212, CA
72 *Trident International Ltd v Barlow & ors* [2000] BCC 602, CA
73 See discussion at **section 8.29(1)–(2)**
74 SI 2003 No 3226; see reg 3, definition of 'security interest', para (e)

the taking of a lien in some circumstances.[75] These matters provide strong evidence that possessory liens relating to securities in accounts are genuine legal constructs.)

10.11 These traditional classifications may need some re-evaluation in light of the Securities Law Directive and its narrower set of rules for effectuation of dispositions of securities. If the SLD is proceeded with, the collateral-provider's property will be acknowledged to be a peculiar species of asset constituted solely by the entry on the account-provider's books. To create a mortgage the account-provider can create new account entries in favour of the collateral-taker, which will constitute a disposition of the collateral-provider's entitlement to the securities. To distinguish this type of disposition from an outright transfer with no equity of redemption, clear documentation will be needed. Charges could be created by means of the 'earmarking' and 'control agreement' techniques, with their differing consequences in terms of priority. The position of liens and the concept of 'possession' may still be difficult.[76]

10.12 Turning now to examine the merits of the various techniques in a clearing and settlement context, the following comments may be made.

(1) In the first place, securities are rarely a static asset in the hands of a person seeking clearing and settlement services. Securities tend to be stock-in-trade for many heavy users of such services, such as hedge funds or investment firms. It is therefore commercially illogical to expect securities to be 'locked away' in the account equivalent of a tin box for the duration of the exposure by these collateral-providers. Rather, securities collateral arrangements need to be dynamic, constituting floating charges or purchase-money security interests. Constant re-evaluation of the amount of collateral required (typically on an intra-day basis) and achieving real-time transfer of title may be operationally impossible for many service providers. The implication is that mortgages and title transfer collateral arrangements may not be feasible for those situations.

(2) Secondly, the need for flexibility can force both parties to a collateral arrangement to the conclusion that they need to have a floating charge. While floating charges are weaker than fixed charges, because of the lower priority accorded to a creditor with a floating charge in the collateral-provider's insolvency, the principal fear about floating charges – that they will be completely void – can be overcome by registration under the Companies Act 2006. But the biggest fear with charges and mortgages should not be want of registration, but unenforceability in administration. In administration, permission of the administrator or of the court is needed to enforce a security interest of any description, whether mortgage, fixed charge or floating charge, and whether or not registered under the Companies Act.[77] If a title transfer collateral arrangement is not feasible (there being no bar in administration to operating the default mechanism under such an arrangement), the only solution to the problem of enforceability is to try to ensure that the collateral arrangement is a 'financial collateral arrangement' as defined in the FCRs. This solution is

---

75 Financial Services Authority, *Handbook of Rules and Guidance, Client Assets Sourcebook* (April 2012), CASS 6.3.5R
76 See **section 10.8(2)**
77 Insolvency Act 1986, Sch B1, para 43(2); cf **section 8.9(10)**

far from easy to come by, as discussed in **section 8.28**. The chances are that a lien cannot be relied upon to detain securities in administration any more than a charge can be enforced, because the administration moratorium prohibited the airport authority in *Bristol Airport v Powdrill*[78] from exercising a right to detain an aircraft.

(3) Thirdly, unlike other countries, English law does not provide under the general law for an intermediary to have a purchase-money security interest. This is sometimes misleadingly referred to as a 'broker's lien', but in the countries where it is available it appears to protect an agent bank as well as a broker against settlement risk where the agent bank has, in effect, paid for the client's purchase of securities. In such a case the broker or account-provider, or a third party, will have paid on the account-holder's behalf, and may wish to reserve title until payment is made. An example is the statutory lien in Italy[79] which allows the unpaid service provider to sell securities received for the account of its client to cover the price paid for them. Similar laws apply in France (which gives the unpaid account-provider ownership rights over the securities).[80]

10.13 Mention should also be made of the unique security arrangements available in the CREST system, which add a further layer of complication to the process of taking security in the United Kingdom. If a collateral-provider holds its securities directly in CREST, that is in an account opened in its own name (typically where a sponsor is appointed to operate the account, ie to give properly authenticated dematerialised instructions in accordance with the Uncertificated Securities Regulations 2001[81] and the CREST Reference Manual), it may create security in a variety of ways:

(1) The most obvious is a legal mortgage, whereby the securities are transferred to the account of another CREST participant. However, collateral-providers shy away from transfer of title even under mortgage terms, and in the clearing and settlement context where a floating charge is essential, this approach is unworkable.

(2) A second option offered in CREST is the 'escrow account', whereby a transfer to the collateral-taker's escrow account visibly preserves the collateral-provider's property interest in the securities; but it is open to the same objection as a mortgage, and, moreover, the escrow account is at risk of being frozen by Euroclear UK & Ireland (EUI), the CREST operator. This is because EUI's practice is to enforce the moratorium in an administration until authorisation by the administrator for the enforcement has been granted. 'In the event of the disablement (suspension) of a member, the CREST system has functionality which … might be utilised, for example, where a bank wishes to enforce its (fixed) charge over the stock held in the escrow balance. However, EUI will not permit the settlement of a [transfer from escrow] in these circumstances without being satisfied that the risk of a bad delivery or of a threat to the security, reputation or integrity of the system has been minimised.'[82] It seems to be immaterial from EUI's

---

78 [1990] Ch 744, CA
79 Civil Code, s 2761(2)
80 Code Monétaire et Financier, arts L. 431–3; Code Civil, art 544
81 SI 2001 No 3755
82 EUI, *CREST Reference Manual* (March 2011), https://www.euroclear.com/site/publishedFile/Reference+Manual+_March+2011_tcm87-120016.pdf?title=CREST+reference+manual, ch 7, s 3

viewpoint that the arrangements might constitute a financial collateral arrangement and therefore be unaffected by a moratorium.

(3) A third possibility, which is of great benefit to settlement service providers, is open to CREST settlement banks only. If EUI is satisfied that the charge documentation is in the appropriate form, a charge securing settlement bank exposures can be noted by EUI as eligible for 'fast track' enforcement notwithstanding the implementation of insolvency proceedings. In brief: if the chargee is a settlement bank, EUI will allow the bank to control the chargor's account in CREST and issue 'properly authenticated dematerialised instructions' pertaining to the chargor's account, provided that the CREST requirements for fast track enforcement[83] are met and (if the chargor is disabled by EUI, due to its insolvency) the charge falls within Regulation 4 of the Financial Markets and Insolvency Regulations 1996 (FM&I Regulations).[84] Regulation 4 requires that the charge is granted to secure debts or liabilities arising in connection with the transfer or issue of uncertificated securities,[85] and refers in its provisions to the CREST system. The FM&I Regulations apply Part VII of the Companies Act 1989,[86] and thereby grant protection against the administration moratorium. Additional protection, to the same effect, applies by virtue of the Settlement Finality Regulations 1999;[87] and the FCRs ought also to be available, although again they are not mentioned by EUI in the CREST Reference Manual. Security provided in this way will typically be a floating charge and will typically encompass all the securities in the account of the collateral-provider.

OWNERSHIP OF PURCHASED SECURITIES

10.14 In the context of clearing and settlement, a burning question is at what moment a purchaser actually acquires ownership of his securities. 'When the purchaser has his name recorded on the shareholders' register' is a trite answer, given that typical scenarios will involve intermediation by a custodian or broker. Furthermore, registration is not conclusive, since long-standing case-law shows that equitable ownership can be transferred without entry on the shareholders' register.[88] The question of time of acquisition of ownership is, at least in the absence of a securities law Directive, a question of when the account-provider intends to hold the securities acquired on trust for the acquirer. This would make it important for the provider of accounts to specify when ownership is intended to pass. In the absence of any express agreement, transfer of beneficial ownership ought to coincide with delivery (or credit to the account), though there does not appear to be judicial authority precisely on this point. The following would be helpful if it applied to securities credited to accounts:

'Where there is a contract for the sale of unascertained or future goods by description, and goods of that description and in a deliverable state are unconditionally appropriated to the contract, ... the property in the goods then passes to the buyer.'[89]

---

83 CREST Reference Manual, ch 6, s 7
84 SI 1996 No 1469
85 Cf FM&I Regulations, reg 3(2)
86 See **sections 8.10ff**
87 Financial Markets and Insolvency (Settlement Finality) Regulations 1999, SI 1999 No 2979; see **section 8.22**
88 *Re Rose, Rose v IRC* [1952] Ch 499, CA
89 Sale of Goods Act 1979, s 18, r 5(1)

The trust construct leaves open the possibility under English law that credit entries might be made to a securities account without the intention of conferring ownership rights on the account-holder, though this theoretical line of reasoning may not be consistent with all operational practices.

10.15 'Conditional credits' (such as arise in connection with contractual settlement)[90] may be a species of credit entry not intended to confer ownership rights. Conditional credits may be used where the securities have been bought to satisfy the order of an account-holder who has not paid for them, as well as to cover the case where delivery has been notified by the CSD but is not legally final. Under English law, equitable title will pass at the moment intended by the parties in creating the trust arrangement. Consequently, in England it is not possible to conclude that an unpaid service provider retains any beneficial interest in the securities once they are credited to a non-payer's account, unless some explicit arrangement to the contrary has been agreed. Given that the non-payer might itself be an intermediary, anomalies can arise. Consider the case where the account-holder is a broker, on whose behalf a custodian has paid the purchase price; and now the broker is unable to pay its debts. The broker's securities account may be a client account, with the result that the broker's client may receive title to the purchased assets regardless of whether the client or the broker has paid for them. A more troublesome example is where the end-investor client did pay the broker, who did not pass the price on to the agent bank. Here, title to the securities may pass to the client, but without the prospect of payment being made to the agent bank, unless somehow the bank can assert the client's rights to any share in the pool of client money which the broker should have set aside.[91] Or it may be that the custodian has successfully reserved title to the unpaid-for securities, and (as the broker is insolvent) the client will get nothing even though the client has paid the broker in full.

OMNIBUS AND NOMINEE ACCOUNTS

10.16 An omnibus account is a single account where the assets of multiple clients are co-mingled. Omnibus accounts have various advantages. The main one is that they allow for net settlement (deliveries in respect of sales can be netted against receipts in respect of purchases) thereby saving cost. Other advantages have been asserted which include the difficulty of establishing large numbers of single-client accounts in the CSD, transfer of shareholder management to the account-provider and internalised settlement.[92] However, there are also disadvantages, first among which is the need for some mechanism for loss-allocation in the event of a shortfall which cannot be rectified. Other disadvantages which have been mentioned are 'forced borrowing' – that is, when securities are debited leaving a temporary shortfall, resulting in credit risk on the account-provider, distancing the issuer from the investor, and unequal treatment on corporate actions.

10.17 A nominee account is typically an account used by a broker for custody of its clients' securities. The nominee is established as a separate corporate

---

90 See **section 18.32**
91 See **section 9.7**
92 Turing, D, *Omnibus Accounts* (August 2005), European Commission Legal Certainty Group working document, http://ec.europa.eu/internal_market/financial-markets/docs/certainty/background/31_8_5_turing_en.pdf

vehicle with limited permissions under the Regulated Activities Order – in particular, not including dealing permissions – with the intention that its function will be restricted to safeguarding and administering the investments of the clients, and where a fully-regulated custodian accepts responsibility for the nominee's activities.[93] The structure will serve to isolate the clients' assets from the insolvency of the broker and thereby provide a second layer of protection (in addition to the trust implicit in the nominee's custody relationship) for the clients. A regulated firm holding a safe custody asset for a client is required to have the security registered in the name of a nominee unless it is registered in the client's name or it is a non-United Kingdom security.[94] Securities held in 'nominee name' are thereby held apart from those in 'street name'. A nominee account does not guarantee to clients that their assets will be returned, as (i) in the ordinary way, the nominee will be under the control of the broker, thereby exposing the assets to the risks associated with fraud and incompetence; and (ii) the nominee's account at the CSD will be an omnibus account. On the other hand, a nominee account will bring to the client the advantages of an omnibus account, anonymity (as the nominee name appears on the public record of shareholders), and, potentially, cost savings associated with dematerialisation.

REHYPOTHECATION

10.18 A right of use of a customer's assets would generally be a violation of the duties of a trustee, or, if the reason that the assets have been entrusted to a third party is because of the existence of a mortgage or charge, a clog on the customer's equity of redemption. However, it is permissible for the terms of a trust to give the trustee unimpeded rights to deal with the trust property, including rights to lend, repo, or dispose outright.[95] Furthermore, since the implementation of the FCRs, it is permitted for a security financial collateral arrangement to include a term creating a binding right of use in favour of a collateral-taker.[96] In the strict sense 'rehypothecation' refers to the latter situation only, in circumstances where the collateral-taker needs to use the securities to secure its own obligations; but in common usage all cases of use of a client's assets for purposes other than the client's own may be meant.

Rehypothecation is a controversial practice because the use of a client's property necessarily involves the conversion of the client's asset, which was a piece of property held in safe custody, into a personal claim against the securities account-provider, and such a claim may be worthless in the event of the account-provider's insolvency. Rehypothecation has also been accused of creating a variety of risks, such as systemic risk, delay in return of client assets, ownership contests between 'bona fide purchaser' and original owner, and exacerbation of runs to withdraw assets from hedge funds in times of stress.[97]

---

93 Yates, M, and Montagu, G, *The Law of Global Custody* (3rd ed, Tottel, February 2009), ISBN 978-1847661425, para 7.20

94 Financial Services Authority, *Handbook of Rules and Guidance, Client Assets Sourcebook*, CASS 6.2.3R

95 *Re Lehman Brothers International (Europe), Pearson and ors v Lehman Brothers Finance SA and ors* [2010] EWHC 2914 (Ch)

96 FCRs, reg 16

97 Deryugina, M, 'Standardization of Securities Regulation: Rehypothecation and Securities Commingling in the United States and the United Kingdom' (Fall 2009) Review of Banking Law, vol 29, pp 253–288

It may be disingenuous for hedge funds and other sophisticated investors to assert that they were unaware of the implications of rehypothecation for their ownership rights, but before the Lehman crisis prime brokers had only weak obligations to be explicit and timely in their disclosures to clients as to the extent of exercise of rehypothecation rights. Since the Lehman episode, and a consultation by H.M. Treasury on the question,[98] FSA rules have been introduced which require prime brokers to provide general information about rights of use,[99] and daily information to their clients on collateral held in respect of transactions where the prime broker has exercised a right of use[100] (though, curiously, no report of the safe custody assets in respect of which a right of use has been exercised is required). All this contrasts with the position in the United States, where a broker or dealer is required to have physical possession of 'excess margin securities', defined as securities having a market value in excess of 140% of the total of the debit balances in the customer's accounts.[101]

CLIENT ASSETS

10.19 Pervading the discussion of ownership of securities has been a recurring theme: that one person may be holding securities for the benefit of another. The investor is thereby placed in a position of dependency on the holder of the securities, that is the provider and operator of the securities account. The weakness of the law of trusts to address fully the needs of the investor implies that there should be a set of regulatory rules to plug the gap.

It is commonly expected that the United Kingdom regulatory regime requires 'segregation' of client assets from house assets. In December 2009, HM Treasury noted 'Although FSMA does not specifically empower the FSA to make rules to create a statutory trust designed to protect clients' assets, CASS imposes requirements on firms to ensure that adequate arrangements are in place to safeguard clients' interests in client assets. These arrangements will generally involve firms holding client assets subject to implied trusts or other proprietary entitlement in favour of the clients.'[102] Even more surprisingly, when introducing custody rules to implement the Markets in Financial Instruments Directive (MiFID),[103] the FSA repealed its general custody rule obliging firms to segregate ('A firm must segregate safe custody investments from its own designated investments except to the extent required by law or permitted by the custody rules').[104]

10.20 What is meant by segregation also causes confusion. The concept means setting up separate accounts *at the firm's account-provider* for the firm's own property and its clients'; it is insufficient that the firm's *own* books show what

---

98 H M Treasury, *Establishing resolution arrangements for investment banks* (December 2009), http://webarchive.nationalarchives.gov.uk/20100407010852/http://www.hm-treasury.gov.uk/d/consult_investmentbank161209.pdf, paras 4.19ff

99 Financial Services Authority, *Handbook of Rules and Guidance, Client Assets Sourcebook* (March 2011), CASS 9.3.1R

100 CASS 9.2.1R

101 Securities and Exchange Commission, 17 CFR §240, r 15c3-3

102 H M Treasury, *Establishing resolution arrangements for investment banks,* para 4.15

103 Directive of the European Parliament and of the Council of 21 April 2004 on markets in financial instruments etc, 2004/39/EC

104 CASS 2.2.3R, which ceased to have effect even for non-MiFID business after 31 December 2008

securities are due to the client, for that is no segregation at all. Yet often one hears the expression 'the assets are segregated on our own books', which is meaningless. As shown above, segregation is not necessary under English law in order to establish a trust in favour of the client. Segregation is, however, a highly desirable adjunct which reinforces the distinction between trust 'client' assets and beneficially-owned 'house' assets. EMIR thus requires CCPs:

- to keep separate records and accounts which enable it to distinguish *on its own books* assets and positions held for the account of one clearing member from those of another;

- to offer to keep separate 'house' and omnibus 'client' accounts for each clearing member;

- to offer to keep a separate individual 'client' account for each client of each clearing member.[105]

EMIR also requires clearing members to keep records on its own books which separate client and house positions, and to offer individual client segregation as well as an omnibus account. Similar obligations to those imposed on CCPs are intended to be imposed on CSDs under the proposed CSD Regulation.[106]

10.21 MiFID states, at article 13(7), that 'an investment firm shall, when holding financial instruments belonging to clients, make adequate arrangements so as to safeguard clients' ownership rights, especially in the event of the investment firm's insolvency, and to prevent the use of a client's instruments on own account except with the client's express consent.' This principle is amplified by specific, more detailed rules in articles 16–20 of the Commission's implementing directive,[107] which cover record-keeping, reconciliation, segregation, use of custodians, use of client securities, and audit. As transposed into FSA rules,[108] the primary provisions may be noted as follows:

(1) A firm must, when holding safe custody assets belonging to a client, made adequate arrangements so as to safeguard clients' ownership rights.[109] This is a direct copy-out of article 13(7) of MiFID. Additionally, firms must 'effect appropriate registration or recording of title … in the name of (1) the client … unless the client is an authorised person acting on behalf of its client, in which case it may be registered in the name of the client of that authorised person; (2) a nominee company which is controlled by (a) the firm; (b) an affiliated company; … (3) any other third party if (a) the … asset is subject to the law … of a jurisdiction outside the United Kingdom … .'[110]

(2) There are detailed rules about the choice and monitoring of third parties with whom safe custody assets are 'deposited' by a firm.[111] 'Depositing' is

---

105 Regulation (EU) No 648/2012 of the European Parliament and of the Council of 4 July 2012 on OTC derivatives, central counterparties and trade repositories, art 39

106 European Commission, *Proposal for a Regulation of the European Parliament and of the Council on improving securities settlement in the European Union and on central securities depositories etc* (March 2012), COM(2012) 73 final, http://eur-lex.europa.eu/LexUriServ/LexUriServ.do?uri=CELEX:52012PC0073:EN:PDF , art 35

107 Commission Directive 2006/73/EC of 10 August 2006 implementing MiFID etc

108 Financial Services Authority, *Handbook of Rules and Guidance, Client Assets Sourcebook* (January 2009), CASS 6

109 CASS 6.2.1R (January 2009)

110 CASS 6.2.3R (January 2009)

111 CASS 6.3.1R – 6.3.4R (January 2009 – April 2012); MiFID implementing directive, arts 16(1), 17(1)

an unhelpful concept which encourages users of the FSA rules to visualise securities as pieces of paper; a 'deposit' of dematerialised securities held in custody, like a 'deposit' of cash, involves the creation of a credit entry in an account, though the legal consequences of a securities 'deposit' thus made are quite different.

(3) A firm is not permitted to allow a third party to have a lien, right of retention or right of sale of safe custody assets belonging to a client, except in limited circumstances.[112] The carve-outs include liens etc which relate to liabilities arising from custody services provided for securities held in the account, arising under the operating terms of a CSD or CCP, and arising under local law in relation to securities held outside the United Kingdom.[113]

(4) A firm is allowed to borrow or lend out a client's safe custody assets but only if the client's consent has been obtained. Where the account used for lending transactions is an omnibus account, all the clients must consent, or the firm must have systems and controls to limit the use of assets to those belonging to clients who have consented.[114] There is no general prohibition on rehypothecation.[115]

(5) There is an exception to all these rules 'in relation to a delivery versus payment transaction through a commercial settlement system' where the securities 'will be due to the client' within one business day of his payment or 'due to the firm' within one day of 'fulfilment of a payment obligation'.[116] This rule enables brokers which can turn over cash and securities quickly to avoid the burdens of client asset segregation.

It may be noted that these rules (apart from the limitation of liens, which was not then in force) were found wanting in the case of the Lehman insolvency. The exercise of rehypothecation rights appears to have delayed and complicated the return of client assets.[117] In response, IOSCO carried out a study of the effectiveness of client asset protection regimes in 16 countries, including five (France, Germany, Italy, Spain and the United Kingdom) in the European Union.[118] Those (all except the United Kingdom) classified as 'custodial regimes', were noted to have deficiencies such as the risk of shortfalls attributable to rehypothecation, pro-rata sharing by clients of any shortfall with the balance to be made up through a claim on the investor compensation scheme, and no mechanism for the transfer of clients' assets to a solvent substitute firm on the insolvency of the client's original investment firm. The United Kingdom was classified as a 'trust regime', whose deficiencies were shortfalls attributable to rehypothecation, the return of client assets only insofar as the assets can definitively be traced back to the claimant, and the absence of a mechanism for transfer of clients' assets to a solvent substitute firm.

10.22 The UK Government's response can be summarised as follows. First, 'investment banks' (which include deposit-taking banks) can go into a form

---

112 CASS 6.3.5R (April 2012)
113 CASS 6.3.6R (April 2012)
114 CASS 6.4.1R – 6.4.3R (January 2009–April 2010); MiFID implementing directive, art 19
115 See **section 10.18**
116 CASS 6.1.12R (January 2009)
117 *In re Lehman Brothers International (Europe), Four Private Investment Funds v Lomas and ors,* [2008] EWHC 2869 (Ch)
118 International Organization of Securities Commissions, *Survey of Regimes for the Protection, Distribution and/or Transfer of Client Assets: Final Report* (March 2011), FR05/11, http://www.iosco.org/library/pubdocs/pdf/IOSCOPD351.pdf

of 'special administration', one of the objectives of which is the distribution of client assets.[119] This would overcome the previous problem that administrators deal with the insolvent company and its own assets, not the trust property the insolvent company holds. The regulations also provided for pro-rata loss-sharing in the event of a shortfall,[120] and allowed administrators to impose a 'bar date' to block late claims by clients for the return of their assets.[121] Secondly, the FSA has introduced transparency obligations relating to rehypothecation practice[122] and restricting the availability of third-party liens and rights affecting client assets.[123] These reforms are admirable in that they do not substantially restrict what firms and their clients were previously able to do, but introduce greater clarity and remove needless obstacles inherent in the old insolvency process. They can, however, be criticised for failing to address all the points made in the IOSCO study and in not re-introducing a clear concept of segregation.

Client asset protection vs investor compensation

10.23 IOSCO points out the link between client asset protection and investor compensation schemes. The Investor Compensation Schemes Directive (ICS Directive)[124] obliges member states to have schemes which provide cover for claims arising out of an investment firm's inability to return financial instruments belonging to investors and held, administered or managed on their behalf in connection with investment business.[125] Consequently, any gap in the client assets regime ought, at least from a financial perspective, to be plugged by the compensation scheme. The reality is that there are differences. First, coverage of the two regimes is different: professional and institutional investors can be excluded from the compensation scheme, but not client asset protection. Secondly, agreement by a client to rehypothecation or use of its assets converts the client's claim into a monetary claim, not a claim on the compensation scheme for inability to return assets (though it may be a claim on the scheme for inability to repay money owed in connection with investment business). Thirdly, a claim on the scheme is subject to a monetary limit. Fourthly, compensation schemes themselves may be poorly financed, and despite the ICS Directive's three-month time-limit for claims handling[126] it may be impossible to deliver compensation to investors as quickly as, in theory, assets can be handed over.

GIOVANNINI BARRIER 9

10.24 The Giovannini Reports[127] identified 'national restrictions on the location of securities' as a barrier to efficient cross-border clearing and settlement. The question of 'location of securities' in this context is sometimes

---

119 Investment Bank Special Administration Regulations 2011, SI 2011 No 245, reg 10
120 Regulation 12
121 Regulation 11
122 CASS 9.2.1R, CASS 9.3.1R; see **section 10.18**
123 CASS 6.3.5R (April 2012); see **section 10.21**
124 Directive 97/9/EC of the European Parliament and of the Council of 3 March 1997 on investor-compensation schemes
125 ICS Directive, art 2(2)
126 ICS Directive, art 9(2)
127 See **section 1.26**

difficult to understand, and some commentary may be desirable. The first Giovannini report said:

> 'National restrictions often apply to the location of securities. Such restrictions can limit the choices for issuers when placing their securities and/or make it more complicated to hold and settle those securities in Member States other than the place of issuance. In this context, two types of restrictions have been identified:
>
> 'First, there is a requirement in some Member States that issues in listed securities be deposited exclusively in the local settlement system and/or that transactions in such securities be capable of settlement exclusively on the books of the local settlement system. This seems also to be the market practice in countries where it is not enshrined in law.
>
> 'Second, there may be a connection between listing on the regulated market and registration with a local registrar. This can constrain the choice of settlement location available to users because the selection of a foreign settlement system will be less attractive, particularly when the local settlement system is the approved local registrar or has already an established network of links with local registrars.'[128]

After a period of more than ten years the European Commission issued a proposal for a Regulation on CSDs, which will include a statutory right for issuers to choose a CSD established in any Member State.[129] In this way, freedom of choice of 'location' for securities will be granted. 'Location' in this sense means choice of CSD. It does not have the same meaning as '*situs*' for the purposes of property law questions.[130]

10.25 It would, however, be naïve to assume that this provision alone is capable of creating a single market in which issuers are scattered around CSDs in other member states. The factors which will tend to encourage issuers to favour their local CSD notwithstanding the proposed CSD Regulation include the following.

(1) *Company law*. The rules under company law for issue of securities, maintaining shareholders' registers, handling corporate actions, and who is entitled to be regarded as a shareholder, are left to the company law of Member States. These laws are not identical. Local CSDs have grown up to specialise in handling with great efficiency the local company law requirements. A challenger may profess to offer equally good or better services of this nature, but the capabilities required to move into another jurisdiction may discourage foreign CSDs from expanding outside their home country.[131]

---

128 Giovannini, A, et al, *Cross-Border Clearing and Settlement Arrangements in the European Union* (November 2001), http://ec.europa.eu/internal_market/financial-markets/docs/clearing/first_giovannini_report_en.pdf, pp 49–50

129 European Commission, *Proposal for a Regulation of the European Parliament and of the Council on improving securities settlement in the European Union and on central securities depositories etc* (March 2012), COM(2012) 73 final, http://eur-lex.europa.eu/LexUriServ/LexUriServ.do?uri=CELEX:52012PC0073:EN:PDF , art 47

130 See **section 10.6**

131 Cf European Central Securities Depositories Association, *ECSDA's Answer to the Commission Consultation on CSDs and the harmonisation of certain aspects of securities settlement in the EU* (March 2011), http://www.ecsda.eu/site/uploads/tx_doclibrary/2011_03_01_ECSDA_Answer_to_CSDL_consultation.pdf

(2) *Market connectivity*. The issuer's primary concern is likely to be to find a liquid market on which its securities can be traded. The quality of the link between the market and the CSD will be well-established in the case of the issuer's home state regulated market (which may well be the most relevant market in terms of liquidity, owing to the familiarity of local investors with the issuers); these links would need to be established if a new CSD were used. Again, the difficulty is not insuperable, but local stockbrokers serving domestic investors would typically not have in place settlement arrangements with foreign (or newcomer) CSDs.

(3) *Business case*. Issuers may not see an obvious business case in selecting a different CSD even when a free choice is offered. CSDs might be able to offer enhanced investor-relations services for issuers anxious to stay close to investors: ECSDA identified a variety of services potentially provided by CSDs to issuers relating to corporate actions, information supply, general meetings, and securities numbering.[132] The limited range of business activities permitted to CSDs may constrain development of such services.

(4) *Tax*. CSDs are typically interwoven into the transaction tax recovery process.[133] It may be difficult for challenger CSDs to overcome the difficulties which acting as the tax authority's policeman and collector may involve.

(5) *Multiple connections*. If securities traded at a single venue settle in various places, the brokers serving investors using that venue will need to be connected to all the CSDs, either directly or through agent banks. This is commonplace for MTFs on which all manner of liquid securities are traded. But the implication is that service providers connected to all the CSDs which are relevant will be needed. This could be achieved by CSDs providing 'interoperable' services (in other words themselves taking the role of agent banks[134]); but however this is structured, multiple links or intermediation introduces cost.

(6) *Dually rooted securities*. Insofar as two or more CSDs hold the root of title to a single issue of securities, some form of balancing mechanism akin to the 'bridge' between the ICSDs[135] would be needed.

132 European Central Securities Depositories Association, *Issuer Services* (January 2008), Report, http://www.ecsda.eu/site/uploads/tx_doclibrary/2008_01_ECSDA_Issuer_Services_Report. pdf
133 See **sections 22.5ff**
134 See **section 13.46**
135 See **section 2.24**

11 Regulation of Infrastructures under English law

CONTEXT OF REGULATION IN ENGLAND

11.1   English law follows the pattern noted in **Chapter 6** for the regulation of infrastructures; indeed English law may be regarded as the precedent which is followed at an international level. Thus, payment systems are subject to regulation of the lightest sort, with only minimal statutory content and remarkably little detail; CSDs occupy a middle space where the detail of regulation is largely an accidental consequence of settlement finality legislation and its English cousin, Part VII of the Companies Act 1989, and the focus of the regulatory statute is on operational aspects of transferring shares by means of a computerised system; and CCPs are subject to a high degree of detailed regulation. It may be remarked that as the effect of European legislation, in the form of EMIR[1] and the proposed CSD Regulation,[2] becomes felt in England, the regulation of both CCPs and CSDs is bound to change.

At the outset it should be noted that infrastructures are likely to be outside the scope of 'ordinary' financial services regulation as applied to banks and investment firms. In England, CCPs and CSDs are typically organised as 'recognised clearing houses' which accords them an exemption from the general corpus of financial services regulation.[3] The implications of 'exemption', and the factors influencing the choice between exemption and full authorisation, are discussed in **sections 12.4–12.5**. Here it may merely be noted that, as recognised but not authorised persons, CCPs and CSDs are subject to a much narrower scope of regulation than banks or investment firms – for example there is next to nothing corresponding to the 'Conduct of Business' (or customer-facing) Sourcebook of the FSA's Handbook – and that the degree of detail surrounding such issues as are covered by regulation is considerably lower, as for example in relation to prudential standards.

Payment systems may not need to be structured as banks in order to carry on their activities. So, for example, CHAPS operates as a system without itself taking deposits from its participants, rather relying on their accounts at the

---

1   Regulation (EU) No 648/2012 of the European Parliament and of the Council of 4 July 2012 on OTC derivatives, central counterparties and trade repositories
2   European Commission, *Proposal for a Regulation of the European Parliament and of the Council on improving securities settlement in the European Union and on central securities depositories etc* (March 2012), COM(2012) 73 final, http://eur-lex.europa.eu/LexUriServ/ LexUriServ.do?uri=CELEX:52012PC0073:EN:PDF
3   Financial Services and Markets Act 2000, s 285(2)

Bank of England,[4] and as it carries on no regulated activities prescribed in the Regulated Activities Order,[5] CHAPS does not need any authorisation under the Financial Services and Markets Act 2000 (FSMA). Neither CLS Bank nor EBA Clearing had FSMA authorisation in 2011, presumably because neither of them accepts deposits in the United Kingdom.

In consequence of the financial market infrastructure falling outside the mainstream of regulation, the approach of the regulators has been somewhat different from that in the case of authorised firms. The structure of the FSA Handbook, which has five general blocks of rules dealing with general principles and authorisation conditions, prudential standards, business conduct standards, regulatory processes, and redress, is not carried across into the English practice of infrastructure regulation. The FMI Principles[6] are arranged around eight blocks, dealing with organisation, credit and liquidity risk, settlement, CSDs and exchange-of-value systems, default management, business and operational risk management, access, efficiency, and transparency. The Bank of England's Principles for oversight of interbank payment systems (Bank of England Principles)[7] follow this outline, but the regulatory standards applied by the FSA to CCPs and CSDs derive from the Recognition Requirements Regulations (RRRs),[8] and do not.

PAYMENT SYSTEMS

11.2   In a critical assessment of the English approach to regulation of payment systems, it might first be noted that much of the literature strikes a faintly apologetic note. The tone of Bank of England publications over many years has been to justify the need for any oversight of payment systems.[9] In a more febrile financial climate the desirability of effective regulation of payment systems is perhaps self-evident, and the introduction by the Banking Act 2009 of formal statutory powers of oversight of payment systems followed the financial crisis of 2007–2008.

Part 5 of the Banking Act 2009

11.3   Part 5 of the Banking Act 2009 (Part 5) created a statutory regime in the United Kingdom for the oversight of 'inter-bank payment systems', meaning 'arrangements designed to facilitate or control the transfer of money between financial institutions who participate in the arrangements.'[10] For these purposes,

---

4   Cf CHAPS criteria for membership (2010), http://www.chapsco.co.uk/chaps_company/-/page/337/

5   Financial Services and Markets Act 2000 (Regulated Activities) Order 2001, SI 2001 No 544

6   Bank for International Settlements Committee on Payment and Settlement Systems and Technical Committee of the International Organization of Securities Commissions, *Principles for Financial Market Infrastructures* (April 2012), http://www.bis.org/publ/cpss101a.pdf; see **section 6.41**

7   Bank of England, *The Bank of England's oversight of interbank payments systems under the Banking Act 2009* (September 2009), http://www.bankofengland.co.uk/publications/other/financialstability/oips/oips090928.pdf, p 4

8   Financial Services and Markets Act 2000 (Recognition Requirements for Investment Exchanges and Clearing Houses) Regulations 2001, SI 2001 No 995

9   Bank of England, *Oversight of Payment Systems* (November 2000), http://www.bankofengland.co.uk/publications/psor/ops.pdf; Haldane, A, and Latter, E, 'The role of central banks in payment systems oversight' (Spring 2005) Bank of England Quarterly Bulletin, vol 45, http://www.bankofengland.co.uk/publications/quarterlybulletin/qb0501.pdf, pp 66–71

10   Banking Act 2009, s 182

'financial institutions' means only banks and building societies, but the inclusion of other types of person as participants does not rule the system out of scope.

An inter-bank payment scheme becomes subject to supervision under Part 5 if the Treasury specifies the system as a 'recognised system'.[11] The Treasury may do so if satisfied that deficiencies in the design of the system, or disruption of its operation, would be likely to threaten the stability of, or confidence in, the UK financial system, or to have serious consequences for business or other interests throughout the United Kingdom.[12] The Treasury must consult with the Bank of England, and, if the operator of the system is an authorised person, the Prudential Regulation Authority; and it must notify the operator and consider any representations made.[13] According to the Bank of England's Payment Systems Oversight Report for 2011, the following systems had been recognised: Bacs, CHAPS, CLS, the Faster Payments Service, and the embedded payment arrangements within CREST, LCH.Clearnet Ltd and ICE Clear Europe.[14]

Once a system is 'recognised', it becomes subject to rules and guidance made by the Bank of England, which are referred to in Part 5 as 'principles' and 'codes of practice' respectively.[15] The Bank of England is also able to require the operator of a recognised system to establish rules for operation of the system or change them, and to notify the Bank and obtain pre-approval of proposed rule changes;[16] the Bank has statutory power to give directions to the operator to take or refrain from taking specified action;[17] the Bank can set operational standards;[18] and it can appoint an inspector.[19] The Bank did not propose to issue a code of practice when it created its Principles.[20] Part 5 also describes a statutory framework of supervision which is similar to that applicable to financial firms authorised under FSMA. The Treasury may also apply Part 5 to persons who are service providers in relation to a recognised inter-bank payment system.[21]

Bank of England Principles

11.4   The Bank's Principles[22] are based on the CPSS Core Principles for Systemically Important Payment Systems,[23] a predecessor of the FMI

---

11 Banking Act 2009, s 184
12 Banking Act 2009, s 185
13 Banking Act 2009, s 186, as modified by Financial Services Act 2012, s 88
14 Bank of England, *Payment Systems Oversight Report 2010* (April 2012), http://www.bankofengland.co.uk/publications/psor/psor2012.pdf, p 3; for HM Treasury's recognition orders see http://webarchive.nationalarchives.gov.uk/+/http://www.hm-treasury.gov.uk/fin_payment_bankingact.htm
15 Banking Act 2009, s 188
16 Banking Act 2009, s 190
17 Banking Act 2009, s 191(2)(a)
18 Banking Act 2009, s 191(2)(b)
19 Banking Act 2009, s 193
20 Bank of England, *The Bank of England's oversight of interbank payment systems under the Banking Act 2009* (September 2009), http://www.bankofengland.co.uk/publications/other/financialstability/oips/oips090928.pdf, p 4
21 Banking Act 2009, s 206A; see **section 11.6**
22 Bank of England, *The Bank of England's oversight of interbank payment systems under the Banking Act 2009* (September 2009), http://www.bankofengland.co.uk/publications/other/financialstability/oips/oips090928.pdf
23 Bank for International Settlements Committee on Payment and Settlement Systems, *Core Principles for Systemically Important Payment Systems* (January 2001), http://www.bis.org/publ/cpss43.pdf

Principles. The Bank's Principles Numbers 1 to 10 are identical to the ten CPSS Core Principles.[24] Numbers 11 to 14 are brief and can be set out in full here as they may be worthy of comment:

11. The system should manage its business risks so that its users can rely on continuity of its services.
12. The system should regularly review the risks it bears from, and poses to, other infrastructures as a result of interdependencies, and should implement controls adequate to manage those risks.
13. The system should understand and manage risks that are brought to the system as a result of participants' relationships with indirect participants.
14. The system should manage its outsourced relationships prudently, ensuring that contractual and risk management arrangements are clear, appropriate and robust.

These can each be mapped to the FMI Principles, though equally one might observe that some aspects of the FMI Principles have been given different, or no, emphasis in the Bank's Principles. (It may also be noted that the Bank's Principles pre-date the FMI Principles.) Business continuity, interdependency, tiering and outsourcing are evidently major concerns for infrastructure regulators. The FSA's rules applicable to 'recognised clearing houses' – its REC Sourcebook, discussed at **sections 11.17–11.18** – cover business continuity,[25] interdependency[26] and outsourcing,[27] though primarily as 'notification rules' rather than 'recognition requirements', and the subject of tiering has not yet received explicit treatment.

Interdependency is an issue which became prominent in regulators' thinking after the 2008 financial crisis. The Bank of England's 2010 Payment Systems Oversight Report (2010 PSO Report)[28] points out that all UK infrastructures are dependent on the RTGS system operated by the Bank. The 2010 PSO Report also classifies interdependencies[29] as 'system-based', of which the reliance by systems on each other is an example, 'environmental' (SWIFT and payment schemes are said to be part of the environment in which recognised systems operate) and 'institution-based', meaning that participants are common to several systems. The Bank suggests that once a system has identified interdependencies, it could aim to manage them jointly, for example through joint business continuity exercises.

11.5 Tiering is a risk issue more likely to be relevant for payment systems than other types of infrastructure;[30] and it attracted detailed comment in the 2010 PSO Report.[31] In the first place, an indirect participant in a payment system may expose the direct participant to risk, particularly where the indirect participant's business is large in terms of the credit extended by the direct participant relative to the direct participant's ability to withstand a shock. In this context it may be

---

24 See **box 6.1**
25 Financial Services Authority, Handbook of Rules and Guidance, *Recognised Investment Exchanges and Recognised Clearing Houses* (June 2001), REC 3.16.2R, REC 3.16.3R
26 REC 2.8.3G, REC 3.13.3R
27 REC 3.13.2R
28 Bank of England, *Payment Systems Oversight Report 2010* (March 2011), http://www.bankofengland.co.uk/publications/psor/psor2010.pdf
29 PSO Report, p 19
30 See **section 6.41(7)**
31 Page 6

observed that the ordinary measures for assessing capital adequacy may fail to identify the risk assumed by the direct participant, since the risk is usually assumed and settled intra-day, whereas exposures are measured overnight for capital adequacy assessments. The 2010 PSO Report also highlighted liquidity and operational risks arising in the context of tiered participation structures. Regulatory distaste for large-scale indirect participation may manifest itself either by encouraging designated systems to seek designation for indirect participants under the settlement finality regime,[32] or, perhaps more probably, to encourage systems to allow indirect participants with inappropriately large-scale activity referable to the system to become direct participants. The latter solution raises difficult questions as to the degree to which regulators should intervene in the commercial relations between financial institutions, and the manner in which eligibility criteria for systems are set, given that these have to balance factors arising from risk, competition law,[33] and the need (where relevant) to preserve designation under the Settlement Finality Directive (SFD).[34]

11.6   The degree of attention given to business continuity and outsourcing may deserve some comment. Neither subject receives more detailed treatment in the Bank of England's Principles document – the statement of principle itself stands as a complete statement of policy. It is presumably thought self-evident that the operator of a recognised payment system will be aware of the general regulatory standards applicable in these areas and will adhere to them. Concerns arising from business continuity and outsourcing are common to all financial institutions; perhaps the issues are more acute when the institution operates an infrastructure, but the regulator has not thought it necessary to issue yet more duplicative rules. It may also be noted that the Banking Act 2009 was amended in 2010[35] to enable the Treasury to apply Part 5 to a person who is a 'service provider' to a Part 5 recognised payment system. To fall within this provision the services must 'form part of the arrangements constituting the system,' and to allow for flexibility the Treasury's order applying Part 5 to a service provider may modify Part 5 in its application to the person affected.[36] In this way a computer systems provider, or a communications network provider, may become subject to financial sector supervision and direction. It is for debate whether the direction given to such a service provider could prevent the provider terminating its services for good cause, in similar vein to the 'continuity powers' applicable when a property transfer is imposed on an ailing bank under the Banking Act 2009.[37]

Designation under the Settlement Finality Regulations 1999

11.7   Payment systems may also be regulated by reason of having been designated under the Settlement Finality Regulations 1999 (SFRs).[38] Assuming a system is eligible for designation,[39] the SFRs impose various 'requirements'

---

32 See sections **2.42**, **6.16**, **16.7**
33 See **Chapter 7**
34 Directive 98/26/EC of the European Parliament and of the Council of 19 May 1998 on settlement finality in payment and securities settlement systems
35 Financial Services Act 2010, s 20, inserting s 206A into the Banking Act 2009
36 Banking Act 2009, s 206A(2)(a), (7)(a)
37 See **section 8.4**
38 Financial Markets and Insolvency (Settlement Finality) Regulations 1999, 1999 SI No 2979
39 See **section 8.19**

for designation of a system which must be observed if the system is to obtain and retain its designated status.[40] These are set out in the Schedule to the SFRs; insofar as they do not replicate the requirements of the SFD as to eligibility of systems for designation and revocability of transfer orders, they cover the following topics:

(1) The system must have adequate arrangements and resources for the effective monitoring and enforcement of compliance with its rules.[41]

(2) The system operator must have financial resources sufficient for the proper performance of its functions as a system operator.[42]

(3) The system operator must be able and willing to co-operate, by the sharing of information and otherwise, with the FSA,[43] the Bank of England, any relevant insolvency office-holder or other person having responsibility for the default of a participant.[44]

(4) The rules of the system must require each participant to provide, within fourteen days of a request being made, details of the other designated systems in which the participant participates, including information about the main rules of those systems.[45]

(5) The system must have default arrangements which are appropriate for that system in all the circumstances.[46]

Recognition vs designation

11.8 It will at once be noted that these requirements do not at all coincide with the Bank of England's Principles. In fact, they are closer to the recognition requirements for clearing houses, discussed below, from which they appear to be derived. It may therefore be asked whether a recognised payment system will invariably be designated, and vice versa. The Part 5 regime has broader reach than the SFD: payment systems in which investment firms or payment institutions participate are not eligible for SFD designation and are thereby ineligible for the insolvency protections which a designated system can enjoy.[47] There is also no numerical lower limit on the number of participants in a Part 5 recognised payment system, whereas a designated system must have at least three (unless an exception is made on the grounds of systemic risk).[48] By providing that persons who are not 'financial institutions' can participate in a Part 5 recognised payment system, section 182(2) of the Banking Act 2009 envisages that a Part 5 recognised payment system might not be eligible for designation. So, in theory, the two classes of system might be wholly distinct. In practice, this is not the case, as illustrated in **table 11.1**. Evidently, for payment systems properly so called,[49] there is close correspondence; the main point emerging from the comparison is that the United Kingdom authorities have found 'inter-bank payment systems' embedded in three 'recognised clearing

---

40 SFRs, regs 4(1)(c) and 7(1)(a)
41 SFRs, Schedule, para 2
42 Paragraph 3
43 Expected to be modified to refer to the Prudential Regulation Authority and Financial Conduct Authority by subordinate legislation made under the Financial Services Act 2012
44 Paragraph 4
45 Paragraphs 5(2) and (3)
46 Paragraph 6
47 See **section 8.20**
48 Settlement Finality Directive, art 2(a)
49 See **section 1.17**

houses' (two of which are CCPs and one of which is a CSD), and have brought them under the regulatory control of the Bank of England by this device.

Table 11.1   Comparison of recognition and designation of UK payment systems

Payment System	Whether 'recognised'[50]	Whether 'designated'[51]
Bacs	Yes	Yes
CHAPS	Yes	Yes
Cheque and Credit Clearing	No	Yes
CLS	Yes	Yes
CREST embedded system	Yes	No (designated as securities settlement system)
LCH.Clearnet Ltd embedded system	Yes	No (designated as securities settlement system)
Faster Payments	Yes	No
ICE Clear Europe	Yes	No (designated as securities settlement system)

Supervision of designated systems

11.9   A designated system will be answerable to its designating authority. In the case of a payment system, the designating authority will usually be the Bank of England. But, at least until the Financial Services Act 2012 is given full effect, where the system or its operator is a recognised investment exchange or recognised clearing house, or a listed money market institution,[52] or a system through which securities transfer orders are effected, the designating authority is the FSA.[53] The FSA (unlike the Bank) has issued guidance to applicants,[54] though this adds little to the content of the SFRs. In particular, there is no commentary on what is meant by having 'financial resources sufficient for the proper performance of its functions as a system operator.' There is, however, some limited guidance:

- The FSA will require to be given information about various matters at the time of application for designation. Apart from the things specified in the Schedule to the SFRs, the FSA will need to see (a) details of the applicant's constitution, structure, ownership and management, (b) details of the design and function of the system, and (c) copies of the last three annual reports

---

50   PSO Report, p 5
51   European Commission, *Designated Payment and Security Settlement Systems: Article 10 of Settlement Finality Directive 98/26/EC* (April 2012), http://ec.europa.eu/internal_market/financial-markets/settlement/dir-98-26-art10-national_en.htm#ukingdom
52   Regulated under FSMA, s 301; see **section 8.17**
53   SFRs, reg 2(1)
54   Financial Services Authority, *Guidance to Applicants: Designated Systems under the Financial Markets and Insolvency (Settlement Finality) Regulations 1999* (December 1999), http://www.fsa.gov.uk/pubs/policy/p27.pdf

and accounts (with any auditor's reports) and, for the current financial year, quarterly financial statements and management accounts.[55]

- The FSA will also require information on an ongoing basis. The information comprises the list of participants, changes to the system's rules (including advance notice of changes to default rules), and ad hoc information to assure the FSA of the system's continuing ability to satisfy the designation requirements in the SFRs.[56]

This approach to supervision – supervision by gathering information – is not unique to designated payment and settlement systems. Recognised clearing houses operate under a very similar regime,[57] and there are strong parallels between the statutory structures of supervision applicable to these two cases. The list of information which the regulator may call for gives little insight into the issues which will be of particular concern to the regulator of a designated system, or how the regulator is expected to exert powers of supervision to ensure that those concerns are addressed. Those issues are presumably those set forth in the FMI Principles and the Bank of England's Principles. Historically, supervision of banks was done by informal extra-statutory cajoling (the 'cup of tea' approach to regulation[58]), and it seems as if the same idea has been continued for designated payment systems.

However, where a system is also a recognised Part 5 system, a formal supervision mechanism exists by virtue of the Banking Act 2009. The Bank of England and the FSA have entered into a Memorandum of Understanding (MoU) with the objective of avoiding regulatory duplication in cases where both authorities have oversight of a payment system.[59] Recalling that section 192 of the Banking Act 2009 requires the Bank to have regard to any action that the FSA has taken[60] or could take when the Bank wishes to exercise its powers, the MoU sets out a procedural timetable. If the FSA is taking action, the Bank 'may not take action unless the FSA consents or the notice is withdrawn. The FSA will give such notice only if it reasonably expects that the action it is considering taking would address the Bank's concerns ... .'[61] Whether, and if so in what form, this arrangement will survive the Financial Services Act 2012's reorganisation of regulatory responsibilities, is unclear.

Payment Services Regulations

11.10 The Payment Services Regulations 2009 (PSRs)[62] complement the supervisory arrangements under the Banking Act 2009 with rules relating to access to payment systems which are not designated systems under the SFRs. Regulations 96–105 of the PSRs implement article 28 of the Payment Services

---

55 FSA *Guidance to Applicants*, para 10
56 FSA *Guidance to Applicants*, paras 32–35
57 See **section 11.18**
58 Cf **section 6.14**
59 Financial Services Authority and Bank of England, *Memorandum of Understanding between the Bank of England and the Financial Services Authority regarding the oversight of payment systems* (February 2010), http://www.fsa.gov.uk/pubs/mou/fsa_boe.pdf
60 After s 88, Financial Services Act 2012 takes effect, the Financial Conduct Authority or the Prudential Regulation Authority
61 MoU, para 12
62 SI 2009 No 209

Directive,[63] prohibiting restrictive rules on access to affected payment systems.[64] Designated systems are outside the scope of this prohibition, presumably because the criteria for designation, deriving from the SFD, impose severe limitations on who can participate in a designated system.[65] It is, however, possible for a payment system to impose access criteria which are necessary to safeguard against settlement risk or to protect the financial stability of the system.[66] The Office of Fair Trading (OFT) is given extensive investigatory and penal powers.[67] However, not being considered systemically worthy enough to deserve designation, a payment system which is covered by the PSRs regime would fall outside the limited oversight prescribed by the SFRs, and it may not be recognised under section 185 of the Banking Act 2009 either with the consequence that it would fall wholly outside the scope of English supervision.

RECOGNISED CLEARING HOUSES

11.11   Part XVIII of FSMA (Part XVIII) provides the statutory basis for the licensing of investment exchanges and clearing houses in the United Kingdom. The concept with which Part XVIII commences[68] is the idea that 'recognised' investment exchanges and clearing houses obtain an exemption from the 'general prohibition', that is the provision of FSMA[69] which prohibits the carrying on of a regulated activity without authorisation. CCPs and CSDs may seek recognition as clearing houses and thus step outside the general regulatory regime. They are likely to choose to do so for the reasons discussed in **section 12.5**.

It may be noted here that any body (regardless of its country of establishment) can apply to be recognised. Some differences apply to a recognised overseas clearing house, notably that statutory obligations with regard to default management are waived for overseas bodies.[70]

11.12   Much of Part XVIII is taken up with the process of obtaining recognition, the circumstances and process for revocation of recognition, ownership and control of investment exchanges (but not, curiously, clearing houses), and obsolescent rules on competition.[71] Before the Financial Services Act 2012, the collection of statutory provisions relating to the oversight of clearing houses might have been thought rather sparse, and can be summarised as in the list which follows. The detail of regulation is left to the RRRs, which are discussed in **section 11.15**.

(1)   The qualifying conditions for becoming a recognised body are to be set out in regulations made by the Treasury;[72] those regulations are the RRRs.

(2)   The regulator (the FSA until transfer to the Bank of England under the Financial Services Act 2012) may not make a recognition order if a

---

63   Directive 2007/64/EC of the European Parliament and of the Council on payment services in the internal market, etc
64   See **section 7.15**
65   See **section 8.19**
66   PSRs, reg 97(1)(b)
67   PSRs, regs 98–105
68   Section 285
69   Section 19
70   Cf **section 14.60**
71   In relation to the competition provisions, see **section 7.12**
72   FSMA, s 286

'regulatory provision' of the applicant imposes an excessive requirement on the persons affected by it.[73] Furthermore, a recognised body proposing to make a 'regulatory provision' must notify the regulator,[74] and the regulator may direct that the proposed provision must not be made if it appears to the regulator that the proposed provision will impose an excessive requirement on persons affected by it.[75] Various sections provide supplementary procedural and related detail.

(3) Recognised clearing houses must also give notice of changes to their rules, guidance and criteria for participation to the regulator:[76] these notices can, however, follow the making of the change, unlike the case of 'regulatory provisions' which must be pre-notified. Given the breath of the meaning of 'regulatory provisions' in relation to the notification requirement, the need for these extra notices seems superfluous.

(4) The regulator is empowered to make rules requiring recognised bodies to give it notice of events and information.[77] Recognised clearing houses can ask for waivers.[78] The old rules about rules are significant: the FSA noted, in its consultation on regulation of recognised bodies when FSMA was introduced, that 'the FSA will have no power to make rules applying to recognised bodies (apart from notification rules). It will only be able to give guidance on the interpretation it proposes to follow in respect of each [recognition] requirement, and the factors which it is likely to consider in its assessment of a recognised body's compliance with a requirement. ... Guidance cannot bind recognised bodies and they will be free to meet the recognition requirements in other ways than that implied by the FSA's guidance.'[79]

(5) The regulator has the power to direct a clearing house to take specified steps if it appears that the clearing house has failed, or is likely to fail, to satisfy the recognition requirements set out in the RRRs, or has failed to comply with any other obligation imposed by or under FSMA.[80] A direction is enforceable by injunction.

(6) There are sections dealing with complaints[81] and enabling the Upper Tribunal to take jurisdiction in relation to 'disciplinary proceedings' of a clearing house (that is, proceedings under its rules, in relation to market abuse by persons subject to the rules).[82]

(7) A recognised body, its officers and staff are not to be liable in damages for anything done or omitted in the discharge of the recognised body's 'regulatory functions' unless it is shown that the act or omission was in bad faith.[83]

11.13 With the Financial Services Act 2012, a change in approach to supervision of recognised clearing houses can be seen. The new statute heralds

---

73 Section 290A; see **section 11.14** for 'regulatory' provisions
74 Section 300B
75 Section 300A
76 Section 293(5), (7)
77 Section 293(1), (2)
78 Section 294
79 Financial Services Authority, *CP39: RIE and RCH Sourcebook* (January 2000), http://www.fsa.gov.uk/pubs/cp/cp39.pdf
80 Section 296
81 Section 299
82 Section 300
83 Section 291

the demise of the 'cup of tea' approach to supervision,[84] reflecting a wider trend in regulation of the post-trade industry away from soft law approaches.[85] The 2012 Act brings in the following new measures:

(1) Regulatory responsibility for clearing houses (but not, curiously, self-clearing investment exchanges) is moved to the Bank of England.[86]

(2) The Bank of England will have more comprehensive rule-making powers. These will be conferred under the RRRs.[87]

(3) The Bank of England will have disciplinary powers previously available in respect of authorised persons, but not 'recognised' (exempt) bodies. These include the ability to issue public censure,[88] to levy a fine,[89] to gather information and carry out formal investigations,[90] to issue a direction to a UK-incorporated parent undertaking,[91] the ability to obtain information from auditors,[92] and the power to apply for an injunction or a restitution order.[93]

(4) EMIR can be given effect through notification rules[94] and the power to give directions, and action can be taken for non-compliance with EMIR.[95]

Regulatory functions of clearing houses

11.14 In light of the emphasis given to regulatory provisions and regulatory functions of recognised bodies by FSMA, one question which arises in this context is which functions and rules of a recognised clearing house would be 'regulatory' in nature. Section 300E, which relates to disapplication by the regulator of 'excessive requirements', states that a regulatory provision means 'any rule, guidance, arrangements, policy or practice.' Section 302 provides a further definition for the old competition-related sections of FSMA, which impose requirements in respect of a recognised body's 'regulatory provisions' which may have a significantly adverse effect on competition: this defines regulatory provisions as the rules, guidance, clearing arrangements with any recognised investment exchange, and criteria for providing clearing services to persons other than recognised investment exchanges. However, no definition is provided in relation to the exemption from liability in damages. Moreover, no guidance is available from the predecessor legislation: the Financial Services Act 1986 did not confer immunity from liability in damages to recognised bodies; its provisions on competition scrutiny of rules did not make a distinction between 'regulatory' and other rules or practices; and the sections dealing with 'excessive requirements' were inserted by the Investment Exchanges and Clearing Houses Act 2006.

---

84 See **section 6.14**
85 See **section 6.3**
86 FSMA, s 285A, as modified by Financial Services Act 2012, s 27
87 FSMA, s 286(4F), as modified by Financial Services Act 2012, s 28
88 FSMA, s 312E, inserted by Financial Services Act 2012, s 30
89 FSMA, s 312F, inserted by Financial Services Act 2012, s 30
90 FSMA, Sch 17A, paras 11–13, inserted by Financial Services Act 2012, s 27
91 FSMA, ss 192B–192E, and Sch 17A, para 17, inserted by Financial Services Act 2012, ss 25 and 27
92 FSMA, Sch 17A, paras 18ff, inserted by Financial Services Act 2012, s 27
93 FSMA, Sch 17A, paras 24–26, inserted by Financial Services Act 2012, s 27
94 See **section 11.18**
95 FSMA, ss 293A, s 296(1A), 297(2A) as modified by Financial Services Act 2012, s 32 and Sch 8

It may be unfair to conclude that the draftsman was confused about the nature of regulatory activities carried out by a clearing house; but since the reader of these provisions is quite likely to be confused, some discussion may be appropriate. It is worth remembering that Part XVIII is primarily about regulation of investment exchanges: clearing houses have historically received less attention from legislators than exchanges. Until the 2012 Act, Part XVIII had 54 sections, of which 17 applied only to United Kingdom recognised investment exchanges. All the provisions referring to regulatory provisions or regulatory functions of clearing houses also apply to exchanges. That investment exchanges have regulatory functions has been extensively written about;[96] typically exchanges are concerned with matters such as oversight of listing, corporate disclosure and transparency, market abuse, and their participants' business conduct.[97] These roles reflect the RRRs applicable to recognised investment exchanges, which aim to ensure that business is conducted on an exchange in an orderly manner and so as to afford proper protection to investors.[98] The regulatory functions just described are unlikely to apply to clearing houses which are operated independently of investment exchanges. Nonetheless, a clearing house is also required to 'ensure that its facilities are such as to afford proper protection to investors'[99] and to be 'able and willing to promote and maintain high standards of integrity and fair dealing in the carrying on of regulated activities by persons in the course of using the facilities provided.'[100] The functions thereby required of clearing houses would appear to be regulatory in nature, so it may be concluded that the reference to 'regulatory functions' in relation to immunity in damages is likely to be to these, rather than other activities, of the clearing house. The courts are likely to be sparing in their grant of immunity, so it is fair to conclude that a narrower (and for clearing houses, very much narrower) view of 'regulatory functions' will be taken in that context than in relation to the duties of clearing houses to pre-notify their rules.

Recognition Requirements Regulations

11.15 The RRRs, together with the FSA's interpretative guidance set forth in its REC Sourcebook,[101] are the principal regulatory instruments applicable to clearing houses themselves. Two things are immediately striking about the RRRs, insofar as they apply to recognised clearing houses: the almost complete lack of overlap with the FMI Principles, and the idea that both a CCP and a CSD could be a recognised clearing house. These observations are, when put into their historical context, apparently connected.

Clearing houses were exempted from the regulatory requirements of the Financial Services Act 1986 (the predecessor to FSMA, which imposed a requirement for authorisation upon persons carrying on investment business in the United Kingdom). Under section 39 of the 1986 Act, it was necessary for a clearing house desiring recognised status to show that it would provide clearing

---

96 For a comprehensive review, see Lee, R, *Running the World's Markets: The Governance of Financial Infrastructure* (Princeton University Press, 2011), ISBN 978-0-691-13353-9
97 Cf Lee, pp 86, 115
98 RRRs, Schedule, para 4
99 RRRs, Schedule, para 19(1)
100 RRRs, Schedule, para 20(1)
101 Financial Services Authority, Handbook of Rules and Guidance, *Recognised Investment Exchanges and Recognised Clearing Houses (REC)*, ch 2

arrangements for a recognised investment exchange.[102] Recognised investment exchanges had to satisfy a list of recognition requirements,[103] which are largely reproduced (albeit in modernised, expanded form, and supplemented as a result of the implementation of MiFID[104]) in Part 1 of the Schedule to the RRRs, which specifies the current recognition requirements for investment exchanges. By contrast, a clearing house did not have to satisfy the recognition requirements listed in the 1986 Act; it simply had to show that

(1) it had financial resources sufficient for the proper performance of its functions (see now paragraph 16 of the Schedule to the RRRs).

(2) it had adequate arrangements and resources for the effective monitoring and enforcement of compliance with its rules (see now paragraph 22).

(3) it was able to provide clearing services which would enable a recognised investment exchange to make arrangements with it that satisfied the recognition requirements – note in particular that these included 'the exchange must either have its own arrangements for ensuring the performance of transactions effected on the exchange or ensure their performance by means of services provided under clearing arrangements made by it with a recognised clearing house.'[105] By the time of re-enactment of the eligibility criteria in the RRRs, clearing of OTC products had already begun, and the precondition of providing clearing services to a recognised investment exchange was not retained in the RRRs.

(4) it was able and willing to promote and maintain high standards of integrity and fair dealing in the carrying on of investment business and to co-operate, by the sharing of information and otherwise, with the Secretary of State and any other authority, body or person having responsibility for the supervision or regulation of investment business or other financial services (see now paragraph 20).

Further, when the Companies Act 1989 came into force, a recognised clearing house was required to have default rules[106] (see now paragraphs 24–28; though it should be noted that clearing houses which do not enter into contracts 'with a member of the clearing house for the purpose of enabling the rights and liabilities of that member under transactions in investments to be settled' do not have to have default rules[107]).

In 2001, the RRRs introduced the following additional recognition requirements for clearing houses:

(1) to be a fit and proper person (paragraph 17).

(2) to ensure that its systems and controls are adequate (paragraph 18).

(3) to ensure that its facilities afford proper protection to investors, including access criteria designed to protect orderly functioning of its facilities, the timely discharge of rights and liabilities to parties to transactions, record-keeping, avoidance of market abuse and financial crime, and satisfactory arrangements for safeguarding and administration of users' assets, where relevant (paragraph 19).

---

102   Financial Services Act 1986, s 39(2), (4)
103   Financial Services Act 1986, Sch 4
104   Directive 2004/39/EC of the European Parliament and of the Council of 21 April 2004 on markets in financial instruments, etc
105   Financial Services Act 1986, Sch 4, para 2(4)
106   Companies Act 1989, s 156 and Sch 21, paras 8–14
107   RRRs, reg 8

(4) to have rule-making and review procedures (paragraph 21).

(5) to have complaints arrangements (paragraph 23).

Finally, the implementation of MiFID introduced a requirement for transparent and non-discriminatory participation criteria (paragraph 21A).

These again reflect the development of thinking as regards investment exchanges: equivalent extensions were made to the recognition requirements for those bodies at the same time. The origin of the RRRs is thus firmly rooted in the regulation of investment exchanges, and may best be seen as an adjunct to that. Consequently, it may be less surprising that the issues which currently exercise regulators of CCPs were not being considered at the time the RRRs were formulated. The places to look for modern concerns are, as regards counterparty risk borne by CCPs, the FSA's REC Sourcebook, and as regards the role of CSDs as guardians of the root of title to dematerialised securities, the Uncertificated Securities Regulations 2001 (USRs).[108]

CCPs and CSDs as 'clearing houses'

11.16 The other feature remarked on with regard to the origin of the RRRs is their applicability to both CCPs and CSDs. There was no definition of 'clearing house' in the Financial Services Act 1986, nor is there one in the Financial Services and Markets Act 2000. The FSA's Glossary unhelpfully says that a clearing house is 'a clearing house through which transactions may be cleared.'[109] It was remarked earlier that terminological confusion is endemic in the post-trade space, and that 'clearing' is a term which causes more confusion than most.[110] The draftsman of the Financial Services Act 1986 presumably envisaged that post-trade services, whatever they might be, would be provided by 'clearing houses'; at the time, the CREST settlement service did not exist, and settlement of wholesale market transactions in equities was mediated by the London Stock Exchange under the aegis of its TALISMAN service. When CREST was created in 1996, a regulatory pigeon-hole was needed, and the advantages of becoming recognised were, first, that an exemption from the need for a formal regulatory authorisation under the 1986 Act was available, and, secondly, that protection from the vagaries of insolvency law was also available – CREST being established before the Settlement Finality Directive was passed in 1998. Fortunately the eligibility criteria for recognition as a clearing house were (and remain) sufficiently vague to enable CREST to make a successful application. But, as the need for a separate regulatory regime for central counterparties becomes more apparent, and the distinct role of a CSD as operator of a root of title and settlement system becomes better understood, the anomalies of lumping both together in the same regulatory group are becoming more obvious: hence regulation 8 of the RRRs, which exempts CSDs from having default rules.

Regulatory rules for clearing houses

11.17 It was noted above that the rule-making powers of the regulator as regards recognised bodies have historically been much weaker than the powers

---

108 SI 2001 No 3755; see **section 11.21**
109 Financial Services Authority, Handbook of Rules and Guidance, *Glossary* (June 2001)
110 See **section 1.4**

applicable to authorised persons: the regulator could only issue *guidance* on its interpretation of the RRRs, and *rules* relating only to notifications. It may be that the Bank of England reshapes the regulatory rules for clearing houses when it assumes responsibility for their regulation under the Financial Services Act 2012, and in light of the new international regime imposed under EMIR. Meanwhile the rules are those made by the FSA under the old regime. In that context, the following additional comments may be made on the RRRs.

(1) *The financial resources requirement.* It is fair to say that policy on the financial resources requirements for recognised bodies is evolving. The FSA's 2000 consultation stated 'First, [recognised bodies] will need to have sufficient capital to cover market and counterparty risk. This will obviously be more significant for those recognised bodies which are central counterparty clearing houses ... Second, all recognised bodies will have [to] demonstrate that they have sufficient financial resources to cover other risks (e.g. operational risks).'[111] Yet the leading item of guidance on financial resources under the REC Sourcebook states that the FSA 'may have regard to (1) the operational and other risks to which the UK recognised body is exposed'[112] and there is little discussion in the REC guidance on counterparty risks, which are surely the most significant risks to which a CCP is exposed. A 2011 consultation by the FSA[113] repeated the theoretical objective of covering both counterparty risk and operational risk, but devoted very little space to the question of counterparty risk, even stating that its proposals were 'not intended to address the risks that arise as a result of the RCH as a counterparty to transactions.'[114] In this respect the FSA followed the lead of the CPSS and IOSCO in the FMI Principles.[115] The problem can be broken up as follows:

● Because 'recognised bodies' include investment exchanges and CSDs, which carry little counterparty risk, it is difficult to come up with one-size-fits-all capital standards for counterparty risk assumed by recognised bodies.

● There is a question (notwithstanding repeated assertions by the FSA) whether the role of capital in a CCP is to provide only for transfer or wind-down of a going concern, or a fund for payment of creditors (participants, in the case of a CCP). Until the resolution of the debate about who should pay losses when the margin and default fund of a CCP are exhausted,[116] it will be impossible to devise a coherent uniform model for capitalisation of CCPs.

Consequently the regulatory pronouncements on financial resources tend to look at operational risks, wind-down costs, and liquidity requirements. That is not to say that the FSA ignored the issue of counterparty risk in CCPs; its guidance to CCPs, is, however, not in the REC Sourcebook, but a 'Finalised Guidance' paper.[117]

---

111 Financial Services Authority, *CP39: RIE and RCH Sourcebook* (January 2000), http://www.fsa.gov.uk/pubs/cp/cp39.pdf, paras 5.20, 5.21
112 REC 2.3.3G
113 Financial Services Authority, *CP11/19: Financial resources requirements for Recognised Bodies* (October 2011), http://www.fsa.gov.uk/pubs/cp/cp11_19.pdf
114 *CP 11/19*, para 1.13
115 See **section 6.41**
116 See **sections 17.12–17.14**
117 Financial Services Authority, *FSA Reviews of Counterparty Credit Risk Management by CCPs* (January 2012), http://www.fsa.gov.uk/static/pubs/guidance/fg12-03.pdf,

(2) *A fit and proper person.* The REC Sourcebook gives helpful detail on what the FSA will look out for in assessing the suitability of a person to perform the functions of a recognised clearing house.[118] The focus is on governance arrangements and on issues which in banking regulation are called 'close links' – that is the question whether any person with close links to the recognised body could prevent the effective exercise of supervisory functions.[119] In this, as in other respects apart from capital requirements, the direction of supervision is indicated by the policy taken with regard to banks.

(3) *Systems and controls.* The FSA set considerable store by effective systems and controls, and close parallels exist between the guidance given in REC 2.5 and the rules for authorised firms in its SYSC Sourcebook.[120] Two matters on which the REC Sourcebook adds detail are safeguarding and administration of assets belonging to users,[121] and information technology.[122] Some matters which receive significant attention in the case of operational risk management by authorised firms, such as employees, outsourcing, relationship with other group companies, and remuneration of key individuals, do not attract the level of detail found in the SYSC Sourcebook.

(4) *Investor protection.* Several provisions in the Schedule to the RRRs are directed towards protection of investors.

- Paragraph 19(2)(b) requires the timely discharge of rights and liabilities of parties to transactions. The manner in which this requirement is applied by CREST in cases of participant default is discussed in **section 15.16**. The guidance in the REC Sourcebook does not cast light on the FSA's opinion of CREST's practice.

- Paragraph 19(2)(d) requires a recognised clearing house to adopt 'appropriate' measures to reduce the extent to which its facilities can be sued for a purpose connected with market abuse or other financial crime. The REC Sourcebook's guidance does not distinguish between the approach to be taken by investment exchanges and that to be taken by clearing houses. In practice one would expect the differences to be substantial.

- Paragraph 19(2)(e) requires satisfactory arrangements to be made for safeguarding and administration of assets belonging to users of the clearing house's facilities. For a CCP, this may include margin (and potentially deliverable assets to which title has been transferred); for a CSD, it should include everything, the very heart of its role as operator of the fundamental record of title. REC 2.11.3G sets out ten items of guidance which do not distinguish between the very different functions of CCPs and CSDs.[123] These ten items mirror the custody obligations imposed on authorised persons in the FSA's CASS Sourcebook.[124]

---

118 REC 2.4
119 Cf Directive 2006/48/EC of the European Parliament and of the Council of 14 June 2006 on the taking up and pursuit of the business of credit institutions, art 12(3)
120 Financial Services Authority, Handbook of Rules and Guidance, *Senior Management Arrangements, Systems and Controls (SYSC) Sourcebook*
121 REC 2.5.9G
122 REC 2.5.18G
123 See also **table 11.2**
124 Financial Services Authority, Handbook of Rules and Guidance, *Client Assets (CASS) Sourcebook*; see **sections 10.19–10.22**

(5) *Rules about rules.* The REC Sourcebook makes it clear that a recognised body should consult on proposed rule changes (except 'minor changes to any rules of an administrative or commercial character'[125]); consultees should include members and other users of the body's facilities. Guidance is given on the consultation process and on the level at which rule changes should be signed off within the organisation.[126] Section 157 of the Companies Act 1989 also confers on the Bank of England a power of veto over changes to the default rules of the recognised clearing house.

(6) *Access.* The RRRs underline the general principle of competition law that a recognised clearing house must have 'transparent and non-discriminatory rules, based on objective criteria, governing access to central counterparty, clearing or settlement facilities provided by it.'[127] Access criteria are discussed at **section 7.9**.

(7) *Default rules.* Recognised clearing houses which are CCPs must have default rules, which are a vital component of counterparty risk management.[128] However, if the recognised body does not enter into contracts with members for the purpose of enabling the rights and liabilities of members under transactions to be settled, or for the purpose of providing CCP services – in other words, if the 'clearing house' is a CSD rather than a CCP – the requirement for default rules is disapplied.[129] (Nor may contracts be entered into for either of these two purposes with other recognised bodies if the disapplication is to be available.)

Notification rules

11.18 The rules adopted by the FSA are set out in Chapter 3 of its REC sourcebook, and oblige a recognised body only to give certain information to the FSA. Supervision by notification is a species of regulation of the 'cup of tea' type.[130] It facilitates the periodic assessment of risk, which is the extra-statutory tool used by the FSA to carry out supervision of recognised bodies.[131] The statutory tools available before the 2012 Act are only to give directions,[132] or to revoke recognition,[133] which (being weapons of regulatory destruction) are unsuitable for most everyday supervisory purposes. Additional prescriptive rules, which say what recognised bodies may or may not do, might be *ultra vires.* Instead, the apparent 'gaps' in the guidance relating to the RRRs are plugged using notification rules. Section 293 of FSMA sets out the scope of the FSA's rule-making powers: namely, to require a recognised body to give it notice of events and information in respect of those events;[134] and to give it information relating to the recognised body itself.[135] Section 293 also imposes notification obligations upon recognised bodies directly: they must give written notice to the FSA without delay if they alter, revoke, or create rules or

---

125 REC 2.14.4G
126 REC 2.14.6G and REC 2.14.3G
127 RRRs, Schedule, para 21A
128 RRRs, Schedule, Part IV; see **section 8.12**
129 RRRs, reg 8
130 See **section 6.14**
131 REC 4.3
132 FSMA, s 296
133 FSMA, s 297
134 Section 293(1)
135 Section 293(2)

guidance;[136] and (in the case of a recognised clearing house) if it changes the recognised investment exchanges for whom it provides clearing or the criteria it applies to whom, other than recognised investment exchanges, it will provide clearing services.[137]

In this context, the following specific notification and information rules of the FSA might deserve comment:

(1) *Organisation and personnel* (REC 3.4). For authorised persons, the management structure is carefully regulated. Firms must appoint persons to carry out certain mandatory functions, in particular the function of 'apportionment and oversight';[138] they must establish reporting lines to ensure that these responsibilities are allocated among senior managers in a clear manner in order that 'the business and affairs of the firm can be adequately monitored and controlled';[139] and the personnel who are appointed to senior positions must meet certain standards of fitness and propriety, and abide by a code of conduct while being subject to personal regulation (and the risk of sanction) by the FSA directly.[140] With only notification powers, in the REC Sourcebook the FSA can only require notification of appointments and resignations of 'key individuals', including particulars of the role to which an appointment is made, and notification of composition of standing committees.

(2) *Litigation* (REC 3.12). Authorised firms are under a duty to 'disclose to the FSA appropriately anything relating to the firm of which the FSA would reasonably expect notice.'[141] The REC Sourcebook singles out civil or criminal legal proceedings instituted against a recognised body for immediate notification to the FSA. Litigation need not be notified where the amount of damages claimed would not significantly affect the recognised body's financial resources or adversely affect the reputation and standing of the body, and it does not relate to its 'regulatory functions'.[142] For these purposes 'regulatory function' means 'any function of a recognised body so far as relating to, or to matters arising out of, the obligations to which the body is subject under or by virtue of [FSMA]',[143] which is so broad as to encompass everything other than ancillary businesses which the operator of the clearing house may be engaged in incidentally.[144]

(3) *Outsourcing* (REC 3.13). Above, in relation to payment systems, it was noted that outsourcing poses a significant risk to infrastructures, unless competently managed. Outsourcing is discussed in more detail in **sections 14.5** and **15.18**, to which reference may be made for a more detailed assessment of regulatory expectations in general. It may in particular

---

136 Section 293(5)
137 Section 293(7)
138 Financial Services Authority, Handbook of Rules and Guidance, *Supervision (SUP) Sourcebook*, SUP 10
139 Financial Services Authority, Handbook of Rules and Guidance, *Senior Management Arrangements, Systems and Controls (SYSC) Sourcebook*, SYSC 2.1.1R
140 Financial Services Authority, Handbook of Rules and Guidance, *The Fit and Proper test for Approved Persons (FIT) Sourcebook*; *Statements of Principle and Code of Practice for Approved Persons (APER) Sourcebook*
141 Financial Services Authority, Handbook of Rules and Guidance, *Principles for Businesses (PRIN) Sourcebook*, PRIN 2.1.1R(11)
142 REC 3.12.2R
143 Financial Services Authority, Handbook of Rules and Guidance, *Glossary*
144 See **section 11.14**

be noted that the outsourcing of risk management functions by CCPs is frowned upon. Against that background, the FSA's rules look meagre. The FSA must receive a copy of an invitation to tender, and a copy of an outsourcing agreement. The FSA must also be informed of the reasons for a proposed delegation of an 'exempt activity' or a 'regulatory function' and the reasons why the recognised 'is satisfied that it will continue to meet the recognition requirements following that delegation.'[145] Exempt activities are activities which would require authorisation under FSMA, but for the recognised body's status as an 'exempt' person;[146] regulatory functions are defined in the broad manner just described. Finally, the FSA must be notified where the recognised body is an *in*sourcer (supplier) for another UK recognised body.[147] Given that the clearing functions are outsourced among recognised bodies, such as the outsourcing of 'certain clearing functions to LCH.Clearnet Ltd, including the provision of risk management activities and clearing guarantee arrangements' by NYSE Liffe,[148] it might fairly be asked how the warnings of the Hay Davison report have been borne in mind, given that a CCP once failed as a direct result of inappropriately structured outsourcing.

(4) *Suspension of services* (REC 3.15, 3.17). Inability to operate is self-evidently a matter of the utmost seriousness in the case of an infrastructure, whereas in the case of an authorised person it may be of limited significance. Accordingly, the FSA requires to be notified of: suspension of clearing services[149] or of arrangements for safeguarding other persons' assets,[150] and in either case the reasons for the action taken; and it also requires to be notified of force majeure events which cause it to be unable to operate its facilities[151] or to extend its hours of operation,[152] and in the former case what the recognised body is doing to enable it to recommence operations. A recognised body must also immediately notify the FSA if it is unable to discharge any 'regulatory function'[153] – again with 'regulatory function' having the wide meaning which would encompass all activities of the recognised body which have anything to do with its clearing house function.

(5) *Membership* (REC 3.18, 3.20). The FSA requires to be notified if a recognised body admits a person who is not authorised (ie, does not hold a FSMA permission to carry on a regulated activity), or who is foreign, to its membership.[154] The explanation for this is that 'the information required ... is relevant to ... the enforceability of compliance with the UK recognised body's rules. It is also relevant to the FSA's broader responsibilities concerning market confidence and financial stability and, in particular, its functions in relation to market abuse and financial crime. It may also be necessary in the case of members based outside the United Kingdom to examine the implications for the enforceability of default rules or collateral

---

145 REC 13.3.2R
146 See **sections 12.4ff**
147 REC 13.3.3R
148 NYSE Euronext, *NYSE Liffe Clearing* and *London Notice 3174* (July 2009), http://globalderivatives.nyx.com/en/clearing/nyse-liffe
149 REC 3.15.3R
150 REC 3.15.4R
151 REC 3.15.6R
152 REC 3.15.7R
153 REC 3.17.1R
154 REC 3.18.2R, 3.18.3R

and the settlement of transactions, and thus the ability of the UK recognised body to continue to meet the recognition requirements.'[155] The FSA also wishes to know about disciplinary action taken against members.[156]

11.19   The FSA has added to the formal rules in REC by issuing extra-statutory 'finalised guidance' for CCPs on counterparty credit risk management.[157] This covers many issues studied in more detail in **Chapter 14**, and the FSA states that it aims to follow the FMI Principles.[158] Here it may be noted that the finalised guidance explains that the FSA carries out a risk management review focused on risk management governance, initial margin models, variation margin calculation, default fund, stress testing, wrong way and concentration risk, collateral, and validation and back-testing.

OPERATORS UNDER THE UNCERTIFICATED SECURITIES REGULATIONS

11.20   The main source of regulation of CSDs in the United Kingdom is not the financial services legislation. The operator of a CSD is an Operator appointed in respect of regulations made under the Companies Acts. This is because the Operator's core function is to provide a computerised system under which title to securities can be transferred without a written instrument. From a legal viewpoint, the CSD is not seen as part of the financial markets infrastructure, rather as a centralised system under which public companies can streamline the method of keeping their registers of members. Hence, under section 785 of the Companies Act 2006, regulations may be made 'for enabling title to securities to be evidenced and transferred without a written instrument';[159] and 'the regulations may make provision ... for the regulation of ... procedures [for recording and transferring title to securities] and the persons responsible for or involved in their operation.'[160]

Under section 93 of the Financial Services Act 2012, the regulations may be expanded to confer the functions of giving guidance or issuing a code of practice, or making rules, on 'any person'. The quantity of regulation applicable to CSDs and their users may therefore change as and when this power is activated.

The Regulations in question are the Uncertificated Securities Regulations 2001 (USRs).[161] Under regulation 4, a person may apply to the Treasury for approval as Operator of a relevant system. The Treasury may approve an applicant if the requirements of Schedule 1 to the USRs are satisfied: Schedule 1 therefore sets out the fundamental regulatory requirements for an Operator in the same way as the Schedule to the RRRs does in the case of a recognised clearing house. Indeed in some cases the recognition requirements for clearing houses and the approval requirements for operators are identical. The only system in place is

---

155   REC 3.18.1G(3)
156   REC 3.20
157   Financial Services Authority, *FSA Reviews of Counterparty Credit Risk Management by CCPs* (January 2012), http://www.fsa.gov.uk/static/pubs/guidance/fg12-03.pdf
158   Cf FMI Principle 4
159   Section 785(1)
160   Section 785(2)
161   SI 2001 No 3755

in fact CREST, and the approved Operator of the system is Euroclear UK & Ireland (EUI), which was approved under its former name of Crestco.[162]

Regulation under the Uncertificated Securities Regulations

11.21 The USRs set out a regulatory regime which contains the following elements. First, regulatory powers are nominally conferred upon the Treasury, but under regulation 11 the Treasury may delegate these functions to the FSA, which has been done.[163] Secondly, the regulator may withdraw approval[164] and issue directions,[165] obtain injunctions,[166] and require the operator to provide specified information, including in particular notification of rule changes.[167] Thirdly, provision is made for scrutiny of the operator's rules for their compatibility with competition law.[168] The second and third elements of this structure are familiar: they closely resemble Part XVIII of FSMA, in relation to the regulation of recognised clearing houses. Perhaps noteworthy is the requirement in regulation 11(4) that the FSA should send to the Treasury a copy of any guidance issued by it: no publicly available guidance would appear to have been issued. This may be because EUI is already rather heavily regulated:

'[Euroclear UK & Ireland] is incorporated in the UK as a private limited company, and as such is subject to UK company law. It is regulated by the FSA:
- as a Recognised Clearing House (RCH) under [FSMA];
- subject to the [RRRs];
- according to the FSA's specialist [REC] Sourcebook...;
- as an approved operator under the [USRs]; and
- designated under the Financial Markets and Insolvency (Settlement Finality) Regulations 1999 ... .'[169]

11.22 But the conclusion to which this leads is that the principal regulatory instrument specific to EUI's role as operator of a CSD is in the approval requirements of Schedule 1 to the USRs. The central functions of a CSD are to safeguard the integrity of the securities in issue – in other words, to ensure that the number of shares in existence at any one time equals with precision the number of shares actually issued – and to provide for DvP. As to these, the following comments may be made:

---

162 EUI, *CREST Glossary of Terms* (September 2009), https://www.euroclear.com/site/publishedFile/2009-09-01_Glossary_September_2009_tcm87-119879.pdf?title=CREST+Glossary+of+Terms

163 Euroclear UK & Ireland, *Regulatory environment* (April 2008), https://www.euroclear.com/site/public/EUI/!ut/p/c5/hY7LDoIwEEW_hS_o2ArFZW1NeRSoQgqyMSwMaSLgwvj9lp0hsc5dnpx7B_XIZR7edhxedpmHB-pQH92i8FwrmmCA-sgBNyI2RXjZwR4cv35xWcgQcEmqDAQnsqB_7Hbd8_srhx_HYOPHRsVugelDUwnIDfH3n_CGVlq5DzPJTa4ITnPq7YeMoDJZpjt6Th3Y1OqRBcEHgQytfQ!!/dl3/d3/L2dJQSEvUUt3QS9ZQnZ3LzZfNjVRU0w3SDIwTzRSNDAySkk5NDFFBTzNLMzI!/

164 USRs, reg 7

165 USRs, regs 8 and 12

166 USRs, reg 9

167 USRs, reg 10

168 USRs, regs 11(5), 11(6), 13 and Sch 2

169 Financial Services Authority and Bank of England, Assessment of CRESTCo Limited against the *CPSS-IOSCO recommendations for Securities Settlement Systems* (June 2006), http://www.fsa.gov.uk/pubs/other/crestco.pdf, pp 4–5

(1) *Integrity of the issue.* Paragraphs 7 and 8 of Schedule 1 to the USRs tackle this subject, in a manner which is potentially open to criticism. Before registering a transfer of title, the operator is obliged to check that the transferor has enough units of the security; and before sending an update instruction to the issuer's registrar, the system must check that the transferor has title to the number of units to be transferred. But these rules do not go to the heart of the problem: that the operator should not be allowed to record credits, on its own books, of an aggregate number of securities greater than the number actually in issue. Indeed the statutory framework of the USRs is to expect the issuer's registers to give way to the operator's.[170] The policy is that the issuer's obligations, and the investors' entitlements, are determined by the operator; while this might seem perverse, the operator is liable to give compensation for losses occasioned by forged transfer instructions.[171] Comparison may be made with the system for land registration, which includes a detailed set of arrangements for adjudication of alleged registration errors.[172]

(2) *Delivery versus payment.* Paragraph 13 of Schedule 1 to the USRs provides that 'a relevant system must be able to establish, where there is a transfer of uncertificated units of a security to a system-member for value, that a settlement bank has agreed to make payment in respect of the transfer, whether alone or taken together with another transfer for value.' This is all well, as far as it goes. But it may be noted that the USRs do not provide for simultaneity between the transfer and the assumption by the settlement bank of its payment obligation; they do not provide for settlement of the cash leg in central bank money, even at the end of the day; and the mere 'agreement' of a settlement bank to make payment may not actually constitute a payment.[173]

11.23 The USRs also cover a number of other topics. Much attention is given to the technical requirements (such as security, operating procedures, content of rules) for a system which must allow for high volumes of settlement instructions which require due authentication in order to safeguard the property interests of those whose assets are recorded in the Operator's books, and whose ownership rights are at risk to mis-processing or fraud. The following additional matters might be worthy of specific comment as regards the regulatory regime for CSDs:

(1) *Overlap with RRRs.* Paragraphs 1–3 and 28 of Schedule 1 to the USRs cover familiar ground: an Operator must have adequate arrangements and resources for monitoring and enforcing compliance with its rules; an Operator must have sufficient financial resources for the proper performance of its functions; an Operator must be able and willing to promote and maintain high standards of integrity and fair dealing in the operation of the system; an Operator must have transparent and non-discriminatory access criteria. These paragraphs mirror with close exactitude some of the requirements for recognition of clearing houses.[174] A discussion as to why there are differences between the remainder of the requirements is probably

---

170 Cf USRs, regs 20(6), 24(2), 25(1), 26, etc
171 USRs, reg 36
172 Cf Land Registration Act 2002, Part 11
173 Cf **section 9.2**
174 RRRs, Schedule, paras 22, 15, 20 and 21A respectively

valueless, as the legislation is in any case confused as to the functions of 'clearing houses'.

(2) *Outsourcing.* Unlike the RRRs, the USRs cover outsourcing specifically. Paragraph 4 of Schedule 1 requires an Operator which outsources 'a part of the relevant system which is not the Operator-system' to monitor performance and have arrangements for information and assistance to enable compliance with the USRs. The tortuous drafting of this requirement suggests that even these weak constraints will not apply if an Operator chooses to outsource any part of the 'relevant system' (that is, the computer-based system which enables title to securities to be transferred without a written instrument[175]) other than the 'Operator-system' (that is, the part of the relevant system which generates and receives transfer instructions[176]). As with clearing houses, the formal regulation of outsourcing is significantly diluted by comparison with banks and payment systems, for reasons which are far from apparent.

(3) *Maximising settlement success.* Paragraph 19(2)(b) of the RRRs requires a recognised clearing house to ensure that its 'clearing services involve satisfactory arrangements for securing the timely discharge (whether by performance, compromise or otherwise) of the rights and liabilities of parties to transactions in respect of which it provides such services.' The USRs contain no similar provision, implying that a high success rate in settlements is not a policy priority. Indeed, the policy seems to be that in difficult cases it is better *not* to transfer: regulation 27(2) of the USRs oblige an Operator to refuse to register a transfer of title 'if he has actual notice that the transfer is – (a) prohibited by an order of a court in the United Kingdom; (b) prohibited or avoided by or under an enactment; (c) a transfer to a deceased person.' Rather than let transferor and transferee sort out the consequences of court orders, other legal issues, and death, the Operator is expected to intervene. Operators will be cautious; asking them to become policeman introduces friction into the settlement process. One example of friction arises in insolvency cases. Section 127 of the Insolvency Act 1986[177] renders void transfers of property, and transfers of shares, after the presentation of a winding-up petition affecting the transferor and issuer respectively; section 127 is presumably an example of avoidance under an enactment, and the consequence is that insolvency events are treated by CREST as grounds for discontinuing settlements. Comment is made in **section 15.16** on the actual practice of CREST in processing settlement instructions in cases of default by participants.

(4) *Liability.* It was noted above that recognised clearing houses enjoy a certain degree of statutory immunity from liability in damages. Operators can put on a further layer of bullet-proof clothing. Regulation 23 of the USRs provides that the obligations imposed by the USRs '(a) shall not give rise to any form of duty or liability on the Operator, except such as is expressly provided for in these Regulations or as arises from fraud or other wilful default, or negligence ... ; and (c) shall not give rise to any form of duty or liability enforceable by civil proceedings for breach of statutory duty.' On the other hand, as mentioned above, an Operator is liable for compensation for losses caused by forged dematerialised instructions.

---

175 USRs, reg 2(1)
176 USRs, reg 3(1)
177 See **section 8.9(15)**

Table 11.2   Comparison of custody requirements for recognised clearing houses and operators

Recognised clearing houses	Operators under the USRs Sch 1	Comment
Protection against risk of theft and other loss Assets to be transferred only in accordance with owner's instructions	Para 20 requires that a relevant system only respond to properly authenticated dematerialised instructions	Broadly comparable; Operator is liable under USRs reg 36
Assets not to be used to settle owner's debts without valid instructions	No equivalent	FSA guidance seems inappropriate for a CSD
Corporate actions handled in accordance with owner's instructions	Para 22 requires that a relevant system have procedures to deal with corporate action instructions	Broadly comparable
Segregation of assets belonging to recognised body from those of users of its facilities	No equivalent	See **section 6.38** as regards the proposed CSD Regulation
Procedures for selection, etc of sub-custodians	No equivalent	FSA guidance seems inappropriate for a CSD
Agreements with users to include terms and conditions of custody	No equivalent	1. The USRs themselves are, in a sense, custody terms and conditions 2. FMI Principles suggest that a formal transparency rule would be desirable
Records to identify legal and beneficial owners, charges, to record additions, reductions and transfers in each account, and separately identify different owners (including clients of members)	Para 7 requires an Operator to check transferor has sufficient securities Para 10 requires a relevant system to maintain records of all dematerialised instructions	The purpose of the USRs is to establish a record of legal ownership and transfers between legal owners, not these other matters
Reconciliation with users	Para 23 requires reconciliation with issuers	The approach of the USRs seems more appropriate than the FSA guidance
Provision of statements	Para 11 requires a relevant system to enable system-members to obtain and correct records	Broadly comparable

(5) *Custody rules*. The FSA's REC Sourcebook[178] sets out ten items of guidance on the provision in the RRRs[179] which requires recognised clearing houses to make provision for safeguarding and administration of users' assets. In some cases the guidance works well for a CSD, and can be validly compared with the USRs; in others it does not. A comparison is set out in **table 11.2**. This implies that a revision of the FSA's guidance is desirable in relation to Operators.

COMPARISON OF UNITED KINGDOM LEGISLATION WITH INTERNATIONAL STANDARDS

11.24 **Table 11.3** attempts to map the FMI Principles to the United Kingdom legislation reviewed in this chapter. Accepting that the United Kingdom legislation has to be brought up to date to reflect the new international standards, it may not be surprising that there are evident gaps in the national framework. There is also duplication, owing to the confused regulatory status of infrastructures, some of which arises in areas which seem to be of little current relevance. It has also been mentioned[180] that the FMI Principles are a one-size-fits-all solution to a complex problem which demands different solutions to different risk profiles. Some of the matters demanded by the FMI Principles can rightly be said to be covered by more general legal provisions inherent in the supervisory framework. With all those caveats in mind, the following comments might be made:

(1) The United Kingdom legislation is excessively focused on market abuse, high standards of integrity and fair dealing in its markets, and oversight. To be concerned about these issues is not a bad thing: but it is questionable whether post-trade infrastructures which are not specifically designed to have these roles should have market oversight duties thrust upon them, particularly when there are other bodies who can, and should, perform them better. Any future revision of infrastructure legislation in the United Kingdom should distinguish more clearly between the functions of a trading platform operator and those of infrastructures providing clearing or settlement services.

(2) The United Kingdom legislation rightly places significant emphasis on outsourcing as a source of risk to infrastructures. Outsourcing is covered in the Bank of England's Principles for recognised inter-bank payment systems,[181] in the RRRs,[182] and in the USRs.[183] In adopting international standards, it would not be right for the authorities to abandon the good parts of the legislative programme along with any outdated or superfluous parts, out of a desire to avoid gold-plating.

(3) The British habit of regulation through notification rules, coupled with 'nuclear' weapons, was not found adequate to regulate banks, which have since the adoption of the Banking Act 1987 been expected to comply with

---

178 REC 2.11.3G
179 Schedule, para 19(2(e)
180 See **section 6.41(1)**
181 Principle 14
182 Regulation 6
183 Schedule, para 4

a rulebook containing graduated disciplinary powers (including personal responsibility for senior managers) and a range of requirements expressed at various levels of detail. The deficiency of the old system came to light only in connection with failed banks which had found ways to manipulate the softer regulatory system. The FSA's REC Sourcebook is a valiant attempt to use the feeble rule-making powers it has to ensure effective regulation across the board. If the attempt is unsuccessful, though, it will likely be shown up in the afterlight of an infrastructure failure. That is a risk which the United Kingdom legislature (and the regulators who will be criticised) should not allow to continue.

Table 11.3   Mapping of FMI Principles to United Kingdom legislation on infrastructures

FMI Principle	Payment systems	CCPs	CSDs
1. well-founded legal basis in all relevant jurisdictions	RPS Principle 1		
2. clear and transparent governance arrangements that promote safety, efficiency, financial stability etc	RPS Principle 10	REC 2.4, 3.6	REC 2.4, 3.6
3. framework for managing legal, credit, liquidity, operational, and other risks		RRRs Para 18(2)(b)	RRRs Para 18(2)(b)
4. measure, monitor, and manage credit risk; sufficient financial resources to cover credit exposure	RPS Principle 3	FG para 6	
CCPs: additional financial resources to cover stress scenarios including default of two participants with largest exposures in extreme conditions	not applicable	FG para 15 [but does not specify 2-participant requirement]	not applicable
5. accept collateral with low credit, liquidity, and market risk; set conservative haircuts and concentration limits		FG para 24	
6. CCPs: risk-based and regularly reviewed margin system	not applicable	FG paras 8, 26, 27	not applicable
7. measure, monitor, and manage liquidity risk	RPS Principles 3, 5		

FMI Principle	Payment systems	CCPs	CSDs
CCPs: sufficient liquid resources to effect settlement of payment obligations under stress scenarios including default of 1–2 participant(s) with largest aggregate payment obligation in extreme conditions	not applicable	REC 2.3.5G [but does not specify quantitative test]	not applicable
8. final settlement by the end of value date if not intraday or in real time	RPS Principle 4	RRRs Para 19(2)(b) [as to timely discharge of obligations]	RRRs Para 19(2)(b) [as to timely discharge of obligations]
9. money settlements in central bank money where practical; otherwise control credit and liquidity risk with commercial bank money	RPS Principle 6		
10. physical delivery: state obligations, and identify, monitor, and manage risks	not applicable		USRs Para 18 [as to rights of re-materialisation]
11. CSDs: rules to ensure the integrity of securities issues and manage safekeeping and transfer risks; maintain securities in immobilised or dematerialised form for book entry transfer	not applicable	not applicable	USRs generally
12. settlement of two linked obligations: final settlement of one to be conditional upon final settlement of the other			USRs Para 13
13. rules to manage participant default, to contain losses and liquidity pressures, and continue to meet obligations	SFRs Para 6	RRRs Part IV SFRs Para 6	SFRs Para 6
14. CCPs: rules for segregation and portability of positions of customers of a participant and associated collateral	not applicable		not applicable

FMI Principle	Payment systems	CCPs	CSDs
15. manage general business risk; hold sufficiently liquid net assets funded by equity to continue operations and ensure recovery or orderly wind-down	RPS Principle 11 [as to general business risk] SFRs Para 3 [as to financial resources]	RRRs Para 15, SFRs Para 3 [as to financial resources]	USRs Para 2, RRRs Para 15, SFRs Para 3 [as to financial resources]
16. safeguard own and participants' assets; invest in instruments with minimal credit, market and liquidity risks		RRRs Paras 18(2)(d), 19(2)(e) [as to safeguarding]	USRs Para 5, RRRs Para 19(2)(e) [as to safeguarding]
17. identify and mitigate operational risk; use systems, policies, procedures and controls; systems to have high security, reliability and scalable capacity; business continuity plans for timely recovery, including in wide-scale or major disruption	RPS Principle 7 [as to security, reliability and business continuity]	RRRs Para 18 [as to systems and controls] REC 3.15 [as to continuity]	RRRs Para 18 [as to systems and controls] USRs Paras 5, 6 [as to security and scalability] REC 3.15 [as to continuity]
18. objective, risk-based, and publicly disclosed criteria for participation, which permit fair and open access	RPS Principle 9	RRRs Paras 19(2)(a), 21A	USRs Para 28, RRRs Paras 19(2)(a), 21A
19. identify, monitor, and manage risks arising from tiered participation arrangements	RPS Principle 13		
20. identify, monitor and manage risks from links with other FMIs	FMI Principles state not applicable RPS Principle 12		
21. efficient and effective in meeting the requirements of participants and markets	RPS Principle 8		
22. accommodate internationally accepted communication standards to facilitate efficient payment, clearing, settlement and recording			

FMI Principle	Payment systems	CCPs	CSDs
23. clear and comprehensive rules and procedures; provide information for participants to understand risks, fees and costs; rules to be publicly disclosed	RPS Principle 2 [as to understanding] SFRs Para 5(2) [as to disclosure]	RRRs Para 21(1) [as to requirement for rules] SFRs Para 5(2) [as to disclosure]	USRs Para 25, RRRs Para 21(1) [as to requirement for rules] SFRs Para 5(2) [as to disclosure]
24. TRs: provide timely and accurate data to authorities and public	not applicable	not applicable	not applicable

Notes:
- Shaded cells refer to FMI Principles which will rarely be relevant to the infrastructure in question; darkly shaded cells are expressly deemed inapplicable by the FMI Principles; blank cells are where the United Kingdom legislation does not appear to cover the issue expressly
- Comments in square brackets indicate limited coverage of the United Kingdom legislation
- The FMI Principles refer separately to CSDs and SSSs (securities settlement systems) – in this table both CSDs and SSSs are covered under the heading CSDs

RPS = Bank of England's Principles for recognised payment systems
SFRs = Schedule to the Settlement Finality Regulations 1999
RRRs = Schedule to the Recognition Requirements Regulations 2001
REC = FSA Guidance and Rules in the REC Sourcebook
FG = FSA Finalised Guidance on REC 2.3
USRs = Schedule 1 to the Uncertificated Securities Regulations 2001

12 Legal form and governance of infrastructures

LEGAL FORM OF INFRASTRUCTURES

12.1　Whether an infrastructure is required to opt for a particular legal form, and if so what that form might be, are questions with a perplexing variety of answers. It depends partly on the way that the law views those operations and thus the characteristic regulated activities of the entity carrying them out. As the law struggles to distinguish clearing from settlement, and as European policy struggles to wean infrastructures from dependency on the state and to promote competition, it is not surprising that different countries have different solutions to the problem.

Yet a grounding in the legal requirements for form is crucial in order to determine the governance requirements to which an infrastructure will be subject. For example, if an infrastructure needs to be a bank, that fact may require the infrastructure to take a different corporate form, and will almost everywhere subject the infrastructure to special rules as to its ownership, management and organisation. Furthermore, the legal requirements for form determine other aspects of the infrastructure's strategy and development: the ability to merge, to outsource, to capitalise, to expand into new activities will all be affected by the choice of form.

CSDs AND CCPs INCORPORATED IN THE UNITED KINGDOM

12.2　The law of the United Kingdom does not specify a legal status for CCPs or CSDs. As to infrastructures generally: 'any body corporate or unincorporated association may apply to the Bank of England for an order declaring it to be a recognised clearing house.'[1] And for CSDs in particular: 'any person may apply to the Treasury for their approval of him as Operator of a relevant system.'[2] Nor does the law of the United Kingdom specify a particular kind of corporate entity for a bank or any other type of financial institution, though a person accepting deposits must be a body corporate or a partnership, and a person effecting or carrying out contracts of insurance must be a body corporate, a friendly society or a member of Lloyd's of London.[3] This would imply total freedom of choice:

1　Financial Services and Markets Act 2000, s 288(1), as amended by the Financial Services Act 2012, Sch 8, para 4
2　Uncertificated Securities Regulations 2001, SI 2001/3755, reg 4(1)
3　Financial Services and Markets Act 2000, Sch 6, para 1

the normal form of joint-stock company (a registered company with liability limited by shares, either private or public) is typically favoured by UK financial institutions. The registered company is also the form of company chosen by most UK infrastructures – for example, LCH.Clearnet Limited and Euroclear UK & Ireland Limited are both private companies limited by shares.[4] However, a free choice is in practice illusory. While the choice of *corporate* form may be unrestricted in the United Kingdom, the regulatory regime which applies – and thus, the question whether the infrastructure is characterised as a bank, an investment firm, or something else – is more constrained.

Financial Services and Markets Act 2000 – recognised clearing houses

12.3   The fount of law on the subject of regulatory status of infrastructures is the Financial Services and Markets Act 2000 (FSMA). The central provision as regards infrastructures is section 285(3), which confers an 'exemption' from the 'general prohibition' for 'recognised clearing houses'. The general prohibition[5] states that no person may carry on a regulated activity unless he is authorised or exempt, and section 23 of FSMA makes it an offence to contravene the general prohibition. If you are a 'clearing house', then, you will not need to obtain authorisation – the licence which enables banks and investment firms to carry on regulated activities – but authorisation may technically be available if for some reason 'exemption' is unattractive.[6]

FSMA contains no definition of 'clearing house', but there is a roundabout way of finding a meaning. Recognised clearing houses are required to comply with the Recognition Requirements Regulations (RRRs),[7] which specify that a recognised clearing house must ensure that 'its clearing services involve satisfactory arrangements for securing the timely discharge (whether by performance, compromise or otherwise) of the rights and liabilities of the parties to transactions in respect of which it provides such services (being rights and liabilities in relation to those transactions).'[8] So it would appear that the essence of being a 'clearing house' is to *secure the discharge* of obligations arising under market transactions. Using language in its everyday sense, this is what CSDs and payment systems do: act as settlement systems so as to facilitate the fulfilment of market participants' promises to deliver securities and make payments. Thus, CREST is a 'recognised clearing house'.[9] You can also argue that this is what CCPs do: through multilateral netting, and through close-out in default scenarios, CCPs also discharge obligations of market participants. At first blush it is curious that the Recognition Requirements Regulations should describe for 'clearing houses' a function which is more apposite to CSDs; but then it is reassuring to observe that the United Kingdom's CCPs are also

---

4   LCH: registered number 4743602; EUI: registered number 2878738
5   FSMA, s 19
6   See **section 12.4**
7   Financial Services and Markets Act 2000 (Recognition Requirements for Investment Exchanges and Clearing Houses) Regulations 2001, SI 2001/995
8   RRRs, Schedule, Part III, para 19(2)
9   Financial Services Authority list of recognised clearing houses (August 2010), http://www.fsa. gov.uk/register/exchanges.do

'recognised clearing houses'.[10] But no ACHs or other payment systems have been recognised as clearing houses under section 290 of FSMA.

Exemption

12.4   Thus far, there is no indication that the system is anything other than flexible for an entity which is a clearing house: there is apparently a free option to avoid the regulatory regime for banks and investment firms, which makes sense given the differences between the respective activities of market participants and market infrastructures. Exempt firms will be freed from the shackles of the Capital Requirements Directives[11] and the conduct of business requirements of MiFID,[12] though they are subject to the regulatory regime described in **Chapter 11**. However, the protections potentially available under Part VII of the Companies Act 1989 (Part VII) complicate the story. As discussed in **sections 8.12–8.15**, Part VII makes a range of immunities from attack under insolvency legislation available to contracts entered into by participants of recognised investment exchanges and recognised clearing houses, but not participants of a system operated by any other category of regulated person.[13] To obtain the protection, one would therefore wish to become recognised; and insofar as the clearing activity involves a regulated activity, one would be exempt and therefore not have to apply for authorisation.

12.5   Exemption then raises the question whether it is actually possible to be authorised as, say, a bank or investment firm, and still carry on the activities of a recognised clearing house. At this final stage in the analysis, section 42(4) of FSMA comes into play, and unbalances the apparent freedom of choice between regulatory regimes. Section 42(4) deals expressly with the case of applicants for authorisation who are exempt because they are recognised clearing houses. The application for authorisation is to be treated as relating only to regulated activities which the exemption does not cover. Thus, insofar as a CSD or CCP is a recognised clearing house, it cannot obtain authorisation for the regulated activities for which it has recognition: to put it less technically, a single legal entity *can* be both a bank and a recognised CCP/CSD, but its banking licence will not cover the CCP/CSD activities unless it surrenders its Part VII benefits. In **table 8.2**, the apparent advantage of Part VII protection over financial collateral protection – the only alternative available to banks and other regulated entities – is compared. Together with the other benefits of being exempt, this would appear to have driven the United Kingdom's infrastructures to choosing 'recognised' status in preference to authorisation.

12.6   Having concluded that clearing and settlement systems need to choose between recognition and authorisation, and noted that the United Kingdom's

---

10   European Central Counterparty Limited, ICE Clear Europe Limited and LCH.Clearnet Limited are also on the FSA list
11   Directive 2006/48/EC of the European Parliament and of the Council of 14 June 2006 relating to the taking up and pursuit of the business of credit institutions; and Directive 2006/49/EC of the European Parliament and of the Council of 14 June 2006 on the capital adequacy of investment firms and credit institutions
12   Directive 2004/39/EC of the European Parliament and of the Council of 21 April 2004 on markets in financial instruments, etc
13   Companies Act 1989, s 155

systems have elected for recognition, it may be useful to examine the disadvantages which they have chosen to suffer. These include:

(1) *Cross-border activity.* A UK firm which is merely 'recognised' and therefore exempt will not be eligible for a passport under either the Banking Directive[14] or MiFID, because it has no valid authorisation under those directives and is thus neither a 'credit institution' nor an 'investment firm'. Worse, where another country requires that a CCP or CSD take the form of a bank, it will be impossible for the UK firm to obtain local authorisation in order to carry on its business there. Accordingly, consolidation of activities between the UK and French entities of the LCH.Clearnet group, each carrying out CCP functions, has been impossible.[15] It may be assumed that the passporting provisions of EMIR[16] and the proposed Regulation on CSDs[17] will cure this deficiency, but the label 'exempt' will continue to be unhelpful unless FSMA is modified in order to show that CCPs and CSDs respectively enjoy 'authorised' status in the United Kingdom.

(2) *Interoperability.* In order to participate in another system which is designated under the Settlement Finality Directive,[18] it will generally be necessary to be a credit institution, an investment firm or a government body. Not having this status will impair the ability to interoperate with a peer CCP or CSD, to settle payments directly (or in the case of a CCP, to settle securities delivery obligations directly at a CSD) without hiring an agent bank.

(3) *Central bank funding.* Commentators have underscored the importance of CCPs having access to central bank liquidity to help them manage defaults.[19] Banks have access to central bank liquidity. Non-banks may not, though this is a matter for the policy of the central bank in question. The chief executive of LCH.Clearnet, giving evidence to the House of Lords Select Committee on the European Union in February 2010 said:

> 'The other reason why [a CCP] may need access to central bank money could be as a means of providing some backstop liquidity in the event of a real crisis ... the answer ... is there are some situations where temporary liquidity could be beneficial. Again, each of the clearing houses really is designing their business model to prevent the need for that, but in the event that it was necessary then it would be a sensible measure to take. I am very nervous, however, about the sort of moral hazard associated

---

14 Directive 2006/48/EC of the European Parliament and of the Council of 14 June 2006 relating to the taking up and pursuit of the business of credit institutions
15 Lamb, A, *Roadmap to the future* (June 2004), conference presentation, 12th ISSA symposium http://www.issanet.org/pdf/issa12_lamb.pdf
16 Regulation (EU) No 648/2012 of the European Parliament and of the Council of 4 July 2012 on OTC derivatives, central counterparties and trade repositories, art 14(2)
17 European Commission, *Proposal for a Regulation of the European Parliament and of the Council on improving securities settlement in the European Union and on central securities depositories etc* (March 2012), COM(2012) 73 final, http://eur-lex.europa.eu/LexUriServ/LexUriServ.do?uri=CELEX:52012PC0073:EN:PDF, art 21
18 Directive 98/26/EC of the European Parliament and of the Council of 19 May 1998 on settlement finality in payment and securities settlement systems, art 2
19 Fleuriot, P, *Rapport au Ministre de L'Economie, de l'Industrie et de l'Emploi sur la révision de la directive sur les Marchés d'Instruments Financiers* (February 2010), http://www.economie.gouv.fr/directions_services/sircom/100217_rap_fleuriot.pdf; Langen, W, *Report on derivatives markets: future policy actions* (June 2010), European Parliament Committee on Economic and Monetary Affairs document A7-0187/2010, http://www.europarl.europa.eu/sides/getDoc.do?pubRef=-//EP//NONSGML+REPORT+A7-2010-0187+0+DOC+PDF+V0//EN&language=EN; see also **section 14.59**

with explicit guarantees to organisations like ours. I really believe that in principle we should not feel we have any guarantee from anybody at all, and should be operating on that basis.'[20]

PAYMENT SYSTEMS IN THE UNITED KINGDOM

12.7   Payment systems in the United Kingdom are mercifully free from this evil choice. Payment systems can obtain protection akin to that under Part VII via section 301 of FSMA without becoming recognised – see **section 8.17**. Furthermore, they (like CCPs and CSDs) can get most if not all of the wished-for insolvency protection under the settlement finality legislation, which was designed specifically with payment systems in mind.[21]

Payment systems will, instead, need to consider the implications under the Regulated Activities Order[22] of receiving their participants' money. This might constitute deposit-taking and therefore require a banking permission under FSMA. Or, oddly, it might not: article 6(1)(a)(ii) of the Regulated Activities Order deems sums paid by persons who are banks or insurers not to constitute 'deposits', so it may be that a payment system never needs such a permission. On the other hand the processing of payment instructions – including even the discharge of payment orders and replacing them with other payment orders, which is what happens at an ACH[23] – would not appear to be a regulated activity under the Regulated Activities Order and could thus be carried out without any authorisation under FSMA. Likewise payment transactions which are 'carried out within a payment or securities settlement system between settlement agents, central counterparties, clearing houses and/or central banks and other participants of the system, and payment service providers' are excluded from the scope of the Payment Services Directive,[24] and thus a person providing services as a payment system ought not to require authorisation or registration as a payment institution.

12.8   A payment system which finds it does not need a banking permission under FSMA may, however, be at a disadvantage. Without a banking authorisation the passport under the Banking Directive[25] will be unavailable. Access criteria to other payment systems may be denied, not least because the Settlement Finality Directive requires that participation in designated settlement systems be restricted to credit institutions and other types of regulated and public entity.[26] Thus payment systems seeking to operate outside the United Kingdom might wish to take steps to become regulated as banks; though none of Bacs or VocaLink (between them operating the UK's primary ACH), CLS Bank (a US bank operating a settlement system in the United Kingdom) or

---

20 House of Lords European Union Committee, HL Paper 93: *The future regulation of derivatives markets: is the EU on the right track?* (March 2010), 10th Report of Session 2009–10, Oral Evidence of Mr Roger Liddell, p 48, Q137

21 See **section 8.18**

22 Financial Services and Markets Act 2000 (Regulated Activities) Order 2001, SI 2001 No 544

23 See **section 2.27**

24 Directive 2007/64/EC of the European Parliament and of the Council of 13 November 2007 on payment services in the internal market, etc, art 3(h)

25 Title III

26 Directive 98/26/EC of the European Parliament and of the Council of 19 May 1998 on settlement finality in payment and securities settlement systems, art 2; and see **section 8.19**

EBA Clearing (the operator of a Pan-European ACH) were authorised to take deposits in the United Kingdom, either directly by the FSA or indirectly via a Banking Directive passport.

LEGAL FORM OF INFRASTRUCTURES IN CONTINENTAL EUROPE

12.9   Across the EU, regulatory authorities approach the unusual position of infrastructures in a variety of ways. The Committee of European Securities Regulators (CESR) studied the question whether CSDs and CCPs were required to have a particular regulatory form as part of its assessment of barriers to interoperability in 2009.[27] CESR notes that some member states require all CCPs operating in their territory to hold a banking licence; notably, these states include France[28] and Germany.[29] Likewise, CSDs may have to have a banking licence, notably in Germany;[30] CESR's report also observed in relation to Germany that acting as a CSD will constitute custody business (which may therefore require a banking licence), and that other services provided by the CSD such as the grant of credit may equally require a banking licence. The responses for Germany indicated that passporting of CSD business, being custody, was possible, in contrast to CCP business.[31] But, in most member states, there is either special legislation applicable to CSDs and CCPs, or a special set of regulatory rules which are peculiar to the infrastructure business. For similar reasons, interbank payment systems may need banking licences; but, apparently, in France neither payment systems nor securities settlement systems are subject to a threshold licence requirement.[32]

Belgium may be worthy of special note. CSDs are licensed under the Royal Decree No 62 of 10 November 1967 on the promotion of the circulation of securities. As well as the National Bank of Belgium (which provides the CSD for Belgian government bonds) and Euroclear Belgium (equities), Euroclear Bank has been licensed as a CSD, in relation to its activities as ICSD for Eurobonds.

OVERSIGHT OF GOVERNANCE

12.10   It almost goes without saying that the regulator of an infrastructure should set the rules for governance of infrastructures, and to have oversight of the infrastructure's compliance with the mandated approach to governance.

---

27   Committee of European Securities Regulators, *Preliminary Technical Advice by CESR in response to the Mandate from the European Commission on Access & Interoperability Arrangements* (February 2009), CESR document 08-870, http://www.esma.europa.eu/system/files/1-08_870.pdf

28   Article L. 440-1 of the Code Monétaire et Financier states: 'Les chambres de compensation ... doivent avoir la qualité d'établissement de crédit'

29   Section 1(1) of the Gesetz über das Kreditwesen (Kreditwesengesetz) states 'Kreditinstitute sind Unternehmen, die Bankgeschäfte gewerbsmäßig oder in einem Umfang betreiben ... . Bankgeschäfte sind ... die Tätigkeit als zentraler Kontrahent ... .'

30   Section 1(3) of the Gesetz über die Verwahrung und Anschaffung von Wertpapieren (Depotgesetz) states 'Wertpapiersammelbanken sind Kreditinstitute'

31   CESR document, p 29

32   Cf Code Monétaire et Financier, art L 330-1

Unfortunately there are at least two complications: first, infrastructures tend to be members of groups; secondly, they can have multi-country presence.

Where there is a group of companies, one of which is an infrastructure, there may be a tension between the traditional approach to consolidated supervision and the presence of the infrastructure in the group. Consolidated supervision under the Banking Directive[33] and the Capital Adequacy Directive[34] starts from the presence of a credit institution or investment firm within a group. A CCP or a payment system may be a bank, in which case consolidated supervision may apply; but if it is not a bank, it may not. A CSD is unlikely to be a bank or an investment firm. A CCP or a CSD may be in the same group (silo) as a trading venue; if that venue is an MTF it will have an investment firm licence, but a regulated market may not need to have that status. So different groups containing infrastructures are likely to be differently regulated.

The practical solution for this, and also to tackle multi-country presence, is for the home country authority of the parent regulated entity, or of the infrastructure, to act as the 'lead coordinator' of interested regulators. Dr Elias Kazarian has pointed out[35] various deficiencies with this arrangement: in particular, that their objectives of supervision may differ, and that problems developing outside the home country may be disregarded by both home and host state regulators. Indeed this is the situation which obtained when Bank of Credit and Commerce International SA failed in 1991, leading to a specific directive on consolidated supervision.[36]

12.11 There are specific provisions in the proposed Regulation on CSDs and in EMIR for coordinated regulation. It may be noted that neither of these legislative measures deals with the problem of groups, but they do address the multi-country aspect:

(1) The proposed CSD Regulation follows the approach of the Banking Directive and MiFID as regards cross-border activity. The home state regulator must notify the regulators of countries in which the CSD intends to provide services under the CSD Regulation passport. The host state regulators may demand reports and carry out inspections of branches. If the activities of the CSD reach a level of 'substantial importance' in the host state, the two regulators much establish cooperation arrangements for supervision.[37]

(2) EMIR requires the establishment of a highly elaborate 'college' of regulators.[38] A college comprises, in addition to the home state regulator and ESMA, the regulators supervising the clearing members with the three largest default fund contributions, the regulators supervising trading venues cleared by the CCP, the regulators of interoperating CCPs and linked CSDs, the ESCB members responsible for the oversight of the CCP and interoperating CCPs, and the central banks of 'the most relevant Union

---

33 Article 72
34 Directive 2006/49/EC of the European Parliament and of the Council of 14 June 2006 on the capital adequacy of investment firms and credit institutions, art 2
35 Kazarian, E, *Integration of the Securities Market Infrastructure in the European Union: Policy and Regulatory Issues* (October 2006), IMF Working Paper WP/06/241, p 21
36 Council Directive 92/30/EEC of 6 April 1992 on the supervision of credit institutions on a consolidated basis
37 Proposed Regulation, arts 21, 22
38 EMIR, art 18(2)

currencies of the financial instruments cleared'. In some cases, this will be a gathering of as many as two dozen regulators. The role of the college is to assess and potentially to veto a CCP's application for authorisation, to consider potential withdrawal of authorisation from non-compliant CCPs, to consider extensions of authorisation, to receive reports from the home state regulator on compliance and emergencies facing the CCP, and to determine procedures and contingency plans for emergencies.[39]

12.12 There are no legislative rules for consolidated or cross-border supervision of payment systems.

Location requirement for CCPs

12.13 In the context of a single market in which CSDs and CCPs are expected to be able to operate in any Member State, mention may be made of an apparent residence requirement of the European Central Bank (ECB) for CCPs. In July 2007 the ECB issued a set of policy principles on the location of euro-denominated payment systems.[40] These principles stated that '[p] ayment infrastructures settling euro-denominated PvP and/or non-PvP payment transactions ... that have the potential to reach systemic relevance for the euro area should, as a matter of principle ... be incorporated in the euro area.' Subsequently the ECB concluded that it was 'in line with the Eurosystem's location policy for payment, clearing and settlement systems for euro-denominated financial instruments' that '[t]he location of such key market infrastructures within the euro area enables the Eurosystem to directly fulfil its responsibilities with regard to financial stability, the smooth functioning of payment, clearing and settlement systems and the implementation of monetary policy.'[41] The logic deployed is that CCPs which clear derivative products which are cash-settled in euro constitute the CCP a payment system within the ECB's oversight jurisdiction; and it is important for such payment systems to be located within the eurozone to facilitate effective supervision. In earlier policy, which is cited in the more recent ECB statements, the ECB said:

'The logical geographical scope of a market infrastructure is in practice the currency area ... . Indeed, payment, clearing and settlement systems may trigger liquidity problems, which can only be addressed by competent local authorities, in particular central banks. ... Now that the need for securities clearing is growing rapidly in the euro area, it would appear that a coherent domestic infrastructure for the euro will have to develop. Such an infrastructure should logically be located in the euro area, as is the case with core infrastructures in other monetary areas. This would be preferable from a regulatory perspective and would help the Eurosystem, as the "central bank" of the euro, to ensure the smooth functioning of payment systems, efficient monetary policy implementation and financial stability. Existing agreements among central banks give a prominent role to "domestic" authorities, as do the international agreements among central banks and possibly with securities regulators. The existence of such agreements would

---

39   EMIR, arts 18(4), 19–21
40   ECB, *The Eurosystem policy principles on the location and operation of infrastructures settling euro-denominated payment transactions* (July 2007), http://www.ecb.eu/pub/pdf/other/eurosystem_policy_principlesen.pdf
41   ECB, *OTC Derivatives and Post-trading Infrastructures* (September 2009), http://www.ecb.eu/pub/pdf/other/overthecounterderivatives200909en.pdf, p 27

make it easier to achieve effective oversight of central counterparties established in the euro area. Furthermore, the location of central counterparties in the euro area would facilitate the provision, when deemed necessary and appropriate, of central bank money in euro.'[42] The ECB's policy is formalised in two further papers: the Eurosystem Oversight Policy Framework,[43] which states the ECB's oversight objectives and standards in relation to payment and settlement systems; and the Standards for CCPs in Eurosystem foreign reserve management operations,[44] which requires a CCP which clears interest rate swaps denominated in foreign currencies to comply with 'Eurosystem policies ... which includes the Eurosystem's location policy for non-euro-area CCPs with sizeable amounts of euro-denominated business.'[45] These requirements can be criticised on various grounds: fears of inadequate access to liquidity and uncooperative Member State regulators are believed to be groundless;[46] and that they are inconsistent with the principle of freedom of establishment in the Treaty on the Functioning of the EU. The United Kingdom has brought actions against the ECB seeking the annulment of the requirements.[47]

PRINCIPLES OF GOVERNANCE

12.14 How an infrastructure is managed is a question of public importance as well as matter of vital interest to the owners, directors, employees and users of the infrastructure. There is, accordingly, a good deal of literature, mainly at supra-national level, on the subject of governance of clearing and settlement systems. These precepts can, however, be criticised for lack of specificity and rigour: it is therefore worth starting from first principles, to determine what the governance arrangements of infrastructures should look like.

'The traditional definition of corporate governance refers to relations between a company's senior management, its board of directors, its shareholders and other stakeholders, such as employees and their representatives. It also determines the structure used to define a company's objectives, as well as the means of achieving them and of monitoring the results obtained. Due to the nature of their activities and interdependencies within the financial system, the bankruptcy of a financial institution, particularly a bank, can cause a domino effect, leading to the bankruptcy of other financial institutions. This can lead to an immediate contraction of credit and the start of an economic crisis due to lack of financing, as the recent financial crisis demonstrated. This systemic risk led governments to shore up the financial sector with public funding. As a result, taxpayers are inevitably stakeholders in the

---

42 ECB, *The Eurosystem's Policy Line with regard to Consolidation in Central Counterparty Clearing* (September 2001), http://www.ecb.eu/pub/pdf/other/centralcounterpartyclearingen. pdf, p 2

43 ECB, *Eurosystem Oversight Policy Framework* (July 2011), http://www.ecb.eu/pub/pdf/other/ eurosystemoversightpolicyframework2011en.pdf, p 10

44 ECB, *Standards for the use of Central Counterparties in Eurosystem Foreign Reserve Management Operations* (November 2011), http://www.ecb.eu/pub/pdf/other/ standards201111en.pdf

45 ECB Standards, p 11

46 Jones, L, *Current Issues Affecting the OTC Derivatives Market and its Importance to London* (April 2009), City of London Research Report, http://server-uk.imrworldwide.com/cgi-bin/b?c g=downloadsdo&ci=cityoflondon&tu=http://217.154.230.218/NR/rdonlyres/252E99A2- 7329-4C3A-B923-A3E7060A0AC2/0/OTCDerivativesReportv2.pdf

47 *United Kingdom v ECB*, cases T-496/11 (September 2011) and T-45/12 (January 2012)

running of financial institutions, with the goal of financial stability and long-term economic growth.'[48]

The objective of corporate governance is thus to balance the interests of the relevant stakeholders. This task falls to the board of directors of the infrastructure: the owners cannot do it, neither can the regulator, nor the users, as in all cases their involvement is too remote to have immediate effect on the tactical decision-making of the organisation or to be able to address the practical details of implementing a strategy on which they may have been consulted or exercised some power of approval. It is curious, then, that so little emphasis is given in the existing regulatory standards to these key concepts of balancing of interests, and the effectiveness of the board. Even the European Commission's Green Paper (the Green Paper) on corporate governance in financial institutions, from which the above passage was quoted, devotes as much space to questions on shareholder involvement, regulators and auditors as to the key issues of directors, risk and conflicts of interest.

12.15 The ideal governance structure should, it is suggested, have in place each of the following four building blocks in order to ensure high quality decision-making in a corporate environment:

- setting of corporate objectives and measuring their attainment
- selection, training, appraisal and removal/retirement of board members and senior managers
- internal controls and reporting lines, and the flow of relevant, timely and high-quality information to senior management and the board
- checks and balances in decision-making and ensuring due account is taken of stakeholder concerns.

Until recently, these matters have received little official attention in the post-trade space, and thinking is still in development. This may be in part because historically clearing and settlement infrastructures were seen as adjuncts to exchanges and markets; the leading study on governance of infrastructures amalgamates debate on governance of clearing and settlement systems with that on governance of exchanges,[49] assessing governance arrangements in the context of core principles for securities regulation issued by the International Organization of Securities Commission (IOSCO).[50] While those principles are the right starting point for assessment of governance of exchanges, being focused on cleanliness of markets, investor protection and systemic risk avoidance in that context, they are less useful in relation to post-trade infrastructures, upon the soundness of which peoples' money and property rights, and the protection of the financial system, all depend.

International standards

12.16 In 2004 the Organisation for Economic Co-operation and Development published a revised version of its Principles of Corporate Governance (the

---

48 European Commission, *Corporate governance in financial institutions and remuneration policies* (June 2010), Green Paper COM(2010) 284 final, http://ec.europa.eu/internal_market/company/docs/modern/com2010_284_en.pdf

49 Lee, R, *Running the World's Markets: The Governance of Financial Infrastructure* (Princeton University Press, 2011), ISBN 978-0-691-13353-9

50 IOSCO, *Objectives and Principles of Securities Regulation* (June 2010), http://www.iosco.org/library/pubdocs/pdf/IOSCOPD329.pdf

OECD Principles).[51] These principles are grouped under six headings, namely: ensuring the basis for an effective corporate governance framework; the rights of shareholders and key ownership functions; the equitable treatment of shareholders; the role of stakeholders in corporate governance; disclosure and transparency; and the responsibilities of the board. The OECD Principles provide a useful reference point for assessing the way in which market infrastructures should be run. Similarly, the UK Corporate Governance Code[52] provides another useful source of best practice recommendations, particularly focusing on the composition and role of the board.

More specific precepts are set forth in the Principles for Financial Market Infrastructures (the FMI Principles) issued by the Committee on Payment and Settlement Systems (CPSS) of the Bank for International Settlements and IOSCO.[53] These have, to a large degree, been reflected in EMIR and the proposed CSD Regulation. But there is no European-level regulatory statute for payment systems, and soft-law models for payment system oversight will need to catch up with the FMI Principles.[54]

Governance of infrastructures in the United Kingdom

12.17 Very limited governance arrangements are required by the Recognition Requirements Regulations, which require a recognised clearing house to have appropriate rule-making procedures, which must include consultation of users in appropriate cases.[55] The FSA have supplemented this with regulatory 'notification' rules[56] which are entitled 'Constitution and governance' and require a recognised clearing house to give the FSA notice of changes to its constitutional documents and any agreement which relates to its constitution or governance. In this way the governance arrangements for clearing and settlement systems which fall under the 'recognition' regime will be kept under close scrutiny; but what the FSA is looking for remains hidden beneath the surface.

The position of payment systems is complicated. A payment system which is to be designated for the purposes of the Settlement Finality Directive[57], and would therefore apparently be 'systemically important', must only comply with the designation criteria set out in the Schedule to the Settlement Finality Regulations,[58] which say nothing about governance. While the Bank of England is careful to say that it assesses an applicant for designation against the criteria set forth in the Settlement Finality Regulations, its publications on

---

51 Organisation for Economic Co-operation and Development, *Principles of Corporate Governance* (April 2004), http://www.oecd.org/dataoecd/32/18/31557724.pdf

52 Financial Reporting Council, *The UK Corporate Governance Code* (June 2010), http://www.ecgi.org/codes/documents/uk_cgc_june_2010_en.pdf

53 CPSS and IOSCO, *Principles for financial market infrastructures* (April 2012), http://www.bis.org/publ/cpss101a.pdf

54 See **section 6.10**

55 RRRs, Schedule, para 21

56 FSA, Handbook of Rules and Guidance, *Recognised Investment Exchanges and Recognised Clearing Houses Sourcebook* (June 2001), REC 3.6

57 Directive 98/26/EC of the European Parliament and of the Council of 19 May 1998 on settlement finality in payment and securities settlement systems

58 Financial Markets and Insolvency (Settlement Finality) Regulations 1999, SI 1999/2979

payment systems oversight[59] make it clear that, once designated and therefore under the Bank's eye, the CPSS Core Principles for Systemically Important Payment Systems[60] will be applied. More convincingly, the Bank of England has a statutory power to oversee any 'recognised'[61] interbank payment system, which must comply with 14 principles set out by the Bank.[62] Those principles closely mirror the CPSS Core Principles and, as regards governance, include the relevant Core Principle (X) verbatim.

Infrastructures are vital. If they are badly run, investors and others stand to lose their wealth, and the impact on the wider economy could be devastating. It is not right that the rules for governance of infrastructures should be vague or mysterious. What this evaluation shows is that the governance of infrastructures requires particular attention: it is therefore appropriate to look in more detail at the FMI Principles and how EMIR and, in due course, the regulation of CSDs will measure up. Unfortunately, governance of payment systems will remain more malleable due to the absence of a European regulatory instrument, as only the soft-law precepts of the FMI Principles will apply.

FMI Principles

12.18   The first 'key consideration' of the FMI Principles is that infrastructures 'should have objectives that place a high priority on the safety and efficiency of the FMI and explicitly support financial stability and other relevant public interest considerations.'[63]

In formulating objectives, the infrastructure will need to undertake the complex balancing process between the concerns of management, owners and other interested parties. It is not surprising, given the diversity of existing practices and governance models within the clearing and settlement industry, that regulators (and, *a fortiori*, supra-national bodies) are shy of spelling out how infrastructures should balance these concerns. But public interest factors should, apparently, outweigh private factors (reduction of cost, increase of profit, marketability of ownership stakes, protection of franchise). Where the infrastructure is run on a for-profit basis – a topic considered further in **section 12.25** – this balance will be difficult to achieve.

12.19   The content of an infrastructure's governance arrangements is described as follows:

'Governance arrangements, which define the structure under which the board and management operate, should be clearly and thoroughly documented. These arrangements should include certain key components such as the (a) role and composition of the board and any board committees, (b) senior management structure, (c) reporting lines between management and the board, (d) ownership structure, (e) internal governance policy, (f) design of risk management and

---

59   For example, Haldane, A, and Latter, E, 'The role of central banks in payment systems oversight' (January 2005) Bank of England Quarterly Bulletin, Spring 2005, p 66

60   CPSS, *Core Principles for Systemically Important Payment Systems*, http://www.bis.org/publ/cpss43.pdf

61   By virtue of the Banking Act 2009, part 5; see **section 11.3**

62   Bank of England, *The Bank of England's oversight of interbank payment systems under the Banking Act 2009* (September 2009), http://www.bankofengland.co.uk/publications/other/financialstability/oips/oips090928.pdf; see **section 11.4**

63   FMI Principles, Principle 2, Key consideration 1

internal controls, (g) procedures for the appointment of board members and senior management, and (h) processes for ensuring performance accountability. Governance arrangements should provide clear and direct lines of responsibility and accountability, particularly between management and the board, and ensure sufficient independence for key functions such as risk management, internal control, and audit. These arrangements should be disclosed to owners, the authorities, participants, and, at a more general level, the public.'[64]

12.20 EMIR broadly reflects these principles, imposing requirements for organisational structure, board composition, reporting lines, risk management, controls and criteria for senior management. EMIR also provides a degree of independence for the risk management function and requires transparency of governance arrangements and rules.[65] By and large, the proposed Regulation on CSDs will cover similar ground.[66]

It may be convenient to examine several of these issues in turn.

BOARD AND COMMITTEES

12.21 The board of directors is where the strategic direction of the company is seated; it is also the body which determines the structure and controls applicable to the day-to-day management of the business. The board may delegate its powers to individual managers or to committees, but it is the board which decides whether and how this should be done. Moreover, the board will effectively control the timing and business agenda of shareholders' meetings, and the communications with users and the wider community. In short, the board is at the centre of the governance web. If the balance between the different interest groups is to be successfully achieved, with the optimum outcome in terms of risk management, delivery of service, profitability (where a profit-based strategy is being pursued) and efficiency in terms of value for money, the board must be composed of persons who are able to see and weigh these different objectives, articulate their decisions on that balance clearly, set day-to-day management goals and impose controls to ensure that the objectives are satisfied, and at the same time handle crises and resist inappropriate external pressures.

12.22 The following points regarding boards may be mentioned:

(1) *Composition of the board.* Detailed rules on board composition have not typically featured in regulators' requirements about governance of infrastructures. Traditionally the FSA expected the board of a recognised body to include at least two 'strictly independent' non-executive directors,[67] and that 'normally a majority of the board should be non-executive directors, ie either independent directors or other non-executive directors (including those directors who represent users).'[68] In similar vein,

---

64 FMI Principles, para 3.2.3
65 EMIR, arts 26–28
66 Proposed Regulation, arts 24–26
67 Financial Services Authority, *Corporate Governance of Recognised Bodies* (March 2004), Dear Chief Executive letter, http://www.fsa.gov.uk/static/pubs/ceo/ceo_recbod_31mar04.pdf
68 Financial Services Authority, *Corporate Governance of Recognised Bodies* (June 2007), Dear Chief Executive letter, http://www.fsa.gov.uk/static/pubs/ceo/corp_governance.pdf

for corporates of all descriptions, the European Commission recommends that '[t]he presence of independent representatives on the board, capable of challenging the decisions of management, is widely considered as a means of protecting the interests of shareholders and other stakeholders.'[69] EMIR now requires not less than one-third (and no fewer than two) of the directors of a CCP to be 'independent',[70] as will the CSD Regulation.[71] This is clearly desirable, but there are difficult questions about who is independent, and the extent to which users and other stakeholders should be represented (and indeed whether they would count as 'independent' directors if they are). A long list of factors relating to independence set out in the European Commission's Recommendation on non-executive directors will be valuable guidance, but is unlikely to be conclusive.[72] Dr Ruben Lee[73] cites, in relation to exchanges, a rule of the United States' Securities Exchange Act[74] for ensuring 'fair representation' on the board of an exchange, which requires that at least one director is to be a representative of issuers and investors. Dr Werner Langen MEP[75] has urged that key market participants should not have a controlling influence on the governance and risk management of CCPs.

In practice, infrastructures may assert that they already observe these rules. CCPs, CSDs and the ICSDs include outsiders among their board members, typically drawing on the user community to provide senior-level expertise from within the industry. Yet even this practice could be criticised. The Commission's Recommendation specifies that independent directors ideally should not 'have, or have had within the last year, a significant business relationship with the company or an associated company, either directly or as a partner, shareholder, director or senior employee of a body having such a relationship,'[76] a notion which is reflected in the FMI Principles.[77] This could appear to disapprove, if not prohibit, the practice of appointing senior industry specialists who are still serving as senior managers of users or suppliers of the infrastructure concerned. A second criticism is that holding a non-executive directorship of an infrastructure can be seen as a position of prestige for long service to the industry, more in the nature of a lifetime-achievement award than a specialist role requiring substantial commitment of time and thought which may not be compatible with a full-time demanding job for another financial institution. Further, the usefulness of non-executives for the governance of infrastructures may be limited: Dr Lee[78] gives numerous reasons why independent directors may not be effective, including management influence over the nomination

---

69 Commission Recommendation 2005/162/EC of 15 February 2005 on the role of non-executive or supervisory directors of listed companies and on the committees of the (supervisory) board (February 2005), recital (7)
70 Article 27(2)
71 Article 25(2)
72 Recommendation 2005/162, Annex II
73 Lee, *Running the World's Markets*, p 247
74 Securities Exchange Act 1934, PL 73-291, 48 Stat 881, s 6(b)(3)
75 Langen, W, *Report on derivatives markets: future policy actions* (June 2010), European Parliament Committee on Economic and Monetary Affairs document A7-0187/2010, http://www.europarl.europa.eu/sides/getDoc.do?pubRef=-//EP//NONSGML+REPORT+A7-2010-0187+0+DOC+PDF+V0//EN&language=EN, para 26
76 Recommendation 2005/162, Annex II, para 1(e)
77 FMI Principles, para 3.2.9
78 Lee, OFG Report, Vol 1, pp xvii–xviii

process, lack of commitment by the independent directors, deference to management, lack of clarity of the organisation's objectives, the primary loyalty of a person to the employer, and the inherent difficulty in balancing the conflicting interests of stakeholders.

(2) *Conflicts of interest.* The Companies Act 2006 imposes a general duty to avoid conflicts of interest, but conflict situations can be disclosed to the other directors and the conflict waived by a board resolution.[79] Conflict management arrangements are (in relation to recognised clearing houses) subject to guidance from the FSA.[80] The (now withdrawn) guidance notes on Core Principle X for systemically important payment systems had this to say:

> 'Because directors are usually nominated by participants, they may have conflicts of interest in overseeing or governing a payment system that arise because (1) they represent organisations that compete with other owners and/or (2) the interests of the company operating the payment system may not coincide with those of the director's employer. It is possible that this problem cannot be fully avoided, but it can be addressed by adopting clear and transparent policies in this area.'[81]

Although the Core Principles have been superseded by the FMI Principles, the guidance is likely to be of continuing validity where an infrastructure is governed exclusively by participants' nominees.

User representatives may encounter significant risk of conflicts in carrying out their role on the board or committee of an infrastructure. Examples could be decision-making about declaring a competitor to be in default; obtaining information about other participants' volume of business or other confidential information; or where the infrastructure receives, or is about to issue a tender for, services which the representative's organisation might supply. To manage these cases, it might be better for the representative concerned to resign, or to absent herself from the relevant part of the meeting and to ensure that information is suitably filtered before it reaches her. Sharing of participants' data among selected participants who have privileged access due to their board position is dangerous from the viewpoint of competition law.[82]

It has also been suggested that CCPs might be directed by powerful clearing members to limit the range of cleared products, so as to preserve the uncleared businesses of those firms or their affiliates.[83] Whether or not the economic incentives would actually work that way, concerns such as this indicate that a good balance between interests is needed on the board.

79 Companies Act 2006, ss 175, 180(4)

80 Financial Services Authority, Handbook of Rules and Guidance, *Recognised Investment Exchanges and Recognised Clearing Houses (REC)*, http://fsahandbook.info/FSA/html/handbook/REC, REC 2.5.10G – REC 2.5.16G

81 CPSS, *Core Principles for Systemically Important Payment Systems* (January 2001), http://www.bis.org/publ/cpss43.pdf?noframes=1, para 7.10.14

82 See **section 4.12**; and European Commission, *Commission approves the Volbroker.com electronic brokerage joint venture between six major banks* (July 2000), Press Release IP/00/896, http://europa.eu/rapid/pressReleasesAction.do?reference=IP/00/896&format=HTM L&aged=1&language=EN&guiLanguage=en

83 Pirrong, C, *The Economics of Central Clearing: Theory and Practice* (May 2011), ISDA Discussion Paper No 1, http://www2.isda.org/attachment/MzE0NA==/ISDAdiscussion_CCP_Pirrong.pdf, p 29

Another source of conflict is the risks inherent in the vertical silo structure,[84] which may distort the formation of suitable 'objectives' because of the desire to protect a franchise in an adjacent economic space (for example, to protect the revenue of an exchange, by operating a wholly-owned CCP in a particular manner which would not necessarily be explicable if the CCP were fully independent). The question of conflicts was explored by the ECB in a paper which reached three conclusions.[85] These were, in the first place, that to contain the potentially detrimental effects of conflicts arising in CSDs and CCPs offering banking services, decisions concerning risk management should be taken independently of other management decisions. This finding would explain the contemporaneous recommendation of the CPSS[86] that CCPs should have independent reporting lines for risk management, now enshrined in article 28 of EMIR. The other two conclusions of the ECB on conflicts were that mechanisms were needed to resolve conflicts between the different entities in a vertically or horizontally integrated group comprising more than one clearing or settlement system; and that where multiple markets are served, the interests of foreign customers and shareholders should be taken into account.

One further comment can be made about conflicts of interest. Sometimes the conflict rules under MiFID[87] are mentioned in the context of corporate governance[88], but these are about conflicts which adversely affect clients, rather than the misalignment of different 'objectives' of infrastructure management, and are of limited relevance. The ECB/CESR Recommendations for CCPs mentioned the risk of misuse of sensitive information on participants' positions:[89] this *is* an example of a MiFID-style conflict, but the concern of the authorities seems to be misplaced. A CCP is likely to have non-clearing relationships with its participants, for example for the purposes of treasury management (deposit placement, repo-based liquidity facilities, etc); it would be odd if the CCP were not permitted to have an overall view of its total clearing- and non-clearing-based exposures and to take risk decisions accordingly. CCPs should act with integrity, but to elevate the remote possibility of improper use of information into a principle of corporate governance while ignoring far more serious issues is an error of emphasis.

(3) *Board members' skills*. The criteria for fitness and propriety of directors are very weak under EU legislation: directors of credit institutions, investment firms and payment institutions must be of 'sufficiently good repute' and have 'adequate expertise' (EMIR)[90] or have an 'appropriate mix of skills, experience and knowledge of the entity and of the market' (Proposed CSD

---

84 See **section 7.20**
85 Russo, D, et al, *Governance of Securities Clearing and Settlement Systems* (October 2004), European Central Bank occasional paper No. 21, http://www.ecb.int/pub/pdf/scpops/ecbocp21.pdf
86 CPSS and Technical Committee of IOSCO, *Recommendations for Central Counterparties* (November 2004), http://www.bis.org/publ/cpss64.pdf, para 4.13.4
87 Article 18 of MiFID requires investment firms to identify conflicts of interest and article 13(3) requires them to take steps to prevent conflicts adversely affecting clients' interests
88 European Commission, Corporate Governance Green Paper COM(2010) 284 final, para 3.1
89 ECB and Committee of European Securities Regulators, *Recommendations for Securities Settlement Systems and Recommendations for Central Counterparties in the European Union* (May 2009), http://www.ecb.eu/pub/pdf/other/pr090623_escb-cesr_recommendationsen.pdf, Recommendation 13, para C.5
90 Article 27(2)

Regulation).[91]These rules reflect the thinness of the requirements of the Banking Directive, MiFID and the Payment Services Directive on directors' skills.[92] The FSA has gone much further in the United Kingdom, having an entire sourcebook devoted to the fitness and propriety of directors of authorised firms[93] – but as infrastructures are generally not authorised, this does not imply that UK infrastructures have to abide by it.

(4) *Duties of the board.* The FMI Principles list the directors' duties as follows:

'(a) establishing clear strategic aims for the entity; (b) ensuring effective monitoring of senior management (including selecting its senior managers, setting their objectives, evaluating their performance, and, where appropriate, removing them); (c) establishing appropriate compensation policies (which should be consistent with best practices and based on long-term achievements, in particular, the safety and efficiency of the FMI); (d) establishing and overseeing the risk-management function and material risk decisions; (e) overseeing internal control functions (including ensuring independence and adequate resources); (f) ensuring compliance with all supervisory and oversight requirements; (g) ensuring consideration of financial stability and other relevant public interests; and (h) providing accountability to the owners, participants, and other relevant stakeholders.'[94]

In contrast, the starting point in the United Kingdom is the Companies Act 2006, which has codified the duties of directors of companies. Section 172 sets out one of the primary duties, which is to 'act in the way, he considers, in good faith, would be most likely to promote the success of the company for the benefit of its members as a whole,' and here at once is exposed a primary problem for independent directors of infrastructures. Their job is focused around the 'benefit of the members' – that is (to eliminate a piece of potential confusion, given that participants in infrastructures are sometimes referred to as 'members') the benefit of the *shareholders*. Certainly, the director is required to 'have regard (amongst other matters) to – (a) the likely consequences of any decision in the long term, (b) the interests of the company's employees, (c) the need to foster the company's business relationships with suppliers, customers and others…'[95] but these are just factors to consider in assessing the benefit of the members.

The Companies Act is a general statute and not focused on the financial sector, let alone systemically crucial parts of that sector, so it is not a surprise that the directors are supposed to treat the shareholders as their constituents – but the statutory duty puts non-executive directors of infrastructures in a quandary. If all else is equal, the interests of the shareholders win out, not the public interest of the financial system. The UK Corporate Governance Code[96] is full of useful guidance on induction,

91 Article 25(4)
92 Banking Directive, art 11; MiFID, art 9(1); Directive 2007/64/EC of the European Parliament and of the Council of 13 November 2007 on payment services in the internal market etc (November 2007), art 5(i)
93 Financial Services Authority, Handbook of Rules and Guidance, *The Fit and Proper Test for Approved Persons (FIT)*, http://fsahandbook.info/FSA/html/handbook/FIT
94 FMI Principles, para 3.2.8
95 Companies Act 2006, s 172(1)
96 Financial Reporting Council, *The UK Corporate Governance Code* (June 2010), http://www.ecgi.org/codes/documents/uk_cgc_june_2010_en.pdf

skills, information, performance evaluation, re-election and more which will assist any company in appointing a high-quality board. But the Code, being again a general measure, cannot assist on this specific problem.

(5) *Committees.* EMIR requires CCPs to have a risk committee,[97] and the proposed CSD Regulation will require CSDs to have a user committee.[98] It would also be common for an infrastructure to have some or possibly all of the following committees, to allow full debate at policy-forming level, of the relevant issues: a nominating committee, to refresh and ensure balance at board level; a remuneration committee, to determine the salary and other emoluments of management; a rules committee; and an audit committee. Committees can also be used as a device for introducing outside interest into governance. Committees may be 'committees of the board' – in other words, committees which exercise the power of the board through formal delegation – or 'management committees' whose status is more nebulous. Typically a company is constitutionally empowered to establish committees which include non-directors in their constitution, which allows for the possibility of outsiders to join in the governance. In some organisations, the drive for inclusiveness can lead to a proliferation of committees and chairmanships without in practice enhancing the decision-making processes.

MANAGEMENT, INTERNAL CONTROLS AND AUDIT

12.23   While it is clear that the centre of power within a corporate organisation is the board, it is also clear that a governing body comprised largely of non-executive members will be highly dependent for due execution of their decisions on effective and responsible managers who are acting in line with the policy of the board, not just in what they do but also in what they do not do. The processes for keeping a grip on management assume that the board controls management, and not the other way around. Some infrastructures may operate on the practical footing that management is the permanent secretariat answering to a government which is subject to political change from time to time – that approach may lead to insufficient self-criticism of the effectiveness of management.

Systems and controls are at the heart of an effective management structure. In the United Kingdom, the RRRs provide:

'The clearing house must ensure that the systems and controls used in the performance of its functions are adequate, and appropriate for the scale and nature of its business. This requirement applies in particular to systems and controls concerning – (a) the transmission of information; (b) the assessment and management of risks to the performance of the clearing house's functions; (c) the operation of the [arrangements for timely discharge of obligations of participants]; and (d) (where relevant) the safeguarding and administration of assets belonging to users of the clearing house's facilities.'[99]

This is amplified by the FSA's guidance, which requires responsibilities to be clearly apportioned among staff, but also calls for management of conflicts of interest, demands internal and external audit, and states that the FSA 'may have

---

97   Article 28
98   Article 26
99   RRRs, Schedule, para 18

regard to' the clearing house's information technology systems.[100] EMIR and the proposed Regulation on CSDs contain similar rules.[101]

There is a great deal of literature on design and implementation of systems and controls for financial institutions, sometimes falling under the heading of management of operational risk.[102] Any attempt to summarise this is bound to select some issues at the expense of others of equal importance. Nevertheless, at minimum a clearing or settlement infrastructure should have the following in place: clear, written, available organisation charts showing reporting lines; clear, written, available job descriptions explaining the role of each person in the organisation; monitoring of automated processes, including reconciliation with participants; double-checks by a second person on non-automated processes; external audit of systems and controls as well as accounts; and a structure for review of its controls and reporting on control breaches and exceptions.

One means of ensuring management do not become autocratic is the mechanism of audit. This is an ex-post control, and therefore of limited preventive value in relation to crises or unpredicted events. However, the principle of control through audit is acknowledged at European level. European company law has, in the Statutory Audit Amending Directive identified a certain type of organisation known as the 'public-interest entity', which includes listed companies and banks[103]. It is open to member states to designate other types of entity as public-interest entities; and as Recital (23) to the directive notes, 'public-interest entities have a higher visibility and are economically more important,' it might seem appropriate for unlisted post-trade infrastructures to be subject to the same strictures. These would include having an audit committee and having external auditors certify their independence;[104] these requirements are, however, not imposed on CCPs or CSDs by European law. But auditors have much more to offer than the mere vetting of accounts. They can, in particular, probe the effectiveness of control and management systems, and it might be suggested that such discipline should be routine for this type of organisation. Historically, when responsible for banking supervision, the Bank of England would commission an annual report from a bank's auditors on a selected control issue under section 39 of the Banking Act 1987,[105] but since the banking supervisory functions were assumed by the FSA the use of this power has been reserved for more exceptional circumstances. However, it is being introduced (alongside other audit-related powers) as a supervisory tool in relation to recognised clearing houses under the Financial Services Act 2012.[106]

OWNERSHIP, CAPITAL AND CONTROL

12.24 Control may be exercised over the board, and, indirectly, over management, by the shareholders or owners of the company which operates the

---

100 Financial Services Authority, Handbook of Rules and Guidance, *Recognised Investment Exchanges and Recognised Clearing Houses Sourcebook (REC)* (November 2007), REC 2.5.3G
101 EMIR, art 26; proposed CSD Regulation, art 24
102 See Turing, D, and Cramb, E, *Managing Risk in Financial Firms* (Tottel Publishing, March 2009), section 6.11
103 Directive 2006/43/EC of the European Parliament and of the Council of 17 May 2006 on statutory audits of annual accounts and consolidated accounts, etc, art 2(13)
104 Articles 41ff
105 Re-enacted as Financial Services and Markets Act 2000, s 166
106 Schedule 7, paras 11–16, 18–21

infrastructure. Engagement of shareholders in governance is challenging, as the European Commission has noted.[107] But in the case of infrastructures to expect shareholders to control the company's operations in the wider public interest may be wishful thinking.

For profit or not for profit

12.25 There are broadly three models for ownership of clearing and settlement infrastructures. The first, which is for the infrastructure to be owned by the state or the central bank, is largely historical, and the mainstream model for ownership of infrastructures in Europe is for them to be in private hands. The other two choices are: (a) for the organisation to be a not-for-profit concern, typically owned by its participants, and charging fees on the principle that any surplus after meeting operating expenses will be rebated to participants (rather than paid out as dividends); and (b) a for-profit undertaking of which its owners and its participants are likely to belong to different constituencies (though there may be some overlap). Important among the second group are the 'vertical silos', where the clearing or settlement undertaking is owned by an exchange. Dr Lee gives statistics for ownership of clearing and settlement organisations in September 2006, which are reproduced in **table 12.1**,[108] together with data on payment systems in six selected countries gleaned from the ECB's 'blue book'.[109]

Table 12.1   Control of infrastructures

	Number analysed	**Not for profit**		**For profit**	
		Government control	**User control**	**Independent**	**Exchange control**
Clearing houses	87	12	35	7	33
Settlement systems	82	13	37	9	23
		Government owned or central bank operated		**User owned (whether or not for profit)**	
Payment systems	17	8		9	

The motivations of these different types of owner are likely to be self-evident: the user-owners are likely to be protective of their franchise and wary of innovation; the independent owners and, possibly, the exchanges, may be tempted to maximise short-term profitability at the expense of longer-term risk-focused considerations. There is, of course, no hard evidence for any such motivations – a study by the CPSS was unable to draw any conclusions as to a

---

107 European Commission, Corporate Governance Green Paper COM(2010) 284 final, para 3.5
108 Lee, *Running the World's Markets*, pp 156, 160
109 ECB, *Payment and securities settlement systems in the European Union* (4th edn, August 2007), http://www.ecb.eu/pub/pdf/other/ecbbluebookea200708en.pdf and http://www.ecb.eu/pub/pdf/other/ecbbluebooknea200708en.pdf

possible correlation between user-ownership and reduced risk[110] – and to quote Dr Lee again:

> 'There is no evidence that any one of the main governance models a market infrastructure institution may adopt best delivers investor protection. There is no evidence that any one of the main governance models a market infrastructure institution, and particularly a CCP, may adopt best reduces systemic risk.'[111]

Professor Pirrong argues, in relation to CCPs, that there ought to be 'alignment of ownership and control rights on the one hand, and the incidence of risk on the other. That is, those who bear the counterparty risks assumed by a CCP should have the power to make decisions that affect the riskiness of the CCP.'[112] The risk in a CCP is borne primarily by the contributors to the default fund; unless the ownership and control is also vested in its participants, there would appear to be no such alignment.

Nevertheless – absent any specific law to the contrary – it is a requirement of company law that a company be run in the interests of its members, and the shareholders of a for-profit company who can quickly sell if their investment is not performing as well as other investments are likely to encourage their board to take a short-term view. This line of reasoning suggests that, if it is appropriate for an infrastructure to build up and retain significant reserves to manage the risk of a low-probability but high-impact event, it will struggle to do so if it is structured as a for-profit entity. However, the same can be argued in relation to an infrastructure organised as a non-profit entity: if the net surplus over operating costs is always rebated to participants, there is never an opportunity to build reserves.

12.26 Who should own the post-trade infrastructure, and whether an infrastructure should operate on a for-profit basis, are questions which have generated intense debate. There are several factors at work.

(1) *Public-interest utility status.* 'Clearing and settlement is seen as a utility function and there is a concern that exchanges – particularly for-profit exchanges – could keep clearing and settlement prices high, cross-subsidise trading fees or control access to the process chain so as to prevent entry by competitors. This view is supported by the joint statement of principles issued by trade organisations in the UK, France, Sweden and Italy in February 2005.'[113] The first part of this statement sets out a principle of general philosophy supported by many market users – that infrastructures provide a common good, and should not seek to make a profit.

(2) *User power.* One has to interpret the commentaries with care, because public-interest 'utility' arguments may be used to support continuation of 'mutual' ownership structures where control is firmly vested in the users of the infrastructure. User power may be inimical to optimal management of risk;[114] other disadvantages of 'mutual' structures include the brake

---

110 CPSS, *Market structure developments in the clearing industry: implications for financial stability* (September 2010), http://www.bis.org/publ/cpss92.pdf
111 Lee, OFG Report, p xxiii
112 Pirrong, ISDA Discussion Paper, p 26
113 Bourse Consult, *The Future of Clearing and Settlement in Europe* (December 2005), City Research Series No 7, p 28 and Appendix D
114 Langen Report, para 26

on decision-making needed to achieve consensus among diverse interest groups, and that 'management may be able to pursue its own interests by dividing and ruling among the various user interests.'[115]

(3) *Profit motivation*. If an organisation is run for profit, its decision-making is more likely to be 'agile, flexible, streamlined and swift,' 'provide a good incentive for management to perform well,' and 'respond to the demands of all market participants, independent of whether they are members of the institution or not.'[116]

(4) *Capital requirements*. CCPs and CSDs are to be required by regulatory rules to maintain a certain amount of capital. If the capital requirement is high relative to the organisation's ability to generate a return on investment, there is likely to be little reason to choose a for-profit model. The capital requirements of EMIR and the proposed Regulation on CSDs are, however, too limited to constitute any real constraint on choice.[117]

12.27 EMIR requires a pre-authorisation check to be made on the suitability of shareholders of a CCP. A competent authority must take appropriate action, including potentially withdrawal of authorisation from a CCP, if a shareholder with 10% or more of the shares or voting rights exercises an influence which is likely to be prejudicial to the sound and prudent management of the CCP.[118] EMIR also has rules, similar to those applicable to banks, for notification and vetting of increases and decreases of control by shareholders.[119] The proposed Regulation on CSDs has more limited provisions of a similar nature.[120]

Vertical silos

12.28 Finally, in this context, it is essential to mention 'vertical silos'. Exchanges, which faced competition from crossing networks and alternative trading platforms before competition became a reality in the post-trade space, may have been keen to retain ownership of infrastructures – vertical silos – for operational and financial reasons. Operationally, there may be straight-through processing benefits of vertical silos where a one-stop-shop provides comprehensive trade-through-to-settlement service; since the adoption of standardisation agendas across Europe, and since trading markets are no longer organised on national lines in Europe, the operational argument in favour of vertical organisation would appear to have weakened significantly. As to finance, it can be suggested that ownership of an infrastructure provides a source of easy profit, as infrastructures can exploit their quasi-monopolistic position to set prices at whatever level they choose, and pass the benefits to the exchange and enable it to lower its own prices and compete more easily. However, in monopolistic or foreclosed market-places, the ability of a person with the monopoly to charge fees which enable other businesses in competitive markets to be cross-subsidised is wrong.[121] Other anti-competitive practices

---

115 Lee, OFG Report, p xv
116 Lee, OFG Report, pp xiii–xiv
117 See **sections 6.28, 6.36**
118 EMIR, art 30
119 EMIR, art 31(2)
120 Proposed CSD Regulation, art 25
121 See **sections 7.18, 7.22**

might include denial of access and bundling of services.[122] Some commentators have argued that vertical silos should be broken up.[123] Accordingly, the European Code of Conduct for Clearing and Settlement demands accounting separation between trading venues, CCPs and CSDs (albeit that disclosure of the separate accounts is to regulators, not users, competitors or the general public).[124] Furthermore, the introduction of competition, at least as regards clearing services, would drive down cost.[125] On the other hand, operators of vertical silos have argued that cost is independent of structure and indeed of whether there is a for-profit or a non-profit model.[126]

USERS AND OTHER STAKEHOLDERS

12.29   A running theme throughout the discussion of board and owner control of clearing and settlement systems is the notion that the participants, end-users, and beneficiaries of the financial system at large all have an interest in the effective, balanced governance of those systems. The Group of 30 included among its 20 recommendations: 'Ensure equitable and effective attention to stakeholder interests', stating 'efficient and safe operation of clearing and settlement infrastructure providers is central to the effective operation of securities markets. Consequently, a variety of stakeholders have a significant and legitimate interest in the operation of these institutions.'[127] A number of observations may be made:

(1) *Laws and regulations.* EMIR mandates user involvement to a limited degree: a CCP is obliged to have a risk committee, which must be composed of representatives of clearing members and clients, and independent members of the board. But the risk committee's role is advisory only, and EMIR states expressly that the advice of the risk committee is not required for the daily operations of the CCP.[128] The proposed CSD Regulation will require the establishment of an independent advisory user committee.[129] Furthermore, regulatory powers 'typically' include the power to review 'the operational plan, internal control arrangements, system rules and risk management programme of the system operator' as well as other oversight of its board, management, shareholders, operations and fees.[130] Whether the power to inspect and oversee needs to be backed up by a power to intervene or other supervisory powers can be debated, but regulators almost invariably have the ultimate sanction of de-licensing a delinquent, so a range of disciplinary remedies may be unnecessary.

---

122 Russo, D, et al, *Governance of Securities Clearing and Settlement Systems* (October 2004), European Central Bank occasional paper No. 21, http://www.ecb.int/pub/pdf/scpops/ecbocp21.pdf, p 24

123 Cf Bourse Consult report, p 28

124 FESE, EACH and ECSDA, *European Code of Conduct for Clearing and Settlement* (November 2006), http://ec.europa.eu/internal_market/financial-markets/docs/code/code_en.pdf, paras 42–43; see **section 7.18**

125 See **section 1.29**

126 Deutsche Börse Group, *The European Post-Trade Market – An Introduction* (February 2005), http://deutsche-boerse.com/dbag/dispatch/de/binary/gdb_content_pool/imported_files/public_files/10_downloads/80_misc/WP_European_Post-Trade_Market_final.pdf, p 27

127 Group of Thirty, *Global Clearing and Settlement: A Plan of Action* (January 2003)

128 Article 28

129 Article 26

130 Russo et al, p 16

(2) *Rule-making*. Involving users and others in the rule-making process is also important. In the United Kingdom, a recognised clearing house 'must ensure that appropriate procedures are adopted for it to make rules, for keeping its rules under review and for amending them. The procedures must include procedures for consulting users of the clearing house's facilities in appropriate cases.'[131] The FSA's guidance on this requirement indicates that it will look at the level at which decisions are taken and the range of persons to be consulted on a change, and includes detailed process requirements for the conduct of consultations including cost-benefit analysis.[132] Finally, a clearing house must bear in mind that introducing anything which could be an 'excessive' regulatory provision may fall foul of sections 300A–300E of the Financial Services and Markets Act 2000, which enables the regulator to veto such a provision.

(3) *Transparency for end-users*. Transparency is important as it provides a natural means of ensuring optimum practice, allowing end-users and even a wider community to become comfortable with the way things are done. EMIR requires that CCPs make their governance arrangements, rules and membership criteria publicly available without charge.[133] The proposed CSD Regulation will make CSDs publish their governance arrangements and rules.[134] In fact, many European CCPs and CSDs complied with these principles already. CPSS Core Principle X for systemically important payment systems also recommended public disclosure of governance arrangements and rules,[135] though oddly, the FMI Principles are less prescriptive. Some clearing and settlement systems do not publish their rulebooks on their websites – and payment systems are the worst offenders on transparency, interpreting their compliance obligation as being fulfilled if they provide their rules to their participants. (CHAPS was assessed only as 'broadly observed' in relation to Core Principle X by the IMF in 2011.[136])

(4) *The wider interest*. One stakeholder, normally overlooked in a discussion of governance of infrastructures, is the taxpayer. Clearing and settlement systems are systemically important institutions, whose risk profile is unusual: risk events are rare, but potentially devastating in their impact. A CSD which fails would wipe out the property entitlements of ordinary citizens to the tune of many trillions of euros: Euroclear reports that in the UK alone it holds title to over £3 trillion of worth.[137] A payment system which failed would cause unimaginable disaster: 'in 2008, the value passing through UK payment systems was around £200 trillion, about 140 times

---

131 RRRs, Schedule, para 21
132 FSA, Handbook of Rules and Guidance, *Recognised Investment Exchanges and Recognised Clearing Houses Sourcebook* (November 2007), REC 2.14
133 Article 26(7)
134 Article 24(4)
135 CPSS Core Principles (January 2001), para 7.10.10
136 IMF, *United Kingdom: Observance by CHAPS of CPSS Core Principles for Systemically Important Payments Systems Detailed Assessment of Observance* (July 2011), IMF Country Report No 11/237, p 29
137 Euroclear UK and Ireland, *Performance Statistics* (July 2010), https://www.euroclear.com/site/publishedFile/Newsletter+Stats+1007_tcm87-174323.pdf?title=EUI+and+market+statistics

UK annual gross domestic product.'[138] And a CCP acts as credit insurer to the participants it serves (and reinsurer to the end-users of the markets), so that a failure of a CCP would imply failure of the margining system used by its participants. The dire consequences would preclude any post-trade infrastructure being allowed to fail without at least a managed wind-down closely supervised by the regulators and, presumably, the relevant central bank. Ultimately, any cost will be borne not by the shareholders of the failed infrastructure – the loss of whose equity investment will bear no relationship to the risks in question – but by the taxpayers in the country whose economy would not without intervention withstand the shock.

12.30 Perhaps this last is the sobering point about all facets of clearing and settlement system governance. Whatever the decisions taken about boards, ownership, or user-involvement, nobody has yet devised a model which adequately reflects the risk profile of an infrastructure. There is no right way to arrange the fees or dividend profile of an infrastructure if its mismanagement can jeopardise an economy.

---

138 Bank of England website, payment systems oversight page (September 2010), http://www.bankofengland.co.uk/financialstability/role/risk_reduction/payment_systems_oversight/index.htm

13 Interoperability

INTEROPERABILITY DESIGNED, INTEROPERABILITY DEFINED

13.1 The G30's report on Clearing and Settlement in 2003 (the G30 Report)[1] made 20 recommendations on clearing and settlement. These were grouped into three sections, of which the first, with eight recommendations, is called 'Creating a Strengthened, Interoperable Global Network.' 'Promoting competition and innovation is not simply a matter of removing specific barriers, but also of creating compatible systems that permit seamless operations on a global basis.'[2] The G30 Report defines interoperability in the following terms:

> 'Interoperability refers to the ability of participants along the clearing and settlement value chain to communicate and work with service providers and other participants without special effort on the part of users. Interoperability involves more than technical compatibility of systems, although standardized communication, messaging, data, and timing are clearly essential. The ability of systems to interoperate also requires like or compatible processes, business practices, controls, technologies, products, access arrangements, and fee structures.'[3]

The G30's eight recommendations for interoperability cover automation of data capture and trade matching, harmonisation of messaging standards, development of reference data standards, synchronisation of timing, use of CCPs and securities lending, and automation and standardisation of asset servicing processes, corporate actions, tax claims and so forth. These recommendations are aimed at one aspect of interoperation of systems: compatibility, connectivity, and standardisation. Historical examples were given in the G30 Report about railway gauges, air traffic control arrangements, and telecommunications, all of which have been made internationally compatible. The securities industry needs equivalent measures.

Structural interoperability v standards

13.2 Having a single standard for post-trade services is clearly beneficial. The costs and delays in having to cope with multiple standards and local idiosyncrasies slow down processes and inhibit growth and international trade in investments. Without technical interoperability, it is difficult to achieve

---

1   Group of Thirty, *Global Clearing and Settlement – A Plan of Action* (January 2003)
2   G30 Report, p 26
3   G30 Report, p 14

300

straight-through-processing, and manual interventions or bespoke technical solutions may tend to introduce errors. Furthermore, 'interoperation will enable competition between payment processors, so that payment service providers can easily connect to or switch processing partners, or, if they desire to do so, to connect easily to other payments service providers directly. Technical interoperability will enable the payment processors to reach new markets. Interoperability will potentially create accessibility to and from all, thus realising a level playing field for all involved.'[4] While this statement was made in the context of technical interoperation between payment systems, the concepts and rationale translate readily into other post-trade environments.

Interoperability would thus appear to be about standards and technical matters, and a long discussion about the details would be out of place here. But in Europe, the concept of 'interoperability' has taken on a distinct meaning, referred to here as 'structural' interoperability, which is not primarily about the securities equivalent of railway gauges, telecommunications or other aspects of technical interoperability. Structural interoperability is needed because of the European policy to promote competition between infrastructures. And, because infrastructures need links in order to compete, structural interoperability is about obligations owed by one infrastructure to another.

Europe's post-trade infrastructure is still fragmented. The proliferation of trading platforms stimulated by MiFID, and the focus on central clearing since the financial crisis of 2008, have together allowed numerous CCPs to develop in Europe. CSDs are still organised on national lines, despite the efforts of the post-crisis legislation. Yet there is a 'single market' which this infrastructure is supposed to serve. It is in theory possible for an Irish investor to sell a French share to an Italian fund on a UK-based MTF, clear the trade through a Dutch CCP, and, with the implementation of Target2-Securities, settle the trade through a Polish CSD. But the counterparty who has bought the French share may wish to clear the trade using a UK CCP and settle in the French CSD. Somehow those differences must be aligned: the fragments must be joined up. Joining the pieces requires the infrastructures to be 'interoperable'. In practice, that means that links have to be forged between the interoperating entities. Structural interoperability is thus a matter of creating those links and making them work.

Definitions of interoperability – vertical and horizontal

13.3 'Interoperability' is curiously defined in the European Code of Conduct for Clearing and Settlement[5] (the Code). It means 'advanced forms of relationships amongst Organisations where an Organisation is not generally connecting to existing standard service offerings of the other Organisations but where Organisations agree to establish customised solutions. Amongst its objectives, Interoperability will aim to provide a service to the customers such that they have choice of service provider. Such agreement will require Organisations to incur additional technical development'. This verbiage is

4   European Automated Clearing House Association, *Technical Interoperability Framework for SEPA-Compliant Payments Processing* (March 2009), EACHA Taskforce Report v4.1, http://www.eacha.org/downloads/EACHA%20Framework%204.1%20CV.pdf, para 2.2
5   FESE, EACH and ECSDA, *European Code of Conduct for Clearing and Settlement* (November 2006), http://ec.europa.eu/internal_market/financial-markets/docs/code/code_en.pdf

unhelpful and by being opaque it is unlikely to engender rapid development of links between infrastructures.

13.4   It is probably better to think of structural interoperability in the following terms:

- Interoperability is needed where trading members of the same marketplace (or their agents) wish to use different infrastructures from each other to clear or settle their trades.
- Interoperability implies that there is either more than one CCP or more than one CSD providing post-trade services for a single marketplace.
- Interoperability requires that the different infrastructures agree on common standards and processes in order to provide efficient post-trade services to the satisfaction of all trading members according to their choice.
- Interoperability also implies that the interoperating infrastructures provide services to each other.
- Interoperability may be needed between infrastructures providing the same service (horizontal interoperability, as between two CCPs or between two CSDs) or between infrastructures providing different services (vertical interoperability, as between a CCP and a CSD).

Interoperability can thus mean 'access conditions' – in other words, the basis upon which one infrastructure allows another to participate in it or to enjoy the right to provide services to its participants: for example, the right of a CCP to clear for a platform, or the right of a CSD to settle transactions emanating from a platform or CCP.[6] This chapter is not concerned with those types of vertical inter-operation. Interoperability in the sense used here means horizontal interoperability between CCPs, between CSDs, and between payment systems.

13.5   The following points may be made at the outset, because they are central to the understanding of the issues arising in relation to horizontal structural interoperability:

(1) Where two *CCPs* are to clear the same marketplace, some traders will select one CCP and others will select the other. Since each CCP needs to have a matched book, there needs to be a sale-and-purchase contract between the two interoperating CCPs. Interoperability is thus about far more than standards: it is about counterparty risk and the terms on which CCPs are permitted to become participants in each other's system.

(2) Where two *CSDs* are to settle the same securities, the problem is different. Here the fundamental consideration is that in the majority of cases one CSD will have the 'root of title'[7] whereas the other will not. The CSD which does not have the root of title will only be able to settle transactions in securities to the extent that it has a securities account at the CSD which is the Issuer CSD, and debit and credit entries are made to that account whenever one of the trading parties participates in the Issuer CSD. Interoperability between CSDs is not about counterparty risk but it is about the terms on which participation in Issuer CSDs may be granted to other CSDs. (The exceptional case where the Issuer/Investor CSD dichotomy

---

6   See **section 7.21**
7   See **section 2.17**

over root of title does not arise is where two CSDs rely on a 'common depository' to provide a common root.[8])

Merits of horizontal interoperability

13.6 Philosophically, horizontal structural interoperability is not straightforward. It requires infrastructures which are competing with each other for business to reach agreements among themselves about cooperation. At the heart of a horizontal interoperability arrangement is an agreement by one party to assist the other party in its effort to take away part of the first party's business. One party is likely to be an incumbent, and to wish to continue in that position, and so to be tempted to impose its own standards or in other ways to control the relationship; yet the objective of interoperability is equivalence of result for market users. Interoperability is, therefore, a somewhat unnatural order of things.

One might thus be tempted to ask whether fragmentation and re-connection is efficient or desirable. Other single markets – notably the United States – seem to manage quite well with a single, integrated infrastructure. But in Europe it is deliberate policy to have fragmentation. Competition between infrastructures is still believed to have beneficial, cost-reducing effects, notwithstanding that the complexities of interoperability introduce other costs and risks, as this chapter will explain. Consolidation of infrastructures, either horizontally (by mergers of CCPs with each other or CSDs with each other) or vertically (by mergers of CCPs with CSDs) faces regulatory and competition-driven obstacles which discourage a move towards a US model, notwithstanding a sheaf of market-user propaganda arguing for it.[9]

The following further observations might be made:

(1) Interoperability is in theory pro-competitive. By enabling market participants to choose their preferred infrastructure, a variety of service offerings might be made available, so that investor A can choose cheap but cheerful, and investor B can choose proud but pricey. That theory, however, does not withstand the regulatory environment, which normalises the behaviour of infrastructures in the interests of reducing systemic risk. Cheap and cheerful, to put it simply, may not be allowed.[10]

(2) Having multiple interchangeable infrastructures should provide for redundancy and thereby protect against systemic risk. Dr Manmohan Singh says, in relation to CCPs, that '[a]ll else being equal, interoperability reduces both (i) the probability of default of CCPs since the overall netting will be higher, which results in smaller tail risks at CCPs, and (ii) the sizable collateral needs associated with offloading derivative risks to multiple CCPs.'[11]

(3) Where competition does occur, the cheapest or most efficient provider may indeed win out, but the consequence may be the elimination of the other interoperating infrastructures, resulting in a dominant winner or monopoly.

---

8   See **section 2.24**
9   See **sections 7.23–7.26**
10 Cf **section 13.19**
11 Singh, M, *Making OTC Derivatives Safe – A Fresh Look* (March 2011), IMF Working Paper WP/11/66; see also Caserta, S, 'Systemic Risk in Central Counterparties Clearinghouses', in Engelen, P-J, and Lannoo, K, eds, *Facing New Regulatory Frameworks in Securities Trading in Europe* (Intersentia, 2010), ISBN 978-90-5095-973-5, pp 147–158

But there is no incentive to infrastructures remaining small, and indeed this is potentially inefficient.

(4) Not all commentators agree that a multiplicity of interoperating CCPs is optimal.[12]

(5) All commentators agree that interoperability between CCPs is extremely hard to bring about.[13] Competition among CSDs is also very difficult to achieve through interoperability owing to the Issuer/Investor CSD 'root of title' issue. Investor CSDs act as intermediaries and introduce a layer of cost.[14] Whether CSD interoperability constitutes 'competition' among peers is, to put it mildly, debatable. Consequently, CSD interoperability does not provide for redundancy or systemic risk protection.

In 2008 the Committee of European Securities Regulators (CESR) conducted a comprehensive survey of regulatory reasons why, in practice, structural interoperability was not actually happening.[15] CESR points out in its report that it has no powers to deal with requests for interoperability, and included the following barriers to interoperability in the summary of its findings:

● CCPs may be unable to carry on business in some member states unless they hold a banking licence.

● CCPs and CSDs will typically have to go through a local process of obtaining authorisation or recognition in order to carry on business in a host member state – in other words, there is no 'passport' for CCP or CSD activity.

● CCPs and CSDs impose criteria for participation which may be difficult for other CCPs/CSDs to fulfil, such as membership of the local stock exchange.

EUROPEAN LAW OF INTEROPERABILITY

13.7 Legal rules conferring rights whereby structural interoperability might be achieved have historically been weak. The Markets in Financial Instruments Directive (MiFID)[16] tried to encourage them, but ultimately failed. Article 34 of MiFID requires member states to give *investment firms* a right of choice between CCPs and clearing and settlement systems, and articles 35 and 46 of MiFID require member states to allow *MTFs* (trading platforms) and *regulated markets* to use CCPs and settlement systems in other member states. But these apparent rights are restricted, in that there must be 'such links and arrangements between

---

12 See Evanoff, D, Russo, D, and Steigerwald, R, *Policymakers, Researchers, and Practitioners discuss the role of central counterparties* (July 2007), http://www.ecb.int/pub/pdf/other/rolecentralcounterparties200707en.pdf, p 10

13 See, for example, Pirrong, C, *The Economics of Central Clearing: Theory and Practice* (May 2011), ISDA Discussion Paper No 1, http://www2.isda.org/attachment/MzE0NA==/ISDAdiscussion_CCP_Pirrong.pdf, p 43; Chlistalla, M, 'OTC derivatives – a new market infrastructure is taking shape' (April 2010) Deutsche Bank Research, http://www.dbresearch.com/PROD/DBR_INTERNET_EN-PROD/PROD0000000000256894.pdf, p 10; Kalogeropoulos, G, Russo, D, and Schönenberger, A, *Link arrangements of Central Counterparties in the EU – results of an ESCB survey* (July 2007), http://www.ecb.int/pub/pdf/other/rolecentralcounterparties200707en.pdf, pp 50–58

14 See **section 13.42**

15 Committee of European Securities Regulators, *Preliminary Technical Advice by CESR in response to the Mandate from the European Commission on Access & Interoperability Arrangements* (February 2009), http://www.cesr.eu/index.php?docid=5572

16 Directive 2004/39/EC of the European Parliament and of the Council of 21 April 2004 on markets in financial instruments etc

the designated settlement system and any other system or facility as are necessary to ensure the efficient and economic settlement of the transaction in question' and the agreement of the competent authority responsible for supervision of the regulated market that 'technical conditions of settlement of transactions ... are such as to allow the smooth and orderly functioning of financial markets.'[17] The rights are not unfettered, therefore. But actually, the rights are given to the wrong people. The 'choice' was assumed by the policy-makers to lie with the investment firm or the trading platform/market, but the person with power to block the exercise of a choice is more likely to be the incumbent, without whose cooperation structural interoperability is doomed to fail. MiFID is silent on the duties of incumbents. The Commission recognised this in its 2004 paper on clearing and settlement, acknowledging that CSDs should have the right of access to CSDs, and CCPs to CCPs, in other member states; unfortunately its belief that these rights were to be conferred by MiFID were misplaced.[18]

13.8   Since MiFID, there have been further legislative provisions dealing with interoperability, in the amended Settlement Finality Directive (SFD)[19], EMIR[20] and the proposed CSD Regulation:[21]

(1) The SFD was amended in 2009[22] to ensure that the insolvency protections made available to designated systems[23] would apply effectively where the parties to a transfer order participate in different, interoperable systems. The operators of interoperating systems are also required to coordinate their rules on the moment of entry and irrevocability in their systems. Bearing in mind that all three main types of infrastructures (CCPs, CSDs and payment systems) may be designated under the SFD, this development has the broadest scope. The SFD is, however, not prescriptive as to the outcomes which interoperability should achieve. Indeed, the SFD says that one interoperable system's rules as to (i) the moment of entry of a transfer order into its system and (ii) the moment of irrevocability of a transfer order are *not* affected by any rules of the other systems with which it is interoperable.[24] The proposed CSD Regulation goes further in terms of requiring interoperable systems to achieve simultaneous finality.

(2) EMIR contains an entire Title[25] on interoperability arrangements between CCPs which clear transactions in transferable securities and money-market instruments.[26] This provides for the CCPs' risk management to be adapted to the link arrangements, which must be the subject of an agreement;

---

17   MiFID, art 34(2), applied under arts 35(2) and 46(2) to MTFs and regulated markets respectively
18   European Commission, *Clearing and Settlement in the European Union – The way forward* (April 2004), http://eur-lex.europa.eu/LexUriServ/LexUriServ.do?uri=COM:2004:0312:FIN:EN:PDF, p 15
19   Directive 98/26/EC of the European Parliament and of the Council of 19 May 1998 on settlement finality in payment and securities settlement systems
20   Regulation (EU) No 648/2012 of the European Parliament and of the Council of 4 July 2012 on OTC derivatives, central counterparties and trade repositories
21   European Commission, *Proposal for a Regulation of the European Parliament and of the Council on improving securities settlement in the European Union and on central securities depositories (CSDs) etc* (March 2012), COM(2012) 73 final, http://eur-lex.europa.eu/LexUriServ/LexUriServ.do?uri=CELEX:52012PC0073:EN:PDF
22   Directive 2009/44/EC of the European Parliament and of the Council of 6 May 2009 amending Directive 98/26/EC on settlement finality, etc
23   See **section 8.19**
24   SFD, arts 3(4) and 5 respectively
25   Title V
26   EMIR, art 1(3)

and for inter-CCP margin to be segregated and excluded from any 'right of use' otherwise available to a CCP.[27] CCPs must obtain regulatory approval for interoperability arrangements. ESMA is to create guidelines or recommendations, which may in due course supplant the Code. It is recognised that the trading venues hold many of the cards which control the effectiveness of an interoperability arrangement. Accordingly, CCPs are granted 'non-discriminatory access' to data needed for performance of its functions, subject to compliance 'with the operational and technical requirements established by the trading venue.' Non-discriminatory access to settlement systems is also granted. Unfortunately the relevant provisions are written in the passive voice, making it unclear on whom the relevant legal obligations lie, and thereby complicating the process of enforcement.[28]

(3) The proposed CSD Regulation, in addition to various provisions dealing with vertical interoperability, would give a CSD a right to become a participant in any other CSD, subject to regulatory approval.[29] There are also various risk management provisions:[30] links would have to assure finality of transfer; linked CSDs would have to have robust reconciliation; DvP would have to be achieved across a link 'wherever practical and feasible'; and linked CSDs would have to have identical moments of entry of transfer orders, irrevocability of transfer orders, and finality of transfers of securities and cash, if they use a common settlement infrastructure.

13.9   As to CSDs, the European Central Bank's Eligibility Criteria for CSDs in Target2-Securities (T2S)[31] require a CSD which wishes to join T2S to do two things to assure interoperability: an Issuer CSD must make every security available to each other T2S CSD, and it must offer a basic custody service to each other T2S CSD. Interoperability between CSDs requires that the Issuer CSD allows the Investor CSD to become its client, and for CSDs participating in T2S there are no grounds on which the Issuer CSD could refuse.

Soft law

13.10   The Principles for Financial Market Infrastructures (FMI Principles) set out a code of soft law.[32] Principle 20 covers all types of horizontal link between infrastructures. It recommends identification and management of all link-related risks, including legal, operational and financial risks, and spells out matters of particular concern in relation to CSD-to-CSD links and CCP-to-CCP links.

13.11   The Code of Conduct[33] also applies to interoperability among CSDs and CCPs. The Code was brought into being as a device for self-regulation,

---

27 Cf **section 13.22**
28 EMIR, art 51(2)
29 Articles 17, 48–50
30 Proposed CSD Regulation, art 45
31 Decision of the European Central Bank of 16 November 2011 establishing detailed rules and procedures for implementing the eligibility criteria for central securities depositories to access TARGET2-Securities services (ECB/2011/20), OJ L 319/117
32 Bank for International Settlements Committee on Payment and Settlement Systems and Technical Committee of the International Organization of Securities Commissions, *Principles for Financial Market Infrastructures* (April 2012), http://www.bis.org/publ/cpss101a.pdf
33 FESE, EACH and ECSDA, *European Code of Conduct for Clearing and Settlement* (November 2006), http://ec.europa.eu/internal_market/financial-markets/docs/code/code_en.pdf

perceived at the time to be more desirable and more rapidly achievable than a directive (as had first been proposed by the European Commission[34]). The Code is the product of the Federation of European Securities Exchanges, the European Association of Central Counterparty Clearing Houses (EACH), and the European Central Securities Depositories Association (ECSDA). It is voluntary in the sense that no statutory, regulatory or contractual arrangements make it enforceable by any person, whether or not that person is a member of one of the sponsoring associations. The Code has been supplemented by an Access and Interoperability Guideline (the A&I Guideline).[35] The A&I Guideline contains additional detail on access rights and obligations of the interoperating parties. Both the Code and the A&I Guideline address a range of permutations of access and interoperation among trading, clearing and settlement infrastructures: not only are the horizontal arrangements between CCPs, or between CSDs, covered, but also the linkages between trading platforms on the one hand and CCPs and CSDs on the other, or between CCPs and CSDs.

13.12 The Code's provisions on access are as follows:

'25. Requests for access will be dependent upon considerations relating to the business case only of the requesting Organisation.

26. Standard unilateral access and transaction feed access shall be provided on a non-discriminatory price basis; any customised component of a unilateral access or transaction feed access should be paid for by the Organisation requesting access on a cost-plus basis unless otherwise agreed between the parties.

27. Access should be granted on the basis of non-discriminatory, transparent criteria and prices.

28. Requests for access should be treated expeditiously.

29. The process under which access requests are to be treated should be publicly available.

30. Refusals of access should only be based on risk related criteria or exemptions to access rights as detailed in MiFID. They should be explained in writing and communicated to the requesting Organisation promptly.

31. In case of disputes, the undersigning Organisations undertake to settle the dispute expeditiously.

32. In the event of a potential dispute, a mediation mechanism will be set up.

33. An Organisation requesting access to another Organisation should, in principle, comply with the legal, fiscal and regulatory arrangements applicable to the receiving Organisation.'

It might be noted that there is, *ex hypothesi*, no business case for the *receiving* organisation to allow the requesting organisation to share in the spoils of its quasi-monopoly. The purpose of this set of rules is to eliminate that as an excuse for the receiving organisation to deny interoperability. That is all very well for CSDs, but links between CCPs are not solely within the control of the incumbent CCP; in order to establish a link, a requesting CCP needs to be

---

34 European Commission, *Clearing and Settlement in the European Union – The way forward* (April 2004), http://eur-lex.europa.eu/LexUriServ/LexUriServ.do?uri=COM:2004:0312:FIN:E N:PDF, p 11

35 FESE, EACH and ECSDA, *Access and Interoperability Guideline* (June 2007), http:// ec.europa.eu/internal_market/financial-markets/docs/code/guideline_en.pdf

engaged by the trading platform as well as to establish a link to the incumbent CCP. The Code applies to platforms as receiving organisation as well as CCPs. But access is not simply a matter of request and acceptance. As this chapter goes on to show, there are myriad technical and operational issues to address in making interoperability work, and as there is no business case for the receiving organisation to devote time, money and effort to solving them, the receiving organisation can claim to be complying with all of the above rules and still have no interoperability arrangements in place. The Code does not provide any machinery for enforcement of the access rights which it apparently gives or to test the behaviour of a receiving organisation which is failing to resolve difficulties in implementing interoperability where it has accepted a competitor's request. Without the legislative force of EMIR it is no surprise that interoperability has been difficult to get started.

13.13 In relation to conditions of interoperability, the Code says the following:

> '34. Establishment of Interoperability is subject to the business case of the entities concerned and on proper risk control.
> 35. To achieve such an optimised design both Organisations seeking interoperability, with the involvement of relevant stakeholders and the respective regulators in particular, need to have discretion in the design of the Interoperability relationship and not be limited in their solutions.
> 36. Against this background, the Organisations seeking Interoperability commit to the following:
>   • Any Organisation receiving a proposal for Interoperability will expeditiously enter into discussions with the proposing Organisation about the most appropriate design and procedures for establishing such an Interoperability relationship.
>   • They will conduct these discussions and negotiations in good faith and will avoid any undue delay.
>   • Organisations will consider appointing a mediator to facilitate these discussions and negotiations and to support the resolution of conflicts between Organisations.
> 37. An Organisation requesting access to another Organisation should, in principle, comply with the legal, fiscal and regulatory arrangements applicable to the receiving Organisation. To the extent that the proposed Interoperability arrangement requires either organisation to access the other, that Organisation should, in principle, comply with the legal, fiscal and regulatory arrangements applicable to the other Organisation.'

The spectre of the business case is raised again, but this time with more baneful effect. The *establishment* (that is to say, the implementation) of interoperability can apparently be blocked legitimately on business case grounds. Only 'against this background' will organisations commit to expedition, conflict resolution and so forth. In case that were unclear, the A&I Guideline emphasises the point: 'The Receiving Organisation cannot be forced to change its own market practices and standards towards its own participants, unless mutually agreed.'[36] And then applicable legal, fiscal and regulatory arrangements can be used to make the course even harder to run. With these difficulties it is a tribute to those

---

36 A&I Guideline, para 52

infrastructures which, in the years following the adoption of the Code, actually managed to establish link agreements with their competitors.

The interoperability provisions of the Code seem unlikely to survive in their 2006 form after the adoption of EMIR and the proposed CSD Regulation.

13.14 There is further soft law in the form of an EACH publication, the Inter-CCP Risk Management Standards.[37] There are seven standards, the most important of which is the prohibition of competition on risk grounds, which is analysed below. The others are: compliance with the CPSS-IOSCO recommendations for risk management; 'recognition' of the nature and regulatory status of CCPs, which is to say that, since CCPs have a different risk profile from ordinary participants (as discussed below), concessions on admission criteria are appropriate; measurement and management of inter-CCP exposure, in line with the A&I Guideline; performing an assessment of counterparty risk on the other CCP in order to inform a decision to interoperate or to continue with a link; transparency (information exchange); and operational flexibility on questions such as business hours and holidays.

13.15 Finally, in relation to CCPs and CSDs, mention should be made of the Recommendations issued by the European Central Bank and the Committee of European Securities Regulators (ECB-CESR Recommendations) in 2009.[38] These may be superseded by the FMI Principles, or more probably, by guidelines and recommendations issued by ESMA under article 54 of EMIR. Recommendation 11 for CCPs followed closely the equivalent Recommendation for CCPs issued by the CPSS and IOSCO,[39] which have now been replaced by the FMI Principles.

13.16 Soft law rules relating to interoperating payment systems are discussed at **section 13.53**.

STRUCTURE OF INTEROPERATION BETWEEN CCPs

13.17 Interoperability between CCPs is dictated by the essential function of a CCP, which is to replace the original counterparty on the trade: the CCP becomes buyer to the seller, and seller to the buyer. If the original buyer and seller participate in different CCPs, the buyer's CCP becomes its seller, and the seller's CCP becomes its buyer, but how will the CCPs manage their now unmatched books? Interoperability involves some structure whereby buyer's CCP buys from the seller's CCP – the clearing process, which ordinarily replaces one trade with two trades, will in a case of interoperation of CCPs create a longer chain of three back-to-back trades.

37 European Association of CCP Clearing Houses, *Inter-CCP Risk Management Standards* (July 2008), http://www.eachorg.eu/each/

38 European Central Bank and Committee of European Securities Regulators, *Recommendations for Securities Settlement Systems and Recommendations for Central Counterparties in The European Union* (June 2009), http://www.ecb.int/pub/pdf/other/pr090623_escb-cesr_recommendationsen.pdf

39 CPSS and IOSCO, *Recommendations for Central Counterparties* (November 2004), http://www.bis.org/publ/cpss64.htm

13.17   *Interoperability*

To achieve this objective, an interoperability arrangement can be structured in one of several ways:

(1) *Mutual participation.* Most commonly, each CCP will become a participant in the other CCP, albeit on modified terms. Each CCP will enter into the relationship expecting or demanding certain performance from the other, which would ordinarily be provided by a CCP's participants. But CCPs are one-way creatures in their normal clearing existence, receiving margin

Models of interoperability

(1) Mutual participation

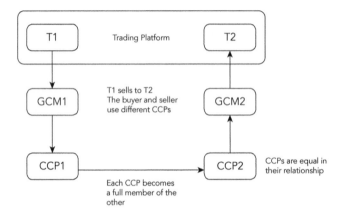

(2) Unidirectional participation

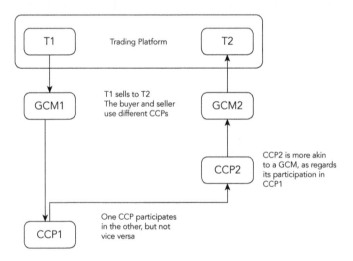

Fig 13.1

and default fund contributions from their participants and imposing rules and procedures upon them. To put the same proposition differently: CCPs do not ordinarily *give* margin or default fund contributions to third parties and do not expect to have to *obey* a third party's rules. A CCP which is itself a participant is not likely to be willing to be dictated to, when it is itself expecting to act as dictator. A compromise will be needed, hence the modified terms associated with mutual participation. This form of interoperability is referred to as a 'peer-to-peer link' in FMI Principle 20.

(2) *Unidirectional participation.* Alternatively, one CCP can become a participant in the main CCP, and the main CCP will be able to distance itself from the clearing arrangements of the participant-CCP. The link between LCH.Clearnet and X-Clear for clearing trades on the virt-x market

(3) Facilitated transfer

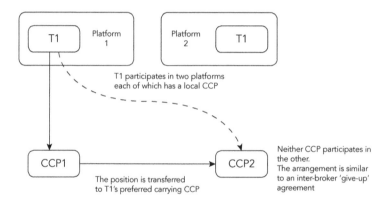

(4) Cross-margining

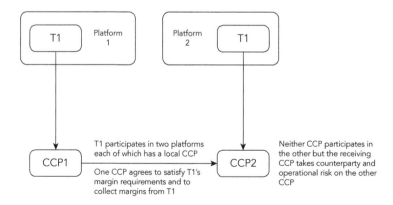

Fig 13.1

historically worked in this way.[40] Notwithstanding that the participant-CCP is a CCP, and may have been admitted to participation in the main CCP in a special membership category, the participant-CCP is acting as a GCM. The risks faced by the participant-CCP are the risks faced by GCMs[41], and the main CCP is able to remain aloof in the same way as it remains aloof from the clearing arrangements entered into by its GCMs. No doubt the participant-CCP will have to adjust its behaviour in order to provide margin and to be dictated to in relation to the positions which it holds with the main CCP, but that is the effect of the subordinate role which this structure presumes. This option may involve some degree of bespoke service provision to the participant-CCP, and may thus grow into something closer to full interoperability. This form of interoperability is called a 'participant link' in FMI Principle 20.

13.18   Three further possibilities ought briefly to be mentioned, although neither would completely solve the central problem identified, namely that different traders may wish to clear through different CCPs.

(3) *Facilitated transfer.* A link may be 'designed to facilitate the transfer of positions between CCPs ... In such links, market participants may open positions in a product cleared by one CCP (the "host" CCP) but subsequently all these positions are transferred to the "home" CCP for that product. The "host" CCP takes on the counterparty risk of its participants until the positions are transferred to the "home" CCP, generally at the end of the trading day. After the transfer, the "home" CCP becomes the counterparty to the participant of the "host" CCP for the positions that are transferred.'[42]

(4) *Cross-margining.* The second example is 'cross-margining', a structure more common in the United States, where CCPs exist to serve different market segments, than in Europe.[43] Cross-margining enables a single participant, who participates in two CCPs, to amalgamate the margin calls made into a single flow, so that one CCP effectively acts as a conduit or agency for the delivery of margin to the other. Cross-margining may work so as to enable surpluses of margin in the participant's account at one CCP to be routed to the other CCP, to help the participant with its liquidity needs. This kind of interoperability arrangement may develop in Europe as specialist CCPs grow up to satisfy the demands of EMIR for OTC derivatives clearing.[44]

(5) *Choice without full interoperability.* For a brief period BATS, a trading platform, offered its participants a choice between clearing at its incumbent CCP, or a trio of (different) interoperating CCPs. The default situation was for the clearing to occur at the incumbent CCP, but if both parties to the transaction selected clearing at one of the three CCPs able to interoperate,

---

40   Kalogeropoulos et al, p 54
41   See **sections 18.17–18.21**
42   CESR and ECB, *Recommendations for Securities Settlement Systems and Recommendations for Central Counterparties in the European Union* (May 2009), http://www.ecb.int/pub/pdf/other/pr090623_escb-cesr_recommendationsen.pdf, p 205
43   See, for example, Kalogeropoulos et al, p 50
44   See **section 13.38**

their choice would prevail.[45] After six months, the incumbent CCP was fully interoperable with the other three.[46]

Competition, but not on risk

13.19 It is often suggested that CCPs should compete with each other, but not on questions of risk management. Various industry associations have warned that where CCPs compete for business, there is danger when they compete on quality of risk management.[47] This theme has been reflected in comments from the authorities, too: the European Central Bank says that competition between CCPs creates a risk of a 'race to the bottom',[48] and a joint presentation by regulators from the United Kingdom, the Netherlands and Switzerland on interoperability says that competition between CCPs on risk 'is not envisaged'.[49]

The response from the CCPs themselves is rather vague. The Code says nothing. The A&I Guideline states that 'competition between CCPs must not have a significantly detrimental effect on risk management standards in place.'[50] This is more an article of faith than practical guidance. The EACH Standards tackle the problem with more vigour than the Code, the A&I Guideline, or any official pronouncement. In summary, Standard 2 states categorically that risk management practices cannot be used as a competitive tool among CCPs. EACH itself considers that its Standards were 'adopted in order to prevent competition between CCPs leading to a decline in risk management standards.'[51]

It may therefore be appropriate to examine why and how competition between interoperating CCPs might give rise to a 'race to the bottom'. If CCPs were to compete on risk grounds, 'it is clear that the market would see a downward spiral of risk protections which would be to the detriment of all the CCPs concerned and the financial system as a whole. This must be avoided at all costs as a consequence of interoperability.'[52] Several illustrations are given as to what the standard prohibits and what it does not. First, a CCP must not set its initial margin at an imprudently low level to attract more participants. But that does

---

45 BATS press release (July 2011), http://www.batstrading.co.uk/resources/press_releases/ BATS_Go_Live_Pref_Interop_FINAL.pdf

46 BATS-Chi-X press release (January 2012), http://www.batstrading.co.uk/resources/chi-x_ press_releases/batschi-x-full-interop-go-live-final.pdf

47 See, for example: European Repo Council, response to the ESCB/CESR consultation on recommended standards for CCPs (January 2009), http://www.ecb.int/paym/pdf/cons/escb_ cesr/ERC_P.pdf?32e22db295b6a7d66a8d2d78ca87a1ef, p 11; Bundesverband der Deutschen Volksbanken und Raiffeisenbanken, Bundesverband deutscher Banken (BdB), and Deutscher Sparkassen und Giroverband, response to the same consultation (January 2009), http://www. ecb.int/paym/pdf/cons/escb_cesr/BVR_BDB_DSGV.pdf?ba6c59ebdc9ae1224b8b5ab13951a 6c5, p 4; European Banking Federation, *CCP for CDS User Requirements* (February 2009), slide presentation, http://www.ecb.int/events/pdf/conferences/ccp_cds/AGENDA_ITEM3_ EBF.pdf?ba0bd8065956f6f33d7c8b9796883b59, p 9

48 Schönenberger, A, *CCP Interoperability* (July 2009), ECB slide presentation, http://www.ecb. int/events/pdf/conferences/ccp_cds2/ECBInteroperability.pdf?691775cae468c3406c75acd8f3 488d2a

49 AFM, DNB, and FSA, *Interoperability: Regulatory Expectations* (March 2010), slide presentation, http://ec.europa.eu/internal_market/financial-markets/docs/code/mog/20100315_ afm_dnb_fsa_en.pdf, p 2

50 A&I Guideline, para 13

51 European Central Bank, minutes of the 18th meeting of the Contact Group on Euro Securities Infrastructures (June 2008), http://www.ecb.int/paym/groups/pdf/COGESI_minutes_18th_ meeting_0608.pdf?d640863fa86e8773f441cec24f7aa22a , p 2

52 EACH Standards, Standard 2, para 2.2

not mean that all CCPs have to impose the same level of initial margin – the EACH Standards indicate that the balance of backing between initial margin and default funding may legitimately differ between CCPs. EMIR imposes only a floor on margin levels.[53] Secondly, CCPs cannot make exceptions to their margin policy so as to treat markets where there is interoperability with another CCP differently from markets where there is no interoperability. But, thirdly, CCPs can change their margin policy, and changes should be publicised. This exception is important: who is to decide whether a reduction in margin requirements, or a shift to alternative methods of risk protection, or a change in risk quantification algorithms, is 'imprudent' or whether the aim of the CCP was to attract more custom. It is naïve and unrealistic to suppose that a CCP would volunteer to withhold an innovation which would economise on margin requirements for its participants; competitors might deride the innovation as imprudent or unfair competition; but, since under EMIR the CCP's policy will be subject to technical standards designed by ESMA,[54] and regulators of infrastructures are likely to be conservative, there may be little incentive to innovate.

In a report for the European Parliament it was stated: 'CCPs will be restrained by regulation from competing on margins (also called race to the bottom) since this behaviour would weaken CCPs' risk mitigation mechanisms. However, it has been found that the major existing CCPs have demonstrated remarkable skill and conservatism in managing risk. It rather seems that CCPs compete on prudential risk management and financial integrity instead of attracting OTC-cleared derivatives volume.'[55]

Thus 'no competition on risk' is, however, more a slogan than a reality. To deny CCPs the 'right' to compete on risk grounds is absurd as well as unachievable. In the first place, CCPs should on principle be allowed to compete on risk grounds: if my risk model is better than yours, I should be permitted to advertise this, and the users of the market will benefit. Secondly, the reason why participants will choose one CCP over another is heavily influenced by the competing CCPs' approaches to risk management. Participants understand that the raison d'être of a CCP is management of counterparty risk – they will inevitably make their choice based upon their assessment of the competing CCPs' effectiveness at risk management. Rather than there being a 'race to the bottom', with CCPs vying to reduce margin and default fund levels to a dangerous level of cheapness, participants are just as likely to eschew a bargain-basement CCP. Competition on the price of clearing or the apparent efficiency of a CCP is likely to take second place to this consideration. To say that there must be no competition on the quality of this essential function is the same as saying there must be no competition on quality between two restaurants.

CCP INTEROPERABILITY AND RISK

13.20 The real danger in the slogan of 'no competition on risk' is that it distracts attention from another feature of having competition between CCPs:

---

53 Article 41(1)
54 Article 41(5)
55 Schröder, M, et al, *Assessment of the Cumulative Impact of Various Regulatory Initiatives on the European Banking Sector* (August 2011), Study for the European Parliament, PE 464.439, http://www.europarl.europa.eu/document/activities/cont/201203/20120313ATT40643/201203 13ATT40643EN.pdf, p 15

that interoperability, without enhancement of the financial resources of each interoperating CCP, actually *increases* risk. Disapplying the carefully-erected fences designed to protect against counterparty risk in order to allow another CCP to become a participant is nothing other than detrimental to risk management standards already in place. Special risk management arrangements have to be crafted in order to address the special issues which arise when a CCP's counterparty is another CCP. The risk of contagion, as a problem in one CCP may, through its participation in another CCP contaminate the other CCP, has led regulators to state that formal links between CCPs increase systemic risk.[56]

In order to understand why interoperability increases risk, a discussion may be helpful on the subject of risk management of inter-CCP transactions. Mutual membership cannot be achieved without some watering-down by each CCP of its standards with regard to its management of counterparty risk. Whether it is appropriate to allow dilution of risk management because a CCP is a special kind of counterparty requires an assessment of whether CCPs are less prone to mishap than 'ordinary' participants. In part this depends on how CCPs are capitalised, governed and regulated, in part on what business they are able to conduct, and in part on how a counterparty risk event – the insolvency of a CCP – could actually arise.

Inter-CCP Counterparty Risk Management

13.21 The basic problem of full interoperability between CCPs is the management of counterparty risk. Normally a CCP will take care of this problem by control at the gate (restriction of participation to entities of adequate capital, operational ability, business profile etc); by collecting margin to secure the positions taken by the participant; and by arranging default backing from resources provided by participants, either in the form of up-front default fund contributions or by having a power to call for additional funding from them in a crisis or to put a defaulter's unwanted positions onto them.[57] In other words, CCPs impose obligations on their participants, they do not accept them. On each of these risk management fundamentals, an interoperability arrangement requires a complete re-think.

(1) *Control at the gate.* EMIR does not oblige CCPs to interoperate, but says that they 'may' do so with regulatory approval, provided that certain preconditions are satisfied. Interoperability is allowable if the CCPs in question have been authorised for at least three years.[58] Nor does EMIR require relaxation of the criteria for participation which a CCP would otherwise wish to impose, but such criteria will typically not be designed with CCPs (as opposed to GCMs) in mind. It has been noted that the risk profile of a CCP differs from that of an ordinary clearing member: CCPs have no 'endogenous risk' (meaning that they have a balanced book from a market risk perspective, every sale being matched by a purchase at the same price), they have special risk controls, and that they typically enjoy a special regime of regulation and oversight, which may include special

---

56 Joint Regulatory Authorities of LCH.Clearnet Group, *Investigation of risks arising from the emergence of multi-cleared trading platforms* (July 2008), http://www.dnb.nl/binaries/Investigation%20of%20risks%20arising%20from%20the%20emergence%20of%20multi-cleared%20trading%20platforms_tcm46-216876.pdf
57 See **Chapter 14**
58 EMIR, art 54(2)

insolvency protections such as those granted under the Settlement Finality Directive.[59] The EACH Standards also mention these points, adding that CCPs have non-speculative business models which do not risk the institution's capital in order to make a profit.[60] This may be true where CCPs are run as non-profit utilities, but CCPs are very commonly run for profit and while they may not speculate in the cleared instruments CCPs are certainly indulging in risk-taking in the centralisation of counterparty risk. All these considerations may point to the conclusion that risk management is not lowered if a CCP is allowed to become a participant; but they do show that different conditions of access for CCPs are almost unavoidable.

(2) *Default funding and loss-sharing.* The A&I Guideline stipulates that 'no CCP is obliged to contribute to the other CCP's participants' default fund or other post default backing schemes.'[61] This is echoed in the FMI Principles.[62] That seems a defensible idea: a default fund is a means of mutualising risk. In other words, the survivors, with gritted teeth, agree to assist the CCP in its attempt to withstand any financial shock caused by another participant's default, even though the problem is not of their own making. But if you accept that the entire purpose of full mutual interoperability between CCPs is to enable participants to choose their preferred CCP – or, to put it the other way round, to escape the consequences of being in a different CCP – then it must follow that participants are deliberately choosing to be shielded from the financial shock caused by the other CCP's default. If a participant's own CCP has to contribute to another CCP's default fund, the viability of the contributing CCP is affected by the quality of risk management of the other CCP, and the participant might as well have joined the other CCP in the first place. And if CCPs do not contribute to each other's default funds, those funds will be relatively under-funded, and the CCPs will need to find other financial resources to plug the gap.[63]

(3) *Margin.* Whether a participant is buying or selling a security, the CCP will call for initial margin[64] – there is always some risk on the position, regardless of the direction of the trade. This means that a CCP is expecting to receive initial margin from both its selling and its buying participant. Where one of those participants is a CCP, the two CCPs are immediately brought into conflict, as each CCP will wish to make a margin demand on the other in respect of the same position. CCPs collect initial margin, they do not deliver it. From where does a CCP which is required to satisfy a margin call source the funds it needs? A CCP will not wish to diminish its financial resources by paying a margin call in respect of a position which, ordinarily, it would have required to be supported by a net inflow of margin. Some other source of funds is going to be required.

Variation margin practices raise similar issues though on less grand a scale. Unlike initial margin, variation margin reflects the daily movement in market prices, and is both received and paid out by CCPs. If the price of a security rises, the value of the seller's contract diminishes, and there is

59 Kalogeropoulos et al, p 50
60 EACH, *Inter-CCP Risk Management Standards* (July 2008), http://www.eachorg.eu/each/, Standard 3.2, paras 4 and 5
61 A&I Guideline, para 84
62 FMI Principles, para 3.20.17
63 Cf FMI Principles, para 3.20.17
64 See **section 14.23**

Margin flows between interoperating CCPs

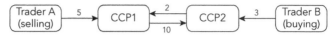

CCPs' assessments of the initial margin requirements for a single trade:

CCP 1:	seller should pay 5;	buyer should pay 2
CCP 2:	seller should pay 10;	buyer should pay 3

Interoperability reduces the total initial margins received by both CCPs

Initial margin totals	CCP1	CCP2
Without interoperability:	7	13
With interoperability:	(3)	11

The more conservative CCP is less badly affected, and a more adventurous CCP with borderline risk management may be significantly impaired by having to provide margin.

Fig 13.2

an increase in the replacement cost to the CCP of the contract in case the seller defaults before settlement. So the seller must pay variation margin to the CCP. But there is a corresponding reduction in the replacement cost of the CCP's contract with the buyer if the buyer defaults, so the CCP will pass through the variation margin to the buyer. If the buyer is another CCP, however, the computation of variation margin may be done according to a different algorithm, and there is a possibility that the amount expected to be paid differs between the CCPs. Where the amount required by the second CCP exceeds that which is collected by the first CCP, the problem of diminution of resources arises again for the first CCP.

13.22 The law and regulatory guidance do not go far to address these practical issues. The A&I Guideline says that CCPs 'have to arrange an adequate collateralisation scheme to cover the exposure of potential losses.'[65] EMIR lays down that CCPs are required to have risk management policies and procedures to address the implications of interoperation. In particular, EMIR mentions that the default of one CCP's participant should not affect an interoperating CCP,[66] and that risk issues requiring particular attention are 'potential interdependencies and correlations' relating to 'clearing member concentrations and pooled financial resources.'[67] Inter-CCP margining differs slightly from the regular margin requirements of EMIR. First, any right of use of margin securities provided by one CCP to another under a security interest must be disapplied;[68] but there is no restriction on the ability of a CCP to demand that margin under an interoperability arrangement is posted by way of title transfer collateral arrangement, and there is no restriction on re-use of margin posted by

---

65   A&I Guideline, para 84
66   EMIR, art 52(1)(c)
67   EMIR, art 52(1)(d)
68   EMIR, art 53(2)

participants as inter-CCP margin. So the restriction on use may be of limited value. The FMI Principles do not expressly forbid the re-use of participants' margin for inter-CCP margining either; and, in contrast to the recommendations dealing with default fund contributions, they do not say that the CCP has to raise supplementary financial resources to cover inter-CCP margin obligations.[69] Secondly, securities collateral must be deposited with a securities settlement system which has been designated under the Settlement Finality Directive,[70] ruling out the use of private sector custodians, but apparently not ruling out the interoperating CCP, which itself is likely to be so designated.[71] Thirdly, if the CCP which has *received* collateral defaults, the collateral 'shall be readily returned to the providing CCP.'[72] This latter provision is unclear. It is tempting to read it as requiring a bankrupt CCP to hand back collateral even though the non-defaulting CCP may still owe obligations to the bankrupt CCP. That reading would, however, be wrong, for two reasons: it would worsen the affairs of the bankrupt CCP if it is required to surrender its collateral at a moment of extreme market shock, that is at a point when the *non*-defaulting CCP is likely to be at its most unstable; and it would probably contravene the 'anti-deprivation' principle of insolvency law.[73]

13.23 Various questions of principle and practice are left unanswered by these rules.

(1) A CCP required to post inter-CCP margin (CCP1) may be able to re-use margin collected from its participants. Cash margin posted to a CCP would not ordinarily be subject to client money protection in the United Kingdom, as CCPs are not subject to the client money rules made under the Financial Services and Markets Act 2000.[74] Cash margin taken in by CCP1 is therefore recyclable to an interoperating CCP (CCP2). If securities collateral has been posted to CCP1 under a financial collateral arrangement, re-use can be agreed with the participant,[75] and thereby recycled as well. The inter-CCP margin must be returnable to CCP1 in the event of CCP2's failure.[76] The mechanism is intended to ensure that CCP1 is in no worse position than if there were no interoperability. That may be true as regards credit risk, but is not true as regards liquidity risk or as regards the default fund. The idea of recycling margin, would, therefore, appear to be the norm, despite at one stage being disavowed by regulators.[77]

(2) CCP2's margin demands may be high relative to the margin receipts of CCP1 in respect of the same trade.[78] If cash is going to flow out of a CCP, rather than into it, there is a question for CCP1 of liquidity management. This question will become acute at times when a market is in stress or when a participant in one or other CCP has defaulted (which may well be

---

69 FMI Principles, paras 3.20.16–17
70 EMIR, art 53(3)
71 EMIR, art 17(4)
72 EMIR, art 53(5)
73 See **section 8.9(14)**
74 See **section 9.13**
75 Financial Collateral Arrangements (No 2) Regulations 2003, SI 2003 No 3226, reg 16.1
76 EMIR, art 53(5)
77 AFM, DNB, and FSA, *Interoperability: Regulatory Expectations* (March 2010), slide presentation, http://ec.europa.eu/internal_market/financial-markets/docs/code/mog/20100315_afm_dnb_fsa_en.pdf, p 3
78 See **figure 13.2**

correlated events). Resources of the CCP1 may become locked up in CCP2 if CCP2 is managing a default and declining to repay margin deposits. Interoperating CCPs are likely to need liquidity facilities.

(3) Inter-CCP margining thus demands an increase in resources, unless CCP1 has sufficient flexibility with re-used margin collected from its participants. The question may then arise as to who pays for the additional resources required. There are two choices: the participants in CCP1, or the shareholders of CCP1. Neither constituency will see why it is right that they should be asked to pay for risk not of their own making and outside their control.

Margin as a tool for managing CCP default risk

13.24 Thinking about margin as the means of managing a default of a *CCP* is likely to be wrong-headed. As noted above, CCPs are rather unusual counterparties/participants. The default of a CCP is a systemic risk event. Despite the awareness of these factors, the authorities have not found any recipe for risk management other than collateralisation of exposure. This approach is, unfortunately, fallacious. The purpose of margin is to cover the replacement cost of a defaulting participant's positions. But margin is calculated by reference to the expected loss in the event of a default by an entity which *does* have endogenous risk, and by observing market conditions in such events (including extreme market reactions such as that which followed the Lehman Brothers failure in 2008, and other non-default related conditions). These are the wrong scenarios against which to assess the loss suffered if a CCP defaults. Precisely because a CCP takes on no endogenous risk, the failure of a CCP must be entirely attributable to exogenous events – catastrophic failure both of one or more of its participants coupled with failure of the CCP's margining and default-management methodologies. Ordinary measures of expected post-default loss are inappropriate for such circumstances. The failure of a CCP implies a fundamental error by that CCP in either its risk management model or its operational support to give effect to the model: for example, the CCP either miscalculated the amount of margin or default funding it needed to contain the risk it was assuming, or if it calculated correctly it was unable to collect on the margin or default funding in order to support itself. These are catastrophically bad scenarios. 'Margin' in ordinary parlance is protection against ordinary market movements, not total failure of an infrastructure. It is arguable that margin is a red herring in the interoperability debate. Yes, admittedly, collecting some margin from a CCP will provide a modicum of financial protection against such a catastrophe – but it is like insuring your life for £100: your dependants will not find the contribution particularly helpful. The joint regulators of LCH.Clearnet themselves acknowledged the issue of getting the risk measure wrong.[79] It seems perverse that, although there is no consensus as to who should bear the losses when a single CCP defaults,[80] there is a settled view as to how the exposures arising between two CCPs should be covered.

---

79 Joint Regulatory Authorities of LCH.Clearnet Group, *Investigation of risks arising from the emergence of multi-cleared trading platforms* (July 2008), http://www.dnb.nl/binaries/ Investigation%20of%20risks%20arising%20from%20the%20emergence%20of%20multi-cleared%20trading%20platforms_tcm46-216876.pdf, p 9
80 See **sections 17.12ff**

13.25 Default fund contributions should, under the A&I Guideline and the FMI Principles, not be made by one CCP to another. Presumably this is because it is not right for CCPs to provide contributions towards mutualisation of risks outside the CCP's control, though the FMI Principles are not explicit on the point. Non-contribution could, however, leave both CCPs short of financial resources. Supplementary funding may be needed to plug the gap. Yet default backing, rather than margining, might be the more appropriate tool for management of CCP-default risk: it may be that the paying-CCP has in fact collected little or no margin from its own participant, and, because margin is computed to manage a completely different risk from a CCP's default, the amount collected will have no relationship to the size of the loss. EuroCCP has argued that each CCP should augment its own default fund, from contributions by its non-CCP participants, to cover losses in the event of default by the interoperating CCP.[81] An objection to EuroCCP's proposal is that it imposes the financial burden on the participants in the surviving CCP, de-linking the cost from the risk. EuroCCP also argue that a better solution is to establish a super-CCP, which acts as CCP to all the CCPs and reduces the inter-CCP exposure by multilateral netting; while this solution may reduce the exposures, it does not solve the problem of how to quantify and manage the residual counterparty risk. By contrast, EMCF suggested that CCPs should rely on margin, and indeed should follow the 'current practice' of using participants' collateral contributions.[82]

Regulatory views on inter-CCP risk management

13.26 In considering the problem in early 2010, a group of regulators from the United Kingdom, the Netherlands and Switzerland (countries in which three CCPs then seeking to interoperate were domiciled) issued a statement on inter-CCP credit exposures. This statement was presented to the European Commission's Monitoring Group, which had responsibility for oversight of the operation of the Code.[83] In summary, the regulators concluded:

- Inter-CCP credit exposures should be measured, monitored and mitigated with collateral.

- The collateral so provided should be extra collateral – it should not be sourced from the margin contributions made by other participants. It could, for example, be paid for by an increase in the default fund contributions made by other participants or a special levy on participants. (The notion that the cost is borne by the non-defaulting CCP's participants, and that this upsets the normal principle that the introducer of risk should pay the insurance premium or perverse incentives will follow, seems not to have troubled the regulators.)

---

81 European Central Counterparty Ltd, *Recommendations for Reducing Risks Among Interoperating CCPs – A discussion document* (January 2010), http://www.euroccp.co.uk/docs/leadership/EuroCCP_InteroperatingCCPs.pdf
82 European Multilateral Clearing Facility, *Interoperability for CCPs – a way forward* (undated, Spring 2010), http://www.euromcf.nl/images/emcfpositionpaperoninteroperability.pdf
83 For a summary of the statement, see papers submitted to the Monitoring Group: AFM, DNB and FSA, *Interoperability and Regulatory Expectations*, slide presentation, http://ec.europa.eu/internal_market/financial-markets/docs/code/mog/20100315_afm_dnb_fsa_en.pdf, and FESE, EACH & ECSDA, *Joint Status Update of the Code of Conduct* (March 2010), slide presentation, http://ec.europa.eu/internal_market/financial-markets/docs/code/mog/20100315_fese_each_ecsda_en.pdf, p 8

- The collateral so provided should be pre-funded. Standby arrangements would not be acceptable.

- The interoperating CCPs should ensure that their assets do not become trapped in the other CCP in the event of that CCP's failure.

The regulators also drew attention to several other risks faced by interoperating CCPs: in particular operational/technical risks, legal risks, settlement risk and liquidity risk. These risks were also elaborated in a paper on CCP interoperability prepared by the regulatory college then responsible for oversight of the LCH.Clearnet group.[84] The paper points out in particular that the process of registration of contracts (typically novation)[85] by which the CCPs become interposed between buyer and seller may be less reliable when there is a link, for example if the point of irrevocability is differently defined by the two CCPs. It also explains that settlement risk can arise if the buy-in structures at the two CCPs require one CCP to deliver securities which it has not yet received. These are just two examples of the many operational issues which arise in establishing a link: the majority of the points which arise follow from the unusual nature of the link in the chain of transactions where both buyer and seller are CCPs (the inter-CCP contract). Operational and legal issues require compromise by both interoperating CCPs; as with the counterparty risk issues, compromise erodes the integrity of both CCPs' containment of risk. The operating and legal issues thus need to be considered in fuller detail.

Insolvency protection

13.27 To accommodate interoperability, various modifications have been made to the protective legislation designed to block the effect of insolvency laws which might interfere with the management of defaults. In the first place, changes to the SFD were made in order to deal with the following case: if a participant A in system A fails, and participant A had entered a transfer order in favour of a participant B in system B, it should not be possible to challenge the finality of the transfer to participant B on the grounds that participant A had nothing to do with system B.[86]

Secondly, revisions were made to the Part VII Companies Act regime.[87] These changes allowed for inter-CCP transactions to be characterised as 'market contracts' and thereby protected.[88] In addition, the segregation rules were changed in a rather confusing way. Regulation 16 of the Financial Markets and Insolvency Regulations 1991[89] elaborates on when different transactions entered into by the same person should be treated as if they were entered into by different persons: this is to ensure that transactions booked to a GCM's 'client account', and the margin money which supports those transactions, are ring-fenced and not intermingled with losses or margin booked to the GCM's 'house' or 'proprietary' account. The regulation has been amended to cater for

---

84 Joint Regulatory Authorities of LCH.Clearnet Group, *Investigation of risks arising from the emergence of multi-cleared trading platforms* (July 2008), http://www.dnb.nl/binaries/ Investigation%20of%20risks%20arising%20from%20the%20emergence%20of%20multi-cleared%20trading%20platforms_tcm46-216876.pdf
85 See **section 2.3**
86 SFD, art 3(1), as amended
87 Financial Markets and Insolvency Regulations 2009, SI 2009 No 853
88 See **section 8.10**
89 SI 1991 No 880

inter-CCP transactions, and it appears that the intention[90] was to provide that, on default by a CCP which is party to an interoperability arrangement, market contracts entered into by the failed CCP will be treated by the surviving CCP as if they were booked to a 'client account' and not intermingled or set off against other transactions.[91] Unfortunately, the drafting cannot be described as lucid, it is not error-free even if this is the correct interpretation, and the convoluted interplay of the sub-paragraphs leaves it open to other, less helpful, constructions.

OPERATING ISSUES WITH CCP INTEROPERABILITY

13.28   If margin is to be posted between CCPs, it creates operational issues as well as points of principle. The issues on which the interoperating CCPs will need to compromise include eligibility criteria and concentration limits for particular margin types and the timetable for postings. Eligibility criteria differ quite widely between CCPs and product lines. Even cash, which is universally accepted, can be complicated: what currencies are accepted, other than the receiving CCP's home state currency; what limits are imposed; should cash be posted to an account maintained by the CCP at the central bank? Timings can also be troublesome, particularly if the CCPs are in different time-zones and thus have different opening hours, or operate under different holiday schedules, quite apart from the question of grace periods. A CCP which is required to post margin to another CCP out of hours or at times when its liquid resources are low will need to put in place special, possibly expensive, liquidity management arrangements.

13.29   CCPs will need to receive a flow of trade data from the relevant trading venue. Where the venue is already served by a CCP, one possible method for a new CCP aiming to clear the same marketplace is to receive the flow from the incumbent CCP (L-shaped flow) rather than the venue itself (Λ- or inverted-V-shaped flow). L-shaped arrangements are more risky for the new CCP, because they expose it to a range of IT and connectivity risks which do not arise with the Λ-shaped model.

13.30   Settlement of the inter-CCP transactions raises a number of issues where the products cleared are not invariably cash-settled. The settlement issues include similar points to margin as regards timetables and, as noted above, tolerances referable to buy-in schedules. Additionally, the technical arrangements adopted by the interoperating CCPs may differ. Settlement instructions may be routed direct from the trading venue or created by the CCP: in the former case, the instructions need to cope with the extra link in the chain where the trading entities participate in different CCPs; in the latter, which CCP's instructions to the CSD will prevail? Operational practices at CCPs may also allow (or they may not allow) splitting of trades for settlement when a clearing member has only a partial quota of securities available for delivery; they may (or they may not) aggregate and net the participants' obligations before sending settlement

---

90   HM Treasury, *Summary of responses to consultation on amendments to Part 7 of Companies Act 1989* (December 2008), http://www.hm-treasury.gov.uk/d/companiesact1989_responses. pdf, p 10
91   Regulation 16(1A)

instructions to the CSD; and they may (or they may not) use the same systems interface to generate and reconcile settlement information.

13.31 Corporate actions will arise on securities which have passed through the CCPs' hands. Record dates may occur shortly before settlement, with action needing to be taken by the original holder of securities now transferred to one or more buyers. Exceptionally, the record date may occur while one or other of the CCPs is in actual possession of the securities. In any of these cases a decision may be needed as to which CCP owes duties in relation to the corporate action, how any rights or obligations are to be apportioned among buyers of the securities, and what limits there are on the requirement of each CCP to take action.

LEGAL ISSUES WITH CCP INTEROPERABILITY

13.32 The primary legal issue identified by the LCH.Clearnet joint regulators is the risk introduced by different moments of novation or registration at the two CCPs. This would create an imbalance: one CCP might consider that it has a valid pair of trades, one with its participant and the other with the interoperating CCP, whereas the interoperating CCP may consider that the transaction is not yet registered. The point is picked up by the FMI Principles[92] and legislated for (in slightly different ways) in both the Settlement Finality Directive[93] and EMIR.[94] The wider point at issue here is that, in a case of full mutual interoperability, neither CCP can dictate to the other that its own rules are better than the other's, and either a CCP will have to bear the risk of mismatch or change its own procedures wholesale (no doubt to the general disgruntlement of its participants). Related points will derive from the CCPs' respective rules on reconciliation of trade data, criteria for and timing of rejection of trades for registration, and (where the CCP is a designated system for settlement finality purposes) the moment of finality. Perhaps oddly, the ECB-CESR Recommendations state that 'differences between the criteria and timing of finality also creates risks as transfers regarded as final in one system are not necessarily final in the linked CCP.'[95] (This recommendation also features in the FMI Principles,[96] but is not directed specifically to CCPs.) As finality of securities trade settlement is the preserve of CSDs rather than CCPs, this comment is difficult to apply to CCPs clearing cash market transactions, but for CCPs clearing derivatives trades or other cash-settled transactions where netting equates to settlement it is a valid thought.

13.33 The rules of each CCP would be the ordinary starting point for determining how the operating issues should be handled. Each CCP will prefer its own rulebook to apply to the inter-CCP relationship, but this will not usually be possible where there is a conflict between the two CCPs' rules. In practice it may be that the CCPs agree that neither CCP's rulebook will apply, and

---

92 FMI Principles, para 3.20.3
93 SFD, art 3(4)
94 EMIR, art 52(1)
95 European Central Bank and Committee of European Securities Regulators, *Recommendations for Securities Settlement Systems and Recommendations for Central Counterparties in The European Union* (May 2009), http://www.ecb.int/pub/pdf/other/pr090623_escb-cesr_recommendationsen.pdf, Recommendation 11 for CCPs, para C5
96 FMI Principles, para 3.20.3

instead a bespoke set of arrangements will be created to achieve interoperability without the wholesale overhaul of either CCP's rules and procedures vis-à-vis all participants. If a CCP admits a third party to participate in its system, but that person is not bound but the CCP's rules, there is a question whether that might affect the ability of the CCP to rely on the protective settlement finality and market protection legislation:[97] article 2(a) of the SFD requires a system to have 'common rules', and the protective legislation in Part VII of the Companies Act 1989 hinges on the application of 'default rules', which are 'rules of a ... recognised clearing house which provide for the taking of action in the event of a person appearing to be unable ... to meet his obligations ... .'[98] Interoperating CCPs will need to take care not to abandon completely the idea that 'rules' apply to each other, even if special processes need to be put in place. The ECB-CESR Recommendations also mention the possibility that the interoperating CCP's rules, contracts and procedures may no longer be enforceable on the default or insolvency of a participant (which presumably includes the other CCP).[99]

13.34 CCPs will typically have powers to suspend registration and to take other action (including making emergency rule-changes) in the event of market disruption or other internal or external events which make it desirable for the CCP to take self-preservatory steps. Suspension by one, but not both, CCPs, can lead to mismatch; and any other self-preservatory steps could disrupt the interoperating CCP because of their effect on the inter-CCP contracts. Furthermore, if a CCP wished to change its rules in an act of self-preservation, and the inter-CCP contract is outside the scope of the rule changes, special arrangements between the CCPs may be needed to facilitate rapid modification of the inter-CCP obligations.

13.35 Liability is an extremely delicate topic. CCPs almost invariably exclude liability for everything in their dealings with their participants, and take indemnities from them.[100] The converse is demanded in an interoperability arrangement: that CCPs accept some degree of liability to each other. But where to draw the line is challenging. Clearly each CCP should be obliged, without exclusions, to perform its inter-CCP contract obligations. But even that simple proposition does not withstand close scrutiny, because a CCP can argue that consequential or indirect losses, or losses reasonably foreseeable in the peculiar circumstances of an inter-CCP contract which is not being performed, ought not to be passed between CCPs. Other obligations of CCPs might withstand a mutual exclusion of liability, but then the question will arise 'what binds CCPs to comply with their contract if they have agreed that no liability follows from its breach?'

MULTIPLE INTEROPERATING CCPS

13.36 The FMI Principles urge extra caution where more than two CCPs are interoperating.[101] Certainly the problems listed above will become even

---

97 See **sections 8.10–8.23**

98 Companies Act 1989, s 188(1)

99 ECB-CESR Recommendation 11 for CCPs (June 2009), para C4

100 See, for example, LCH.Clearnet Limited, General Regulation 39; Eurex Clearing AG, Clearing Conditions number 1.9; European Central Counterparty Ltd, Rule 24; European Multilateral Clearing Facility, Clearing Rulebook art 8.5

101 FMI Principle 20, Key consideration 7

more complicated. Quite apart from the number of bilateral interoperability agreements needed (EuroCCP has pointed out that the number of agreements needed for n interoperating CCPs is $(n - 1) + (n - 2) + (n - 3) + ... + (n - n)$),[102] the difficulties of achieving compromise between two players will scale up proportionately when a third and a fourth CCP seek to come into the same marketplace.

INTEROPERABILITY OF DERIVATIVES CCPs

13.37 Title V of EMIR is limited to CCPs providing clearing services in relation to transferable securities and money market instruments.[103] This means that interoperability is not legislated for in relation to OTC derivatives clearing, despite (a) OTC derivatives clearing being a main rationale for the adoption of this legislation and (b) the likely need for transatlantic links (and other links to and from the European Union) owing to the slightly differing clearing requirements under the various items of legislation mandating OTC derivatives clearing.

13.38 It may be that interoperability is harder for OTC derivatives CCPs than for cash securities CCPs. The following points can be put forward in support of interoperability of OTC derivatives CCPs:

(1) The operational difficulties discussed in relation to securities should not arise.

(2) The demand for collateral which is a side-effect of OTC clearing would be mitigated, improving market liquidity conditions, provided that the additional risk introduced by the link did not swamp the netting benefit of increased clearing levels.[104]

(3) If party A, who participates in CCP1, enters into a transaction with party B, who participates in CCP2, in the absence of interoperability between the CCPs it may be necessary for A or B to seek to participate in the other CCP, or employ a GCM, either of which would involve extra cost. Market pressure may build to force some interoperation of CCPs, at least as regards fungible products.

On the other hand, the following points might be mentioned:

(4) The inter-CCP margin requirements may be very large, and the need to fund these margin payments independently of margin collected from participants[105] would render interoperability economically unviable.

(5) Another difficulty with interoperation of derivatives CCPs is product fungibility. Derivatives CCPs need to be very careful how they select products for clearing.[106] Because OTC products do not emanate from an

---

102 European Central Counterparty Ltd, *Reducing Risks Among Interoperating CCPs* (January 2010), slide presentation, http://www.euroccp.co.uk/docs/leadership/EuroCCP_ Interoperability_Reducing_Risks.pdf, p 18

103 EMIR, art 1(3)

104 Bank for International Settlements Committee on the Global Financial System, *The macrofinancial implications of alternative configurations for access to central counterparties in OTC derivatives markets* (November 2011), http://www.bis.org/publ/cgfs46.pdf, p 17

105 FMI Principles, para 3.20.16; see **section 13.21(3)**

106 See **sections 14.16–14.18**

exchange or other trading platform, there is no guarantee that a product accepted for clearing by CCP1 is fungible with a product cleared by CCP2.

(6) Transatlantic interoperable clearing may be harder than European interoperable clearing owing to differences in the risk management and regulatory regimes applicable to CCPs in different continents. Interoperating CCPs must take special care to manage the risk of CCP default, which involves novel and complex analysis. Regulatory approval of a transatlantic link is likely to be slower to achieve than for intra-EU cross-border link.

13.39 Official statements give guarded support for interoperability of OTC derivatives CCPs.[107] A variety of interoperability options for exchange-traded derivatives was discussed by the European Central Bank in a paper from 2002,[108] and revived in an IMF paper from 2010.[109] In particular, cross-margining[110] seems to find favour as a potential route towards interoperability. Full mutual interoperability is noted to be designed 'to promote competition among marketplaces,'[111] whereas cross-margining might provide benefits where this kind of full interoperability is unnecessary, or difficult to achieve. One possible benefit would be to reduce the inefficiency that participation in multiple CCPs creates for use of collateral. Cross-margining approaches could, for example, have the effect that one CCP acts as collateral agent for the other CCP as well as taking margin on its own account, so that a single aggregate net margin call could be made, and the need to transfer margin from CCP1 to CCP2 would be eliminated. However, it may also be noted that cross-margining has been used in the futures clearing space because of a natural symmetry: where a product is traded in two different markets, traders wishing to arbitrage between the markets will typically be long in one while they are short in another, so that margin calls at two CCPs will naturally offset. It is less clear that such logic would apply to OTC derivatives clearing.

INTEROPERABILITY OF CSDs

13.40 Interoperability between CSDs is different from interoperability between CCPs. This is because securities have a 'home' CSD – the CSD which provides the root of title[112], and referred to in the literature as the 'Issuer CSD' – and any user selecting a CSD other than the 'home' or 'root' CSD will need, ultimately, to connect through to it. Interoperability between CSDs has the purpose of facilitating this type of selection.

---

107 CGFS paper 46, s 3.3
108 Russo, D, Hart, T, and Schönenberger, A, *The Evolution of Clearing and Central Counterparty Services for Exchange-Traded Derivatives in the United States and Europe: a Comparison* (September 2002), ECB Occasional Paper No 5, http://www.ecb.eu/pub/pdf/scpops/ecbocp5.pdf
109 Kiff, J, et al, 'Making Over-the-counter Derivatives Safer: The role of Central Counterparties',in IMF, *Global Financial Stability Report* (April 2010), http://www.imf.org/external/pubs/ft/gfsr/2011/01/pdf/text.pdf, ch 3
110 See **section 13.18(4)**
111 IMF paper, p 24
112 See **section 2.17**

Regulation and competition

13.41 Unlike CCPs, it is impossible for competing CSDs to provide true equivalence of service, precisely because the Issuer CSD provides an essential function which no other CSD can match. As described in **section 2.16**, CSDs have two key roles: to keep the ultimate (root) record of entitlement to securities, and to provide a settlement engine which effects transfers between the accounts of persons entitled to securities.

- As to the root of title function, investors have no choice. The ultimate title to the securities in which they are investing is inherent in the security itself. The root of title is not a matter of 'choice' for the investor: to say that you bought a share in a French company but you really wish that it was the same company, but German, is to wish for the moon to be painted blue. But there *can* be choice in this matter: the issuer of the securities could, in theory, select the German root of title system rather than the French, if this is permitted by the company law of the issuer's country. But until the full roll-out of a European practice under the proposed CSD Regulation, this type of choice will remain purely theoretical.

- It is different as regards the settlement function. Whether or not a CSD has outsourced its settlement engine functionality to T2S, it is possible for a non-Issuer CSD (referred to in the literature as an 'Investor CSD') to offer to act in a quasi-custody role,[113] holding a pool of securities at the Issuer CSD and then offering, as between its participants, a settlement service purely dependent on the functionality and efficiency of its own settlement service offering. That does introduce an element of choice for investors. Some investors may, of course, choose a different CSD – possibly the Issuer CSD, or even a different Investor CSD – which means that there needs to be some means of supporting cross-system settlements. It is these scenarios which give rise to the need for CSD interoperability.

13.42 The purpose of competition between CSDs should therefore be explained. It is not possible, just because there is interoperability, for an investor to choose to use CSD2 in preference to CSD1 as a device to cut costs. This is true even if CSD2's prices are a fraction of those of CSD1. Transactions in a given security must always (subject to internalised settlement, which is fortuitous[114]) settle across the books of the Issuer CSD. If the Issuer CSD is bound to be involved, the involvement of a second CSD is bound to add a layer of *extra* cost. Competition may, in the long run, reduce CSD costs, but this would appear to require one of two things happen: a single, cheap, Investor CSD scoops the entirety of the Issuer CSD's clientèle and internalises the entire settlement flow relating to the Issuer CSD's securities; or an Investor CSD absorbs the costs of the Issuer CSD as part of its own pricing programme – essentially offering a loss-leader service for securities domiciled at expensive Issuer CSDs.

13.43 At this point a few comments may be made about competition and dependency. Where both investors participate in an Investor CSD, the selection of

---

113 See, for example, European Commission, *Clearing and Settlement in the European Union – The way forward* (April 2004), http://eur-lex.europa.eu/LexUriServ/LexUriServ.do?uri=COM :2004:0312:FIN:EN:PDF, p 5
114 See **section 2.21**

the Investor CSD may be done for operational convenience – typically to enable the investors to use their 'local' CSD, with whose operational and connectivity requirements they will be familiar, for holding title to and transferring 'foreign' securities. Simplification of this type is to be commended, but it can be achieved in other ways (notably via T2S[115] or Link Up Markets, discussed below, or by using an agent bank); and where an Investor CSD is employed, the investors are taking custody risk on the Investor CSD, but without excising the Issuer CSD from the chain because it retains its fundamental role as holder of the root of title. Where a party to a trade participates in an Investor CSD, the dependency on the Issuer CSD is not eliminated: if the trade counterparty participates in the Issuer CSD, there must be a title transfer at that level, so the settlement engine of the Issuer CSD is being used notwithstanding one investor's choice of Investor CSD. If both investors participate in different Investor CSDs, the Investor CSDs are merely passive recipients of settlement instructions which are passed on to the Issuer CSD – they are functionally carrying out the role of agent banks.

Dual listing has been an important reason for creating links between CSDs. Owing to the want of technical interoperability – incompatible systems, communications, data requirements and so forth – it is easier for traders and their service providers using a particular stock exchange to plug into the local post-trade infrastructure built to serve that exchange, even where the security being bought or sold is not a local security for which the infrastructure was designed. This shifts the problem of connectivity and technical inter-operation to the Investor CSD to solve. Many inter-CSD links were developed to enable dually-listed securities to be conveniently settled. Competition was involved – but competition between trading platforms, and this type of link between CSDs was not about a 'choice' of settlement venue. Traders and their service providers have, through the absence of technical interoperability, historically been denied a real choice owing to the costs of switching to settlement in a different CSD.

Link up Markets

13.44   Connectivity and technical interoperation can be viewed as an exercise in 'translation' between the language used by one CSD for data requirements and formats, timetables and other operational matters, and that used by another CSD. A central translation engine could, in theory, take the text used for settlement in one market and modify it so as to be comprehensible and effective in another. This is the idea developed by Link up Markets to facilitate cross-border settlement of transactions. No structural interoperability is needed between CSDs if CSD participants are able to use Link up Markets to connect to a foreign CSD; nor is any technical interoperability, since Link up Markets exists only because of the absence of a lingua franca for settlement.[116] Whether there is a need for a translation engine after Target2-Securities becomes live remains to be seen.

---

115   See **section 2.22**

116   For information, see Link up Markets, slide presentation (May 2010), http://www. linkupmarkets.com/pdf/LinkUpMarkets_May2010.pdf

The settlement function

13.45 The principal function of a CSD apart from its root of title function is to provide for settlement. Despite the inescapable fact that an Issuer CSD holds the root of title and an Investor CSD does not, it is possible to devise an interoperable system between the two CSDs for settlement of securities transactions. Interoperability will thereby allow a participant in the Investor CSD to settle transactions in securities for which the Issuer CSD is the root CSD without the need to open an account at the Issuer CSD. Both CSDs could be Investor CSDs for the securities for which the other CSD is the Issuer CSD – providing reciprocal interoperability, if not fully mutual interoperability as between CCPs.

CONCLUSIONS ON INTEROPERABILITY AND COMPETITION BETWEEN CSDs

13.46 The following conclusions might be stated.[117]

(1) True horizontal interoperability among CSDs for their root-of-title functionality is, if not impossible, very difficult to achieve. Although issuers will be permitted by the proposed CSD Regulation to have dually rooted securities, there will be formidable challenges. The example of the ICSDs may be followed.[118] But the fundamental dichotomy between a central root of title (connoting a single guardian of integrity of the issue) and competition between providers of that service is likely to be too difficult to resolve, at least in the first few years of operation of the CSD Regulation.[119]

(2) Interoperability in relation to the root-of-title function can thus be ruled out, in relation to a single issue of securities. There is, however, no theoretical or practical objection to competition between CSDs seeking to provide the root-of-title function for *different* securities issues in the same market-place. If securities of series A are held at CSD1 and securities of series B at CSD2, there is no need for interoperability between the two CSDs. They need to be linked to the relevant trading platforms and CCPs, but those are vertical links rather than 'interoperable' links as discussed in this chapter.

(3) Mutual participation by CSDs is a form of interoperability which may bring about a degree of 'competition' between CSDs. This will be competition for the settlement function. However, it will not constitute horizontal interoperability in the manner of competition between CCPs, but vertical competition: a CSD which cannot provide the root of title, but which offers a settlement service, is an Investor CSD providing 'internalised' settlement, akin to that potentially offered by an agent bank,[120] or an access service to facilitate settlement which takes place on the books of the Issuer CSD. These services take the Investor CSD into another marketplace, namely that occupied by agent banks, even though Investor CSDs may be given privileges not available to non-CSDs, such as a statutory right to open an

---

117 See also **section 7.6**
118 See **section 2.24**
119 Cf **section 10.25**
120 See **section 2.21**

account.[121] In theory, a highly successful internaliser (Investor CSD) might capture all the settlement activity for a given issue onto its own books, and reduce the role of the Issuer CSD to a cipher; but whether that can happen in practice will depend on the pricing arrangements of the two CSDs.

Settlement between linked CSDs

(1) Investors both participate in an Investor CSD

(2) One Investor only participates in Investor CSD

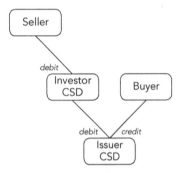

(3) Investors each participate in different Investor CSD

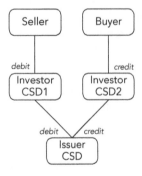

Fig 13.3

---

121 Cf section 7.26

DvP IN INTEROPERABLE CSDs

13.47 Structural interoperability between CSDs – where the buyer is a participant in one CSD, and the seller a participant in another – requires that the settlement engines of the two CSDs are coupled together. To express the problem differently, links between CSDs require a solution to the DvP problem – how to ensure, for both participants, that there is simultaneous delivery and payment, when there are two infrastructures occupying the space between them. The ECB-CESR Recommendations state, in respect of links between CSDs, that 'DvP should be achieved. CSDs should achieve DvP for links that process transactions against cash. The length of the settlement cycle and the achievement of DvP with intraday finality should not be jeopardised by the establishment of a link.'[122]

The problem is this: each delivery versus payment transaction involving a single CSD requires four accounting entries to take place simultaneously: the seller's securities account is to be debited at the moment that seller's cash account is credited, while the buyer's cash account is debited at the moment that the buyer's securities account is credited. Tying up the payment and securities settlement systems is complicated enough, but solved technologically in most European countries. When you introduce two CSDs into the picture, and accept that one of the CSDs must hold the root of title to all securities (ie, one CSD must act as Issuer CSD) so that the other CSD is no different from an agent bank in the eyes of the Issuer CSD, the number of book entries to occur simultaneously has been increased: the Investor CSD's accounts at the Issuer CSD are also involved, so there must be at least a debit (if the seller is a participant in the Investor CSD) or a credit (if the buyer is a participant in the Investor CSD) to the Investor CSD's account, and countervailing credit/debit entries to a cash account held somewhere in the Investor CSD's name.

The first point to note from this is that the Investor CSD, if acting as an agent bank, would ordinarily need to hold a cash account. Vanilla CSD functions do not necessarily require a CSD to hold cash for the purposes of settlement. Indeed CSDs can and generally will run securities settlement on their own books in parallel with cash settlement across the books of a central or commercial bank: DvP is a question of linking these systems up to achieve simultaneity of settlement.[123] The accounts at the central bank would ordinarily be in the names of the CSD participants (or their settlement agents) – there is no need for the CSD itself to handle any cash. But to achieve structural interoperability, Investor CSDs may need to have cash – they cannot buy securities on behalf of their participants if they do not have cash, because the Issuer CSD could not transfer securities to the Investor CSD without a cash payment from the Investor CSD. Of course, the Investor CSD will obtain the cash by getting it from the buyer of the securities. But why would the buyer, who wants DvP – that is, not to take settlement risk – advance cash to the Investor CSD? To do so would violate the central principle of DvP, which is that transfer of title should be simultaneous with transfer of money, not behind it.

This central principle is reinforced by the proposed CSD Regulation.[124] This will require that any interoperable CSDs using a common settlement infrastructure

---

122 Recommendation 19 for CSDs, para B2
123 FMI Principles, para 3.12.2
124 Article 45(8)

must establish identical moments of finality of transfers of securities and cash. Where buyer and seller participate in different CSDs using T2S, it is therefore not to be allowed for seller to part with her securities before she is paid, or for buyer to part with his cash before he receives the securities with finality. There are two possible answers to this conundrum. The first is for cash liquidity to be made available to support a CSD link; the second is to rely on a cash bypass.

(1) *Cash liquidity.* The cash leg of the DvP can be addressed if the Investor CSD is allowed credit by the Issuer CSD, or maintains its own cash account using its own funds, or requires its participants to grant the Issuer CSD access to their cash accounts.[125] Each of these mechanisms has the drawback that one CSD is taking credit risk on another, or on the other's participants. The ECB-CESR Recommendations prescribe that 'credit extensions between CSDs should be fully secured by securities, letters of credit, other high-quality collateral or other means that ensure the same level of protection and should be subject to limits.'[126] This option may, however, be achievable where a CSD is itself a bank. As a bank, an Investor CSD can offer a bank account to an Issuer CSD. So, if the Investor CSD has a participant acting as buyer, the Issuer CSD can transfer securities to the Investor CSD's account against a credit to its bank account with the Investor CSD. This involves the Issuer CSD taking credit risk on the Investor CSD; as the Investor CSD is a bank, this might be acceptable; but for the Issuer CSD it is 'settlement in commercial bank money,' which is not the preferred arrangement according to the ECB-CESR Recommendations.[127] This option may not be consistent with the proposed CSD Regulation unless both transfers are so close in time as to be indistinguishable, because buyer and seller do not receive simultaneous DvP, and one of them is forced for a short time to take credit risk on a CSD.

(2) *Cash bypass.* If the CSDs share a settlement engine, associated functionality may be able to identify that a particular transaction is to be settled across CSDs. This may enable a direct cash payment between the buyer and the seller without the need for an Investor-CSD cash account. Using an example where the seller participates in the Issuer CSD: instead of the expected account entries, there would be a debit of the seller's securities account; a credit to the Investor CSD's securities account, and a credit to the buyer's securities account, all occurring simultaneously, and at the same time as a debit to the buyer's cash account and a credit to the seller's cash account. This option may be achievable in T2S.

13.48 A final word may be appropriate on cash accounts and CSDs. Article 15(1)(d) of the T2S Guideline[128] requires CSDs in T2S to offer a basic custody service to other participating CSDs. No detail is given as to what is comprised in a basic custody service, either in the T2S Guideline itself or in the ECB's

---

125 ECSDA, *Cross-border Clearing and Settlement through CSD Links* (October 2006), https://www.ecsda.com/attachments/working_groups/settlement_links_%28wg3%29/WG3%20 report%20Vs.%201-0.pdf, p 48
126 ECB-CESR Recommendation 19 for CSDs, para C6
127 ECB-CESR Recommendation 10 for CSDs
128 ECB, Guideline of the European Central Bank of 21 April 2010 on TARGET2-Securities (ECB/2010/2), http://www.ecb.eu/ecb/legal/pdf/en_gui_ecb_2010_2_f_sign.pdf?d273a26be9 382d3edeecc848515a410d

Cash bypass for DvP in interoperating CSDs

(1) Traditional situation: intermediary is agent bank

(2) Cash bypass: intermediary is a CSD with no cash account

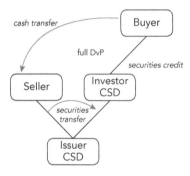

Fig 13.4

more elaborate Decision on eligibility criteria for CSDs.[129] However, providing a custody service without an accompanying cash account is difficult to imagine: dividend and other cash payments will pass through a custodian's hands, so it would appear that a CSD complying with the T2S Guideline would need to have the capability of providing cash accounts. This may lead to the CSD acquiring the ability to offer DvP on one of ECSDA's models, described below, if T2S itself does not support the cash bypass model.

ECSDA models of cross-CSD DvP

13.49 There is only limited regulatory guidance on interoperability between CSDs in Recommendation 19 of the ECB-CESR Recommendations.[130] Likewise, the A&I Guideline says little about CSD-to-CSD interoperability, citing a number of technical issues (cut-off times, synchronicity, contingency

---

129 Decision of the European Central Bank of 16 November 2011 establishing detailed rules and procedures for implementing the eligibility criteria for central securities depositories to access TARGET2-Securities services (ECB/2011/20), OJ L 319/117
130 Recommendation 19 for CSDs

plans, etc) to be overcome.[131] But it does not prescribe requirements or propose solutions. These are left to the European Central Securities Depositories Association (ECSDA). Two models have been developed by ECSDA to facilitate DvP in the context of a link, with different implications for liquidity and credit.[132]

(1) In the 'Issuer CSD' model, the Issuer CSD controls the moment of settlement.

If the Issuer CSD's participant is buying, there is no real problem: the settlement will not proceed until the buyer is ready with the cash and the seller is ready with the securities. The seller is (as far as the Issuer CSD is concerned) the Investor CSD, and the Issuer CSD can segregate/identify (or 'earmark' or 'block') the securities to be sold so that DvP can happen immediately upon that cash being ready in the buyer's cash account at the central bank. As far as the Investor CSD is concerned, it needs to debit the seller's securities account immediately on having its own account debited at the Issuer CSD level. That leaves the cash leg at the seller's account to be tied up, either through direct credit, or a credit to the Investor CSD's cash account at the central or commercial bank it uses for payments, or even (where the Investor CSD is a bank using the first option described above) by the Investor CSD making a debit entry to the Issuer CSD's account on its own books while it makes a credit entry to the seller's cash account. As the cash is coming in, the Investor CSD can time the DvP on its own books so as to follow instantly upon the movements it sees in its own cash and securities accounts.

However, if the Issuer CSD's participant is selling, things are more complicated. The Issuer CSD will not transfer the securities to the Investor CSD's account until it can simultaneously transfer cash to the seller, and until there is cash in the Investor CSD's cash account nothing will happen. But the Investor CSD needs to offer DvP to its buyer participant. In order to decide whether chicken or egg will happen first, the Investor CSD needs to have a liquidity arrangement to ensure its cash account is credited, then the settlement can occur on a DvP basis at the Issuer CSD and, finally, hard on the heels of that DvP, the Investor CSD can credit the securities to the buyer, take the buyer's cash, and replenish its own cash resources. In practice, this will work if the Investor CSD has funds of its own, or its settlement bank is willing to extend the Investor CSD intra-day credit. To grant intra-day credit is a reasonable risk as the Investor CSD should finish each day with a net zero cash position, having no personal interest in any of the trades settling: danger only arises if the Investor CSD allows trades to proceed to settlement where its buyer participant will not pay. ECSDA suggests that pre-funding will only be needed if a settlement is due to take place overnight, which implies that intra-day credit is the norm.[133]

(2) The alternative to the Issuer CSD model is the 'Buyer CSD' model. In this case, which appears to be used by few, if any CSD links,[134] the buyer's CSD controls the moment of settlement. If the buyer participates in the Issuer CSD

---

131 FESE, EACH and ECSDA, *Access and Interoperability Guideline* (June 2007), http://ec.europa.eu/internal_market/financial-markets/docs/code/guideline_en.pdf, para 102
132 ECSDA links paper, p 34
133 ECSDA links paper, pp 48–49
134 ECSDA links paper, p 34

ECSDA Models of DvP

(1) Issuer CSD model

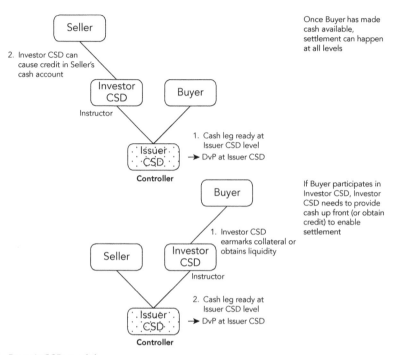

Once Buyer has made cash available, settlement can happen at all levels

If Buyer participates in Investor CSD, Investor CSD needs to provide cash up front (or obtain credit) to enable settlement

(2) Buyer's CSD model

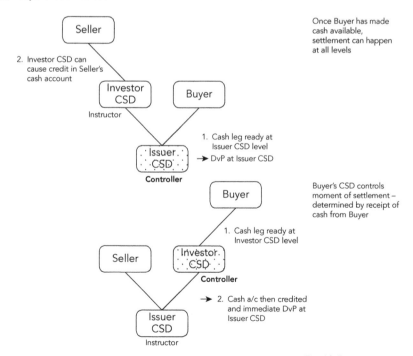

Once Buyer has made cash available, settlement can happen at all levels

Buyer's CSD controls moment of settlement – determined by receipt of cash from Buyer

Fig 13.5

the arrangements are the same as for the Issuer CSD model. If the buyer participates in the Investor CSD, though, the Investor CSD can call for settlement across the books of the Issuer CSD at any time if it is a bank or has a liquidity facility with its settlement bank, and the transfer of securities will be made to the account of the Investor CSD even if the Investor CSD's buyer participant is not yet ready to settle. This approach decouples the settlements at Issuer and Investor CSD levels, with the Investor CSD taking a position in the instrument being settled. To address the credit issue the Investor CSD can pledge the securities received to cover its overdraft. To have to take a position might seem unattractive for the Investor CSD, which probably explains why the model has not proved popular.

Other intermediary issues

13.50 Because a CSD which takes on the role of Investor CSD is acting as intermediary, in a quasi-custody role, the issues which such a CSD must confront will be similar to those faced by agent banks and which are discussed in **Chapter 18**. Among the most important are the following:

(1) *Omnibus account risk.* As explained in **section 18.15(3)**, an account provider who holds the securities for which it is responsible to its account-holders in an omnibus account (such as an Investor CSD holding foreign securities for its own participants at an Issuer CSD) may face the risk that a settlement system (the Issuer CSD) will identify securities in the omnibus account as available to satisfy the Investor CSD's settlement obligations, without regard to the identity of the client (participant) to whom they in fact belong. The settlement system may thus unwittingly use the 'wrong' securities to effect settlement, leaving the account provider (Investor CSD) with a shortfall which it must rectify. This problem is referred to in the ECSDA Links paper as 'borrowing from the pool'. Borrowing from the pool is disallowed under the FMI Principles.[135] The solution is to adopt a 'settlement control mechanism'[136] to prevent instructions for settlement being submitted to the Issuer CSD before the Investor CSD has been supplied with the securities for the account of the selling participant.

(2) *Corporate actions.* A CSD acting as custodian would need to process corporate actions as if it were an agent bank. CSDs may not offer full-service corporate actions services.[137]

(3) *Fees.* A CSD acting as intermediary will wish to charge a fee for its pains. This cannot realistically be done at the expense of the Issuer CSD, so, if the principles of fee separation outlined in article 31(1) of the proposed CSD Regulation and the Code of Conduct[138] are to be followed, it should ordinarily be the case that use of a CSD link entails greater cost than direct participation in an Issuer CSD. That 'ordinary case' might prove to be wrong where both CSDs' fee tariffs are volume-based, so that a participant can get a cheaper rate by concentrating its business in an Investor CSD

---

135 FMI Principles, para 3.20.7
136 ECSDA links paper, p 20
137 European Central Securities Depositories Association, *Issuer Services*, Report (January 2008), http://www.ecsda.eu/site/uploads/tx_doclibrary/2008_01_ECSDA_Issuer_Services_Report.pdf
138 See **section 7.18**

than from multiple Issuer-CSD participations, or where the technical costs of set-up for multiple Issuer-CSD participations outweigh the savings from disintermediation.

(4) *Contractual matters.* CSDs entering into links are invited to sign up to standardised contracts prepared by ECSDA.[139] Given that interoperating CSDs must accept a degree of counterparty risk in dealing with each other, many of the issues discussed above in relation to interoperating CCPs will also be relevant; for example, liability, rules, suspension of operations, etc. In particular, the point made in relation to CCPs – that infrastructures classically reject the notion of liability, which leads to a stand-off in a link arrangement – needs careful thought. The ECSDA model agreements include provisions addressing force majeure and liability as well as a number of technical issues; inter-CCP liability is sidestepped by envisaging that the Issuer CSD's 'general rules and business conditions ... (including, without limitation, liability arrangements) shall be applicable.'[140] Presumably if the link is reciprocal the principle applies in either direction. The solution adopted by ECSDA on liability neatly illustrates a vital difference between CSD links and CCP links: the Issuer CSD is at the head of the title chain and will always dominate the relationship as regards the securities for which it is ultimate keeper of title; CCPs are, where adopting full mutual interoperability, in a partnership of equals.

Operational issues with CSD links

13.51 Finally, mention should be made of two operational issues which interoperating CSDs are likely to have to consider.

(1) *Matching and reconciliation.* The data flow from trading platforms or CCPs which generates settlement instructions needs to be handled carefully. If the flow is routed through one CSD to the other, that creates a dependency on the CSD which initially receives the data. If the data arrive at the two CSDs separately, that creates a need for reconciliation. Either way, there is risk for participants, who 'should be informed of the risks they are assuming.'[141]

(2) *Role of the CCP.* Settlement instructions may be sent direct from the trading platform or its participants, or they may come from a CCP. If they come from a CCP they may be net or gross; the fact that CCPs carry out multilateral netting does not always mean that the CCP sends net settlement instructions, so that it is possible for CCPs to delegate netting for settlement purposes to the CCP.[142] One of the linked CSDs may be set up to handle gross settlement instructions and the other net; this will complicate the link and the reconciliation process. On the other hand, as ECSDA points out, where a single CCP is used as the clearing house for trades by participants in both CSDs, it is possible for the CSDs to eliminate the risk they would otherwise take on each other: this is because the CCP

---

139 European Central Securities Depositories Association, *Model Agreements* (March 2001), https://www.ecsda.com/portal/working_groups/public_policy_%28wg_2%29/model_agreements/
140 Model Agreement between European Central Securities Depositories, art 8
141 ECB-CESR Recommendation 19 for CSDs, para C7
142 ECSDA links paper, para 4.2.3

can maintain accounts in both CSDs, and carry out a free-of-payment transfer between the CSDs without compromising the quality of DvP in either CSD.[143]

PAYMENT SYSTEMS

13.52 Where payment systems such as ACHs interoperate, this is to enable a participant in system 1 to make a payment to a participant of system 2. If the ACHs join each other's systems as participants, the pay-out from system 1 can constitute a pay-in to system 2, and the objectives of the ultimate payer and payee will be achieved.[144] From this very short description, the following conclusions can be drawn: first, that the type of interoperability experienced by payment systems is horizontal and mutual, unlike with CSDs (because the problem of hierarchy attributable to the 'root of title' to securities is absent); secondly, that ACHs will take risk on each other in the same way that they assume risk to their participants; and thirdly, that many of the risk and other issues previously identified in this chapter will be as relevant to payment systems as they are to other types of infrastructure.

These features make the study of payment system interoperability more similar to that of CCPs interoperating than CSDs. But some distinguishing factors should be noted at the outset:

(1) CCPs manage counterparty risk during the pre-settlement period, which means that they are exposed to their participants (and an interoperating CCP) for an extended time, requiring margin and more elaborate default-management processes. Also, because CCPs are responsible for contractual performance, they have a much wider range of obligations to each other when they interoperate, driven by the characteristics of the transactions being cleared. Payment systems may not need these features, and consequently interoperation may be simpler.

(2) Payment systems may aim to avoid taking risk on their participants; instead the participants take risk on each other, albeit in a form dictated by the rules of the system.[145] Accordingly, the credit and liquidity risks which a system operator can avoid – by having them assumed by the participants – in a case where it is operating alone have to be confronted head-on when the operator, or the system itself, is becoming a participant in another system.

13.53 There is little literature on competition between payment systems, suggesting that competition may not be the driving force behind interoperability in this sector. There are various reasons for this. Until the development of the single European currency, there was no need for payment systems to establish links in order to compete with each other for business. Within a single country different payment systems developed for particular purposes; settlement of payment transactions would take place ultimately across the books of the country's central bank or selected commercial banks. Competing systems attempting to win the same business were rare.

---

143 ECSDA links paper, para 4.2.5.1
144 Cf Kokkola, T, ed, *The Payment System* (European Central Bank, September 2010), ISBN 978-92-899-0632-6, Chart 29
145 See **section 2.27**

The eurozone has in theory brought competition into the marketplace as payment systems doing economically equivalent functions could extend their offering into other countries. Such development has, however, been hampered by the diversity of standards for payment instruments such as credit transfers and direct debits: until the adoption of the SEPA schemes and their uniform payment methodologies there was really no need for pan-European payment systems. The two main regulatory pronouncements – a set of Oversight Expectations from the ECB,[146] and a self-regulatory initiative from the trade association (EACHA) representing ACHs[147] – post-date SEPA. As is common in SEPA documentation, the acronym 'CSM' (clearing and settlement mechanism) is used to refer to payment systems – and thus to distinguish them from payment 'schemes' – in all the relevant European standards.

The European Payments Council has also issued a 'PE-ACH/CSM Framework',[148] which sets out the minimum standards which CSMs must adhere to in order to be regarded as SEPA-compliant. The framework specifies goals rather than technical standards, and does not give recommendations on management of risk issues arising from interoperability arrangements.

Finally, the ECB issued 'Terms of Reference' for SEPA-compliance of infrastructures[149] which include two relevant criteria:

'Criterion 2 – Interoperability. To promote the SEPA-compliance of infrastructures, infrastructures are asked to adopt interoperability rules, i.e. interface specifications and business procedures for the exchange of SEPA credit transfers and SEPA direct debit payment orders between banks and infrastructures, and between infrastructures, that are preferably mutually agreed upon by the relevant CSMs, and undertake to establish a link with any other infrastructure upon request, based on the principle that the cost for establishing the link is borne by the requesting infrastructure.

'Criterion 3 – Reachability. To promote the SEPA-compliance of infrastructures, infrastructures are asked to be able to send or receive euro payments to and from all banks in the euro area, either directly or indirectly through intermediary banks, or through links between infrastructures (in other words, to provide full reachability).'

Reachability and the SEPA Regulation

13.54 SEPA has brought the development of pan-European clearing and settlement systems for payments, and in particular the concept of 'reachability'. A payer participating in a payment scheme in its home country may need to reach a payee participating in another scheme in another country, and if the payer's local payment scheme is limited in its geographical scope, the objective of reachability requires arrangements between the systems so that the payment

---

146 ECB, *Oversight Expectations for Links between Retail Payment Systems* (March 2012), http://www.ecb.eu/pub/pdf/other/eurosystemconsultation-oversightexpectations-rps-linken.pdf

147 European Automated Clearing House Association. *EACHA Interoperability Framework 5.0* (May 2010), http://www.eacha.org/downloads/EACHA_Framework_5_0.pdf

148 European Payments Council, *PE-ACH/CSM Framework v1.2* (June 2008), http://www.europeanpaymentscouncil.eu/documents/EPC170-05%20v1%202%20CSM%20Framework%20approved.pdf; see **section 6.15**

149 ECB, *Terms of reference for the SEPA-compliance of infrastructures* (April 2008), http://www.ecb.eu/paym/sepa/about/compliance/html/tor.en.html

can get through. Indeed, the SEPA Regulation[150] stipulates that a payee's payment service provider which is 'reachable' for a national credit transfer must be reachable for credit transfers initiated by a payer through a payment service provider located in any Member State, and also makes a similar rule for direct debit transfers. Attaining reachability has been a more important driver of interoperability of payment systems in Europe than competition theory. Thus, the EACHA Interoperability Framework specifies as its first goal 'creating reach in SEPA'. EACHA also explains that there are two sub-species of reachability:

(1) As to payment service providers, there is a need for a 'reachability directory' which works like the 'get directions' function on an electronic map, enabling a payer who needs to reach a payee to choose a route for this purpose. One such directory is provided by SWIFT.[151]

(2) As regards payment systems, there is a 'reach table' annexed to the EACHA Interoperability Framework which specifies the payment service providers which a particular payment system can reach, together with information such as cut-off times and the conditions under which payment service providers can be reached. Where payment systems are interoperable, the information extends to the payment service providers in the interoperable system.

Risk issues for interoperating payment systems

13.55 The risk issues may be similar to those facing CCPs which intend to interoperate. Contract and liability issues are likely to be very similar. Access criteria are likely to need adaptation, since payment systems will ordinarily restrict their membership to banks of sufficiently high credit, liquidity and operational standing, which are requirements other system operators may be unable to meet. Fees will have to be considered. The ECB's Oversight Expectations also mention legal risk, operational risk, efficiency, governance and relayed links as sources of risk, and these could equally be applied to links between CCPs.

13.56 Interoperating payment systems are, however, exposed to several particular risk issues which may deserve attention.

(1) *Stepwise reachability*. The guiding principle of the EACHA Interoperability Framework is 'Settlement before Output': the sending CSM does not even send settlement messages to the interoperating CSM until the settlement cycle at the sending CSM has completed, and its ability to satisfy a pay-out (pay-in, from the viewpoint of the receiving CSM) is thereby assured. This may be prudent in order to limit credit risk for the receiving CSM, but introduces technical delays in attaining full reachability. The requirement to complete each step with finality before even instructions can be submitted to the next CSM makes a successful and timely payment dependent on the coordination of each payee-CSM's cut-off time with the completion of the payer-CSM's earlier settlement cycle. If a payee can only be reached through a long chain of CSMs, the coordination exercise

---

150 Regulation (EU) No 260/2012 of the European Parliament and of the Council of 14 March 2012 establishing technical and business requirements for credit transfers and direct debits in euro, etc, art 3
151 SWIFT, *SEPA Routing Directory* (May 2012), https://www2.swift.com/directories/

may be difficult. Payments may clog up in the interoperating systems.[152] The Payment Services Directive (PSD)[153] imposes a next-day deadline for many cash transfers, which means that a leisurely approach to this problem is not permitted.

(2) *Cash trapped between systems.* The ECB Oversight Expectations stipulate that the asset used for settlement across a link should carry little or no credit or liquidity risk.[154] EACHA's Interoperability Framework explains that each interoperating CSM should have an account in TARGET-2, so that pay-ins and pay-outs between the two systems are settled in that system. Thus, when the payer-CSM1 has completed its processing cycle, and is poised to submit settlement instructions to the payee-CSM2, a cash balance will exceptionally remain on CSM1's TARGET-2 account after the completion of CSM1's processing cycle.

This approach results in money being 'in limbo', which represents a pay-out from CSM1 which has not yet become a pay-in to CSM2. If CSM1 were to fail at this moment, there is a difficult question to answer as to whose money this is. The contenders for ownership might legitimately include CSM1 itself, CSM2, participant(s) in CSM2 claiming to be entitled to share in the net receivable expected from CSM1, and even (though this would require a challenge to the finality of settlement in CSM1) the participants in CSM1 who claim to have contributed towards this amount by virtue of being transferors in favour of payees participating in CSM2. The legal answer to who is entitled is not straightforward. There is little illumination from the sparse case-law on the failure of a bank in a chain of payments;[155] but it seems that there is little prospect of a successful claim that the funds in the CSM's account are held by it as agent, or trustee, or on some other fiduciary basis,[156] or as a non-party beneficiary of a contract – at least unless some special arrangement is put in place under the CSM's rules. The answer would therefore appear to be, in the absence of such rules, that CSM1 is entitled, and so the money would be lost to the creditors of CSM1.

In practice, the credit risk problem may be controlled by ensuring that the gap between the settlement cycles of the CSM which is the net payer and the CSM which is the net payee is reduced as far as possible. EACHA specifies that funds are only held by a CSM intra-day. The intra-day principle helps, in that the SFD[157] will ensure that transfer orders processed on the day of insolvency cannot be attacked under insolvency laws; but it may not be enough to keep the funds outside the estate of an insolvent system operator, since the SFD also requires that the system operator was unaware of the insolvency proceedings.

---

152 Renault, F, et al, *Congestion and Cascades in Coupled Payment Systems* (October 2007), Conference paper, http://www.ecb.int/events/pdf/conferences/pmfs/theme2_2.pdf?aee71c829 ed989e02d7c77188dfc6ac1

153 Directive 2007/64/EC of the European Parliament and of the Council of 13 November 2007 on payment services in the internal market, etc, art 69

154 ECB Oversight Expectations, p 6

155 Cf *Royal Products v Midland Bank* [1981] 2 Lloyd's Rep 194; *Abou-Rahmah v Abacha* [2006] EWCA Civ 1492

156 Brindle, M, and Cox, R, eds, *The Law of Bank Payments* (4th edn, Sweet & Maxwell/ Thomson Reuters, November 2010), ISBN 978-1847035516, paras 3-087 to 3-097

157 Article 3

Accordingly, the ECB also requires that funds needed for settlements are segregated, and EACHA says that the account in which funds in transit are credited should be a 'Fiduciary Account which means the funds are legally shielded from insolvency.' That statement is, however, a policy objective, not a legal mechanism, and interoperating payment systems will need to consider how it is achieved in practice.

Even if the payee-CSM2's entitlement to the funds in limbo is legally assured, it is not at all clear that the non-defaulting system operator has operational control over the funds in transit. The result of that will be that the payee-CSM2 will have to wait for these funds to be disbursed by the insolvency officer of the payer-CSM1 in the slow fullness of time. That means that, even if CSM2 ultimately avoids the credit risk of CSM1, it has a liquidity problem.

One final consideration relating to funds in limbo is that links between payment systems could involve a commercial bank rather than TARGET-2 as the account-provider for inter-system settlement. Such an arrangement clearly exposes the interoperating systems to commercial bank credit risk, and does not provide the finality protection of the SFD if the commercial bank fails and its settlement action is challenged. This type of arrangement is referred to by EACHA as a 'Liquidity Bridge'; EACHA says 'there is some risk in this model and hence it is not the preferred EACHA model.'[158]

(3) *Liquidity and credit risk.* The EACHA principle of Settlement before Output means that CSM2 would not ordinarily be exposed to liquidity risk if the pay-out from CSM1 is delayed or cancelled, because the settlement instructions from CSM1 should not have been submitted until the funds are known to be available. But, as has been seen, this outcome is at risk if CSM1 fails during the processing day; and the principle itself may come under commercial or operational pressure in a long chain owing to the conflicting needs of safety and timely processing to meet the PSD deadline.

For these reasons CSM2 may need to have exceptional arrangements to cover the non-performance of the counterpart system. Payment systems typically have liquidity back-up lines and loss-sharing rules,[159] and an immediate question for interoperating systems is whether the commitments made by ordinary participants to these arrangements would be waived in respect of a participant which is another system. If they are waived (cf the non-participation of interoperating CCPs in each other's default funds), this may not be fatal: the bank participants in the non-defaulting system may be able to supply the needed liquidity and/or to absorb the losses, but the risk-sharing is distributed among fewer members. Supplementary or alternative arrangements (such as a guarantee fund) may be considered desirable to provide an additional buffer against the extra costs and risk introduced by interoperability.

(4) *Cross-system finality.* The moment of finality of settlement for a cross-system payment will depend on the finality of both settlement cycles. The EACHA Framework is based on serial attainment of finality for each step in the chain of payments: this is a different approach to that taken in relation to interoperating CSDs or CCPs, where finality coordination is expected.

---

158 EACHA Interoperability Framework, p 11
159 See **sections 16.12(6)–16.13**

The ECB Oversight Expectations note a number of considerations which affect finality. In the first place, legal risk is higher for linked systems, because the rules applicable in the interoperating systems will be different, and the applicable laws may also differ. Second, if the moments of finality differ between the systems, there may be difficulty. EACHA does not (unlike the ECB) expressly stipulate that interoperating systems must coordinate their finality arrangements, but if this is not done it would be theoretically possible for the sending CSM to transmit funds to a receiving CSM before the moment of legal finality, thereby exposing the receiving CSM to unwind risk. Thirdly, the ECB says that the moment of finality and irrevocability of a payment transmitted via a link should be clearly defined;[160] failing this, a payment sent via a series of routing links carries a higher degree of finality risk than a payment sent across a single CSM.

Finality within interoperating systems under the SFD is assisted by a provision which allows a system operator to be regarded as a 'participant' in a system,[161] thereby avoiding the result that a system which interoperates with another ceases to be eligible for designation on the grounds that it has admitted a non-qualifying person as a participant.

(5) *R-transactions.* R-transactions are exception processing, 'where the letter "R" can signify "reject", "refusal", "return", "reversal", "revocation", or "request for cancellation".'[162] R-transactions may be a source of risk in interoperating systems, as the rules for processing, including such matters as cut-off times and pre-conditions for use of the R-service, may differ between systems. Some R-transactions affect the finality of a payment, but others are processed after final settlement and have some characteristics similar to an independent payment transaction.

(6) *Access criteria.* Payment systems are typically risk-managed on the assumption that the payer-in is a bank or other regulated financial institution meeting high standards of credit-worthiness and ability to settle in central bank money, because of the credit risk taken by the other participants in a netting system. Payment system operators will not typically be able to meet such standards, yet by becoming participants (as opposed to operators) they become part of the chain of payers and payees and therefore exposed to each other. The ECB Oversight Expectations include familiar provisions[163] as to non-discriminatory access for interoperating systems.

---

160 ECB Oversight Expectations, p 4
161 SFD, art 2(f)
162 Regulation (EU) No 260/2012 of the European Parliament and of the Council of 14 March 2012 establishing technical and business requirements for credit transfers and direct debits in euro, etc, recital (20)
163 ECB Oversight Expectation No 5; see **sections 7.11–7.15**

14 Risk Management at CCPs

COUNTERPARTY RISK

14.1   The raison d'être of a CCP is the management of counterparty risk. This task can be divided into phases, which inform the structure of this chapter. In first place is the idea that participants who pose undue counterparty risk should not be admitted to the club. Secondly, there is the problem of product eligibility, which requires careful selection of products whose risk profile can be confidently predicted by the CCP, as when a participant defaults the CCP will itself have to shoulder the market and delivery risks until the defaulter's account is closed out. Once these choices have been made, there is the need to protect against credit risk, which is done by taking margin. The CCP will also need to consider its ability to survive in the event that the margin received is insufficient to cover the exposure to a defaulting participant: the default fund, loss-sharing among survivors, capital and other backing will need to be considered. If the participant defaults, the CCP will need to implement a default handling strategy, which will, in particular, shape the margining algorithm adopted by the CCP. Transfer of a defaulter's positions to a surviving participant may be an important service provided by a CCP, in the interests of the wider market. Finally, in order to help the CCP over the various obstacles which these activities may encounter, there is the benefit of statutory protection against insolvency-law challenge, which forms the last piece of the CCP's risk management armour.

The general principles of risk management for CCPs were first set down in Recommendations made by the Bank for International Settlements' Committee on Payment and Settlement Systems (CPSS).[1] These were adopted in modified form by the Eurosystem (the ECB-CESR Recommendations), the modifications largely but not exclusively considering the issues associated with OTC clearing.[2] OTC clearing informed the wholesale revision of the CPSS Recommendations and their amalgamation into the Principles for Financial Market Infrastructures (FMI Principles).[3]

---

1   Committee on Payment and Settlement Systems, *Recommendations for Central Counterparties* (November 2004), http://www.bis.org/publ/cpss64.pdf
2   European Central Bank and Committee of European Securities Regulators, *Recommendations for Securities Settlement Systems and Recommendations for Central Counterparties in the European Union* (May 2009), http://www.ecb.eu/pub/pdf/other/pr090623_escb-cesr_recommendationsen.pdf
3   CPSS and Technical Committee of the International Organization of Securities Commissions, *Principles for Financial Market Infrastructures* (April 2012), http://www.bis.org/publ/cpss101a.pdf

Hard law exists in the form of EMIR, which imposes mandatory standards within the European Union on exposures management, margin, default funds, client asset segregation, default procedures, investment risk, model risk and settlement risk.[4] EMIR's rules reflect generally-held standards in place elsewhere in the world.[5] The most comprehensive set of rules on CCP risk management is arguably that of the Commodity Futures Trading Commission in the United States, which additionally expects CCPs to have admission standards, contract eligibility standards, documented plans for managing extreme market events, and automated systems oversight and disaster recovery.[6] The approach of the CFTC implies that more than counterparty risk is at stake, and indeed various other regulators recognise this.

OTHER RISKS

14.2   While counterparty risk is the most obvious risk for a CCP to manage, and the management of counterparty risk may encapsulate a wide range of other subsidiary risks such as model and liquidity risk, it is worth a short foray into the other types of risk frequently encountered by financial institutions, to examine what else CCPs should have in consideration, and how they are expected to manage them.

14.3   Typically a bank would be expected to manage the three 'Pillar 1' risks (credit, market and operational risks) set out in the Basel II framework.[7] But then regulators also expect banks to manage other risks under 'Pillar 2' of the Basel II framework, and those other risks include matters as diverse as underwriting risk and pension risk. Taking the FSA's list of Pillar 1 and 2 items for consideration,[8] together with the FMI Principles, it is suggested that CCPs should have regard to the following matters in addition to counterparty risk. Curiously, few of these aspects are directly covered in the United Kingdom's regulatory rulebook for CCPs.[9]

(1) *Operational risk.* The operational matters which may require careful attention by the CCP include, at least, its IT systems (including disaster recovery), its staff, its control structure, and outsourcing. The subject of outsourcing is considered further in relation to the risk management function of a CCP at **section 14.5**.

(2) *Concentration risk.* This question is touched on in **sections 14.11** and **14.17(6)**. The CCP needs to consider its exposure not just in respect of a participant acting as such, but as part of a wider financial group (which may include deposit-taking banks which the CCP uses to hold its margin

---

4   Regulation (EU) No 648/2012 of the European Parliament and of the Council of 4 July 2012 on OTC derivatives, central counterparties and trade repositories, Title IV, ch 3
5   For example, Reserve Bank of Australia, *Financial Stability Standard for Central Counterparties* (February 2009), http://www.rba.gov.au/payments-system/clearing-settlement/standards/ctrl-counterparties-std.html
6   Commodity Futures Trading Commission, *Regulations,* Part 39
7   For a set of documentation on Basel II, see http://www.bis.org/list/bcbs/tid_22/index.htm
8   Financial Services Authority, *Our Pillar 2 assessment framework* (May 2007), http://www.fsa.gov.uk/pubs/other/Pillar2_framework.pdf
9   Financial Services Authority, Handbook of Rules and Guidance, *Recognised Investment Exchanges and Recognised Clearing Houses sourcebook* (June 2001–November 2011), REC 2.5

deposits, or for access to payment or settlement systems or in other business-critical ways). Concentration risk may also manifest itself in relation to product types and geographical factors.

(3) *Liquidity risk.* The FMI Principles specify that a CCP needs sufficient liquid resources to settle its obligations and to make variation margin payments, under a wide range of stress scenarios. A CCP should have liquidity to withstand the default of the participant (or, if it is involved in complex activities or systemically important in multiple jurisdictions, the default of two participants) which, together with its or their affiliates, have the largest aggregate payment obligation.[10] Liquidity issues are considered further, in **sections 14.17(3), 14.28** and **14.59**.

(4) *Settlement risk.* Guidance for CCPs is somewhat variable. The United Kingdom's statutory framework[11] and the Reserve Bank of Australia[12] focus on the need for the CCP's exposures to be extinguished on settlement, and (in the latter case) whether settlement is done using DvP and RTGS modalities.[13] Similarly the CFTC requires that the CCP has the ability to complete settlement on a timely basis in different circumstances.[14] The FMI Principles strongly recommend that cash obligations referable to CCPs are settled in central bank money.[15] Whether this means that CCPs need to have access to central bank liquidity is discussed in **section 14.59**.

(5) *Investment risk.* Investment risk is not something special to CCPs: investments give rise to similar risk considerations for banks as they do for CCPs – namely, risk of loss of value, and risk of illiquidity – and those risks can be managed in the same way, though no regulatory guidance recommends capital adequacy regulation for CCPs analogous to banks. Investment risk is the subject of various strictures, considered in **section 14.11**.

(6) *Capital adequacy.* Whether the function of capital of a CCP is for protection of its creditors – in other words, to be a backup to the default fund – is considered in **sections 6.26–6.28**. Further discussion of capital top-ups for CCPs is in **section 17.12**.

(7) *Legal risk.* Legal risk is noted to be particularly relevant to the ability to close out or transfer positions and to liquidate a defaulting participant's positions and margin. Legal risk issues of this nature are considered below in the context of default management and legislative protection against insolvency-law-based challenges.

14.4   Mention may also be made of the Standards of Risk Management Controls issued by the European Association of CCP Clearing Houses (the EACH Standards).[16] These standards include recommendations on a variety of risk issues not otherwise discussed later in this chapter. Notable are the following:

---

10 Principle 7, key consideration 4
11 Financial Services and Markets Act 2000 (Recognition Requirements for Investment Exchanges and Clearing Houses) Regulations 2001, SI 2001 No 995, Schedule, para 19(2)(b)
12 Reserve Bank of Australia, *Financial Stability Standard for Central Counterparties* (February 2009), http://www.rba.gov.au/payments-system/clearing-settlement/standards/ctrl-counterparties-std.html, para 5
13 See **sections 2.27ff**
14 CFTC Regulations, Part 39, Core Principle E
15 Principle 9; Annex E
16 EACH, *Standards of Risk Management Controls used by Central Counterparty Clearing Houses* (November 2001), http://www.eachorg.eu/each/cm/

(1) *Custody*. CCPs should ensure that its collateral is securely held, that cash is deposited only with selected banks and subject to appropriate limits, or secured under reverse repos.[17] The same subject is also covered in FMI Principle 16.

(2) *Risk Management Function*. CCPs should have adequate, qualified risk management staff who are independent from the business development and commercial function of the CCP.[18] Independence of the risk management function is also mandated by EMIR.[19]

(3) *Transparency*. CCPs should publish a comprehensive description of its risk management practices.[20]

Outsourcing

14.5 In **section 6.41(6)**, it is noted that the FMI Principles might be considered too thin as regards their prescriptions on outsourcing. It is generally thought that financial institutions should not be permitted to outsource the part of their activities which require a regulatory licence, and in particular that they may not delegate to a third party the decision-making and responsibility for ensuring that such activities are duly conducted in accordance with the requisite regulatory standards:

'The outsourcing of core management functions is considered generally to be incompatible with the senior management's obligation to run the enterprise under their own responsibility. Core management functions include, inter alia, setting the risk strategy, the risk policy, and, accordingly, the risk-bearing capacity of the institution. Hence, management functions such as the setting of strategies and policies in respect of the authorised entity's risk profile and control, the oversight of the operation of the entity's processes, and the final responsibility towards customers and supervisors should not be outsourced.'[21]

This robust statement is not repeated in the FMI Principles, but there is no fundamental reason why this basic rule should not be observed by an infrastructure of systemic importance.

For a CCP, the basic rule has been emphasised in authoritative commentary. In a speech, Mr Paul Tucker, the Bank of England's Deputy Governor for Financial Stability, said: 'the core risk management functions of CCPs should not be outsourced. Regulators have been slow to embrace this. But I am glad to say that it does get some recognition in the EMIR text, perhaps not as unambiguously as is warranted in my view.'[22] EMIR in fact has a whole article devoted to outsourcing,[23] which does indeed state that a CCP which is outsourcing operational functions must ensure that: '(a) outsourcing does not

---

17 EACH Standard C9
18 EACH Standard F12
19 Article 28
20 EACH Standard H14
21 Committee of European Banking Supervisors, *Guidelines on Outsourcing* (December 2006), http://www.eba.europa.eu/getdoc/f99a6113-02ea-4028-8737-1cdb33624840/GL02OutsourcingGuidelines-pdf.aspx, Guideline 3, para 1; see also Guideline 4
22 Tucker, P, *Central counterparties: the agenda* (October 2011), Speech, http://www.bankofengland.co.uk/publications/Documents/speeches/2011/speech524.pdf
23 Article 35

result in the delegation of its responsibility;' and '(e) outsourcing does not result in depriving the CCP from the necessary systems and controls to manage the risks it faces;' but these obligations are potentially ambiguous because they leave it open to a CCP to agree contract terms with a supplier of risk management services which leave 'responsibility' and 'controls' with the CCP.

14.6   The basic rule would suggest that a CCP should particularly be wary of outsourcing any of the following aspects of its activities, which might be regarded as central to its regulated activity: the creation and maintenance of its register of cleared transactions; the assessment of applicant participants; the choice of cleared products; the margin and default fund methodology; and the management of defaults. Furthermore, given that the contributors to the default fund, rather than the owners of the CCP, stand to suffer from mismanagement in relation to these questions, it would suggest that where the governing body of a CCP does not answer to the default fund contributors, a decision to outsource any critical part of the operational functions underpinning these core activities should be subject to a veto by those contributors.

14.7   The outsourcing of the risk management function of a CCP seems to have been one of several main causes of the failure of the Hong Kong futures clearing system in 1987. The structural arrangements in place there, which were criticised by the Hay Davison inquiry,[24] can be summarised as follows. The Hong Kong Futures Exchange used ICCH (Hong Kong) Ltd (ICCH) as its clearing house and Hong Kong Futures Guarantee Corporation Ltd (FGC) as a separate guarantor of the trades. ICCH did not act as central counterparty, but calculated margin requirements and managed FGC.[25] FGC had very low – less than $2 million – capital, and no default fund. Although ICCH had a 20% ownership stake in FGC, an error by ICCH in risk management would primarily affect market participants and FGC, but not ICCH itself. The Hay Davison report concluded that this structure was unworkable; that the clearing house should be the guarantor and manage its own risks; and that the clearing members of the Exchange should stand behind the clearing house by contributing a default fund.[26]

14.8   In view of this discussion, it might be expected that regulators would generally find it inappropriate for a CCP to delegate the risk management function of its operations to a third party, wholly or in part; or if partial delegation can sometimes be acceptable, to set firm boundaries. Curiously, however, the position seems to be rather flexible. Examples of outsourcing of risk management by CCPs indicate a range of approaches:

● NYSE Liffe received approval from the FSA to become a self-clearing recognised investment exchange in June 2009.[27] Until development of its own clearing functionality, NYSE Liffe continued to employ LCH.Clearnet Limited as supplier of its clearing service, but not as CCP in the traditional sense:

---

24 Hay Davison, I, et al, *The Operation and Regulation of the Hong Kong Securities Industry, Report of the Securities Review Committee* (May 1988), http://www.fstb.gov.hk/fsb/ppr/report/davison.htm

25 Hay Davison report, paras 7.3–7.9

26 Paragraphs 7.32, 7.48

27 NYSE Liffe London Notice No 3174 (July 2009)

'LIFFE has appointed LCH as provider of certain clearing services, including the management of positions of any LIFFE Clearing Member that is declared a defaulter. These arrangements provide that, in the event of a Clearing Member default, each outstanding Registered Exchange Contract between the defaulting Clearing Member and LIFFE is automatically novated so as to substitute LCH as party in place of LIFFE (the Default Novation), thus enabling LCH to undertake its default management services.'[28]

LCH.Clearnet Limited was also to provide margin calculation and collection services and to manage settlement and delivery obligations. In other words, the outsourcing was a complete delegation of the whole clearing function.

● EuroCCP stated that it 'leverag[es] DTCC's technology and processing capacity' while also noting that '[r]isk management is the core competence of a central counterparty.'[29] From these remarks it would appear that some degree of outsourcing takes place, though the risk management function would appear to reside with EuroCCP itself since EuroCCP has its own risk committee and head of risk.[30]

● CC&G delegated its netting calculations to Monte Titoli, 'blurring the functions between the CSD and CCP.'[31] Calculation of net settlement positions might, however, be a mechanical rather than discretionary function, and thus not regarded as a delegation of risk management.

Investment risk

14.9 Given the expected influx of margin assets into CCPs in consequence of mandatory clearing, it may be thought remarkable that the FMI Principles contain only one paragraph on investment policy for infrastructures.[32] This states that investments should be claims on, or secured by, high-quality obligors, and be easily liquidated. The FMI Principles also warn of the risk of entering into repos with participants, and proscribe investment in participants or their affiliates.

14.10 Article 47 of EMIR essentially repeats the FMI Principles, but adds the following:

● Financial instruments deposited as margin or default fund contributions must if possible be held with 'operators of securities settlement systems that ensure the full protection of those financial instruments.'[33] The assumption underlying this rule is that custody risk is reduced if intermediation is

---

28 NYSE Liffe London Notice No 3159 (June 2009), para 2.4
29 Depository Trust & Clearing Corporation, *Annual Report 2008* (2009), http://dtcc.com/downloads/annuals/2008/2008_report.pdf, p 26
30 European Central Counterparty, *Corporate Governance* webpage (May 2012), http://www.euroccp.co.uk/about/governance.php
31 Comotto, R, *A white paper on the operation of the European repo market, the role of short-selling, the problem of settlement failures and the need for reform of the market infrastructure* (July 2010), White Paper for the International Capital Market Association's European Repo Council, http://icmagroup.org/assets/documents/Maket-Practice/Regulatory-Policy/Repo-Markets/ICMA%20ERC%20European%20repo%20market%20white%20paper%20July%202010%20%282%29.pdf, para 8.14
32 FMI Principles, para 3.16.4
33 EMIR, art 47(3)

disallowed; while that may be true, there may be disadvantages to direct holdings in CSDs, such as a reduced range of ancillary services which might more commonly be available from commercial custodians than from CSDs.[34] Arrangements with other authorised financial institutions are the fall-back, and must be 'highly secure.' Assets belonging to clearing members have to be held separately from the CCP's own assets.[35]

- Cash, by contrast, can be held 'through highly secure arrangements with authorised financial institutions, or alternatively, through the use of the standing deposit facilities of central banks or other comparable means provided for by central banks.'[36] This is, then, the other way round from non-cash assets, reflecting the relative difficulty which CCPs may have (particularly if they are not banks) in opening accounts at central banks.[37] Access to central bank liquidity may go hand-in-hand with the ability to hold cash directly in central bank funds, and the question whether CCPs need (or should be permitted to have) access to central bank liquidity is considered further in **section 14.59**.

- Reinvestment policy is covered in article 39. CCPs are allowed to have a right of use of margins and default fund contributions collected under a security financial collateral arrangement, and title transfer[38] margin and default fund arrangements are not disallowed. If re-use takes place, article 47 applies, so that the CCP may only invest in cash or highly liquid financial instruments with minimal market and credit risk, and which are capable of being liquidated rapidly with minimal adverse price effect.[39]

14.11   The investment restrictions might be thought superficial, if a sound investment policy for a CCP should be to avoid, as far as possible, any correlation between the loss of value on its investments and movement in the prices of products which the CCP is clearing. However, the FMI Principles emphasise the need of a CCP to liquidate assets in managing defaults, and in a contest between preservation of value and liquidity, liquidity would appear to be the winner.

CCPs which repo out non-cash assets, and deposit cash with their participants, would be regarded as behaving imprudently. Another factor to consider is how a reinvestment might be structured so as to minimise concentration risk in a wider sense – that is, to minimise exposure to the banking sector, which will be the sector in which defaults arise. EMIR requires that CCPs consider their overall credit risk exposures to individual obligors and to ensure that exposures remain within acceptable concentration limits.[40] There are, however, no quantitative limits as there are for banks in the Banking Directive.[41] The Chair of ESMA has said that 'CCPs need to be safer than banks, and for this reason they fully collateralise their exposure. Now all this collateral cannot be returned to banks through unsecured arrangements, otherwise we will be back to square one.

---

34 See **section 6.34**
35 EMIR, art 47(5)
36 EMIR, art 47(4)
37 Cf European Commission Services
38 See **section 10.10(2)**
39 EMIR, art 47(1)
40 EMIR, art 47(7)
41 Directive 2006/48 of the European Parliament and of the Council of 14 June 2006 relating to the taking up and pursuit of the business of credit institutions, Title V, ch 2, s 5

We will therefore need to establish strict rules on CPs' investment policies.'[42] EMIR also gives ESMA the duty to develop regulatory technical standards on concentration limits as well as what constitute 'highly secure arrangements.'[43]

MEMBER ELIGIBILITY

14.12 The first step in risk management is to keep the door barred against unwanted intruders. The function of the CCP is to manage counterparty risk, so it must ensure that its counterparties are robust, or it will simply be writing off the default fund contributions of its stronger participants.

The FMI Principles aim to balance the objective of fair and open access with the need to bar the doorway on grounds of risk.[44] Legitimate risk-based criteria are said to include operational, financial and legal requirements, and requirements relating to indirect (tiered) participation.[45] ECB-CESR Recommendation 2 is slightly more prescriptive, specifying that 'a CCP should establish requirements for participation to ensure that participants have sufficient financial resources and robust operational capacity, including a sufficient level of relevant expertise, necessary legal powers and business practices.'[46] This statement, and the next, which says that a CCP should have procedures to monitor that participation requirements are met on an ongoing basis 'either through timely access to reports ... or directly if such reports are not available or do not contain the required information'[47] are weaker than the criteria commonly expected of banks for extending ordinary loan credit.[48] However, the supplementary notes to the ECB-CESR Recommendation emphasise financial and operational capacity, but list the following additional matters in a non-prescriptive way:

- Capital adequacy
- Credit rating
- Parent guarantee
- Risk management in respect of non-clearing clients whose positions are cleared
- Collateral, payment and delivery arrangements
- Fitness and properness of senior management
- Obligations to participate in default management processes.

The Recommendation notes that many of these things may have been vetted by the regulator already, which then raises the question whether it is safe for a CCP to rely on the fact that its own membership criteria correspond to the regulator's assessment criteria to reduce the admission burden on new applicants for membership, or to reduce the level of duplicate supervision which it might otherwise feel obliged to carry out. There is no official sanction of such a

---

42 Maijoor, S, *Keynote Address at the AFME Market and Liquidity Conference* (February 2012), http://www.esma.europa.eu/system/files/2012-76.pdf,
43 EMIR, art 47(8)
44 FMI Principle 18
45 FMI Principles, para 3.18.5
46 ECB-CESR Recommendation 2, Key Issue B1
47 ECB-CESR Recommendation 2, Key Issue B2
48 Cf Basel Committee on Banking Supervision, *Sound credit risk assessment and valuation for loans* (June 2006), http://www.bis.org/publ/bcbs126.pdf

policy, and regulatory standards have been shown to be inconsistently applied in the past,[49] so it may be unwise for a CCP to do so.

14.13   It may be of interest to consider the participant eligibility rules of the United States' Commodity Futures Trading Commission (CFTC) for CCPs ('derivatives clearing organizations') under its jurisdiction.[50] These require fair and open access, forbidding restrictive standards if less restrictive requirements would achieve the same objective without materially increasing risk; they require that participants have access to sufficient financial resources to meet their obligations in extreme but plausible market conditions; they insist on capital and operational capacity requirements; and they require monitoring of and reporting by participants to the 'derivatives clearing organization'. The CFTC also forbids a 'derivatives clearing organization' requiring its participants to be swap dealers or to maintain a swap portfolio of a given size, or imposing a capital requirement of over $50 million for a swap clearing participant.[51]

As the CFTC criteria suggest, it may be tempting for a CCP to impose very burdensome admission criteria. However, as discussed in **sections 7.9–7.12**, this may be deemed to be an anti-competitive practice unless the criteria can be shown to be proportionate and risk-based.

14.14   LCH.Clearnet Ltd's membership criteria for its SwapClear service[52] impose various requirements which are not found in ECB-CESR Recommendation 2. These include (in addition to the standard requirements for capital, participation in the CCP's margin collection system called PPS, non-contravention of the United Kingdom rule prohibiting carrying on of regulated activities without authorisation,[53] and a functional back office arrangement) a minimum credit rating, a minimum interest rate swaps portfolio size, signing up to the default management process and participation in a default management fire-drill, having a bank or investment firm in the group, and being able to receive data on SwapClear contracts in particular formats. These supplementary criteria illustrate what a CPSS Consultative Report said in relation to clearing of OTC derivatives: 'If an OTC derivatives CCP uses procedures which introduce specific roles for its participants in the default procedures, it may need to consider if and to what extent additional participation requirements are necessary in order to ensure that the participants are able to perform their roles as expected.'[54]

14.15   Having admitted a participant, a CCP takes on the burden of monitoring and, if necessary, ejection of participants who do not keep up to the standard. The EACH Standards state:

49   Cf Financial Services Authority, *The supervision of Northern Rock: a lessons learned review* (March 2008), http://www.fsa.gov.uk/pubs/other/nr_report.pdf, paras 16ff

50   CFTC, *Final Rules for derivatives clearing organizations* (November 2011), 76 FR 69334, §39.12(a)

51   Cf **section 5.6(3)**

52   LCH.Clearnet Limited, *Clearing House Procedures* (July 2010), s 1.2

53   Financial Services and Markets Act 2000, s 19

54   CPSS and Technical Committee of the International Organization of Securities Commissions, *Guidance on the application of the 2004 CPSS-IOSCO Recommendations for Central Counterparties to OTC derivatives CCPs – consultative report* (May 2010), http://www.bis.org/publ/cpss89.pdf, Recommendation 2

'Having admitted a firm to membership, the clearing house should ensure that the firm continues to meet the membership requirements, and should evaluate and keep under review the financial health of members – so that it is in a position to take any additional steps to protect its risks and therefore the integrity of the market or markets that it clears.

'Clearing house procedures should ensure that:
a) members' adherence to the membership requirements is monitored and enforced;
b) there is an evaluation of the standing of each member as an aide to the monitoring of exposures by the clearing house;
c) there is at least daily review of the member-specific exposures run by the clearing house;
d) there is liaison and information-sharing with statutory regulators, as appropriate and permitted;
e) there are information channels with other clearing houses/exchanges, as appropriate and permitted.'[55]

The old CPSS Recommendations for CCPs explained further:

'A priority, of course, should be to avoid defaults. ... A CCP's participation requirements should include financial requirements that reduce the likelihood of defaults. Furthermore, a CCP should identify situations that it determines may pose a threat of default and develop early warning pre-default plans and procedures, such as increasing monitoring or imposing restrictions on a participant. These procedures should provide an incentive to participants for early notification of potential financial, liquidity or systems problems that could lead to a default.'[56]

The FMI Principles emphasise the need to monitor ongoing compliance with membership criteria, and recommend additional collateral and reduced credit limits for participants who pose heightened risk; but do not reiterate this specific guidance.[57]

CCPs may thus need powers to require participants to reduce their positions. Whether it is sufficient for such powers to exist under the rules or the participation agreement is questionable: safer practice may be to ensure that the trading platform from which the positions emanate can constrain the trading activity which gives rise to the cleared positions (which may be challenging, if the CCP participant is a GCM clearing a number of NCMs' trades) and is willing to intervene at the CCP's behest.

PRODUCT RISK

14.16 The amount of credit risk assumed by a CCP is not solely a function of the quality of its participants. The other principal factors in this equation are the type of transaction which the CCP accepts for clearing, and the question whether transactions have become binding between the CCP and both participants. It is thus, perhaps, curious that neither the FMI Principles, nor the older CPSS and ECB-CESR Recommendations, devote significant space to the question how a

---

55 EACH Standard A2
56 CPSS paper No 64, Recommendation 6, para 4.6.1
57 FMI Principles, para 3.18.8

CCP should approach the topic of transaction eligibility. Furthermore, EMIR contains no specific rules on product selection by CCPs.

The FMI Principles note that the amount of margin needed by a CCP will be affected by the product cleared, and give a list of product risk issues, viz: price volatility and correlation, non-linear price characteristics, jump-to-default risk, market liquidity, liquidation procedures, and wrong-way risk.[58] But there is no real attempt to guide CCPs on how to approach the question of product eligibility. This may perhaps be attributed to the fact that political considerations are dictating that certain products be cleared, and that it would be unhelpful for the FMI Principles to complicate other policy objectives.[59] EMIR stops short of mandating the clearing of particular products, but it is implicit in the creation of a 'top-down' list of products which ESMA wishes to see cleared that such products are deemed, by a regulator, to be safe enough to clear.[60]

A CCP could, therefore, be forgiven for thinking that careful selection of products for clearing should be a relatively straightforward process. However, the CFTC Rules for 'derivatives clearing organizations' are prescriptive, listing seven factors which should at minimum be considered: trading volume; liquidity; availability of reliable prices; ability of market participants to use portfolio compression;[61] market access to create, liquidate, transfer, auction or allocate positions; measurability of risk for margin setting; and operational capacity of the derivatives clearing organisation to address unusual risk characteristics of the product.[62] In relation to the last point, it may be noted that for clearing of OTC products the ability of a CCP to see a complete view of the market is not assured.[63] The Bank of England also emphasises the importance of liquidity and standardisation in product selection.[64]

It might also be noted that the regulatory principles for CLS also contain a chapter on product choice,[65] even though CLS is not a CCP (though it does operate a netting function and does take on counterparty risk vis-à-vis its participants). The omission of the subject from European hard and soft law on CCPs does not mean the topic should be disregarded.

14.17 Professor Craig Pirrong makes a number of comments regarding product eligibility, from a perusal of which the following observations might be made:[66]

(1) *Standardisation.* Standardisation helps, because it facilitates disposal by a CCP of a defaulter's portfolio in that there is greater prospect of a deep market. On the other hand, Professor Pirrong notes that standardisation does not necessarily entail simplicity: standardised products such as credit default swaps can behave in complex ways.

---

58 FMI Principles, para 3.6.3
59 See **Chapter 5**
60 EMIR, art 5(3); see **section 5.14**
61 See **section 4.14**
62 CFTC Rules, 76 FR 69437, §39.12(b)(1)
63 See **section 5.2(5)**
64 Sidanius, C, and Wetherilt, A, *Thoughts on determining central clearing eligibility of OTC derivatives* (March 2012), Bank of England Financial Stability Paper No 14, http://www.bankofengland.co.uk/publications/Documents/fsr/fs_paper14.pdf
65 Board of Governors of the Federal Reserve System, *Protocol for the Cooperative Oversight Arrangement of CLS* (November 2008), http://www.federalreserve.gov/paymentsystems/cls_protocol.htm, paras 19–21
66 Pirrong, C, *The Economics of Central Clearing: Theory and Practice* (May 2011), ISDA Discussion Paper No 1, http://www2.isda.org/images/file_exts/fileext_pdf.png, pp 17–20

(2) *Complexity.* Complexity is an enemy of clearing, as it complicates the accurate computation of margin requirements and increases the risk of the CCP being a victim of information asymmetry. Complex instruments may be difficult to hedge or liquidate.

(3) *Liquidity.* Illiquid products are difficult to price accurately, and give rise to a problem which CCPs may be ill-equipped to deal with, namely the responsibility of holding an unhedged position in a financial instrument for a period until the market frees up and a disposal can be arranged.[67] The liquidity of a product is not constant throughout its life – in particular, a credit default swap may become illiquid as it approaches maturity – and may change markedly at times of market stress, for example immediately after a participant default. Where cleared products are illiquid, position measurement may be doubtful, and the CCP may have to model a 'reasonable daily settlement price' where marking to market is not informative.[68]

(4) *Price behaviour.* Some products may experience exacerbated volatility or even discontinuities in price movement in particular circumstances. The 'jump-to-default' characteristic of credit default swaps (the risk that a credit event occurs too suddenly to have been reflected in the price of a credit derivative) has already been mentioned in relation to the FMI Principles. Jump-to-default risk has been noted to require immediate payments from potentially illiquid counterparties, presenting CCPs with acute liquidity issues if the CDS pay-out coincides with a participant default.[69]

(5) *Correlations.* Some products may behave in a way which is related to the risk of participant default or the loss of value of margin (ie, they engender wrong-way risk – that is, the risk that the CCP's exposure increases in tandem with the risk of default of a participant[70]). To give a simplistic example, a CCP should not clear a credit derivative referenced on its own participant, since there is wrong-way risk either if the participant trades in such products itself, or indeed if any other participant defaults (because the surviving participants' ability to price the derivative is affected by their assessment of the impact of the default on the referenced participant in its capacity as such). Professor Pirrong notes that dependencies of this sort are hard to model, and may also change dramatically during periods of market stress. Exposure to participants can increase rapidly as a result of change in prices or the participant having taken a more entrenched position.

(6) *Concentration risk.* It may be noteworthy that the FSA considers issues of concentration risk as related to wrong-way risk.[71] CCPs cannot avoid concentration risk, because their function is to centralise the management of counterparty risk for cleared products, and the need for rigorous product selection implies that they will have a less diversified investment portfolio than ordinary investors – albeit that in ordinary market conditions they will undertake no market risk. Concentration risk may be exacerbated because

67 Cf **section 14.43**
68 ECB-CESR Recommendation 3, para C2
69 Kress, J, 'Credit Default Swaps, Clearinghouses, and Systemic Risk: Why centralized counterparties must have access to central bank liquidity' (May 2011) Harvard Journal on Legislation, Vol. 48, No. 1, pp 47–93
70 See **section 5.6(2)(c)**
71 Cf Financial Services Authority, *FSA Reviews of Counterparty Credit Risk Management by Central Counterparties* (January 2012), Finalised Guidance, http://www.fsa.gov.uk/static/pubs/guidance/fg12-03.pdf, paras 19–23

a particular participant, or group of participants, or a participant together with its clients, builds up a certain position in a product. The FSA's guidance to CCPs says that concentration risk could be mitigated by calls for additional margin,[72] though this seems a less appropriate tool than, for example, position limits, which might differ by product.

Evidently the question of product choice overlaps with a discussion of measurement and management of credit risk and margining.

14.18 CPSS Recommendation 3 included a brief discussion on the impact of the product settlement cycle on credit risk management. In cash equities markets where the duration of risk is both short and (subject to contingencies)[73] fixed, CCPs can 'employ risk control mechanisms other than margin requirements,' such as trading limits imposed by the market in which the participant operates. The implication is that trading limits will not be effective if the settlement period is longer or variable, or in relation to OTC clearing. The following comments may be made in this context.

(1) *Settlement period and risk.* Evidently the duration of the settlement period is relevant: the longer the time for which the position remains open, the greater the risk of a price movement which is troublesome enough to make the participant unable to meet the consequential margin call. However, it does not follow that short settlement periods make alternative risk control strategies more, rather than less, appropriate. Consider, for example, the futures markets, which have been cleared markets for many years.[74] Futures contracts have long life-spans, but CCPs which clear futures have a range of risk management options which may be better suited to long-tenor transactions, such as the power to require a participant to reduce its positions, fix settlement prices,[75] or even to 'invoice back' (reverse)[76] a transaction. But the general point is that different products have different risk profiles, and different mechanisms are needed: slavish reliance on margin, with all the risk that entails in terms of quantification and collectability, may be imprudent.

(2) *Absence of an organised market.* OTC products raise particular problems of product eligibility. In the first place, similar contracts may in fact differ in a significant risk-related parameter (consider, for example, past deliberations among market participants about which types of 'restructuring' constitute a credit event in relation to a credit derivative). Secondly, even when standardised, OTC products require some form of matching mechanism to ensure that the CCP is not bound vis-à-vis the seller but not vis-à-vis the buyer; pre-existing mechanisms may exist in relation to some trade types but not others. Thirdly, the liquidity of OTC products is likely to be more variable than where there is an organised trading venue; the policy drive to have all standardised products and instruments traded on regulated markets,

---

72 FSA Finalised Guidance, para 23
73 For the effects of settlement fails, see **Chapter 21**
74 Kroszner, R, 'Central Counterparty Clearing: History, Innovation, and Regulation' in European Central Bank and Federal Reserve Bank of Chicago, *The Role of Central Counterparties* (July 2007), http://www.ecb.eu/pub/pdf/other/rolecentralcounterparties200707en.pdf, p 30
75 Dale, R, 'Risk Management in US Derivative Clearing Houses' (September 1998) Essays in International Financial & Economic Law, vol 14, http://www.jscc.co.jp/en/ccp12/materials/docs/0416/1.pdf
76 Cf LCH.Clearnet Limited, *General Regulations* (January 2011), reg 28

MTFs and OTFs in Europe will exacerbate this.[77] Finally, the default management arrangements for OTC positions will be more elaborate than where there is an organised marketplace, as discussed below. These considerations show that it would be wrong to draw the inference that position limiting is an inappropriate risk management tool in relation to OTC products.

REGISTRATION RISK

14.19 A more subtle problem than the self-evident risk of taking on a contractual position which is unwanted by the CCP is the question whether the contractual position *has* actually been taken on. The process by which a CCP becomes bound in a transactional relationship with a participant is referred to as 'registration'. There are two main reasons why registration might not be as easy as it might seem. First, the CCP needs to have an operational set-up which is effective in bringing about binding contractual relations in respect of each newly registered transaction. Secondly, the CCP will need to ensure that its registration system assures that there will always be a matched book – in other words that there is no risk of being bound by the buyer without being bound to the seller, or vice versa.

The effectiveness of the registration process is thus a mixed question of operational practice and law. As regards operational risk, where the transactions emanate from an exchange or other organised trading platform, it should be operationally straightforward to ensure that there is a matching engine in effect which feeds transaction data to the CCP only where it is certain that both buyer and seller are agreed on the essential terms of the bargain. The CCP can register the transaction without danger of mismatch, provided that the platform is willing to accept responsibility for the effectiveness of the matching engine. Where the platform is cleared by more than one CCP, the simplicity of this analysis breaks down, because data needs to flow from the matching engine to more than one destination.[78] One option is for the data to be sent to both CCPs (the $\wedge$ or inverted-V structure), risking communications breakdown on one of its journeys, but not both, so that one CCP believes the trade to be registrable whereas the other is unaware of its existence. Another is for the platform to send all the matched data to one CCP on which the interoperating CCP is dependent (the L structure). The L structure has communications risk as well as introducing this dependency. Other mismatch errors arising in interoperability contexts include where the CCPs' registration systems process identical data differently and require reconciliation.

OTC clearing also introduces difficulty into the registration process because of the absence of a single market operator from which a definitive feed of transaction data can be obtained. This problem may be solved in typical OTC clearing service through the use of a matching service supplier such as MarkitSERV. The CPSS has also drawn attention to the consequences of participants' activities being spread across different time-zones, which may include mismatch of timing of margin calls in relation to the opening hours of the participant's applicable settlement systems.[79]

---

[77] See **sections 3.6, 5.13**
[78] See **section 13.29**
[79] CPSS-IOSCO Consultative Report CPSS 89, Guidance 4.1

14.20 From a legal perspective the important consideration is to ensure that the rules and operational processes of the CCP are effective to create binding relations and (where novation, rather than open offer, is used[80]), to discharge the old transaction. Both registration techniques rely on a degree of 'finality' protection in a manner similar to settlement systems. Here the question of finality is not about whether a payment or delivery has been done in a manner which cannot give rise to any risk of unwind or claw-back, but whether the creation of the contractual relationship is subject to such a challenge. For this reason the protection given by the Settlement Finality Directive[81] is of value to CCPs in their armoury against risk. By virtue of the Settlement Finality Regulations,[82] a designated system must specify in its rules the point at which a 'transfer order' takes effect as having been entered into the system and the point after which a transfer order may not be revoked by a participant or any other party, and prohibit revocation by a participant or any other party of a transfer order from the point of no revocation. For this purpose, UK CCPs typically have special chapters of 'settlement finality regulations' in their rulebooks.

Further, both registration techniques raise issues regarding the proper law of the contract. Formalities required for contract formation are determined by the proper law of the contract.[83] Where novation is involved, the requirements for a successful discharge of the original contract will be determined by the proper law of the original contract.[84] The interplay between the rules of the CCP, and the proper law of the bargain (particularly where this involves performance of obligations in other jurisdictions) may be non-trivial. Where open offer is the technique, the principal issue is likely to be whether the operational methodology satisfies the requirements for contract formation under the proper law of the transactions intended to become binding.

Drs Bliss and Papathanassiou[85] have identified other legal problems associated with novation. These include certainty over the moment of novation, so as to limit the risks associated with unexpected continuing exposure to the original trading counterparty, and the extinction of security rights or other rights in rem when the original contract is dissolved. Where OTC derivative trades are novated to a CCP, any credit support associated with the pre-novation trade is thus at risk of falling away.

MARGIN

14.21 Two of the FMI Principles are devoted to subjects relevant to margining. Principle 6 is directed to CCPs specifically, and sets out the fundamental rules with regard to quantification of margin. Principle 5 has more general provisions relating to collateral. These can be summarised as follows:

---

80 See **sections 2.3** and **2.4**
81 Directive 98/26/EC of the European Parliament and of the Council of 19 May 1998 on settlement finality in payment and securities settlement systems
82 Financial Markets and Insolvency (Settlement Finality) Regulations 1999, SI 1999 No. 2979, Schedule, para 5
83 Regulation (EC) No 593/2008 of the European Parliament and of the Council of 17 June 2008 on the law applicable to contractual obligations (Rome I), art 11
84 Rome I Regulation, art 12(1)(d)
85 Bliss, R, and Papathanassiou, C, *Derivatives clearing, central counterparties and novation: the economic implications* (March 2006), Wake Forest University Working Paper, http://www.wfu.edu/~blissrr/PDFs/Bliss-Papathanassiou%20-%202006,%20CCPs.pdf

(1) CCPs should cover credit exposures with margin commensurate with the product, portfolio and markets served.[86] (It may be noted that CCPs are *not* expected to vary margin levels in accordance with the credit-worthiness of the participant.)

(2) CCPs require reliable and timely price data for margin-setting, and contingency arrangements for when regular price sources are unavailable.[87]

(3) The amount of initial margin[88] should 'meet an established single-tailed confidence level of at least 99 per cent with respect to the estimated distribution of future exposure.'[89]

(4) Build-up of exposures should be limited by the collection of variation margin[90] at least daily.[91]

(5) Margin offsets between products are allowed if the risk on the products is significantly and reliably correlated.[92]

(6) Models should be back-tested daily. Models should be subjected to sensitivity assessment at least monthly against a wide range of possible market conditions, including extreme volatility and extreme changes in price correlation.[93] The margin system should be reviewed and validated regularly.[94]

(7) Collateral should have low credit, liquidity and market risks.[95]

(8) Collateral should be market to market daily.[96]

(9) Haircuts should be regularly tested, take into account realisable value and time to liquidate in stressed market conditions, and be stable and conservative in order to avoid procyclical adjustments.[97]

(10) Infrastructures should diversify holdings of collateral.[98]

(11) Foreign collateral should be useable promptly and its use should take account of foreign exchange risk.[99]

(12) Collateral management should be flexible enough to accommodate changes in margining, substitution, and re-use.[100] Re-use of collateral is expressly permitted during default management in order to access liquidity; in other circumstances, it is not forbidden, except 'as an instrument for increasing or maintaining ... profitability;' but rules on re-use should be clear and transparent.[101] Cash collateral can be invested subject to management of custody and investment risks.[102]

---

86 FMI Principle 6, key consideration 1
87 FMI Principle 6, key consideration 2
88 See **section 14.26**
89 FMI Principle 6, key consideration 3
90 See **section 14.24**
91 FMI Principle 6, key consideration 4
92 FMI Principle 6, key consideration 5
93 FMI Principle 6, key consideration 6
94 FMI Principle 6, key consideration 7
95 FMI Principle 5
96 FMI Principles, para 3.5.5
97 FMI Principle 5, key considerations 2 and 3 and para 3.5.5
98 FMI Principle 5, key consideration 4
99 FMI Principles, para 3.5.8
100 FMI Principles, para 3.5.9
101 FMI Principles, para 3.5.10
102 FMI Principle 16

14.22 Given the importance of margin in a CCP's defence against participant default, it is perhaps surprising how brief and undemanding the previous set of CPSS Recommendations were:

'If a CCP relies on margin requirements to limit its credit exposures to participants, those requirements should be sufficient to cover potential exposures in normal market conditions. The models and parameters used in setting margin requirements should be risk-based and reviewed regularly.'[103]

The CPSS explained their previous recommendation in terms of the balance of convenience between opportunity cost for participants[104] and protection for the CCP. The question of the degree of prudence which should be adopted in setting margin requirements is discussed below, but while CCPs compete for business it is unavoidable that there will be some degree of competition among them on the (expensive to participants) level of margin collected. In a competitive market, the official regulatory standard becomes the floor in the 'race to the bottom',[105] and CCPs will assess the degree of prudence of their protective measures by reference to their default funds. These considerations, together with the move to mandatory clearing of OTC derivatives, may have influenced the more prescriptive approach taken in the 2012 FMI Principles.

Initial margin and variation margin compared

14.23 In a discussion of margining, it is vital to distinguish between 'initial' and 'variation' margin. Initial margin is the buffer of collateral collected by the CCP to assist it in avoiding loss following a default. All new transactions registered at the CCP will thus require the posting of initial margin, unless the effect of the new transaction is to cancel, partly or wholly, an existing registered position. The CCP collects initial margin from both buyer *and* seller in respect of the same market transaction, since either might default. Most of the discussion which follows is devoted to *initial* margin, being the first financial line of defence in the event of a participant's failure.

Variation margin

14.24 Variation margin, by contrast, is not part of the CCP's protective mechanism for managing defaults. It is merely the mechanism whereby the CCP keeps pace with price movements in the market. So, if the buyer agreed to pay 100 for some securities when the trade was done on Monday, but by Tuesday the price of the securities fell to 99, the CCP is exposed to the buyer by an additional 1 in the event of the buyer's failure unless the CCP collects 1 in variation margin from the buyer. Similarly, if the price had risen, the CCP's exposure to the buyer would have fallen, but its exposure to the seller would have risen. So variation margin is a conduit payment, paid to the CCP by the participant with the loss-making position and paid on by the CCP to the participant with the gain-making position. Being a throughput, variation margin is almost invariably paid in cash.

---

103 CPSS Recommendation 4
104 See Kalavathi, L, and Shanker, L, 'Margin Requirements and the Demand for Futures Contracts' (April 1991) Journal of Futures Markets, vol 11, pp 213–237
105 See **section 13.19**

Variation margin raises few technical issues because its quantification is a matter of observed fact, unlike initial margin determination, which requires predictive guesswork. Apart from risks associated with non-collection, the principal difficulty with variation margin arises from the accounting treatment in the books of participants of variation margin payments made to a CCP. The issue is this: if variation margin is merely collateral, held by the CCP on the title transfer basis, then it represents a debt owed by the CCP to the participant who has paid it. The participant might therefore need to show, in its accounts, that it had an obligation to the CCP, representing the losses accrued but not yet due on its transaction, and an offsetting entitlement or exposure to the CCP, in the form of the CCP's obligations regarding the variation margin. For some participants this may be less desirable than the alternative characterisation, which is that the payment of variation margin represents a settlement payment. The General Regulations of LCH.Clearnet Limited[106] indicate that open exchange contracts are settled daily to market, meaning that LCH.Clearnet opens a 'settlement contract' on the same terms as the open contract but opposite in sense at the official exchange price for the day, and will then calculate a settlement amount which results from the offsetting of the settlement contract against the open contract. This amount is the variation margin which is paid one way or the other. LCH.Clearnet then opens a new contract in the participant's account at the official exchange price.

14.25 The FSA, in its finalised guidance for CCPs on credit risk management, says this on the subject of variation margin:

'The FSA considers the ability to calculate and promptly call variation margin a key aspect of [counterparty credit risk] mitigation. In considering the adequacy of the variation margin process the FSA may typically consider to what extent: the CCP has the operational capacity and authority to call variation margin on an intraday basis; and when a minimum threshold to call variation margin is reached, the materiality of this threshold is compared to the size of the position cleared.'[107]

The subject of variation margin is thus closely connected with that of intra-day margin calls, considered further at **section 14.27(4)**. However, an intra-day call for variation margin is still a call based on previous price movements; it may be coupled with an intra-day call for additional *initial* margin, because a sizeable change in prices during the course of a day indicates a time of extreme volatility, and may imply that an adjustment to the CCP's initial margin model is needed.

Initial margin

14.26 As to initial margin, the issues are manifold and complex. The starting point is to examine what 'initial margin' is supposed to cover. The EACH Standards explain that 'the clearing house should establish prudent initial margin requirements that measure the latent market risk of the positions held by members – so that, should a member default, the clearing house has, in all

---

106 LCH.Clearnet Limited, *General Regulations* (January 2011), reg 15
107 Financial Services Authority, *FSA Reviews of Counterparty Credit Risk Management by Central Counterparties* (January 2012), Finalised Guidance, http://www.fsa.gov.uk/static/pubs/guidance/fg12-03.pdf, para 14

but the most extreme market circumstances, sufficient margin to cover default losses without recourse to other financial resources at its disposal.'[108] The losses will arise in the following way. A participant who has defaulted will leave the CCP with an unmatched book, obliging the CCP to ensure performance to the non-defaulting participants but without the expectation of performance being rendered by the defaulter. Strategies for handling this mismatch are discussed in **sections 14.40–14.46**. Whichever is chosen, the size of the CCP's potential loss is predominantly driven by the market price at which the CCP can close off its mismatched book. The simplest way to envisage the problem is that the CCP must buy a replacement contract to plug the gap left by the defaulter. The cost of that exercise is a function of three variables: the duration of the period before the replacement exercise is completed, the steps taken to mitigate loss during that period, and the volatility of the market.

The duration of market risk which initial margin is intended to cover – what may be called the 'default holding period' – is the period between the last valuation of the position or portfolio being managed and the moment of its liquidation, assuming all variation margin has been paid up. (The old CPSS Recommendation timed the start-point at the last delivery of variation margin.[109]) Regulatory standards about the price movement during the default holding period which margin is supposed to cover are undemanding. Professor Richard Dale[110] observed in 1998 that US CCPs clearing futures contracts set margin levels to cover the maximum one-day price movement on 95% of the days during selected historical observation periods. It may be that a one-day default holding period is (or at one time was) prudent for the US futures markets, but for other transaction types such a standard might be regarded as lax.[111]

EMIR does not prescribe the default holding period but sets a 99% confidence interval standard, in line with the FMI Principles: 'margins shall be sufficient ... to cover losses that result from at least 99% of the exposures movements over an appropriate time horizon.'[112] If it is generally accepted that market volatility increases at times of stress, and that stress is highly correlated with default by CCP participants, the 99% standard also looks casual. The explanation is presumably this: 'Margin requirements impose opportunity costs on CCP participants. So, a CCP needs to strike a balance between greater protection for itself and higher opportunity costs for its participants. For this reason, margin requirements are not designed to cover price risk in all market conditions.'[113] This approach – that is, to collect margin on the basis that even on about 12 'ordinary market conditions' days each year it will be insufficient – may still be prudent if there is enough in the default fund to fill the gap. The apportionment of CCP protection between the default fund and margin is considered further below.

---

108 EACH Standard B4
109 CPSS Recommendations, para 4.4.3
110 Dale, R, 'Risk Management in US Derivative Clearing Houses' (September 1998) Essays in International Financial & Economic Law, vol 14, http://www.jscc.co.jp/en/ccp12/materials/docs/0416/1.pdf
111 Cf FMI Principles, footnote 76
112 EMIR, art 41(1)
113 CPSS Recommendations, para 4.4.3; see also EMIR, recital (66)

14.27 Other factors may also affect the sufficiency of initial margin:

(1) *Product risk.* This subject is considered in **sections 14.16–14.18**.

(2) *Collection risk.* CCP participants will usually pay variation margin in cash, as described above, but initial margin will be locked away for longer periods, and CCPs will be expected by their participants to allow for alternative forms of collateral to be deposited as initial margin. LCH. Clearnet Limited lists the following as acceptable types of collateral, in principle: cash, certain government bonds, performance bonds and certificates of deposit.[114] Insofar as margin consists of cash, there may be some risk associated with the timetable for collection of the cash: the EACH Standards state 'the clearing house should ensure that members' cash liabilities are finally settled as quickly and securely as possible, bearing in mind the currency mix of its business – so that money settlement risk is kept to a minimum.'[115] LCH.Clearnet Limited requires its participants to have accounts at one of a number of selected banks which allow LCH. Clearnet to draw cash from them by book transfer – ie without the need for transfer across any independent payment system – immediately. Securities collateral is clearly subject to collection risk, and on a larger scale owing to the duration of settlement cycles. Letters of credit and performance bonds may be useful in a default as a source of immediate liquidity, not involving the problems of sale, but are relatively inflexible after the point of receipt.

(3) *Valuation risk.* Securities collateral and cash collected in a different currency from that in which the exposure arises will involve market and currency risk, which will be reflected in a haircut applied by the CCP. Further, the need to liquidate securities or foreign currency will have an impact on the default holding period, unless the CCP has a liquidity line sufficient to tide it over until the margin is realised (but even this will entail some cost). Various studies show that it is unwise for a CCP to model the value realisable from collateral on the basis of Value-at-Risk methodology, and that haircuts should prudently be set so as to take account of more unusual price behaviour in extreme market conditions.[116] There is an unavoidable trade-off between complete protection and market acceptability of haircutting practice. If it is accepted that *both* the measure of risk to be collateralised *and* the value of the collateral collected are subject to this type of compromise, it follows logically that margin cannot be expected to be sufficient to cover the CCP for all circumstances. Another danger is wrong-way risk:[117] collateral should not fall in value at the moment it is most needed, or if the exposure it is supposed to cover increases, but this is what could happen if a CCP were to rely too heavily on equities as collateral for cash equities clearing, or government bonds as collateral for clearing of interest rate products.

(4) *Changed market conditions.* Intraday margin calls – that is, increments to the amount of initial margin considered prudent to support a given

---

114 LCH.Clearnet Ltd, *Clearing House Procedures,* s 3 (April 2008)
115 EACH Standard C7
116 Saardchom, N, 'Collateral Valuation in Clearing and Settlement System' (December 2010) Journal of Business and Policy Research, vol 5, pp 36–53; García, A, and Gençay, R, *Risk-Cost Frontier and Collateral Valuation in Securities Settlement Systems for Extreme Market Events* (May 2006), Bank of Canada Working Paper 2006-17
117 See **section 14.17(5)**

position – may be needed if the market conditions have changed since the participant registered the positions with the CCP. Professor Dale's 1998 study indicated that intraday margin calls could be expected at the Options Clearing Corporation when initial margin was eroded by 50% during the trading day, or when the circumstances of an individual participant merited action; it may be questioned whether the 50%-erosion approach is prudent in the modern clearing environment. Intraday margining was studied in 2006 by Ms Froukelien Wendt, who discerned that three intraday margining practices were prevalent in Europe: routine intraday calls are made, as well as price-driven non-routine calls, and non-routine participant-specific calls attributable to the size of a participant's positions and, presumably, the CCP's opinion of that participant's financial standing.[118] (Routine intra-day calls would reflect changes in the portfolios of participants which have occurred since the beginning of the day, and would therefore not be attributable to changed market conditions.) Ms Wendt also observed that intraday calls can have 'side-effects', including alteration of trading behaviour (geared to the timing of routine calls), liquidity impact, investment in systems both by CCP and participants, the size of the default fund, and the risk assumed by a participant on its client (to whom an intraday margin call might not easily be passed on).

(5) *Model risk.* Model risk is an acute problem for CCPs setting their parameters for margin collection. The EMIR test of 'sufficient to cover losses that result from at least 99% of the exposures movements' inevitably means that CCPs' margin models will be based on 'normal' market conditions, it is easy to design models which predict 'normal' market price movements and 'normal' post-default holding periods. But the numbers generated by such models are unlikely to do valuable duty in a market upset by the default of a participant which was robust enough to be allowed into the sanctum of (ex hypothesi high-quality credit) CCP participants. Two consequences flow: CCPs do not, in practice, design models which are that simplistic; and CCPs do not assume that margin alone would be good enough to protect them in times of disturbance.

Model risk is a well-studied problem in relation to OTC derivatives exposures, where for many years financial institutions have had to manage their own potential future credit exposure to each other. The Basel Committee on Banking Supervision has written extensively on prudent practices for model validation,[119] but the read-across to CCPs' margining practices is not explicitly made in the FMI Principles.

As regards CCPs and margin, there have been some theoretical studies, and a few empirical studies which really test the sufficiency of margin actually

---

118 Wendt, F, *Intraday Margining of Central Counterparties: EU Practice and a Theoretical Evaluation of Benefits and Costs* (July 2006), DNB Working Paper No 107, http://www.dnb.nl/binaries/Working%20Paper%20No%20107-2006_tcm46-146764.pdf;h=repec:dnb:dnbwpp:107

119 Bank for International Settlements Basel Committee on Banking Supervision, *International Convergence of Capital Measurement and Capital Standards* (June 2006), http://www.bis.org/publ/bcbs128.pdf, Part 2, s VI; *Findings on the interaction of market and credit risk* (May 2009), http://www.bis.org/publ/bcbs_wp16.pdf; *Revisions to the Basel II market risk framework* (July 2009), http://www.bis.org/publ/bcbs158.pdf; *Sound practices for backtesting counterparty credit risk models* (December 2010), http://www.bis.org/publ/bcbs185.pdf

collected.[120] One study back-tested various modelling techniques in relation to the Brent and FTSE-100 futures contracts, with the conclusion that margins provided a coverage level generally in excess of 99%, over a one-day time horizon.[121] It is clear that models become less robust in disturbed market conditions, owing to the problem of 'fat tails' (the probability of an actual price being a long way from the expected price being higher than predicted under a Normal or Gaussian distribution). Furthermore, the studies rely to a greater or lesser extent on G-ARCH modelling[122] to determine the behaviour of prices, so the reliability of the conclusions depends on the validity of this choice of starting-point.

(6) *Portability of client positions and margin.* It is a requirement of EMIR[123] as well as an expectation of the FMI Principles[124] that CCPs make arrangements so that the positions, and accompanying margin deposits, supporting transactions entered into by clients of clearing members can be transferred to a second participant if the client's original clearing member defaults. Insofar as transfer is successful, the CCP may not need the margin to manage the default of the first clearing member. A high proportion of client clearing may in theory enable a CCP to reduce margin levels. On the other hand, ESMA notes that a low margin level makes it more likely that transfer would be impeded, because of the greater risk that a top-up of margin, or default fund contribution, would be needed by the transferee participant.[125]

It might be noted that the factors discussed in this and the previous section are, in general (and with the notable exception of certain intra-day margin calls observed by Ms Wendt), ones which are independent of the credit quality of the CCP's participants. Counterparty-specific credit risk is managed by control at the gate;[126] the role of initial margin is to manage the potential future credit exposure specific to the participant's cleared portfolio.

Liquidity

14.28 Liquidity risk introduces a handful of troublesome considerations into the margining debate. First, the margin itself may be illiquid, as noted above. Secondly, the positions being closed out or managed may be illiquid, lengthening the default holding period, and imposing a requirement for more margin and exacerbating the impact of any volatility in the margin. Thirdly, regulators are rightly concerned that a CCP's ability to manage a default is as

---

120 Bates, D, and Craine, R, 'Valuing the Futures Market Clearinghouse's Default Exposure during the 1987 Crash' (May 1999) Journal of Money, Credit and Banking, Vol 31, No 2, pp 248–272; Knott, R, and Mills, A, 'Modelling risk in central counterparty clearing houses' (December 2002) Bank of England Financial Stability Review, pp 162–174; Heller, D, and Vause, N, *Collateral requirements for mandatory central clearing of over-the-counter derivatives* (March 2012), BIS working paper No 373, http://www.bis.org/publ/work373.pdf

121 Knott, R, and Polenghi, M, *Assessing central counterparty margin coverage on futures contracts using GARCH models* (January 2006), Bank of England Working Paper No.287

122 Cf Turing, D, and Cramb, E, *Managing Risk in Financial Firms* (Tottel, March 2009), ISBN 978-1-84766-3030-0, s 2.2

123 Articles 39 and 48

124 FMI Principle 14

125 European Securities and Markets Authority, *Draft Technical Standards for the Regulation on OTC Derivatives, CCPs and Trade Repositories* (February 2012), Discussion Paper ESMA/2012/95, p 26

126 See **section 14.12**

much about the liquidity pressures it faces in the post-default period as about the crude assets-versus-liabilities solvency of the CCP:

> '[A] CCP that is involved in activities with a more-complex risk profile or that is systemically important in multiple jurisdictions should consider maintaining additional liquidity resources sufficient to cover a wider range of potential stress scenarios that should include, but not be limited to, the default of the two participants and their affiliates that would generate the largest aggregate payment obligation to the CCP in extreme but plausible market conditions.'[127]

The problem is that the CCP needs to continue to meet its obligations (in particular, but not exclusively, variation margin obligations) to the surviving participants in the CCP in the interim before the positions of the defaulter are closed out. These obligations need to be met from liquid assets. The post-default thirst for liquidity means that the CCP will need to maximise the amount of collateral it obtains in the form of cash, and probably to have a liquidity facility with its bankers to provide for contingencies.

In its extreme form regulatory thinking suggests that CCPs should have access to central bank emergency liquidity.[128]

Other risks affecting margin

14.29 Brief mention may be made of a few other risks related to margin.

(1) There is the possibility that the participant fails to pay, or that delivery of securities collateral is thwarted by a settlement failure. Those risks may be operational or they may be indicators of insolvency. CCPs may aim to eliminate operational risks by requiring participants to have redundant back-up structures for making margin deliveries. In times of stress, when intra-day margin calls may be made, the CCP is likely to have a low tolerance for non-delivery of margin in a timely fashion.

(2) Secondly, the CCP may be the victim of custody failure. FMI Principle 16 warns that CCPs should use regulated custodians and be sure that the assets held in custody are safe from claims of the custodian's creditors, and EMIR states a preference for non-cash assets to be held directly at a CSD.[129] If a custodian fails, the CCP should be immune from the effect of the insolvency of the custodian if the custody structure is legally robust, but there may nevertheless be delays in retrieving the collateral assets: even client assets held on trust may not be immediately accessible in the event of the custodian's failure.[130]

(3) Thirdly, there is a risk to the CCP's cash. Cash margin has to be at a commercial bank somewhere unless the CCP is privileged to have a central bank deposit account (which may be the case if the CCP has bank status). If a commercial deposit-taker fails, the CCP will lose a part of its risk protection. Bank failure is potentially catastrophic for CCPs: banks are likely to be (or to be affiliated to) CCP participants; bank failures are

---

127 FMI Principle 7, key consideration 4
128 See **section 14.59**
129 Article 47(3)
130 See **sections 10.21–10.22**

market-threatening events. The combination of extreme volatility busting margin models, default of a bank-affiliated participant, and loss of margin at a failed bank may be one which can be contemplated only with terror, but in the event of failure of a major bank must prudently be regarded as highly correlated.

Gross v net margining

14.30 One further concept relating to margining needs mention, not because it creates risk for the CCP, but because it is relevant to the handling of defaults in cases where the CCP participant has cleared trades entered into by its clients. The historical practice, before EMIR, was for CCPs to provide a 'house' and a 'client' account for each participant, with the intention, supported by the law, that in the insolvency of the participant the 'client' account transactions and margin would be handled separately from the 'house' account.[131] Client money and client asset protections were structured so as to keep the client account transactions and margin away from the insolvent estate of the participant. All client transactions were, however, bundled together into a single omnibus account.

If an omnibus account is used, the question whether the CCP receives margin on a 'gross' or a 'net' basis becomes important. If the defaulting participant had two clients who had taken opposite positions in the market, as between the CCP and the participant there would be offsetting, mutually cancelling trades, and no margin would be called by the CCP. The margin collected by the participant would be in the participant's client account, not at the CCP. Net margining occurs because the CCP regards the participant, not the client(s), as its counterparty. In the alternative, a CCP may allow or require 'gross' margining: in such a case the two opposite market positions would each be registered with the CCP and would not be offset, and a margin call would be made in respect of both transactions. This is obviously more expensive for the participant and (assuming costs to be passed through to the clients) for the clients as well. Gross margin does, however, have a beneficial effect in the case where the participant defaults. It is much easier for the CCP to identify both the positions, and the margin, referable to each of the clients, and thus it is much easier for the CCP to allow the combination of positions and margin to be transferred to another participant. Since the coming into force of EMIR it has become obligatory for European CCPs to offer individual per-client account gross-margined option in respect of cleared client transactions.[132]

DEFAULT BACKING

14.31 It is evident from the discussion about margining that margin cannot reasonably be expected to be the sole line of defence against default of a CCP participant, even if it is rightly regarded as the first line of defence. Once a margin-exhausting event happens, the ordinary parameters for determination of price movement cease to be reliable. The FMI Principles state:

---

131 See **section 9.13**
132 EMIR, art 39(5)

'A CCP should cover its current and potential future exposures to each participant fully with a high degree of confidence using margin and other prefunded financial resources… . In addition, a CCP that is involved in activities with a more-complex risk profile or that is systemically important in multiple jurisdictions should maintain additional financial resources to cover a wide range of potential stress scenarios that should include, but not be limited to, the default of the two participants and their affiliates that would potentially cause the largest aggregate credit exposure for the CCP in extreme but plausible market condition. All other CCPs should maintain additional financial resources sufficient to cover a wide range of potential stress scenarios that should include, but not be limited to, the default of the participant and its affiliates that would potentially cause the largest aggregated credit exposure for the CCP in extreme but plausible marked conditions.'[133]

It may be noteworthy that this standard is not setting a level of protection to be covered by margin alone, but by the totality of the CCP's financial resources.

EMIR is slightly different from the FMI Principles: it obliges a CCP to maintain a pre-funded default fund to cover losses which exceed those covered by margin. It must 'at least enable the CCP to withstand, under extreme but plausible market conditions, the default of the clearing member to which it has the largest exposures or of the second and third largest clearing members, if the sum of their exposures is larger.'[134] Different funds may be established for different asset classes.

Size of default fund

14.32 The default fund must be appropriately sized to protect the CCP from the exceptional risks for which it is provided. While the FMI Principles lay down rules about testing sufficiency of resources, little guidance is given on the level of additional resources required. But stress-tests, like statistical techniques for quantifying margin, cannot guarantee a 'right answer' to the level of default fund needed for what is essentially an unpredictable set of circumstances. Professors David Bates and Roger Craine[135] assessed the implications of a price move which exhausts the margin and sought to measure the 'conditionally expected additional required funds' to ensure that the CCP could perform its obligations on all contracts. Their study modelled the funds needed by the CME during the 1987 crash, and using various techniques calculated that the CME could have required between $1.2 billion and $10 billion of additional funds, if a price movement extreme enough to exhaust its margin – $2.5 billion in total – had occurred. They also concluded that a false sense of security may be given by 'aggressive margin requirement increases in October 1987' which by traditional margining methodology had 'reduced clearinghouse exposure to pre-crash levels by or before the end of November.' In another study of the 1987 stock market crash, it was found that with the level of margining then used, the exposure of the International Commodities Clearing House (now LCH.Clearnet Limited) might exceed £40 million about once per year and £200 million once per thirty years.[136]

---

133 FMI Principle 4,key consideration 4
134 EMIR, art 42
135 Bates, D, and Craine, R, 'Valuing the Futures Market Clearinghouse's Default Exposure during the 1987 Crash' (May 1999) Journal of Money, Credit and Banking, vol 31, pp 248–272
136 Gemmill, G, 'Margins and the Safety of Clearing Houses' (October 1994) Journal of Banking and Finance, vol 18, pp 979–996

In 2012 a study using G-ARCH models to quantify margin shortfalls with respect to clearing of imaginary portfolios of interest rate swaps and credit derivatives concluded that a default fund could be set at 'a small fraction of dealers' equity' if margin is adjusted to reflect prevailing level of volatility.[137] This would imply that default funds can be kept low if margining is dynamically adjusted; but the FMI Principles indicate that margining should not have negative procyclical effects,[138] and dynamic margin model adjustment would appear to violate that recommendation.

14.33 All in all, it is a difficult question for a CCP to decide on the optimum balance between default fund and margin. If the cost of collateral, the probability of default, and the risk-mitigating effect of posting margin to the CCP are the only factors taken into account, there would appear always to be a case for having some element of non-margin default funding.[139] Default fund contributions are less dynamic than margin contributions. Default fund readjustments as between contributors are done quarterly at Eurex Clearing AG[140] and LCH.Clearnet Limited.[141] Default fund contributions might be preferable over margin contributions in order to reduce liquidity stress on participants in times of high market volatility. On the other hand, there may be moral hazard if there is no margin component.

14.34 The following further considerations may be relevant in creating supplementary financial backing for a CCP beyond what is available through margining.

(1) A default fund is not the only option: other structural possibilities include 'assessment' – that is, the power to levy financial contributions, and insurance. Assessment has commonly been used by US-based CCPs, though it may expose the CCP to unacceptable liquidity risk given the potential difficulty in enforcing guarantee obligations in times of market stress. Insurance is expressly contemplated by the LCH.Clearnet Limited Default Fund Rules but may also raise equivalent liquidity concerns. For these reasons, together with the EMIR requirement for pre-funding, pre-funded default funds have become the norm for default backing in Europe. But a combination of pre-funding and assessment may be found in some CCPs: EuroCCP states '[t]o provide nevertheless for the possibility that a Participant's margin amount and contributions to the Guarantee Fund are insufficient to cover EuroCCP's losses in the event of the Participant's default, EuroCCP rules enable loss sharing among the surviving Participants according to their respective levels of recent activity.'[142]

(2) Financial backing not consisting of margin implies that someone other than the defaulter is paying for the losses. Default fund contributors may note that, in effect, they already contribute to the post-default recovery of the CCP through their availability as counterparties accepting the defaulter's

137 Heller, D, and Vause, N, *Collateral requirements for mandatory central clearing of over-the-counter derivatives* (March 2012), BIS working paper No 373, http://www.bis.org/publ/work373.pdf
138 FMI Principle 6, key consideration 3
139 Haene, P, and Sturm, A, *Optimal Central Counterparty Risk Management* (June 2009), Swiss National Bank Working Papers 2009-7
140 Eurex Clearing AG, *Clearing Conditions* (January 2011), s 6.1.1
141 Default Fund Rule 20
142 European Central Counterparty, *EuroCCP Risk Management Approach and Processes* (January 2012), http://www.euroccp.co.uk/docs/leadership/risk_mgmt_updated_12_2011.pdf

closed-out positions – explicitly so in the case of OTC derivatives clearing, which entails the agreement by the survivors to bid for parts of the defaulter's book,[143] but also implicitly in the case of products traded on organised markets. Mutualisation of risk tends, with effective governance, to ensure that the CCP adopts prudent standards of risk management. These factors may result in a shift towards a higher proportion of contingency funding being in the form of margin, or other risk-reduction techniques, as opposed to default fund contributions, notwithstanding that it may be more costly for participants to provide margin than default fund backing.

(3) If survivors are paying, they will wish to ensure that their contributions are fair. The amount of contributions may be assessed by reference to their volume of usage of the CCP. More complex systems of contribution can be devised where the default fund is divided up according to product types (as with the LCH.Clearnet Limited default fund).[144] As to application of the survivors' contributions, while it might superficially seem appropriate to share losses by reference to the size of each survivor's trading relationship with the defaulter, this is inherently unfair in a CCP, because (even where OTC trading is involved) a survivor's choice of counterparty is not, in a cleared market, influenced by the probability of default of the counterparty: the job of counterparty risk assessment is for the CCP.

14.35 The 'survivors will pay' principle raises the question not just of how to balance the risk between the defaulter and the survivors, but also which group of survivors should pay. As CCPs do not have to be owned by their participants, the shareholders might legitimately be regarded as a group of survivors who should suffer if the risk management of the CCP has been imprudent.[145] Default backing may thus be provided through the capital of the CCP. Regulatory capital requirements for European CCPs are discussed in **sections 6.23–6.26**; suffice it to say here that the rules have not been set with default management in mind. Default funding is more flexible than share capital, but it exposes the CCP to competitive disadvantage. A CCP which sets low default fund levels might be more attractive to participants than a more conservatively-managed CCP. However, in a market shock, the CCP with the smaller default fund may struggle to survive without a capital injection from its shareholders or requesting the surviving participants for further funds. The notion that the CCP might have to seek consent of the participant-survivors in order to continue in business will allow flexibility both in the structuring of default backing and in its quantification. In practice, any usage of the default fund will necessitate a call for top-up funding from the surviving participants, and major CCPs do not oblige survivors to commit to honour top-up requests,[146] though they may have to cease to participate as clearing members.[147]

Structure of default funds

14.36 A default fund will typically be structured as a contribution by CCP participants of cash or securities collateral, which will be added to the

---

143 See **section 14.45**

144 See LCH.Clearnet Limited Default Fund Rules (July 2009), http://www.lchclearnet.com/ Images/default%20fund%20rules_tcm6-43735.pdf

145 See **section 6.26**

146 See for example LCH.Clearnet Limited Default Fund Rule 32

147 See for example Eurex Clearing AG Clearing Condition 6.3

contributor's margin in the event of the participant's own default, but which is also available in the event of another participant's default if the margin (and own default fund contribution) provided by the defaulter are insufficient to cover the losses sustained by the CCP in consequence of the default.[148] Default fund contributions are treated, as regards the contributor itself, as a supplement to margin: under Part VII of the Companies Act 1989 the protections given to margin are also extended to 'default fund contributions', defined, in relation to a recognised clearing house as 'contribution by a member of a recognised clearing house to a fund which (i) is maintained by that clearing house for the purpose of covering losses arising in connection with defaults by any of the members of the clearing house, and (ii) may be applied for that purpose under the default rules of the clearing house.'[149] To benefit from such protection, the rules about the application of the default fund must constitute part of the CCP's default rules.

DEFAULT HANDLING

14.37   The FMI Principles relating to default handling are clear and correct. 'An FMI should have appropriate policies and procedures to handle participant defaults. ... Further, a CCP needs an appropriate segregation and portability regime to protect customer positions in the event of a participant default or insolvency.'[150] The explanatory paragraphs cover, among other matters, suggested content for default rules,[151] waterfall of usage of financial resources,[152] and portability arrangements.[153]

14.38   Being a one-size-fits-all document, the FMI Principles can be criticised for avoiding some of the more troublesome detail with regard to default management, which, together with the older CPSS Recommendations targeted at CCPs, can be summarised as follows.

- CCPs should strive to avoid defaults happening in the first place, through monitoring and (if necessary) imposing restrictions.

- CCPs should have powers promptly to close out or effectively manage a defaulting participant's positions and to apply collateral. Close-out, hedging and transfer are all contemplated as possible techniques, but it is expected that CCPs will prefer to liquidate positions quickly rather than hold and manage.

- CCPs should have procedures for dealing with the positions and margin of customers. Customer and proprietary assets should be handled separately. CCPs should structure its portability arrangements for customer positions and margin in a way that makes it highly likely that they will be transferred to one or more other participants.

- CCPs should be able to utilise promptly the financial resources maintained to cover losses and liquidity risk arising from defaults. The rules should specify the order in which resources will be utilised (the waterfall): a CCP

---

148   See, for example, LCH.Clearnet Limited, Default Fund Rule 16 (July 2009)
149   Companies Act 1989, s 188(3A)(b)
150   FMI Principles 13–14, introductory text
151   FMI Principles, para 3.13.2
152   FMI Principles, para 3.13.3
153   FMI Principles 14, key consideration 3

will 'typically' look first to assets posted by the defaulting participant. Beyond that there is no prescription as to order of utilisation. The rules should specify the obligations of non-defaulting participants to replenish the CCP's resources.

- The rules and powers of the CCP should be able to withstand challenge under the insolvency regime applicable to the defaulting participant. In particular, collateral application should not be subject to a stay or reversal under applicable law.

- CCPs should manage defaults in a manner which causes minimal disruption to the market.

- Default events and procedures should be publicised. In this respect, it may be noted that the European Association of CCP Clearing Houses has issued a Guideline[154] which specifies that the following six matters should be made 'available to market participants': Events of default; Waterfall of resources; Impact of default on settlement; Legal relationship between the CCP and customers; Treatment of house and client positions; Post-default news updates. Each of these is covered in a degree of detail and contains sub-recommendations. Why publicity should be confined to 'market participants' only is unclear – certainly the Recommendations make it clear that the whole market, not just the participants of the CCP is meant – but a review of the public websites of leading CCPs suggests (perhaps surprisingly, given that default risk management is the raison d'être of a CCP) that giving wider publicity about default procedures is not regarded as a priority.

14.39 EMIR covers these matters in the following way.

(1) A CCP must have detailed default procedures.[155]

(2) A CCP must take prompt action to contain losses and liquidity pressures resulting from defaults. Close-out should not expose non-defaulting clearing members to losses they cannot anticipate or control.[156] (In relation to the default handling of cleared OTC products, meeting this requirement may be challenging.[157])

(3) A CCP must notify its regulator before implementing the default procedure.[158] EMIR is silent on wider communications.

(4) A CCP must ensure that its default procedures are enforceable,[159] but EMIR stops short of providing the type of legal protection seen in Part VII of the Companies Act 1989 or the Settlement Finality Directive (SFD).[160] It is, however, envisaged that CCPs will be designated under the SFD.[161]

(5) A CCP must trigger the transfer procedures for individually-segregated or collectively-segregated client positions on request, assuming there is a replacement GCM which has previously committed to accept them.[162]

---

154 European Association of CCP Clearing Houses, *Default Procedures Publication Guideline* (May 2010), http://www.eachorg.eu/each/each-info-100527-default-procedure-publication.pdf
155 EMIR, art 48(1)
156 EMIR, art 48(2)
157 See **sections 5.4** and **14.40–14.44**
158 EMIR, art 48(3)
159 EMIR, art 48(4)
160 See **sections 8.9–8.23**
161 Cf EMIR, recital (51), art 17
162 EMIR, art 48(5), (6)

(6) A CCP may use clients' collateral only to cover positions held for their account.[163]

In the following sections, the following core aspects of default management, as well as certain practical issues, are studied in more detail: close-out and managing a defaulter's positions; transfer and portability; liquidity; and legal obligations imposed on CCPs managing defaults.

RE-ESTABLISHING A MATCHED BOOK

14.40 Upon an event of default, the CCP will have two considerations to manage: staunching the losses attributable to the failure of a participant which will no longer be able to satisfy its obligations; and ensuring performance continues vis-à-vis the surviving counterparties. At its most simplistic, a trade entered into by the defaulter with a survivor, which has been novated to the CCP, is a trade which is not going to be performed by the defaulter but which continues as regards the CCP's obligations to the survivor. The duality of duties means that a CCP cannot adopt the model of close-out followed in OTC bilateral arrangements such as the ISDA master agreement.[164] (That model involves the termination of all open transactions, a valuation process to establish the replacement cost or loss (or as the case may be, gain) of the terminated transactions, and an aggregation and netting to establish a single overall net monetary amount payable by one party to the other.[165]) To close out in this fashion will deal with the first problem, viz. terminating ongoing relations with, and quantifying a claim against, the defaulter; but it does not deal with the second.

Close-out by CCPs

14.41 Accordingly the CCP's method of close-out will typically require some form of 'trading out' in order to re-establish a matched book, where each obligation owed by the CCP to a surviving participant is matched by another, opposite obligation owed to the CCP by another surviving participant. The result can be achieved by the CCP instructing a broker to take a new position on behalf of the defaulter in the market-place, as illustrated by the following example.

X has defaulted with a single transaction recorded in its account at the CCP: X has contracted to buy 1000 shares of Mega PLC at a cost of £1 a share. CCP is obligated to pay its selling participant Y the £1000 for these shares on the delivery date. CCP instructs broker B to enter the market and, in its own name but on behalf of CCP, to sell 1000 shares of Mega PLC at the prevailing market price. B duly achieves a bargain at today's market price of 90p a share; B's market counterparty uses Z as its clearing member who is from this moment obliged to buy 1000 Mega shares from CCP. CCP can now match the obligation of Z to buy with the obligation of Y to sell. B's obligation to sell will be booked by CCP to the account of X, as if X had been B's client, with the consequence that X is now obliged to buy 1000 Mega from CCP at £1 and also to sell 1000 Mega to CCP at

---

163 EMIR, art 48(7)
164 See http://www.isda.org/publications/isdamasteragrmnt.aspx
165 ISDA master agreement (2002 Multi-currency Cross-border version), s 6

90p; the delivery obligations net out to zero and the cash obligations net out at a loss to CCP of £100, which CCP can set off against X's margin deposit.

14.42   While this example uses a cash securities trade, the logic is the same even for cash-settled and derivative products. The need for the CCP to re-establish a matched book makes it imperative to trade out rather than simply terminate. The processes of the CCP which achieve this are, however, theoretically at risk of challenge under insolvency laws:[166]

(1) One fear is section 127 of the Insolvency Act 1986. Section 127 renders void any disposition of a company's property after the commencement of winding-up unless the sanction of the court is obtained. The fear is that section 127 may render void the entry by the defaulter into a new contract in the manner envisaged by the process of trading-out. However, it does not appear that the cases relating to section 127 prohibit new contracts unless the contract creates a specifically enforceable obligation to deliver property.[167] Property transfer obligations under clearable contracts are unlikely to be specifically enforceable, owing to the fungibility of the property concerned. Any actual delivery or payment made by the defaulter may, however, be at risk. Nonetheless, the residual problem under section 127 is disapplied by section 164 of the Companies Act 1989.

(2) New contracts are more a problem of agency: the loss of agency is perhaps more troublesome than section 127. Insolvency proceedings may terminate the agency of the CCP, with the result that the CCP cannot enter into closing-out positions on the defaulter's behalf and book them to the defaulter's account. This is the primary mechanism for neutralising the defaulter's obligations other than payment obligations. However, there are alternative devices for achieving this result, such as treating the cost of the closing-out contract as the gain or loss made by the CCP as a result of termination of the defaulter's pre-default positions; and any residual problem should be dispelled by section 159 of the Companies Act 1989.

(3) Another threat is the rule against build-up of set-offs set out in the statutory insolvency set-off code.[168] The rule renders ineligible for set-off any obligation entered into by the insolvent person after a certain cut-off time, which is broadly the time of opening of insolvency proceedings. This cut-off rule is designed precisely to stop counterparties 'building up' set-off rights.[169] This rule is disapplied by section 163 of the Companies Act 1989.

Hold and manage

14.43   An alternative for the CCP is to manage the defaulter's book for itself. In relation to cash equities positions, an obligation of the defaulter to pay for securities could possibly be covered by margin deposits, leaving the CCP with an unwanted long position in securities when delivered by the surviving

---

166   See **section 8.8** for a more comprehensive range of possible challenges
167   *Re French's Wine Bar Ltd* (1987) 3 BCC 173; *Sowman v David Samuel Trust Ltd* [1978] 1 WLR 22
168   Insolvency Rules 1986, SI 1986 No 1925, rr 2.85(2), 4.90(2); Bank Insolvency (England and Wales) Rules 2009, SI 2009 No 356, r 72(1); Investment Bank Special Administration (England and Wales) Rules 2011, SI 2011 No 1301, r 164(2)
169   See Turing, D, 'Set-off' in Marks, D (ed), *Tolley's Insolvency Law* (looseleaf, December 2010), paras S6038ff

selling participant. Those securities could be liquidated by the CCP at its leisure. Similarly, if the defaulter's position was that of seller, the CCP could rely on the exchange's or MTF's buy-in procedures to be operated at the end of the conventional buy-in period, thus satisfying the entitlement of the CCP's surviving buying participant, with the costs of the buy-in being booked to the account of the defaulter. In essence the CCP would rely on the exchange or MTF to operate the default management procedure. This may be less effective if the relationship between the CCP and the MTF or exchange is not close, as it cannot be assumed that the exchange or MTF would exercise its powers in a way designed to protect the interests of the CCP.

The hold-and-manage option may, however, be less prudent in the case of markets with long buy-in periods where the CCP is exposed to volatility following a high-profile default, or for derivative instruments which can convert from being an asset to a liability. In either of these cases there is a risk that holding and managing may leave the CCP with a loss which increases over time and could eventually exceed the value of margin held.

On the other hand, there remain a variety of possibilities for handling more complex products such as derivatives. Partial hedging, which will limit or contain the risk if not eliminate it altogether, may be possible. Hence the CPSS's focus on the CCP's ability to deal in the underlying products to which a cleared OTC derivative relates. 'To manage the hedging and macro-hedging process, a CCP should consider (1) its ability and the timeframe required to obtain individual hedges for portfolio positions; (2) the cost of obtaining those hedges; and (3) its ability and the associated cost to actively manage the associated risks (including basis risk) of the hedging strategy up to the disposition of the portfolio of a defaulting participant.'[170]

Holding and managing OTC derivative positions may present particular complexities. On the one hand, liquidity may dry up, leaving the CCP with an unmatched holding whether it likes it or not. To force the surviving participants into an auction or to exercise put-option rights against survivors[171] may deepen an existing financial crisis or even begin one – the CCP will need to balance its wider duty to the market under article 48(2) of EMIR against its own need to mitigate loss deriving from the default. Another danger is that the default itself may have had an adverse effect on the prices attributable to the positions to be closed out or managed: for example, wrong-way risk may be exacerbated in times of CDS volatility.[172]

Transfer

14.44 A third option for a CCP is to transfer the defaulter's trades to survivors. Transfer is commonly considered in relation to clients' positions, on the basis that clients would prefer to be allowed to keep their positions open; this subject is discussed in **sections 14.47–14.58**, and some of the issues discussed there may be relevant even where no client is involved. The outcome of a transfer in a simple case, where no client is involved, will be similar to that achieved

---

170 CPSS-IOSCO Consultative Report CPSS 89, Guidance 6.2
171 See **section 14.45**
172 Brigo, D, and Chourdakis, K, 'Counterparty Risk for Credit Default Swaps – Impact of spread volatility and default correlation' (November 2009) International Journal of Theoretical and Applied Finance, Vol. 12, No. 7, pp. 1007–1026

by trading out, with two differences: the CCP will be saved broking charges; and there may be market-integrity issues to be managed. On the latter point, considerations will include whether the price agreed with the survivor for the transferred positions is fair and whether any questions of market abuse could arise;[173] and whether the CCP is obliged to offer the positions for acquisition among its participants generally.[174]

On these questions of fairness, it may be noted that the Swaps and Derivatives Market Association objects to the practice of limiting transfers to a select group of bidders, as is the practice with OTC derivatives CCPs:

> 'Another clearinghouse rule requires clearing members to utilize their own internal dealer desks to participate in auctions of the portfolios of any distressed clearing members. This rule limits broader auction participation. The true measure of success of an auction is achieving a clearing price and to achieve the optimal clearing price it is better to have more participants in the auction than fewer participants.
>
> 'Moreover, there is precedent in the OTC marketplace for rapid and highly organized auctions. For example, ISDA currently manages a default auction process when an event triggers a payout on a default swap and these auctions include many, not a limited few, participants. There were over 400 participants in the Lehman Brothers auction, which clearly yielded better prices than if there were less than 10 participants.
>
> 'Speed is also not a legitimate excuse to restrict auctions to only a few select bidders as speed is already present in other auction scenarios. For example, successful auctions in CDS for bid wanted in comp/offers wanted in comp ("BWIC/OWIC") exist. For BWICs, institutional investors enter the market with multiple swap positions for auction by submitting them to dealers for bid with time frames as short as 60 to 90 minutes. Market auction participants then bid on these BWICs accordingly and the auctions proceed efficiently. Electronic platforms provide auction venues: Creditex and IDX are such platforms already capable of managing such an auction and other players are likely to follow.'[175]

It may also be noted in this context that the CME managed the preponderance of its close-out of Lehman Brothers' book of cleared energy, foreign exchange, interest rate and equity derivatives through limited-participation auctions and transfer. Of these asset classes, the prices required from successful bidders exceeded the margin referable to them in two cases, though in the other two cases the margin referable was more than required. Overall the CME had a surplus of margin. But the Examiner's report considered the availability of 'colorable claims' against the CME and the firms which 'bought [the] positions a steep discount during the liquidation ordered by the CME' for losses sustained by Lehman Brothers as a result of the forced sales.[176]

173 Cf Directive 2003/6/EC of the European Parliament and of the Council of 28 January 2003 on insider dealing and market manipulation

174 Cf EMIR, art 36(1)

175 Swaps and Derivatives Market Association, *Lessening Systemic Risk: Removing Final Hurdles to Clearing OTC Derivatives* (September 2010), http://www.thesdma.org/pdf/skirmish_paper_091610.pdf, p 4

176 Valukas, A, *Lehman Brothers Holdings Inc. Chapter 11 Proceedings Examiner Report* (March 2010), http://jenner.com/lehman/, pp 1841–1871

OTC derivatives

14.45 Clearing of OTC derivatives or other transactions for which there is no commonly accepted market price gives rise to the special difficulty of liquidity risk in the market immediately after an event of default has occurred with regard to an OTC clearing participant. There is *ex hypothesi* no organised market or platform to which the CCP can go to replace closed-out positions and re-establish its matched book. There may, moreover, be no guarantee that the participants in the OTC market who were active before the event of default will wish to continue to make a market after that event. Prices quoted by surviving market participants may be well away from what was expected under 'normal' trading conditions; participants willing to trade may have no relationship with the CCP which is managing the default. CCPs which clear OTC products thus need to ensure the existence of a pool of market participants willing to take over the book of the defaulter, as an alternative to the market-based trading out strategy illustrated by the example given above. Consequently, 'an OTC derivatives CCP may need to consider having participants sign up ex ante to bid in an auction of the defaulting participant's portfolio, and, in extremis (ie if the auction process fails), accept an allocation of the portfolio to surviving participants.'[177]

The typical arrangement is to oblige survivors to take on undisposed-of transactions (or positions which represent aggregate transactions or sub-portfolios) under a pre-determined pricing mechanism. One example of this approach is found in the Clearing Rules of ICE Clear Europe:

> 'To the extent that the Clearing House does not terminate, transfer or close out all of the CDS Contracts of a Defaulter, the Clearing House may at its discretion require the entry into of new CDS Contracts between the Clearing House and CDS Clearing Members that are not Defaulters which CDS Contracts replace any remaining CDS Contracts of the Defaulter at a price determined by the Clearing House, taking into account the minimum target price determined in accordance with the Procedures, on a pro rata basis (or as near as practicable, with odd lots determined by the Clearing House and assigned randomly) in proportion to the size of each CDS Clearing Member's required CDS Guaranty Fund Contribution relative to the aggregate of all required CDS Guaranty Fund Contributions.'[178]

The ICE Clear model presumes the effectiveness of a pricing methodology agreed to by the survivors. The approach of LCH.Clearnet Limited involves an auction under which participants submit a best offer for each portfolio of transactions by sealed bid. LCH.Clearnet does not undertake to solicit bids from all its participants and indicates that non-participants may also be permitted to bid, stating that its aim is to 'ensure sufficient competitiveness to provide the best reasonable price.'[179] Both approaches assume that the survivors would prefer to see the survival of the CCP rather than resign from participation so as to escape having to assume unwanted transaction obligations. All involve

177 CPSS-IOSCO Consultative Report CPSS 89, Guidance 6.1

178 ICE Clear Europe, *Clearing Rules* (May 2010), https://www.theice.com/publicdocs/clear_ europe/rulebooks/rules/ICE_Clear_Europe_Clearing_Rules_att.pdf, r 903(a)(xii)

179 LCH.Clearnet, *Default Management Overview – Exchange and Commodity Derivatives Markets* (June 2010), http://www.lchclearnet.com/Images/Default%20Management%20 overview%20June%202010_tcm6-54499.pdf mutualisation of risk, thus encouraging CCPs to adopt highly conservative transaction eligibility criteria.

14.46 The following description by LCH.Clearnet Limited of its handling of the Lehman Brothers default illustrates what may be done:

'The total notional value of the portfolio was $9 trillion, encompassing a total of 66,390 trades across 5 major currencies. This was achieved through the risk neutralisation and competitive auctioning of the Lehman OTC interest rate swap portfolio among the SwapClear members.... The management of the default involved:

'At default (Monday, 15 September 2008) the default management group (member firms form part of this group on a rotating basis) seconded preassigned and experienced traders to work alongside LCH.Clearnet's risk management team to apply hedges and neutralise the macro level market risk on the defaulter portfolio. All participants adhered to strict confidentiality rules throughout the process.

'The risk positions were reviewed daily and further hedges were executed in response to changing market conditions.

'From Wednesday, 24 September to Friday, 3 October, the competitive auctions of the five hedge currency portfolios were successfully completed.

'The default was managed well within Lehman margin held and LCH. Clearnet will not be using the default fund in the management of the Lehman default.'[180]

CLIENT CLEARING – TRANSFER (PORTABILITY) OF CLIENT POSITIONS

14.47 Where a surviving participant is willing to take on the transactions of the defaulter, it will be expected that the CCP will have the ability to transfer positions from the defaulter's client accounts to the survivor's. Transfer will preserve the clients' investments from premature termination or from settlement in cash rather than by physical delivery. The CPSS Consultative Report noted that portability of client positions may also have a stabilising influence, reducing the risk of a 'run on a counterparty' which may otherwise happen if a GCM's financial position deteriorates.[181] There are views to the contrary.[182] It has been said that segregation and portability can have economic effects which may seem odd: whereas use of an omnibus account involves a degree of loss-sharing among the clients using the account,[183] use of single-client accounts at the CCP 'effectively transfers the risk of customer default ([concurrent] with a clearing member default) to other clearing members via the default fund.'[184]

The technique for successful transfer of a client's transactions to a new GCM, following the default of the previous GCM, will depend on the structure of

---

180 LCH.Clearnet Limited, Press Release (October 2008), http://www.lchclearnet.com/images/2008-10-08%20swapclear%20default_tcm6-46506.pdf
181 CPSS-IOSCO Consultative Report CPSS 89, Guidance 6.4
182 See **section 6.29(3)**
183 See **section 9.11**
184 Pirrong, C, *The Economics of Central Clearing: Theory and Practice* (May 2011), ISDA Discussion Paper No 1, http://www2.isda.org/attachment/MzE0NA==/ISDAdiscussion_CCP_Pirrong.pdf, p 31

clearing arrangements at the CCP. The variables which determine the outcome are the counterparty and account structure allowed by the CCP, whether the CCP collects margin on a net or gross basis, and how the client transfers margin to the GCM. The last factor, in particular, may not be controlled by the CCP, and the success of the transfer may be affected by the adequacy of the client money and client asset protection regime applicable in the insolvency of the GCM.

Agency model

14.48 A fundamental precept of clearing is that a CCP needs to have certainty as to its participants' ability to fulfil their obligations. For this reason, and because of the risk that agency structures pose to multilateral netting under the rule in *British Eagle*,[185] CCPs tend to favour a principal-to-principal basis for their dealings with participants.[186] However, when it comes to transfer, an agency structure would be much simpler. The CCP could just ignore the defaulter, and the CCP and the client could agree on the appointment of a new agent.

As it is, pure agency, where the GCM is no more than a transfer agent, is not regarded as a feasible option by European CCPs. But a mixed model is sometimes encountered, which combines features of the purist principal-to-principal approach to risk management with the client-facing advantages of agency. In the mixed model, the GCM is the party which owes obligations to the CCP, but the CCP may, in the event of the GCM's demise, be entitled to perform its own obligations to the client direct. Where the CCP has this option, it can readily return margin to the client (and then the client can re-use it to support the same transactions, once they have been transferred in the CCP's books to a replacement GCM).

14.49 The following observations may be made about a mixed-agency model for assisting transfer.

- While better for the client than a strict principal-to-principal model, a significant number of the same issues arise as in a principal-to-principal case. In particular, the client's positions and the margin associated with them will need to be separately identifiable; and the basis on which margin is provided needs to be structured so as to avoid any risk that the margin is not part of the insolvent estate of the failed GCM. Furthermore, even under the mixed-agency model, the client may owe obligations to the GCM, which will have to be satisfied somehow. These points are considered below in relation to the principal-to-principal model.

- The ability of the CCP to leapfrog over the failed GCM needs, even in an agency case, to be legally robust against possible insolvency challenge. If the GCM is liable to the CCP for any net *obligation* to the CCP in respect of client transactions, it seems asymmetric that the *benefit* of the GCM's positions will be removed from the GCM's estate. This effect will have to be tested and proved against insolvency laws which restrict 'deprivation' clauses or cherry-picking.[187]

---

185 See **box 2.1** and **section 8.8(3)**
186 See **section 2.13**
187 See **section 8.9(14)**

Portability under the principal-to-principal model

14.50 Under the principal-to-principal model, there are obligations owed by the CCP to the GCM, and vice versa; and there are obligations owed by the GCM to the client, and vice versa. The obligations arising between the GCM and the client may not match those between the CCP and the GCM, despite them being referred to frequently as 'back-to-back'. Accordingly, any portability analysis needs to consider the transfer of four types of obligation, two of which are more readily under the control of the CCP:

(1) *The obligations owed by the GCM to the CCP.* These obligations are those which the margin posted by the GCM is supposed to satisfy. In theory, then, the transfer of these obligations can be achieved without loss to either CCP or GCM, since the margin can be used to meet any loss sustained by the CCP. If the position is to be transferred as an open contract to a replacement GCM, the margin previously posted by the defaulting GCM could, in some arrangements, be transferred to the margin account of the replacement GCM. Evidently such a transfer will require the positions being transferred, and the associated margin, to be clearly separable from any other transactions. But there are residual issues to consider: in particular, whether the transfer of margin would violate any proprietary rights of the defaulting GCM, for example an equity of redemption (the right to recovery of the excess over the value of the secured obligations).

(2) *The obligations owed by the client to the GCM.* If the transaction, or portfolio of transactions, which the client has with the defaulting GCM is out-of-the-money, or the client is behindhand with margin payments, the client will still have to satisfy its obligations. The defaulting GCM can, to the extent that posted margin is represented by a payment obligation owed to the client, utilise margin for this purpose. But such an approach would amount to close-out rather than transfer. Transfer (from the client's perspective) of out-of-the-money transactions will deprive the GCM's estate of an asset; selecting the in-the-money transactions for transfer, leaving behind the out-of-the-money transactions is cherry-picking, and exacerbates the risk for the GCM's estate, as the portfolio is likely to have been margined on a net basis. In practice, the solution is likely to be that as between the client and its former GCM, full close-out, application of margin, and payment of any balance owed by the client will be needed, and as between the client and the replacement GCM, a portfolio of positions reflecting the transfer at CCP level will be created anew at prevailing prices. If there is a surplus of margin due to the client from the defaulting GCM, this can be handled as outlined below at sub-section (4) below (obligations owed by the GCM to the client).

(3) *The obligations owed by the CCP to the GCM.* These obligations form part of the estate of the GCM and raise similar issues to those discussed under sub-section (2) above (obligations owed by the client to the GCM), namely deprivation of an asset or cherry-picking, if transferred to another GCM. In practice one solution adopted by European CCPs may be to confer upon the *client* a proprietary entitlement to whatever the CCP owes the GCM, so as to neutralise the argument that transfer interferes with an asset of the estate. There are, however, residual issues to consider. The first is the effectiveness of the proprietary solution (charge or trust). Also, given that the value of the GCM's obligations to the client may not be an exact match with the value of the property hypothecated, there is still a danger of the arrangement being treated as a deprivation for the GCM's estate.

(4) *The obligations owed by the GCM to the client.* If what is due to the client can be satisfied through hypothecation of the CCP's obligation to the defaulting GCM, the client will be able to seize that item of property, and transfer it to the replacement GCM. While slightly odd, what is happening in such a case is that the client does not *actually* seize this property, but authorises the CCP to make use of it as collateral for the account of the replacement GCM.

Transfer of client transactions

(1)

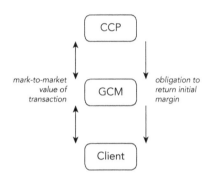

Transfer of a client's position will need to take account of both (1) the client's obligations and entitlements as against the GCM and (2) the GCM's obligations and entitlements as against the CCP. Typically the CCP will owe margin-return obligations to the GCM (which, in turn, the GCM will owe to the client); and the CCP may owe, or be owed, the net loss or gain on the transactions (and again the GCM may owe, or be owed, the same by the client).

(2)

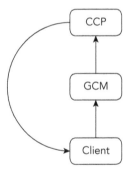

Where an agency model is in effect at the CCP, the CCP may owe its obligations direct to the client (albeit that while the GCM is solvent, this obligation can be satisfied by payment and delivery to and from the GCM). But the client will owe obligations to the GCM, because the CCP requires the GCM to be its own obligor.

(3)

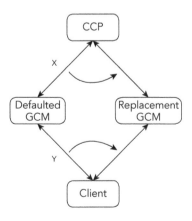

If the CCP deals with its GCM participants as principal, the GCM's position vis-à-vis the CCP as regards the client (X) has to be transferred, as does the client's position vis-à-vis the GCM (Y)

Fig 14.1

Mechanism for transfer of client positions

14.51 In a case where the CCP deals exclusively with its participant GCMs as principal, the success of an attempt to transfer client positions will, therefore, depend on a large number of matters. A detailed study by OTC Derivatives Dealers for the Board of Governors of the Federal Reserve System and other supervisors (the Fed Report)[188] divides the subject into two classes of issue: 'segregation' issues and 'portability' issues. The importance of segregation issues is emphasised by the distilled version of the Fed Report,[189] which states:

> 'The presence of the following factors related to the Segregation Analysis could significantly enhance the Portability Analysis: (i) margin being held away from the CMs; (ii) margin not being commingled with the property of the CMs, and if possible, not commingled with the property of other custodial claimants of the CMs; (iii) the existence of a direct contractual relationship between customers and the margin holder; (iv) margin being free from liens and setoff rights (except liens and setoff rights in favor of the CCP and the CMs in respect of customer trades); and (v) margin not being subject to rehypothecation or on-transfer by the CMs (except to the CCP as margin for customer trades).'

14.52 The segregation issues can be summarised as follows.

(1) The transactions between the failed GCM and the CCP need to be clearly identified. This is not always the case. The principal obstacle is that CCPs may allow their GCMs to operate 'omnibus accounts' in which the transactions attributable to several, or indeed all, of the GCM's clients, have been collectively recorded. The omnibus account may contain transactions which are offsetting as a result of one client having bought a particular product which another client has sold, for the same delivery date. These offsetting transactions may be netted out by the CCP's risk management processes, making it impossible to achieve a transfer to the replacement broker of a replica position unless all clients participating in the omnibus account wish to transfer and can all agree with the replacement broker for the creation of the new relationship, in particular as regards the positions to be transferred. Even if the offsetting issue can be overcome, a further issue with regard to identification of transactions is that the interests of the underlying clients in specific transactions may not have been recorded, given that the CCP was dealing with the GCM as principal, notionally disregarding that the GCM had entered into transactions in the capacity of an intermediary.

(2) The transactions between the failed GCM and the CCP which are to be transferred need to be margined separately from other transactions. In relation to an omnibus account, the CCP may collect margin on a 'net' basis, acknowledging that the account reflects offsetting positions. The GCM, dealing with the CCP as principal, may obtain some cost savings, which it may be willing to share with its clients. But the downside of that

---

188 AllianceBernstein et al, *Report to the Supervisors of the Major OTC Derivatives Dealers on the Proposals of Centralized CDS Clearing Solutions for the Segregation and Portability of Customer CDS Positions and Related Margin* (June 2009), http://www.newyorkfed.org/markets/Full_Report.pdf

189 http://www.newyorkfed.org/markets/Distilled_Report.pdf (July 2009)

arrangement is that the CCP will be able to deal with the positions and the supporting margin only as a single unit. Although the omnibus position at the CCP can be transferred to the new GCM, the result will likely be a margin shortfall for the new GCM, because it needs to dis-aggregate the clients in order manage its own risk, and it will not have access to the pool of surplus margin called by the failed GCM but not passed to the CCP. The omnibus clients will be unwilling to have to produce margin afresh in order to achieve the transfer. But if the GCM has retained the surplus margin called from clients and held it in a manner which is both outside the insolvent estate of the GCM and also immediately accessible to the clients for transfer to the replacement GCM, transfer of an omnibus net-margined portfolio is possible.[190]

This analysis leads to the conclusion that individually segregated client accounts at the CCP, as envisaged by article 39(3) of EMIR, will be the simplest way to facilitate transfer of client transactions. An omnibus account (as envisaged by article 39(2)) is not fatal, but it will only work if the whole account transfers across as a single unit (as envisaged by article 48(5) of EMIR), and that will require the consent of all clients who use the omnibus account, and some additional structuring if net margining is used.

14.53 The portability issues can be summarised as follows.

(1) The positions (transactions and associated margin) registered in the name of the defaulting GCM must be transferable by the CCP to the account of the replacement GCM. Potential obstacles to this apparently simple requirement may be that the request for transfer is made after the CCP has closed out the positions, as at Eurex,[191] or that there is an objection under the insolvency law regime applicable to the GCM that to carry out the transfer would deprive the insolvent estate of an asset. Typically, insolvency law objections can be overcome via protective legislation such as Part VII of the Companies Act 1989 or the Settlement Finality Regulations.[192]

(2) The positions between the client and the GCM must be transferable to the account of the replacement GCM. Unless the CCP has some sort of contractual or other jurisdiction over the client (which, *ex hypothesi*, is not a participant in the CCP) this part of the transfer is more challenging. The protective legislation which neutralises insolvency law objections is unlikely to be effective at this level either, though as regards the default mechanisms of some exchanges operating their own clearing infrastructure, there is an option to extend coverage of Part VII to 'designated non-members'.[193] Another theoretically possible manner of extending protection to clients is to have them designated as 'indirect participants' in a designated settlement system on grounds of systemic risk.[194] If the client's transactions are in-the-money for the client, then they will represent a liability of the insolvent estate,

---

190 See also Rasheed, TZ, and Zebregs, B, 'Can a house divided between itself stand? Segregation in derivatives clearing' (May 2012) 5 JIBFL, pp 293–300

191 Fed Report, p 10

192 See **Chapter 8**

193 Companies Act 1989, s 155(2); EDX London, *Rulebook* (December 2010), http://www. londonstockexchange.com/edx/documents/rulebook.pdf, r 5.4

194 Financial Markets and Insolvency (Settlement Finality) Regulations 1999, SI 1999 No 2979, reg 9; see also **section 8.24**

and if the corresponding transactions between the GCM and the CCP are transferred, it is unlikely that the insolvency officer of the failed GCM would object to the estate being relieved of that liability. But the insolvency officer will not be likely to be in a position to respond to a request for transfer until long after the client had hoped for a result – a self-help remedy is needed. In practice, though, the issue with transfer of the client's positions with the failed GCM is not that the client seeks to transfer a liability, but an asset of the estate: the net amount of the margin retained by the failed GCM after satisfying the contractual obligations on both sides.

(3) The margin deposited by the client with the GCM needs to be separable from the insolvent estate. The client will need to overcome the objections of insolvency law that the margin deposited with the failed GCM can be extracted from the insolvent estate and transferred to the replacement GCM. If the margin was initially transferred to the GCM on the title transfer basis for provision of collateral,[195] which will be the case in relation to cash if the GCM is a bank, and may also be the case even if the GCM is not a bank or if the collateral comprises securities, the client's claim is merely an unsecured monetary claim, and the problem is not with unreasonable insolvency law stipulations but with a poorly chosen structure. If an omnibus account is used with net margining at the CCP level, surplus margin will have been left with the GCM and may be recoverable only with difficulty.[196] Alternatives which enable the client to extract its asset with varying degrees of practical difficulty include the creation of a trust or a charge to ensure that the client has a proprietary entitlement over the margin. The following may be considered:

- *Title was transferred by the client to the GCM.* If the client transferred title in the margin absolutely to the GCM, the client's claim against the GCM is an unsecured claim; the client's hope for a transfer looks, on the face of it, doomed. However, it may be possible to leapfrog over the GCM. If the GCM has passed on the margin to the CCP, the margin may be returnable to the client provided that it does not fall into the GCM's insolvent estate. This can be achieved by the GCM entering into a charge in favour of its client in relation to any entitlement of the GCM to a return of margin from the CCP. The obligation secured by the charge is the GCM's net obligation to the client. Upon transfer, the client will notionally seize the security (the margin return entitlement due from the CCP) and hand it to the client's replacement GCM, where it can be used to satisfy the replacement GCM's margin obligations to the CCP. In this way both the transactions, and the collateral supporting them, can be moved to the replacement GCM's account. This model has been used by LCH.Clearnet Limited.[197]

- *Margin was charged by the client direct to the CCP.* Another option, which is also used by LCH.Clearnet Limited,[198] is for the client to hand the collateral to the GCM only for the purpose of charging it to the CCP on account of the GCM's obligations to the CCP. This style

---

195 See **section 10.10(2)**
196 Cf. Fed Report, footnote 11
197 LCH.Clearnet Ltd, *Notice to End-users of SwapClear Client Clearing Services* (undated), http://www.lchclearnet.com/Images/Notice%20to%20End-users%20of%20SwapClear%20Client%20Clearing%20Services_tcm6-52978.pdf
198 LCH.Clearnet Ltd, *Procedures,* s 4.2.1

Transfer of client's entitlement vis-à-vis clearing member

(1) Before default:

(2) Upon operation of transfer rules:

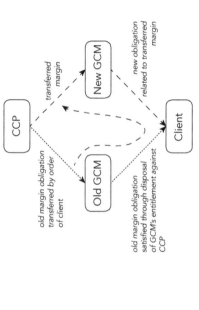

The GCM may create security over the CCP's obligation to transfer margin back to the GCM. The security will secure the GCM's own obligations to the client. If the GCM defaults, the client can take possession of the security, and order it transferred to the replacement GCM to satisfy the new GCM's margin obligation to the CCP.

Fig 14.2

of margining would be effective to isolate the margin deposit from the insolvency of the GCM if the CGM has no interest in the margin assets. Unfortunately, the GCM will usually wish to have such an interest in order to protect the GCM in case the client defaults, when the GCM will itself need recourse to the margin; and so the GCM will usually take a second-ranking interest in the collateral behind the CCP. Transfer of the margin without regard to the GCM's interest again runs the risk of a deprivation argument being made.

Client clearing – portability in practice

14.54   The arrangements to facilitate the transfer of a client's transactions to a replacement GCM will thus typically include the following components.

(1) First, a replacement GCM must be lined up to take on the positions; this cannot be done overnight, as the replacement GCM will need to be persuaded to take on the new client and indeed the portfolio of transactions. A pre-arranged standby clearing relationship will be prudent.

(2) Secondly, if an event of default occurs, the client will need to notify the CCP that it wishes to have its transactions moved to the replacement GCM before the CCP takes action to close them out.

(3) Thirdly, the client will need to extricate any surplus margin from the failed GCM, either through the client asset and client money protection mechanisms or through the arrangements provided under the auspices of the CCP.

(4) Fourth, the client may need to close out its position with the failed GCM. As it will typically be impossible, against the constraints of insolvency law, to have the failed GCM assign the book of transactions associated with the client to the replacement GCM, the client will need to close out those transactions and open up new transactions with the replacement GCM. As to close-out, the client may need contractual rights (for example under a netting agreement) to terminate its obligations to the failed GCM and to establish a net obligation.

(5) Finally, the replacement GCM will register the transferred positions and margin to the account of the client once details have been notified, and may need to make a top-up margin call to reflect price movements during the period between the last margin payment and the completion of transfer.

Other issues related to transfer

14.55   The Fed Report[199] observed that where a defaulting GCM's book can be transferred wholesale to a bridge bank under bank special resolution procedures,[200] there is little problem. However, special resolution procedures typically need to be implemented before a formal insolvency regime is in place. And, in Europe, there is a question whether special resolution procedures would be classified as 'reorganisation measures' – this is important, because only winding-up proceedings and reorganisation measures qualify for automatic

---

199 Footnote 9
200 See **section 8.4**

recognition between member states under the EU Insolvency Regulation[201] and the Settlement Finality Directive.[202] Without this certainty, the procedures of the CCP for resolving the default may not have to be recognised in other member states.

14.56 Given the challenges in extricating client assets and client money from an insolvency officer – which may be practical rather than proprietary challenges – any portability solution needs to be operable by the CCP and the client without involvement by the defaulting GCM. The protections granted to CCPs by Part VII of the Companies Act 1989 (Part VII) and the Settlement Finality Regulations are not coercive in nature, and do not empower the CCP to take steps beyond what is set out in its default rules. In particular, these legislative measures do not enable the CCP to interfere with third party property rights or to require an insolvency officer to disregard his or her statutory duties.

14.57 In relation to the effectiveness of segregation, some parts of the United Kingdom's protective legislation under Part VII may be of assistance. GCMs which operate separate 'house' and 'client' accounts at the CCP would risk having the distinction ignored in their insolvency, because statutory insolvency set-off indiscriminately lumps together mutual debts. Although debts entered into in different capacities ought not to be regarded as mutual, the position is put beyond doubt by section 187 of the Companies Act 1989, which provides that the rest of Part VII applies as if market contracts entered into in different capacities were entered into by different persons.[203]

14.58 One final consideration is whether the ability of the client to 'cherry-pick' transactions to be transferred is legitimate. Cherry-picking is usually a concept which is considered with regard to a *defaulting* party – that is, the fear that a liquidator will selectively choose to perform transactions which are in-the-money for the insolvent estate, but repudiate the others. ('The term 'cherry picking' refers to a power that some insolvency officials have under the insolvency laws of certain jurisdictions to reject certain contracts burdensome to the insolvent company while affirming contracts beneficial to the insolvent company.'[204]) In this context, however, the problem arises from the other perspective: a client with a portfolio of transactions may prefer to transfer the transactions which are in-the-money from the client's perspective, leaving the remainder closed out. Under English insolvency law, such a strategy might not be unlawful. There is no deprivation to the estate of the value of the closed-out transactions, since the client cannot escape his obligation to pay up the close-out amount once the election to close out rather than transfer has been made. On the other hand, market standard documentation requires that if close-out is to be done, it should be for all transactions, and not some only.[205] This is presumably because of a concern that if cherry-picking is to be denied to the insolvent party, on grounds of fair reciprocity it should also be denied to the solvent party.

201 Council Regulation (EC) No 1346/2000 of 29 May 2000 on insolvency proceedings, art 9
202 Directive of the European Parliament and of the Council of 19 May 1998 on settlement finality in payment and securities settlement systems, 98/26/EC, art 8
203 Cf **section 9.13**
204 204 International Swaps and Derivatives Association, various publications, http://www.isda.org/
205 Securities Industry and Financial Markets Association, Cross-Product Master Agreement, version 1, s 2.1; European Federation of Energy Traders, Master Netting Agreement, s 4.1

LIQUIDITY

14.59 Liquidity risk has been particularly identified as an issue for CCPs in managing defaults. '[A] CCP may need to maintain sufficient liquid resources to meet payments to settle required margin and other payment obligations over multiple days to account for multiday hedging and close-out activities as directed by the CCP's participant-default procedures.'[206] CCPs will therefore wish to ensure that their margin assets are in suitably liquid form, and that repo or other investment operations can be unwound rapidly if needs be.

The introduction of mandatory clearing of OTC derivatives has shone a light on one aspect of liquidity availability, namely the ability of CCPs to tap a central bank's lender-of-last-resort function. Nothing inherent in the liquidity needs of a CCP suggests that only a central bank can fulfil the role of liquidity-provider: commercial banks could, in theory, provide this service. Both commercial and central banks are likely to wish to have any loans made in the exigencies of default-management supported by collateral. Thus, the liquidity question for a CCP is principally whether there is a repo lender willing to provide liquidity on demand. Pre-arranged commercial standby facilities may be satisfactory. But the risk is that market circumstances at the time of a default may make such arrangements difficult or expensive to arrange, and difficult to enforce at the time of need. The most troublesome issue is the adequacy of such facilities, and that is likely to be what has prompted the 'central bank' debate in relation to OTC derivatives clearing.

It has been argued that CCPs 'must' have access to central bank funds in order to clear these products.[207] The argument runs that jump-to-default risk on credit default swaps exposes CCPs to acute liquidity pressures, since participants' liquidity could dry up precisely at the time these derivative products generate a need for large volumes of payments, thus bringing about a nasty cocktail of defaults, high cash-flow needs, disrupted markets and reluctant lenders. A lender of last resort is accordingly highly desirable.[208] These arguments have been echoed in various quarters, notably prompting a suggestion that CCPs should be required to be established as banks in order to have access to central bank accounts.[209] But non-bank CCPs may be allowed to open central bank accounts in consequence of the FMI Principles' strong preference for CCPs to settle in central bank money.[210]

On the other hand, it is suggested that central banks might not be the preferable source of liquidity for CCPs. If CCPs' liquidity problems arise because the CCP has reinvested cash under repos which cannot easily be unwound, it would be better for the repo counterparties to be required to unwind them, even if this involves them going to the central bank for liquidity to do so.[211]

---

206 FMI Principles, para 3.7.9
207 Kress, J, 'Credit Default Swaps, Clearinghouses, and Systemic Risk: Why centralized counterparties must have access to central bank liquidity' (May 2011) Harvard Journal on Legislation, Vol. 48, No. 1, pp 47–93
208 See also **section 12.6(3)**
209 Fleuriot, P, *Rapport au Ministre de l'Économie, de l'Industrie et de l'Emploi sur la revision de la directive sur les Marchés d'Instruments Financiers (MIF)* (February 2010), http://www.tresor.economie.gouv.fr/File/333690, p 5
210 FMI Principle 9
211 Singh, M, *Making OTC Derivatives Safe – A Fresh Look* (March 2011), IMF Working Paper WP/11/66, pp 9–10

It should also be borne in mind that no lender of last resort will guarantee to prop up a failed institution. If the CCP in liquidity difficulties has no assets to pledge as collateral, it may be insolvent as well as illiquid, and needs a more radical resolution.

LEGAL OBLIGATIONS IN DEFAULT MANAGEMENT

14.60 A CCP's principal sources of protection in United Kingdom from insolvency laws are found in Part VII of the Companies Act 1989 (Part VII) and the Financial Markets and Insolvency (Settlement Finality) Regulations 1999 (SFRs),[212] with some support from the Financial Collateral Arrangements (No.2) Regulations 2003.[213] The insolvency protections given by these pieces of legislation are discussed in **Chapter 8**. In broad terms, the law of insolvency is subordinated to the default rules of the CCP in relation to market contracts and market charges.[214]

The provisions of Part VII go rather further than the insolvency protection, however. They supplement the provisions of the Recognition Requirements Regulations[215] by regulating the behaviour of CCPs as regards their management of defaults, and by protecting CCPs against certain property law dangers which might arise in connection with the handling of margin. These statutory rules apply to CCPs incorporated in the United Kingdom, but not recognised overseas clearing houses.

14.61 In summary, Part VII imposes the following obligations and privileges on a CCP managing a default.

(1) The Bank of England[216] may give directions to a recognised UK clearing house about the conduct of default proceedings.[217] In particular, the regulator can direct the CCP to take default action or to desist from action, and may do so to facilitate the use of special resolution powers under the Banking Act 2009.[218] Directions to desist lapse, and may not be given afresh, if the defaulter is subject to insolvency proceedings. A direction may include sub-directions about the exercise of specific powers under the default rules. Conversely, an insolvency office-holder can apply to the regulator in a case where a 'relevant insolvency event' has occurred in relation to a CCP participant, but the CCP has not taken default action, the consequence of which is that the insolvency law disapplications of Part VII will cease to have effect, unless within three business days the CCP initiates default action or informs the regulator that it proposes to do so forthwith.[219]

(2) A recognised UK clearing house is required to certify to the Bank of England the net sum payable under the default rules to or from the

---

212 SI 1999 No 2979
213 SI 2003 No 3226
214 Companies Act 1989, ss 158; cf **sections 8.11–8.13**
215 Financial Services and Markets Act 2000 (Recognition Requirements for Investment Exchanges and Clearing Houses) Regulations 2001, SI 2001 No 995
216 Following the transfer of functions from the FSA under the Financial Services Act 2012
217 Companies Act 1989, s 166, as amended by Financial Services Act 2012, s 92
218 Section 166(3), as modified by Financial Services Act 2012, s 92; see **section 8.4**
219 Companies Act 1989, s 167

defaulter in respect of each creditor or debtor on completion of the default proceedings.[220] This rule emphasises the duty of the CCP under the Recognition Requirements Regulations to have default rules which provide for all rights and liabilities of the defaulter under unsettled market contracts to be discharged, and the sums payable by or to the defaulter to be set off so as to produce a net sum.[221] Creditors and debtors of the defaulter can inspect the reports made to the Bank, insofar as the report relates to the sum certified to be due to or from him or its calculation.[222] The net sum is treated as a provable debt and can thus be set off against other sums due to or from the defaulter which have nothing to do with the default proceedings.[223] The insolvency office-holder must reserve against the outcome of the default proceedings.[224]

(3) The CCP and its officers receive certain exemptions from liabilities,[225] and failure by a CCP to comply with its own rules do not prevent the matter being treated as done in accordance with the rules for the purposes of Part VII, subject to the failure not substantial affecting rights of any person (essentially a participant) entitled to require compliance with the rules.[226]

Practical implications of the Part VII regime

14.62 The FSA has issued a brief guide, after consulting with various accounting firms whose partners have taken the role of insolvency practitioner in various clearing member defaults, on the interplay between the Part VII regime and the duties of insolvency officers.[227] This document discusses the following, among other points:

(1) The obligation of the insolvent clearing member (and thus its insolvency officers) to give information and assistance to a CCP handling a default. The broad conclusion is that the insolvency officer cannot resist information requests despite a demanding timescale imposed by the CCP and despite the newly-appointed officer struggling to get to grips with the affairs of the defaulter.

(2) The cancellation of settlement instructions.[228] Where the CCP wishes to cancel a settlement, and this cannot be done unilaterally, the insolvency officer will issue matching cancellation instructions to the relevant CSD.

(3) The problem of the insolvency officer's personal liability. It is suggested that information might be forthcoming with greater alacrity if the insolvency practitioners are released from personal liability. The problem is surely wider than the supply of information; but the intention is clear, that individuals cannot be expected to shoulder the financial risks of assisting with snap decisions in troubled markets.

---

220 Companies Act 1989, s 162(1), as modified by Financial Services Act 2012, Sch 18, para 63
221 Recognition Requirements Regulations, Schedule, para 25(1)(a) and (b)
222 Companies Act 1989, s 162(5), (6)
223 Companies Act 1989, s 163(2)
224 Companies Act 1989, s 161(2)
225 Companies Act 1989, s 184(3), (5)
226 Companies Act 1989, s 184(2)
227 Financial Services Authority, *Cooperation Guidance between Recognised Bodies and Insolvency Practitioners to Assist Management of Member Defaults by Recognised Bodies (Recognised Clearing House Version)* (May 2011), http://www.fsa.gov.uk/pubs/other/cooperation_guidance.pdf
228 Cf **section 15.16**

14.63   One issue not covered by the FSA is one alluded to by the Examiner of Lehman Brothers Inc., who reported as follows:

'The CME did not give "liquidation only" instructions to LBI because it was in default with respect to any CME margin requirements, but rather for general financial insecurity reasons related to LBHI's bankruptcy filing … . The CME also was concerned that JPMorgan might cease acting as LBI's settlement bank with the CME Clearing Division. Although it was technically possible to conduct transactions with the CME without a settlement bank, no CME clearing member had ever done so. [Tim Doar, Managing Director of Risk Management in the CME Clearing House Division] stated that it would have presented an unprecedented situation and additional risk to the CME and noted that on Wednesday, September 17, [Bank of America] ceased acting as LBI's settlement bank with respect to the other dominant domestic derivatives clearing organization, the Options Clearing Corporation.'[229]

In this respect, it might be noted that neither Part VII nor the Settlement Finality Regulations empower a CCP to disallow an agent bank from exercising a termination right under its settlement agreement. The nearest thing under English law is a power in the Banking Act 2009,[230] which might, at a stretch, be used insofar as the CCP is treated as a payment system.

229 Valukas report, pp 1848–1849
230 See **section 11.5**

15 Risk Management at CSDs

CSDs' ROLE AS SETTLEMENT SYSTEMS

15.1 CSDs have two principal functions, as discussed in **section 2.16**: the operation of a settlement system for transfer of securities, and the provision of a central register of ultimate title to the securities in issue.

The risks faced by CSDs, as settlement systems causing the transfer of title to securities by means of book entries, are similar to those faced by payment systems. In particular, aspects of finality, credit, liquidity and operational risk are common to all central settlement system operators. There is no need to repeat here what is said in **Chapter 16**, which considers each of those topics in detail. This chapter focuses on those matters which stem from the special operations of a CSD as an exchange-of-value system, and as ultimate custodian for an issue of securities.

However, unlike a payment system, a CSD's role as keeper of the ultimate record of title places it, among securities intermediaries, adjacent to the issuer of the securities. Many of the functions assumed by CSDs in addition to their basic roles of settlement system operator and ultimate title registrar will be attributable to this proximity: those functions are commonly referred to as 'issuer services' or 'asset servicing', and involve the processing of actions engaged in by an issuer with its investors.[1] The risk issues which arise will frequently overlap with those arising in relation to corporate actions processing and those experienced by agent banks, which are discussed in **Chapters 20** and **18** respectively.

The other differentiating aspect of a CSD is its central role as guardian of the integrity of the issues of securities. In this respect, the problem faced by a CSD is essentially a problem of custody risk. A CSD may seek to pass on the burden of losses of securities to its participants. Euroclear, which operates a group of CSDs, has as part of the 'ESES Terms and Conditions' a set of rules which enable any of Euroclear's 'ESES' network of CSDs to determine that there has been a 'Securities Loss' and then to take actions which include reduction of the holdings of the clients with securities of the affected issue.[2]

---

1   See **section 10.25(3)** and European Central Securities Depositories Association, *Issuer Services* (January 2008), Report, http://www.ecsda.eu/site/uploads/tx_doclibrary/2008_01_ECSDA_Issuer_Services_Report.pdf
2   Euroclear, ESES Terms and Conditions (August 2011), https://www.euroclear.com/site/publishedFile/2011-08-T-and-C-conditions-BOOK-I-FR_tcm91-130281.pdf?title=Conditions+G%C3%A9n%C3%A9rales+%E2%80%93+Livre+I, art 10

DELIVERY VERSUS PAYMENT

15.2   The central issue for risk management by a CSD is how to ensure that it can achieve simultaneous exchange of cash for securities, or delivery versus payment (DvP). Indeed, in 2000, the International Securities Services Association's recommendations for management of risk in securities settlement systems specified reduction of settlement risk through 'the implementation of real delivery versus payment' as its priority.[3] Failure to achieve DvP leaves the payer with settlement (or Herstatt) risk:[4] the risk of having paid its money to a buyer who has suffered the opening of an insolvency procedure before delivering the securities, or a seller having delivered securities to a buyer who becomes insolvent before paying. Either of these situations may leave the first mover in the unwelcome position of an unsecured creditor for the whole gross value of the transaction.[5] DvP eliminates the risk by ensuring that there is no first mover.

Unfortunately the subject of DvP is cluttered with political jumble. Two political sub-topics may thus require analysis: the 'three models of DvP' and the question of 'central versus commercial bank money'.

Models of DvP

15.3   In 1992 the Committee on Payment and Settlement Systems (CPSS) issued a report describing three 'models' of DvP:

'The Study Group has thoroughly reviewed most of the securities transfer systems in use or under development in the G-10 countries. On the basis of this review, the Study Group has identified three broad structural approaches to achieving DVP (or more generally, to creating a strong linkage between delivery and payment in a securities settlement system):

Model 1:   systems that settle transfer instructions for both securities and funds on a trade-by-trade (gross) basis, with final (unconditional) transfer of securities from the seller to the buyer (delivery) occurring at the same time as final transfer of funds from the buyer to the seller (payment);

Model 2:   systems that settle securities transfer instructions on a gross basis with final transfer of securities from the seller to the buyer (delivery) occurring throughout the processing cycle, but settle funds transfer instructions on a net basis, with final transfer of funds from the buyer to the seller (payment) occurring at the end of the processing cycle;

Model 3:   systems that settle transfer instructions for both securities and funds on a net basis, with final transfers of both securities and funds occurring at the end of the processing cycle.'[6]

In truth, only the first of these is DvP. Model 2 implies that there continues to be risk on the payment leg until the processing of the funds transfers is final. Model 3 implies that both legs are at risk until, separately, they achieve finality. The

---

3   International Securities Services Association, *ISSA Recommendations 2000* (June 2000), http://www.issanet.org/pdf/rec2000.pdf, Recommendation 5

4   See **box 2.3**

5   For further examples of potential gross risk, see **section 18.15**

6   Bank for International Settlements Committee on Payment and Settlement Systems, *Delivery versus Payment in Securities Settlement Systems* (September 1992), http://www.bis.org/publ/cpss06.pdf, para 1.9

purpose of the report in 1992 was to 'enhance central bank understanding of issues relating to securities settlement systems,' rather than to criticise existing methodologies, with the result that terminology was adapted to enable a greater number of systems to claim to be delivering DvP than a purist approach would have allowed. A 2004 study by the European Central Bank showed that a wide range of approaches to DvP was practised in Europe.[7] Nowadays, only Model 1 should be recognised to deliver DvP. Yet in 2012 the European Central Bank (ECB) reported that six EU securities settlement systems (Austria, Denmark, Greece, Hungary, Italy and Latvia) still used Model 3.[8]

The CPSS report pointed out that Model 1 systems provided their enhanced protection against Herstatt risk at some cost. Real-time gross settlement requires higher levels of liquidity in both cash and securities than net settlement: Model 1 systems are therefore vulnerable to higher fail rates, and credit extensions may be needed for their participants, and the credit risk thus taken was assessed to be potentially of the same magnitude as the principal risk – that is, the Herstatt risk intended to be avoided by a choice of Model 1.[9] These concerns are not to be dismissed lightly.

However, whether Model 1 DvP can be achieved is likely to be a question of technical feasibility. In the first place, Model 1 requires the processing of securities transfers and payments to be done using RTGS methodology. Secondly, the two transfers must be linked so that each is a *sine qua non* relative to the other. Thirdly, if the securities settlement system is operated independently of the payment system, the link between the systems needs to be utterly robust so that there is no danger of mismatch in terms of timing or conditionality. The closer the payment and securities settlements are, from an organisational perspective, the easier it will be to fulfil these objectives.

Central v commercial bank money

15.4 A closely connected issue relates to the 'cash asset' in which the payment leg is settled. Proximity between payment and securities transfer systems can readily be achieved if both systems are operated by the central bank, as has typically been the case where the securities settlement system is exclusively devoted to the settlement of government bonds. Such a structure has led to an orthodox view that the cash leg ought, for preference, to be settled in 'central bank money', which is to say by transfer across the books of the central bank.[10] However, it is equally possible to settle the cash leg across the books of a commercial bank in order to achieve the same result – that is the approach at Euroclear Bank and Clearstream Banking Luxembourg, the two ICSDs which operate Eurobond settlement systems.

The CPSS and IOSCO Principles for Financial Market Infrastructures (FMI Principles) indicate that the advantage of central bank money for settlement is

---

7 European Central Bank, *The Use of Central Bank Money for Settling Securities Transactions* (May 2004), http://www.ecb.eu/pub/pdf/other/useofcbmoneyforssten.pdf
8 European Central Bank, *Settlement Fails – Report on Securities Settlement Systems (SSS) Measures to Ensure Timely Settlement* (April 2011), http://www.ecb.eu/pub/pdf/other/settlementfails042011en.pdf, p 9
9 CPSS report on DvP, para 1.10
10 CPSS and Technical Committee of the International Organization of Securities Commissions, *Principles for Financial Markets Infrastructures* (April 2012), http://www.bis.org/publ/cpss101a.pdf, Principle 9

the avoidance of credit and liquidity risks.[11] However, the CPSS and IOSCO acknowledge that there are limits to this advantage: not all CSD participants may be eligible to hold accounts at the central bank, forcing them to use, and thus to take credit risk on, an agent bank (with all that implies for DvP, as discussed in **sections 13.47** and **18.30**); and, as regards liquidity, central banks should not be regarded as a limitless supply of liquidity, since central banks tend to regulate, and require collateral for, the release of liquidity. Nevertheless, linkage of CSDs to central banks is the norm for equities settlement in Europe: France, Germany and the United Kingdom all use this structure, as well as many other countries.

Commercial bank money, on the other hand, is not an unmitigated panacea.[12] Where the CSD is not itself a bank across whose books the cash transfers take place, the CSD will typically have a settlement bank, or a group of settlement banks to provide this service. Selecting a single commercial bank concentrates risk and is dubious practice on competition policy grounds. On the other hand, an oligarchy spreads the risk at the cost of DvP and immediate finality. The effect of having several banks involved can be illustrated with an example. CSD participant B is buying securities. B banks with settlement bank X, whereas his counterparty seller S banks with settlement bank Y. At the moment of settlement, the CSD records the transfer of title from S to B, and immediately takes steps to record that X owes funds to Y. In CREST, where US dollar cash settlement arrangements take this form,[13] Banks X and Y reckon up with each other on a net basis at the end of the settlement day. Evidently this is 'Model 2 DvP', or to put it more bluntly, the settlement banks are taking risk on each other owing to the absence of true DvP. Moreover, since the cash leg settlement in Model 2 is a DNS system,[14] it is vulnerable to unwind if one of the settlement banks fails, potentially affecting the finality of all settlements effected on that day.

A CSD which wishes to open its doors to immediate Model 1 DvP to its whole constituency, without the constraints of central bank eligibility criteria, may wish to provide the cash accounts itself, which implies that the CSD operator may become a bank itself. Apart from the ICSDs, this model has not typically been followed in Europe. But having a banking licence will enable a CSD to conduct credit operations, which may be attractive in light of the proposed CSD Regulation.[15]

PROCESSING OF SETTLEMENTS

15.5 It is apparent that efficient processing and true DvP are forces pulling in opposite directions. CSDs need to adopt processing algorithms which enable immediate finality for both securities and cash transfers without, if

---

11 FMI Principles, para 3.9.3
12 See also **section 9.14**
13 Euroclear UK & Ireland, *CREST Reference Manual* (April 2012), https://www.euroclear.com/site/publishedFile/Reference+Manual+-+April+2012_tcm87-120016.pdf?title=CREST+Reference+Manual+, s 6
14 See **section 2.30**
15 European Commission, *Proposal for a Regulation of the European Parliament and of the Council on improving securities settlement in the European Union and on central securities depositories etc* (March 2012), COM(2012) 73 final, http://eur-lex.europa.eu/LexUriServ/LexUriServ.do?uri=CELEX:52012PC0073:EN:PDF; see **sections 6.33** and **15.12**

at all possible, exposing their participants to intolerable liquidity pressure. The problems are similar to those faced by payment systems, with the added complication that the participants' liquidity pressures arise in relation to their cash requirements as well as their securities delivery obligations.

Processing of securities transfers on an RTGS model[16] may be unachievable in practice if the agent banks responsible for settlement of the cash leg are unable to proceed owing to shortage of cash liquidity. Similarly, a participant who is a seller of securities may be unable to proceed to settlement until another transaction in respect of which the same participant is buyer has settled, which may in turn depend on timeliness of a receipt from a third participant or the cash liquidity constraints of the first participant. Efficient processing algorithms will be able to look intelligently at the queue of transactions and identify cases where allowing one transaction to settle first will free up many more transactions for settlement. Likewise, as with payment systems processing, techniques such as circles processing, partial settlement, and multilateral netting will all speed up efficiency.[17]

Cyclical and net settlement

15.6 Multilateral netting borrows from CCPs and ACHs the idea of taking all transactions in the queue, and working out the overall single net delivery or receipt for each participant for each security. However, multilateral netting implies a cyclical system for settlement, and requires that multilateral netting is able to withstand attack, in the event of insolvency of one of the participants, under the rule in *British Eagle* or its non-English equivalent.[18]

If cyclical processing is used, the cycles at the CSD and the linked payment system must be tied together, so that the use of cycles does not introduce Herstatt risk.[19] Cyclical settlement systems would also appear to be examples of Model 3 DvP. However, this may not be a disaster, depending on how the cycle operates. One example of a cyclical system which poses little or no Herstatt risk is where the queuing algorithm selects a group of transactions which neatly match, so that no net delivery or receipt is needed, and 'nets them out' so that only net cash payments are due, and the moment of finality is when the cash payments are settled in the payment system. This example is referred to as circles processing. Typically a circles process and the coupled payments will settle in a fraction of a second. A more interesting variant is where the algorithm simply operates a multilateral netting cycle very rapidly, so that only net securities and cash transfers are made, but with completion occurring in a fraction of a second. Where this degree of rapidity is achievable, there is little danger to the participants in terms of Herstatt risk, because the algorithm can check that the net payers will, at the moment the cycle is completed, be able to fulfil their obligations: unlike the classic Herstatt problem, the participants are not asked to part with their asset in the hope that their counterparty, or another user of the system, will at some later stage in the day be able to perform.

Modern processing algorithms freely adopt miniature processing cycles along these lines, and because finality is assured in real time, they are characterised as 'RTGS' rather than 'DNS' systems (despite settlement being achieved through

---

16 See **section 2.33**
17 See **section 16.15**
18 See **box 2.1** and **section 8.9(3)**
19 See **box 2.3**

multilateral netting rather than gross, trade-by-trade). An alternative model is used by Monte Titoli in Italy, which operates an overnight DNS cycle, followed by a daytime RTGS cycle. This allows participants to choose between the RTGS arrangement, which may be demanding in terms of liquidity, to achieve immediate settlement with finality, or to defer the settlement to the overnight batch run, where finality will be assured at a later time.[20]

As to *British Eagle* risk, the Settlement Finality Directive (SFD)[21] ought to ensure that, from the moment determined under the rules of the system, multilateral netting is effective and proof against insolvency attack.[22] Depriving the insolvency officer of his weapons, however, is not a guarantee that things will go smoothly from an operational perspective. If a multilateral netting system requires that a net payer or net deliverer must make a payment or delivery, and the payer or deliverer fails to perform, there will not be enough cash or securities to go round, and no amount of legal stipulations can plug the hole. So the system must either (a) have failsafe components to eject from the batch of settlement instructions any transactions which would be compromised owing to the absence of securities ready for delivery from any net transferor, or insufficiency of funds on the part of any net payer, or (b) have standby liquidity arrangements so that the gap is filled by other participants. For these reasons, CSDs – or, more accurately, their participants – are exposed to liquidity and credit risks.

Partial settlement

15.7   Partial settlement is a further processing technique which may be used by CSDs to improve settlement rates. Where a participant is due to transfer 100 securities but has only 80 available, it may be possible for the participant to settle his obligations in part and receive the equivalent proportion of the purchase price. Whether this is legally permitted will depend on the terms of the contract between the buyer and seller of the securities; under the general English law, partial non-delivery would not discharge the seller's delivery obligation, unless trading platform rules have provided for different results. Market commentators dislike partial settlements as 'operationally inefficient'.[23]

LIQUIDITY RISK MANAGEMENT

15.8   Guidance on liquidity risk issues is set forth at Principle 7 of the FMI Principles, based on which the following comments might be made:

(1) Modern, fast, frequent batch processing reduces liquidity demands. It is suggested that CSDs might introduce incentives to submit transactions early into the system.[24] The issue which the latter recommendation seeks to address is a temptation to which participants may be exposed, namely to hoard their own liquidity (in cash or securities) by submitting settlement instructions only when they are rich in the asset which they are due to

20 Thomas Murray, *Monte Titoli, Public CSD Rating Report* (June 2007)

21 Directive 98/26/EC of the European Parliament and of the Council of 19 May 1998 on settlement finality in payment and securities settlement systems

22 SFD, art 3

23 International Securities Services Association, *ISSA Recommendations 2000* (June 2000), http://www.issanet.org/pdf/rec2000.pdf, p 23

24 FMI Principles, para 3.7.7

transfer. Participants can also be assisted in the task of liquidity risk management through the provision of information about their positions.

(2) Failure by a participant to deliver securities (and failure to pay, which may in fact be default) may have to be covered by a combination of fallback liquidity provision by one or more other participants. Such services will have to be paid for, and for that reason it may be appropriate for the CSD to hold collateral posted by each participant. CSDs, being account providers for their participants, are well-placed to take collateral by asserting a security interest over the securities recorded to the credit of their participants' accounts, and may also be able to treat the transactions themselves as self-collateralising. The techniques of fails coverage through securities loans and self-collateralisation to manage cash liquidity are discussed in **sections 15.9** and **15.15**.

(3) Sources of liquidity risk include the banks and service providers on whom the CSD may be dependent for cash deposits, liquidity loans, and securities lending. CSDs may wish to have counterparty limits or other risk limiting strategies to reduce dependency and concentration risk.

(4) Rules and procedures are desirable to deal with the possibility that the liquidity risk management arrangements fail to address the problem completely. Default management procedures should be explicit, and should aim to avoid the risk of unwinding settlements. Default rules are considered in **section 15.16** in connection with credit risk management.

Securities lending

15.9   A highly important technique for addressing liquidity issues is to enable participants who are short of deliverable securities to borrow them from others who are long. Securities loans might be privately arranged – participants ought, generally, to be at liberty to seek loans in the private marketplace – or they might be more swiftly and efficiently brokered by the CSD itself. Issues related to securities lending are explored in **Chapter 21**.

A CSD is uniquely in a position to organise a loan between the long and short participant, as it can see where the shortfalls will arise and where no liquidity pressure will be introduced for the long participant in making the loan. The CSD may invite participants to join its lending programme on standardised terms, which provide for fees, collateralisation and automation, assuring a relatively low degree of risk for lender as well as benefit for the borrower. However, the arrangements are not risk-free. A securities loan involves a transfer of ownership of the lent securities, and thus the assumption by the lender of credit risk on the borrower. Collateral provided should be valued according to the totality of the credit risk, which includes not just the value of the securities lent, plus change in market price over the likely buy-in period, but buy-in costs, the loss of any corporate action such as a dividend during the loan, the lending fee, and the costs (including market risk of fall in the value of the collateral) of liquidation of the collateral. Collateral would usually be selected and valued by the CSD as part of its service, and a lender will thus assume risk on the CSD's agency lending processes. A further area of risk arises in relation to the legal uncertainties connected with taking collateral over securities held in accounts.[25]

---

25   See **sections 8.28** and **10.12**

The FMI Principles specify that a CSD which re-invests its participants' assets should adopt a risk management strategy for investing participants' assets which is consistent with its own overall risk-management strategy, and fully disclose its approach to its participants.[26]

The proposed Regulation on CSDs (CSDR)[27] will enable authorised CSDs to act as a securities lending agent as an 'ancillary service'.[28] But the CSDR, as proposed by the European Commission, does not address the points just alluded to, and fails to include any regulatory restriction (other than a general duty to manage conflicts of interest[29]) to combat the risk that a CSD acting as securities lending agent with a view of the whole market could exploit a dominant position unfairly. The position of a CSD at the centre of a market, where it has sight of all possible candidates for fails-coverage assistance and many potential lenders of securities, gives rise to a competition policy concern. CSDs compete in this field with agency lenders, who are typically agent banks offering a range of securities services to their clients including fails-coverage and securities lending services. CSDs might aim to profit from their whole-market view, by arranging stock loans the agent banks would wish to intermediate themselves, if only they had the same market knowledge. Abusive exploitation of the whole-market view may in some circumstances be actionable under article 102 of the European Union Treaty unless duly justified.[30]

As discussed in **section 15.14**, a role as lending agent may also expose the CSD itself to credit risk.

Alternative measures for streamlining settlement

15.10 In theory, a CSD might be willing to allow its participants some leeway in relation to shortfalls incurred in the course of a settlement cycle. An overdrawn securities account would, if allowed, enable a participant to settle a transaction notwithstanding that it has insufficient deliverable securities, and to cover the overdraft with collateral in the form of the credit balances in respect of other types of security. Provided that the overdrawn participant does not transfer its collateral securities, this might be considered legitimate risk management by the CSD. However, the CSD also has a role as guardian of the integrity of the issue – in other words, the CSD may not allow the number of securities credited to its accounts to exceed the number issued by the issuer.[31] Allowing an overdraft violates that principle, since the transferee of the securities represented by the overdraft has obtained securities out of thin air, and the total number credited to the accounts provided by the CSD would exceed the number in issue. Thus, 'a CSD should prohibit overdrafts and debit balances in securities accounts.'[32]

Actual practice may be more nuanced. CSDs may allow for 'provisional' settlement where a cyclical net settlement process is adopted. Provisional

---

26 FMI Principles, para 3.16.4

27 European Commission, *Proposal for a Regulation of the European Parliament and of the Council on improving securities settlement in the European Union and on central securities depositories etc* (March 2012), COM(2012) 73 final, http://eur-lex.europa.eu/LexUriServ/LexUriServ.do?uri=CELEX:52012PC0073:EN:PDF

28 CSDR, Annex, Section B, para 1(a)

29 Article 24(3)

30 Cf **sections 7.2** and **7.16**

31 Cf proposed CSDR, art 34

32 FMI Principles, Principle 11, Key consideration 2; proposed CSDR, art 34(3)

settlement implies that the CSD has allowed transactions to proceed to 'settle' in the cycle even though one or more participants had not made available the net deliverable amount of securities required ahead of time. The settlement remains provisional until the last security is delivered by the net transferor: in other words, until the state of finality is attained, securities perceived to have been credited to transferees may not actually exist.

Cash leg liquidity risk – self-collateralisation

15.11 If a securities overdraft is not permitted, there is less likely to be a constraint on cash overdrafts, at least as far as settlement in commercial bank money is concerned. Even central banks may be willing to lend money to certain participants short of ready money, provided that adequate collateral is provided. Collateral is, again, something which the CSD can very simply deliver on the borrowing participant's behalf, and thus a CSD may be in a position to broker an automatic repo facility for its participants, whereby collateral is delivered automatically on standardised terms to the central bank (or other cash lender). Collateral management services are also 'ancillary' services under Section B of the Annex of the proposed CSDR. The risks will be similar to those described in relation to securities loans.

Securities settlements against cash provide an inherent source of collateral – a loan of the purchase price of securities can be seen to be covered by the securities received. Such a loan might be considered to be 'self-collateralising' if the arrangements for treating the securities received as collateral are effective. However, the value of the securities received may be insufficient to cover the gross value of the loan, and once the other factors are taken into account (market risk, cost of enforcement, and interest) it may often be thought that the cover is insufficient. Risks faced in connection with purchase-money security interests are discussed further in **sections 18.24** and **10.12(3)**.

From the foregoing discussion it will be apparent that management of liquidity risk can transform liquidity risk into credit risk. Accordingly, credit risk is the next topic for analysis.

CREDIT OPERATIONS OF CSDs

15.12 Credit operations by a CSD raise the stakes in the risk game of securities settlement. Participants in a CSD, and investors in securities, do not expect the operation of a CSD to be a risk-taking activity. Commercial considerations may intrude, however, and in a marketplace where CSDs cannot compete on the efficiency of the settlement engine after the introduction of Target2-Securities,[33] CSDs may have to offer credit in order to differentiate their settlement services. Accordingly:

> 'Where they are permitted to do so, CSDs often extend intraday credit to participants (either as principal or as agent for other participants) to facilitate timely settlements and, in particular, to avoid gridlock. In a gross settlement system, where credit extensions occur, they are usually extended by the CSD as principal and take the form of intraday loans or repurchase agreements. In

---

33 See **section 2.22**

net settlement systems these credit extensions are usually in effect extended by the CSD as agent for other participants and take the form of net debit positions in funds, which are settled only at one or more discrete, pre-specified times during the processing day.'[34]

CSDs following the lead of agent banks in the range of services which they offer will potentially be subject to a similar set of risks. There is no need to repeat here the assessment of credit-related risks commonly confronted by agent banks.[35] What follows is a discussion of issues most likely to be encountered by CSDs; some of the points identified may indeed be applicable to agent banks.

CSDs as lenders of cash and securities

15.13 It was noted in **section 15.3** that true DvP may impose challenging liquidity pressures on CSD participants. CSDs are expected to attain high standards of efficiency in the interests of their users.[36] A CSD operator may thus arrange, or even itself extend, credit for participants to assist them with liquidity management.[37] If it provides the credit directly, the CSD will need to adopt the usual credit risk management devices available to lenders: restricting the class of participants eligible for credit to those of the highest standing; imposing limits and ejecting trades from the queue if the limit would be exceeded; taking collateral and other credit support; and having a loss-sharing system which protects the CSD in the event that other controls should fail.

Arranging for credit to be provided between participants would not expose the CSD itself to its participants, and would thus present less of a public policy question than a CSD offering the credit directly.

15.14 Liquidity pressures are not confined to the cash leg of transactions, and CSDs will equally wish to smooth the way for their participants on the securities side. If the CSD acts as lending agent for securities loans between participants, the CSD ought to be able to step aside if either participant fails, allowing the principals to bear the residual risk. Where the loans are collateralised, that risk might be small. But often the CSD itself will be responsible for selection of the collateral supporting the loan, and notwithstanding the disclaimers of liability commonly found in CSDs' rulebooks there may be some residual liability for the CSD if the collateral arrangements are deficient in some way. For example, if the collateral were subject to wrong-way risk (the value of the collateral falls when the collateral-provider fails) this could be attributed to a failure by the CSD to manage the collateral effectively.

Furthermore, CSDs may have assets of their own: they are obliged to invest their capital prudently, and the possibility arises that CSDs will have own-account holdings of government bonds or other financial instruments in respect of which the CSD is both CSD and investor.[38] As investor the CSD may wish

---

34 Committee of European Securities Regulators and European Central Bank, *Recommendations for Securities Settlement Systems* (May 2009), http://www.ecb.eu/pub/pdf/other/pr090623_escb-cesr_recommendationsen.pdf, Recommendation 9, para C1
35 See **chapter 18**
36 FMI Principle 21
37 Cf Russo, D, et al, *Prudential and Oversight Requirements for Securities Settlement* (December 2007), ECB Occasional Paper No 76, http://www.ecb.eu/pub/pdf/scpops/ecbocp76.pdf, pp 25–28 and Annex 1
38 Cf FMI Principles, para 3.16.4

to engage in lending as principal. Quite apart from the obvious implications for the CSD from a credit perspective of participating in a lending market as principal, such activity would require the careful management of conflicts of interest. The proposed CSDR will require such conflicts to be managed, and ESMA is to create related technical standards.[39]

Collateral arrangements

15.15   A CSD which extends credit to its participants is expected to cover the exposure with collateral.[40] That practice implies that the CSD should adopt all prudent means to manage and control the risks associated with collateral: the FMI Principles mention limiting the types of asset treated as acceptable collateral, valuation and haircutting, avoidance of concentration, legal risk in taking collateral across borders, and operational issues related to timing of liquidation of collateral, and management.[41]

CSDs have, of course, a primary source of collateral assets in their immediate control, namely the assets in respect of which it acts as CSD. For example, Clearstream Banking Frankfurt relies on collateral for claims.[42] Those assets may, however, fail some of the tests identified by the FMI Principles, which may lead to the imposition of tight limits on the amount of credit made available.

Further, the CSD will need to have regard to the possibility that the beneficial interest in the securities provided as collateral may be vested in a person other than the participant to whom credit is being granted. Except in 'beneficial owner' or direct-holding markets, the local legal practice will usually disregard the ultimate account holder's interest,[43] and the CSD may find it impossible to know for sure whether the collateral assets belong beneficially to the recipient of credit; representations and warranties are not proof against operational error or fraud by the participant making them.

DEFAULT RULES AND DEFAULT MANAGEMENT

15.16   One, possibly striking, feature of the limited literature on regulation and risk management of CSDs is the rarity of discussion of default by a participant in a CSD. By contrast, this subject occupies much of the discussion relating to operation of payment systems, and is the major focus of debate around management of CCPs. In the United Kingdom the CSD is configured as a 'recognised clearing house', which is a regulatory status shared with CCPs.[44] The Recognition Requirements Regulations (RRRs),[45] which set forth the basic regulatory regime for recognised clearing houses, make no distinction between CSDs and CCPs except this: that recognised clearing houses which do not enter into market contracts need not have default rules.[46]

---

39   Article 24(3) and (8)
40   FMI Principles, Principle 4, key consideration 3
41   FMI Principles, Principle 5, key considerations
42   Clearstream Banking AG Frankfurt, *General Terms and Conditions* (October 2010), s XXVI
43   See **section 6.39**
44   Cf **section 11.16**
45   Financial Services and Markets Act 2000 (Recognition Requirements for Investment Exchanges and Clearing Houses) Regulations 2001, SI 2001 No 995
46   Regulation 8

However, CSDs are subject to paragraph 19 of the Schedule to the RRRs, which specifies that '[a] clearing house must ensure that ... its clearing services involve satisfactory arrangements for securing the timely discharge (whether by performance, compromise or otherwise) of the rights and liabilities of the parties to transactions in respect of which it provides such services.'[47]

Moreover, a CSD is likely to wish, or need, to have the status of a designated system under the SFD.[48] Under paragraph 6 of the Schedule to the Settlement Finality Regulations,[49] a system to be designated in the United Kingdom must have default arrangements which are appropriate for that system in all the circumstances. Thus, a CSD which is a recognised clearing house will need default rules. The content or objective of such rules is, however, not spelled out. Although the ordinary expectation of a recognised clearing house with default rules would be that their purpose is to achieve the discharge of unsettled market contracts,[50] that expectation is not explicit for recognised clearing houses which are not themselves party to the market contract. So, it seems, a CSD is free to make whatever default rules it considers prudent.

The default rules of CREST are limited in scope and content. The principal power which Euroclear UK & Ireland (EUI, the operator of CREST) asserts in a default situation is disablement of the defaulting participant.[51] Notes (which are not part of the Rules) explain the process, and are worth quoting extensively, since they show how different the approach to default management is from that in a CCP:

'EUI can be expected to take the following actions under its default arrangements in the event that it is notified that insolvency proceedings have commenced against a CREST member (a "defaulting participant") ...

1. Initial disablement. Unless a defaulting participant's participation is already suspended, EUI will in normal circumstances immediately suspend its participation on receiving notification that insolvency proceedings have commenced against the defaulting participant. This will result in all settlement involving the defaulting participant immediately being suspended.

2. Conditions for re-enablement. EUI will not re-enable the defaulting participant's participation, unless EUI is satisfied that:

   (a) systemic or other types of risk that arise by reason of the participation of the defaulting participant in [CREST] would be limited or otherwise mitigated by re-enabling its participation;

   (b) ... re-enablement ... will not cause EUI to be in breach of any direction or requirement of any regulatory authority or body to whose jurisdiction it is subject;

   (c) ... re-enablement ... will be consistent with the effect and operation of the default rules ... of any relevant exchange or clearing house;

   (d) ... re-enablement ... can be effected without material interference with or disruption to the efficient operation of [CREST]; and

   (e) the defaulting participant (or its insolvency office-holder) has complied with all requirements and conditions that may be imposed by EUI ... .'

---

47 Paragraph 19(2)(b)
48 See **sections 8.18ff**
49 Financial Markets and Insolvency (Settlement Finality) Regulations 1999, SI 1999 No 2979
50 RRRs, Schedule, para 25(1)
51 CREST Rules (June 2011), r 13, s 6.2

The Notes were added as guidance following the default of Lehman Brothers to clarify the likely behaviour of EUI in a default of a participant.[52] However, the guidance does not explain why EUI chooses to exercise its discretion in this manner; disablement seems to prevent discharge of market contracts through settlement – which may be thought surprising, in light of the general philosophy expressed in the RRRs – and the need to persuade EUI to engage in the cautious process of re-enablement in order to carry out a settlement may be regarded as an unnecessary impediment, especially where a participant is in administration and dispositions of its property are permitted by insolvency law.

CREST takes the process one step further as regards unsettled trades which are in its system. In these cases the practice is to impose a requirement on both the defaulter and all market counterparties to 'match delete' pending settlement instructions of all types.[53] This idea can be reconciled with the RRRs only if the 'otherwise' option for timely discharge of market contracts is regarded as including tearing up the contracts, which for the reasons given seems to stretch a point.

OPERATIONAL RISKS

15.17 A CSD's approach to management of operational risks will probably not differ greatly from that of other infrastructures or indeed from that of agent banks. The proposed CSD Regulation singles out IT security, reliability, and capacity, as well as business continuity and disaster recovery (including a standard that recovery should take place fast enough to enable settlement to complete on the scheduled date).[54] A useful guide to business continuity planning has been issued in the United States by the Depository Trust & Clearing Corporation, setting out in detail arrangements for back-up facilities, redundant functionality, communications and human resource issues, keeping people informed, and testing.[55]

Outsourcing and T2S

15.18 In one particular, operational risk for CSDs in Europe has a significant difference from other types of infrastructure. This is in the area of outsourcing.

A CSD will typically be dependent on external providers for a range of services, in particular software. Again, managing outsourcings is an experience which will not be widely different from that of other infrastructures. A list of relevant considerations can be briefly set out, based on the principal sets of regulation,

---

52 EUI, *Guidance for CREST Rule 13* (March 2009), https://www.euroclear.com/site/publishedFile/crest_rule_13_additional+guidance_tcm87-146136.pdf?title=New+guidance+to+CREST+Rule+13

53 Cf Euroclear UK & Ireland, *MF Global UK Limited in special administration – matched deletion and settlement discipline* (December 2011), Operational Bulletin No 1819, https://www.euroclear.com/site/publishedFile/Operational_Bulletin_1819+_tcm87-240057.pdf?title=Operational+bulletin+1819+-+MF+Global+UK+Limited+in+special+administration+%E2%80%93+matched+deletion+and+settlement+discipline+%2B+more

54 Article 42

55 Depository Trust & Clearing Corporation, *Safe, Secure, Setting New Standards – An Updated Report to the Industry on Business Continuity Planning* (October 2011), http://www.dtcc.com/downloads/leadership/whitepapers/BusinessContinuityPlanning.pdf; see also **section 16.20**

viz. the Joint Forum's guidance (1),[56] the Commission Directive implementing MiFID (2)[57] and the guidelines issued by the Committee of European Banking Supervisors (CEBS) (3).[58]

- Regulated firms should notify their regulator of a material outsourcing. (2, 3)
- Outsourcing may not result in a delegation of responsibility by senior management for the core competence or regulated activity which the regulated firm undertakes. (1, 2, 3)
- The supplier should have the ability and capacity to perform the outsourced functions, and may in some instances have to be regulated itself. (1, 2, 3)
- The contract with the supplier should address service quality, monitoring, sub-contracting, termination, and other key issues. (1, 2, 3)
- The supplier should be monitored so that corrective measures can be taken. (1, 3)
- The supplier should protect confidential information. (1, 2, 3)
- The regulated firm should be able to terminate the outsourcing without detriment to service, and able to transfer the service back to itself or a third party. (1, 2, 3)
- The regulated firm should have contingency plans, including an exit strategy. (1, 3)

Where a CSD is configured as a bank, the national rules on outsourcing which apply to banks will also apply to the CSD. However, these are not harmonised in the case of a bank which is not providing investment services and to which MiFID is irrelevant. Furthermore, not all CSDs are banks. The European Central Bank (ECB) noted in 2007 that there was significant diversity of regulatory approaches to outsourcing by CSDs.[59] The lack of uniformity is unlikely to change with the implementation of the CSD Regulation, as that is very thin on the subject.

15.19 However, the freedom of movement of CSDs has been cut back very significantly by the development of the Target2-Securities (T2S) project. This project requires participating CSDs to outsource to the ECB the service of providing the settlement engine, which is the functional software which the CSD needs to carry out its main business activity.

The ECB has explained that the basis for outsourcing involved in the T2S project has to be different from a private bilateral supply contract. In the first place, the T2S service is provided on a homogeneous basis to many CSD clients: 'T2S will be an open and shared infrastructure that promotes equal access to all CSDs.' Secondly, the formal definition of an outsourcing is the provision of a service which the outsourcer would otherwise provide for itself,[60] whereas 'T2S entails... the provision of integrated settlement in central bank money

---

56 The Joint Forum, *Outsourcing in financial services* (February 2005), http://www.bis.org/publ/joint12.pdf

57 Commission Directive 2006/73/EC of 10 August 2006 implementing Directive 2004/39/EC of the European Parliament and of the Council as regards organisational requirements and operating conditions for investment firms and defined terms for the purposes of the Directive

58 CEBS, *Guidelines on Outsourcing* (December 2006), http://www.eba.europa.eu/getdoc/f99a6113-02ea-4028-8737-1cdb33624840/GL02OutsourcingGuidelines-pdf.aspx

59 Russo et al, Table 4, pp 39–40

60 CEBS, *Guidelines on Outsourcing*, Guideline 1.a

[which] entails Eurosystem activities, which by no means would otherwise be undertaken by the CSDs.'[61]

The terms and conditions on which the outsourcing is to be done will, therefore, not be as freely negotiated as they would with a free-market supplier of software. The ECB has also published a Memorandum of Understanding which summarises (at a very high level of generality) what the contracts will cover.[62] However, the issues which arise for CSDs in outsourcing to T2S (notwithstanding the distinctions that the ECB notes) will typically be more complex and troublesome than the Memorandum of Understanding might suggest. In particular, one might note that the following provisions are normally heavily negotiated in an outsourcing agreement:

(1) *Service levels.* It would be ordinary practice for an outsourcing firm to require its supplier to adhere to agreed service levels, and for some form of credits to be provided to the firm in cases where those levels are not met. The Eurosystem, as a public organisation, is likely to be reluctant to make such commercial concessions. The CSDs, as sole providers of central settlement services for users, are likely to wish to insist.

(2) *Liability for breach, and indemnity for losses.* Heavy negotiation will often take place, even in a private context, about the degree to which the supplier should be liable for losses sustained by the outsourcer. Where the outsourcer is wholly dependent on the supplier for the centrepiece of the service provided by the outsourcer, which is the case with T2S, the expectation is that the supplier will assume a significant level of liability. Indemnities may be requested to cover cases where negligence or other default by the supplier cannot be proved, but the outsourcer suffers loss nonetheless. Conversely, the supplier may demand an indemnity from the outsourcer in cases where the provision of the service exposes the supplier to liabilities which are not attributable to the supplier's fault. Both the Eurosystem and the CSDs will be unused to conceding the assumption of liability for losses sustained by any other person. The liabilities for mis-performance could be large, as they involve potentially the loss by an investor of its assets.

(3) *Compliance with international standards.* Of the eight key matters identified above from international regulatory standards relating to outsourcing, T2S looks problematic in at least four cases: delegation of governance and control, monitoring of service performance with a view to corrective action, termination rights, and exit strategies.

(4) *Pricing.* The rationale for the T2S project is reduction of cost of settlement. But the T2S project is costly, and the Eurosystem has asserted that the project should be self-reimbursing.[63] CSDs cannot be compelled to adopt a particular pricing structure, and the adoption of a new, outsourced, system for settlement and keeping of registers cannot be assumed to involve a saving of cost, even if it does involve an increase in efficiency. Participating

---

61 ECB, *The nature of outsourcing in T2S* (October 2009), http://www.ecb.eu/paym/t2s/pdf/natureofoutsourcing.pdf

62 ECB, *Target2-Securities Memorandum of Understanding* (July 2009), http://www.ecb.eu/paym/t2s/pdf/T2S_MoU.pdf?1bf03f283a6afd10535d18b1a9e140c1

63 ECB, Governing Council Decision (November 2010), http://www.ecb.eu/press/pr/date/2010/html/pr101119.en.html

CSDs will nevertheless have no choice but to accept the pricing imposed by the Eurosystem.

15.20 The proposed CSDR sets out various conditions for an outsourcing by an authorised CSD which can, more or less, be benchmarked to the international standards for financial institutions mentioned in **section 15.18**.[64] Also it does not ignore T2S. The result is to jettison the international standards altogether:

'Paragraphs 1 to 4 [ie the basic set of conditions for outsourcing] shall not apply where a CSD outsources some of its services or activities to a public entity and where that outsourcing is governed by a dedicated legal, regulatory and operational framework which has been jointly agreed and formalised by the public entity and the relevant CSD and agreed by the competent authorities on the basis of the requirements established in this Regulation.'[65]

Corporate actions and asset servicing

15.21 Another area of operational risk which perhaps deserves better attention is asset servicing. The processing of corporate actions is considered in more detail in **Chapter 20**. Here, however, it may be noted that the feature which will distinguish the services offered by competing CSDs is their approach to asset servicing.[66] Asset servicing is believed to be a potent source of operational risk, largely because of the wide range of possible corporate actions,[67] the fact that the issuers are free to invent their own types of corporate action and services they need, and the constant struggle of intermediaries to evolve their systems and controls to keep pace with what issuers and markets are doing. Automation of corporate actions processing is, therefore, more of a challenge than for other securities processes.

In comments on the draft FMI Principles, Thomas Murray pointed out that it was a 'significant oversight' that the FMI Principles contain no recommendations on asset servicing. Thomas Murray give independent 'risk ratings' to CSDs in order to assess risk exposures arising in relation to settlement, safekeeping and asset servicing. For asset servicing risk, Thomas Murray consider that risk factors include 'corporate action and proxy arrangements, centralised information source, obligations on issuers to provide information to the CSDs and CSDs' liability for the accuracy, completeness and timeliness of corporate action information and the processing of corporate action instructions.'[68] Neither the FMI Principles nor the proposed CSD Regulation seeks to address any of these matters in any detail.

---

64 Proposed CSDR, art 28
65 Article 28(5)
66 Cf **section 2.22**
67 Cf Loader, D, *Clearing, settlement and custody* (Butterworth-Heinemann, 2002), ISBN 0 7506 5484 8, pp 141–154
68 Thomas Murray, consultation response letter (July 2011), http://www.bis.org/publ/cpss94/cacomments/thomasmurray.pdf, pp 1, 15

16 Risk Management in Payment Systems

RISK MANAGEMENT GUIDANCE

16.1   Although risks for payment systems have been described at the international level, notably by the Committee on Payment and Settlement Systems (CPSS) of the Bank for International Settlements in its seminal 2001 publication 'Core Principles for Systemically Important Payment Systems' (the Core Principles),[1] now incorporated into the Principles for Financial Market Infrastructures (FMI Principles),[2] it is perhaps remarkable that at European level there is no comprehensive pronouncement on risk management from the European Central Bank (ECB) equivalent to the joint publications by the ECB and the Committee of European Securities Regulators on CSDs and CCPs.[3] The absence of a consolidated European regulatory text cannot be explained by the absence of a formal regulatory regime for payment systems, since the equivalent standards for other types of infrastructure pre-date the European legislation applicable to CCPs and CSDs. Rather, the reason is more likely to be that the Core Principles have served as an effective and intelligible international handbook.[4]

The European System of Central Banks is obliged to promote the smooth operation of payment systems,[5] and the ECB is empowered to make regulations to ensure efficient and sound clearing and payment systems within the European Union.[6] The ECB's approach has been set forth in a number of documents,[7] principal among which are:

---

1   CPSS, *Core Principles for Systemically Important Payment Systems* (January 2001), http://www.bis.org/publ/cpss43.pdf
2   CPSS and Technical Committee of the International Organization of Securities Commissions, *Principles for Financial Markets Infrastructures* (April 2012), http://www.bis.org/publ/cpss101a.pdf
3   ECB and CESR, *Recommendations for Securities Settlement Systems and Recommendations for Central Counterparties in the European Union* (May 2009), http://www.ecb.eu/pub/pdf/other/pr090623_escb-cesr_recommendationsen.pdf?77b7a9f4e503479614e3f524f6b0d3d6
4   See **box 6.1**
5   Treaty on the Functioning of the European Union (May 2008), OJ(C) 115 pp 47–388, art 127(2)
6   Protocol (No 4) on the Statute of the European System of Central Banks and of the European Central Bank (May 2008), OJ(C) 115 pp 230–250, art 22
7   For a full list, see Kokkola, T, (ed), *The Payment System* (European Central Bank, September 2010), http://www.ecb.eu/pub/pdf/other/paymentsystem200909en.pdf, pp 274–275

- the Core Principles, which were formally adopted by the ECB Governing Council in January 2001,[8]

- oversight standards for retail payment systems operating in euro (the ECB Oversight Standards),[9] and

- a policy document on business continuity.[10]

Although the Core Principles have been superseded by the FMI Principles, there is valuable detail specific to payment systems in the Core Principles which has been truncated in the process of assimilation into the FMI Principles. All the above sources are thus relevant, and have to be taken together, for a study of the management of risk in payment systems in Europe.

16.2   In the United Kingdom, the Bank of England acquired express statutory responsibility for oversight of payment systems under Part 5 of the Banking Act 2009. In exercise of its powers the Bank of England has issued a policy statement[11] which sets out 14 Principles for recognised payment systems.[12] These Principles predate, but closely reflect, the FMI Principles, with some differences of emphasis in relation to operational risks.

The Bank of England's principles apply to 'recognised' payment systems, which are systems where disruption of operations would be likely to threaten the stability of, or confidence in, the United Kingdom financial system or to have serious consequences for business or other interests throughout the United Kingdom.[13] This is, of course, a description of systemic importance. The other guidance on payment systems referred to above is also directed at systemically important payment systems. It may therefore be helpful, for the purposes of context and limitation, to note that the ECB has issued commentary which explains how to determine, in respect of retail payment systems, which are of systemic importance: the indicators the ECB identifies are market penetration exceeding 75%, high aggregate value of processed payments, and the risk of a domino effect.[14] The ECB Oversight Standards disapply four of the original ten Core Principles in respect of 'economically prominent' retail payment systems, presumably because such systems will typically be organised as ACHs, and those Principles would not be relevant. Systems which do not meet the tests for economic prominence are exempt from any obligation to comply with the Core Principles.[15]

As the ECB Oversight Standards implicitly recognise, payment systems come in a variety of forms, considered in **section 2.27**. A few preliminary observations, pertaining to variety, may be appropriate before launching the

---

8   ECB, *Eurosystem Oversight Policy Framework* (February 2009), http://www.ecb.eu/pub/pdf/other/eurosystemoversightpolicyframework2009en.pdf?2340d93806dc0f85c19f338338a1f5d3, p11

9   ECB, *Oversight Standards for Euro Retail Payment Systems* (June 2003), http://www.ecb.eu/pub/pdf/other/retailpsoversightstandardsen.pdf?a87b13ebceee1957d4a3a534d1fab8c0

10   ECB, *Business Continuity Oversight Expectations for Systemically Important Payment Systems (SIPS)* (June 2006), http://www.ecb.eu/pub/pdf/other/businesscontinuitysips2006en.pdf?fc59335973d7e1054939600f55897d1e

11   Bank of England, *The Bank of England's oversight of interbank payment systems under the Banking Act 2009* (September 2009), http://www.bankofengland.co.uk/publications/other/financialstability/oips/oips090928.pdf

12   Cf **section 11.4**

13   Banking Act 2009, s 185

14   ECB Oversight Standards, para 2.1; see **section 6.12**

15   ECB Oversight Standards, para 3.1

description of risks faced within payment systems. Much of the guidance for infrastructures conflates two distinct risk problems: the risks faced by the payment system operator itself, and the risks faced by the system's participants. Some regulatory recommendations addressed to systems might better be addressed to participants and completely disapplied in relation to the system operator. However, a payment system operator may be in a similar position to a central counterparty, taking on its shoulders the risk associated with the handling of cash. In such cases the risk issues it faces may be very similar to those confronted by participants. Or it may be a processor, merely handling information – critically important information, of course – but without handling the asset of value. Both types of payment infrastructure need to have regard to the impact their operations will have on their participants and the wider economy. Failure to distinguish the essential differences between a value-transfer system and a processor will confuse the story of how the infrastructure should approach the problem of safeguarding the interests of its participants. Given the variety of structures, a uniform approach to risk management cannot be expected.

LEGAL RISK – FINALITY

16.3   Legal risk can be defined as the risk of inability to enforce rights or obligations;[16] though regulators tend to say it is the unexpected application of a law or regulation, or the unenforceability of contracts. In the context of financial market infrastructures, 'legal risk is the risk of the unexpected application of a law or regulation, usually resulting in a loss. Legal risk can also arise if the application of relevant laws and regulations is uncertain. For example, legal risk encompasses the risk that a counterparty faces from an unexpected application of a law that renders contracts illegal or unenforceable. Legal risk also includes the risk of loss resulting from a delay in the recovery of financial assets or a freezing of positions.'[17]

Legal risks facing operators of payment systems include the danger of an action in tort for misuse of discretion, particularly in circumstances involving participant failure. System operators who reserve discretion to (say) re-order settlement queues or to extend credit at the cost of participants may find that action can be taken against them. Damages in tort may be measured differently from damages for breach of contract; statutory immunity may not apply to payment system operators[18] for action taken under default conditions.

In the European Central Bank's book entitled 'The Payment System',[19] legal risks faced by payment systems are itemised as finality risk, netting risk, and robustness of rules against insolvency challenge. These issues are reflected in the focus of the FMI Principles. Netting and insolvency issues are considered in **chapter 8**. For the present discussion that leaves the question of finality, insofar as that subject is not covered there as well.

---

16   Turing, D, and Cramb, E, *Managing Risk in Financial Firms* (Tottel, March 2009), ISBN 978-1-84766-303-0, p 9
17   FMI Principles, para 2.4
18   Cf Financial Services and Markets Act 2000, s 291, in relation to recognised clearing houses
19   Kokkola, T, (ed), *The Payment System* (European Central Bank, September 2010), http://www.ecb.eu/pub/pdf/other/paymentsystem200909en.pdf

16.4   The topic of settlement finality is introduced in **section 9.16**, where it was concluded that a payment which is 'final' is one which is irrevocable by the participants and irreversible under the rules of the system. It should perhaps be noted that settlement finality is *not* about guaranteeing that transactions which are submitted to a system and are irrevocable by the system must unavoidably proceed to final settlement. Confusion on this score was rife after the collapse of Lehman Brothers in 2008: unfortunately 140,000 trades failed, notwithstanding that many were ostensibly protected by settlement finality legislation.[20] Settlement finality is not the same concept as settlement certainty. Provided that the participants know whether the securities or payment transfer has settled, and that the transfer cannot be reversed, finality is achieved. It has, perhaps surprisingly, not been a policy objective to assure participants about certainty. The FMI Principle on finality states:

'An FMI should provide clear and certain final settlement, at a minimum, by the end of the value date. Where necessary or preferable, an FMI should provide final settlement intraday or in real time.
Key considerations

1. An FMI's rules and procedures should clearly define the point at which settlement is final.

2. An FMI should complete final settlement no later than the end of the value date, and preferably intraday or in real time, to reduce settlement risk. [A large value payment system or securities settlement system] should consider adopting RTGS or multiple-batch processing during the settlement day.

3. An FMI should clearly define the point after which unsettled payments, transfer instructions, or other obligations may not be revoked by a participant.'[21]

16.5   Finality risk arises for as long as *reversal* is still possible; typically when a challenge, aiming to reverse the payment, can be made under the insolvency law applicable to one of the participants. The following five possible threats to finality have been identified: revocation risk (legitimate cancellation of settlement instructions under the rules of a system); illegality risk (the very transfer is unlawful, for example because it is in breach of sanctions legislation); attachments and tracing risk (the money did not belong to the payer and must be given back to its rightful owner); preference risk (insolvency challenge based on unfair selection of one creditor for payment by an insolvent payer); and zero-hour and void disposition risk (insolvency challenge to prevent any asset disposals after a cut-off time).[22] These can generally be dealt with either by rule changes within the system or litigation outside the system to establish the true entitlement to funds being transferred. The insolvency-based challenges, however, are more troublesome, given that insolvency laws tend to be classified

---

20 PricewaterhouseCoopers, *Lehman Brothers International (Europe) (in administration) – Unsettled trades – Market Update* (November 2008), http://www.pwc.co.uk/eng/issues/lehmans_stakeholder_failed_trades.html
21 FMI Principle 8
22 Turing, D, and Cramb, E, *Managing Risk in Financial Firms,* (Tottel, March 2009), ISBN 978-1-84766-303-0, pp 222–3

as being for the public good and therefore to override contractually agreed provisions where incompatible.[23] The following comments may be made:

(1) *Preference risk.* A payment will often be open to challenge as a preference because it is made to a creditor after the payer's assets were less than its liabilities, and as a result the payee has received an unfair advantage over other creditors who will have to make do with a dividend. The payee may be ordered by the court exercising insolvency jurisdiction to return the payment. However, this does not mean that the payment originally made was not final: the return ordered by the court can take place outside the system, and no lack of clarity or effectiveness of the system's rule is implied. One issue to consider is whether the system operator can become implicated in the challenge. This is technically possible (if, in practice, unlikely) under sections 239(3) and 241(2) of the Insolvency Act 1986, which make it clear that an order restoring the pre-preference position can be 'such order as the court thinks fit' and may 'impose any obligation on any person whether or not he is the person with whom the company in question entered into the transaction or (as the case may be) the person to whom the preference was given.'

(2) *Zero hour and void disposition rules.* Zero hour rules deem insolvency proceedings to have begun at the stroke of midnight at the beginning of the day when the insolvency order was made. Void disposition rules render void and of no effect a disposition of any property of an insolvent company after a cut-off time, which is typically the opening of insolvency proceedings, and may thus be back-dated to zero hour. Void disposition rules, to the extent deemed part of the overriding public policy aspect of insolvency laws, represent a potent threat to finality.[24]

(3) *Netting challenges.* It is explained in **section 8.9(3)** how a multilateral netting system may be incompatible with the *pari passu* system of distribution of assets in an insolvency. (The same is true of bilateral netting, since the non-defaulting party invariably receives a higher percentage of recovery than if he paid up in full and proved for a dividend in the insolvency proceedings.) Application of these challenges to ACH or other payment systems dependent on netting for their efficiency algorithms could lead to an unwind of payments, such as that narrowly averted in the case of failure of Barings.[25]

Settlement Finality Directive

16.6   In Europe, blocking laws, which aim to disempower the ability of insolvency officers to make successful attacks of this nature, are available to designated settlement systems under the Settlement Finality Directive (SFD).[26] The blocking effect of these laws is discussed in detail in **sections 8.18–8.22**.

---

23 Cf Council Regulation (EC) No 1346/2000 of 29 May 2000 on insolvency proceedings, art 4(2)(3); Directive 2001/24/EC of the European Parliament and of the Council of 4 April 2001 on the reorganisation and winding up of credit institutions

24 See **section 8.9(7)** and **(15)**

25 CPSS, *Settlement Risk in Foreign Exchange Transactions* (March 1996), http://www.bis.org/publ/cpss17.pdf, pp 7–8; and see **box 2.2**

26 Directive 98/26/EC of the European Parliament and of the Council of 19 May 1998 on settlement finality in payment and securities settlement systems

16.7 The SFD is divided into three principal sections. The first sets out its scope, specifying which systems will benefit from its protective umbrella. 'Systems' are defined by the need to have at least three external 'participants', by the fact that they must be governed by the law of a Member State, and by the requirement to be 'designated' and notified to the European Commission.[27] The Commission publishes a list of designated systems.[28] Some payment infrastructures, such as card schemes, could not readily satisfy the conditions needed to become designated. (It may be worthy of note that the system operator itself is a 'participant', so that the insolvency protections granted by the SFD apply to the insolvency of the system as well as external participants.[29])

In this context a comment may be made on the concept of an 'indirect participant', who is an institution, settlement agent or infrastructure with a contractual relationship with a 'participant' which enables the indirect participant to pass transfer orders through the system.[30] The purpose of the definition is, however, limited: the protective provisions of the SFD apply to participants only, except where a Member State has decided that an indirect participant can be considered a participant on grounds of systemic risk.[31] So, in general, a participant is not protected against the insolvency of its client, only the insolvency of the system itself or other full 'participants'.

16.8 The second section of the SFD grandiosely states that 'transfer orders' and 'netting' shall be legally enforceable,[32] and that transfer orders may not be revoked after the moment defined by the rules of the system.[33] For the purposes of a payment system, a transfer order is payment instruction.[34] Netting has a less abstruse definition: 'the conversion into one net claim or one net obligation of claims and obligations resulting from transfer orders which a participant or participants either issue to, or receive from, one or more other participants with the result that only a net claim can be demanded or a net obligation be owed.'[35] The legal enforceability of these things is assured notwithstanding insolvency events affecting a participant, provided that the transfer order was entered into the system before the opening of insolvency proceedings. The moment of opening of insolvency proceedings is defined so as to exclude the operation of zero-hour and other retroactive timing rules.[36] The rule underpinning irrevocability is intended to nullify mandatory rules of law which might empower participants to disregard system rules which specify the point of no return for revocation of instructions.[37]

16.9 The third section of the SFD tackles some, but not all, troublesome issues arising from insolvency law.

---

27 SFD, art 2(a)
28 http://ec.europa.eu/internal_market/financial-markets/settlement/dir-98-26-art10-national_en.htm
29 SFD, art 2(f)
30 SFD, art 2(g)
31 SFD, art 2(f)
32 SFD, art 3
33 SFD, art 5
34 See **section 8.19**
35 SFD, art 2(k)
36 SFD, art 6
37 Vereecken, M, 'Directive 98/26/EC on the European Union Payment Systems and Securities Settlement Systems' in Vereecken and Nijenhuis, para 5

- Article 4 provides that insolvency proceedings cannot automatically result in a freeze on a participant's funds on a settlement account, so that they remain available to be utilised by the system.

- Article 7 neutralises zero hour rules and other rules of law which would have retroactive effects on a participant's rights and obligations. Many 'anti-avoidance' rules of insolvency law, such as preference rules, have retroactive effects, and unlike other protective legislation[38] article 7 is not limited to void disposition rules.

- Article 8 provides for supremacy of the governing law of the system, and thus of its rules, in the event of insolvency proceedings against a participant.

- Article 9 protects the rights of system operators and participants to 'collateral security', which is widely defined to mean 'all realisable assets' provided under a pledge, a repo or otherwise, to secure rights and obligations arising in connection with a system.[39]

CREDIT RISK

16.10 Not all payment systems involve the assumption of credit risk by the system operator. Pure ACHs do not involve the assumption of credit risk for the operator, as no money changes hands within the system, unlike in the case of a value-transfer system such as a multilateral netting DNS system, an RTGS, or an exchange-of-value system,[40] each of which requires a pay-in of funds to the operator. In these latter cases, the operator (or, in the case of a fully mutualised system such as the EBA's EURO-1 system, the other participants collectively) takes both credit and liquidity risk on each payer in relation to the payer's pay-in obligation.

16.11 The Core Principles noted that the credit risk issues are likely to arise primarily for the participants in the system rather than the operator itself.[41] However, this is not invariably the case:

(1) In a DNS system, where the system operator is in effect a central counterparty, a participant's failure to meet its pay-in obligation is a question of credit as well as liquidity risk. If the system is not to unwind the entire cycle of netted payment obligations it will need to have assurance that the paying-in participant will meet its obligations – the very netting mechanism impliedly involves the extension of credit. Failure to acknowledge this truth nearly led to the failure of the precursor to the current EBA Clearing system on the collapse of Barings in 1995.[42]

(2) In an RTGS, efficiency in liquidity management by participants may require that the system operator make available credit to participants. It is inherent in the RTGS model that payments are made gross, thereby demanding that participants pay in the whole of the gross amount of each transaction which needs to settle. Where large volumes and large sizes are involved even the largest participants will be constrained to meet the demands of the system at all times of the day. Typically, therefore, RTGSs will allow credit extensions

---

38 See **table 8.2**
39 SFD, art 2(m)
40 See **section 2.27**
41 Paras 7.3.4, 7.3.5
42 CPSS, *Settlement Risk in Foreign Exchange Transactions* (March 1996), http://www.bis.org/publ/cpss17.pdf, para 2.2.5; see also **box 2.2**

to their participants to avoid congestion and to enable transactions to settle. Credit typically takes the form of a repo facility.[43]

(3) In an exchange-of-value system, improved efficiency of processing may involve the extension of credit. If a participant has paid in an amount of currency ϕ in anticipation of settling a transaction with a counterparty who has not yet paid in, so that that settlement remains queued, it may be possible for a different transaction of the same participant to settle, even though that other transaction involves a payment of currency ψ which the participant has not yet paid in. The system may be able to lend the participant currency ψ, thus allowing the second transaction to settle, and leaving the participant with a credit balance of the countervalue received on the second transaction (say in currency Ω). At all stages in the process the system will have 'collateral' recorded to the credit of the participant's account which, allowing for market fluctuations, should be sufficient to protect the system operator in the event the participant fails to pay in currency ψ altogether. Note that the system operator would rarely be satisfied that the countervalue received in currency Ω is enough to cover the credit risk involved in lending currency ψ, owing to the market risk on the collateral, so it is usually essential for each participant to pay in a small amount of some currency to cover that risk – in effect, the payment-in of currency ϕ was to 'prime the collateral pump'.

16.12 Credit risk may be managed in a number of familiar ways. Classically the techniques for credit risk management are:

(1) *Barring the gate.* Keeping the right to participate in the system is the first line of defence. The issues which arise in relation to payment systems are the same for all types of infrastructure, save that in relation to undesignated payment systems there are legal constraints. These arise under article 28(1) of the Payment Services Directive,[44] which provides that payment systems' access criteria must be objective, non-discriminatory and proportionate, may not discriminate between 'authorised' and 'registered' payment service providers, and may not impose any restriction on the basis of institutional status. (Article 28(2)(a) of the Directive disapplies article 28(1) in relation to systems designated under the SFD.) RTGS systems may be operated by central banks, which require the participant to have a settlement account at the central bank. Central banks may have restrictive conditions for opening accounts, limiting the ability of some participants in the payments market to obtain access to the system. For other issues relating to exclusion of participants, see the discussions in **sections 7.11** and **14.12**.

(2) *Capital and guarantees.* Payment system operators may, like other forms of infrastructure, rely on their participant having large amounts of capital or being supported by a guarantee from a person (such as the parent bank) who does.

(3) *Position limits.* A typical approach to limiting the amount of credit risk which participants assume against each other in a DNS system is described,

---

43 European Central Bank, *Payment and Securities Settlement Systems in the European Union* (the Blue Book) (August 2007), http://www.ecb.eu/pub/pdf/other/ecbbluebooknea200708en. pdf, vol 2, p 375
44 Directive 2007/64/EC of the European Parliament and of the Council of 13 November 2007 on payment services in the internal market etc

curiously, in a report on RTGS (the Lucas Report).[45] This approach allows each participant to set bilateral limits against each other participant: bank X decides how much credit exposure it is willing to tolerate in relation to bank Y. The amount which a payer can be obliged to pay is calculated as the sum of the limits referable to that payer which have been agreed by all other participants. That payer may then be required to post collateral to cover the agreed aggregate amount. This model is adopted, for example, by the EBA's EURO-1 system.[46] The EURO-1 system allows for two credit limits: the *credit cap*, which limits the credit risk which the participant (P) is willing to take on other participants, and the *debit cap*, which is the maximum obligation which P can incur at any time. The credit cap is set by P, and is the aggregate of all the individual credit exposures which P has set on the other participants. The debit cap is set by the other participants, and (subject to a minimum) is the total of all the individual credit exposures which the other participants are willing to bear on P. A payment will be queued and not fed into the netting cycle if it would breach the receiving bank's credit cap or the paying bank's debit cap. The payment system operator will need to ensure that the caps are appropriate: in the 2011 Payment Systems Oversight Report, the Bank of England noted that the net debit position of a defaulter in the Bacs system could, at that time, have exceeded the amount of liquidity committed by surviving members.[47]

(4) *Netting*. Netting is inherent in a multilateral netting system. But the credit risk can be cut by increasing the number of cycles per day.

(5) *Collateral*. The FMI Principles specifically require financial market infrastructures to take collateral to cover current and potential future exposures to each participant.[48] This may be done, as in the EBA's EURO-1 system, by requiring each participant to contribute to what is essentially a cash default fund (although described as a liquidity pool) covering the maximum possible debit position of a participant.[49] Or it may be done, in an exchange-of-value system like CLS, by relying on the paid-in balances of the participant, which constitute the asset to be transferred or received, as a form of collateral in relation to credit extension. Where credit is extended by a central bank to cover intra-day liquidity it will often be done in conjunction with the central bank's overnight collateralised lending.[50] Issues (2) to (5) discussed in **section 14.27** are also likely to be relevant to collateral management by a payment system operator.

(6) *Loss-sharing*. The FMI Principles also require infrastructures to have rules and procedures for allocation of uncovered credit losses.[51] This may arise, for example, if collateral values are insufficient to cover the credit extended. Kokkola notes that loss-sharing structures have three components: an agreement as to whether it is 'defaulter pays' or 'survivors

45 CPSS, *Real-time Gross Settlement Systems* (March 1997), http://www.bis.org/publ/cpss22. htm, pp 40–41

46 Kokkola, T, (ed), *The Payment System* (European Central Bank, September 2010), ISBN 978-928990632-6, http://www.ecb.eu/pub/pdf/other/paymentsystem200909en.pdf, p 181

47 Bank of England, *Payment Systems Oversight Report 2011* (April 2012), http://www.bankofengland.co.uk/publications/Documents/psor/psor2011.pdf, para 1.2.3

48 FMI Principle 4, key consideration 3

49 ECB Blue Book, http://www.ecb.eu/pub/pdf/other/ecbbluebookea200708en.pdf, vol 1, p 44

50 Allsopp, P, Summers, B, and Veale, J, *The Evolution of Real-time Gross Settlement – Access, Liquidity and Credit, and Pricing* (February 2009), World Bank Working Paper No 49002

51 FMI Principle 4, key consideration 7

pay'; collateralisation; and practical arrangements to activate the structure so as to ensure settlement when there is a loss.[52] The Lucas Report notes that loss-sharing is only effective where the position limits are robust.[53]

16.13 When there is a robust collateral or loss-sharing arrangement in place, alongside position limits which apply in operational practice, the liquidity risk recommendation of the FMI Principles will be adhered to, namely that:

'A payment system … including one employing a DNS mechanism, should maintain sufficient liquid resources in all relevant currencies to effect same-day settlement, and where appropriate intraday or multiday settlement, of payment obligations with a high degree of confidence under a wide range of potential stress scenarios that should include, but not be limited to, the default of the participant and its affiliates that would generate the largest aggregate payment obligation in extreme but plausible market conditions.'[54]

Tiering (indirect participants)

16.14 One further consideration pertinent to credit risk management in payment systems is the question of 'tiering'. Tiering occurs when a system's potential participants are in fact clients of the direct participants in the system, so that they do not participate directly. Some systems may have 'indirect' participants, such as the EBA Clearing. The explanatory note to FMI Principle 19 states that '[the risks] are most likely to be material where there are indirect participants whose business through the FMI is a significant proportion of the FMI's overall business or is large relative to that of the direct participant through which they access the FMI's services.'[55] There is a tension between (on the one hand) the desirability of a payment system protecting itself, and its participants, by having suitable rules to limit the amount of third-party business undertaken by its participants to what can practically be handled by the participant without undue risk, and (on the other) the social and regulatory need[56] for large-volume providers of payment services to have access to the system, either directly or indirectly. Indirect participants (who, subject to the right to input instructions directly, and to the elusive possibility of protection under the SFD, are not participants at all) are at a disadvantage when their service-provider fails; however, this is a matter not for the system operator but for contingency planning by the indirect user of the system. Where the indirect user is a significant user, switching of service providers rapidly ought to be facilitated by the system operator.[57]

LIQUIDITY RISK

16.15 Liquidity risk is another issue which is predominantly one that affects the participants in payment systems, but where a duty is imposed upon the system-operator to minimise liquidity burdens and disruptions upon the

---

52   Kokkola, p 117
53   Page 40
54   FMI Principle 7, key consideration 3
55   FMI Principles, para 3.19.3
56   Cf FMI Principle 21
57   Allsopp et al

participants. The sources of liquidity risk in payment systems depend on the type of system:

(1) *RTGS.* RTGS structures inherently made demands on participants for significant amounts of liquidity. This is because each payment instruction is, in principle, settled as a separate unit, requiring pre-funding in full unless the system operator is willing to take credit risk on the payer participant. DNS systems, by contrast, do not require pre-funding of each payment transaction, and only a net pay-in per cycle is needed, thereby substantially reducing the liquidity demands made on participants.

The liquidity pressure imposed on participants may have the following adverse consequences. First, a payer participant may find that its payment instructions are indefinitely queued, while the system waits for the payer's account to accumulate a credit balance sufficient to enable a large payment to be processed. If the system operates a first-in, first-out (FIFO) processing algorithm, smaller payments in the queue will also not be processed. Other participants awaiting transfers from the payer may find themselves unable to settle outgoing payments because they are dependent on the incoming funds which are stuck in the queue. This phenomenon is called gridlock. Secondly, if market conditions are impaired, participants in a payment system may be untrusting of the ability of others to honour their obligations. RTGS systems tend not to be supported by guarantee mechanisms such as loss-sharing arrangements (because the credit risk inherent in the system is zero: failed settlements just fail, they do not proceed at a cost, as is the case with DNS settlement), so bank X may prefer to postpone submitting transfer instructions into the RTGS system until after transfers due from bank Y, whose ability to survive may be in question, have arrived with finality. Bank X's self-protective behaviour (which may be copied by all other participants) may also lead to gridlock.[58]

RTGS systems will thus typically have various liquidity mitigants built in. These can include avoiding the FIFO principle where appropriate, enabling other payments due from other participants to be freed up. Sophisticated queuing algorithms will pick irrevocable payment instructions from the queue and process them in the order which maximises the number of successful settlements.

> 'Complex algorithms consider the queues of several participants and search those queues for a set of payments between those participants that largely offset one another. Those payments are then settled by means of offsetting – i.e. either the individual payments are all effected simultaneously on a gross basis at the same legal and logical second, or net balances are settled. These algorithms can work on a multilateral or bilateral basis and can be run at discrete intervals (either at designated times or following a decision by the system operator) or be event-driven (being run, for instance, every time a participant's account is credited with an incoming payment or every time a payment is added to the queue).'[59]

One option for queue management is to identify a circle of payments (A→B→C→A) which can be taken out of the queue and be deemed to

---

58 Cf Kokkola, p 122
59 Kokkola, p 53

have settled.[60] Another queue management technique which frees up liquidity is to break up large payments into smaller units which stand a greater chance of success. Partial processing may be necessary in order to give effect to circles processing, since the chances of identical amounts flowing all the way round a circle will be low. (Whether a partial settlement can be regarded as *pro tanto* final may, of course, be a difficult question, but in Europe clear system rules will assist with legal certainty.)

The simplest solution for liquidity problems is for the participants to borrow to cover their liquidity needs. They may borrow from each other or in the money market generally, or they may be able to borrow from the central bank. Where the central bank is the RTGS operator, the question of central bank funding is wrapped up with questions about monetary policy and the central bank's role as lender of last resort. The Lucas Report suggests that smooth operation of the RTGS will be assisted if the participants do not have to go to the market for intra-day funds; the speed of the RTGS could become dependent on the effectiveness of interbank collateral settlement.[61] Central banks typically allow RTGS participants to access intra-day liquidity via repo facilities.[62]

(2) *DNS.* DNS structures may, notwithstanding that the liquidity pressures they induce, have some liquidity features. A DNS system will typically impose position limits for the reasons discussed in relation to credit risk management. The old Core Principles explained that position limits can lead to large payments being rejected by the system;[63] in a DNS environment the would-be recipient of the blocked transfer will therefore suffer an increase in the funds required to achieve effective settlement of its own outgoings in that cycle, and run the risk of blockings owing to its own credit limit being reached; and these blockings will affect other participants in that cycle as the same logic is applied iteratively. Again, to address the risk, a DNS system can adopt mitigants similar to those described in relation to RTGS systems.

Having dealt with the problems in this analytical way, it is worth noting that in practice payment systems are typically hybrid systems – very short processing cycles will make DNS systems more similar to RTGS systems; and RTGS systems will typically adopt algorithmic solutions, including circles processing, which borrow DNS methodologies. So many modern payment systems should not be crudely classified as 'RTGS' or 'DNS', and should be recognised to need risk management features relevant to both categories.

16.16 Liquidity risk management is not exclusively about the operational rules of the system. Incentives may be built in to minimise the risk of gridlock, such as a pricing incentive (time-varying tariff) for early payers, or the classically-British threat of being asked to explain bad behaviour over a cup of tea in front of your peers.[64] It has also been noted that the policy of the central bank with

---

60 Lucas Report, pp 24ff
61 Page 37
62 Cf Bank of England, *A Guide to the Bank of England's Real Time Gross Settlement System* (September 2010), http://www.bankofengland.co.uk/markets/paymentsystems/rtgsguide.pdf
63 Paragraph 7.3.8
64 Ball, A, et al, *Intraday liquidity: risk and regulation* (June 2011), Bank of England Financial Stability Paper No 11, http://www.bankofengland.co.uk/publications/Documents/fsr/fs_paper11.pdf, pp 19, 17

regard to intra-day liquidity is important: liquidity problems have been lower in Japan, where the central bank offered free (but collateralised) liquidity facilities than in the United States, where the Federal Reserve offered paid-for (but uncollateralised) facilities.[65] If the central bank is able to allow liquidity coverage assets, which must be retained by banks against the risk of general cash outflows, to do 'double duty' as a source of collateral for the central bank to extend liquidity, this may help, though at the risk that the prudential buffer may be needed for other liquidity coverage such as a run on deposits.[66]

16.17 The following further comments may be made in the context of liquidity risk management in payment systems:

- Intraday revocability may affect queue management, and may be forbidden in some RTGS systems, even though revocability will typically be revived for transfers remaining unsettled at the end of the processing day. A receiving bank may take the view that a queued transfer from another bank is highly likely to settle (as it cannot be revoked) and decide to treat it as 'as good as received'. The result could be a 'contractual settlement' as far as the bank's customer is concerned – in other words a decision by the bank to credit the customer's account notwithstanding that the funds have not yet been received by the bank itself with finality.[67]

- Regulatory rules on liquidity coverage may have a perverse effect. One possible consequence is that banks might manage their liquidity tightly for fear of regulatory attention; another is that banks might act so as to manage the regulatory obligations, rather than 'normally' or in the way which is best for general systemic safety and efficiency.[68]

- Where liquidity is scarce, the system's approach may come under pressure. Any weaknesses in liquidity management may translate into real problems if there is a default. The role of the central bank as liquidity provider of last resort will be crucial in this situation.[69]

OPERATIONAL RISK

16.18 Operational risk is as important as – arguably even more important than – the risks already considered. Systemically important payment system operators are, as noted at the beginning of this chapter, responsible to the wider economy for their smooth running. All payment systems, whatever their structure, have this responsibility, even if they have successfully arranged their affairs to avoid the problems of legal, credit and liquidity risk for themselves. Operational risk is not something that can be shifted outwards to be borne by the community of participants. Nevertheless an operational risk failure will be felt in that wider community more than it is at home.

---

65 Shirakawa, M, *'Liquidity' and 'Payment and Settlement Systems'* (November 2008), Conference speech, http://www.boj.or.jp/en/announcements/press/koen_2008/ko0811f.htm
66 Ball et al, p 12
67 Lucas Report, p 27; see also **sections 18.30ff**
68 Ball et al, p 14
69 Cf Bernanke, B, *Clearinghouses, Financial Stability, and Financial Reform* (April 2011), Conference speech, http://www.federalreserve.gov/newsevents/speech/Bernanke20110404a.htm

There is a wide literature on operational risk and its management. Selecting the parts which specifically apply to payment systems operators is a challenging and ultimately fruitless task. Operational risk is defined as 'the risk of loss resulting from inadequate or failed internal processes, people and systems or from external events. This definition includes legal risk, but excludes strategic and reputational risk.'[70] Given the breadth of the subject, it is hardly surprising that official guidance on management of operational risk is set out at a high level of generality, focusing on governance, management information, policies and such like. Little insight is derived from these on what operational issues should be of concern to infrastructure providers.

Perhaps the starting point, in the context of payment systems, is that any business needs to have a rigorous approach to systems and controls in order to prevent operational risks. All businesses are exposed to the threat of fraud, HR problems, data losses, new business teething problems, and the fallout from mergers. The Basel Committee has issued guidance for banks on how to handle these day-to-day issues, including the following:

'In addition to segregation of duties and dual control, banks should ensure that other traditional internal controls are in place as appropriate to address operational risk. Examples of these controls include:
(a) clearly established authorities and/or processes for approval;
(b) close monitoring of adherence to assigned risk thresholds or limits;
(c) safeguards for access to, and use of, bank assets and records;
(d) appropriate staffing level and training to maintain expertise;
(e) ongoing processes to identify business lines or products where returns appear to be out of line with reasonable expectations;
(f) regular verification and reconciliation of transactions and accounts; and
(g) a vacation policy that provides for officers and employees being absent from their duties for a period of not less than two consecutive weeks.'[71]

These ideas are not peculiar to banks, or indeed infrastructures or payment systems, and do not need special treatment here. Instead this section approaches the subject by attempting to select those operational risks which appear to have specific relevance to payment system. Literature looking at infrastructures homes in on three types of operational risk.

IT systems

16.19 Infrastructures depend critically on IT systems for their operation. Being specialist processors of high volumes of transactions there is likely to be no manual alternative, as may exist for businesses with smaller volumes and more diversified activities. International guidance emphasises the virtues of capacity, reliability, scalability, and adaptability:

● 'Management should ensure the bank has a sound technology infrastructure that meets current and long-term business requirements by providing sufficient capacity for normal activity levels as well as peaks during

---

70 Basel Committee on Banking Supervision, *Principles for the Sound Management of Operational Risk*, (Bank for International Settlements, June 2011), http://www.bis.org/publ/bcbs195.pdf, footnote 5
71 Basel Committee on Banking Supervision, *Principles for the Sound Management of Operational Risk* (Bank for International Settlements, June 2011), http://www.bis.org/publ/bcbs195.pdf, para 50

periods of market stress; ensuring data and system integrity, security, and availability.'[72]

- 'Operational performance objectives and service-level targets should define both qualitative and quantitative measures of operational performance and should explicitly state the performance standards the FMI is intending to meet.'[73]

- '[A]n FMI's operational objectives should be periodically reviewed to incorporate new technological and business developments.'[74]

- 'An FMI should ensure that it has scalable capacity adequate to handle increasing stress volumes and to achieve its service-level objectives, such as the required processing speed.'[75]

- 'An FMI's arrangements with participants, operational policies, and operational procedures should be periodically, and whenever necessary, tested and reviewed, especially after significant changes occur to the system or a major incident occurs. In order to minimise any effects of the testing on operations, tests should be carried out in a "testing environment." This testing environment should, to the extent possible, replicate the production environment (including the implemented security provisions, in particular, those regarding data confidentiality).'[76]

Business continuity and disaster recovery

16.20 The ability of the financial market infrastructure to keep functioning in the face of major incidents such as the terrorist attacks of 11 September 2001 has caused a good deal of anguish.

'The attacks on the World Trade Centre caused widespread destruction of physical infrastructure supporting financial institutions and extensive telecommunications breakdowns throughout the region. US equity markets were closed for four days and most bond trading ceased for two days. The clearing and settlement mechanisms for government securities, repurchase agreements and commercial paper were all disrupted. While payment systems continued to work well, operational and telecommunications breakdowns among major financial firms led to liquidity problems for several days. All major payment systems remained open past their normal closing times to help institutions trying to send funds or waiting to receive funds. Some institutions borrowed substantial amounts from the central bank discount window to obtain sufficient liquidity to meet their obligations. Others built up large cash balances or held on to government securities for precautionary reasons, thereby increasing market liquidity imbalances. Prudential regulatory requirements were relaxed in the face of credit and liquidity disruptions and unreconciled transactions.'[77]

---

72 BCBS 195, para 53
73 FMI Principles, para 3.17.9
74 FMI Principles, para 3.17.9
75 FMI Principles, para 3.17.11
76 FMI Principles, para 3.17.6
77 HM Treasury, Bank of England, and FSA, *UK Financial Sector Continuity*, http://www.financialsectorcontinuity.gov.uk/section.asp?catid=650

'Some of the key steps the Federal Reserve has taken to improve our infrastructure and the delivery of critical central-bank and financial services include the following:

- We have developed plans to ensure that critical central-bank activities, supervisory functions, and financial services operations have sufficient redundancy in facilities and staff. We have enhanced and tested business-continuity arrangements for critical functions and business lines.

- Our facilities for providing critical financial services are backed up at fully operational, geographically diverse sites to ensure a speedy recovery even if the critical infrastructure is disrupted across multistate areas.

- We have enhanced our resiliency for discount window lending and cash services provided by the Reserve Banks.

- We have improved our tools and authority to provide liquidity in a crisis. In 2003, the Board established the primary credit program, as well as special arrangements for rapidly reducing the primary credit rate to the federal funds rate in an emergency. We also have improved the ability of the Board to approve the extension of emergency discount window credit.'[78]

Business continuity thus assumes a high profile among the operational risk concerns of regulators. General guidance on business continuity[79] emphasises the need to develop recovery objectives, to communicate effectively, and to test the effectiveness of business continuity plans. That general guidance is echoed in the ECB's Business Continuity Oversight Expectations for Systemically Important Payment Systems,[80] which mention the importance of secondary processing sites, ensuring that not all critical staff are in the same place at the same time, and avoiding over-dependence on single components or service providers. Similar issues are covered in documentation issued by other infrastructure types.[81]

On secondary sites, the FMI Principles set out detailed guidance, adding that the locations of secondary sites should have different risk profiles from the primary site:

'The objectives of an FMI's business continuity plan should include the system's recovery time and recovery point. An FMI should aim to be able to resume operations within two hours following disruptive events; however, backup systems ideally should commence processing immediately. The plan should be designed to enable the FMI to complete settlement before the end of the day even in case of extreme circumstances.'[82]

---

78 Olson, M, *Protecting the financial infrastructure* (September 2004), Testimony before the US House of Representatives Committee on Financial Services, http://www.federalreserve.gov/boarddocs/testimony/2004/20040908/default.htm

79 Eg The Joint Forum, *High-level principles for business continuity* (August 2006), http://www.bis.org/publ/joint17.pdf

80 ECB, *Business Continuity Oversight Expectations for Systemically Important Payment Systems (SIPS)* (June 2006), http://www.ecb.eu/pub/pdf/other/businesscontinuitysips2006en.pdf?fc59335973d7e1054939600f55897d1e

81 Cf **section 15.17**

82 FMI Principles, para 3.17.14

The ECB paper also discusses the dependency of the system on its participants. The technical failure of a participant may have adverse consequences for the system itself, and the ECB recommends that participants have their own back-up processing sites which should re-enable them to attain operational effectiveness within one business day. Of course most participants will be banks and therefore subject to direct regulatory scrutiny; but the inclusion of specific recommendations targeted at participants in the ECB's supervisory 'expectations', directed at system operators, tends to encourage the insertion of rules directed at participants into systems' rulebooks.

Outsourcing

16.21 Being dependent on IT, an infrastructure will at some level be dependent on external suppliers for equipment, systems, power, data storage, communications media, software, maintenance and possibly staff. These external links may be classified as 'outsourcing', another subject on which there is an extensive regulatory literature, the general principles of which again do not need reiteration here.[83] Aspects of outsourcing which appear to be relevant to payment system operators include:

(1) *Custodians.* Systems may use custodians to hold collateral. Specific guidance in the FMI Principles focuses on custody risk and concentration risk (given that custodians may also be participants).[84]

(2) *Regulatory oversight of suppliers.* The FMI Principles indicate that the regulator of the system may wish to regulate the supplier directly, or to insist that the system operator obtain suitable assurances from the service provider that the provider complies with the regulator's requirements.[85] Annex F of the FMI Principles sets out five rules to be complied with by critical service providers, covering risk management, information security, operational resilience, technology upgrades and and supply of information to the system and its users.

(3) *Emergency providers.* Systems may depend on their participants to provide liquidity or to buy collateral or otherwise support them in moments of turmoil. Turmoil which is serious enough to affect the infrastructure is likely to be having disruptive effects in the wider financial world, and the participants in question may be impaired in their ability to respond or even in a state of personal crisis management. The system operator needs to be satisfied that its ability to implement emergency provision is resilient in the face of such disruption, and has adequate redundancy to ride out the non-performance of one or more participants.

---

83 Cf The Joint Forum, *Outsourcing in Financial Services,* http://www.bis.org/publ/joint12.pdf (February 2005)
84 FMI Principles, paras 3.16.2–3
85 FMI Principles, para 3.17.20

17 Insolvency of Infrastructures

INFRASTRUCTURES, AND THE TECHNIQUES FOR RESOLUTION OF CRISES, COMPARED

17.1 Insolvency, as it affects infrastructures themselves rather than their participants, is a poorly-documented subject. This is partly because there are few infrastructures relative to the number of participants, and still fewer insolvencies. In fact, the cases of infrastructure failure have typically been resolved without recourse to insolvency proceedings, no doubt because of the potentially devastating systemic consequences of an infrastructure being forced into a formal insolvency process. Necessarily, therefore, much of what is set forth in this chapter is of a speculative nature. Nevertheless, the subject is important, for without a study of it the implications of an insolvency process cannot be fully understood, and appropriate planning cannot be carried out.

At the outset one might note that the risk profiles of different types of clearing and settlement infrastructures are different, and the mechanisms for resolving problems which arise in those different types of infrastructure will vary accordingly. Two classes of infrastructure can be specified: those where the infrastructure is exposed to counterparty or credit risk in respect of its participants on a routine basis, and those where such exposures are exceptional. In the first class will be CCPs and payment systems. In the second will be CSDs. In the second class, a problem threatening the solvency of the CSD is unlikely to originate with the participants in the CSD – it is more likely to stem from an operational failure which is wholly internal to the infrastructure.

17.2 The mechanism for resolving an internally-generated or operational failure of proportions significant enough to threaten the viability of the infrastructure itself would probably be the following. Assuming that the technical platform on which the infrastructure operates is not fatally compromised, the business of the infrastructure could be assumed within a reasonably short timescale by a substitute service provider, who could take over the entire undertaking and operations without the liabilities of the predecessor entity. The Committee on Payment and Settlement Systems' (CPSS) Principles for Financial Market Infrastructures (FMI Principles) state:

'An FMI should hold liquid net assets funded by equity (such as common stock, disclosed reserves, or other retained earnings) so that it can continue operations and services as a going concern if it incurs general business losses. The amount of liquid net assets funded by equity an FMI should hold should be determined by its general business risk profile and the length of time required to achieve a recovery or orderly wind-down, as appropriate, of its critical operations and services if such action is taken.' [1]

This approach might be termed a 'lift-out' of the failed infrastructure. Where a lift-out cannot be achieved, or is inappropriate because the infrastructure's systems have been shown by the failure to be flawed, the options would appear to be either to close out the relationships between the infrastructure and its participants, and deal with the residual problems in a manner similar to a conventional financial-sector insolvency, or to close the infrastructure to new business (switching such new business to an alternative infrastructure) and run off the remaining exposures. Close-out and run-off are considered in the next section, in which the impact of a formal insolvency procedure is explored. Realistically, though, these options will be irrelevant to an infrastructure where lift-out is achievable before the implementation of an insolvency procedure.

LIFT-OUT

17.3 Lift-out is a desirable solution for all infrastructure types, but may be difficult to achieve. Unlike the case of an insolvent bank, it is unlikely that a crisis in an infrastructure which takes on counterparty risk can be managed so as to peak during or immediately before a weekend, during which the authorities have time (even though a weekend is not a generous amount of time) to arrange the least disruptive outcome. CCPs and payment systems which are in crisis will be in crisis because of abnormal things happening during the working week; at least, suddenness is likely for infrastructures, whereas a problem in a failing bank or investment firm is likely to have a longer gestation. Another difference from the 'recovery' options mooted for banks in the post-Lehman era, which is a recapitalisation based on trigger events and the conversion of certain classes of debt into equity, is equally improbable. This is because infrastructures do not typically issue debt securities, and do not have other classes of liability which can or ought to be convertible into equity. Furthermore, if crises break suddenly, the occurrence of the trigger event would rapidly be overtaken by complete and catastrophic breakdown before the actions designed to be implemented following the trigger event could actually take place. Lift-out is therefore a leisurely option, designed to deal with slowly-developing management failure and where orderly transfer is possible – it is not a feasible option in a crisis, unless done under the umbrella of an insolvency procedure.

17.4 The following aspects of a lift-out would need to be considered in any circumstance, regardless of whether an insolvency procedure has been implemented.

(1) The operations, accounts, systems, and assets of the failed infrastructure must be detachable and transferable to the substitute service provider. The difficulties which will be encountered include the application of termination rights of contract counterparties, including providers of IT and communications equipment. Where a failed bank or 'investment bank' is

---

1   Bank for International Settlements Committee on Payment and Settlement Systems and Technical Committee of the International Organization of Securities Commissions, *Principles for Financial Market Infrastructures* (April 2012), http://www.bis.org/publ/cpss101a.pdf, Principle 15, key consideration 2

concerned, termination rights may be curtailed;[2] but if the infrastructure provider is not configured as a bank or investment bank, this tool of resolution will be unavailable. There are non-legal difficulties too, such as the ability of the substitute service provider to retain staff able to operate the systems of the failed infrastructure and to interpret its records. Transfer restrictions may also apply, and may impair the transfer of vital contracts such as the provision of liquidity facilities.

(2) Risks and their mitigants must not be separated. The common worries in this area are that payables and receivables, which were intended to be set off, are left in different legal vehicles; or that the same fate occurs to collateral and the obligation it was intended to secure. Transferring the assets (including the benefit of contractual provisions and debt obligations) to the substitute service provider, and leaving the liabilities behind, is unlikely to be a solution. Again, in contrast to bank resolution, it is unlikely to be feasible to identify some 'bad assets' which could be ring-fenced and left behind in the failed infrastructure entity while 'good assets' are transferred.

(3) Liabilities may need to be transferred without the consent of the persons to whom they are due. English law does not allow for non-consensual transfer of a liability,[3] although there are various statutory ways to navigate around this rule.[4] While it might be pragmatic for many creditors to accept the promise of a transferee, in the circumstances of an infrastructure failure where the creditors are also likely to be the users of, providers of capital to, and in other ways connected with the failed entity and the replacement entity, this outcome cannot in all circumstances be relied on. An example of a challenge in this area is the ability to transfer the failed infrastructure's membership of other infrastructures (such as a CCP's participation in payment and securities settlement systems), which comprises both rights and obligations.

(4) The transferee entity will need to have appropriate regulatory status, including in the United Kingdom compliance with the full range of requirements discussed in **Chapter 11**. These matters cannot realistically be put in place overnight, which may limit the transferees to those, if any, who are competitors of the transferor. Where the infrastructure has multinational reach, the regulators of other jurisdictions will have powers which may also be relevant.

17.5 For these reasons, a lift-out may not be successful in an emergency. The complexity of the issues listed above, and other practical difficulties which would become apparent only on the day, effectively foreclose the ability to use this option for anything other than a pre-planned switchover.

Some aspects of a lift-out may be easier to achieve where the infrastructure operator is configured as a bank, since the toolkit available under the Banking Act 2009 will be available.[5] Alas, where the United Kingdom is concerned, a banking structure is unlikely except in the case of a payment system, since

---

2   Cf Banking Act 2009, s 38; Investment Bank Special Administration Regulations 2011, SI 2011 No 245, reg 14
3   *Tolhurst v Associated Portland Cement Mfrs (1900) Ltd* [1902] 2 KB 660, CA
4   Cf Banking Act 2009 s 34; Financial Services and Markets Act 2000, s 112
5   See **section 8.4**

the legislation does not currently favour a CCP or CSD taking any form as an authorised firm under the Financial Services and Markets Act 2000.[6]

APPLICATION OF INSOLVENCY LAW TO FAILED INFRASTRUCTURES

17.6 Where an infrastructure has failed to the point where an insolvency procedure is inevitable, the various risk issues discussed in **chapter 8** will need to be considered. In addition to the formal powers of insolvency office-holders and the possible application of special risk mitigants under Part VII of the Companies Act 1989 (Part VII) and the Settlement Finality Regulations (SFRs),[7] the likely behavioural responses of the participants in the failed infrastructure should be considered. The last of these matters is unavoidably a matter of conjecture, as there is no historical record of infrastructures to which formal legal insolvency processes have been applied. Case histories of failed infrastructures are considered in **sections 17.8–17.11**; if a conclusion can be drawn it is that the avoidance of a formal insolvency procedure has constituted the primary objective of the authorities. That can no longer be regarded as a foregone conclusion, as repeated utterances from regulators aim to show.[8]

17.7 The features of a formal insolvency process for an infrastructure which may be worth special attention include the following.

(1) *Status of infrastructures as 'participants'*. By virtue of regulation 2(1) of the SFRs, a CCP, a 'settlement agent' and a 'clearing house' are each to be regarded as a 'participant' in a designated system. A 'central counterparty' is defined as a person 'interposed between the institutions in a designated system and which acts as the exclusive counterparty of those institutions with regard to transfer orders.' In relation to payment and securities settlement systems, the system operator is likely to be a 'clearing house' (defined as a person 'responsible for the calculation of the net positions of institutions and any central counterparty or settlement agent in a designated system') or a 'settlement agent' (a person 'providing settlement accounts to the institutions and any central counterparty in a designated system for the settlement of transfer orders within the system and, as the case may be, for extending credit to such institutions and any central counterparty for settlement purposes.')[9] In addition, Part VII provides that the modified version of insolvency law applies where a recognised body is subject to insolvency proceedings.[10] Consequently the insolvency officer of the infrastructure operator itself will be subject to the constraints which would apply in the case of an insolvent direct user of the infrastructure – including the inability to challenge transfer orders on various insolvency-law grounds,[11] and the disapplication of the administration moratorium as it would otherwise apply to collateral security provided in connection

6 See **section 12.5**
7 Financial Markets and Insolvency (Settlement Finality) Regulations 1999, SI 1999 No 2979
8 Cf Tucker, P, *Central counterparties: the agenda* (October 2011), Conference speech, http://www.bankofengland.co.uk/publications/Documents/speeches/2011/speech524.pdf
9 SFRs, reg 2(1)
10 Companies Act 1989, s 158(2)
11 SFRs, regs 14, 16, 17, 19; see further **section 8.9**

with the system.[12] These constraints will not give any immediate relief to other participants in the failed system beyond the knowledge that perverse challenges under insolvency law are ruled out.

(2) *However, an infrastructure is not a 'defaulter'.* Under Part VII, special protection from insolvency-law challenge is given to action taken in relation to a 'defaulter'.[13] However, the definition of 'defaulter' does not include the recognised body, so that (for example) there is no obligation on the insolvency officer of the failed infrastructure to produce computations of net sums with regard to each participant,[14] and the statutory obligation on the part of persons who have control of the infrastructure's assets to give assistance for the purposes of default proceedings will not apply;[15] but perhaps the most important thing is that there is no explicit obligation to cater for the insolvency of the infrastructure in its default rules.[16] The SFRs are less clear on whether the infrastructure itself can be a 'defaulter', since the word 'participant' embraces the system operator itself, but the system operator's duty as regards default rules is only 'to have default rules which are appropriate for the system in all the circumstances.'[17] The perverse consequence of all this is that the right of a user of the infrastructure to terminate its relationship with the insolvent service provider is left for the rules of the infrastructure to decide, and those rules may approach the subject in a wide variety of ways.

(3) *Performance by the infrastructure is not assured.* Although there is no universal right to close out and rule off the financial aspects of the uncertainty which an infrastructure's failure will cause, the inevitable consequence of an insolvency proceeding is that the infrastructure operator will cease to perform most of its obligations. Thus: payments will not be made and unsecured obligations will remain unperformed with impunity; deposits (including margin and default fund contributions) will suffer the same fate; securities collateral will not be returned immediately even if it has been provided under a security interest rather than transferred outright; and contractual obligations to deliver securities or other property will not be performed. These reactions are not simply unfortunate; they are necessary, the legally required responsibility of the insolvency officer whose duty it is to maximise the estate for *pari passu* distribution among the creditors. Continuation of normal operations would be incompatible with that preservative function.

(4) *Client segregation is compromised.* An obligation to segregate client cash and contracts applies to CCPs,[18] and will be imposed on CSDs under the proposed Regulation on CSDs.[19] 'Segregation' of client cash and

---

12 SFRs, reg 19
13 See **section 8.12**
14 Cf Companies Act 1989, s 163
15 Cf Companies Act 1989, s 160
16 Cf Financial Services and Markets Act 2000 (Recognition Requirements for Investment Exchanges and Clearing Houses) Regulations 2001, Schedule, para 25
17 SFRs, Schedule, para 6
18 Regulation (EU) No 648/2012 of the European Parliament and of the Council of 4 July 2012 on OTC derivatives, central counterparties and trade repositories (EMIR), art 39
19 European Commission, *Proposal for a Regulation of the European Parliament and of the Council on improving securities settlement in the European Union and on central securities depositories etc* (March 2012), COM(2012) 73 final, http://eur-lex.europa.eu/LexUriServ/ LexUriServ.do?uri=CELEX:52012PC0073:EN:PDF, art 35

contractual entitlements depends on recording the cash and contractual entitlements in different accounts. As regards CCPs, the objective of segregation is not to protect the clients against the failure of a participant in a CCP, rather than failure of the CCP itself, so the accounts in question will exist only on the books of the CCP. This kind of segregation does not imply insulation from the insolvency of the account-provider: the 'segregation' may withstand the insolvency, in the sense that the client claims will remain distinguishable from the non-client claims, but this will not give the client claimants any priority in the insolvency process. The CCP will be liable as debtor in relation to cash claims and contractual entitlements, and its insolvency will reduce these claims to an entitlement to dividend only. The general law of insolvency poses a further threat to segregation, since agreements not to set off cease to be effective once statutory insolvency set-off comes into operation;[20] this rule would imply that an insolvent CCP is no longer able to honour the firewall between house and client accounts. As regards CSDs, there is no guarantee that the segregation requirements in the proposed Regulation would be any more effective than with CCPs. There is no help (in either case) from section 187 of the Companies Act 1989, which, together with regulation 16 of the Financial Markets and Insolvency Regulations 1991,[21] requires that the provisions of Part VII be applied as if client and house positions were entered into by different persons when Part VII applies. But only selected provisions of Part VII apply when the clearing house is subject to insolvency proceedings,[22] and they do not include section 187.

(5) *Client and non-client assets may be trapped.* A CCP is likely to hold non-cash assets at a third party custodian, who may be required to provide separate 'client' and non-client accounts, but within that crude bifurcation all clients may have an interest in common in an omnibus account. Non-cash assets should therefore avoid falling into the insolvent estate, though as ever with omnibus accounts there may be a complex and protracted reconciliation effort to identify each claimant's true entitlement. Insolvency of a CSD ought not to jeopardise the integrity of the CSDs' records of entitlement either; but the circumstances which cause a CSD to become so fatally compromised before lift-out is implemented are highly likely to imply failure of record-keeping. Moreover, the insolvency regimes available to insolvent investment banks, designed to enable client assets to be returned speedily through a special administration process, do not apply to CCPs or CSDs in the United Kingdom, as they do not hold the regulatory permissions necessary to qualify as 'investment banks'.[23]

(6) *Close-out will not be uniform.* Solvent participants will take such action as they consider suitable to protect their own interests. Where they have the power to do so they will cease to make payments and post collateral. If they can close out contractual obligations to minimise loss they will do so; but this does not imply that all the obligations would be closed out, or all at the same time. One solution to this problem is found in the rules of CME Clearing Europe, which provide that the insolvency of the CCP deems all participants to be defaulters, so that the whole of the CCP's operations

---

20 *National Westminster Bank v Halesowen Presswork and Assemblies Ltd* [1972] AC 785, HL
21 SI 1991 No 880
22 Companies Act 1989, ss 159–165, by virtue of Companies Act 1989, s 158
23 Banking Act 2009, s 232

are closed out and the operation of its default rules will apply across the board.[24] But this is not universally true of CCPs: the rules of LCH.Clearnet Limited allow its members a discretionary power to close out and net their positions if the CCP is subject to insolvency proceedings,[25] and it is likely that LCH.Clearnet members would not wish to close out if their contracts would tend to come more into-the-money if left open. Where margin is irretrievable, leaving contracts open so as to defer and reduce a loss may be the more logical approach. The upshot is that the insolvency procedure for a CCP such as LCH.Clearnet could be very complex and slow to resolve. Regulators may seek to intervene to avoid these consequences, but the outcome cannot be assured.

CASE HISTORIES – FAILURES OF PAYMENT AND SECURITIES SETTLEMENT SYSTEMS

17.8   One example of failure of a settlement process may be the 'paper crunch' of securities settlement in the late 1960s and early 1970s.[26] Briefly, what happened was due to the complete absence of any settlement 'system', with broker-dealers left to sort out the problems of delivery of paper certificates and collection of payments from counterparties in the absence of any form of delivery-versus-payment assurance. When volumes rose, so did the unprocessed backlog in back-offices, and some firms were driven into bankruptcy. The outcome was the creation of the Euroclear system in Europe and the DTC in the United States.

Reports of collapses of systemically important payment and settlement systems are mercifully absent from the literature. This may be because many payment and settlement systems have historically been operated by central banks. However, there are privately operated systems, and there have been some near-misses, of which a useful illustration comes from the collapse of Baring Brothers in 1995.[27] The CPSS noted that the case

'demonstrates the potential problems ... . If the sending bank had not eventually agreed to borrow in order to cover its payment ... [t]he clearing would have had to be unwound, so that no payments between any of the 45 ECU clearing banks would have been settled on the due day, even though less than 1% of those payments had anything to do with Barings. The failure to settle could have had very serious consequences for the banks, and for their customers.'[28] This case study illustrates that the impact of a failure of an ACH participant may be felt by the other participants rather than the system operator itself. However, a modern ACH like EBA Clearing, or an exchange-of-value payment system such as CLS,

---

24 CME Clearing Europe Limited, *Clearing Rules* (March 2011), http://www.cmeclearingeurope. com/membership/files/CMECE-Rulebook.pdf, Definitions of 'Defaulting Clearing Member' and 'Clearing House Insolvency Event'

25 LCH.Clearnet Ltd, *General Regulations* (July 2011), http://www.lchclearnet.com/Images/ General%20Regulations_tcm6-43737.pdf, reg 39A

26 See Norman, P, *Plumbers and Visionaries* (Wiley, 2007), ISBN 978-0-470-72425-5, pp 20–23; Donald, D, *Heart of Darkness: the problem at the core of the US proxy system and its solution* (December 2010), http://works.bepress.com/david_donald/3/

27 See **box 2.2**

28 Bank for International Settlements Committee on Payment and Settlement Systems, *Settlement risk in foreign exchange transactions* (March 1996), http://www.bis.org/publ/cpss17.pdf, s 2.2.5

is more likely to accept cash pay-ins. Nowadays if the system's loss-sharing mechanism failed to address any problem so that the bank became insolvent, it could be dealt with using the remedies available for resolution of any other systemically-important bank. In addition, and apparently notwithstanding the implementation of insolvency proceedings, the Bank of England could give directions to the operator of a recognised inter-bank payment system under section 191 of the Banking Act 2009.[29] Such remedies may be available to mitigate the worst consequences of insolvency of a payment system operator; though even the Bank of England does not have power to give direction to the *participants* in a payment system to keep it functioning notwithstanding its operator's insolvency.

CASE HISTORIES – FAILURES OF CCPs

17.9 There have been several failures of CCPs: the Caisse de Liquidation des Affaires en Marchandises in France in 1974, the Kuala Lumpur Commodity Clearing House in 1983, and the Hong Kong Futures Guarantee Corporation (the Guarantee Corporation) in 1987.[30] The case in regard to which the most salutary detail is available is that of the Guarantee Corporation. In understanding the unfolding of events it should first be explained that the infrastructures involved in the crisis were the Guarantee Corporation, whose function was to act as guarantor of contracts entered into on the Hong Kong Futures Exchange, though the CCP risk management function was carried out by ICCH (Hong Kong) Limited. This duality left the Guarantee Corporation, rather than ICCH, with the financial exposure to defaulters, although ICCH was a shareholder in the Guarantee Corporation.[31]

The backdrop to this spectacular CCP failure was the global plunge in stock prices which took place during the period 15–20 October 1987. This is not the place to analyse the causes of that plunge, but the following distinguishing facts may be noted in respect of Hong Kong. Of the indexes tracking the behaviour of the world's major financial markets, the Hang Seng Index (HSI) fell the furthest – a 45% drop over a three-week period. Secondly, the Hong Kong Stock Exchange was closed to trading for a period of four days, as was the Hong Kong Futures Exchange, and when trading re-opened the fall in prices significantly exceeded the worst predictions. No other major market took the radical step of an extended closure. Thirdly, the members of the Hong Kong Futures Exchange were thereby exposed to an extreme price movement in the spot HSI future contract, reportedly the world's second-largest traded index contract at the time: as stock prices fell 33% on the day cash-market trading resumed, so the futures contract fell from 3529 to 1975 (a 44% drop).[32]

During the period of the suspension, life had not been quiet in the futures market. Failures to post margin were predicted in respect of brokers exposed to the HSI

---

29 See further **section 11.3**
30 Hills, B, Rule, D, and Parkinson, S, 'Central counterparty clearing houses and financial stability' (June 1999) Bank of England Financial Stability Review, http://www.bankofengland. co.uk/publications/fsr/1999/fsr06art6.pdf; Norman, P, *The Risk Controllers* (Wiley, 2011), ISBN 978-0-470-68632-4, pp 131–146
31 Norman, p 144; see also **section 14.7**
32 Cremer, R, and Zepp, R, *Stock Market Crash 1987: A Hong Kong Perspective* (UEA Press, November 1987), ISBN 962-308-003-4, pp 49, 88, 113

contract, and ICCH had made intra-day margin calls. Owing to the financial weakness of the Guarantee Corporation, a support package of HK $2 billion was put together in time for the re-opening of the markets. This took the form of a loan by the Hong Kong Government (diverted from the Exchange Fund – sums intended for stabilising the Hong Kong dollar in the money markets), the Guarantee Corporation's shareholders, and members of the Futures Exchange. The expectation was that HK $2 billion would be sufficient to protect against a 1000 point fall in the HSI.[33] Special legislation was passed to remove doubt as to the ability of the Guarantee Corporation to recover funds for repayment of the loans: this was achieved by a special levy on transactions in the HSI and on transactions done on the Stock Exchange, as well as from Futures Exchange members who had defaulted on margin calls.[34]

Unfortunately the fall in the HSI was greater than expected. Although some defaults had been expected,[35] the problem was worse than the authorities had bargained for: 43 Futures Exchange members were suspended for failure to meet margin calls, writs were issued against 39 brokers, and the newspapers carried reports of bounced cheques.[36] The Guarantee Corporation requested a further bail-out of HK $2 billion, this time to be split between the Hong Kong Government's Exchange Fund and three major banks. In the event, it was not needed.

17.10 Regardless of the causes of the Guarantee Corporation's failure, it may be remarked that the Guarantee Corporation did not suffer an insolvency event. However, the following comments might also be made. Special legislation was needed to ensure that the Guarantee Corporation could be restored to solvency. It is no solution to a problem of solvency to lend the insolvent person money. The loan must be repaid, so what is needed is a source of permanent funding. While the appearance of the process to resurrect the Guarantee Corporation is that the shareholders were asked to bear the pain, the reality is different: the market users were the ultimate sufferers. This may be fairer than leaving the problem with the Government (and the taxpayer) but the surviving market users, who had already sustained substantial losses in many cases owing to the collapse in equity prices, were being asked to plug the gap left by defaulters in a mutualisation scheme imposed on them, without their consent, after the event. There is much to criticise in this ad hoc manner of dealing with the problem.

17.11 The CCPs in the United States also had to deal with similar problems of large margin calls affecting the solvency of their participants in October 1987. The effect was as follows:

'Under normal conditions, banks typically extended short-term credit to clearing members to permit them to meet margin calls and to deal with the mismatch between the time that members had to post variation margin with the clearinghouse and the time that customers paid variation margin to the members. Given the huge amount of margin payments pending, and the

33 Cremer and Zepp, pp 78–9
34 Jacobs, P, speech to the Hong Kong Legislative Council moving the second reading of the Exchanges (Special Levy) Bill 1987 (28 October 1987)
35 Hay Davison, I, *The operation and regulation of the Hong Kong securities industry – Report of the Securities Review Committee* (May 1988), http://www.fstb.gov.hk/fsb/ppr/report/davison. htm, para 6.14
36 Cremer and Zepp, pp 95, 101, 102

uncertainty about the effect of the crash in prices on the financial condition of clearing members, many banks were reluctant to extend credit as normal. Absent credit, some CCPs' members would have been unable to meet margin calls, and the margin shortfalls would have exceeded the ability of the clearinghouses to meet their obligations to those with winning trades, thereby forcing the closure of the clearinghouses — and of the markets. Moreover, concerns about the solvency of clearing members sparked rumours about the solvency of the CCPs. These rumours sparked additional panic selling that contributed to the magnitude of the crash.

'Disaster was averted at the last minute due, in large part, to the intervention of the Federal Reserve. The Fed assured the market that it would supply sufficient liquidity to market members. It pressured banks to lend to securities firms and clearing members. It also permitted a large bank to absorb the liabilities of a subsidiary that was a major clearing firm, thereby preventing its default. In the end, it was a close-run thing.'[37]

TOO BIG TO FAIL

17.12 It may be concluded from the preceding discussion that the failure of a CCP would have, in the modern world, unthinkably dangerous consequences for the economies of those countries and regions which make extensive – and following the G20 agenda developed after the 2008 crisis in the financial sector, state-sponsored – use of CCPs as a tool for financial stability.[38] 'Of course, increased reliance on clearinghouses to address problems in other parts of the system increases further the need to ensure the safety of clearinghouses themselves. As Mark Twain's character Pudd'nhead Wilson once opined, if you put all your eggs in one basket, you better watch that basket.'[39]

Unfortunately, the special tools developed for resolving the situation of a failing bank[40] will not be available for a failing CCP unless, as in some continental European countries, the CCP is configured as a bank. The situation in relation to CCPs incorporated in the United Kingdom is therefore less than satisfactory, as has been pointed out by the Deputy Governor of the Bank of England with responsibility for financial stability:

'In the case of a distressed CCP … two strategies come to mind … . The first would be "recapitalising" the CCP so that it can carry on. The second would be to aim to bring off a more or less smooth unwinding of the CCP's book of transactions.

'On the former route … the only options are [recapitalisation by] the surviving clearing members themselves or a new "owner". On the face of it, the clearing members would have to be involved, as surely the stricken CCP's default fund would also need replenishing in order for it to continue. If the default fund were to be replenished by its surviving clearing members, that

---

37 Pirrong, C, *The Inefficiency of Clearing Mandates* (July 2010), The Cato Institute, Policy Analysis No.665, http://www.cato.org/pub_display.php?pub_id=11990; see also Norman, pp 135–143

38 See G20 Leaders Statement: The Pittsburgh Summit (September 2009), http://www.g20. utoronto.ca/2009/2009communique0925.html

39 Bernanke, B, *Clearinghouses, Financial Stability, and Financial Reform* (April 2011), Speech, http://www.federalreserve.gov/newsevents/speech/Bernanke20110404a.htm

40 See **section 8.4**

could in principle be sorted out at the time or it could be pre-programmed. In practice, making it up at the time must be dangerous. A pre-programmed allocation of losses would be akin to the old "Down to the Last Drop" rule that used to be employed by a Chicago clearing house, under which surviving clearing members ultimately had collectively to absorb all losses: mutualisation.'[41]

17.13 Disposing of the CCP's books of business is the other issue mentioned by the Deputy Governor. In theory, they could be transferred to another CCP, or they could be 'de-cleared', that is to say treated as bilateral uncleared contracts. Neither of these options is likely to work. There is unlikely to be a CCP available to take on the failed CCP's portfolio: *ex hypothesi* the failed CCP's risk management system was flawed, and other CCPs probably never wanted this business on the failed CCP's terms (and maybe not at all). De-clearing is impossible for practical reasons: you cannot just 'unwind' multilateral netting of a complex portfolio of trades: (a) there would have to be some mechanism for allocating trades among participants, and recreating their pre-registration bilateral positions is not a solution since some original dealers will have netted off and closed out their positions by trading with other participants; (b) the participants will not be ready and willing to deal with each other bilaterally, since this is a cleared market where they have not risk-assessed each other; and (c) the margin has gone, so de-clearing involves taking unsecured counterparty risk.[42]

17.14 Further work on the question of how to resolve a failing CCP, and the tools needed to bring about a resolution, is expected.[43] In the meantime, the following observations may be made.

(1) An open-ended (Down to the Last Drop) obligation to recapitalise and replenish the default fund, even if it were granted favourable regulatory capital treatment,[44] would not be attractive to clearing members, who expect CCPs to be more robust than their participants in all market conditions. Furthermore, CCPs do not depend on traditional capital arrangements but on margin and default funding for their robustness. If it is inappropriate for a CCP to be revived through an injection of capital, it is necessary to disjoin the control of CCPs from the provision of capital in its traditional form, and reallocate control to the providers of default funding. An open-ended obligation imposed upon clearing members is incompatible with any governance structure which allows the short-term rewards of operating a clearing business to be shared by management and owners of CCPs who are different from the clearing members with the ultimate liability, if the clearing members do not have the power to control the decision-making and distribution of profits. Boards of CCPs in Europe are required to have 'independent' members,[45] but it is unclear whether clearing members

---

41 Tucker, P, *Clearing Houses as System Risk Managers* (June 2011), Speech, http://www. bankofengland.co.uk/publications/speeches/2011/speech501.pdf

42 See further Pirrong, C, *The Economics of Central Clearing: Theory and Practice* (May 2011), ISDA Discussion Paper No 1, http://www2.isda.org/attachment/MzE0NA==/ISDAdiscussion_CCP_Pirrong.pdf, p 38

43 Financial Stability Board, *Effective Resolution of Systemically Important Financial Institutions* (November 2011), http://www.financialstabilityboard.org/publications/r_111104dd.pdf, p 2

44 Cf **section 19.12(1)**

45 EMIR, art 27

will be regarded as having the requisite independence.[46] Where there is unlimited liability, it could be suggested, it is inappropriate to have decision-making controlled by those who do not have to pay.

(2) Other types of loss-absorbing instrument and layers of capital could be structured which (albeit at cost) could be utilised.[47] Examples recommended by the Guarantee Corporation inquiry included credit protection in the form of bank guarantees or an insurance policy, before invoking the Down to the Last Drop principle.[48] In older guidance, the CPSS said that a CCP should not rely 'primarily' on insurance, guarantees or letters of credit, but certainly did not rule them out.[49] Another possibility is a loss-sharing rule, reducing the liabilities of the CCP: by cutting the in-the-money amount due to, but not yet settled with, non-defaulting participants; or in a more extreme case along the lines of what the participants would receive as a dividend in a bankruptcy.[50] It is far from obvious that the right, or only, solution for a CCP which has suffered a loss which has depleted the default fund is to have the CCP recapitalised by its participants. Down to the Last Drop will worsen a severe crisis, and it may be that only some participants are actually good to the last drop needed to recapitalise the CCP. CCPs should be encouraged to purchase these additional types of protection and, if their risk management strategy is unsuccessful, to fail if they suffer exceptional losses.

(3) It is not necessarily fatal that a CCP should fail, as a matter of principle. Notwithstanding that the consequences of failure may be bad, those consequences would be limited if the failed CCP is not of systemic importance. Limiting the systemic importance of a CCP would be as valuable as a toolkit to resolve failing CCPs. Redundancy among CCPs clearing particular products, and fostering of decentralised approaches (uncleared – also called 'bilaterally cleared' – transactions) as an alternative to clearing, will facilitate switching of business away from a failing CCP. Redundancy also implies interoperability, which in turn implies that a solution be found to the complexities of establishing interoperability among CCPs.[51]

17.15 At least there is a debate with regard to the insolvency of CCPs. What is perhaps curious is that there is no equivalent debate with regard to other types of market infrastructure. The distinction may be attributable to the difference in risk profile between a CCP, on the one hand, and a payment or settlement system, on the other: a CCP voluntarily assumes future credit exposure to its participants, whereas, for the most part, payment and settlement systems do not. But, as **chapters 15** and **16** illustrate, it is naïve to suppose that payment and settlement systems do not take credit risk on their participants. They may

---

46 Cf Langen, W, *Report on derivatives markets: future policy actions* (June 2010), European Parliament Committee on Economic and Monetary Affairs document A7-0187/2010, http://www.europarl.europa.eu/sides/getDoc.do?pubRef=-//EP//NONSGML+REPORT+A7-2010-0187+0+DOC+PDF+V0//EN&language=EN, para 26
47 See further **sections 6.22–6.28**
48 Hay Davison report, para 7.51
49 CPSS and Technical Committee of the International Organization of Securities Commissions, *Recommendations for Central Counterparties* (November 2004), http://www.bis.org/publ/cpss64.pdf, p 27
50 Pirrong, ISDA Discussion Paper, p 39
51 See **chapter 13**

be limited-purpose organisations, but this fact does not put their survival beyond doubt in a crisis. It is suggested that a more organised approach to the possibility of payment and settlement system failure is warranted, particularly as the increased complexity of those organisations may increase the possibility of something going wrong.

17.16 At a minimum, all systemically important infrastructures should be subject to the following precepts:

- There should be formal regulatory oversight of the risk-taking of infrastructures, with realistic rules about coverage of those risks through collateral or other mitigants.

- The policy for ensuring survival of infrastructures should not depend exclusively on the ability of participants to pour in financial resources without limit at times of crisis.

- The powers of competent authorities to intervene and remedy the problems of ailing banks should be made available to deal with infrastructures, regardless of their form.

- Redundancy should be encouraged, so that there is always an alternative available in case of failure of an infrastructure.

- Participants in infrastructures should have contingency plans to ensure they are equipped and ready to handle an infrastructure failure.

18 Risk Management at the Agent Bank

18.1 For a private provider of clearing and settlement services – that is to say, a service provider who is a participant in, rather than an operator of, clearing and settlement infrastructure – the central problem of risk management is that the service provider (in this chapter called the 'agent bank' for simplicity) faces in two directions. As a participant, the agent bank will be under obligations to the clearing or settlement infrastructure, which will expose the agent bank to liabilities. And as a service provider, the agent bank will in consequence take credit, liquidity and operational risk on its client.

In this chapter the duties and obligations imposed on the agent bank by the infrastructure are first examined, followed by the implications the agent bank's relationship with the infrastructure has for its relationship with its client.

RISK ISSUES RELATED TO THE INFRASTRUCTURE

18.2 An agent bank assumes numerous obligations to an infrastructure operator when it accepts the responsibilities that accompany the status of participant in the infrastructure system. Those obligations manifest themselves as risks, of which the following may be identified.

Liquidity risk

18.3 Infrastructures will impose strict timetables upon their participants as regards payment and delivery. All clearing and settlement systems require adherence to such rules, for the efficiency of operation of the system depends on it. Under the Principles for Financial Market Infrastructures (FMI Principles),[1] systems are expected to comply with basic standards of efficiency and effectiveness;[2] 'to mitigate and manage liquidity risks from the late-day submission of payments or other transactions, an FMI could adopt rules or financial incentives for timely submission.'[3] Thus, payment and securities settlement systems will typically have cut-off times by which transaction data must be submitted if the transfer is to take place on a particular day; payment systems will typically have pay-in schedules, failure to comply with which will

---

1   Bank for International Settlements Committee on Payment and Settlement Systems and Technical Committee of the International Organization of Securities Commissions, *Principles for Financial Market Infrastructures* (April 2012), http://www.bis.org/publ/cpss101a.pdf

2   Principle 21

3   FMI Principles, para 3.7.7

lead to queued transfers being bunked out of the queue, and CSDs may operate similar timetables with regard to deliverable securities; and CCPs will have strict pay-in timetables for margin calls.

Participation in the system means that the agent bank assumes a duty to comply with these operational requirements, and must manage the liquidity risk that that entails. The FMI Principles set forth numerous precepts which, while ostensibly addressed to infrastructure operators, actually constitute guidance to participants on the issues to be considered:

● Participants may be explicit liquidity providers to an infrastructure, for example as settlement service provider to a CCP, or in the event of settlement failure by, or insolvency of, another participant.[4] Infrastructures are expected to carry out due diligence on the liquidity provider's ability to understand and manage these risks.[5]

● Participants may be exposed to liquidity risk on each other in a DNS settlement environment,[6] owing to the threat of unwinding of settlements in the event of another participant's failure.[7] DNS systems are expected to provide information and tools to assist participants in managing these risks.[8]

● Participants may be subject to allocation of uncovered liquidity shortfalls.[9]

In addition to these considerations, participants will wish to have regard to the general guidance on management of liquidity risk, which will be as relevant here as in other areas of financial sector endeavour.[10]

Credit and lock-in risk

18.4 Participants are typically exposed to infrastructures in a direct sense (participants may have sums on deposit, either intra-day or on a longer-term basis, with payment system operators and CCPs) and contingently (participants may be obliged to contribute funds, such as margin and default funding). GCMs are exposed as principal to CCPs; only in some cases do CCPs' rules allow GCMs to close out their positions with the CCP on the CCP's own default and manage the risk as they would with a defaulting client.[11] Where a CCP's rulebook does not contemplate its own default, the GCM will need to consider how such a default would in practice be managed; the GCM could be locked-in to non-performing contracts.

Other sources of credit risk may arise because of the manner of operations of the system. For example, a DNS system involves a time interval between

---

4   FMI Principles, para 3.7.1
5   FMI Principles, para 3.7.5
6   See **section 2.30**
7   FMI Principles, para 3.7.3
8   FMI Principles, para 3.7.4
9   FMI Principles, paras 3.7.18–19
10   See, for example, Turing, D, and Cramb, E, *Managing Risk in Financial Firms* (Tottel, March 2008), ISBN 978 1 84766 303 0, ch 8; Institute of International Finance, *Principles of Liquidity Risk Management* (March 2007); Committee of European Banking Supervisors, *Second Part of CEBS's Technical Advice to the European Commission on Liquidity Risk Management* (September 2008), http://www.eba.europa.eu/getdoc/bcadd664-d06b-42bb-b6d5-67c8ff48d11 d/20081809CEBS_2008_147_%28Advice-on-liquidity_2nd-par.aspx; Bank for International Settlements Basel Committee on Banking Supervision *Principles for Sound Liquidity Risk Management and Supervision* (September 2008), http://www.bis.org/publ/bcbs144.pdf
11   See **section 17.7(6)**

processing and finality: a recipient of funds in a DNS system takes credit risk on the other participants until the moment of finality is reached.[12] Again, a delivery obligation may be converted to a payment obligation under buy-in rules if it is not complied with.

18.5 The conditions of participation may indirectly involve the assumption of credit risk. For example, a system operator may be able to pass on costs which it incurs through indemnity provisions, including through loss-sharing rules; it may be empowered to claim damages for rule breaches or to levy fines; and it may be able to 'assess' the participant for top-up contributions to replenish default backing following a market crisis. In relation to these matters, the participant will wish to understand its ability to exit the system so as to avoid or limit the future application of liability. Participants may be locked-in under the system rules so that they cannot resign, or if they can resign, they cannot exempt themselves from liability by doing so. Careful scrutiny of the system operator's ability to impose liability on ex-participants will be desirable.

18.6 A further example of lock-in risk arises where a CCP may impose default management duties on its participants, so that participants are obliged to bid at auction for portfolios of the defaulter's book of cleared transactions. As well as committing the participant to bid for (and thus potentially acquire, at the price which is best for the CCP, and thus worst among the bidding participants) a book of unwanted transactions, it is possible that in the market conditions prevailing after a default the ability to on-sell or hedge is impaired. For example, credit default swaps may be subject to wrong-way risk (the risk that the exposure on the instrument increases with deterioration of the credit quality – so that the risk assumed is greater after the default than before it, even if the reference credit is not the credit of the defaulter), so that the locked-in risk is greater than the participant may have assumed before the default.[13]

Custody, settlement and finality risk

18.7 Participants 'deposit' securities with CSDs and thereby depend on the integrity of the registration system operated by the CSD in carrying out its root-of-title function[14] in the same way as a custody client depends on its custodian. The risk includes not only that static holdings of securities become erased through operational error or (if the CSD does not create records which are legally the definitive indicator of title) shortfall, but also that upon a transfer there is a mis-recording.

Another facet of custody risk is the danger that securities become trapped in the system. A system operator may have a lien or security interest in relation to any liabilities of the participant, so that securities or funds to which the participant may be entitled cannot be immediately withdrawn owing to the existence of actual or even contingent liability to the system operator. CCPs which accept securities collateral under a charge or security interest ought in theory to return those securities if the secured obligations are discharged or alternative acceptable collateral is tendered. However, if the CCP is itself in

---

12 Kokkola, T, *The Payment System* (European Central Bank, September 2010), ISBN 978-92-899-0632-6, p 116
13 Cf **section 14.44**
14 Cf **section 2.16**

financial difficulties, the ability to extract unencumbered assets is not assured to any greater extent than any securities placed with an insolvent custodian: the experience of the Lehman Brothers clients seeking to recover their proprietary assets was that this was extremely slow and uncertain.[15]

18.8 Settlement risk is, classically, distinct from custody risk. Settlement (or Herstatt) risk arises when a participant pays or delivers what it is obliged to, but does not receive the countervalue in return.[16] The system is expected to be designed so as to eradicate this risk.[17] But even where the system does not purport to be an 'exchange of value' system, there is finality risk if the receiving participant is led to believe that the funds or asset have been transferred, but there is still the possibility of unwind. Hence a settlement system is expected to provide final settlement, at latest by the end of the value date.[18]

A further settlement-related issue is that a guarantee of settlement finality does not equate to a guarantee that settlement will happen. The distinction between these two concepts is vital but frequently overlooked. Settlement finality is simply an assurance that a settlement which has taken place will not be reversed. There is, however, no obligation on the settlement system to carry out a settlement, other than obligations which the system has assumed voluntarily under its rules. Some systems do not assume any absolute duty to process transactions queued for settlement and may unilaterally decide to freeze unprocessed settlement instructions.[19] Unsettled transactions represent market risk for participants, who may be limited in their ability to pass on the costs and risk to their clients.

18.9 Finally, mention may be made of the liquidity-risk management device used in the CLS system, known as the In/Out Swap. It may be observed that the pay-in and pay-out timetables of CLS put the participating banks under liquidity pressure. Ahead of settlement, and by looking at the net positions of its participants for the forthcoming settlement day, CLS Bank is able to observe that Bank A is due to pay in a large quantity of currency ϕ and that Bank B is due to pay in a large quantity of currency ψ; but CLS Bank can see also that Bank A is due to receive a large quantity of currency ψ and Bank B to receive a large quantity of currency ϕ. The pay-in requirements of both banks would be significantly reduced if A and B had entered into a foreign exchange transaction between them under which A paid Y to B in return for B paying X to A. Such a transaction would help their liquidity positions but not their overall economic one, so the In/Out Swap involves both the proposed FX transaction, which is booked into the CLS system, and the creation of its mirror image (whereby B pays Y to A in return for A paying X to B), which cancels out the effect of the 'In' transaction, which is settled outside CLS.[20]

In/Out Swaps are an example of how a prudent device for managing one risk can open up another category of risk. The 'Out' transaction is settled outside CLS,

---

15 See **section 10.4(10)–(11)**]
16 See **box 2.2**
17 FMI Principle 12
18 FMI Principle 8
19 See **sections 8.21(4)** and **15.16**
20 Mägerle, J, and Maurer, D, *The Continuous Linked Settlement foreign exchange settlement system (CLS)* (November 2009), Swiss National Bank Report, http://www.snb.ch/en/mmr/reference/continuous_linked_settlement/source/continuous_linked_settlement.en.pdf

and for that reason it cannot be settled on a Payment versus Payment basis and involves exactly the type of foreign exchange settlement risk which CLS was designed to limit. This may not, of course, be a bad thing: in the first place there will be the saving in liquidity risk; and secondly, when the multilateral netting effect of CLS[21] is taken into account, the overall reduction in settlement risk across the portfolio of Bank A or Bank B's FX settlements is likely to be substantial.

Concentration risk

18.10 Participants frequently constitute an inner circle of multi-service banks, to whom the operator of market infrastructure is likely to turn for its own financial services needs. Infrastructures may need deposit-takers, cash managers, repo and other credit facilities, brokers and buyers of securities, custody and depositary services, registration and record-keeping, hedging and so forth. Participants will often find themselves carrying out functions where the infrastructure acts as the client of the participant. The infrastructure may be under duties to ensure that services provided to it comply with the FMI Principles' guidelines relating to custody[22] and outsourcing of critical services.[23]

Furthermore, participants may also be owners of the infrastructure operator or capital providers. Ownership may not invariably imply limited liability. These roles may increase the degree of exposure which a participant has to the infrastructure, including potentially express or implied obligations to recapitalise the infrastructure following a serious loss. Such risks may be compounded when participants are encouraged to nominate employees to carry out governance roles, including directorships, within the infrastructure organisation.[24] Careful monitoring and management of conflicts of interest will be essential where the relationship between a participant and an infrastructure is multi-faceted.

RISK ARISING FROM STRAIGHT-THROUGH PROCESSING AND INDIRECT PARTICIPATION

18.11 Many of the risk issues described above derive from the expectation that modern financial market infrastructures will be fast and, to that end, will support straight-through processing (STP). 'An FMI should be efficient'.[25] Speed and STP give infrastructures little ability to intervene and recalibrate in response to disruptive events, so the result is to transfer the associated risk to participants. Participants, however, may have even less control over the obligations they assume. The most important risk issue for participants is arguably that STP removes the ability of the participant to pull the plug – that is, to terminate the provision of services to a client before the exposure which those services involves becomes unacceptable.

All activities of an agent bank involve, to a greater or lesser degree, the provision of access to a clearing or settlement system to a client who is not a

---

21   See **section 2.38**
22   FMI Principle 16
23   FMI Principles, Annex F
24   Cf **section 12.22**
25   FMI Principle 21

direct participant in that system. The client relies on the agent bank to satisfy the system's conditions of access, which will in all cases involve minimum criteria for financial and operational robustness. But the client may wish to have a speedier service than that which is implied by submission of clearing or settlement instructions to an agent bank and waiting on the agent bank to pass on those instructions to the infrastructure – STP will be more immediate and provide the client with a post-trade experience which is more akin to direct participation in the infrastructure than the basic two-step model. And, where infrastructures are all linked in a value chain involving the trading platform, the CCP, and the payment and securities settlement systems, it may be that the booking of a matched trade at the moment of trading automatically generates both clearing and settlement instructions which go immediately, and irrevocably, to the clearing and settlement infrastructures concerned. The agent bank may be unable to intervene in this process, and until the client's ability to commit the agent bank is disabled, the agent bank's commitment may continue.

Tiering issues for the agent bank

18.12 FMI Principle 19 exhorts market infrastructures to consider the risks which 'tiered participation arrangements' may engender.[26] It seems that tiering comprises any arrangement for service provision by a participant to a client. The following issues which can arise from indirect participation:

(1) In ordinary usage an 'indirect participant' is a special type of client who can submit instructions or data directly to the infrastructure, and thus receive a service similar to any other participant. In this type of indirect participation, narrower than that envisaged by the FMI Principles which expect indirect participants not to be bound by the system's rules,[27] the infrastructure requires the indirect participant's obligations (in particular in terms of credit and liquidity) to be satisfied by a direct participant as a condition of the indirect participant's access. Whether or not the indirect participant is bound by the rules, failure by the indirect participant to comply may expose the direct participant to liabilities.

(2) Infrastructures may impose criteria relating to how direct participants manage their client relationships, particularly where the volume of business transacted through the infrastructure by the client is significant. Infrastructures' rulebooks should allow the infrastructure to

> 'gather basic information about indirect participants in order to identify, monitor, and manage any material risks to the FMI arising from such tiered participation arrangements. This information should enable the FMI, at a minimum, to identify (a) the proportion of activity that direct participants conduct on behalf of indirect participants, (b) direct participants that act on behalf of a material number of indirect participants, (c) indirect participants with significant volumes or values of transactions in the system, and (d) indirect participants whose transaction volumes or values are large relative to those of the direct participants through which they access the FMI.'[28]

---

26 Cf **sections 6.41(7)** and **11(5)**
27 FMI Principles, footnote 148
28 FMI Principles, para 3.19.5

A direct participant may not have the whole-market view of its client's activities. Insofar as the direct participant is not the exclusive supplier of services, the overall amount of risk being assumed by the client relative to its resources may be difficult to determine.

(3) An indirect participant may default; related issues will include whether the direct participant has to any extent internalised the flow of instructions,[29] whether the indirect participant's business is large in scale relative to the resources of the direct participant, whether the relationship of principal and agent in relation to the transactions will survive the insolvency of the indirect participant,[30] and the availability of the mechanisms of the infrastructure to provide effective and risk-minimising default management in the case of a person who is not a direct participant.[31]

(4) Indirect participants may themselves be agent banks. One difference for risk purposes from other clients is that the degree of straight-through processing may be greater, thus implying that the direct participant may wish to insist on vigilance and control on the part of its client.

(5) The Settlement Finality Directive (SFD)[32] allows for 'institutions' (banks, investment firms, and certain public authorities) and 'settlement agents' who have contractual relationships with system participants enabling them to pass transfer orders through the system – that is, who are indirect participants – to be considered by a Member State as full 'participants' on systemic risk grounds.[33] Where this status is granted, other participants in the system will be given the insolvency protections of the SFD if the indirect participant were to fail. Except where this is the case, participants have no protection against the risk of legal challenges, attributable to the insolvency of their clients, including other indirect participants.[34]

Straight-through processing

18.13 The crucial question with any STP-related arrangement is how to limit the ability of a client to commit its agent bank to assume the client's risk. To answer the question it is first essential to understand the moment at which the commitment arises: in a case where the agent bank is clearing or settling the client's trades, it may well be the moment of trading, where there is an organised trading platform. Where trades are executed over the counter (that is, away from an organised platform), the payment and settlement instructions may have to be specially generated, which limits the degree of STP-related risk. Where STP-related risk is unavoidable, agent banks may wish to have regard to market guidance[35] on limiting risk in cases where access to markets is granted

---

29 See **sections 2.10** and **2.21**
30 See **section 8.9(4)**
31 Cf **sections 14.47ff** in relation to 'client clearing'
32 Directive 98/26/EC of the European Parliament and of the Council of 19 May 1998 on settlement finality in payment and securities settlement systems
33 SFD, arts 2(f) and (g)
34 Cf **section 8.21**
35 Cf Futures Industry Association, *Market Access Risk Management Recommendations* (April 2010), http://www.finextra.com/finextra-downloads/newsdocs/FIAMarket_Access-6.pdf; Financial Services Authority, *Good Practices for Settlement Bank management of potential risk exposures to customer banks* (January 2011), Finalised Guidance FG11/02, http://www. fsa.gov.uk/static/pubs/guidance/fg11_02.pdf

by intermediaries who assume risk in respect of their client' positions: the recipes for limiting the risk include position limits, real-time monitoring, fat-finger quantity limits, kill buttons and so forth.

In the next section, the ways in which STP-related risks can arise for a participant providing access services for any client, whether or not an indirect participant, are explored in more detail. All involve exposure of the participant to its client.

EXPOSURES TO THE CLIENT

18.14   The topics considered below are those which describe the origins of the agent bank's potential exposure to its client. However the risk originates, the agent bank will have in mind that most issues can be sorted out if the client is still solvent. The threats to the agent bank's ability to limit its exposure in the event of a formal insolvency procedure, or steps being taken under a 'special resolution regime' applicable to failing financial institutions, are considered in **Chapter 8**. Other related risks are operational: how the agent bank might deal with everyday issues, typically while the client remains in good financial health, is considered in **Chapters 20–22**.

Securities settlement risk – gross or net risk

18.15   Agent banks which settle securities transactions may be exposed to their clients in respect of the value of the transactions concerned. If managed, the size of the risk ought to be a market risk amount – that is to say, the difference between the contractually agreed price for the securities and their actual present value. However, there is a danger that the agent bank can be exposed to the full (gross) value of the transaction being settled. The risk can materialise in one of three ways:

(1) *Client buying.* If the client is buying securities, the agent bank which is responsible for settling the cash leg of the transaction will find that the STP settlement instructions are sent to the system automatically, with the result that its cash account at the payment system is to be debited, whether or not the agent bank's client has paid the agent bank. Consequently, the agent bank is (unless the client has paid up front) committing to provide credit to the client if the client does not pay before the moment of settlement; and this commitment is irreversible from the moment at which the STP instructions are initiated. That moment will, in relation to modern trading platforms, typically be the moment of matching on the platform, or (to express it differently) imperceptibly after the moment of trading. Where the trade-to-settlement cycle is of two (T+2) or three (T+3) days duration, the agent bank carries a contingent future credit exposure to all clients who do not wish to tie down cash for the duration of the cycle. In such a case, the theoretical size of the agent bank's exposure is the (gross) payment obligation on the trade; but in some markets (such as France[36]) there is a statutory lien over the securities purchased at the agent bank's expense, and at common law a similar lien can be implied, at least in favour of a bank.[37] Prudent agent banks back this up with contractual liens and security

---

36   Code Monétaire et Financier, art L. 211-18
37   *Brandao v Barnett* (1846) 12 Cl & F 787, HL; see **section 10.10(4)**

interests, thereby reducing the risk to the (net) difference between the price contractually agreed by the client and the actual saleable value of the securities delivered. However, the right to rely on the countervalue to offset the purchase price of the transaction may be at risk of challenge under insolvency laws, which raises further questions of 'gross risk' explored in **section 18.24**.

(2) *Client selling.* If the client is selling securities, two different scenarios need to be considered. In some cases, the client will hold securities at the CSD in an account in its own name (in which case the agent bank acts as account operator). If the client has insufficient securities in its account, the settlement will fail partially or wholly, and the agent bank should not ordinarily be liable for its client's failure. There may be exceptions where the settlement system or market operator insists on a 'Model B' structure under which the agent bank is required to underwrite its clients' obligations.[38] However, the client may have asked the agent bank, for regulatory or other reasons, to open an account at the CSD for the client, but in the agent bank's name. In such a case the agent bank may be liable, even without a formal Model B obligation, to make good any losses suffered by the buyer of the securities for failure to make timely delivery. Evidently the size of the risk in this situation is net (difference between contract price and replacement cost). Where the market has buy-in rules there is a risk that the agent bank can be required to underwrite the buy-in process; in most of Europe the buy-in periods[39] are, before the CSD Regulation, between four and eight days after scheduled settlement; but in the United Kingdom the buy-in period is 35 days, which in times of stress could represent a significant degree of market risk. The proposed CSD Regulation would impose a 4-day buy-in period for the whole of the EEA.[40]

(3) *Borrowing from the box.* The other situation which falls to be discussed where a client is selling is where the client holds its securities in an omnibus account. If the agent bank holds several clients' securities in a single account at the CSD, the settlement may not fail when the client has not provided sufficient securities to satisfy its obligation. This is because the bank's other clients may hold securities of the same description, and the settlement system operator cannot of course distinguish the selling client's securities from those of clients who have static holdings. In such a case the settlement will proceed in accordance with the STP instructions, but the agent bank will now be left with a duty to its other clients to replenish the missing securities. (This problem of using another client's securities is sometimes called 'borrowing from the box', or 'borrowing from the pool'.) Again, this duty represents a credit risk on the client who failed to provide the securities, but theoretically the size of this risk is the (gross) price paid for the replacement securities. In practice the agent bank will ordinarily be the cash leg settlement agent as well as the securities leg settlement agent, and will have either a banker's right of set-off[41] or explicitly agreed set-off

38 See **section 18.26**
39 European Central Counterparty, *Procedures* (March 2012), http://www.euroccp.co.uk/docs/EuroCCP_Proc.pdf, p 5
40 European Commission, *Proposal for a Regulation of the European Parliament and of the Council on improving securities settlement in the European Union and on central securities depositories etc* (March 2012), COM(2012) 73 final, http://eur-lex.europa.eu/LexUriServ/LexUriServ.do?uri=CELEX:52012PC0073:EN:PDF, art 7(3)
41 For review, see *Halesowen Presswork & Assemblies Ltd v National Westminster Bank* [1971] 1 QB 1

rights so that the cash price received can be set off against the liability of the client to refund the agent bank for buy-ins carried out by the agent bank or other losses, and in such cases the risk is reduced to a net risk.

The agent bank may be powerless to eliminate these risks unless the bank can defer the moment at which irrevocable settlement instructions are submitted to the system concerned. Where STP governs the submission of instructions, the process may be wholly outside the agent bank's control. Even where STP does not govern the process of submitting instructions, the agent bank will have to comply with the cut-off times of the system, after which timely settlement will be unachievable. The longer the interval between the cut-off time and the moment of settlement imposed by the system operator, the longer the period for which the agent bank is at risk, unless of course the agent bank has insisted on up-front payment (or, in relation to securities, delivery) before agreeing to submit any instructions for settlement.

Payment system settlement risk

18.16 Agent banks which submit transfer instructions to a payment system take credit risk more openly if they do so at a time when they have not received adequate funds from their client.

A more subtle variant of the problem arises in relation to a payment system such as CLS which operates an 'exchange of value' system.[42] Here the issue is similar to that described above with regard to securities settlement. Transactions which fall to be settled by CLS may include foreign exchange transactions which do not originate from any trading platform and are not subject to the tyranny of STP; nevertheless CLS Bank, like other system operators, has cut-off times after which submitted instructions are rejected for the next day's settlement cycle, so that the agent bank will be committed to paying into CLS Bank the payable amounts due in respect of all instructions submitted before the cut-off. Again, if the agent bank has not received funds from its client in the payable currency before that time, it will be taking credit risk on the client. It may be impracticable to obtain up-front funds from its client, because (a) the amount of currency due from the client will be in part a function of the amount of that currency potentially receivable from other CLS participants, some of which might be single-leg payments, and the details of which may not be known to the agent bank in time, and (b) where the currency payable by the client is Asian, the payment systems in the Asian markets will have closed relatively early in the European processing day, so that the client would effectively have to tie up funds more than a whole day before settlement in order to provide up-front funding.

A further variant arises in relation to the Bacs payment system in the United Kingdom. Bacs operates on a three-day settlement cycle, so that an agent bank must submit instructions to Bacs three days before the settlement date. The agent bank is committed under Bacs rules to make the payment once the instructions have been submitted to Bacs, but it is not permitted to earmark funds then standing to the credit of the client's account, since the FSA interprets regulations 65 and 70(1) of the Payment Services Regulations[43] to mean that the

---

42 Cf FMI Principle 12; see also **section 2.37**
43 SI 2009 No 209

'point in time of receipt' of a payment order must be no later than the moment at which the funds cease to be available to the client.[44]

Principal risk with CCPs

18.17 GCMs are, as described in **section 2.13**, typically placed in a principal-to-principal position vis-à-vis the CCP. In all typical European structures the GCM will be obliged to undertake liability to the CCP in respect of any registered transactions entered into by its client. So, if the client defaults, the GCM will still be obliged to perform its obligations in respect of the client's transactions even if, as between the GCM and the client, the GCM can close out and collateralise its client-facing risk. The ongoing liability to the CCP will involve continuing with an obligation to post variation margin, initial margin on any transactions entered into by the client on the day of its default and in respect of intra-day margin calls (the risk of which may be correlated to markets disrupted by defaults), and to perform contracts which reach maturity without having been closed out. All of these duties imply credit risk on the client.

The GCM will expect to be able to cover the risk concerned by margins collected from the client. Post-default liability for ongoing margin calls is considered below. The GCM will wish to close out the positions taken by the client by taking opposite positions in the marketplace and applying any margin received (including margin returned by the CCP once close-out is completed and any settlement amount paid) in a similar manner to that in which a CCP manages a participant default.[45] The GCM may, however, let transactions proceed to maturity, in which case a (gross) liability to deliver securities or make payment for securities will arise, which will not be covered by margin, margin being quantified by reference to (net) close-out methodology.[46] As with an agent bank providing settlement services, the GCM will wish to retain the payment received for securities delivered, or vice versa; as principal, this ought in theory to be the outcome, subject to considerations of ownership of securities in markets where the role of GCM as principal does not preclude a question of ownership or where a GCM has a mixed principal-and-agent role. Any (net) market risk remaining ought to be covered by margin, assuming it has been received and is of adequate quantum.

Margin risk with CCPs

18.18 GCMs will be obliged to meet margin calls issued by CCPs in very short timeframes, and as regards routine daily margin calls, the margin collection arrangement is likely to be by way of direct debit from the GCM's bank account. The amount of margin due from the client may be unexpected, owing to the ability of the CCP to impose an exceptional intra-day margin call, or because it is a function of the day's trading by the client and there is limited time between the close of the relevant market and the closure of the payment systems during which the GCM must calculate the client's contribution to the margin call due to be satisfied the next morning, and collect the contribution

---

44 Financial Services Authority, *The FSA's role under the Payment Services Regulations 2009* (August 2011), http://www.fsa.gov.uk/pubs/other/PSD_approach_latest.pdf, para 8.123
45 See **sections 14.41–14.42**
46 See **section 14.26**

from the client. Evidently the GCM takes credit risk on its client in respect of the margin likely to be due in respect of the client's open positions. The duration of the risk period is from the moment that the client last satisfied a margin call to the moment when all the client's positions can be closed out, which may be several days (or in relation to cleared OTC products, significantly longer).

18.19 GCMs may offer a 'collateral transformation' service to clients, under which the GCM is able to post eligible collateral to the CCP in respect of the client's cleared transactions even though the client is unable to provide such collateral itself. If the client can furnish the GCM with some other species of collateral, this may be an acceptable arrangement for all parties. The GCM will need to be wary of the basis and wrong-way risks that it might entail.[47]

18.20 Margin risk may also involve a species of borrowing from the box, as became evident in the default of Griffin Trading. Where clients of a GCM which is not a bank accept an omnibus account arrangement in respect of their cleared transactions, the cash margin which they have contributed will be held in a client money bank account under the client money rules. The CCP will debit margin calls from this bank account in respect of the omnibus account to which all client transactions are recorded. As with the securities settlement system, the CCP cannot tell which clients have contributed margin to this bank account and which have not, so the risk is that the CCP takes funds which belong to clients other than the one whose trades gave rise to the margin call. The GCM will be in the position of having to make whole the client money bank account even if the client in question fails to honour its own margin obligations. As in the case of Griffin, the obligation to top up the client money bank account may cause the insolvency of the GCM.[48]

Additional issues for GCMs

18.21 Various other points for GCMs to consider in the context of 'client clearing' of OTC derivatives transactions (but which are of broader application) have been identified: need for parity between the infrastructure's rules and the clearing agreement between GCM and client; issues relating to indirect access, and the need for clients to regulate the behaviour of their own customers, in conjunction with 'onboarding' rules about new customers; collateral management; treatment of transactions which fail to clear; and harmonisation of operational requirements between the CCP and the GCM, and dovetailing all that with the client's own arrangements.[49] GCMs should also consider their ability to withdraw from the services provided to their clients, including whether this is permitted under the contractual arrangements agreed with the client, the rules of the CCP, and the insolvency law applicable to the client.

Settlement agents' risk with CCPs

18.22 An agent bank which is not acting as GCM might assume that there is little to fear in providing a settlement service to a client which is itself a

---

47 See **sections 14.17(5)** and **14.27(3)**
48 See **box 9.1**
49 Cf AllianceBernstein et al, letter to the Federal Reserve Bank of New York (March 2011), http://www.newyorkfed.org/newsevents/news/markets/2011/SCL0331.pdf, p15

participant in a CCP. However, the usual settlement-related risks, described in **section 18.15**, will apply. So, there is the potential for settlement risk when an agent bank provides services a client who has contracted to buy securities in a cleared market, and clears its own trades. The client may need, for example, an agent bank to settle the securities trades, and for these purposes the agent bank is in no different a position from the agent bank providing a settlement service in relation to an uncleared trade. If the client fails to pay for securities bought, the agent bank will (by virtue of the STP instructions issued at the moment of trading) be unable to avoid paying the CCP for the securities, and will have the securities delivered by the CCP to its account. This scenario has the following results, which might be thought curious:

- the CCP, which had taken margin from the self-clearing client in respect of the trade, no longer needs the margin because the trade has settled; the CCP's pool of margin is thus augmented.

- the agent bank, by contrast, who will ordinarily not have taken 'margin' to cover itself in respect of settlement risk, will be left to cover the difference between the price paid for the securities and their actual value.

- the margin is thus in 'the wrong place'; whereas if the agent bank had provided a GCM service as well as a settlement service, it would have received margin in respect of its GCM function, which would have provided a pool of collateral from which to cover the loss.

Void dispositions risk

18.23 Several of the situations described expect that the agent bank will be able to rely on a payment or securities received (the countervalue), coupled with rights of set-off or security, to reduce the size of the risk from a 'gross' to a 'net' amount, exposing the agent bank to market risk on the client's trade for a period but not the whole principal amount. While the agent bank may be able to create contractual set-off rights and ensure it has an effective security interest over in relation to securities it holds, there are nonetheless significant remaining insolvency issues which may conspire to convert the risk back to a gross risk.

18.24 The problem is that frameworks of insolvency law regard payments or deliveries of property belonging to the insolvent person as being void if they occur after, or in some cases even before, the moment of opening of insolvency proceedings. These rules of law are referred to as 'void disposition rules'[50] and the moment with effect from which a disposition of property is void as 'the critical time'. Void disposition rules may have the following effects on the size of settlement-related risk, and whether it is gross or net:

(1) *Bankrupt seller, securities pre-delivered.* If the client is selling and has pre-delivered the securities to the agent bank, then if settlement takes place after the critical time, there is a void disposition of the securities. Although one might expect that the disposition is in favour of the market counterparty, it may be possible under insolvency law for the agent bank who effected the transfer to be sued for the value of the disposed-of securities by the insolvency officer of the client. This is not a problem – or at least the risk is a net risk – so long as the agent bank can retain the countervalue. Whether

---

50 See **section 8.9(15)**

that is possible may depend on the application of insolvency set-off in relation to post-insolvency receipts.

(2) *Bankrupt buyer, cash pre-paid.* If the client is buying and has pre-paid the agent bank, then the debit made by the agent bank to the client's account may be a void disposition if done after the critical time. Again, if the agent bank may be attacked by the insolvency officer for the amount of cash disposed of, the agent bank would wish to retain the countervalue to keep the risk net in size. Whether this is achievable may depend on a further application of void disposition rules, namely whether it is legally possible for a security interest to bite on an asset coming into the ownership of an insolvent person after the critical time.

(3) *Bankrupt seller, securities* not *pre-delivered.* If the client is selling but did not pre-deliver, any securities which were in fact delivered by the agent bank should not be regarded as a void disposition of the client's property. The risk here is that the countervalue is regarded as being wholly due to the client, rather than the agent bank, notwithstanding that the agent bank provided the securities for the settlement, and that any diversion of sale proceeds to the agent bank for the purposes of reimbursement is regarded as a void disposition. Again, whether the agent bank can retain part or all of the countervalue received is likely to depend on the interplay of void disposition and post-insolvency set-off rules.

(4) *Bankrupt buyer, cash* not *pre-paid.* If the client is buying but did not pre-pay, the agent bank has used its own funds to effect settlement. As with the bankrupt seller scenario, the risk is that the countervalue cannot be retained, unless under the relevant system of property law it is clear that the securities received by the agent bank are owned by the agent bank itself or subject to its security interest despite the fact of receipt after the critical time.[51]

18.25 The following supplementary remarks may be made about gross and net risk arising from the application of void disposition rules:

(1) In practice few systems of insolvency law seem to operate so as to expose agent banks to gross risk in this way.

(2) Similar considerations may apply to participation in any exchange-of-value system, such as CLS; it is immaterial that there are no securities involved.

(3) The operators of infrastructures do not face these problems because they have the protection of the Settlement Finality Directive,[52] which provides that transfer orders are enforceable as between participants notwithstanding the opening of insolvency proceedings.[53] Except in the unlikely event that a client is an 'indirect participant' in a designated system,[54] this safe harbour is not available to a participant in its dealings with a non-participant.

(4) Limited protection against void disposition rules may be available under the Financial Collateral Arrangements (No 2) Regulations 2003.[55]

---

51 Cf **section 10.12(3)**
52 Directive 98/26/EC of the European Parliament and of the Council of 19 May 1998 on settlement finality in payment and securities settlement systems
53 See **section 8.20**
54 Cf **sections 2.40** and **16.7**
55 2003 SI No 3226; see **sections 8.26ff**

(5) Other techniques available to agent banks for management of these risks are the traditional ones available for handing credit risk, such as: refusing to provide services to clients with weak credit status; imposing, monitoring and enforcing position limits; ensuring that there are contractual rights to terminate the services provided at will or in prescribed circumstances; having rights of set-off and netting; taking collateral; taking third-party guarantees. Finally it should be noted that the set-off rights which an agent bank may rely on may also depend on the effectiveness of indemnity rights given by the client to the agent bank in respect of the actions voluntarily or involuntarily taken by the agent bank in relation to the client's transactions.

VOLUNTARILY ASSUMED EXPOSURES TO THE CLIENT

Model B clearing

18.26 Firms offering custody and settlement services may enhance the service by offering 'Model B clearing' services. It is unfortunate that the phrase 'Model B clearing' has no single meaning. In some manifestations the activities of a Model B clearing firm expose it to risks similar to those of a GCM, even in the absence of a CCP. The subject requires some analysis before the risks can be classified.

Before the introduction of a central counterparty to serve the London Stock Exchange (LSE), it was a requirement of the LSE's rules that member firms take steps to ensure that their transactions would settle, and to this end they were required to nominate either a 'Model A' or a 'Model B' clearing agent.[56] Model A agents accepted responsibility for arranging settlement of the member firm's trades, but did so as agent (typically, in a CREST environment, by acting as sponsor or account operator in relation to the firm's own account at CREST). Model B agents accepted responsibility for settlement in their own names, thus taking liability as principal to the rest of the market in respect of their client's transactions. A Model B clearing agent in this old-fashioned sense was, by virtue of exchange rules and practices, obliged to honour its client's trade and was, albeit facing out to a large number of counterparties, acting if it were a GCM.

> 'Model A and Model B clearing are arrangements whereby firms outsource part or all of their back office to a fully regulated third party.
> 'With Model A clearing the clearing firm performs a series of administrative functions such as the movement of stock and cash for settlement purposes, the reconciliation of bank and stock accounts, and the processing of corporate actions and dividends. However, the correspondent firm retains full responsibilities for the functions carried out by the clearing entity from a regulatory basis.
> 'With Model B clearing, the Model B clearing firm becomes the legal counterparty to all trades and adopts the primary settlement risk until the transactions are fulfilled. Correspondent firm records are transferred to the clearing firm's system and a standard suite of dedicated accounts is established specifically for each co-respondent. The clearing firm will still

---

56 Rules of the London Stock Exchange, pre-CCP editions, rr 10.13 and 10.14

undertake functions such as the settlement of transactions, the movement of stock and cash, the reconciliation of bank, trading and custody accounts and the process of corporate actions and dividends.'[57]

18.27 Now that central counterparty clearing has been introduced for LSE trades, the need for this old form of Model B clearing has disappeared, since all trades will be cleared by the trading member itself or by its GCM. Nevertheless, the LSE rulebook still has a definition of 'model B firm',[58] and the use of the term persists more generally. The following observations may be made about Model B clearing in the post-CCP environment.

(1) Under LSE rules, a Model B firm is defined as 'a member firm that takes on all immediate liabilities for trades dealt by an introducing firm' (an introducing firm being a member firm that uses the services of a model B firm).[59] The LSE rules no longer impose counterparty-risk liabilities on Model B firms, even though it is still contemplated that Model B firms persist.

(2) Model B firms offer services in the London market on the basis that their name is 'given up' by the executing broker to the market so that Model B firm is responsible for settlement. The structure is used in particular (but not exclusively) in the bond markets where transactions may not be centrally cleared, and the confidence of the counterparty in a trading firm's ability to perform its obligations needs to be assured.[60]

(3) A typical Model B structure will enable a financial intermediary (the executing broker, that is the Model B firm's client) to advertise to its own customers and to its market counterparties that they are not taking counterparty risk on the intermediary. The customers can avoid taking the risks associated with the intermediary being interposed between the customers and the market counterparty, and the market counterparty can avoid settlement risk on the intermediary.

(4) In a typical Model B structure, the Model B clearing firm will provide individualised settlement accounts for each of the intermediary client's customers, rather than an omnibus account. However, the Model B clearing firm will look to the intermediary client to carry out all regulatory duties owed to customers, such as those arising under the FSA's Conduct of Business Sourcebook,[61] and the firm will also carry out its credit assessment on the intermediary client (not the customers). As settlement agent, the firm will at least have the STP risk described above, and may have a wider duty to the market to settle trades even if the settlement instructions have not yet been submitted to the infrastructure. The implication of this structure is that the Model B clearing firm is exposed to the risk that its intermediary client

57 Association of Private Client Investment Managers and Stockbrokers, *Review of Capital Requirements for Banks and Investment Firms – Response to Commission Services Third Consultation Paper 1st July 2003* (October 2003), http://ec.europa.eu/internal_market/bank/docs/regcapital/cp3/contributors-list/association-private-client-investment-managers-stockbrokers_en.pdf, Annex 3

58 London Stock Exchange, *Rules of the London Stock Exchange* (August 2010), Definitions

59 London Stock Exchange, *Rules of the London Stock Exchange* (July 2011), Definitions

60 International Capital Market Association, *Rules and Recommendations* (October 2009), Rule 322.1

61 Financial Services Authority, *Handbook of Rules and Guidance, Conduct of Business Sourcebook*; see in particular COBS 2.4.3R

does not pay or deliver securities, and cannot persuade its customer(s) to do so either.

(5) As there is no market rule to require a Model B firm to undertake obligations to an unknown population of potential counterparties of its clients, it would appear to follow that (a) the Model B firm can agree to limit the circumstances in which it is willing to undertake settlement responsibility by contract with its intermediary client, and (b) the ability of the market counterparty to take direct action against the Model B firm is limited. To these conclusions it may be remarked that Model B firms will, upon submission of settlement instructions to the relevant CSD and/ or payment system, find themselves exposed to STP risks as described in **section 19.12** in respect of their own client's possible non-performance.

(6) LSE rule 5000 and the associated guidance state that a member firm, whether acting as agent or principal, is responsible for ensuring each trade effected by it is settled. Thus a Model B firm could be compelled to perform to the market counterparty if the firm's client has failed and if the firm has not issued irrevocable settlement instructions. It is, however, less obvious that a Model B firm is liable to perform to its client if the market counterparty fails. Model B firms may seek to limit or eliminate this liability in their client documentation.

Margin shortfalls and lending

18.28 GCMs should also consider their degree of control over the quantum of margin taken from clients. It is tempting to follow the margin amount prescribed by the CCP for a given position, assuming that this is an accurate sizing of the risk. But in normal conditions CCPs assess margin requirements by reference to the product being cleared, not the credit quality of the CCP's counterparty;[62] a GCM may need to take a more nuanced view, and in particular take account of the likely time-line for closing out a failed client's positions. Those considerations might suggest that GCMs could consider levying higher margin calls than the CCP levies itself.

Approaching the issue from the other direction entirely, a GCM may, where permitted to do so by CCP and market rules, wish to take care of margin calls from the CCP while reducing the frequency or amount of calls made on the client, or even without making any demand at all on the client. A GCM may thus offer a liquidity facility to its client in respect of margin calls made by the CCP in respect of the client's trading. The facility will oblige the GCM to allow the client to run an overdraft in respect of margin calls satisfied by the GCM in respect of the client's account.

EMIR[63] does not disallow such a practice, but where a facility is entered into it will expose the GCM to credit and liquidity risks. Evidently, the client may be unable to meet the potential future losses against which the margin requirement was imposed. A GCM may be willing to forgive the timely payment of margin calls, or even to forgo margin calls altogether if trading is kept within agreed parameters, with regard to a high-grade client. Liquidity risk may also arise

---

62 See **sections 14.26–14.27**
63 Regulation (EU) No 648/2012 of the European Parliament and of the Council of 4 July 2012 on OTC derivatives, central counterparties and trade repositories

where the client's trading pattern is volatile, as the liquidity facility will be drawn upon heavily in times of heightened market activity by the client.

A more sophisticated variant of lending of margin arises where the GCM agrees to accept collateral from the client which is ineligible to be delivered onwards to the CCP. Here the GCM accepts the market risk on the collateral received. The risk is a basis (imperfect correlation) risk, between the collateral posted to the CCP and the collateral received, subject to the overriding consideration that only if the client fails will the risk materialise.

GCM accessing multiple CCPs

18.29 A GCM may also offer to act as a point of access to many CCPs for a single client. Clients carrying out arbitrage strategies involving the simultaneous trading of single product on many exchanges will be attracted to this service, in particular while different CCPs are used to clear for different trading platforms. The bonus which using a single GCM provides, over and above the simplicity of aggregated margin calls and relationship management, is the possibility of margin offsets. A client who is long on market A but short on market B would have dual margin obligations if it participated directly in the CCPs for those markets, but a GCM who sees the whole portfolio may accept that the client's net position is flat, and rationalise that if both trades were cleared at the same CCP the margin requirement would be zero.

To take such a view may require the GCM to consider a variety of issues. First, there may be market rules which disallow the practice altogether. Secondly, the GCM will have to meet margin calls from both CCPs, paying initial margin to both CCPs, but collecting nothing from its client – that is effectively an extension of credit, albeit credit given to the CCPs. Thirdly, if the client defaults, the GCM will need to manage the close-out of both long and short positions in such a way as to minimise loss; because the trades were done in different market-places there is no guarantee that the trades actually do offset perfectly, with the result that actual market differences will add to the overall cost of close-out. The prudent GCM will factor these considerations into its combined-access service and demand at least some margin from the client in addition to compensation for its funding costs.

Contractual settlement

18.30 An agent bank will wish to create for its client a clearing and settlement service which is, as near as possible, equivalent to the service which the client would experience if it were a direct participant in the clearing or settlement system concerned. This near-imperative may lead the agent bank into areas of risk which it is not necessary to assume in order to provide the service, but which flow from enhancements which the agent bank offers. 'Contractual settlement' is an example of service enhancement carried out in order to mimic the behaviour of the settlement system.

As a direct participant in a settlement system, the agent bank will be a beneficiary of the DvP assurance which the system provides.[64] The system's rules and operations will be designed to ensure that there is no risk that any

---

64   See **section 15.2**

participant can deliver without receiving payment, or pay without receiving payment (or in a PvP system like CLS, pay without receiving the countervalue). The fundamental concept underlying DvP and PvP is simultaneous debits and credits of participants' accounts, in both directions. However, for the clients of the direct participant, simultaneity is not achievable. Unless the client's counterparty is the agent bank itself, or another client of the agent bank – a situation considered below – the counterparty's delivery can at best be simultaneous with the agent bank's payment, or vice versa.[65] The interposition of the agent bank ensures that the client is shielded from settlement risk as regards the counterparty, but it does not provide the client with complete freedom from settlement risk: it has substituted the agent bank for the counterparty in this respect. So, the client can ask the agent bank to carry out a simultaneous debit and credit on the agent bank's books: in other words, not to debit the client's account until the moment when a corresponding credit of the countervalue is made.

This structure does not yet give the client an equivalent experience to direct participation in the settlement system. There may be timing delays – for example, in CLS, the pay-out schedule in favour of the agent bank will be timed to follow on from the bulk of the day's settlement activity, and may be later in the client's working day than commercially desired by the client. To defer the simultaneous debit-and-credit across the agent bank's books until the pay-out from the system may be unacceptable; and the agent bank may therefore offer to anticipate settlement by making the relevant entries on its own books in favour of the client at an earlier stage in the day, possibly even before the transaction in question has settled with finality. This service is referred to as 'contractual settlement'.

18.31   An agent bank which is willing to provide a contractual settlement service undertakes additional settlement risk. The settlement system typically avoids settlement risk for its participants by requiring them to pay in ahead of settlement, in order that the central settlement accounts which it provides or operates are in credit (or covered by collateral) at the time of simultaneous debit-and-credit across the books it controls. The pre-requisite of pre-payment will thus put the agent bank of a paying client into a position where it must choose between (a) deferring the moment of contractual settlement, but committing its own funds to the settlement process before the moment arrives when it can debit its client's account on its own books, and (b) giving immediate contractual settlement, but awaiting the payout or delivery from the system and meanwhile assuming the risk that the client withdraws the cash or securities which the client, looking at its account, considers duly received.

An agent bank which chooses option (b) may not be assured that the pay-out in the desired currency will occur; or indeed that the transaction will settle at the system. If either of these problems were to materialise, the agent bank would have credited its client's account with something it does not yet have, exposing itself to liquidity and market risk in relation to its voluntarily assumed obligations. An agent bank which chooses option (a), on the other hand, is making a credit extension to the client, and may wish to ensure that it has

---

65   Cf **section 13.47**

effective rights to the countervalue received in the settlement in order to reduce its risk to a net, rather than a gross, risk.[66]

(From the client's perspective the risk is different: while the agent bank has its cash, the client takes credit risk on the agent bank, and simultaneous debit-and-credit does not alleviate this risk. A client whose agent bank opts for (b) assumes custody-shortfall risk[67] on the agent bank who may not have the securities promised. At least contractual settlement ensures that the client has something, even if it is only an unsecured claim, at all stages in the process. Without contractual settlement, the agent bank would debit the client's account at the time of making the pre-payment or pre-delivery to the system, and the client would have nothing until the countervalue is credited to its account following settlement at the system.)

18.32 Under the suggestion for a Securities Law Directive, contractual settlement would be tolerated, but only if the credits made by the account-provider agent bank were specially marked as conditional. How an agent bank could assume the risk of a failure of finality at the settlement system but still honour its obligation to the client – which is, in effect, how contractual settlement should work – is not clear from the proposal.[68]

On-us settlement

18.33 A variation on the theme of contractual settlement is 'internalised', or 'on-us' settlement. This term is used where the agent bank acts for both buyer and seller in the transaction, and by operational dexterity it is possible to achieve settlement across the books of the agent bank without the need to send settlement instructions to the central system. Whether this is frequently achievable is the subject of debate.[69] Clearly the parties to on-us settlement assume risk on the agent bank, but avoid the timing mismatch issues which flow from having additional steps in the chain. The agent bank will escape many of the STP-related issues described above, but still faces void disposition risk from its clients.

Primary issues

18.34 Another variation is where the client is unable to achieve DvP without the assistance of the agent bank. This may happen where the agent bank assumes the role of issuing agent or, within the Euroclear and Clearstream context, common depository. In any primary issue of securities there needs to be a moment when the subscribers' payments, having been collected, are delivered to the issuer, and the securities being issued become 'live' and registered as held by the subscribers or their nominees. The situation just described commonly involves the issuing agent providing the DvP role, shielding both issuer and

---

66   See **section 18.15**
67   See **section 10.7(7)**
68   European Commission Services, *Legislation on legal certainty of securities holding and dispositions* (November 2010), Consultation Document DG Markt G2 MET/OT/acg D(2010) 768690, http://ec.europa.eu/internal_market/consultations/docs/2010/securities/consultation_paper_en.pdf, p 13
69   See **section 2.21**

subscribers from settlement risk. In a multi-entity chain it is not possible for all parties to enjoy DvP, as the following example illustrates.

A Eurobond issued for settlement in both Euroclear and Clearstream will be held by a common depository.[70] Subscription monies will be collected by or for the lead manager of the issue, and the global note will be delivered to the common depository. The steps that are still needed are for the monies to reach the issuer and for the common depository to record the bond as in issue and held, as to the appropriate number of individual notes each, by Euroclear and Clearstream. There is, accordingly, a chain of four: lead manager acting for subscribers, ICSD, common depository, and issuer. The problem of DvP is solved by the common depository shouldering the settlement risk, as follows. The lead manager confirms that it wishes the issue to occur; the ICSDs undertake to pay the common depository; the common depository then issues the bond to the ICSDs and simultaneously makes a payment to the issuer; and subsequently the common depositary receives its funding. The common depository is free to agree to pay the issuer as paid, but this transfers the settlement risk to the issuer, who may be unwilling to accept it.

PRICE REGULATION

18.35 Given that the origins of much legislative activity in the field of clearing and settlement lie in a concern that the cost of these activities is too high,[71] it would be natural to ask whether there has been any attempt to regulate the price of clearing and settlement services provided by agent banks. Although there have been inroads into freedom of pricing of some financial services – notably for card payments[72] – there are few restrictions likely to affect providers of clearing and settlement services. The following may, however, be mentioned:

(1) Pricing structures agreed on a multilateral basis are likely to be challenged on competition law grounds. Numerous investigations and decisions took place in the 1990s over eurocheques and credit transfer systems in particular.[73] Card schemes and direct debit arrangements are tightly regulated.[74]

(2) Passing on charges for a payment service to another person may not be permitted. 'OUR' and 'BEN' coded credit transfers (under which the costs are paid by the transferor and the transferee respectively), and indeed interbank pricing for payments generally, are likely to be limited by article 52 of the Payment Services Directive (PSD).[75] Where a payment

---

70 See **section 2.24**
71 See **sections 1.28–1.29**
72 Cf European Commission, *Sector Inquiry under Article 17 of Regulation (EC) No 1/2003 on retail banking* (January 2007), COM(2007) 33 final
73 For review, see Gyselen, L, *EU Antitrust Law in the Area of Financial Services* (October 1996), Fordham Corporate Law Institute, 23rd Annual Conference on International Antitrust Law and Policy
74 Case COMP/34.569 – Mastercard, *Summary of Commission Decision of 19 December 2007 relating to a proceeding under Article 81 of the EC Treaty and Article 53 of the EEA Agreement* (November 2009), OJ (C) 264, page 8; Regulation (EU) No 260/2012 of the European Parliament and of the Council of 14 March 2012 establishing technical and business requirements for credit transfers and direct debits in euro, etc, art 8
75 Directive 2007/64/EC of the European Parliament and of the Council of 13 November 2007 on payment services in the internal market etc

does not involve a currency conversion, the rule is that the payee pays the charges levied by his payment service provider (PSP), and the payer pays the charges levied by his PSP. Article 52 can be opted out of by a non-consumer by agreement with his PSP, but of course even a non-consumer cannot control the agreement between his counterparty and the PSP of that counterparty, so the self-denying 'OUR' structure has been effectively killed off.[76] It may be noted, however, that for the purposes of the PSD payment services do not include 'payment transactions carried out within a payment or securities settlement system,' or 'payment transactions related to securities asset servicing.'[77]

(3) Article 67 of the PSD requires that PSPs and their intermediaries transfer the full amount of a payment and refrain from deducting charges from the amount transferred. A payee may agree with its PSP that charges made by the payee's PSP can be deducted before the payee's account is credited.

(4) Article 3 of the Cross-border Payments Regulation[78] requires that charges levied by a PSP in respect of cross-border payments are the same as charges for corresponding national payments of the same value and in the same currency. It is not clear that the limitations of scope regarding payments within settlement systems or payments related to securities asset servicing, mentioned above in relation to the PSD, apply to the Regulation.

(5) Article 38(1) of EMIR requires disclosure by clearing members of the prices and fees associated with the services provided; these have to be disclosed separately for each service and function, including discounts and rebates, and the conditions to benefit from the reductions.

(6) If the suggestions made in the consultation on a possible Securities Law Directive are pursued, a principle equivalent to article 3 of the Cross-border Payments Regulation would be introduced for certain custody services in respect of cross-border holdings of securities.[79]

(7) Article 19(2) of the Short Selling Regulation[80] allows regulators to require notification by securities lenders of significant changes in fees in exceptional market conditions.

76 European Commission services, *Your questions on PSD* (October 2008), response to question 104, http://ec.europa.eu/internal_market/payments/docs/framework/transposition/faq_en.pdf
77 Articles 3(h) and (i)
78 Regulation (EC) No 924/2009 of the European Parliament and of the Council of 16 September 2009 on cross-border payments in the Community, etc
79 European Commission Services, *Legislation on legal certainty of securities holding and dispositions* (November 2010), Consultation Document DG Markt G2 MET/OT/acg D(2010) 768690, http://ec.europa.eu/internal_market/consultations/docs/2010/securities/consultation_ paper_en.pdf, Principle 18; see **section 10.8**
80 Regulation (EU) No 236/2012 of the European Parliament and of the Council of 14 March 2012 on short selling and certain aspects of credit default swaps

19 Prudential Regulation

PRINCIPLES OF PRUDENTIAL REGULATION

19.1   Prudential regulation of financial institutions is built on five main foundations. Three are the 'pillars' of the Basel II international framework for capital adequacy of banks.[1] The other two are limits on exposures and management of liquidity risk. The five foundations differ markedly in the amount of detail, day-to-day relevance and attention paid to them by regulators. They should also not be regarded as the only issues relevant to the management of risk in financial institutions. This chapter looks briefly at the components of each of the five foundations, insofar as likely to be considered relevant to the field of clearing and settlement, before assessing their impact on the different activities of agent banks. (Prudential regulation of infrastructures is discussed in **Chapters 6** and **11**.)

It may be helpful at the outset to review briefly the objectives and tools of prudential supervision. Ideally, prudential regulation is concerned with the financial management of a regulated firm: ensuring that its clients do not suffer loss because the firm becomes subject to an insolvency procedure. Financial institutions deserve (and are subjected to) greater oversight intended to reduce the risk of insolvency because of the devastating effects which a financial sector insolvency can have for the livelihoods and solvency of a firm's clients, and for the wider economy. Many things may cause insolvency: imprudent investment or business decisions, a change in the business environment which invalidates a successful business model, and inadequate internal controls are all examples. In the broadest sense, prudential supervision is about sound business management in a financial institution.

Stated thus, the objective is too broad to be pursued effectively; regulators need more manageable goals. These might be summarised as qualitative goals directed towards the prudent management of business risks as encountered in the financial sector, and quantitative goals directed at the balance sheet and investment decisions of the firm. The qualitative goals may include specific standards relating to operational risks, implementation of systems and controls, and other matters. At an international level, the supervisory assessment of these matters is dealt with in Pillar 2 of the Basel II framework, though operational risk is now accorded quantitative treatment, discussed further below. The quantitative goals are to ensure that the firm has adequate capital to underpin

---

1   Bank for International Settlements Basel Committee on Banking Supervision, *International Convergence of Capital Measurement and Capital Standards – A Revised Framework* (comprehensive unrevised edition, June 2006), http://www.bis.org/publ/bcbs128.pdf

its activities, adequate access to liquidity, and that its investments are not imprudently concentrated.

Regulatory Capital as the main prudential supervisory tool

19.2   The role of regulatory capital in this process should not be overstated. Since the publication in 1988 of the Basel Committee's first Capital Accord,[2] it has been tempting to think of capital adequacy as the only measure for prudential regulation. No doubt capital has a vital role to play: by ensuring that there are investors who will rank behind depositors and other creditors, capital is designed to allow a solvent bank to burn through a certain proportion of its assets and still leave enough behind for those senior claimants. But what it cannot do is turn a liability into an asset. Students of prudential regulation find it confusing that the science of capital adequacy assesses the 'adequacy' of a *liability* of a bank (its capital), and in doing so it requires assets to be risk-weighted, in other words to treat some assets as *bad* – they expect it would work the other way round, by treating assets as good, and liabilities as bad. Let it be said that the students are not wrong. Assets are good. But the teachers are not wrong either: poor quality assets may not be reliable to be converted into hard cash to pay off the senior claimants, and should be discounted. Capital adequacy is an attempt to provide a counterpoint to going-concern accounting: in a sense, it tries to forecast the financial shape of a failed bank.

Capital adequacy is a good defence, then, against some assets becoming devalued; or, indeed, against other losses which manifest themselves in a timescale which enables them to be made good through other more profitable activities or through recapitalisation. Capital does not seek to address the fundamental mismatch in all banking businesses: the danger following from taking in short-term deposits and lending money on long-term loans – that is, liquidity risk. No amount of capital can guarantee a bank against a liquidity crisis.[3] Banks also face other risks: operational risk, reputational risk, systemic risk, political risk and so forth. Having vast amounts of capital cannot protect a bank against all of these without the bank becoming uncompetitive and finding it impossible to provide a reasonable return to its investors – the providers of the capital.

19.3   Capital, then, cannot be the exclusive answer to prudential supervision of financial institutions. Nevertheless, the most detailed rules agreed at an international level now address capital adequacy. Together with the rules relating to large exposures, capital adequacy rules make up Pillar 1 of the Basel II framework. Quantitative standards relating to leverage and liquidity were added through the Basel III framework.[4] That leaves Pillars 2 and 3. Under Pillar 2, bank regulators are expected to develop supervisory regimes which assess the

---

2   Bank for International Settlements Basel Committee on Banking Supervision, *International Convergence of Capital Measurement and Capital Standards* (July 1988), http://www.bis.org/publ/bcbsc111.pdf

3   Cf Turing, D, and Cramb, E, *Managing Risk in Financial Firms* (Tottel, March 2009), ISBN 978-1-84766-303-0, p 179

4   Bank for International Settlements Basel Committee on Banking Supervision, *Basel III: International framework for liquidity risk measurement, standards and monitoring* (December 2010), http://www.bis.org/publ/bcbs188.pdf; *Basel III: A global regulatory framework for more resilient banks and banking systems* (June 2011), http://www.bis.org/publ/bcbs189.pdf; for a summary table see http://www.bis.org/bcbs/basel3/b3summarytable.pdf

generality of a bank's approach to risk management, and take appropriate action – very often, to increase the capital requirement for the bank. Pillar 3 deploys the self-discipline of the market: banks are required to make public disclosure of certain risk-related issues, in the expectation that customers, investors, and competition from peer group members will all inexorably work to impose higher standards. The requirements of Pillars 1 and 2, and the rules relating to liquidity and leverage, as applied to agent banks, are examined in more detail below. In Europe, the recommendations of the Basel frameworks are, at the date of publication, being transcribed into the Capital Requirements Regulation (CR Regulation)[5], which applies to both credit institutions and investment firms.

PRUDENTIAL REQUIREMENTS OF THE BASEL FRAMEWORKS

Capital adequacy

19.4   Capital adequacy is a huge topic. Necessarily, therefore, this introductory discussion is selective.

(1) *Risk weighting of loan assets.* Banks make money by taking deposits and extending credit to their clients. Loans are assets which may prove worthless at the moment they are needed to repay depositors. The centrepiece of the capital adequacy calculation is the principle that each loan should be weighted according to its riskiness – that is, according to the likelihood of the borrower failing to repay – and that the bank should have an amount of capital to support the risk-weighted amount of each loan.[6] The basic requirement is thus for banks to evaluate the probability of default by each borrower, and to compute a risk-weighting for all credit extended to that borrower. Two methodologies are available for determining risk weightings: if a bank has sufficient statistical information it may be allowed to use its own data to calculate a probability of default, which is plugged into a mathematical formula devised by the Basel Committee (these banks will be using the internal-ratings-based approach, and are called 'IRB banks');[7] or failing that the bank can rely on credit rating agency ratings, and look up the associated risk weighting in a table also devised by the Basel Committee (these banks are using the 'standardised' approach).[8]

(2) *Credit for clearing and settlement.* It will immediately be seen that, as many clearing and settlement services involve the extension of credit, there is likely to be a capital adequacy impact of such services. However, many settlement-related credit extensions are intra-day only, and capital

---

5   European Commission, *Proposal for a Regulation of the European Parliament and of the Council on prudential requirements for credit institutions and investment firms* (July 2011), COM (2011) 452 final, http://eur-lex.europa.eu/LexUriServ/LexUriServ.do?uri=SPLIT_CO M:2011:0452%2801%29:FIN:EN:PDF,   http://eur-lex.europa.eu/LexUriServ/LexUriServ. do?uri=SPLIT_COM:2011:0452%2802%29:FIN:EN:PDF,   http://eur-lex.europa.eu/ LexUriServ/LexUriServ.do?uri=SPLIT_COM:2011:0452%2803%29:FIN:EN:PDF; Interinstitutional file 2011/0202 (COD)

6   Directive 2006/48/EC of the European Parliament and of the Council of 14 June 2006 relating to the taking up and pursuit of the business of credit institutions, art 75(a)

7   Banking Directive, art 84(1), Annex VII Part 4

8   Banking Directive, Annex VI

requirements apply only to end-of-day positions, because banks are required to follow accounting standards in ascertaining the size of exposures.[9] Overdrafts which run overnight, as a result of failed settlements or for other reasons such as the lending of margin, will have to be taken into account for capital adequacy purposes.

(3) *Committed credit lines.* Commitments to make loans also require the support of capital. The thinking here is that, once drawn, a lending facility becomes an asset which requires to be risk-weighted. Not all facilities will be drawn, though, and a conversion factor is applied to reflect the probability that the facility may or may not be utilised.[10] So the outcome is similar to actual lending: entering into a commitment to lend will attract a capital requirement which varies according to the credit-worthiness (probability of default) of the client. Again, in the clearing and settlement world, many credit facilities will be able to avoid adverse capital treatment, because the facility is unconditionally cancellable at any time without notice. Such facilities have a conversion factor of zero.[11]

(4) *Collateral.* Lending exposures may be covered, and the size of the risk-weighted assets to which they give rise reduced, by collateral. Clearing and settlement services typically rely on financial collateral in the form of cash or securities, which in almost all cases will be eligible under regulatory capital rules to mitigate the capital requirement associated with an unsecured loan.[12] The Basel II framework provides a variety of approaches to banks, depending on their degree of sophistication. Typically agent banks will use the 'comprehensive' method, which enables them to reduce the value of the credit outstanding by the value of the collateral; the collateral value will be adjusted to reflect its volatility.[13] Various conditions must also be met if collateral is being relied on for reduction of capital requirements: these focus on the absence of correlation between the borrower's credit quality and the collateral value, the legal reliability of the collateral arrangements, and the bank's policies and operational processes related to calling, valuing, and liquidating the collateral.[14]

Trading book business

19.5 Some credit exposure will arise indirectly: not as a result of a conscious advance of money on the client's behalf, but as a consequence of the business being cleared or settled for the client's account. The Basel II framework requires a different approach to capital calculation where the agent bank is engaged in 'trading book' business. Examples of trading book business include transactions in derivatives and equities. These transactions require separate assessments of the market risk (called 'position risk') and credit risk (called 'counterparty credit risk', to distinguish it from non-trading credit) implications of the trades, with capital requirements arising from each assessment. The following comments may be made with regard to trading book activity:

9 Banking Directive, art 74(1)
10 Banking Directive, art 78 (standardised), Annex VII Part 3 (IRB)
11 Banking Directive, arts 78(1) and Annex II (standardised), Annex VII Part 3 para 9 (IRB)
12 Banking Directive, Annex VIII Part 1
13 Banking Directive, Annex VIII Part 3 para 1.4.2
14 Banking Directive, Annex VIII Part 2

(1) Securities position risk is unlikely to arise in relation to clearing and settlement services.

- Offsetting positions (even if involving different counterparties) will allow the market risk component to be netted to zero.[15] So a GCM, which acts as buyer to its selling client and seller to a CCP, should be able to avoid a position risk requirement arising from its clearing service.

- Settlement services which leave an agent bank with a short securities position will be regarded as securities loans, which are considered at paragraph (4) below.

(2) Counterparty credit risk will potentially arise from cleared and unsettled transactions. Clearing members will be exposed to the risk of failure by their client or by the CCP, and so have to consider the counterparty credit risk capital requirements of two exposures in relation to each cleared transaction.

- The value of equities which are owned on a long-term basis will be in the 'banking book' rather than the trading book; but even when they are in the trading book, a bank which handles equities as settlement agent only should not be regarded as having taken a position in them. For a GCM, equities transactions will not attract a counterparty credit risk requirement unless they involve settlements which are overdue. The Basel II framework sets out what counts as overdue; an increasing scale of capital charges applies to transactions that are upwards of 5, 16, 31, or 46 days past the due settlement date.[16]

- Derivatives transactions which are in-the-money entail current exposure and a degree of 'expected exposure', because the transaction may go, or move further, into the money. Banks may calculate the capital requirement using one of three methods;[17] typically, though, they will use an internal model. Netting under a master agreement can be used to mitigate the exposures and thus reduce the capital requirements arising,[18] though in order to encourage banks to spread their derivatives business widely the number of transactions which can be included in a 'netting set' without triggering adverse capital treatment will be limited to 5000.[19] It should also be mentioned that a 'credit valuation adjustment' will be applied to acknowledge the risk that the counterparty's credit status could deteriorate and affect the valuation of the portfolio of transactions.[20]

(3) Settlement fails and 'free deliveries' (where the delivery is made without simultaneous inward transfer of cash) will attract a counterparty credit risk capital requirement for the client which is exposed to the risk following from the fail or mismatch in DvP.[21] But the agent bank is not exposed to these risks, and should not bear the costs.

---

15 Directive 2006/49/EC of the European Parliament and of the Council of 14 June 2006 on the capital adequacy of investment firms and credit institutions, Annex I
16 Capital Adequacy Directive, Annex II para 1
17 Banking Directive, Annex III, Part 2
18 Banking Directive, Annex III, Part 7
19 CR Regulation as proposed, art 279(2)
20 CR Regulation as proposed, Part Three, Title VI
21 Capital Adequacy Directive, Annex II

(4) Margin lending transactions include transactions where an agent bank lends securities from its own investment portfolio to its client to cover what would otherwise be a failed settlement.[22] Counterparty credit risk is present in such transactions since the borrower of securities (the client) may fail, leaving the agent bank with a loss if the value of collateral received from the client is insufficient to cover the replacement cost for the securities.

19.6 Finally, operational risk is subject to a capital requirement under the CR Regulation. Once again, a variety of approaches is available to banks. If a bank is using the standardised approach, it will have to calculate its average gross income for each of eight business lines; for each business line there is a corresponding percentage which reflects the official view of the degree of operational risk associated with that line. The capital required is the gross income multiplied by the percentage. The percentages are 12, 15 or 18; payment and settlement is in the 18% bracket, and agency services, including custody, are in the 15% bracket.[23] Banks may instead calculate their operational risk requirement based on a model if they have the regulator's permission to use an 'advanced measurement approach.'[24]

Adequate liquidity

19.7 The Basel III amendments to the Basel II framework introduced two new prudential requirements into the structure of financial institution supervision. These are the liquidity coverage requirement (LCR) and the net stable funding requirement (NSFR).

LCR measures the predicted net outflow of cash over a 30-day period in stressed market conditions.[25] The Basel III framework ascribes weightings to certain kinds of asset and liability to determine what will lead to an outflow of cash. Having ascertained that amount of outflow, the bank must ensure that it sets aside sufficient liquid assets meeting various narrowly-defined quality criteria to cover the predicted net outflow. Certain deposits are assumed to be more likely to be withdrawn than others. The Basel Committee suggested that non-retail deposits placed by 'customers with specific operational relationships' are weighted at 25% (that is, it is assumed that 25% of such deposits will be withdrawn during the stress period).[26] The 'operational relationships' referred to include clearing and custody:

> 'A clearing relationship, in this context, refers to a service arrangement that enables customers to transfer funds (or securities) indirectly through direct participants in domestic settlement systems to final recipients. Such services are limited to the following activities: transmission, reconciliation and confirmation of payment orders; daylight overdraft, overnight financing and maintenance of post-settlement balances; and determination of intra-day and final settlement positions … .
>
> 'A custody relationship, in this context, refers to the provision of safekeeping, reporting, processing of assets and/or the facilitation of the

---

22 Banking Directive, Annex III Part 1 para 4
23 Banking Directive, art 104, Annex X Part 2
24 Banking Directive, art 105, Annex X Part 3
25 CR Regulation as proposed, Part Six, Titles I, II
26 Basel III framework, BCBS 188, para 72

operational and administrative elements of related activities on behalf of customers in the process of their transacting and retaining financial assets … . Such services are limited to the settlement of securities transactions, the transfer of contractual payments, the processing of collateral, the execution of foreign currency transactions, the holding of related cash balances and the provision of ancillary cash management services. Also included are the receipt of dividends and other income, client subscriptions and redemptions, scheduled distributions of client funds and the payment of fees, taxes and other expenses.'[27]

In the CR Regulation as proposed by the European Commission, the language differs somewhat from the Basel III framework, to give the 25% weighting to 'deposits … maintained … in order to obtain clearing, custody or cash management services from the institution … . Clearing, custody or cash management services … only covers such services to the extent that they are rendered in the context of an established relationship on which the depositor has substantial dependency.'[28]

Furthermore, committed liquidity facilities will be assumed to be fully drawn; uncommitted facilities are left to national regulators to evaluate, but 'may nevertheless have the potential to cause significant liquidity drains in times of stress. For this standard, each supervisor and bank should consider which of these "other contingent funding obligations" may materialise under the assumed stress events.'[29]

The concept of stable funding lies behind the NSFR. This is that some bases on which banks fund their credit activities are less likely to be withdrawn in moments of stress than others. So, for example, retail deposits are relatively stable, compared with commercial deposits and funding derived from the issue of short-term debt instruments such as commercial paper. Banks will need to demonstrate that long-term assets are funded through relatively stable liabilities.[30] To achieve this, each asset and each liability is weighted according to a table mandated by the CR Regulation. Non-retail deposits are given a 50% stability weighting (as contrasted with capital instruments, which achieve 100%);[31] on the assets side, loans to non-financial corporates have a required stable funding weighting of 50%, whereas loans to corporates are weighted at 100%.[32]

Large exposures, leverage and Pillar 2

19.8   Banks should not become over-dependent on a single borrower, or collection of borrowers related in some way. The CR Regulation accordingly sets limits, referable to the amount of capital of the bank, on the amount of credit which can be granted to any one person (or group of connected persons). As far as credit granted to clients not affiliated to the bank is concerned, the limit is 25% of the bank's eligible capital.[33]

---

27   Basel III framework, BCBS 188, paras 75–76
28   CR Regulation as proposed, art 410(4)
29   Basel III framework, BCBS 188, para 102
30   CR Regulation as proposed, Part Six, Title III
31   Basel III framework, BCBS 188, para 128 and Table 1
32   Basel III framework, BCBS 188, para 133 and Table 2
33   Banking Directive, art 111(1)

The other tool, introduced by the Basel III rules, to limit the amount of lending done by banks is the leverage ratio. This simple calculation involves only a comparison of the amount of tier 1 capital invested in the bank and the gross (that is, un-weighted for risk) amount of its loans and commitments.[34] Banks will not be permitted to allow the amount of credit exposure they take on to exceed a certain multiple of capital to be determined by the Basel Committee in due course.[35] Pillar 2 of the Basel II framework is intended to pick up all other risks which Pillar 1 ignores or treats with insufficient gravity. At its most basic, Pillar 2 gives a bank regulator power to impose supplementary capital requirements where the regulator's review process identifies additional risk.[36] Long lists of the types of risk to be assessed are available.[37] Little in these lists implicates clearing and settlement services directly. Pillar 2 may, of course, be a ground on which a regulator could investigate and impose capital requirements on account of intra-day credit extensions; but the difficulty of measuring intra-day credit exposure reliably perhaps makes this unlikely.

CASH AND SECURITIES SETTLEMENT SERVICES

19.9   For an agent bank providing access to payment and securities settlement systems, the application of the rules outlined above poses few problems. Capital rules relating to securities lending and operational risk have been mentioned already. It may then be sufficient to mention the following additional matters:

(1) *Deposits placed with major financial institutions.* In some cases, providing a settlement service requires an agent bank to deposit funds with a payment system. Funds in the home currency on deposit with a central bank attract a risk-weighting of zero for a bank using the standardised approach.[38] Deposits placed with an agent bank, or a bank operating a payment system on its own books, will not have this benefit and sums deposited would be treated as other cash exposures to a bank. Furthermore, the regulations introduced by the Basel III framework have increased the risk-weighting applicable to IRB banks which have credit exposures to large regulated financial sector entities.[39] Consequently, it will be desirable to minimise the amount of any funds left overnight with a payment system operator which is treated as a large regulated financial entity.

(2) *Liquidity facilities ('pay before you pay me').* Clients may need their agent bank to transfer funds to or through a payment system before the moment in time when the client can make funds available to the agent bank. If the refund is to be made on the following day, the agent bank will have made a loan or overdraft available; and accordingly an arrangement which commits the bank to an obligation to do so will be a risk-weighted

---

34   CR Regulation as proposed, Part Seven
35   Basel III framework, BCBS 189, para 153
36   Banking Directive, arts 123, 136 (to be re-enacted in the proposed Capital Requirements Directive: cf European Commission, *Proposal for a Directive of the European Parliament and of the Council on the access to the activity of credit institutions and the prudential supervision of credit institutions and investment firms etc* (July 2011), COM (2011) 453 final, http://eur-lex. europa.eu/LexUriServ/LexUriServ.do?uri=COM:2011:0453:FIN:EN:PDF;   interinstitutional file 2011/0203 (COD))
37   Cf Turing and Cramb, pp 94–97
38   Banking Directive, Annex VI, Part 1, para 1.2, number 4
39   CR Regulation as proposed, art 148(2)

asset, count towards any large exposure which the bank has to the client, count in the bank's computation of leverage ratio, and require the bank to set aside liquid assets to meet its liquidity coverage requirement. These adverse consequences may be avoided if the terms of the facility are that it is unconditionally cancellable at any time without notice.

(3) *Commitments ('match before you pay me').* Some settlement services require an agent bank to enter into a commitment to the payment or securities settlement system one or more business days before the settlement date; under the commitment the agent bank will be obliged to make a payment on the settlement date regardless of whether its client has by that stage paid the agent bank. Once the bank has entered the settlement instructions into the system it is, to all intents and purposes, committed to make the payment. (In theory, the commitment will usually be irrevocable only when a matched instruction is put into the system by the transaction counterparty. However, the agent bank has no control over this, and the risk is that a matching instruction is already in the system when the agent bank puts in its own instruction. Also, there may be a possibility of a bilaterally-agreed cancellation of matched instructions, but again this is outside the agent bank's control. So, in prudent risk-management practice, the moment at which instructions are submitted, or in some cases such as platform-traded equities transactions, automatically generated, should be regarded as the moment of commitment.) A prior-date commitment of this type cannot properly be regarded as a commitment which is unconditionally cancellable, and is therefore likely to attract the treatment discussed above.

(4) *Self-collateralisation.* Agent banks which make available liquidity without requiring pre-funding from their clients may rely on the transaction countervalue as security: in a DvP system, the purchased securities which the agent bank has paid for may be collateral for the purchase price,[40] and in a PvP system such as CLS, the received currency may be collateral for the paid-away currency. Securities and cash will ordinarily qualify as eligible collateral, but the agent bank will need to ensure that the other requirements of the collateral rules (including the need for legal review on the effectiveness of the arrangements) have been complied with. Collateral will be useful to reduce the size of a risk-weighted asset, but will ordinarily not assist with the mitigation of other prudential regulatory burdens discussed above.

CLEARING

19.10 The activities of a clearing member are varied and give rise to a corresponding range of prudential regulatory issues. First, it should be recognised that a clearing member faces both its client and the CCP as principal. This duality of exposure obliges the clearing member to repeat the analysis of its prudential position, looking in both directions, for each item of cleared business. Secondly, the analysis facing the CCP is likely to differ from that facing the client, owing to the special treatment of credit exposures to CCPs. Before looking at specific issues relating to clearing services, then, it is appropriate to describe the prudential treatment of exposures to CCPs.

---

40   Cf **sections 10.10(4)** and **10.12(3)**

Historically, exposures to CCPs were valued at zero, provided that the CCP ensured full collateralisation with all participants on a daily basis.[41] Latterly that treatment has been considered to be too liberal, and a methodology for risk-weighting credit exposures to CCPs has been developed. The Basel III framework is supplemented with a set of rules[42] imposing special counterparty credit risk rules for a bank with credit exposure to a CCP. The new methodology applies only to exposures resulting from financial derivatives, repos and securities lending transactions.[43] Exposures to CCPs benefit from a lower risk-weighting if the CCP satisfies the criteria set out for CCPs in the FMI Principles developed by the Basel Committee's sister committee, the Committee on Payment and Settlement Systems.[44]

19.11 Exposures to CCPs are divided into two categories:

(1) *Trade-related exposures.* A portfolio of transactions with a CCP ought to be fully margined by the CCP. Consequently a clearing member will, on any given day, expect to have a net exposure to the CCP, representing the aggregated net mark-to-market value of the transactions and margin entitlement due from the CCP (insofar as margin deposited takes the form of cash or title-transfer securities collateral). The net exposure is calculated in the same way as the clearing member would calculate exposure under a portfolio of uncleared transactions,[45] with one difference: the penal treatment of netting sets containing more than 5000 transactions does not apply.[46] The clearing member will be allowed to apply a risk-weighting of 2% to this net exposure if the CCP is a EMIR-authorised CCP.[47] If the clearing member has posted securities collateral under a charge or in any other way which is 'bankruptcy remote from the CCP', the risk weighting applied to the collateral is zero.[48] (The latter treatment ought to be self-evident, as there is no credit exposure to the CCP for such collateral.)

(2) *Default fund exposures.* Curiously, given the close linkage between margin policy and default fund sizing,[49] a different, risk-sensitive approach is mandated for the calculation of default fund exposures. It may be noted that the approach differs from the usual method of computing a risk-weighting for credit exposure; rather the approach calculates an amount of capital required to support the default fund contribution. The riskiness of a default fund contribution is assessed by comparing the financial resources of the CCP (its actual capital, plus the amount of its default fund left over assuming two average participants have failed so that their default fund contributions have been used up) with the 'hypothetical capital requirement' of the CCP.

---

41 Banking Directive, Annex III, Part 2, para 6
42 Basel Committee on Banking Supervision, *Capitalisation of bank exposures to central counterparties* (November 2011), Consultative Document BCBS 206, http://www.bis.org/publ/bcbs206.pdf
43 BCBS 206, para 15
44 Committee on Payment and Settlement Systems and Technical Committee of the International Organization of Securities Commissions, *Principles for Financial Market Infrastructures* (April 2012), http://www.bis.org/publ/cpss101a.pdf
45 CR Regulation as proposed, art 297(3)
46 CR Regulation as proposed, art 279(2)(i)
47 CR Regulation as proposed, art 297(1)
48 CR Regulation as proposed, art 297(2)
49 See **sections 14.31ff**

(The hypothetical capital requirement of a CCP is calculated by assuming that the CCP has to calculate a counterparty risk requirement in respect of all its exposures to participants, taking into account initial margin collected, default fund contributions made, and variation margin payable, and assuming that the participants could all be risk-weighted at 20%. The CCP will be expected to have 'hypothetical capital' of 8% of the aggregate risk-weighted exposure arrived at in this way.[50] This methodology is controversial, and if the Basel Committee changes it in response to criticisms made,[51] it is unclear whether its adoption under the CR Regulation would be sustained. It should be noted here that the Basel Committee emphasises that the hypothetical capital requirement is not intended to 'quantify the riskiness of a CCP' – that is, presumably, an indication that the hypothetical capital requirement is not a measure of the actual capital which ought to be held by CCPs.[52])

The purpose of this comparison is to select one of three formulae for computation of the clearing member's default-fund-related capital requirement:

- if the CCP's hypothetical capital requirement is fully funded by its actual capital, without needing the default fund at all, a lenient formula applies;
- if the CCP's financial resources (actual capital and available default fund) are insufficient to cover the hypothetical capital requirement, a penal formula applies;
- and if the CCP needs some, but not all, of the available default fund to supplement its actual capital in order to cover the hypothetical capital requirement, a variable formula which reflects reducing risk to participants as the dependency on the default fund reduces, applies.

The regulatory capital which a clearing member needs to have in respect of its default fund contribution is its proportionate share (that is, in proportion to the clearing member's contribution to the total default fund) of the amount yielded by the formula.[53]

19.12 Further issues relevant to clearing members, which may deserve comment in relation to their exposure to CCPs, include the following:

(1) *Default fund top-up obligations.* As well as attracting a capital requirement, a clearing member may have an obligation to contribute further sums to the default fund in the event of a loss event which obliges the CCP to pass round the hat for replenishment of the fund. Such a commitment may have the appearance of an underwriting facility, which would ordinarily attract a capital requirement. The CR Regulation requires capital support for 'contractually committed contributions' which must be paid on a specified event; this would include contributions which might be demanded if the default fund has been partially used. Commitments to top up a default fund are treated for capital adequacy purposes in a similar fashion to actual default fund deposits.[54]

---

50 CR Regulation as proposed, art 299
51 ISDA et al, Response to Consultative Document BCBS 206 (November 2011), http://www.bis.org/publ/bcbs206/isdaiifgfma.pdf
52 BCBS 206, para 23
53 BCBS 206, p 16, proposed Basel Framework text para 116(ii)
54 CR Regulation as proposed, art 298(4)

(2) *Equities CCPs.* The 2% risk weighting does not apply to equities exposures. Accordingly, as regards counterparty risk capital requirements, clearing members will be obliged to calculate their exposures to CCPs as if they were exposures to ordinary banks or corporates, as the case may be. The position as regards default fund contributions to equities CCPs appears to be the same, as the CR Regulation does not make any specific provision for this case.

(3) *Variation margin.* The correct treatment of variation margin is less obvious than might be desirable. OTC derivatives specialists may regard variation margin as a posting of collateral; an alternative analysis is that variation margin is a daily settlement of gains or losses which have accrued since the last exchange of variation margin.[55] If the former analysis were correct, exposures of clearing members to CCPs would need to include all cash variation margin posted on open contracts as well as any net gains (for which variation margin has not yet been paid to the clearing member) and initial margin. The latter (settlement) analysis will be correct if the rules of the CCP provide for daily replacement of the clearing member's contract by a new contract at an opening price which reflects the settlement of the gain or loss since the previous day.[56]

(4) *Netting.* One consequence of the application to clearing members of the ordinary rules for calculating the size of trading exposures to a CCP is that the ordinary rules about netting will apply. Exposures under portfolios of financial derivatives, repos or futures can be aggregated and the accrued but unrealised gains on in-the-money trades offset by accrued but unrealised losses on out-of-the-money trades only if there is a contractual netting agreement complying with various strictures, including that it is supported by a reasoned legal opinion.[57] For clearing members to avail themselves of a regulatory capital treatment based on their net portfolio (rather than the gross unrealised profit on in-the-money trades), it will be necessary for the CCP's rules or membership agreement to contain a legally robust close-out netting clause. Such clauses exist in the rules of some CCPs.[58]

(5) *Large exposures.* Clearing members may have large exposures to CCPs because of the size of their cleared portfolios (likely leaving the clearing member with a net deposit of margin at the CCP) and their default fund contributions. The ordinary rules for limiting large exposures are disapplied in relation to trade exposures and default fund contributions to a CCP.[59]

(6) *Transfer (portability) of client trade portfolios.* The concept of portability of a client's portfolio of transactions to a new clearing member in the event of failure of the client's first clearing member is designed to protect the client from the consequences of default of the clearing member, and will not affect the clearing member's credit exposure to the CCP, or indeed its obligations.[60] Portability may, however, help the client; and the client may therefore consider itself substantially shielded from credit exposure to the

---

55 See further **section 14.24**

56 Cf LCH.Clearnet Limited, *General Regulations* (December 2011), reg 15(b)

57 Banking Directive, Annex III Part 7 para (b)(ii)

58 For example LCH.Clearnet Limited, *General Regulations* (December 2011), reg 39A; Eurex Clearing AG, *Clearing Conditions* (December 2011), Number 9; see **section 17.7(6)**

59 CR Regulation as proposed, art 389(1)(j)

60 See further **sections 14.47ff**

clearing member, and thus regard the credit obligation as that of the CCP. The CR Regulation allows the client to treat its CCP-related transactions for capital purposes as if it were a clearing member exposed to the CCP, provided that two conditions are fulfilled: (a) the client's clearing member must give 'individual client segregation', and (b) the legal and contractual arrangements must facilitate transfer of the client's positions and margin to another clearing member on the original clearing member's default.[61] Provided that the CCP's procedures for transfer are unconditional, and the transferee's offer to receive transferred positions is also unconditional, the requirement to 'ensure' that transfer occurs may be satisfied.

19.13   Three further comments might also be made, in that clearing members must consider their credit exposure to their clients as well as their position vis-à-vis the CCP. First, the portfolio of transactions which the clearing member has with the client may represent a credit exposure to the client, if the client's transactions are out-of-the-money for the client and the clearing member has not obtained collateral to cover them. Clearing members will usually wish to comply with the requirements for netting in order to minimise the amount of effective exposure relevant to computation of regulatory capital requirements. Secondly, collateral posted by the client may serve to mitigate any net credit exposure, assuming it is cash or securities. Securities collateral, and cash collateral constituting a deposit should pose no problems, but if the clearing member is subject to the obligation to segregate client money there may be a question as to whether cash is available to the clearing member in the event of the client's default (rather than vice versa).[62] Thirdly, a clearing member will wish to consider the implications of making available a liquidity facility to its client to enable the client to comply with margin calls. Where the margin has been lent to the client, there is evidently a credit exposure; where the clearing member has simply made available a facility, the prudential treatment will be that of a liquidity facility, as discussed above in relation to settlement services.

---

61   CR Regulation, art 296(5)
62   Cf **section 9.15**

20 Dividends, Corporate Actions and Voting Rights

RELATIONSHIP OF STATIC OWNERSHIP TO CLEARING AND SETTLEMENT

20.1   At the outset of this chapter it is appropriate to explain why it exists at all. The subject of clearing and settlement is, above all, concerned with the transfer of interests in securities which is the very essence of trading. Once the clearing and settlement process is completed, the investor may enjoy the investment that has been acquired, which will entail not just the right and ability to dispose of that thing, but in the meantime to receive income as payable on the securities acquired, to participate in corporate actions, and (where the securities acquired include this right) to vote on the affairs of the enterprise in which the investment has been made. But these attributes just described are properly classified as the ongoing incidents of a static investment, which will occur regardless of any activity amounting to clearing or settlement. Furthermore, risks associated with corporate action processing do not appear to relate closely to clearing and settlement issues.[1]

Accordingly, Giovannini Barrier No 3 identified differences in national rules relating to corporate actions as one of the obstacles to efficient cross-border clearing and settlement:[2]

> 'National differences in the rules governing corporate actions, e.g. the offering of share options, rights issues etc., can be a barrier to efficient cross-border clearing and settlement. As corporate actions often require a response from the securities owner, national differences in how they are managed may require specialised local knowledge and/or the lodgement of physical documents locally, and so inhibit the centralisation of securities settlement and custody. Particular difficulties in respect of corporate actions arise from the inconsistent treatment of compensation and cash accruals and from the differing practices used to apply the effects of corporate actions to open transactions, e.g. different countries apply different treatments to the payment of a dividend on a security involved in an open transaction.'[3]

---

1   Cf Oxera, *Corporate action processing: what are the risks?* (May 2004) http://www.dtcc.com/downloads/leadership/whitepapers/2004_oxera.pdf
2   See **section 1.26**
3   Giovannini, A, et al, *Cross-Border Clearing and Settlement Arrangements in the European Union* (November 2001), http://ec.europa.eu/internal_market/financial-markets/docs/clearing/first_giovannini_report_en.pdf, p 47

The initiatives to dismantle Barrier 3 have been taken by the industry, rather than through legislation. The Corporate Actions Joint Working Group (CAJWG) have issued a definitive guide to Market Standards for corporate actions processing, covering distributions such as dividends, reorganisations and transaction management.[4] The implementation of the Market Standards is monitored by a Broad Stakeholder Group,[5] which is also working on harmonisation of arrangements for general meetings.

The authority of Prof Giovannini is enough to indicate that the subject of corporate actions (including dividend and voting) is unavoidable in the field of clearing and settlement. In order to understand the relevance it is first necessary to describe the relationship, in terms of timing, between corporate events and the transfer of securities.

DIVIDENDS

20.2   Let us imagine that a company whose equity securities are traded on a stock exchange has announced that a dividend is to be paid shortly. The dividend will be paid to those shareholders whose names appear on the register on a particular date, known as the 'Record Date'. An investor who has completed his acquisition of shares by the Record Date will receive the dividend. An investor who has bought the shares a few days later, so that his transfer is not completed until after the Record Date, will not. The price of the shares will thus be lower for trades which settle after the Record Date. The first date on which the trading price of the shares is reduced to reflect the receipt of dividend by the seller, rather than the buyer, is called the 'Ex Date', as the price is 'ex-dividend' (ex-div); where the price includes the dividend element it is a 'cum-dividend' (cum-div) price.

The relationship between the Ex Date and the Record Date depends on the length of the trading cycle. So, if a market operates on a T+3 cycle, and the company's Record Date is on Friday:

- A trade done on Monday will ordinarily settle on T+3, which is Thursday, and the buyer will receive the dividend, because the registration of the buyer's name will occur before the Record Date.

- A trade done on Tuesday will settle on Friday. Assuming that the company does not close its books on the Record Date until after the completion of all settlement activity, the buyer will again receive the dividend.

- A trade done on Wednesday will settle next Monday, that is after the Record Date, and thus no dividend will be received by the buyer; the seller will receive it instead. So the sale price ought to be lower than Tuesday's price. Wednesday is thus the Ex Date.

The mathematical formula is expressed by the CAWG in the following way: Ex Date precedes Record Date by the settlement cycle minus one business day.[6]

---

4   Corporate Actions Joint Working Group, *Market Standards for Corporate Actions Processing* (November 2009), http://www.afme.eu/WorkArea//DownloadAsset.aspx?id=235
5   Cf Broad Stakeholder Group, *Dismantling Giovannini Barrier 3: The Market Standards for Corporate Actions Processing & General Meetings* (March 2012), 4th Implementation Progress Report, http://www.ecsda.eu/site/uploads/tx_doclibrary/2012_03_BSG_implementation_progress_report.pdf
6   CAWG Market Standards, p 14

Evidently the pricing of securities depends on the reliability of the Ex Date/ Record Date arrangement. If all goes according to this plan, then the clearing and settlement of transactions will remain unaffected by the payment of the dividend. But things do not always run according to this plan, and when they do not the providers of clearing and settlement services will become involved in the reconciliation and adjustment process. This is the main reason for a chapter on corporate actions appearing in a book on clearing and settlement.

MISMATCHED DATES AND MARKET CLAIMS

20.3   If the seller has sold cum-div but received a dividend, the seller will in effect be paid the dividend twice: first, because it was reflected in the price received for the shares, and secondly, because the seller was the actual recipient of the dividend distributed by the company. A readjustment is needed to restore buyer and seller to the positions which they should have. Such adjustments are referred to as 'market claims'.

Under the Global Corporate Actions Principles issued by the International Securities Services Association (ISSA), the CSD should be the person responsible for generating market claims.[7] 'The CREST Claims Processing Unit identifies cum-dividend transactions which were not settled by record date for the event, and generates claim transactions to move the associated dividend to the entitled CREST participant.'[8] Thus the payment obligations of the unjustly enriched settlement system participant will be increased by the amount of the dividend (or its payment entitlements reduced) when the dividend is distributed, bearing in mind that the actual dividend payment date is typically some days or even weeks after the actual Record Date.

20.4   There are several commonly-encountered situations where an adjustment is needed. The following may be mentioned:

(1) *Settlement fails*. The principal reason why the seller may receive the dividend twice is that the seller was late in settlement – in other words, the settlement failed to be made on time. The subject of fails is explored further in **Chapter 21**.

(2) *Record date anomalies*. In some markets the concept of the Record Date is a relatively recent innovation. The CESAME group's report noted: 'In most countries, there is a *de facto* record date, not always enshrined in the law or explicitly recognised by market practices (e.g. in Germany the "KV-Stichtag", or in Italy a record date which is calculated from the ex-date). Moreover, the record date timing is not always defined as an "end of day date" (eg as in Estonia, Denmark).'[9] With the introduction of real-time gross settlement of securities transfers, there is a risk that the register

---

7   ISSA, *Global Corporate Actions Principles* (May 2010), http://www.issanet.org/pdf/2010_ ISSA_CA_WG_REPORT.pdf, p 10

8   CREST, *Corporate actions standardisation* (November 2004), https://www.euroclear.com/site/ publishedFile/ca-standardisation_tcm87-119710.pdf?title=Corporate+actions+standardisation, p 58

9   CESAME, *The work of the Clearing and Settlement Advisory and Monitoring Experts' Group ('CESAME' group): Solving the industry Giovannini Barriers to post-trading within the EU* (November 2008), http://ec.europa.eu/internal_market/financial-markets/docs/cesame/ cesame_report_en.pdf, p 95

of shareholders used for the purposes of determining dividend entitlement might be struck at the wrong time relative to the completion of settlement cycles on the Record Date. Careful synchronisation of the records used by the company or its paying agent to the settlement cycle is needed.[10]

(3) *Special trading.* Notwithstanding the convention of pricing cum and ex dividend, it is possible to reverse the conventional arrangement with a 'special cum' or 'special ex' price. Evidently these trades expressly contemplate an adjustment between buyer and seller so that the dividend is paid to the other party to the trade than the one showing as holder on the Record Date.

(4) *Securities Lending.* Where an investor lends securities to a market counterparty it is generally not intended that the loan deprives the investor of the income on the securities. A market claim can be generated in order to restore to the lender the dividend paid to the buyer, as holder of record, on the Record Date.[11]

MORE COMPLEX CORPORATE ACTIONS

20.5 The example discussed in the foregoing sections of this chapter related to the simplest and most predictable of corporate events. Other events, such as bonus and rights issues, distributions with a scrip option, share buy-backs, and share splits and other reorganisations all raise similar questions with regard to transfers close to the Record Date. Complex corporate actions can be divided into various subgroups, according to their impact in terms of clearing and settlement.

Mandatory actions

20.6 Securities distributions and transformations fall into this category. Distributions arise when (for example) there is a bonus issue – the investor does nothing, and additional shares are credited to her account. Transformations arise when a security is replaced by a different asset – such as on a share split, or a merger where shares in company A are replaced by shares in company B. The principal issue in relation to these types of corporate action is the same as that on cash distributions: the record date for the corporate action needs to be followed, so that the trading in the security cum-entitlement, or in the old security, ceases on the day one settlement period ahead of the record date. The issues which can give rise to a mismatch of price and asset traded for dividends are thus equally relevant to securities distributions. The recommendations of the CAJWG regarding market claims are neutral as to the nature of the distributed asset.[12]

Securities distributions and transformations have the potential to give rise to fractional entitlements on settlement of the corporate action. If each investor is

---

10 Cf Clearstream Banking Frankfurt, *Removal of Giovannini Barrier 3* (August 2011), http:// www.clearstream.com/ci/dispatch/en/cicbinary/CICDownloads/Clearstream/Market_ Reference/CSD/Compensations_and_Giovannini_Barrier_3/Functional_concept_CBF_-_ Removal_of_Giovannini_Barrier_3/functionalconcept_e.pdf?yawlang=en

11 CREST, *Extending repo facilities in CREST* (July 2003), https://www.euroclear.com/site/ publishedFile/ec-repo-0703_tcm87-119391.pdf?title=Enhancing+CREST+July+2003++Exten ding+repo+facilities+in+CREST, s 7

12 CAJWG Market Standards, p 41

entitled to three new shares for every hundred shares already held, the chances are low that every investor holds an exact multiple of one hundred shares; and the problem is compounded at each level in the holding chain: so a custodian may hold 1,234,567,890 shares, and get 37,037,036 new shares and cash compensation for its entitlement to seven-tenths of a share. But the custodian has 17 clients who have different holdings of the shares, respectively totalling 123,456,789 shares, 98,765,432 shares, etc, and these clients will each need to receive a whole number of new shares and cash compensation. The result is that the custodian will be left with a small number of nuisance shares which cannot be distributed and thus need to be disposed of in order to fund the cash compensation which the custodian needs to provide.[13]

Elective actions

20.7   Elective actions involve the exercise by the investor of some optional right, such as the opportunity to receive extra shares in lieu of dividend. In some circumstances the optional component of the corporate action may be separately tradeable (in the United Kingdom, such a right may be referred to as a 'renounceable' entitlement), and in markets following the CAJWG Market Standards[14] the optional component will be represented by an 'interim security' with its own ISIN.

20.8   Again the principal issue with regard to clearing and settlement is the relationship between the key dates associated with the corporate action. The dates in relation to elective actions are somewhat different from those applicable to a mandatory action such as a distribution. In place of the Record Date, the date of central importance is the 'Market Deadline', after which the CSD of the issuer will no longer accept notice of elections. Working back from the Market Deadline, the last date on which a buyer of the securities can be assured to receive the right to participate in the elective action along with the securities is the 'Guaranteed Participation Date'. Provided that the transaction settles the day before the Market Deadline, the buyer should have time to exercise the election before the Market Deadline expires. But this is brinkmanship, and a more robust procedure is for a buyer to issue a 'Buyer Protection' instruction to the seller, which requires the seller to exercise the election in accordance with the buyer's wishes before settlement. To give time for the seller to act, the cut-off time for a Buyer Protection instruction (the Buyer Protection Deadline) is one business day before the Market Deadline. Hence the Guaranteed Participation Date is one settlement cycle before the Buyer Protection Deadline.[15] A buyer who has contracted to buy the securities on or before the Guaranteed Participation Date can make his own election on settlement, or issue a Buyer Protection instruction before the Buyer Protection Deadline and have the seller do it for him. If the seller fails to deliver the securities in a timely fashion, there is a risk that a buyer who did not issue a Buyer Protection instruction could lose the benefit of his desired election. The CAJWG Market Standards do not make allowance for a market claim in these cases, presumably because the Buyer Protection machinery[16] ought to be adequate to avoid loss or disappointment.

---

13   Cf CAJWG Market Standards, p 19
14   CAJWG Market Standards, p 23
15   CAJWG Market Standards, pp 27, 37
16   Cf CAJWG Market Standards, pp 45–6

20.9   Where securities transactions are cleared through a CCP, immediately after the trade date a buyer's counterparty will be the CCP. A CCP is therefore likely to receive a number of Buyer Protection instructions which will need to be allocated among its various selling participants. LCH.Clearnet Limited addresses the issue as follows: 'Allocation Notices are created using the Allocation Algorithm that matches Buying Members with Selling Members in the following order: (1) an outstanding settlement obligation of equal size; then (2) an outstanding settlement obligation of greater size; and (3) an outstanding settlement obligation of greatest size (i.e. the largest available if the largest available is smaller than the elected position).'[17] It may also be noted that the EquityClear Procedures of LCH.Clearnet Limited require a clearing member which has issued a Buyer Election Notice to indemnify the CCP in respect of losses suffered by the CCP as a result of any breach of the terms and conditions of the relevant corporate action.[18]

20.10 Reciprocal actions occur when the investor, as well as the issuer, is required to act in order to give effect to the action. Examples are rights issues, and their converse, tender offers. Reciprocal actions involve the added complication for custodians of gathering in the payment required by their clients who elect to participate in the action, but do not otherwise appear to raise any additional issues.

VOTING

20.11 Voting by shareholders of a company is a subject which gives rise to a good deal of comment. The principal area of concern is 'empty voting', by which is meant the separation of the investment interests of the long-term shareholder from the person who is entitled to exercise the voting rights attributable to the share. Empty voting may occur as a result of several types of economic activity:

(1) The record date applicable to the vote may be different from the general meeting at which the vote is taken, and different again from the date on which shareholders are sent voting papers. There was, in 2011, no harmonised law on this subject in the European Union; such law as there is is described below. Shares may be traded during the period between the announcement of the vote and the taking of the vote; in particular, they may be sold between the record date and the date of the vote, meaning that those who voted may not have any continuing interest in the issuer.

(2) Securities may be lent. A securities loan transfers title to the borrower.[19] One potential result is that the borrower does not vote at all, because the borrower has no long-term interest in the fate of the issuer; another is that the loan was taken out with the intention of conferring the voting rights on the borrower. It is open to the parties to agree that the lender should be able to direct the borrower to exercise voting rights in a particular way. However, the International Securities Lending Association points out that its 2010 Global Master Securities Lending Agreement includes a

---

17 LCH.Clearnet Limited, *Procedures* (November 2011), Section 2D.15.6.3
18 LCH.Clearnet Limited, *Procedures* (November 2011), Section 2D.15.3.4
19 See **section 21.2**

borrower's warranty that each loan is not being entered into for the primary purpose of obtaining or exercising voting rights, and that its Securities Borrowing and Lending Code of Guidance states that there is consensus that securities should not be borrowed for voting purposes.[20]

The European Commission consulted on the possible discouragement of borrowing in order to obtain voting rights in 2007,[21] and ESMA called for evidence on the subject again in 2011.[22] The results were mixed.[23]

One further issue arises in relation to securities loans: the risk of operational error, where a custodian is mistaken about the voting entitlement in relation to the securities, and records the vote of the wrong party to the loan, or even records the votes of both parties ('over-voting'). While over-voting has attracted regulatory attention in the United States,[24] it appears not to have been under the spotlight in Europe.

(3) Derivatives transactions may be entered into which confer an economic interest without granting any voting rights. A short position in a derivative may be hedged with a long position in the physical instrument, for which the hedger has no particular interest in exercising voting rights.

20.12   The problem is complex as, until electronic voting methodologies gain widespread currency, the practical effort required to distribute and collect voting papers necessitates a time gap to complete the steps between the announcement of a vote and the taking of the count: the despatch to ultimate investors and receipt by them of voting papers, due time for investors to consider the issues and return their completed voting papers, and the validation and counting of votes. These processes depend on traditional communication methods, whereas share trading takes place in fractions of a second, and settlement is within not more than three business days of trade. The anomalies which arise can include the following:

- an investor may send back physical voting papers, but have sold his shares before the record date, giving rise to reconciliation issues for the registrar or other person responsible for vote counting.

---

20 International Securities Lending Association, *ISLA's Response to ESMA's Call for Evidence on Empty Voting* (November 2011), http://www.esma.europa.eu/system/files/ISLA_Response_to_ESMA_Call_for_Evidence_on_Empty_Voting_Nov_11.pdf

21 European Commission, *Fostering an Appropriate Regime for Shareholders' Rights, Third consultation document of the Services of the Directorate General Internal Market and Services* (April 2007), http://ec.europa.eu/internal_market/company/docs/shareholders/consultation3_en.pdf

22 European Securities and Markets Authority, *Call for evidence – Empty voting* (September 2011), http://www.esma.europa.eu/system/files/2011_288.pdf

23 European Commission, *Synthesis of the Comments on the Third Consultation Document of the Internal Market and Services Directorate-General 'Fostering an Appropriate Regime for Shareholders' Rights'* (September 2007), http://ec.europa.eu/internal_market/company/docs/shareholders/consultation3_report_en.pdf;   http://www.esma.europa.eu/consultation/Call-evidence-Empty-voting#responses

24 NYSE Euronext, *NYSE Regulation Fines Deutsche Bank Securities $1 Million for Failure to Supervise Handling of Customer Proxies* (February 2006), Press Release, http://www.nyse.com/press/1139915694987.html; *NYSE Regulation, Inc. Fines UBS Securities, Goldman Sachs Execution & Clearing, and Credit Suisse Securities (USA) $1.35 Million for Proxy-Handling Violations in Corporate Elections* (June 2006), Press Release, http://www.nyse.com/press/1150107128723.html

- an investor may vote on shares which she has disposed of after the record date but before the general meeting at which the vote is taken; and there is no general system for a 'market claim' by the purchaser of the shares in such a case.

- an investor may acquire shares before the record date and yet fail to receive voting papers, including in cases where the settlement cycle had completed before the record date.

- an investor may not receive voting papers with adequate time to act, or even at all, because the chain of intermediaries is too extenuated, and the challenge of reproducing papers, distribution and translation, and giving time for postage, collection, collation and reporting to the next intermediary in the chain is too difficult to overcome.

20.13   The legal rules which exist to mitigate empty voting, and to reduce the anomalies mentioned above, are few and relatively unsuccessful.

(1) The Shareholders Voting Rights Directive (SVRD)[25] aimed to eradicate 'blocking': that is, shareholders are not to have their right to sell or transfer their shares between the record date and the general meeting restricted.[26] Issuers are required to allow at least 8 days between the convocation of a general meeting and the record date, to set the record date to occur not more than 30 days before the general meeting,[27] and to allow at least 21 days between convocation and the meeting.[28] These timings are variable between Member States,[29] and the CESAME group noted that the SVRD 'did not solve the discussion around a long or short period between record date and date of the general meeting; a long period has the benefit of giving time to intermediaries to process information but the disadvantage of an increased likelihood that the person voting will not be a shareholder by the time the meeting takes place thus requiring many updates of communications; the opposite applies regarding a short period.'[30] The Expert Group on Market Infrastructures considers that a revision of the SVRD is needed to provide for 'operationally feasible' record dates to allow cross-border participation in general meetings.[31]

(2) The SVRD does not deal fully with the blocking of securities for voting purposes. In the fixed income markets, which the SVRD does not address, the practice of 'blocking' is still prevalent. Securities are 'blocked' in preparation for a vote by causing their transferability to be suspended, so that there is identity of voting and ownership interests (but, of course, neither necessarily corresponds to long-term economic interest).[32]

---

25 Directive 2007/36/EC of the European Parliament and of the Council of 11 July 2007 on the exercise of certain rights of shareholders in listed companies
26 SVRD, art 7(2)
27 SVRD, art 7(3)
28 SVRD, art 5(1)
29 European Commission, *List of days provided for according to Article 15 of Directive 2007/36/ EC* (October 2010), OJ C 285/1
30 CESAME group report, p 95
31 Expert Group on Market Infrastructures, *Report* (October 2011), http://ec.europa.eu/internal_market/financial-markets/docs/clearing/egmi/101011_report_en.pdf
32 See Euroclear Bank, *The Operating Procedures of the Euroclear System* (October 2011), https://www.euroclear.com/site/publishedFile/LG001_tcm86-124206.pdf?title=The+Operating+Procedures+of+the+Euroclear+System, s 9

(3) The Transparency Directive[33]requires that shareholders must notify the issuer of the proportion of voting rights they hold where the proportion reaches, exceeds or falls below certain thresholds.[34] The notification requirement applies in a wide variety of circumstances where a transaction involves something other than a simple transfer, including temporary transfer, collateral arrangements, and custody arrangements where the custodian is given voting discretion.[35] It may be considered regrettable that the Transparency Directive uses a different definition of 'shareholder' from the SVRD, but in both cases there is a question, likely to be answered differently in different Member States until the harmonisation of law regarding securities held in accounts, as to whether the ultimate investor or the actual registered nominee should be treated as the shareholder.

(4) If a Securities Law Directive is proceeded with in line with the European Commission Services' 2010 outline,[36] various enhancements to voting rights would be conferred on 'ultimate account holders' (end-investors). These would include an entitlement to receive, without undue delay, information necessary to exercise rights attached to securities, and various entitlements designed to enable the ultimate account holder actually to exercise those rights.[37] In this context, it may be noted that the European Commission's Legal Certainty Group noted that the absence of harmonised rules over when, and whether, an indirect investor in securities becomes the 'owner' of the securities inhibits effective cross-border exercise of voting rights.[38]

---

33 Directive 2004/109/EC of the European Parliament and of the Council of 15 December 2004 on the harmonisation of transparency requirements in relation to information about issuers, etc
34 Transparency Directive, art 9(1)
35 Transparency Directive, art 10
36 European Commission Services, *Legislation on legal certainty of securities holding and dispositions* (November 2010), DG Markt G2 MET/OT/acg D(2010) 768690, http://ec.europa. eu/internal_market/consultations/docs/2010/securities/consultation_paper_en.pdf
37 Principles 16 and 17
38 Wacławik-Wejman, A, *Legal Certainty Group – Report on Core Issues: Part 3 – Corporate Actions and Voting Rights* (March 2006), http://ec.europa.eu/internal_market/financial-markets/docs/certainty/background/28_3_6_waclawik_en.pdf

21 Securities lending

IMPORTANCE OF SECURITIES LENDING

21.1 Securities lending plays a vital role in clearing and settlement. The ability to 'lend' securities, so that they can be put to use where they are needed, ensures that long-term investors can retain the benefits of their investment while short-term needs of market participants are also catered for. Short-term needs include coverage of delivery obligations to settle trades or meet collateral calls, where insufficient stock is available or a transaction counterparty is late in settling its own obligations, hedging, and investment plays which do not envisage a long-term exposure to the investment.[1]

FUNDAMENTAL CONCEPTS

Ownership of lent securities

21.2 At the heart of securities lending in Europe is the fact that the word 'loan' is a misnomer. A securities loan requires the outright transfer of ownership of the securities being 'lent'.[2] The 'borrower' is free to treat the securities in the same way as any other securities in its absolute ownership, and so the borrower can sell, pledge, redeem or otherwise dispose of them. The borrower's obligation at the end of the loan is to transfer back to the lender 'equivalent' securities; if the borrower has disposed of the securities originally lent, then the borrower must obtain the equivalent securities in the market in order to satisfy its re-delivery obligation.

The second fundamental concept relating to securities lending flows from the first. Because the loan involves an outright transfer of title to the securities, the lender has replaced its ownership of a security with a personal (ie, a non-proprietary) claim on the borrower for the duration of the loan. The lender accordingly has a credit exposure on the borrower, since the borrower may at the return date be unable to satisfy its obligation to deliver equivalent securities. Note that, even if the borrower has retained the securities, they belong outright to the borrower, so that if the borrower is insolvent at the return date, the lender cannot claim the securities for itself: they belong to the insolvent estate of the borrower and the lender's claim is for a dividend based on the value of the securities which will no longer be returned. In consequence, the lender will

---

1 Cf Faulkner, M, *An Introduction to Securities Lending* (March 2004), http://www. bankofengland.co.uk/markets/gilts/securitieslending.pdf, ch 3
2 GMSLA 2010, paras 2.3 and 4.2; GMRA 2011, paras 6(e) and (f)

ordinarily take collateral from the borrower, either in the form of cash, or other securities for which the borrower has no current need.

Fees, rates and rebates

21.3   The lender will expect to be paid a lending fee.

Where the lender accepts only cash collateral, it may be convenient to document the securities loan as a repo (sale-and-repurchase) transaction. A repo is typically a form of secured financing under which the borrower of cash puts up securities as collateral on a title-transfer basis, and pays a 'repo rate' which is a species of interest payment to the lender of cash. In the securities lending world, the 'lender' is the lender of securities and the 'borrower' is the borrower of securities; repo terminology dubs the securities lender the 'seller' and the securities borrower the 'buyer' under the notion of sale followed by repurchase.

The desire of the lender to receive a lending fee, and the desire of the cash provider to receive a repo rate, create between them a tension which has implications for securities clearing and settlement. Where the cash provider's desire for specific securities is high, the repo rate which the cash provider is willing to receive may be reduced. A reduced repo rate is typically referred to as a 'specials' rate, referring to the 'special' securities which are the subject of the repo, and contrasting with the (higher) general-collateral rate. In times of low interest rates, the specials rate payable may be very low, even negative. At other times the interest due to the securities borrower will apply as a rebate to the lending fee otherwise expected by the securities lender. Some implications of this tension in relation to fails are explored further below.

Documentation

21.4   Market standard documentation for securities loans and repos is similar to the master agreement structure for derivatives transactions. Securities loans may be documented in a number of ways; since 2011 the Bank of England's Securities Lending and Repo Committee (SLRC) directs interested persons to the 2010 edition of the Global Master Securities Lending Agreement (GMSLA 2010)[3] for securities lending and the 2011 edition of the Global Master Repurchase Agreement (GMRA 2011).[4] As well as the expected clauses dealing with delivery of securities, payment of a rate, return of equivalent securities, and title transfer, both types of market standard documentation also contains the following important provisions:

- Clauses dealing with collateral: delivery of collateral, marking to market, return to the collateral provider of surplus collateral, and substitution.[5]

- Clauses dealing with the effects of insolvency and other events of default by either party. In brief, the non-defaulting party will be given the option to 'close out' the outstanding transactions, in other words to treat the

---

3   International Securities Lending Association, *Global Master Securities Lending Agreement* (January 2010), http://www.isla.co.uk/uploadedFiles/Member_Area/General_Library/ GMSLA%202010%20Final%281%29.pdf

4   Securities Industry and Financial Markets Association and International Capital Market Association, *Global Master Repurchase Agreement, 2011 version* (April 2011), http://www. icmagroup.org/ICMAGroup/files/d0/d0875d90-e4cb-4213-b8d7-4c2c4e7a0bea.pdf

5   GMSLA 2010 para 5; GMRA 2011 paras 4, 8

obligations to deliver equivalent securities, and return equivalent collateral, as accelerated so that they are immediately performable; and, if the obligations of the defaulting party are not performed, the obligations of both parties will each be ascribed a 'default market value' which is payable in money. The default market values are aggregated and set off, to result in a net money amount due one way or the other.[6]

- Clauses dealing with income on the securities lent and collateral.[7] The transferee of the loaned securities or collateral will be the absolute owner and therefore entitled to receive and keep the income; to adjust the position back to the desired economic position of the parties, they are expected to 'manufacture' income payments which are made between them. The documentation also contains provisions dealing with the tax treatment of these manufactured payments.[8]

21.5   One aspect of the documentation which receives little emphasis is the impact of corporate actions which apply to loaned securities. It is a consequence of the absolute transfer of title to the borrower that the borrower may not hold the loaned securities at the time of a corporate event, and furthermore it is difficult to ascertain in general terms what the money value of a corporate action other than an income or restructuring event may be. The GMSLA 2010 allows the provider of securities (lender or collateral provider) to give to the other party a notice that 'it wishes to receive Equivalent Securities or Equivalent Collateral in such form as will arise if the right [under the corporate action] is exercised or, in the case of a right which may be exercised in more than one manner, is exercised as is specified in such written notice.'[9] The GMRA 2011 does not address corporate actions at all.

21.6   Each type of documentation[10] allows for the possibility of a lending agent. Agency lending enables a custodian, who holds securities for long-term investors such as pension funds, to identify borrowers with borrowing needs, and to match lending and borrowing interests. Lenders will authorise their custodians to enter into market standard lending documentation on their behalf with approved lists of counterparty borrowers, and authorise them to accept certain types of collateral according to their risk appetite. Agency lending introduces the following features into securities lending:

- The lender will need to enter into an authorisation agreement with the custodian, enabling the custodian to effect and administer the loans. The agreement may go further, and permit the custodian to reinvest cash collateral received (for example, by entering into repos) in order to recoup, and possibly exceed, the interest paid to the securities borrower.

- The agent/custodian will have authorisation agreements with lenders, each enabling the entry into securities loans with certain borrowers. On the other side, the agent/custodian will have GMSLA or other market standard

---

6   GMSLA 2010 paras 10, 11; GMRA 2011 para 10
7   GMSLA 2010, para 6; GMRA 2011, para 5
8   GMSLA 2010, paras 6.3(b), 12; GMRA 2011, paras 6(b), 11
9   GMSLA 2010, para 6.7
10 GMSLA 2010, Agency Annex; The Bond Market Association and International Securities Market Association, *Global Master Repurchase Agreement (2000 Version) Agency Annex* (October 2000), http://www.sifma.org/Services/Standard-Forms-and-Documentation/MRA,-GMRA,-MSLA-and-MSFTAs/GMRA_Agency-Annex-%E2%80%93-Supplemental-Terms-and-Conditions-for-Agency-Transactions/

lending documentation with each borrower, to which a number of lender clients of the custodian are party as principal. The agent/custodian has a pivotal role in sourcing and aggregating the securities lent out to a particular borrower, ascertaining the collateral due from the borrower, and allocating the collateral to the lenders concerned.

● Collateral received from any particular borrower will belong to a group of lenders who have, between them, provided the securities which have been lent. The collateral account of each lender will need adjustment to reflect the changes in value of the lent securities and the collateral received, as well as the differential appetite of the lenders to receive collateral. Accordingly, the agency annexes to market standard lending documentation allows for pooling by the agent of collateral held, and adjustment as between the accounts of its principal lenders, notwithstanding that the collateral is in the ownership of the lenders.

REGULATION OF SECURITIES LENDING

21.7 In addition to the requirements under the general regulatory regime for investment business flowing from MiFID,[11] the SLRC has issued a non-binding Securities Borrowing and Lending Code of Guidance.[12] This discusses matters such as pre-transaction diligence, tax, confidentiality, compliance with MiFID, and risk. The Code also endorses the use of the GMSLA as the lending agreement of choice.

The Short Selling Regulation constrains 'short sales' of shares and sovereign debt instruments.[13] Although repos and securities loans are not treated as short sales,[14] the restrictions on short selling can affect securities lending in two principal ways:

(1) First, an open securities loan may have the effect that a lender who is also an intending seller of securities does not 'own' the securities at the moment of agreeing to the sale, and is therefore technically engaging in a short sale, even if the securities loan can be unwound in time to deliver against the sale contract.

(2) The converse of this position is where a borrower of securities enters into a sale contract relating to the borrowed securities. The Short Selling Regulation regards this type of activity as a short sale, because the borrower will be economically 'short' after delivering against the sale, owing to his obligation to return equivalent securities at the end of the securities loan.[15]

In these two cases, the short-seller will potentially be obliged to report a significant short position in shares or sovereign debt to its regulator and to disclose its position publicly;[16] and the short sale transaction may be completely

---

11 Directive 2004/39/EC of the European Parliament and of the Council of 21 April 2004 on markets in financial instruments, etc
12 SLRC, *Securities Borrower and Lending Code of Guidance* (July 2009), http://www.bankofengland.co.uk/markets/gilts/stockborrowing.pdf
13 Regulation (EU) No 236/2012 of the European Parliament and of the Council of 14 March 2012 on short selling and certain aspects of credit default swaps, art 12
14 Short Selling Regulation, art 2(1)(b)((i) and (ii)
15 Short Selling Regulation, art 2(1)(b)
16 Short Selling Regulation, arts 5–7

forbidden unless the short-seller has borrowed the asset or made alternative provisions such as standby arrangements.[17]

21.8 The following further regulatory matters might also be noted.

(1) Under the Short Selling Regulation, regulators may look into the pricing of securities loans in times of market turmoil.[18]

(2) There have been various probes into 'empty voting' associated with securities lending, as discussed in **section 20.11(2)**.

(3) The Financial Stability Board has drawn attention to the stability implications of lack of transparency in the securities lending and repo markets, which are viewed as part of the 'shadow banking' system.[19] It seems likely that formal measures to improve regulators' ability to see what is happening in the market will follow, as for example happened with the requirement to report derivatives transactions to a trade repository.

FAILS AND SETTLEMENT DISCIPLINE

21.9 Settlement fails are, from a policy perspective, considered to be undesirable. The European Central Bank (ECB) notes that fails may expose transaction counterparties to credit or liquidity risk, and that the fear of fails encourages financial firms to hoard securities with adverse consequences for market liquidity.[20] It could also be mentioned that a fail may have the result that a corporate event is missed by the intended transferee, and the loss suffered for a missed event may be high; it may be that the high operational risk[21] associated with securities services is in part attributed to corporate actions and fails.

In its 2011 consultation relating to CSDs, the European Commission put forward an explanation for the causes of settlement fails:

'Settlement fails can have different causes. Failed communication can occur all along the chain of communication between trade and settlement ... . Other [causes] can be operational failures, such as computer errors or system breakdowns. Most settlement fails occur because of a seller's inability to deliver securities it expected to receive from an unrelated transaction, which can lead to a "daisy chain" of settlement fails. A final reason for fails can derive from a short selling strategy, where a seller sells a security it does not own, and where there are insufficient incentives to avoid a failed settlement by borrowing it to make delivery.'[22]

---

17 Short Selling Regulation, arts 12, 13, 17
18 Short Selling Regulation, art 19
19 Financial Stability Board, *Securities Lending and Repos: Market Overview and Financial Stability Issues* (April 2012), http://www.financialstabilityboard.org/publications/r_120427. pdf, p 14
20 European Central Bank, *Settlement Fails – Report on Securities Settlement Systems (SSS) Measures to Ensure Timely Settlement* (April 2011), http://www.ecb.eu/pub/pdf/other/ settlementfails042011en.pdf
21 Cf **section 19.6**
22 European Commission, *Public consultation on Central Securities Depositories (CSDs) and on the Harmonisation of certain aspects of securities settlement in the European Union* (January 2011), DG Markt G2 D(201)8641, http://ec.europa.eu/internal_market/consultations/ docs/2011/csd/consultation_csd_en.pdf, p 36

21.10 CREST Rule 6[23] enables Euroclear UK & Ireland (EUI) to impose fines and charge interest to sellers and buyers respectively who fail to perform their obligations on time. These rules derive from the statutory obligations of EUI to promote and maintain high standards of integrity and fair dealing in the operation of its system[24] and in the use of its facilities as a recognised clearing house.[25]

Preventing fails

21.11 The ECB puts forward a number of suggestions for reducing fail rates.[26] These include operational improvements such as straight-through-processing and queue management, to speed up settlement; interposing a CCP; improved matching and securities-flow (hold-release) mechanisms; publication of fails data; and of course securities lending.

21.12 Under the proposed CSD Regulation, infrastructures will be obliged to take steps to minimise fails,[27] although the responsibility for upholding settlement discipline in equity markets is shifting towards CCPs. CSDs will need to put in place a fails monitoring system, report to their regulator and 'to any person with a legitimate interest' on fail rates, and establish procedures to facilitate settlement of failed trades (including penalties). Persistent offenders could be suspended from participation in their CSD, CCP, or trading platform, and publicly named and shamed. The proposed CSD Regulation would also mandate a four-day buy-in period for all transferable securities, money-market instruments, fund units and emission allowances traded on regulated markets, MTFs or OTFs, or cleared by a CCP. Buy-in would be effected by the CCP, where involved.

21.13 As part of the policy drive for settlement discipline, article 15 of the Short Selling Regulation also requires CCPs which clear equities transactions to have buy-in procedures to reduce fails coverage. Buy-in procedures must kick in automatically four business days after the due date for settlement of an unsettled trade, and if delivery is still not possible then financial compensation based on the value of the shares at the delivery date, plus losses incurred as a result of the settlement failure, are due to the buyer. Meanwhile the CCP must collect 'daily payments for each day that the failure continues' – which must be sufficiently high to deter fails, thus presumably exceeding margin payments – from the seller. The Short Selling Regulation reflects (but accelerates) buy-in practices in various markets. In 2011 buy-in periods ranged from two days (Hungary) to 35 (United Kingdom and depositary receipts settling in Euroclear Bank) in European markets cleared by EuroCCP.[28] It has been noted, however,

---

23 Euroclear UK & Ireland, *CREST Rules* (June 2011), https://www.euroclear.com/site/ publishedFile/CREST_rules_2011-05-13_tcm87-119514.pdf?title=CREST+Rules
24 Uncertificated Securities Regulations 2001 (SI 2001 No 3755), Sch 1, para 3
25 Financial Services and Markets Act 2000 (Recognition Requirements for Investment Exchanges and Clearing Houses) Regulations 2001, (SI 2001 No 995), Schedule, para 20
26 ECB paper, Box 1, p 5
27 European Commission, *Proposal for a Regulation of the European Parliament and of the Council on improving securities settlement in the European Union and on central securities depositories etc* (March 2012), COM(2012) 73 final, http://eur-lex.europa.eu/LexUriServ/ LexUriServ.do?uri=CELEX:52012PC0073:EN:PDF, art 7
28 European Central Counterparty Limited, *Procedures* (October 2011), http://www.euroccp. co.uk/docs/EuroCCP_Proc.pdf, Procedure II, EuroCCP Buy-in Schedule

that mandating buy-in is not necessarily appropriate for all types of financial instrument, notably debt securities where there are no corporate events.[29]

21.14 A delivery failure may have risk implications for a CCP. First, the CCP will be unable to fulfil all its delivery obligations to buying participants without borrowing. Secondly, the CCP may be left with a net long position in a security if it is not possible to deliver out all the securities received: for example if participant X has failed to deliver 50 shares, but participant Y has fulfilled its obligation to deliver 50 shares, the CCP will be unable to satisfy its obligation to deliver 100 shares to participant Z. The rules of the CCP and of the market may not allow for partial settlement, or the apportionment of a shortfall may require re-matching of settlement instructions by the affected buying participants, which might not be achievable in the time available. If a CCP is left with a net holding of shares for a day or two there may be corporate actions requiring intervention, expenditure and potentially liability for the CCP. The CCP may adopt 'splitting' or 'shaping' rules to facilitate disposal of shares which are actually delivered.[30]

21.15 Securities lending has a key role to play in management of failed settlements. If a seller can borrow securities in order to fulfil a delivery obligation, a fail can be averted. However, there is a risk of perverse results when interest rates are very low, as the European Repo Council of the International Capital Market Association explains:

'When interest rates fall to low levels, the economic incentives to remedy delivery failures that are created by the generally-accepted market convention are weakened. If repo rates fall to negative levels, the convention can even produce perverse results. A negative repo rate means that the repo seller (cash borrower) is paid by the repo buyer (cash lender). Therefore, if a repo seller fails at the start of a repo, it is the repo buyer who would have to pay the repo rate and who would be penalised, even though it is the repo seller who has failed. This could encourage repo sellers to enter repo transactions with no intention to deliver, in order to profit from a negative rate (a so-called "strategic fail").'[31]

Although the European Repo Council indicated that 'such abusive behaviour has not been reported in the European Market,'[32] it was recommended that a repo seller (securities lender) who fails to deliver in respect of a repo with a negative repo rate should suffer a readjustment of the repo rate to zero or termination of the transaction by the buyer (borrower).

---

29 European Repo Council, *A white paper on the operation of the European repo market, the role of short-selling, the problem of settlement failures and the need for reform of the market infrastructure* (July 2010), http://icmagroup.org/ICMAGroup/files/ac/ac9739eb-6c8b-4d0f-9f5c-d0f13e89bd8e.pdf, p 27

30 Cf LCH.Clearnet Limited, *Procedures* (October 2011), http://www.lchclearnet.com/Images/Section%202D%20-%20EquityClear_tcm6-43745.pdf, Sections 2D.11.4–5

31 European Repo Council white paper, para 6.21

32 Cf, for the US position, Fleming, M and Garbade, K, 'Explaining Settlement Fails' (September 2005) Federal Reserve Bank of New York Current Issues in Economics and Finance, Vol 11, No 9, http://www.newyorkfed.org/research/current_issues/ci11-9.pdf

CLEARING OF SECURITIES LOANS

21.16 A further market development which has been proposed in relation to securities lending is the potential for a CCP to clear securities loans. LCH.Clearnet Limited has operated a repo clearing service since 1999, and SecFinex has provided a securities lending platform cleared by LCH.Clearnet SA and SIX x-clear since 2009. Given that securities lending is typically a fully-collateralised activity (unlike, say, OTC trading of securities) the policy rationale behind a move towards clearing of securities loans may be unclear; the Bank of England has pointed to enhanced transparency,[33] but a CCP is a sledgehammer to crack that particular type of nut.

The International Securities Lending Association (ISLA) found arguments on both sides of the question of desirability of a CCP for securities loans.[34] ISLA's report noted that securities lending is a two-sided market, so that typical lenders are hardly ever borrowers, and that would mean 'opportunities for position netting are low.' Also, ISLA point out that the characteristics of the counterparty, as opposed to the transaction, dictate terms of securities loans: factors such as likelihood of recall of lent securities and tax rates on manufactured dividends are relevant. CCPs eliminate counterparty issues and call margin based on product characteristics; how in practice issues such as tax would be addressed in a cleared environment is not self-evident.

On the other hand, it has been argued that 'proposed regulatory changes have made inevitable the broad adoption of CCPs in securities lending. Notably, proposed changes to capital adequacy guidelines in Basel III would present significant challenges to the existing securities lending business model and would inhibit growth in the industry.'[35] Unlike practice in the uncleared marketplace, where a CCP acts as counterparty the CCP traditionally receives collateral but does not provide it. If this approach were adopted for securities loans, a lender of securities on a cleared loan would no longer receive cash or securities collateral; the borrower, on the other hand, would be expected to provide it. However, for cleared securities loans the cash collateral for the loan (referred to as 'principal collateral') is provided by the borrower as usual and transferred all the way through the CCP to the lender. The principal collateral is treated in the same way as the cash leg on a repo, and the CCP's margining role is then restricted to the variation margin calculation as the respective values of lent securities and collateral provided move with the market. In this model both borrower and lender are liable for margin calls.

33 Tucker, P, *Shadow Banking, Financing Markets and Financial Stability* (January 2010), Speech, http://www.bankofengland.co.uk/publications/speeches/2010/speech420.pdf, p 8

34 International Securities Lending Association, *A Central Counterparty in the European Equity Securities Lending Market? Initial Report of an ISLA Working Group* (May 2009), http://www.isla.co.uk/uploadedFiles/Member_Area/General_Library/CCPISLA.pdf

35 Howieson, A, and Zimmerhansl, R, *Good, Bad or Inevitable? The Introduction of CCPs in Securities Lending* (2010), White Paper, http://www.secfinex.com/assets/Documents/CCPGoodBadInevitable.pdf?1315820205

22 Tax

SCOPE OF DISCUSSION RELATING TO TAX

22.1 Taxation touches our lives in inescapable ways, and it is desirable not simply to dismiss the subject of tax, for two main reasons.

In the first place, the different approaches of Member States to tax issues arising in connection with clearing and settlement are responsible for two of the Giovannini barriers.[1] Giovannini Barrier 11 cited a number of difficulties relating to withholding tax: different approaches to granting relief; and restrictions on which intermediaries are permitted to grant at-source relief, in particular by requiring a local person to carry out or intermediate in this role. Efforts to dismantle this barrier have been made, as further discussed below. The other Giovannini tax barrier (Barrier 12) relates to the role of infrastructures in collection of transaction taxes. Progress in dismantling this particular barrier is less demonstrable; worse, the notion of co-opting clearing and settlement service providers into the fiscal reporting and collection system has expanded. This is the second major reason for a discussion of tax issues.

The two Giovannini tax barriers were studied by the European Commission's Fiscal Compliance Experts Group (FISCO) which produced two reports,[2] leading to a Commission Recommendation on Withholding Tax Relief Procedures.[3] The FISCO reports do not purport to cover all taxation issues relative to clearing and settlement, and are limited in what they propose as solutions. In particular, FISCO's terms of reference[4] did not extend to recommending the abolition of taxes, which reflects a European political reality. In truth, the disharmony in Europe over taxation issues extends well into the field of clearing and settlement, with the inevitable consequence that cross-border investment is complicated and made more expensive owing to differences in the incidence of taxation as well as differences in the procedures for collection and allocation of reliefs. In its examination of the Giovannini barriers, FISCO reported that some (but by no means all) Member State rules relating to withholding tax collection and relief procedures were attributable to

---

1 See **sections 1.26ff**
2 FISCO, *Fact-finding study on Fiscal Compliance Procedures related to Clearing and Settlement within the EU* (April 2006), http://ec.europa.eu/internal_market/financial-markets/docs/compliance/ff_study_en.pdf; FISCO, *Solutions to Fiscal Compliance Barriers Related to Post-trading within the EU* (October 2007), http://ec.europa.eu/internal_market/financial-markets/docs/compliance/report_en.pdf
3 Commission Recommendation of 19 October 2009 on withholding tax relief procedures, COM(2009) 7924 final
4 European Commission, *Mandate for the EU Clearing and Settlement – Fiscal Compliance Experts' Working Group* (April 2005), http://ec.europa.eu/internal_market/financial-markets/docs/compliance/mandate_en.pdf

490

substantive withholding tax rules; and that 11 out of 27 Member States levied transaction taxes on securities transfers, and in a few of the 11 responsibility for collection was in the hands of settlement service providers.[5] Furthermore, FISCO only dipped its toe into the water as regards tax issues not highlighted by Giovannini, so capital gains tax gets only a passing mention.[6]

Both providers of clearing and settlement services and their clients will typically be liable for direct taxes on profits derived from their everyday activities. The tax issues which arise from these ordinary activities, which do not specifically relate to clearing and settlement, are, however, outside the scope of this work.

TAXES

22.2   At the outset one might conveniently seek to identify the taxes which providers of clearing and settlement services might encounter in the course of their intermediation activity. Taxes which one might regard as commonly relevant to clearing and settlement services include the following:

(1) *SDRT and stamp duty*. United Kingdom stamp duty[7] is payable on certain kinds of 'instrument'.[8] These include transfers on sale of property such as securities, and in some cases agreements to transfer. Given that securities can be transferred without either a written agreement or a written instrument of transfer, a more likely transfer tax in the United Kingdom will be stamp duty reserve tax (SDRT), which is payable in respect of agreements to transfer chargeable securities.[9] SDRT at 0.5% of the consideration is usually due from the person who agreed the purchase of chargeable securities for cash (ie, in most cases, the transferee's broker). There is a complex array of exemptions, in respect of securities, transfer types, and transferees. There is also a set of statutory instruments which disapply stamp duty and SDRT in relation to transfers to and from a CCP, to avoid the consequence that multiple transfers would occur by virtue of the chain of principal-to-principal deliveries (including the added problem of interoperability between CCPs, which involve an extra inter-CCP transfer).[10] Thus, provided that the CCP in question is covered by one of the statutory instruments, only one payment of tax is required in respect of cleared transactions. Rather splendidly, section 110(1) of the Finance Act 1990 abolished SDRT, but the 'abolition date' has not yet been set by HM Treasury.[11]

(2) *VAT*. VAT is payable by the supplier on a taxable supply of goods and services. Most financial services are exempt: in particular the transfer

---

5   FISCO Fact-finding study, pp 31, 46

6   FISCO Fact-finding study, p 22

7   Cf description in the FISCO Fact-finding study (April 2006), p 38ff; for a comprehensive essay see also Yates, M, and Montagu, G, *The Law of Global Custody* (3rd Edition, Tottel, January 2009), ISBN 978 1 84766 142 5, ch 10

8   Stamp Act 1891, s 14; Finance Act 1999, Sch 13

9   Finance Act 1986, s 87

10   Stamp Duty and Stamp Duty Reserve Tax ([CCP name]) Regulations 2011: Eurex Clearing AG, SI 2011 No.666; European Central Counterparty Ltd, SI 2011 No 667; European Multilateral Clearing Facility NV, SI 2011 No. 668; LCH.Clearnet Ltd, SI 2011 No 669; SIX x-clear AG, SI 2011 No 670; Cassa di Compensazione e Garanzia SpA, SI 2011 No 2205

11   Finance Act 1990, s 111

or receipt of money and the transfer or receipt of securities.[12] However, some services provided in connection with back-office activities may fall outside these exemptions. Notably, supply of SWIFT electronic messaging facilities for funds transfers is not an exempt financial service.[13]

(3) *Capital Gains Tax.* Clients may be liable for capital taxes due in respect of gains made when the capital value of assets disposed of has increased since the acquisition of the asset.[14] Giovannini noted that some countries' capital gains tax regimes imposed collection or reporting obligations on intermediaries: 'Examples of such difficulties include (i) a national requirement for computation of capital gains tax at the time of settlement for individual transactions, imposing a costly administrative burden on foreign operators in an environment where securities are held through multiple tiers of custodians, central securities depositories and other financial intermediaries; and (ii) the imposition of a minimum custody period on certain securities, which are then heavily taxed if this obligation is breached.'[15] FISCO found that in Hungary, Italy and Spain tax legislation required capital gains tax to be applied at source in relation to securities transactions,[16] but FISCO's mandate did not extend to recommendations to modifying the way in which these taxes are collected.

(4) *Withholding taxes.* Tax authorities in the country where a security is issued will typically require a deduction to be made from any payment of income in respect of the security. To make things complicated, some Member States levy withholding tax on fixed income securities at the moment of transfer, deeming the income to have accrued daily (*pro rata temporis*).[17] The investor in that security may also suffer a tax charge in respect of the same income payment in the investor's own country. To avoid double taxation, some countries have agreed to allow investors relief, or partial relief from withholding tax. Withholding tax relief may be given at source (resulting in a lower deduction) or may have to be claimed in arrears by the investor. The consequence of these rules is that the amount of withholding tax deductible will depend on the withholding tax policy of the country of issue and the country of tax residence of the investor. (Useful tables of reliefs under double taxation treaties are set out in a European Commission Staff Working Document.[18]) All of the above would appear to be of limited relevance to clearing and settlement, apart from two considerations. First, as pointed out in discussions on the Giovannini barriers,[19] impediments to the static holding of securities have an insidious effect on cross-border investment and thereby indirectly raise the costs of clearing and settlement. Secondly, adjustments in the form of 'market claims' need to be made when

---

12 Value Added Tax Act 1994, Sch 9
13 *Nordea Pankki Suomi (Taxation)* [2011] EU ECJ C-350/10
14 In the United Kingdom, under the Taxation of Chargeable Gains Act 1992
15 Giovannini, A, et al, *Cross-Border Clearing and Settlement Arrangements in the European Union* (November 2001), http://ec.europa.eu/internal_market/financial-markets/docs/clearing/first_giovannini_report_en.pdf, p 53
16 FISCO Fact-finding study, p 22
17 FISCO Fact-finding study, p 21
18 European Commission, *The Economic Impact of the Commission Recommendation on Withholding Tax Relief Procedures and the FISCO Proposals* (June 2009), Commission staff working document, http://ec.europa.eu/internal_market/financial-markets/docs/compliance/booklet-simplified_en.pdf, pp13–14
19 Cf **section 20.1**

a security subject to an income event is transferred, and the complications arising from the differential withholding tax treatment of the buyer and seller cannot be ignored. Withholding tax may also be deducted in some Member States from market claims in respect of shares traded cum-div[20] where the buyer receives compensation for dividend paid to the seller; and where the seller purchased ex-div in order to fulfil a delivery obligation on a cum-div trade, the seller's compensation payment may be treated as if it were a dividend.[21] Withholding tax practices, and their impact on post-trade services, have been the subject of continuous analysis since the establishment of FISCO in 2003. These practices are considered further in the following section.

WITHHOLDING TAX RELIEF

22.3 FISCO's mandate was focused on fiscal *compliance* barriers. Accordingly, in its second report, FISCO's recommendations related primarily to tax processes, rather than harmonising tax rates or the existence of taxes. The recommendations were, by and large, transposed into a European Commission Recommendation – that is, the weakest form of European quasi-legislative measure – on withholding tax relief procedures.[22] The Recommendation urges the following action by Member States:

- To grant withholding tax relief at source; and in cases where this is not achievable, to adopt streamlined refund procedures in accordance with the Recommendation's specifications. (By 2009, 14 Member States had procedures for giving relief at source.[23])

- For the securities intermediary proximate to the investor to act as withholding agent (the person who deducts the withholding tax); and in cases where this is not achievable, for information on entitlement to relief to be passed along the custody chain in a pooled (as contrasted with investor-specific) form.

- For criteria for financial intermediaries to act as withholding or information agents to be proportionate and non-discriminatory.

- To adopt alternatives to official certificates of residence to enable investors to claim relief.

One might assess the Recommendation as being a weak response to the issues identified by FISCO. A high degree of generality surrounds the specific recommendations: in particular, it is left to Member States to decide when exceptions arise, and therefore to adopt the more cumbersome routes set forth in it; and (of course) it is a mere Recommendation, which carries no duty of compliance. The Commission chose a Recommendation, rather than a formal legislative act which could actually involve obligations and their enforcement, because 'national withholding tax procedures ... is an area which is political[ly] sensitive.'[24] To create a binding legislative instrument would require unanimity among the Member States, which would appear to have been impossible to

---

20   See **section 20.2**
21   FISCO Fact-finding study, p 22
22   Commission Recommendation of 19 October 2009 on withholding tax relief procedures, COM(2009) 7924 final
23   Commission staff working document, p 18
24   Commission staff working document, p 4

obtain 'within a reasonable timeframe.' Admitting defeat, the Commission says 'it is clear that a Commission Recommendation will not eliminate the Giovannini Barrier 11 totally.'[25]

22.4   The Commission replaced FISCO with a Tax Barriers Business Advisory Group (T-BAG) in 2010. The mandate of T-BAG was to 'suggest workable solutions to implement the principles outlined in the Commission Recommendation.'[26] T-BAG's work was reported to have been completed in September 2011[27] but it was not made publicly available.

CO-OPTING OF INTERMEDIARIES INTO THE TAX PROCESS

22.5   Under regulation 3 of the Stamp Duty Reserve Tax Regulations 1986,[28] an 'accountable person' must give notice to HM Revenue and Customs of each charge to tax, and pay the tax due. 'Accountable persons' are listed in regulation 2, which sets out a hierarchy of buyer's and seller's brokers. Only if there is no other accountable person does the buyer itself become the accountable person. SDRT collection is a responsibility firmly placed on the intermediaries acting in respect of the trade, although it is unlikely that an agent bank is an accountable person.

But, under Regulation 4A, Euroclear UK & Ireland is obliged to notify HM Revenue and Customs of each charge to tax which has arisen and to pay the tax due, when the securities are transferred by means of the CREST system. A curious aspect of the CREST-HMRC reporting regime is that transactions emanating from different trading venues appear not be able to be netted, at least as far as interoperating CCPs are concerned. So, to take an example: imagine that A sells 100 Glaxo shares to B on platform 1, and C sells 100 Glaxo shares to D on platform 2. A and D both use CCP1 as their CCP, and B and C both use CCP2. As between the CCPs, there is no need for a net transfer of Glaxo shares. Unfortunately it seems that the SDRT reporting regime prevents the elimination of the two, opposite, inter-CCP transfers of 100 shares.

22.6   The FISCO Fact-finding study commented on the SDRT regime as follows:

'In relation to paperless transactions, the obligation imposed upon any system operator to collect taxes will give rise to compliance costs. The compliance costs will, however be the same, whether the operator is in the UK or outside the UK – save in relation to any obligation imposed on a non-UK operation to appoint a UK tax representative. In relation to transactions requiring the execution of documents of transfer and the payment of duty on those documents, a non-UK based person will have somewhat greater postage costs in arranging for the documents to be stamped but that cost

---

25 Commission staff working document, p 5
26 European Commission, *Tax Barriers Business Advisory Group, Mandate* (September 2010), http://ec.europa.eu/internal_market/financial-markets/docs/tbbag/mandate_en.pdf
27 Expert Group on Market Infrastructures, *Report* (October 2011), http://ec.europa.eu/internal_market/financial-markets/docs/clearing/egmi/101011_report_en.pdf, p 10
28 SI 1986 no 1711

should not be significantly greater. There is no provision which expressly requires these taxes to be collected only through UK situated persons.'[29]

Because the SDRT process is essentially neutral in terms of cost for both residents and non-residents of the United Kingdom, FISCO's conclusion was that no procedural reforms were needed in order to bring down the Giovannini barriers. The United Kingdom is not alone in levying taxes similar to SDRT: FISCO also named Belgium, France, Greece and Ireland as having tax charges based on exchange-trading of securities, and Finland, Italy, Malta, Poland, Portugal and Slovenia as having other transaction taxes.[30] These taxes are all different in small ways. Without some degree of harmonisation, differences in transaction taxes will continue to keep the complexity of investment within the single European market – particularly cross-border investment – at a high level.

22.7   Finally, it should be mentioned that a complex regime under section 96 of the Finance Act 1986 for levying an SDRT charge of 1.5% on securities transferred to a person whose business was the provision of 'clearance services' has been abolished, following a judgment adverse to the United Kingdom in *HSBC Holdings plc and Vidacos Nominees Ltd v HMRC*.[31] 'In the light of the ruling HM Revenue & Customs (HMRC) accepts that Article 11(a) of Council Directive 69/335/EEC of 17 July 1969 concerning indirect taxes on the raising of capital, as amended by Council Directive 85/303/EEC of 10 June 1985 (now Council Directive 2008/7/EC) ("the EC Capital Directive"), must be interpreted as meaning that it prohibits the levying of a duty such as the charge to SDRT imposed by section 96 Finance Act 1986 on the issue of shares into a Community clearance service.'[32]

Savings tax directive

22.8   'The ultimate aim of the [Savings Tax] Directive is to enable savings income in the form of interest payments made in one Member State to beneficial owners who are individuals resident for tax purposes in another Member State to be made subject to effective taxation in accordance with the laws of the latter Member State.'[33] To achieve that aim, a paying agent making an interest payment to a person resident in a different Member State must notify the competent authority in the payee's Member State.[34] An agent bank is likely to be characterised as a paying agent for these purposes. A proposal to modify the Savings Tax Directive is in part intended to clarify who has the role of paying agent in a multi-intermediary chain.[35]

---

29 FISCO Fact-finding study, p 41
30 FISOC Fact-finding study, s 3.2
31 ECJ, case C-569/07 (November 2009), OJ (C) 282, p 6
32 HMRC, *Stamp Duty Reserve Tax (SDRT): Claims for refund following the decision of the European Court of Justice HSBC Holdings and Vidacos Nominees Ltd v HMRC,* http://www.hmrc.gov.uk/so/sdrt-claims-ecj.pdf
33 Council Directive 2003/48/EC of 3 June 2003 on taxation of savings income in the form of interest payments, art 1(1)
34 Savings Tax Directive, art 8
35 European Commission, *Proposal for a Council Directive amending Directive 2003/48/EC on taxation of savings income in the form of interest payments* (November 2008), COM(2008) 727 final; inter-institutional file 2008/0215 (CNS)

FATCA

22.9   The adoption by the US legislature of the Foreign Account Tax Compliance Act (FATCA)[36] has extended the duties of agent banks in particular. FATCA does not specifically target clearing and settlement activities: its objective is to facilitate the collection by the United States' Internal Revenue Service (IRS) of data on United States' persons' foreign assets and income. At the centre of FATCA is the idea that 'foreign financial institutions' will enter into agreements with the IRS, under which the foreign financial institution undertakes to identify US persons who are beneficially entitled to assets credited to financial accounts which the institution provides. The foreign financial institution will obtain a waiver from its US clients to enable the institution to report holdings, receipts and withdrawals, both of cash and securities, made in respect of the account. Evidently a tax-related reporting obligation in respect of all settlement activity will be required. Failure to enter into an agreement with the IRS brands the institution a 'non-compliant foreign financial institution', with the result that all US-sourced income and proceeds (fixed or determinable annual or periodical income, sales proceeds, and potentially 'passthru' payments) will suffer a withholding of 30% before being transferred to the institution. Failure by a client to give the institution permission to give information to the IRS or a waiver of secrecy laws brands the client a 'recalcitrant account holder', in respect of whom the institution must withhold 30% of US-sourced income and proceeds (such income and proceeds being the 'passthru' payments referred to earlier), and in some cases to terminate the provision of accounts to the client.

---

36 Hiring Incentives to Restore Employment Act of 2010 (March 2010), Pub. L. No. 111–147, 124 Stat. 71, Title V

Index

(All references are to section numbers)